Monetary Theory and Policy

Carl E. Walsh

The MIT Press
Cambridge, Massachusetts
London, England

Second printing, 2000

© 1998 Massachusetts Institute of Technology

This book was set in Times New Roman on the Monotype "Prism Plus" PostScript Imagesetter by Asco Trade Typesetting Ltd., Hong Kong and was printed and bound in the United States of America.

Library of Congress Cataloging-in-Publication Data

Walsh, Carl E.
  Monetary theory and policy / Carl E. Walsh.
     p.   cm.
  Includes bibliographical references and index.
  ISBN 0-262-23199-9
  1. Monetary policy.   2. Money.   I. Title.
HG230.3.W35   1998
332.4′6—dc21   98-20018
                                        CIP

To my parents

Contents

Figures

Tables

Preface

This project originated when I had the opportunity to teach in the macro theory sequence in the economics department at Stanford University during the fall semester of 1995. The topics covered dealt with money and monetary policy, and I decided to provide the students in the class with a more formal set of lecture notes than I had used in the past for similar courses. Foolishly, I thought these notes could then be easily turned into a book on monetary theory and policy; in the end, the transition from those lecture notes to this book took three years. What merit the final product has owes much to the teachers, coauthors, colleagues, and students I have had over the years at the University of California, Berkeley; Princeton University; the Federal Reserve Bank of San Francisco; and the University of California, Santa Cruz. The manuscript has been immensely improved by the thoughtful and helpful comments of many individuals who took the time to read parts of earlier drafts. Luigi Buttiglione, Marco Hoeberichts, Michael Hutchison, Francesco Lippi, Jaewoo Lee, Doug Pearce, Gustavo Piga, Glenn Rudebusch, Willem Verhagen, and Chris Waller provided me with many insightful and useful comments, all of which led to significant improvements. Students at Stanford and UC Santa Cruz gave me important feedback on draft material; Peter Kriz, Jerry McIntyre, Fabiano Schivardi, Alina Stanciu, and especially Jules Leichter deserve special mention. A very special note of thanks is due Lars Svensson and Berthold Herrendorf. Each made extensive comments on an earlier draft. Attempting to address the issues they raised greatly improved the final product; it would have been even better if I had had the time and energy to follow all their suggestions. I would also like to thank Nancy Lombardi for her excellent production assistance. Needless to say, all the remaining weaknesses and errors are my own responsibility.

This project was made much easier by the excellent resources of the research library at the Federal Reserve Bank of San Francisco. I have greatly benefited from a long association with the research department at the San Francisco Fed, first as a senior economist, then as a visiting scholar. The influence of my colleagues at the SF Fed has undoubtedly kept me focused on issues with at least some relevance to the questions and problems faced in the actual conduct of monetary policy. Of course, any opinions expressed are mine and not necessarily those of the Federal Reserve Bank of San Francisco or the Federal Reserve System.

I would also like to thank the National Science Foundation for its generous support of my research on central banking, which is discussed extensively in Chapter 8.

It probably goes without saying that any project such as this one requires the support and understanding of one's family. I have been especially blessed by the encouragement of my wife Judy, and the understanding of my stepdaughters Deborah and Michelle has been fondly appreciated. It was Michelle, however, who noted when MIT Press sent me the reviewers' reports and I began the work of finishing the manuscript, "The book is back!" in a tone that suggested its return was not met with unreserved joy. I hope students of monetary economics will find the result worthwhile.

Notation

Operators

Operators are written as Roman letters.

$E[x]$	unconditional expectation of x
$E_t[x_{t+i}], E_t x_{t+i}$	expectation of x_{t+i} conditional on information at time t
$L^i x = x_{t-i}$	lag operator
$\Delta x_t = x_t - x_{t-1}$	first difference operator

Chapters 2–4

X	aggregate value
x	per capita value
x^{ss}	steady-state value
$\hat{x}$	percentage deviation of x around x^{ss}
M	aggregate nominal money supply
m	per capita real money supply: M/PN
H	high-powered money
P	aggregate price level
B	government debt (one-period aggregate nominal stock)
b	real per capita stock of government debt
s	real seigniorage
z	productivity disturbance
e	productivity innovation
θ	nominal money-growth rate
u	deviation of money growth around steady state: $\theta - \theta^{ss}$
φ	money-growth-rate innovation
ρ	serial correlation coefficient of productivity disturbance
γ	serial correlation coefficient of u
π	inflation rate
Π	$1 + \pi$
$f(k, n, z)$	production function

δ	rate of depreciation
R	$f_k + 1 - \delta$
r	$R - 1$
β	discount factor: $0 < \beta < 1$
t	time index
α	exponent on capital in production function

Chapters 5–10

m	log of the nominal money supply
p	log of the aggregate-price level
y	log output
π_t	$p_t - p_{t-1}$
r_t	one-period expected real rate of return
i_t	$r_t + E_t \pi_{t+1}$ one-period nominal rate of interest
R	long-term real rate of interest
i^f	federal funds rate (short-term policy rate)
S	nominal exchange rate
s	log nominal exchange rate
ρ	log real exchange rate
T	denotes target variable when used as a superscript
a	output effect of surprise inflation
t	time index
superscript $*$	indicates variable refers to foreign country
λ	weight on output in central bank objective function
k	deviation between target output and average equilibrium level

Introduction

Monetary economics investigates the relationship between real economic variables at the aggregate level—such as real output, real rates of interest, employment, and real exchange rates—and nominal variables—such as the inflation rate, nominal interest rates, nominal exchange rates, and the supply of money. So defined, monetary economics has considerable overlap with macroeconomics more generally, and these two fields have, to a large degree, shared a common history over most of the last 50 years. This statement was particularly true during the 1970s after the monetarist/Keynesian debates led to a reintegration of monetary economics with macroeconomics. The seminal work of Robert Lucas (1972) provided theoretical foundations for models of economic fluctuations in which money was the fundamental driving factor behind movements in real output. The rise of real-business-cycle models during the 1980s and early 1990s, building on the contribution of Kydland and Prescott (1982) and focusing explicitly on nonmonetary factors as the driving forces behind business cycles, tended to separate monetary economics from macroeconomics. More recently, the real-business-cycle approach to aggregate modeling has been used to incorporate monetary factors into dynamic general equilibrium models. Today, both macroeconomics and monetary economics share the common tools associated with dynamic, stochastic approaches to modeling the aggregate economy. Despite these close connections, a book on monetary economics is not a book on macroeconomics. The focus in monetary economics is distinct, emphasizing price-level determination, inflation, and the role of monetary policy. This book provides coverage of the most important topics in monetary economics and of some of the models that economists have employed as they attempt to understand the interactions between real and monetary factors. It deals with topics in both monetary theory and monetary policy and is designed for second-year graduate students specializing in monetary economics, for researchers in monetary economics wishing to have a systematic summary of recent developments, and for economists working in policy institutions such as central banks. It can also be used as a supplement for first-year graduate courses in macroeconomics, as it provides a more in-depth treatment of inflation and monetary policy topics than is customary in graduate macro textbooks. The chapters on monetary policy may be useful for advanced undergraduate courses.

Besides incorporating a discussion of the basic empirical approaches to estimating the impact of monetary policy, the major theoretical models are linked to the calibration and simulation techniques commonly used in macroeconomics and to the class of models commonly used for policy analysis. The use of dynamic simulations to evaluate the quantitative significance of the channels through which monetary policy and inflation affect the economy is one innovation of this book. Modern approaches to monetary policy stress the need to understand the incentives facing central banks and to model the strategic interactions between the central bank and the private sector. This approach receives extensive coverage, and this represents a second innovation of the book. A third innovation is the focus on interest rates in the discussion of monetary policy. Few central banks conduct monetary policy oriented toward a quantity of money, yet most treatments of monetary policy continue to emphasize money-supply control and money demand.

When one is writing a book such as this, several organizational approaches present themselves. Monetary economics is a large field, and one must decide whether to provide broad coverage, giving students a brief introduction to many topics, or to focus more narrowly and in more depth. I have chosen to focus on particular models, models that monetary economists have employed to address topics in theory and policy. I have tried to stress the major topics within monetary economics in order to provide sufficiently broad coverage of the field, but the focus within each topic is often on a small number of papers or models that I have found useful for gaining insight into a particular issue. As an aid to students, derivations of basic results are often quite detailed, but deeper technical issues of existence, multiple equilibria, and stability receive relatively little attention. This choice was made not because the latter are unimportant, but instead the relative emphasis reflects an assessment that to do these topics justice, while still providing enough emphasis on the core insights offered by monetary economics, would have required a much longer book. By reducing the dimensionality of problems and by not treating them in full generality, I hoped to achieve the right balance of insight, accessibility, and rigor. The many references will serve to guide students to the extensive treatments in the literature of all the topics touched upon in this book.

Monetary economics today is dominated by three alternative modeling strategies. The first two, representative-agent models and overlapping-generations models, share a common methodological approach in building equilibrium relationships explicitly on the foundations of optimizing behavior by individual agents. The third approach is based on sets of equilibrium relationships that are often not derived directly from any decision problem. Instead, they are described as "ad hoc" by critics and convenient approximations by proponents. The latter characterization is generally more appropriate, and these models have demonstrated great value in helping economists understand issues in monetary economics. In this book, we will deal with models in the representative-agent class and with ad hoc models of the type more common in policy analysis.

There are several reasons for ignoring the overlapping-generations, or OLG, approach. First, systematic expositions of monetary economics from the perspective of overlapping generations are already available. For example, Sargent (1987) and Champ and Freeman (1994) cover many topics in monetary economics using OLG models. Second, many of the issues one studies in monetary economics require understanding the time-series behavior of macroeconomic variables such as inflation or the relationship between money and business cycles. It is helpful if the theoretical framework one uses can be mapped directly into implications for behavior that can be compared with actual data. This mapping is more easily done with infinite-horizon representative-agent models than with OLG models. This advantage, in fact, is one reason for the popularity of real-business-cycle models that employ the representative-agent approach, and so a third reason for limiting the coverage to representative-agent models is that they provide a close link between monetary economics and other popular frameworks for studying business-cycle phenomena. Fourth, monetary policy issues are generally related to the dynamic behavior of the economy over time periods associated with business-cycle frequencies, and here again the OLG framework seems less directly applicable. Finally, OLG models emphasize the store-of-value role of money at the expense of the medium-of-exchange role that money plays in facilitating transactions. McCallum (1983b) has argued that some of the implications of OLG models that contrast most sharply with the implications of other approaches (the tenuousness of monetary equilibria, for example) are directly related to the lack of a medium-of-exchange role for money.

A book on monetary theory and policy would be seriously incomplete if it were limited to representative-agent models alone. A variety of ad hoc models have played, and continue to play, important roles in influencing the way economists, and perhaps more importantly, policy makers, think about the role of monetary policy. These models can be very helpful in highlighting key issues affecting the linkages between monetary and real economic phenomena. No monetary economist's tool kit is complete without them. But it is important to begin with more fully specified models so that one has some sense of what is missing in the simpler models. In this way, one is better able to judge whether the ad hoc models are likely to provide insight into particular questions.

The book divides naturally into chapters on models with flexible prices (Chapters 2–4), chapters on money in the short run when price rigidities are important (Chapters 5–7), and chapters on policy topics (Chapters 8–10). In covering topics of monetary theory, major emphasis is placed on the money-in-the-utility-function (Chapter 2) and cash-in-advance approaches (Chapter 3) to integrating money into general equilibrium frameworks, and on the role of inflation as a tax instrument (Chapter 4). Stochastic versions for the basic models are calibrated, and simulations are used to illustrate how monetary factors affect the behavior of the economy. Such simulations aid in assessing the ability of the models to capture correlations observed in actual data.

The link between the dynamic general equilibrium models of Chapters 2–4 and the models employed for monetary policy analysis in Chapters 8–9 is developed in Chapters 5–7. I have tried to emphasize that the standard models employed in policy analysis can be viewed as linear approximations to general equilibrium models based on firm micro foundations. An extension to the open economy is provided (Chapter 6), and credit channels for monetary policy are also examined (Chapter 7).

A survey of the recent literature on game-theoretic approaches to the study of monetary policy provides the starting point for the main coverage of policy topics (Chapter 8). The details of policy implementation and operating procedures are important, particularly for empirical work that attempts to measure the impact of policy actions (Chapter 9). Since most central banks use interest-rate-oriented procedures to implement policy, the book provides a discussion of interest rates and monetary policy, concluding with a discussion of recent models that are explicit in dropping the quantity of money from monetary policy analysis (Chapter 10).

There is one traditionally important topic missing from this book—money demand. Academic models in monetary economics have, by long tradition, treated the quantity of money as central to the field. Such a focus leads naturally to an emphasis on the links between the direct instruments of monetary policy (open market operation, discount or other interest-rate-setting policy, reserve requirements) and the money supply and on the determinants of money demand. The interaction of money demand and money supply then serves to determine the quantity of money and the economy's price level. A large branch of the literature in monetary economics has concentrated on understanding the determinants of the demand for money and in developing and estimating empirical models of money demand. While attention will be paid to important approaches to treating the demand for money at a theoretical level, the analysis of money demand for the understanding of many issues related to short-run monetary policy is of less relevance now than it has been in the past. This change has occurred because, to a large extent, central banks operate today by employing a short-term interest rate as their policy operating target, with a deemphasis on the quantity of money. Such a focus reduces the importance of money-demand and money-supply analysis, and this reduced relevance is reflected in the coverage of this book.

This book is about monetary theory and the theory of monetary policy. Occasional references to empirical results are made, but no attempt has been made to provide a systematic survey of the vast body of empirical research in monetary economics. Most of the debates in monetary economics, however, have at their root issues of fact that can only be resolved by empirical evidence. Empirical evidence is needed to choose between theoretical approaches, but theory is also needed to interpret empirical evidence. How one links the quantities in the theoretical model to measurable data is critical, for example, in developing measures of monetary policy actions that can be used to estimate the impact of policy on the economy. Because empirical evidence aids in discriminating between alternative theories, it is helpful to begin with a brief overview of some basic facts. Chapter 1 does so, providing a discussion that focuses primarily on the estimated impact of monetary policy actions on real output. Here, as in chapters that deal with some of the institutional details of monetary policy, the evidence comes primarily from research on the United States. However, an attempt has been made to cite cross-country studies and to focus on empirical regularities that seem to characterize most industrialized economies.

Chapters 2–4 emphasize the role of inflation as a tax, using models that provide the basic micro foundations of monetary economics. These chapters cover topics of fundamental importance for understanding how monetary phenomena affect the general equilibrium behavior of the economy and how nominal prices, inflation, money, and interest rates are linked. Because the models studied in these chapters assume that prices are perfectly flexible, they are most useful for understanding longer-run correlations between inflation, money, and output and cross-country differences in average inflation. However, they do have implications for short-run dynamics as real and nominal variables adjust in response to aggregate productivity disturbances and random shocks to money growth. These dynamics are examined by employing simulations based on linear approximations around the steady-state equilibrium.

Chapters 2 and 3 employ a neoclassical growth framework to study monetary phenomena. The neoclassical model is one in which growth is exogenous, and money either has no effect on the real economy's long-run steady state or has effects that are likely to be small empirically. However, because these models allow one to calculate the welfare implications of exogenous changes in the economic environment, they provide a natural framework for examining the welfare costs of alternative steady-state rates of inflation. They also, as the real-business-cycle literature has shown, can be simulated to generate artificial time series to study their implications for short-run cyclical fluctuations. Since policy can be expressed in terms of both exogenous shocks and endogenous feedbacks from real shocks, the models can be used to study how economic fluctuations depend on monetary policy.

In Chapter 4, the focus turns to public finance issues associated with money, inflation, and monetary policy. The ability to create money provides governments with a means of generating revenues. As a source of revenue, money creation, along with the inflation that results, can be analyzed from the perspective of public finance as one among many tax tools available to governments.

Beginning with Chapter 5, issues related to the short-run impact of monetary policy and to a number of topics that are relevant for understanding the conduct of monetary policy take center stage. The critical difference between the models of Chapters 2–4 and those of Chapters 5–10 lies in the price-adjustment mechanism. Understanding the impacts that monetary disturbances have on the real economy over time intervals measured in months or quarters requires one to drop the assumption used in Chapters 2–4 that the aggregate price level immediately adjusts to ensure that equilibrium in all markets is continuously maintained.

Chapter 5 begins by reviewing some attempts to replicate the empirical evidence on the short-run effects of monetary policy shocks while still maintaining the assumption of flexible prices. Lucas's misperceptions model provides an important example of one such attempt. These efforts provide some insights into money-output links, but they are unable to mimic the persistence of the estimated impacts of monetary shocks on output. To do so requires that prices adjust sluggishly in response to economic disturbances. Chapter 5 discusses some important models of price and inflation adjustment and covers the transition from the earlier models of flexible prices and utility-maximizing agents to the traditional framework provided by the aggregate-supply, aggregate-demand models enshrined in most undergraduate textbooks in macroeconomics. These models still provide one of the basic organizing frameworks used in monetary economics, and it is shown how a simple aggregate-supply, IS-LM model can be viewed as an approximation to a money-in-the-utility-function model of the type studied in Chapter 2.

Chapter 6 extends the analysis to the open economy by focusing on two questions. First, what additional channels from monetary policy actions to the real economy are present in the open economy that were absent in the closed-economy analysis? Second, how does monetary policy affect the behavior of nominal and real exchange rates? New channels through which monetary policy actions are transmitted to the real economy are present in open economies and involve exchange-rate movements and interest-rate linkages.

While the channels of monetary policy emphasized in traditional models operate primarily through interest rates and exchange rates, an alternative view is that credit markets play an independent role in affecting the transmission of monetary policy actions to the real economy. The nature of credit markets, and their role in the transmission process, is affected by market imperfections arising from imperfect information. Chapter 7 examines theories that stress the role of credit and credit-market imperfections in the presence of moral hazard, adverse selection, and costly monitoring.

Chapters 8–10 focus more directly on policy topics. These topics include strategic models of monetary policy, operating procedures and policy implementation, and the role of interest rates and interest-rate-oriented policies. Also discussed are some simple frameworks that have proven useful in discussions of short-run monetary policy.

Chapter 8 discusses monetary policy objectives and then turns to consider the ability of policy authorities to achieve these objectives. Understanding monetary policy requires an understanding of how policy actions affect macro variables (the topic of Chapters 2–7), but it also requires models of policy behavior to understand why particular policies are undertaken. A large body of research over the last decade has used game-theoretic concepts to model the monetary policy maker as a strategic agent. These models have provided new insights into the rules-versus-discretion debate, provided positive theories of inflation, and provided justification for many of the actual reforms of central banking legislation that have been implemented in the past few years.

In Chapter 9, the focus turns to monetary policy implementation. Here, the discussion deals with the monetary-instrument-choice problem and monetary-policy operating procedures. A long tradition in monetary economics has debated the usefulness of monetary aggregates versus interest rates in the design and implementation of monetary policy, and Chapter 9 reviews the approach economists have used to address this issue. A simple model of the market for bank reserves is used to stress how the observed responses of short-term interest rates and reserve aggregates will depend on the operating procedures used in the conduct of policy. A basic understanding of policy implementation is important for empirical studies that attempt to measure changes in monetary policy.

Traditionally, economists have employed simple models in which the money stock or even inflation is assumed to be the direct instrument of policy. In fact, most central banks have employed interest rates as their operational policy instrument, so Chapter 10 departs from tradition by emphasizing explicitly the role of a short-term interest rate as the instrument of monetary policy. Issues such as price-level determinacy under interest-rate-policy rules, the term structure of interest rates, and simple simulation models for policy analysis are discussed.

1 Empirical Evidence on Money and Output

1.1 Introduction

In this chapter, some of the basic empirical evidence on money, inflation, and output is reviewed. This review serves two purposes. First, these basic "facts" about both the long-run and the short-run relationships can serve as benchmarks for judging theoretical models. Second, reviewing the empirical evidence provides an opportunity to discuss the approaches monetary economists have taken to estimate the effects of money, and monetary policy, on real economic activity. The discussion will focus heavily on evidence from vector autoregressions (VARs), since these have served as a primary tool for uncovering the impact of monetary phenomena on the real economy. The findings obtained from VARs have been criticized, and these criticisms, as well as other methods that have been used to investigate the money-output relationship, are also discussed.

1.2 Some Basic Correlations

What are the basic empirical regularities that monetary economics must explain? Monetary economics focuses on the behavior of prices, monetary aggregates, nominal and real interest rates, and output, so a useful starting point is to summarize briefly what macroeconomic data tell us about the relationships among these variables. The focus here will be on the correlations between real output on the one hand, and money and inflation on the other.

1.2.1 Long-Run Relationships

A nice summary of long-run monetary relationships is provided by McCandless and Weber (1995). They examine data covering a 30-year period from 110 countries using several definitions of money. By examining average rates of inflation, output growth, and the growth rates of various measures of money over a long period of time and for many different countries, McCandless and Weber provide evidence on relationships that are unlikely to be dependent on unique, country-specific events (such as the particular means employed to implement monetary policy) that might influence the actual evolution of money, prices, and output in a particular country. Based on their analysis, two primary conclusions emerge.

The first is that the correlation between inflation and the growth rate of the money supply is almost one, varying between 0.92 and 0.96, depending on the definition of the money supply used. This strong positive relationship between inflation and money growth is consistent with many other studies based on smaller samples of countries and different time periods.[1] This correlation is normally taken to support one of the basic tenets of the quantity theory of money: a change in the growth rate of money induces "an equal change in the rate of price inflation" (Lucas 1980, p. 1005). This high correlation does not, however, have any implications for causality. If the countries in the sample had followed policies under which money-supply growth rates were exogenously determined, then the correlation could be taken as evidence that money growth causes inflation with an almost one-to-one relationship between the two. An alternative possibility, equally consistent with the high correlation, is that other factors generate inflation, and central banks allow the growth rate of money to adjust. Any theoretical model not consistent with a roughly one-for-one long-run relationship between money growth and inflation, though, would need to be questioned.[2]

The appropriate interpretation of money-inflation correlations, both in terms of causality and in terms of tests of long-run relationships, also depends on the statistical properties of the underlying series. As Fisher and Seater (1993) note, one cannot ask how a permanent change in the growth rate of money affects inflation unless actual money growth has exhibited permanent shifts. They show how the order of integration of money and prices influences the testing of hypotheses about the long-run relationship between money growth and inflation. In a similar vein, McCallum (1984b) demonstrates that regression-based tests of long-run relationships in monetary economies may be misleading when expectational relationships are involved.

McCandless and Weber's second general conclusion is that there is no correlation between either inflation or money growth and the growth rate of real output. Thus, there are countries with low output growth and low money growth and inflation, and countries with low output growth and high money growth and inflation—and countries with every other combination as well. This conclusion is not as robust as the money-growth–inflation one; McCandless and Weber report a positive correlation between real growth and money growth, but not inflation, for a subsample of OECD countries. Kormendi and Meguire (1984) for a sample of almost 50 countries and Geweke (1986) for the United States argue that the data reveal no long-run effect

1. Examples include Lucas (1980), Geweke (1986), and Rolnick and Weber (1994) among others. A nice graph of the close relationship between money growth and inflation for high-inflation countries is provided by Abel and Bernanke (1995, p. 242). Hall and Taylor provide a similar graph for the G-7 countries (Hall and Taylor 1997, p. 115). As will be noted, however, the interpretation of correlations between inflation and money growth can be problematic.

2. Haldane (1997) finds, however, that the money-growth-rate–inflation correlation is much less than one among low-inflation countries.

of money growth on real output growth. Others, most recently Barro (1995, 1996), report a negative correlation between inflation and growth in a cross-country sample. Bullard and Keating (1995) examine the postwar data from 58 countries, concluding for the sample as a whole that the evidence that permanent shifts in inflation produce permanent effects on the level of output is weak, with some evidence of positive effects of inflation on output among low-inflation countries and zero or negative effects for higher-inflation countries.[3] Similarly, Boschen and Mills (1995b) conclude that permanent monetary shocks in the United States made no contribution to permanent shifts in GDP. Thus, there is somewhat greater uncertainty as to the relationship between inflation and real growth, and other measures of real economic activity such as unemployment, in the long run, but the general consensus is well summarized by the proposition, "about which there is now little disagreement, . . . that there is no long-run trade-off between the rate of inflation and the rate of unemployment" (Taylor 1996, p. 186).

1.2.2   Short-Run Relationships

The long-run empirical regularities of monetary economies are important for gauging how well the steady-state properties of a theoretical model match the data. Much of our interest in monetary economics, however, arises because of a need to understand how monetary phenomena in general, and monetary policy in particular, affect the behavior of the macroeconomy over time periods of months or quarters. Short-run dynamic relationships between money, inflation, and output reflect both the way in which private agents respond to economic disturbances and the way in which the monetary policy authority responds to those same disturbances. For this reason, short-run correlations are likely to vary both across countries, as different central banks implement policy in different ways, and across time in a single country, as the sources of economic disturbances vary.

Some evidence on short-run correlations for the United States is provided in Figure 1.1. The figure shows correlations between the detrended log of real GDP and three different monetary aggregates, each in detrended log form as well.[4] Data are quarterly from 1960:1 to 1995:4, and the figure plots the correlation between real GDP_t and M_{t+j} against j where M represents a monetary aggregate. The three

---

3. Kormendi and Meguire (1985) report a statistically significant positive coefficient on average money growth in a cross-country regression for average real growth. This effect, however, is due to a single observation (Brazil), and the authors report that money growth becomes insignificant in their growth equation when Brazil is dropped from the sample. They do find a significant negative effect on growth of monetary volatility.

4. Trends are estimated using a Hodrick-Prescott filter.

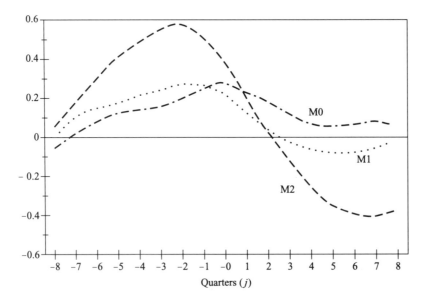

Figure 1.1
Dynamic Correlations GDP$_t$ and M$_{t+j}$

aggregates are the monetary base (sometimes denoted as M0), M1, and M2. The
measure M0 is a narrow definition of the money supply, consisting of total reserves
held by the banking system plus currency in the hands of the public; M1 consists
of currency held by the nonbank public, travelers checks, demand deposits, and
other checkable deposits; and M2 consists of M1 plus savings accounts and small-
denomination time deposits plus balances in retail money-market mutual funds.

As Figure 1.1 shows, the correlations with real output change substantially as one
moves from M0 to M2. The narrow measure M0 is positively correlated with real
GDP at both leads and lags. In contrast, M2 is positively correlated at lags but
negatively correlated at leads. In other words, high GDP (relative to trend) tends to
be preceded by high values of M2 but followed by low values. The positive correlation between GDP_t and M_{t+j} for $j < 0$ indicates that movements in money lead
movements in output. This timing pattern played an important role in Friedman and
Schwartz's classic and highly influential *Monetary History of the United States*
(M. Friedman and Schwartz 1963b). The larger correlations between GDP and M2
arise in part from the endogenous nature of an aggregate such as M2, depending as
it does on the behavior of the banking sector, as well as that of the nonbank private
sector (see King and Plosser 1984; Coleman 1996).

While Figure 1.1 gives one summary of the joint behavior of money and output, at least for the United States, one of the challenges of monetary economics is to determine the degree to which these data reveal causal relationships, relationships that should be expected to appear in data from other countries and during other time periods, or relationships that depend on the particular characteristics of the policy regime under which monetary policy is conducted.

1.3 Estimating the Effect of Money on Output

While almost all economists accept that the long-run effects of money fall entirely, or almost entirely, on prices with little impact on real variables, most also believe that monetary disturbances can have important effects on real variables such as output in the short run.[5] As Lucas puts it in his Nobel lecture: "This tension between two incompatible ideas—that changes in money are neutral unit changes and that they induce movements in employment and production in the same direction—has been at the center of monetary theory at least since Hume wrote" (Lucas 1996, p. 664).[6] The time-series correlations presented in the previous subsection are suggestive of the short-run relationships between money and income, but the evidence for the effects of money on real output is based on more than these simple correlations.

The tools that have been employed to estimate the impact of monetary policy have evolved over time, as the result of both developments in time-series econometrics and changes in the specific questions posed by theoretical models. In this section, we review some of the empirical evidence on the relationship between monetary policy and U.S. macro behavior. One objective of this literature has been to determine whether monetary policy disturbances actually have played an important role in U.S. economic fluctuations. Equally important, the empirical evidence is useful in judging whether the predictions of different theories about the effects of monetary policy are consistent with the evidence. Two excellent recent discussions of these issues are Leeper, Sims, and Zha (1996), where the focus is on the role of identified VARs in estimating the effects of monetary policy, and King and Watson (1996), where the focus is on using empirical evidence to distinguish among competing business-cycle models.

5. For an exposition of the view that monetary factors have not played an important role in U.S. business cycles, see Kydland and Prescott (1990).

6. The reference is to David Hume's 1752 essays *Of Money* and *Of Interest*.

1.3.1 The Evidence of Friedman and Schwartz

Friedman and Schwartz's classic study of the relationship between money and business cycles (M. Friedman and Schwartz 1963b) probably still represents the most influential empirical evidence that money does matter for business-cycle fluctuations. Their evidence, based on almost 100 years of data from the United States, relied heavily on patterns of timing; systematic evidence that money growth rate changes lead changes in real economic activity is taken to support a causal interpretation in which money causes output fluctuations. This timing pattern shows up most clearly in Figure 1.1 with M2.

Friedman and Schwartz concluded that the data "decisively support treating the rate of change series [of the money supply] as conforming to the reference cycle positively with a long lead" (M. Friedman and Schwartz 1963a, p. 36). That is, faster money growth tends to be followed by increases in output above trend, and slowdowns in money growth tend to be followed by declines in output. The inference Friedman and Schwartz drew was that variations in money growth rates cause, with a long (and variable) lead, variations in real economic activity.

The nature of this evidence for the United States is apparent in Figure 1.2, which shows two money-supply measures and detrended real GDP. The monetary aggregates in the figure, M1 and M2, are quarterly observations on the deviations of the actual series from trend. The sample period is 1959–1995, so this figure starts where the Friedman and Schwartz study ends. The figure reveals slowdowns in money leading most business-cycle downturns through the early 1980s. However, the pattern is not so apparent after 1982. B. Friedman and Kuttner (1992) have documented the seeming breakdown in the relationship between monetary aggregates and real output; this changing relationship between money and output has affected the manner in which monetary policy has been conducted, at least in the United States (see Chapter 9).

While suggestive, evidence based on timing patterns and simple correlations may not indicate the true causal role of money. Since the Federal Reserve and the banking sector respond to economic developments, movements in the monetary aggregates are not exogenous, and the correlation patterns need not reflect any causal effect of monetary policy on economic activity. If, for example, the central bank is implementing monetary policy by controlling the value of some short-term market interest rate, the nominal stock of money will be affected both by policy actions that change interest rates and by developments in the economy that are not related to policy actions. An economic expansion may lead banks to expand lending in ways that produce an increase in the stock of money, even if the central bank has not

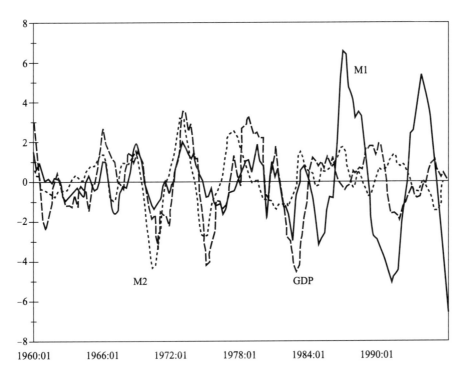

Figure 1.2
Detrended Money and GDP

changed its policy. If the money stock is used to measure monetary policy, the relationship observed in the data between money and output may reflect the impact of output on money and not the impact of money and monetary policy on output.

   Tobin (1970) was the first to model formally the idea that the positive correlation between money and output, the correlation that Friedman and Schwartz interpreted as providing evidence that money caused output movements, could, in fact, reflect just the opposite—output might be causing money. A more modern treatment of what is known as the reverse causation argument is provided by King and Plosser (1984). They show that inside money, the component of a monetary aggregate such as M1 that represents the liabilities of the banking sector, is more highly correlated with output movements in the United States than is outside money, the liabilities of the Federal Reserve. King and Plosser interpret this finding as evidence that much of the correlation between broad aggregates such as M1 or M2 and output arises from the endogenous response of the banking sector to economic disturbances that

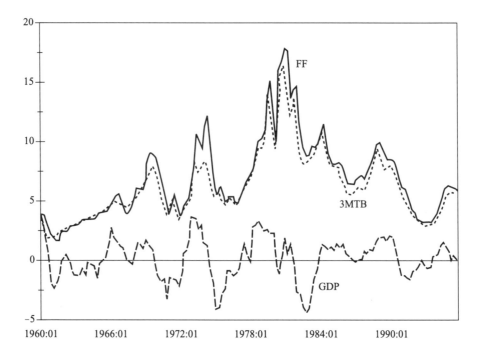

Figure 1.3
Interest Rates and Detrended GDP

are not the result of monetary policy actions. More recently, Coleman (1996), in an
estimated equilibrium model with endogenous money, finds that the implied behavior
of money in the model cannot match the lead-lag relationship in the data. Specifically, a money-supply measure such as M2 leads output, whereas Coleman finds that
his model implies that money should be more highly correlated with lagged output
than with future output.[7]

The endogeneity problem is likely to be particularly severe if the monetary
authority has employed a short-term interest rate as its main policy instrument, and
this has generally been the case in the United States. Changes in the money stock will
then be endogenous and cannot be interpreted as representing policy actions. Figure
1.3 shows the behavior of two short-term nominal interest rates, the three-month
T-bill rate (3MTB) and the federal funds rate (FF), together with detrended real

---

7. Lacker (1988) shows how the correlations between inside money and future output could also arise if
movements in inside money reflect new information about future monetary policy.

GDP. Like Figure 1.2, Figure 1.3 provides some support for the notion that monetary policy actions have contributed to U.S. business cycles. Interest rates have typically increased prior to economic downturns. But whether this is evidence that monetary policy has caused or contributed to cyclical fluctuations cannot be inferred from the figure; the movements in interest rates may simply reflect the Fed's response to the state of the economy.

Simple plots and correlations are suggestive, but they cannot be decisive. Other factors may be the cause of the joint movements of output, monetary aggregates, and interest rates. The comparison with business-cycle reference points also ignores much of the information about the time-series behavior of money, output, and interest rates that could be used to determine what impact, if any, monetary policy has on output. And the appropriate variable to use as a measure of monetary policy will depend on how policy has been implemented.

One of the earliest time-series econometric attempts to estimate the impact of money was due to M. Friedman and Meiselman (1963). Their objective was to test whether monetary or fiscal policy was more important for the determination of *nominal* income. To address this issue, they estimated the following equation:[8]

$$y_t^n \equiv y_t + p_t = y_0^n + \sum_{i=0} a_i A_{t-i} + \sum_{i=0} b_i m_{t-i} + \sum_{i=0} h_i z_{t-i} + u_t \qquad (1.1)$$

where y^n denotes the log of nominal income, equal to the sum of the logs of output and the price level; A is a measure of autonomous expenditures; m is a monetary aggregate; and z can be thought of as a vector of other variables relevant for explaining nominal income fluctuations. Friedman and Meiselman reported finding a much more stable and statistically significant relationship between output and money than between output and their measure of autonomous expenditures. In general, they could not reject the hypothesis that the a_i coefficients were zero, while the b_i coefficients were always statistically significant.

The use of equations such as (1.1) for policy analysis was promoted by a number of economists at the Federal Reserve Bank of St. Louis, so regressions of nominal income on money are often called St. Louis equations (see Andersen and Jordon 1968; B. Friedman 1977a; Carlson 1978). Because the dependent variable is nominal

---

8. This is not exactly correct; because Friedman and Meiselman included "autonomous" expenditures as an explanatory variable, they also used consumption as the dependent variable (basically output minus autonomous expenditures). They also reported results for real variables as well as nominal ones. Following modern practice, equation (1.1) is expressed in terms of logs; Friedman and Meiselmen estimated their equation in levels.

income, the St. Louis approach does not address directly the issue of how a money-induced change in nominal spending is split between a change in real output and a change in the price level. The impact of money on nominal income was estimated to be quite strong, and Andersen and Jordon (1968, p. 22) concluded, "Finding of a strong empirical relationship between economic activity and ... monetary actions points to the conclusion that monetary actions can and should play a more prominent role in economic stabilization than they have up to now."[9]

The original Friedman-Meiselman result generated responses by Modigliani and Ando (1976) and De Prano and Mayer (1965), among others. This debate emphasized that an equation such as (1.1) is misspecified if m is endogenous. To illustrate the point with an extreme example, suppose the central bank is able to manipulate m to offset almost perfectly shocks that would otherwise generate fluctuations in nominal income. In this case, y^n would simply reflect the random control errors the central bank had failed to offset. As a result, m and y^n might be completely uncorrelated, and a regression of y^n on m would not reveal that money actually played an important role in affecting nominal income. If policy is able to respond to the factors generating the error term u_t, then m_t and u_t will be correlated, ordinary least squares estimates of (1.1) will be inconsistent, and the resulting estimates will depend on the manner in which policy has induced a correlation between u and m. Changes in policy that altered this correlation would also alter the least squares regression estimates that one would obtain in estimating (1.1).

1.3.2   Granger Causality

The St. Louis equation related nominal output to the past behavior of money. Similar regressions employing *real* output have also been used to investigate the connection between real economic activity and money. In an important contribution, Sims (1972) introduced the notion of *Granger causality* into the debate over the real effects of money. A variable X is said to Granger cause Y if and only if lagged values of X have marginal predictive content in a forecasting equation for Y. In practice, testing whether money Granger causes output involves testing whether the a_i coefficients equal zero in a regression of the form

$$y_t = y_0 + \sum_{i=1} a_i m_{t-i} + \sum_{i=1} b_i y_{t-i} + \sum_{i=1} c_i z_{t-i} + e_t \qquad (1.2)$$

9. B. Friedman (1977a) argued that updated estimates of the St. Louis equation did yield a role for fiscal policy, although the statistical reliability of this finding was questioned by Carlson (1978). Carlson also contains a bibliography listing many of the papers on the St. Louis equation (see his footnote 2, p. 13).

where key issues involve the treatment of trends in output and money, the choice of lag lengths, and the set of other variables (represented by z) that are included in the equation.

Sims' original work used log levels of U.S. nominal GNP and money (both M1 and the monetary base). He found evidence that money Granger caused GNP. That is, the past behavior of money helped to predict future GNP. However, using the index of industrial production to measure real output, Sims (1980) found the fraction of output variation explained by money was greatly reduced when a nominal interest rate was added to the equation (so that z consisted of the log price level and an interest rate). Thus, the conclusion seemed sensitive to the specification of z. Eichenbaum and Singleton (1986) found that money appeared to be less important if the regressions were specified in log first difference form rather than in log levels with a time trend. Stock and Watson (1989) provided a systematic treatment of the trend specification in testing whether money Granger causes real output. They concluded that money does help to predict future output (they actually use industrial production) even when prices and an interest rate are included.

A large literature has examined the value of monetary indicators in forecasting output. One interpretation of Sims' finding was that including an interest rate reduced the apparent role of money because, at least in the United States, a short-term interest rate, rather than the money supply, provided a better measure of monetary policy actions (see Chapter 9). B. Friedman and Kuttner (1992) and Bernanke and Blinder (1992), among others, have looked at the role of alternative interest rate measures in forecasting real output. Friedman and Kuttner examine the effects of alternative definitions of money and different sample periods, concluding that the relationship in the United States is unstable and has deteriorated in the 1990s. Bernanke and Blinder find the federal funds rate "dominates both money and the bill and bond rates in forecasting real variables."

Regressions of real output on money were also popularized by Barro (1977, 1978, 1979a) as a way of testing whether only unanticipated money mattered for real output. By dividing money into anticipated and unanticipated components, Barro's results suggested that only the unanticipated part affected real variables (see also Barro and Rush 1980 and the critical comment by Small 1979). Subsequent work by Mishkin (1982) found a role for anticipated money as well. Cover (1992) employs a similar approach and finds differences in the impacts of positive and negative monetary shocks. Negative shocks are estimated to have significant effects on output, while the effect of positive shocks is usually small and statistically insignificant.

1.3.3 Policy Uses

Before reviewing other evidence on the effects of money on output, it is useful to ask whether equations such as (1.2) can be used for policy purposes. That is, can a regression of this form be used to design a policy rule for setting the central bank's policy instrument? If it can, then the discussions of theoretical models that form the bulk of this book would be unnecessary, at least from the perspective of conducting monetary policy.

Suppose the estimated relationship between output and money takes the form

$$y_t = y_0 + a_0 m_t + a_1 m_{t-1} + c_1 z_t + c_2 z_{t-1} + u_t \tag{1.3}$$

Consider the problem of adjusting the money supply in order to reduce fluctuations in real output. If this objective is interpreted to mean that the money supply should be manipulated to minimize the variance of y around y_0, then m_t should be set equal to

$$m_t = -\frac{a_1}{a_0} m_{t-1} - \frac{c_2}{a_0} z_{t-1} + v_t$$

$$= \pi_1 m_{t-1} + \pi_2 z_{t-1} + v_t \tag{1.4}$$

where for simplicity we have assumed that the monetary authority's forecast of z_t is equal to zero. The term v_t represents the control error experienced by the monetary authority in setting the money supply. This represents a type of feedback rule for the money supply whose parameters are themselves determined by the estimated coefficients in the equation for y. It implies that output is affected by the systematic response of money to lagged money and lagged realizations of z. A key assumption is that the coefficients in equation (1.3) are independent of the choice of the policy rule for m. Substituting (1.4) into (1.3), output under the policy rule given in (1.4) would be equal to $y_t = y_0 + c_1 z_t + u_t + a_0 v_t$.

Notice that a policy rule has been derived using only knowledge of the policy objective (minimizing the expected variance of output) and knowledge of the estimated coefficients in (1.3). No theory of how monetary policy actually affects the economy was required. Sargent (1976) showed, however, that the use of (1.3) to derive a policy feedback rule may be inappropriate. To see why, suppose that, in fact, real output depends only on unpredicted movements in the money supply; only surprises matter, with predicted changes in money simply being reflected in price-level movements with no impact on output.[10] From (1.4), the unpredicted movement in m_t is just v_t,

10. The influential model of Lucas (1972) has this implication. See Chapter 5.

so let the true model for output determination be

$$y_t = y_0 + d_0 v_t + d_1 z_t + d_2 z_{t-1} + u_t \tag{1.5}$$

Now from (1.4), $v_t = m_t - (\pi_1 m_{t-1} + \pi_2 z_{t-1})$, so output can be equivalently expressed as

$$y_t = y_0 + d_0[m_t - (\pi_1 m_{t-1} + \pi_2 z_{t-1})] + d_1 z_t + d_2 z_{t-1} + u_t$$
$$= y_0 + d_0 m_t - d_0 \pi_1 m_{t-1} + d_1 z_t + (d_2 - d_0 \pi_2) z_{t-1} + u_t \tag{1.6}$$

which has exactly the same form as (1.3). Equation (1.3), which was initially interpreted as consistent with a situation in which systematic feedback rules for monetary policy could affect output, is *observationally equivalent* to equation (1.6), which was derived under the assumption that systematic policy had no effect and only money surprises mattered. The two are observationally equivalent since the error term in both (1.3) and (1.6) is just u; both equations fit the data equally well.

A comparison of (1.3) and (1.6) reveals another important conclusion. The coefficients of (1.6) are functions of the parameters in the policy rule (1.4). Thus, changes in the conduct of policy, interpreted to mean changes in the feedback-rule parameters, will change the parameters estimated in an equation such as (1.6) (or in a St. Louis–type regression). This is an example of the Lucas critique (Lucas 1976): empirical relationships are unlikely to be invariant to changes in policy regimes.

Of course, as Sargent stressed, it may be that (1.3) is the true structure that remains invariant as policy changes. In this case, (1.5) will not be invariant to changes in policy. To demonstrate this point, note that (1.4) implies

$$m_t = (1 - \pi_1 L)^{-1}(\pi_2 z_{t-1} + v_t)$$

where L is the lag operator.[11] Hence, we can write (1.3) as

$$y_t = y_0 + a_0 m_t + a_1 m_{t-1} + c_1 z_t + c_2 z_{t-1} + u_t$$
$$= y_0 + a_0(1 - \pi_1 L)^{-1}(\pi_2 z_{t-1} + v_t)$$
$$\quad + a_1(1 - \pi_1 L)^{-1}(\pi_2 z_{t-2} + v_{t-1}) + c_1 z_t + c_2 z_{t-1} + u_t$$
$$= (1 - \pi_1)y_0 + \pi_1 y_{t-1} + a_0 v_t + a_1 v_{t-1} + c_1 z_t$$
$$\quad + (c_2 + a_0 \pi_2 - c_1 \pi_1) z_{t-1} + (a_1 \pi_2 - c_2 \pi_1) z_{t-2} + u_t - \pi_1 u_{t-1} \tag{1.7}$$

---

11. That is, $L^i x_t = x_{t-i}$.

where we have now expressed output as a function of lagged output, the z variable, and money surprises (the v realizations). If this were interpreted as a policy-invariant expression, one would conclude that output was independent of any predictable or systematic feedback rule for monetary policy; only unpredicted money appears to matter. Yet, under the hypothesis that (1.3) is the true invariant structure, changes in the policy rule (the π_1 coefficients) will cause the coefficients in (1.7) to change.

Note that when we started with (1.5) and (1.4), we derived an expression for output that was observationally equivalent to (1.3). When we started with (1.3) and (1.4), however, we ended up with an expression for output that was not equivalent to (1.5); (1.7) contains lagged values of output and v and two lags of z, while (1.5) contains only the contemporaneous value of v and one lag of z. These differences would allow one to distinguish between the two, but they arise only because this example placed a priori restrictions on the lag lengths in (1.3) and (1.5). In general, we would not have the type of a priori information that would allow us to do so.

The lesson from this simple example is that we cannot design policy without a theory of how money affects the economy. Theory should identify whether the coefficients in a specification of the form (1.3) or in a specification such as (1.5) will remain invariant as policy changes. While output equations estimated over a single policy regime may not allow us to identify the true structure, information from several policy regimes might succeed in doing so. If a policy-regime change means that the coefficients in the policy rule (1.4) have changed, this fact would serve to identify whether an expression of the form (1.3) or one of the form (1.5) were policy invariant.

1.3.4 The VAR Approach

Most recent empirical studies of monetary policy and real economic activity have adopted a vector autoregression (VAR) framework. The use of VARs to estimate the impact of money on the economy was pioneered by Sims (1972, 1980). The development of the approach as it has moved from bivariate (Sims 1972) to trivariate (Sims 1980) to larger and larger systems, and the empirical findings the literature has produced, are summarized by Leeper, Sims, and Zha (1996).[12]

Suppose we consider a bivariate system in which y_t is a measure of real economic activity, such as the natural log of real output at time t or its growth rate and x_t is a candidate measure of monetary policy, such as a measure of the money stock or a

---

12. Two references on the econometrics of VARs are Hamilton (1994) and Maddala (1992).

short-term market rate of interest.[13] The VAR system can be written as

$$\begin{bmatrix} y_t \\ x_t \end{bmatrix} = A(L) \begin{bmatrix} y_{t-1} \\ x_{t-1} \end{bmatrix} + \begin{bmatrix} u_{yt} \\ u_{xt} \end{bmatrix} \tag{1.8}$$

where $A(L)$ is a 2×2 matrix polynomial in the lag operator L, and u_{it} is the time t serially independent innovation to variable i. These innovations can be thought of as linear combinations of independently distributed shocks to output (e_{yt}) and to policy (e_{xt}):

$$\begin{bmatrix} u_{yt} \\ u_{xt} \end{bmatrix} = \begin{bmatrix} e_{yt} + \theta e_{xt} \\ \phi e_{yt} + e_{xt} \end{bmatrix} = \begin{bmatrix} 1 & \theta \\ \phi & 1 \end{bmatrix} \begin{bmatrix} e_{yt} \\ e_{xt} \end{bmatrix} = B \begin{bmatrix} e_{yt} \\ e_{xt} \end{bmatrix} \tag{1.9}$$

The one-period-ahead error made in forecasting the policy variable x_t is equal to u_{xt}, and, since from (1.9), $u_{xt} = \phi e_{yt} + e_{xt}$, these errors are caused by the exogenous output and policy disturbances e_{yt} and e_{xt}. Letting $\sum_u$ denote the 2×2 variance-covariance matrix of the u_{it}'s, $\sum_u = B \sum_e B'$ where $\sum_e$ is the (diagonal) variance matrix of the e_{it}'s.

The random variable e_{xt} represents the exogenous shock to policy. If we wish to determine the role of policy in *causing* movements in output or other macro varia-bles, it is the effect of e_x on these variables that we need to estimate. As long as $\phi \neq 0$, the innovation to the observed policy variable x_t will depend both on the shock to policy e_{xt} and on the nonpolicy shock e_{yt}; obtaining an estimate of u_{xt} does not provide a measure of the policy shock unless $\phi = 0$.

To make the example even more explicit, suppose the VAR system is

$$\begin{bmatrix} y_t \\ x_t \end{bmatrix} = \begin{bmatrix} a_1 & a_2 \\ 0 & 0 \end{bmatrix} \begin{bmatrix} y_{t-1} \\ x_{t-1} \end{bmatrix} + \begin{bmatrix} u_{yt} \\ u_{xt} \end{bmatrix} \tag{1.10}$$

with $0 < a_1 < 1$. Then $x_t = u_{xt}$ and $y_t = a_1 y_{t-1} + u_{yt} + a_2 u_{xt-1}$, and we can write y_t in moving average form as

$$y_t = \sum_{i=0}^{\infty} a_1^i u_{yt-i} + \sum_{i=0}^{\infty} a_1^i a_2 u_{xt-i-1}$$

Estimating (1.8) yields estimates of $A(L)$ and $\sum_u$, and from these we can calculate the effects of u_{xt} on $\{y_t, y_{t+1}, \ldots\}$. If one interpreted u_x as an exogenous policy disturbance, then the implied response of $y_t, y_{t+1}, \ldots$ to a policy shock would be[14]

$$0, \quad a_2, \quad a_1 a_2, \quad a_1^2 a_2, \ldots$$

To estimate the impact of a policy shock on output, however, we need to calculate the effect on $\{y_t, y_{t+1}, \ldots\}$ of a realization of the policy shock e_{xt}. In terms of the true underlying structural disturbances e_y and e_x, equation (1.9) implies

$$y_t = \sum_{i=0}^{\infty} a_1^i (e_{yt-i} + \theta e_{xt-i}) + \sum_{i=0}^{\infty} a_1^i a_2 (e_{xt-i-1} + \phi e_{yt-i-1})$$

$$= e_{yt} + (a_1 + a_2 \phi) \sum_{i=0}^{\infty} a_1^i e_{yt-i-1} + \theta e_{xt} + (a_1 \theta + a_2) \sum_{i=0}^{\infty} a_1^i e_{xt-i-1} \quad (1.11)$$

so that the impulse response function giving the true time pattern of the response of y to the exogenous policy shock e_x is

$$\theta, \quad a_1 \theta + a_2, \quad a_1(a_1 \theta + a_2), \quad a_1^2(a_1 \theta + a_2), \ldots$$

and involves the elements of $A(L)$ *and* the elements of B. And while $A(L)$ can be estimated from (1.8), B and $\sum_e$ are not identified without further restrictions.[15]

Two basic approaches to solving this identification problem have been followed. The first imposes additional restrictions on the matrix B that links the observable VAR residuals to the underlying structural disturbances (see equation 1.9). This approach has been used by Sims (1972, 1988), Bernanke (1986), Walsh (1987), Bernanke and Blinder (1992), Gordon and Leeper (1994), and Bernanke and Mihov (1996), among many others. If policy shocks affect output with a lag, for example, the restriction that $\theta = 0$ would allow the other parameters of the model to be identified. The second approach achieves identification by imposing restrictions on the long-run effects of the disturbances on observed variables. For example, the assumption of long-run neutrality of money would imply that a monetary policy shock (e_x) has no long-run permanent effect on output. In terms of the example that led to equation (1.11), suppose y is the growth rate of real output. Then long-run neutrality of the policy shock would imply that $\theta + (a_1 \theta + a_2) \sum a_1^i = 0$ or $\theta = -a_2$. Examples

---

14. This represents the response to a nonorthogonalized innovation. The basic point, however, is that if θ and ϕ are nonzero, the underlying shocks are not identified, so the estimated response to u_x or to the component of u_x that is orthogonal to u_y will not identify the response to the policy shock e_x.

15. In this example, the three elements of $\sum_u$, the two variances and the covariance term, are functions of the four unknown parameters: ϕ, θ, and the variances of e_y and e_x.

of this approach include Blanchard and Watson (1986), Blanchard (1989), Blanchard and Quah (1989), Judd and Trehan (1989), Hutchison and Walsh (1992), and Galí (1992).

In Sims (1972), the nominal money supply (M1) was treated as the measure of monetary policy (the x variable), and policy shocks were identified by assuming that $\phi = 0$. This approach corresponds to the assumption that the money supply is predetermined and that policy innovations are exogenous with respect to the nonpolicy innovations (see equation 1.9). In this case, $u_{xt} = e_{xt}$, so from the fact that $u_{yt} = \theta e_{xt} + e_{yt} = \theta u_{xt} + e_{yt}$, θ can be estimated from the regression of the VAR residuals u_{yt} on the VAR residuals u_{xt}.[16] This corresponds to a situation in which the policy variable x does not respond contemporaneously to output shocks, perhaps because of information lags in formulating policy. However, if x depends contemporaneously on nonpolicy disturbances as well as policy shocks (i.e., $\phi \neq 0$), using u_{xt} as an estimate of e_{xt} will compound the effects of e_{yt} on u_{xt} with the effects of policy actions.

An alternative approach seeks a policy measure for which $\theta = 0$ is a plausible assumption; this corresponds to the assumption that policy shocks have no contemporaneous impact on output.[17] This type of restriction is imposed by Bernanke and Blinder (1992) and Bernanke and Mihov (1996). How reasonable such an assumption might be clearly depends on the unit of observation. In annual data, the assumption of no contemporaneous effect would be implausible; with monthly data, it might be much more plausible.

This discussion has, for simplicity, treated both y and x as scalars. In fact, neither assumption is appropriate. We are usually interested in the effects of policy on several dimensions of an economy's macroeconomic performance, and policy is likely to respond to unemployment and inflation, as well as other variables, so y would normally be a vector of nonpolicy variables. Then, the restriction that corresponds to either $\phi = 0$ or $\theta = 0$ may be less easily justified. While one might argue that policy does not respond contemporaneously to unemployment when the analysis involves data at a monthly frequency, this is not likely to be the case with respect to market interest rates. And, using the same example, one might be comfortable assuming the current month's unemployment rate is unaffected by current policy actions, but this assumption would not be true of interest rates, since financial markets will respond immediately to policy actions.

In addition, there generally is no clear scalar choice for the policy variable x. If policy were framed in terms of strict targets for the money supply, for a specific

16. This represents a Choleski decomposition of the VAR residuals with the policy variable ordered first.

17. And represents a Choleski decomposition with output ordered before the policy variable.

measure of banking sector reserves, or for a particular short-term interest rate, then the definition of x might be straightforward. In general, however, several candidate measures of monetary policy will be available, all depending in various degree on both policy actions and on nonpolicy disturbances. What constitutes an appropriate candidate for x, and how x depends on nonpolicy disturbances, will depend on the operating procedures the monetary authority is following as it implements policy.

1.3.4.1 Money and Output Sims (1992) provides a useful summary of the VAR evidence on money and output from France, Germany, Japan, the United Kingdom, and the United States. He estimates separate VARs for each country, using a common specification that includes industrial production, consumer prices, a short-term interest rate as the measure of monetary policy, a measure of the money supply, an exchange-rate index, and an index of commodity prices. Sims orders the interest-rate variable first. This procedure corresponds to the assumption that $\phi = 0$; innovations to the interest-rate variable potentially affect the other variables contemporaneously (Sims uses monthly data), while the interest rate is not affected contemporaneously by innovations in any of the other variables.[18]

The response of real output to an interest-rate innovation is similar for all five of the countries Sims examines. In all cases, monetary shocks lead to an output response that is usually described as following a hump-shaped pattern. The negative output effects of a contractionary shock, for example, build to a peak after several months and then gradually die out.

Eichenbaum (1992) presents a comparison of the estimated effects of monetary policy in the United States using alternative measures of policy shocks, discussing how different choices can produce puzzling results, or at least puzzling relative to certain theoretical expectations. He based his discussion on the results obtained from a VAR containing four variables: the price level and output (these correspond to the elements of y in equation 1.8), M1 as a measure of the money supply, and the federal funds rate as a measure of short-term interest rates (these correspond to the elements of x). He considers interpreting shocks to M1 as policy shocks versus the alternative of interpreting funds-rate shocks as policy shocks. He finds that a positive innovation to M1 is followed by an increase in the federal funds rate and a *decline* in output. This result is puzzling if M1 shocks are interpreted as measuring the impact of monetary policy. An expansionary monetary policy shock would be expected to lead to increases in both M1 and output. The interest rate was also found to rise after a

---

18. Sims notes that the correlations among the VAR residuals, the u_{it}'s, are small, so that the ordering has little impact on his results (i.e., sample estimates of ϕ and θ are small).

positive M1 shock, also a potentially puzzling result; a standard model in which money demand varies inversely with the nominal interest rate would suggest that an increase in money supply would require a decline in the nominal rate to restore money-market equilibrium. D. Gordon and Leeper (1994) show that a similar puzzle emerges using total reserves to measure monetary policy shocks, finding positive reserve innovations to be associated with increases in short-term interest rates and unemployment increases. The suggestion that a rise in reserves or the money supply might raise, not lower, market interest rates generated a large literature that attempted to search for a liquidity effect of changes in the money supply (e.g., Reichenstein 1987; Christiano and Eichenbaum 1992a; Leeper and Gordon 1992; Strongin 1995; Hamilton 1996).

When Eichenbaum used innovations in the short-term interest rate as a measure of monetary policy actions, a positive shock to the funds rate represented a contractionary policy shock. No output puzzle was found in this case; a positive interest-rate shock was followed by a decline in the output measure. Instead, what has been called the *price puzzle* emerges; a contractionary policy shock is followed by a *rise* in the price level. The effect is small and temporary (and barely statistically significant) but still puzzling. The most commonly accepted explanation for the price puzzle is that it reflects the fact that the variables included in the VAR do not span the information available to the Fed in setting the funds rate. Suppose the Fed tends to raise the funds rate whenever it forecasts that inflation might rise in the future. To the extent that the Fed is unable to offset the factors that led it to forecast higher inflation, or to the extent that the Fed acts too late to prevent inflation from rising, the increase in the funds rate will be followed by a rise in prices. This interpretation would be consistent with the price puzzle. One solution is to include commodity prices or other asset prices in the VAR. Since these prices tend to be sensitive to changing forecasts of future inflation, they serve to proxy for some of the Fed's additional information (Sims 1992; Chari, Christiano, and Eichenbaum 1995; Bernanke and Mihov 1996). Sims (1992) shows that the price puzzle is not just confined to U.S. studies. He reports VAR estimates of monetary policy effects for France, Germany, Japan, and the United Kingdom, as well as for the United States, and in all cases, a positive shock to the interest rate leads to a positive price response. These tend to become smaller, but do not in all cases disappear, when a commodity price index and nominal exchange rate are included in the VAR.

1.3.4.2   The Funds Rate as a Measure of U.S. Monetary Policy   One difficulty in measuring the impact of monetary policy shocks arises when operating procedures change over time. The best measure of policy during one period may no longer accurately reflect policy in another period if the implementation of policy has changed. Many authors have argued that over most of the last 35 years the federal funds rate has been the key policy instrument in the United States, suggesting that unforecasted changes in this interest rate may provide good estimates of policy shocks. This view has been argued, for example, by Bernanke and Blinder (1992) and Bernanke and Mihov (1996). While the Fed's operating procedures have varied over time,[19] the funds rate is likely to be the best indicator of policy in the United States during the pre-1979 period and during the post-1982 period. Policy during the period 1979–1982 is less adequately characterized by the funds rate.[20] Since our objective in this section is only to give a general sense of the empirical evidence on the impact of policy shocks, we will use the funds rate as an indicator of policy and restrict attention to the 1965–1979 and 1982–1993 periods.

Figure 1.4 and Table 1.1 are based on a VAR estimated using monthly data for the period 1965:01 to 1979:09. The four variables are the log of the CPI,[21] a measure of output, the log of M1, and the federal funds rate. Because GDP is not available at a monthly frequency, standard practice has been to use a variable such as the Federal Reserve's Index of Industrial Production as the monthly measure of real economic activity.[22] This provides a much narrower index of activity than does GDP, so the estimates reported here use instead the log of the Department of Commerce's Index of Coincident Indicators (ICI) as the proxy for real activity.[23] The log of M1 is included as a measure of the money supply, and the funds rate (FF) is included as a measure of short-term market interest rates. By ordering the funds rate last, the identifying restriction is that the other variables do not respond contemporaneously to a shock to the funds rate ($\theta = 0$ in terms of equation 1.9). Given that the results are based on monthly data, this is probably a reasonable restriction.

19. Chapter 9 provides a brief history of Fed operating procedures.

20. During this period, nonborrowed reserves were set to achieve a level of interest rates consistent with the desired monetary growth targets. In this case, the funds rate may still provide a satisfactory policy indicator. Cook (1989) finds that most changes in the funds rate during the 1979–1982 period reflected policy actions. See Chapter 9 for a discussion of operating procedures and the reserve market.

21. The CPI was redefined beginning in January 1983 to incorporate a rental-equivalent measure of housing costs to reduce biases arising from the previous treatment of mortgage interest rates. The official CPI was used in the VAR for 1965:01–1966:12, when inflation was still relatively low, and after 1983:01. From 1967:01 to 1982:12, I use an unofficial series constructed by the Bureau of Labor Statistics designed to be consistent with the post-1983 definition.

22. Bernanke and Mihov (1996) report VAR estimates using a monthly GDP series that they have constructed.

23. See Walsh and Wilcox (1995).

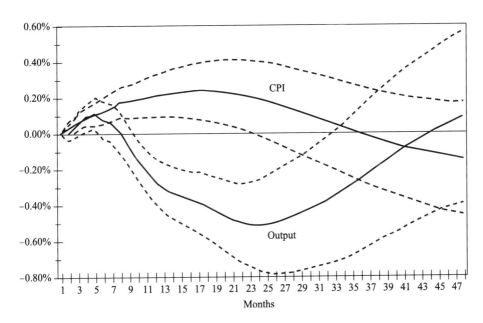

Figure 1.4
Output and Price Response to a Funds-Rate Shock (1965–1979)

Table 1.1
ICI Variance Decompositions (1965:01–1979:09, Percent)

Period	Shock to			
	CPI	ICI	M2	FF
0	0.3	99.7	0	0
6	3.7	76.9	7.6	11.9
12	25.1	49.6	9.8	15.5
18	32.6	33.1	9.2	25.1
24	27.7	26.0	18.9	27.4
36	20.4	23.5	39.5	16.6

Figure 1.4 shows impulse responses of output and the price level obtained when the funds rate is taken as the measure of monetary policy. Exogenous shocks to the funds rate have transitory output effects that die out over time but that leave the funds rate above its baseline for more than a year. Output (as measured by ICI) follows a hump-shaped pattern in response to a contractionary policy shock. Although the response is statistically insignificant for most of the first year after a shock, output then declines below the baseline with the peak effect not occurring until two years after the shock. This humped pattern is a very common finding (see, for example, Leeper, Sims, and Zha 1996 for U.S. evidence, and Sims 1992 for international evidence). The price puzzle is also illustrated in Figure 1.4; contractionary monetary policy is estimated to lead initially to a rise in the price level.

To gauge whether monetary policy shocks have had much role in accounting for movements in the nonpolicy variables, Table 1.1 reports variance decompositions for various time horizons based on the 1965–1979 estimation period. Each row shows the fraction of the n-step ahead forecast error variance for the output measure ICI that is attributed to shocks to the column variable. While policy shocks account for 12% of the output forecast error variance at a six-month horizon, this rises to 27% after two years. Monetary policy shocks, at least as measured by the funds rate during the period in which the Fed employed a funds-rate operating procedure, played an important role in output fluctuations. Both the impulse response functions and the variance decompositions indicate that the major impact of policy shocks, however, only occurs with quite a long lag.

Reestimating the monthly VAR system using data from 1983–1994 yields impulse response estimates whose general qualitative pattern is similar to that for the 1965–1979 period. However, the variance decompositions for the 1983–1994 period, shown in Table 1.2, differ significantly from those reported in Table 1.1. The estimates suggest that exogenous monetary policy shocks have played very little role in

Table 1.2
ICI Variance Decompositions (1983:01–1994:12, Percent)

| Period | Shock to | | | |
	CPI	ICI	M2	FF
0	0.6	99.4	0	0
6	4.8	94.2	0.4	0.7
12	17.0	79.5	0.7	2.8
18	28.5	68.0	1.0	2.5
24	36.3	56.5	1.7	5.5
36	31.7	40.8	3.5	23.9

accounting for U.S. short-run output fluctuations during this period, a conclusion consistent with that of Leeper, Sims, and Zha (1996).

While researchers have disagreed on the best means of identifying policy shocks, there has been surprising consensus on the general nature of the economic responses to monetary policy shocks. A variety of VARs estimated for a number of countries all indicate that, in response to a policy shock, output follows a hump-shaped pattern in which the peak impact occurs several quarters after the initial shock. Monetary policy actions appear to be taken in anticipation of inflation, so that a price puzzle emerges if forward-looking variables such as commodity prices are not included in the VAR.

If monetary policy shocks cause output movements, how important have these shocks been in accounting for actual business-cycle fluctuations? Leeper, Sims, and Zha conclude that monetary policy shocks have been relatively unimportant. However, their assessment is based on monthly data for the period from the beginning of 1960 until early 1996. This sample contains several distinct periods characterized by differences in the procedures used by the Fed to implement monetary policy. As Tables 1.1 and 1.2 suggest, the importance of monetary policy disturbances for fluctuations in U.S. real economic activity may have varied considerably over the past 35 years.

1.3.4.3 Criticisms of the VAR Approach   Measures of monetary policy based on the estimation of VARs have been criticized on several grounds.[24] First, some of the impulse responses do not accord with most economists' priors. In particular, the price puzzle, the finding that a contractionary policy shock, as measured by a funds-rate shock, tends to be followed by a rise in the price level is troublesome. As noted earlier, the price puzzle can be solved by including oil prices or commodity prices in the VAR system, and the generally accepted interpretation is that, lacking these inflation-sensitive prices, a standard VAR misses important information that is available to policy makers. A related but more general point is that many of the VAR models used to assess monetary policy fail to incorporate forward-looking variables. Central banks look at lots of information in setting policy. Because policy is likely to respond to forecasts of future economic conditions, VARs may attribute the subsequent movements in output and inflation to the policy action. However, the argument that puzzling results indicate a misspecification implicitly imposes a prior belief about what the correct effects of monetary shocks should look like. Eichenbaum (1992), in fact, argues that short-term interest-rate innovations have been used to

24. These criticisms are detailed in Rudebusch (1997).

represent policy shocks in VARs because they produce the type of impulse response functions for output that economists expect.

In addition, the residuals from the VAR regressions that are used to represent exogenous policy shocks often bear little resemblance to standard interpretations of the historical record of past policy actions and periods of contractionary and expansionary policy (Sheffrin 1995; Rudebusch 1997). They also differ considerably depending on the particular specification of the VAR. Rudebusch reports low correlations between the residual policy shocks he obtains based on funds rate futures and those obtained from a VAR by Bernanke and Mihov. How important this finding is depends on the question of interest. If the objective is to determine whether a particular recession was caused by a policy shock, then it is important to know if and when the policy shock occurred. If alternative specifications provide differing and possibly inconsistent estimates of when policy shocks occurred, then their usefulness as a tool of economic history would be limited. If, however, the question of interest is how the economy responds when a policy shock occurs, then the discrepancies among the VAR residual estimates may be of less importance. Sims (1996) argues that in a simple supply-demand model, different authors using different supply-curve shifters may obtain quite similar estimates of the demand-curve slope (since they all obtain consistent estimators of the true slope). At the same time, they may obtain quite different residuals for the estimated supply curve. If our true interest is in the parameters of the demand curve, the variations in the estimates of the supply shocks may not be of importance. Thus, the type of historical analysis based on a VAR as in Walsh (1993) is likely to be more problematic than the use of a VAR to determine the way the economy responds to exogenous policy shocks.

While VARs focus on residuals that are interpreted as policy shocks, the systematic part of the estimated VAR equation for a variable such as the funds rate can be interpreted as a policy reaction function; it provides a description of how the policy instrument has been adjusted in response to lagged values of the other variables included in the VAR system. Rudebusch (1997) has argued that the implied policy reaction functions look quite different than results obtained from more direct attempts to estimate reaction functions or to model actual policy behavior.[25] A related point is that VARs are typically estimated using final, revised data and will therefore not capture accurately the historical behavior of the monetary policy maker who is reacting to preliminary and incomplete data. Woolley (1995) shows how the per-

25. For example, Taylor (1993a) has employed a simple interest-rate rule that closely matches the actual behavior of the federal funds rate in recent years. As Khoury (1990) notes in her survey of many studies of the Fed reaction function, few systematic conclusions have emerged from this empirical literature.

ception of the stance of monetary policy in the United States in 1972, and President Richard Nixon's attempts to pressure Fed Chairman Arthur F. Burns into adopting a more expansionary policy, were based on initial data on the money supply that were subsequently very significantly revised.

Finally, at best the VAR approach identifies only the effects of monetary policy shocks, shifts in policy unrelated to the endogenous response of policy to developments in the economy. Yet most, if not all, of what one thinks of in terms of policy and policy design represents the endogenous response of policy to the economy. So it is unfortunate that a primary empirical tool—VAR analysis—used to assess the impact of monetary policy is uninformative about the role played by policy rules. If policy is completely characterized as a feedback rule on the economy, so that there are no exogenous policy shocks, then the VAR methodology would conclude that monetary policy doesn't matter. Yet while monetary policy is not causing output movements in this example, it does not follow that policy is unimportant; the response of the economy to nonpolicy shocks may depend importantly on the way monetary policy endogenously adjusts.

1.3.5   Structural Econometric Models

The empirical assessment of the effects of alternative feedback rules for monetary policy has traditionally been carried out using structural macroeconometric models. During the 1960s and early 1970s, the specification, estimation, use, and evaluation of large-scale econometric models for forecasting and policy analysis represented a major research agenda in macroeconomics. Important contributions to our understanding of investment, consumption, the term structure, and other aspects of the macroeconomy grew out of the need to develop structural equations for various sectors of the economy. An equation describing the behavior of a policy instrument such as the federal funds rate was incorporated into these structural models, allowing model simulations of alternative policy rules to be conducted. These simulations would provide an estimate of the impact on the economy's dynamic behavior of changes in the way policy was conducted. For example, a policy under which the funds rate was adjusted rapidly in response to unemployment movements could be contrasted with one in which the response was more muted.

A key maintained hypothesis, one necessary to justify this type of analysis, was that the estimated parameters of the model would be invariant to the specification of the policy rule. If this were not the case, then one could no longer treat the model's parameters as unchanged when altering the monetary policy rule (as the example in section 1.3.3 shows). In a devastating critique of this assumption, Lucas (1976) argued that economic theory predicts that the decision rules for investment, consumption, and expectations formation will not be invariant to shifts in the systematic behavior of policy. The Lucas critique emphasized the problems inherent in the assumption, common in the structural econometric models of the time, that expectations adjusted adaptively to past outcomes.

While large-scale econometric models of aggregate economies continued to play an important role in discussions of monetary policy, they fell out of favor among academic economists during the 1970s, in large part as a result of Lucas's critique, the increasing emphasis on the role of expectations in theoretical models, and the dissatisfaction with the empirical treatment of expectations in existing large-scale models. The academic literature witnessed a continued interest in small-scale rational-expectations models, both single and multicountry versions (for example, the work by Taylor 1993b), as well as the development of larger-scale models (Fair 1984), all of which incorporated rational expectations into some or all aspects of the model's behavioral relationships. A recent example of a small model based on rational expectations and forward-looking behavior is that of Fuhrer and Moore (Fuhrer 1994a; Fuhrer and Moore 1995a, 1995b). This model is discussed in Chapter 10.

Larger-scale econometric models have proven useful to central banks in providing answers to questions related to the design and implementation of monetary policy, and within the last few years, a new generation of large-scale econometric policy models have come into use. Brayton and Tinsley (1996) and Brayton, Mauskopf, Reifschneider, Tinsley, and Williams (1997) provide a description of the new FRB/US model.[26] Levin, Rogers, and Tryon (1997) discuss the international, multicountry FRB/Global model. These econometric models are designed to address specific questions of relevance for the actual design of monetary policy. The FRB/US model is structured to allow simulations to be conducted under alternative assumptions about expectations formation.

Work reported in R. Bryant, Hooper, and Mann (1992) evaluates the implications for policy experiments of a variety of empirical econometric models. Other countries have also actively developed econometric models for policy work combining both estimated and calibrated relationships. For example, Poloz, Rose, and Tetlow (1994) describe the Bank of Canada's econometric model, while Black et al. (1997) discuss the Core Model employed at the Reserve Bank of New Zealand.

The previous section presented evidence derived from a VAR on the output effects of a funds rate shock. The VAR approach has been criticized for associating policy

---

26. Brayton and Mauskopf (1985) provide a discussion of an earlier-generation FRB model, while Brayton, Levin, Tryon, and Williams (1997) describe the evolution of the Board's macro model.

shocks with VAR residuals that do not closely correspond to other measures of
monetary policy actions. The results from a VAR analysis, such as the impulse response function shown in Figure 1.4, can be compared to the findings from a large-
scale structural model such as the FRB/US. Brayton and Tinsley (1996) report the
output effects of an increase in the funds rate. The funds rate is increased for one
quarter with its subsequent behavior determined by the estimated policy reaction
function embedded in the model. Brayton and Tinsley find an output response that
looks very similar to Figure 1.4, the response function from a simple VAR. Output
follows a hump-shaped pattern, although the peak effect occurs after slightly more
than one year in the FRB/US model simulation, while Figure 1.4 suggests that it
takes two years for output to reach its low point. When the FRB/US model is simulated using a small VAR to generate expectations, the output decline is larger and
the peak decline occurs somewhat later. As a qualitative description of the output
effects of monetary policy, however, the simple VARs give answers that are quite
similar to that of the large FRB/US structural model. The simulation of a change in
the inflation target reported by Black et al. (1997) using the New Zealand model also
yields a qualitatively similar estimate of the output effects of monetary policy.

1.3.6   Alternative Approaches

Although the VAR approach has been the most commonly used methodology in
recent years, and the results that have emerged provide a fairly consistent view of
the impact of monetary policy shocks, other approaches have also influenced views
on the role policy has played. Two such approaches, one based on deriving policy
directly from a reading of policy statements, the other based on case studies of disinflations, have influenced academic discussions of monetary policy.

1.3.6.1   Narrative Measures of Monetary Policy   An alternative to the VAR statistical approach is to develop a measure of the stance of monetary policy from a direct
examination of the policy record. In recent years, this approach has been taken by
Romer and Romer (1989) and by Boschen and Mills (1991), among others.[27]
   Boschen and Mills develop an index of policy stance that takes on integer values
from −2 (strong emphasis on inflation reduction) to +2 (strong emphasis on "pro-
moting real growth"). Their monthly index is based on a reading of the Fed's Federal Open Market Committee (FOMC) policy directives and the records of the
FOMC meetings. This index (multiplied by −1 so that a positive value represents

27. Boschen and Mills (1991) provide a discussion and comparison of some other indices of policy. For a
critical view of the Romers' approach, see Leeper (1993).

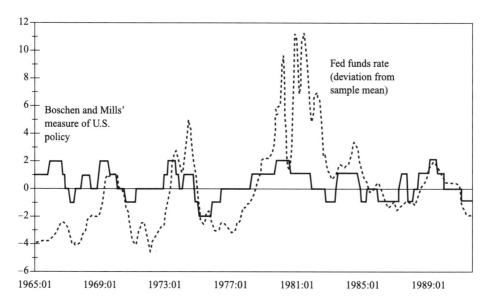

Figure 1.5
Boschen and Mills' Measure of Fed Policy Stance

a contractionary policy stance) is shown in Figure 1.5, together with the federal funds rate. Boschen and Mills show that innovations in their index corresponding to expansionary policy shifts are followed by subsequent increases in monetary aggregates and declines in the federal funds rate. They also conclude that all the narrative indices they examine yield relatively similar conclusions about the impact of policy on monetary aggregates and the funds rates. And, in support of the approach used in the previous section, Boschen and Mills conclude that the funds rate is a good indicator of monetary policy. These findings are extended in Boschen and Mills (1995a), which compares several narrative-based measures of monetary policy, finding them to be associated with permanent changes in the level of M2 and the monetary base and temporary changes in the funds rate.

Romer and Romer (1989) used the Fed's "Record of Policy Actions" and, prior to 1976 when they were discontinued, minutes of FOMC meetings, to identify episodes in which policy shifts have occurred that were designed to reduce inflation. They find six different months during the postwar period that saw such contractionary shifts in Fed policy: October 1947, September 1955, December 1968, April 1974, August 1978, and October 1979. Leeper (1993) has argued that the Romer-Romer index is equivalent to a dummy variable that picks up large interest-rate innovations.

The narrative indices of Boschen and Mills and the dating system employed by Romer and Romer to isolate episodes of contractionary policy provide a useful and informative alternative to the VAR approach that associates policy shocks with serially uncorrelated innovations. The VAR approach attempts to identify exogenous shifts in policy; the estimated effects of these exogenous shifts are the conceptual parallels to the comparative static exercises for which theoretical models make predictions. To determine whether the data are consistent with a model's predictions about the effects of an exogenous policy action, we need to isolate empirically such exogenous shifts. Doing so, however, does not yield a measure of whether policy is, on net, expansionary or contractionary.[28] The narrative indices can provide a better measure of the net stance of policy, but they capture both exogenous shifts in policy and the endogenous response of monetary policy to economic developments. It is presumably the latter that accounts for most of the changes we observe in policy variables such as the funds rate as policy responds to current and future expected economic conditions. In fact, a major conclusion of Leeper, Sims, and Zha, and one they view as not surprising, is that most movements in monetary policy instruments represent responses to the state of the economy, not exogenous policy shifts.

1.3.6.2 Case Studies of Disinflations   Case studies of specific episodes provide, in principle, an alternative means of assessing the real impact of monetary policy. Romer and Romer's approach to dating periods of contractionary monetary policy is one form of case study. However, the most influential example of this approach is that of Sargent (1986) who examined the ends of several hyperinflations. As we will discuss more fully in Chapter 5, the distinction between anticipated and unanticipated changes in monetary policy has played an important role during the past 25 years in academic discussions of monetary policy, and a key hypothesis is that anticipated changes should affect prices and inflation with little or no effect on real economic activity. This implies that a credible policy to reduce inflation should succeed in actually reducing inflation without causing a recession. This implication contrasts sharply with the view that any policy designed to reduce inflation would succeed only by inducing an economic slowdown and temporarily higher unemployment.

Sargent tested these competing hypotheses by examining the ends of the post–World War I hyperinflations in Austria, German, Hungary, and Poland. In each case, Sargent found that the hyperinflations ended abruptly. In Austria, for example, prices rose by over a factor of 20 from December 1921 to August 1922, an annual

---

28. Although Bernanke and Mihov (1996) use their VAR estimates in an attempt to develop such a measure.

inflation rate of over 8800%. Prices then stopped rising in September 1922, actually declining by more than 10% during the remainder of 1922. While unemployment did rise during the price stabilizations, Sargent concluded that the output cost "was minor compared with the $220 Billion GNP that some current analysts estimate would be lost in the United States per one percentage point inflation reduction" (Sargent, 1986, p. 55). Sargent's interpretation of the experiences in Germany, Poland, and Hungary is similar. In each case, the hyperinflation was ended by a regime shift that involved a credible change in monetary and fiscal policy designed to reduce government reliance on inflationary finance. Because the end of inflation reduced the opportunity cost of holding money, money demand grew and the actual stock of money continued to grow rapidly after prices had stabilized.

Sargent's conclusion that the output costs of these disinflations were small has been questioned, as have the lessons he drew for the moderate inflations experienced by the industrialized economies in the 1970s and early 1980s. As Sargent noted, the ends of the hyperinflations "were not isolated restrictive actions within a given set of rules of the game" but represented changes in the rules of the game, most importantly in the ability of the fiscal authority to finance expenditures by creating money. In contrast, the empirical evidence from VARs of the type discussed earlier in this chapter reflects the impact of policy changes within a given set of rules.

Schelde-Andersen (1992) and Ball (1994b) provide more recent examples of the case-study approach. In both cases, the authors examine disinflationary episodes in order to estimate the real output costs associated with reducing inflation.[29] Their cases, all involving OECD countries, represent evidence on the costs of ending moderate inflations. Ball calculates the deviation of output from trend during a period of disinflation and expresses this as a ratio to the change in trend inflation over the same period. The 65 disinflation periods he identifies in annual data yield an average sacrifice ratio of 0.77%; each percentage point reduction in inflation was associated with a 0.77% loss of output relative to trend. The estimate for the United States was among the largest, averaging 2.3 based on annual data. The sacrifice ratios are negatively related to nominal wage flexibility; countries with greater wage flexibility tend to have smaller sacrifice ratios. The costs of a disinflation also appear to be larger when inflation is brought down more gradually over a longer period of time.[30]

---

29. See also R. Gordon (1982) and R. Gordon and King (1982).

30. Brayton and Tinsley (1996) show how the costs of disinflation can be estimated under alternative assumptions about expectations and credibility using the FRB/US structural model. Their estimates of the sacrifice ratio, expressed in terms of the cumulative annual unemployment-rate increase per percentage point decrease in the inflation rate, range from 2.6 under imperfect credibility and VAR expectations to 1.3 under perfect credibility and VAR expectations. Under full-model expectations, the sacrifice ratio is 2.3 with imperfect credibility and 1.7 with full credibility.

The case-study approach can provide interesting evidence on the real effects of monetary policy. Unfortunately, as with the VAR and other approaches, the issue of identification needs to be addressed. To what extent have disinflations been exogenous, so that any resulting output or unemployment movements can be attributed to the decision to reduce inflation? If policy actions depend on whether they are anticipated or not, then estimates of the cost of disinflating obtained by averaging over episodes, episodes that are likely to have differed considerably in terms of whether the policy actions were expected or, if announced, credible, may yield little information about the costs of ending any specific inflation.

1.4 Summary

The consensus from the empirical literature on the long-run relationship between money, prices, and output is clear. Money growth and inflation essentially display a correlation of 1; the correlation between money growth or inflation and real output growth is probably close to zero, although it may be slightly positive at low inflation rates and negative at high rates.

The consensus from the empirical literature on the short-run effects of money is that exogenous monetary policy shocks produce hump-shaped movements in real economic activity. The peak effects occur after a lag of several quarters (as much as two or three years in some of the estimates) and then die out. The exact manner in which policy is measured makes a difference, and using an incorrect measure of monetary policy can significantly affect the empirical estimates one obtains.

There is less consensus, however, on the effects, not of policy shocks, but of the role played by the systematic feedback responses of monetary policy. Structural econometric models have the potential to fill this gap, and they are widely used in policy-making settings. Disagreement over the "true" structure and the potential dependence of estimated relationships on the policy regime have, however, posed problems for the structural modeling approach. A major theme of the next nine chapters is that the endogenous response of monetary policy to economic developments can have important implications for the empirical relationships observed among macroeconomic variables.

2 Money in a General Equilibrium Framework

2.1 Introduction

The neoclassical growth model, due to Ramsey (1928) and Solow (1956), provides the basic framework for much of modern macroeconomics. Solow's growth model has just three key ingredients: a production function allowing for smooth substitutability between labor and capital in the production of output, a capital accumulation process in which a fixed fraction of output is devoted to investment each period, and a labor-supply process in which the quantity of labor input grows at an exogenously given rate. Solow showed that such an economy would converge to a steady-state growth path along which output, the capital stock, and the effective supply of labor all grew at the same rate.

When the assumption of a fixed savings rate is replaced by a model of forward-looking households choosing savings to maximize lifetime utility, the Solow model becomes the foundation for dynamic stochastic models of the business cycle. Productivity shocks or other real disturbances affect output and savings behavior, with the resultant effect on capital accumulation propagating the effects of the original shock over time in ways that can mimic some features of actual business cycles (see Cooley 1995).

The neoclassical growth model is a model of a nonmonetary economy, and while goods are exchanged and transactions must be taking place, there is no medium of exchange—that is, no "money"—that is used to facilitate these transactions. Nor is there an asset, like money, that has a zero nominal rate of return and is therefore dominated in rate of return by other interest-bearing assets. To employ the neoclassical framework to analyze monetary issues, a role for money must be specified so that the agents will wish to hold positive quantities of money. A positive demand for money is necessary if, in equilibrium, money is to have positive value.[1]

Money has been incorporated into general equilibrium models in several ways. All involve shortcuts in one form or another; some aspects of the economic environment are simply specified exogenously in order to introduce a role for money. This can be a useful device, allowing one to focus attention on questions of primary interest without being unduly distracted by secondary issues. But our confidence in the ability of a model to answer the questions we bring to it is reduced if those aspects that are

---

1. This is just another way of saying that we would like the money price of goods to be bounded. If the price of goods in terms of money is denoted by P, then one unit of money will purchase $1/P$ units of goods. If money has positive value, $1/P > 0$ and P is bounded ($0 < P < \infty$). Bewley (1983) refers to the issue of why money has positive value as the "Hahn problem" (Hahn 1965).

simply specified exogenously appear to be critical to the issue of focus. An important consideration in evaluating different approaches will be to determine whether conclusions generalize beyond the specific model or are dependent on the exact manner in which a role for money has been introduced. We will see examples of results that are robust, such as the connection between money growth and inflation, and others that are sensitive to the specification of money's role, such as the impact of inflation on the steady-state capital stock.

Section 2.2 presents a model, originally due to Tobin (1965), that incorporates money into a Solow framework but without incorporating optimizing behavior on the part of economic agents. In this formulation, it is simply postulated that there exists a well-defined demand for money. This approach cannot provide insight into why money is held, but it is useful in highlighting an important channel through which inflation might affect economic welfare—higher inflation induces a substitution away from financial assets and into physical capital.

We then turn in section 2.3 to a model based on optimizing behavior by individual economic agents. In this case, one cannot just assume a demand for money; one needs to show that, given the environment within which they operate, agents will choose to hold positive amounts of money. The basic model is due originally to Sidrauski (1967) and is built on the assumption that money enters directly into the utility function of the representative agent. This "money-in-the-utility-function," or MIU, framework implies a quite different relationship between average inflation and the capital stock in steady-state equilibrium than was implied by Tobin's model. To better understand the role of money in such a framework, a log-linear approximation for which analytic solutions can be derived is also studied. This will allow us to calculate the macro time-series behavior that the model implies. We can then determine whether the model is capable of generating the type of time-series behavior we actually observe in macroeconomic data, as well as assess the quantitative effects of inflation on the real economy.

2.2   The Tobin Effect

The only asset in the Solow neoclassical growth model (Solow 1956) is physical capital, so the decision to save is equivalent to the decision to accumulate physical capital. Tobin (1965) provided a monetary version by introducing money as a second asset; household wealth can take the form of physical capital or holdings of money. Consequently, there is both a savings decision (an asset-accumulation decision) and a portfolio decision (an asset-allocation decision).

As with the Solow model, we begin with the production function, assumed to be linear homogenous so that output per capita can be expressed as a function of capital per capita:[2]

$$y_t = f(k_{t-1}) \qquad (2.1)$$

Note the assumption that output is produced in period t using capital carried over from period $t-1$. The production function is assumed to be continuously differentiable and to satisfy the usual Inada conditions $[f_k \geq 0, f_{kk} \leq 0, \lim_{k \to 0} f_k(k) = \infty, \lim_{k \to \infty} f_k(k) = 0]$.

Households, assumed to be identical, can hold both physical capital (or ownership claims to the economy's physical capital) and money. Real wealth per capita in period t then consists of k_t, and real money balances $m_t = M_t/P_t N_t$ where M_t is the nominal quantity of money, P_t is the price level, and N_t is the population:

$$a_t \equiv k_t + m_t \qquad (2.2)$$

The only role of the government in the model is to make lump-sum transfers of money to the private sector (this introduces a means of changing the money stock). Denote the real value (per capita) of these transfers by τ. Letting uppercase letters denote economy-wide values, real aggregate household income consists of output, the monetary transfer, and any change in the real value of money holdings arising from changes in the price level: $Y_t + \tau_t N_t - \frac{\pi_t}{1+\pi_t} \frac{M_{t-1}}{P_{t-1}}$, where π is the inflation rate, defined as the percentage rate of change in the aggregate price level. The term $-\frac{\pi_t}{1+\pi_t} \frac{M_{t-1}}{P_{t-1}}$ represents the capital loss due to the decline in the real value of the household sector's money holdings as the price level rises.[3]

If we follow Solow's original model and assume there is a fixed savings rate out of real income, asset accumulation will equal the savings rate, s, times household income:

$$\Delta K_t + \Delta \frac{M_t}{P_t} = s \left(Y_t + \tau_t N_t - \frac{\pi_t}{1+\pi_t} \frac{M_{t-1}}{P_{t-1}} \right) \qquad (2.3)$$

where K is the aggregate capital stock and where for any variable x_t, Δx_t denotes

---

2. That is, if $Y = F(K, N)$, where Y is output, K the capital stock, and N labor input, and $F(\lambda K, \lambda N) = \lambda F(K, N) = \lambda Y$, we can write $Y/N \equiv y = F(K, N)/N = F(K/N, 1) \equiv f(k)$. In general, a lowercase letter will denote the per capita value of the corresponding uppercase variable.

3. The capital loss is equal to $(M_{t-1}/P_t) - (M_{t-1}/P_{t-1}) = \left(\frac{P_{t-1}}{P_t} - 1 \right) (M_{t-1}/P_{t-1}) = \left(\frac{1}{1+\pi_t} - 1 \right) (M_{t-1}/P_{t-1}) = -\frac{\pi_t}{1+\pi_t} \frac{M_{t-1}}{P_{t-1}}$. If prices are declining, $\pi_t < 0$ and this term represents a capital gain.

$x_t - x_{t-1}$. We need to rearrange this equation to put it into a more convenient form involving per capita quantities. With $k_t \equiv K_t/N_t$,

$$\Delta k_t = k_t - k_{t-1} = \frac{\Delta K_t}{N_t} - \frac{n_t}{1 + n_t} k_{t-1} \tag{2.4}$$

where $n_t = \Delta N_t/N_{t-1}$ is the population growth rate. Dividing both sides of (2.3) by N_t, and using the result to eliminate $\dfrac{\Delta K_t}{N_t}$ from (2.4), we obtain

$$\Delta k_t = \left[s\left(y_t + \tau_t - \frac{\pi_t}{1 + \pi_t} \frac{m_{t-1}}{1 + n_t} \right) - \left(\Delta \frac{M_t}{P_t} \right)\left(\frac{1}{N_t} \right) \right] - \frac{n_t}{1 + n_t} k_{t-1}$$

Since $y_t = f(k_{t-1})$,

$$\Delta k_t = s\left[f(k_{t-1}) + \tau_t - \frac{\pi_t}{1 + \pi_t} \frac{m_{t-1}}{1 + n_t} \right]$$
$$- \left[\frac{\theta_t - \pi_t}{(1 + \pi_t)(1 + n_t)} \right] m_{t-1} - \frac{n_t}{1 + n_t} k_{t-1} \tag{2.5}[4]$$

where θ_t denotes the growth rate of the stock of nominal money, $\Delta M_t/M_{t-1}$.

Changes in the nominal stock of money are engineered through lump-sum transfers, so τ_t is equal to the real per capita value of the change in the nominal quantity of money, or $\tau_t = (\Delta M_t)/P_t N_t = \dfrac{\theta_t}{(1 + \pi_t)(1 + n_t)} m_{t-1}$. This means we can rewrite (2.5) as

$$\Delta k_t = sf(k_{t-1}) - (1 - s)\frac{\theta_t - \pi_t}{(1 + \pi_t)(1 + n_t)} m_{t-1} - \frac{n_t}{1 + n_t} k_{t-1} \tag{2.6}$$

The change in the capital stock per worker is equal to savings per worker net of additions to real money holdings per worker, minus the investment necessary to equip new entrants to the labor force with the current level of capital per capita. Notice that while real money holdings grow by $\dfrac{\theta_t - \pi_t}{(1 + \pi_t)(1 + n_t)} m_{t-1}$, they "absorb" $(1 - s)\dfrac{\theta_t - \pi_t}{(1 + \pi_t)(1 + n_t)} m_{t-1}$ of real savings. This is because the transfer of money is

4. In deriving (2.15), we have used the fact that $\left(\Delta \dfrac{M_t}{P_t} \right)\dfrac{1}{N_t} = \left(\dfrac{M_t}{P_t} - \dfrac{M_{t-1}}{P_{t-1}} \right)\dfrac{1}{N_t} = \left(\dfrac{M_t P_{t-1}}{M_{t-1} P_t} \dfrac{N_{t-1}}{N_t} - \dfrac{N_{t-1}}{N_t} \right)\dfrac{M_{t-1}}{P_{t-1} N_{t-1}} = \left[\dfrac{1 + \theta_t}{(1 + \pi_t)(1 + n_t)} - \dfrac{1}{1 + n_t} \right] m_{t-1} = \dfrac{\theta_t - \pi_t}{(1 + \pi_t)(1 + n_t)} m_{t-1}.$

viewed as income and therefore raises total savings on the part of households, but only by a fraction $s < 1$ of the rise in money holdings. Thus, real savings are diverted from capital accumulation to the accumulation of real money balances. Here we have the key to the effect that the introduction of money will have on the capital stock. Variations in $\dfrac{\theta_t - \pi_t}{(1 + \pi_t)(1 + n_t)}\, m_{t-1}$ (and we have not yet discussed what might cause such variations) will cause variations in the economy's investment in physical capital.

Now assume that population growth and the growth rate of the nominal money stock are constant and consider an equilibrium in which the per capita quantities of capital and real money balances are constant. Let x^{ss} denote the steady-state value of a variable x. In a steady state, with m and k constant, $\Delta k^{ss} = \Delta m^{ss} = 0$. The fact that

$$\Delta m^{ss} = \left[\frac{1 + \theta}{(1 + \pi)(1 + n)} - 1 \right] m^{ss} = 0 \text{ implies}$$

$$1 + \pi^{ss} = \frac{1 + \theta}{1 + n} \tag{2.7}$$

Thus, the rate of inflation is directly determined by the rate of growth of the nominal supply of money.

With $\Delta k^{ss} = 0$, (2.6) then implies

$$sf(k^{ss}) = (1 - s)\frac{\theta - \pi}{(1 + \pi)(1 + n)}\, m^{ss} + \frac{n}{1 + n}\, k^{ss} \tag{2.8}$$

Letting $\bar{n} = n/(1 + n)$ and substituting (2.7) into (2.8) yields

$$sf(k^{ss}) = (1 - s)\bar{n}m^{ss} + \bar{n}k^{ss} = [(1 - s)\phi^{ss} + 1]\bar{n}k^{ss} \tag{2.9}$$

where $\phi \equiv m/k$ characterizes the portfolio composition of wealth between physical capital and money.[5] When $\phi = 0$, equation (2.9) reduces to the standard steady-state equation in discrete time for the basic nonmonetary Solow neoclassical growth model [$sf(k^{ss}) = \bar{n}k^{ss}$].

Equation (2.9) implies that this model exhibits the property of *monetary neutrality*: proportional changes in the nominal money supply and the aggregate price level leave the real equilibrium unaffected. This property follows from the fact that M

---

5. To obtain (2.9), note that in the steady state $\dfrac{\theta - \pi}{(1 + \pi)(1 + n)} = \dfrac{(1 + \theta) - (1 + \pi)}{(1 + \theta)} = 1 - \dfrac{1}{1 + n} = \dfrac{n}{1 + n} = \bar{n}$ since (2.7) implies $(1 + \pi)(1 + n) = 1 + \theta$.

only appears in the form M/P (actually, it appears in the per capita form $m = M/PN$), and it implies that changes in the level of M affect the level of P and not the real equilibrium.

In the Solow model, the steady-state condition for a constant capital-labor ratio requires that the amount of savings (and therefore, investment) per capita, $sf(k)$, just equals the investment needed to equip the increased population with the existing capital-labor ratio ($\bar{n}k$). In Tobin's model, condition (2.9) includes the term $(1 - s)\bar{n}m$; income is increased by the transfer net of inflation (this is equal to $\bar{n}m$), of which $(1 - s)\bar{n}m$ is consumed. Hence, net savings available for capital accumulation is $sf(k) - (1 - s)\bar{n}m$. When this equals the investment needed to maintain a constant capital-labor ratio ($\bar{n}k$), the economy remains in a steady state.

If the ratio of real money balances to capital is treated for the moment as a parameter, the effect of a change in ϕ can be illustrated using Figure 2.1, which is based on a standard representation of the Solow growth model. The horizontal axis measures the capital labor ratio k. The steady-state value of k is determined by the point where $sf(k) = [(1 - s)\phi + 1]\bar{n}k$. The expression $[(1 - s)\phi + 1]\bar{n}k$ is just the

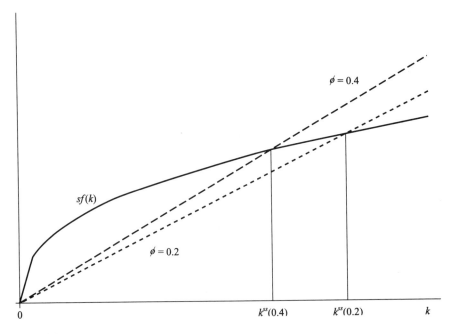

Figure 2.1
Tobin Effect: Constant m/k

equation for a straight line through the origin. Stability of the steady state requires that the $[(1-s)\phi + 1]\bar{n}k$ line cut $sf(k)$ from below; this occurs if $sf_k(k) <$
$[(1-s)\phi + 1]\bar{n}$.[6] A rise in ϕ rotates $[(1-s)\phi + 1]\bar{n}k$ up, leading to a decrease in the
steady-state labor ratio. Totally differentiating (2.9) gives $\dfrac{dk^{ss}}{d\phi} = (1-s)\bar{n}k/$
$\{sf_k - \bar{n}[1 + (1-s)\phi]\} < 0$, where the sign of the denominator (negative) follows
from the fact that the steady state is stable. Thus, the steady-state capital stock is
inversely related to the proportion of aggregate wealth held in the form of money.
Recall that ϕ is the ratio of real money balances to capital in household portfolios; a
portfolio shift toward higher holdings of money reduces investment in real capital
and leads to a decline in the steady-state k.

We do not want to treat ϕ as a parameter, however. The ratio of money holdings
to capital holdings is, for each individual household, a decision variable; the choice
of ϕ is a decision about how to divide total household assets between the two available alternatives, money and capital. Suppose this portfolio choice depends on the
relative real rates of return yielded by the two assets. In particular, let r denote the
real return on capital, and assume that money bears no direct nominal interest return, so that its real return is just $-\pi/(1+\pi)$.[7] Hence, ϕ should depend negatively
on r and positively on $-\pi/(1+\pi)$, or negatively on π. Assume, then, that $m/k =$
$\phi(r,\pi)$, $\phi_r < 0$, $\phi_\pi < 0$, where ϕ_i denotes the partial derivative of ϕ with respect to its
ith argument.

With competitive factor and product markets, the real return on capital will be
equal to the marginal product of capital, $r = f_k(k)$. Hence, $m/k = \phi[f_k(k),\pi]$, and
equation (2.9) becomes

$$sf(k^{ss}) = \{(1-s)\phi[f_k(k^{ss}),\pi] + 1\}\bar{n}k^{ss}$$

This defines k^{ss} as a function of the exogenous parameters (s,θ,n), since (2.7) gives
steady-state inflation as a function of θ and n. It follows that

$$\frac{dk^{ss}}{d\theta} = \frac{(1-s)\phi_\pi \bar{n}k^{ss}}{\{sf_k - \bar{n}[1 + (1-s)\phi + k^{ss}(1-s)f_{kk}\phi_r]\}}\frac{d\pi^{ss}}{d\theta} > 0$$

---

6. From equation (2.6), $\dfrac{\partial \Delta k}{\partial k} = sf_k - [(1-s)\phi + 1]\bar{n}$ evaluated at the steady state. This must be negative to
ensure local stability around the steady state. The Inada conditions on the production function $f(k)$ en-
sure the existence of a stable steady-state equilibrium in this model. See Solow (1956) or Blanchard and
Fischer (1989).

7. The value of a unit of money, in terms of goods, is $1/P$, so the real return on money is just
$\left(\dfrac{1}{P_t} - \dfrac{1}{P_{t-1}}\right)\bigg/\dfrac{1}{P_{t-1}} = \left(\dfrac{P_{t-1}}{P_t} - 1\right) = -\dfrac{\pi_t}{1 + \pi_t}$.

An increase in the rate of money growth, by raising the steady-state rate of inflation, lowers the real return on money relative to capital. By shifting desired portfolios toward greater holdings of capital, the steady-state capital stock is increased. Steady-state output and consumption also rise:

$$\frac{dy^{ss}}{d\theta} = f_k(k^{ss})\frac{dk^{ss}}{d\theta} > 0; \quad \frac{dc^{ss}}{d\theta} = [f_k(k^{ss}) - \bar{n}]\frac{dk^{ss}}{d\theta} > 0$$

where the expression for the effect on consumption comes from the steady-state goods market condition that output equals consumption plus investment. In the steady state, this implies $c^{ss} = y^{ss} - \bar{n}k^{ss}$.

This portfolio substitution effect of inflation on the steady-state capital-labor ratio is known as the Mundell-Tobin effect. The two assets, real money balances and capital, are substitutes in household portfolios. Increases (decreases) in the rate of return on one of the assets decreases (increases) the demand for the other. Higher inflation increases the portfolio demand for capital. Extensions of this basic framework to consider additional assets, growth, short-run dynamics, and fiscal policy include Stein (1969), Levhari and Patinkin (1968), Foley and Sidrauski (1971), and S. Fischer (1972).

There are three major criticisms of this framework. First, the model implies that higher inflation should be associated with higher levels of per capita capital and per capita output. One way to examine this implication is to look at the cross-country relationship between income and inflation. If the effect identified by Tobin is important, one should observe positive correlations between average inflation and per capita measures of income or the capital stock. Alternatively, if higher inflation raises the steady-state level of per capita income, then if two countries start with the same initial level of per capita income, the economy with higher inflation should grow more rapidly as it converges to a higher level of steady-state income. The cross-country comparisons of average growth rates and inflation reported by McCandless and Weber (1995) and discussed in Chapter 1 showed no relationship between the two. Other empirical studies of the relationship between growth and inflation seem to find a negative correlation, at least at moderate to high rates of inflation (Barro 1995, 1996; Motley 1994). Thus, if a Tobin effect is at work, that is, if higher inflation does lead to a substitution away from money and into physical capital, it is dominated by other effects of inflation that, on net, appear to be detrimental to economic growth.

Second, there is really no role for money in the model. What exactly is money doing? Why is money being held? Money serves useful economic purposes in actual economies, and that role is not captured in this framework. In fact, as Levhari and

Patinkin note, "For if the sole result of introducing money into an economy were to reduce k and hence per capita output and consumption, why should it be introduced? Where are the vaunted advantages of a monetary economy?" (Levhari and Patinkin 1968, p. 717).[8]

Third (and this is closely related to criticism number two), the behavioral relationships are *ad hoc* in the sense that they are not explicitly based on maximizing behavior by the agents of the model. This limitation can lead to problems when we try to understand the effects of changes in the economic environment, such as changes in the rate of inflation. The effects will depend, in part, on the way in which individual agents adjust, so we need to be able to predict how they will respond. If the behavioral relationships in the model are simply specified in an ad hoc manner, we will be unable to predict how the demand function for money might shift if the underlying time-series behavior of the inflation process were to change.

The rest of this chapter (and the next two chapters) will deal with alternative approaches to addressing the issues raised by the second and third of these criticisms. That is, we will examine models that propose an explicit role for money and derive behavior consistent with optimizing behavior by the agents in the model. Doing so will also highlight channels through which higher inflation might depress capital accumulation, thereby leading to quite different predictions than Tobin found for the relationship between inflation and per capita income.

2.3 Money in the Utility Function

A fundamental problem in monetary economics is the following: how should we model the demand for money? How do real economies differ from Arrow-Debreu economies in ways that give rise to a valued role for money? Three general approaches have been followed in the literature: (1) assume that money yields direct utility by incorporating money balances into the utility functions of the agents of the model (Sidrauski 1967); (2) impose transactions costs of some form that give rise to a demand for money, either by making asset exchanges costly (Baumol 1952; Tobin 1956), requiring that money be used for certain types of transactions (Clower 1967), or assuming that direct barter of commodities is costly (Kiyotaki and Wright 1989);

---

8. Levhari and Patinkin attempt to address this shortcoming of Tobin's model by assuming that money directly yields utility. However, rather than proceed as we will in the next section by deriving household behavior consistent with utility maximization, they instead modify the definition of disposable income to include the imputed service value of money holdings, equal to the nominal interest rate times the stock of real money balances [see equation (2.23)].

or (3) treat money like any other asset used to transfer resources intertemporally (Samuelson 1958).

In this section, we develop the first of these three approaches by incorporating into the basic neoclassical model agents whose utility depends directly on their consumption of goods *and* their holdings of money. Given suitable restrictions on the utility function, such an approach can guarantee that, in equilibrium, there is a positive demand for money so that money will be positively valued. The money-in-the-utility function, or MIU, model we will develop was originally due to Sidrauski (1967), and it has been used widely to study a variety of issues in monetary economics.[9]

Assuming that money enters the utility function is often criticized on the grounds that money itself is intrinsically useless (as with a paper currency) and that it is only through its use in facilitating transactions that it yields valued services. Approaches that emphasize the transactions role of money will be discussed in Chapter 3, but as will be shown there, transactions models in which money helps to reduce the time needed to purchase consumption goods can also be represented by the money-in-the-utility-function approach.[10]

2.3.1 The Basic Model

Suppose that the utility function of the representative household takes the form

$$U_t = u(c_t, z_t)$$

where z_t is the *flow* of services yielded by money holdings and c_t is time-t per capita consumption. The utility function is assumed to be increasing in both arguments, strictly concave and continuously differentiable. The demand for monetary services will always be positive if we assume $\lim_{z \to 0} u_z(c, z) = \infty$ for all c, where $u_z = \partial u(c, z)/\partial z$.

What constitutes z_t? If we wish to maintain the assumption of rational economic agents, then presumably what enters the utility function cannot just be the number of dollars (or yen or marks) that the individual holds. What should matter is the command over goods that are represented by those dollar holdings, or some measure of the transaction services, expressed in terms of goods, that money yields. In other words, z should be related to something like the number of dollars, M, times their

---

9. The second approach, focusing on the transactions role of money, will be discussed in Chapter 3. The third approach has been developed primarily within the context of overlapping generation models; see Sargent (1987).

10. Brock (1974), for example, develops two simple transactions stories that can be represented by putting money directly in the utility function.

price in terms of goods: $M\left(\dfrac{1}{P}\right) = \dfrac{M}{P}$. If the service flow is proportional to the real value of the stock of money, then we can set z equal to real per capita money holdings:

$$z_t = \frac{M_t}{P_t N_t} \equiv m_t$$

To ensure that a monetary equilibrium exists, it is often assumed that, for all c, $u_m(c,m) \leq 0$ for all $m > \bar{m}$ for some finite $\bar{m}$. This assumption means that the marginal utility of money eventually becomes negative for sufficiently high money balances. The role of this assumption will be made clear later. It is, however, not necessary for the existence of an equilibrium, and some common functional forms that are often employed for the utility function (and that will be used later in this chapter) do not satisfy this condition.[11]

The representative household is viewed as choosing time paths for consumption and real money balances subject to budget constraints to be specified later, with total utility given by

$$W = \sum_{t=0}^{\infty} \beta^t u(c_t, m_t) \tag{2.10}$$

where $0 < \beta < 1$ is a subjective rate of discount.

Equation (2.10) implies a much stronger notion of the utility provided by holding money than simply that the household would prefer having more money than less money. If the marginal utility of money is positive, then (2.10) implies that, *holding constant the path of real consumption for all t*, the individual's utility is increased by an increase in money holdings. That is, even though the money holdings are never used to purchase consumption, they yield utility. This idea should seem strange; we usually think the demand for money is instrumental in that we hold money to engage in transactions leading to the purchase of the goods and services that actually yield utility. All this is just to remind ourselves that putting money in the utility function may be a useful shortcut for ensuring there is a demand for money, but it is just a shortcut.[12]

---

11. For example, $u(c,m) = \log c + b \log m$ does not exhibit this property, since $\lim_{m \to \infty} u_m = 0$.

12. In some environments, money might yield utility, even if never actually spent, if it is held for insurance purposes. For example, Imrohoroglu (1992) studies a model in which agents can insure against income fluctuations only by holding "money."

To complete the specification of the model, assume that households hold both real money balances and physical capital, the two assets in the economy. Physical capital produces output according to a standard neoclassical production function such as was given in equation (2.1). Given its current income, its assets, and any net transfers received from the government (τ_t), the household allocates its resources between consumption, gross investment in physical capital, and gross accumulation of real money balances.

If the rate of depreciation of physical capital is δ, and the rates of inflation and population growth are π_t and n (assumed to be constant), the aggregate economy-wide budget constraint takes the form

$$Y_t + \tau_t N_t + (1 - \delta)K_{t-1} + \frac{M_{t-1}}{P_t} = C_t + K_t + \frac{M_t}{P_t} \tag{2.11}$$

where Y_t is aggregate output, K_{t-1} is the aggregate stock of capital at the start of period t, $\tau_t N_t$ is the aggregate real value of any lump-sum taxes or transfers, and $0 \le \delta \le 1$. Assuming constant returns to scale, per capita output will be a function of the per capita capital stock: $\frac{Y_t}{N_t} = y_t = f(k_{t-1})$. Dividing both sides of the budget constraint (2.11) by the population N_t, the per capita version becomes

$$\omega_t \equiv f(k_{t-1}) + \tau_t + \left(\frac{1-\delta}{1+n}\right)k_{t-1} + \frac{m_{t-1}}{(1+\pi_t)(1+n)} = c_t + k_t + m_t \tag{2.12}$$

where $f(k_{t-1}) = y_t$.

The household's problem is to choose paths for c_t, k_t, and m_t to maximize (2.10) subject to (2.12). This is a problem in dynamic optimization, and it is convenient to formulate the problem in terms of the value function giving the maximized value of utility that the household can achieve by behaving optimally, given its current state.[13] The state variable for the problem is the household's initial resources ω_t. The value function, defined as the present discounted value of utility if the household optimally chooses consumption, capital holdings, and money balances, is given by

$$V(\omega_t) = \max\{u(c_t, m_t) + \beta V(\omega_{t+1})\} \tag{2.13}$$

where the maximization is over c_t, k_t, and m_t and is subject to the budget con-

---

13. Introductions to dynamic optimization designed for economists can be found in Dixit (1990), Chiang (1992), Sargent (1987), or Obstfeld and Rogoff (1996).

straint (2.12) and the definition of ω_{t+1} as equal to $f(k_t) + \tau_{t+1} + \left(\dfrac{1-\delta}{1+n}\right)k_t +$

$\dfrac{m_t}{(1+\pi_{t+1})(1+n)}$.

Using the definition of ω_{t+1} and (2.12) to express k_t as $\omega_t - c_t - m_t$, equation (2.13) can be written as

$$V(\omega_t) = \max \left\{ u(c_t, m_t) \right.$$
$$+ \beta V\left[f(\omega_t - c_t - m_t) + \tau_{t+1} + \left(\frac{1-\delta}{1+n}\right)(\omega_t - c_t - m_t) \right.$$
$$\left. \left. + \frac{m_t}{(1+\pi_{t+1})(1+n)} \right] \right\}$$

with the maximization now an unconstrained maximization over c_t and m_t. The first-order necessary conditions for this problem are

$$u_c(c_t, m_t) - \beta\left[f_k(k_t) + \frac{1-\delta}{1+n} \right] V_\omega(\omega_{t+1}) = 0 \tag{2.14}$$

$$u_m(c_t, m_t) - \beta\left[f_k(k_t) + \frac{1-\delta}{1+n} \right] V_\omega(\omega_{t+1}) + \frac{\beta V_\omega(\omega_{t+1})}{(1+\pi_{t+1})(1+n)} = 0 \tag{2.15}$$

together with the transversality conditions

$$\lim_{t \to \infty} \beta^t \lambda_t x_t = 0, \quad \text{for } x = k, m \tag{2.16}$$

where λ_t is the marginal utility of period t consumption. The envelope theorem implies that

$$\lambda_t = V_\omega(\omega_t) = u_c(c_t, m_t) \tag{2.17}$$

The first-order conditions have straightforward interpretations. Since initial resources ω_t must be divided between consumption, capital holdings, and money balances, each use must yield the same marginal benefit at an optimum allocation. Using equations (2.14) and (2.17), equation (2.15) can be written as

$$u_m(c_t, m_t) + \frac{\beta u_c(c_{t+1}, m_{t+1})}{(1+\pi_{t+1})(1+n)} = u_c(c_t, m_t) \tag{2.18}$$

which states that the marginal benefit of adding to money holdings at time t must equal the marginal utility of consumption at time t. The marginal benefit of additional money holdings has two components. First, money directly yields utility u_m.

Second, real money balances at time t add $\dfrac{1}{(1+\pi_{t+1})(1+n)}$ to real, per capita re-
sources at time $t+1$; this addition to ω_{t+1} is worth $V_\omega(\omega_{t+1})$ at $t+1$, or $\beta V_\omega(\omega_{t+1})$
at time t. From (2.17), $\beta V_\omega(\omega_{t+1}) = \beta u_c(c_{t+1}, m_{t+1})$. Thus, the total marginal benefit
of money at time t is $u_m(c_t, m_t) + \dfrac{\beta u_c(c_{t+1}, m_{t+1})}{(1+\pi_{t+1})(1+n)}$. Equation (2.14) for capital holdings has a similar interpretation; the net marginal return from holding additional
capital, $\beta\left[f_k(k_t) + \dfrac{1-\delta}{1+n}\right] V_\omega(\omega_{t+1})$, must equal the marginal utility of consumption.

Note that we could have, equivalently, assumed the household rented its capital to
firms, receiving a rental rate of r_k, and sold its labor services at a wage rate of w.
Household income would then be $r_k k + w$ (expressed on a per capita basis). With
competitive firms hiring capital and labor in perfectly competitive factor markets
under constant returns to scale, $r_k = f'(k)$ and $w = f(k) - kf'(k)$, so household income would be $r_k k + w = f_k(k)k + [f(k) - kf_k(k)] = f(k)$ as we have in (2.12).[14]

Equations (2.14) and (2.15), together with the budget constraint (2.12) characterize
the household's choice of consumption, money holdings, and capital holdings at
each point in time. While we could use this system to study analytically the dynamic
behavior of the economy (for example, see Sidrauski 1967; S. Fischer 1979b; Blanchard and Fischer 1989), we will instead focus first on the properties of the steady-
state equilibrium. And, since our main focus here is not on the exogenous growth
generated by population growth, it will provide some slight simplification to set
$n = 0$. After we have examined the steady state, we will study the dynamic properties
by examining the time-series behavior of macroeconomic variables implied by a stochastic version of the model that also includes a labor-leisure choice and variable
employment.

2.3.1.1 Steady-State Equilibrium Consider the properties of this economy when it
is in a steady-state equilibrium with $n = 0$. With $V_\omega(\omega_t) = V_\omega(\omega_{t+1}) = V_\omega(\omega^{ss})$,
equations (2.14) and (2.17) imply that $1 = \beta[f_k(k^{ss}) + 1 - \delta]$, or

$$f_k(k^{ss}) + 1 - \delta = \frac{1}{\beta} \tag{2.19}$$

This equation defines the steady-state capital-labor ratio k^{ss}. If the production function is Cobb-Douglas, say $f(k) = k^\alpha$, then $f_k(k) = \alpha k^{\alpha-1}$ and we have that

---

14. This follows from Euler's theorem: if the aggregate constant-returns-to-scale production function is
$F(K, N)$, then $F(K, N) = F_K K + F_N N$. In per capita terms, this becomes $f(k) = F_K k + F_N = rk + w$ if
labor and capital are paid their marginal products.

$$k^{ss} = \left[\frac{\alpha\beta}{1 + \beta(\delta - 1)} \right]^{\frac{1}{1-\alpha}} \tag{2.20}$$

What is particularly relevant for our purposes is the implication from equation (2.19) that the steady-state capital-labor ratio is independent of (1) all parameters of the utility function other than the subjective discount rate β and (2) the steady-state rate of inflation π^{ss}. In fact, k^{ss} depends only on the production function, the depreciation rate, and the discount rate. In contrast to Tobin's result, the steady-state capital-labor ratio is independent of the rate of inflation.

Before examining why this result arises, it is useful to ask what determines the rate of inflation. Just as in the Tobin model, real money balances per capita are constant in the steady state:

$$\frac{\Delta m^{ss}}{m^{ss}} = \frac{\theta^{ss} - \pi^{ss}}{(1 + \pi^{ss})} = 0$$

where $\theta^{ss} \equiv \Delta M^{ss}/M^{ss}$ is the steady-state rate of nominal money growth. So $\Delta m^{ss} = 0$ implies that $\pi^{ss} = \theta^{ss}$.[15] The rate of inflation is determined by the nominal money growth rate. This is the same result obtained in the Tobin model and is simply an implication of the steady-state property that real, per capita money holdings are constant in the steady state.

Now these results can be used to reevaluate the budget constraint (2.12):

$$f(k^{ss}) + \tau^{ss} = c^{ss} + \delta k^{ss} + \frac{\pi^{ss}}{1 + \pi^{ss}} m^{ss}$$

Steady-state transfers are given by $\tau^{ss} = \dfrac{\theta^{ss}}{1 + \pi^{ss}} m^{ss}$, so using the result that $\pi^{ss} = \theta^{ss}$, the budget constraint reduces to

$$c^{ss} = f(k^{ss}) - \delta k^{ss} \tag{2.21}$$

The steady-state level of consumption per capita is completely determined once we know the level of steady-state capital. If we again assume that $f(k) = k^{\alpha}$, k^{ss} is given by (2.20) and

$$c^{ss} = \left[\frac{\alpha\beta}{1 + \beta(\delta - 1)} \right]^{\frac{\alpha}{1-\alpha}} - \delta \left[\frac{\alpha\beta}{1 + \beta(\delta - 1)} \right]^{\frac{1}{1-\alpha}}$$

Steady-state consumption per capita depends on the parameters of the production function (α), the rate of depreciation (δ), and the subjective rate of time discount (β).

---

15. If the population is growing at the rate n, then $1 + \pi^{ss} = (1 + \theta^{ss})/(1 + n)$, as in (2.7).

This model exhibits a property called *superneutrality of money*; the steady-state values of the capital-labor ratio, consumption, and output are all independent of the rate of inflation. This can be seen from the fact that the inflation rate π does not appear in (2.19) or (2.21). That is, not only is money neutral so that proportional changes in the *level* of nominal money balances and prices have no real effects (a result that follows directly from the fact that only the ratio of M and P ever appear in the model, usually in the form $m_t = M_t/P_t N_t$), but changes in the *rate of growth* of nominal money also have no effect either on the steady-state capital stock (or, therefore, on output) or on per capita consumption. Since the real rate of interest is equal to the marginal product of capital, it also is invariant across steady states that differ only in their rates of inflation.

An important distinction is that between changes in the *level* of the nominal supply of money and changes in the *rate of growth* of the nominal money supply. In all the models we will examine, the nominal money stock enters in the form M/P. Thus, proportional changes in the level of M and P, changes that leave M/P unaffected, have no real effects. This is described by saying that the models exhibit *neutrality of money*. If prices do not adjust immediately in response to a change in M, then a model might display nonneutrality with respect to changes in M in the short run but still exhibit monetary neutrality in the long run once all prices have adjusted. In fact, this will be the case with the models used in Chapters 5–10 to examine issues related to short-run monetary policy. A model displays the property of *superneutrality* if the real equilibrium is independent of the rate of growth of the nominal money supply. Thus, the Sidrauski money-in-the-utility-function model possesses the properties of both neutrality and superneutrality. In contrast, Tobin's model of section 2.2 displayed the property of neutrality but not superneutrality.

To understand why superneutrality holds, note that from (2.17), $u_c = V_\omega(\omega_t)$, so using (2.14), $V_\omega(\omega_t) = u_c(c_t, m_t) = \beta[f'(k_t) + 1 - \delta]V_\omega(\omega_{t+1}) = \beta[f_k(k_t) + 1 - \delta]u_c(c_{t+1}, m_{t+1})$, or

$$\frac{u_c(c_{t+1}, m_{t+1})}{u_c(c_t, m_t)} = \frac{1/\beta}{f_k(k_t) + 1 - \delta} = \frac{1/\beta}{1 + r_t} \tag{2.22}$$

where $r_t \equiv f_k(k_t) - \delta$ is the net real rate of return to capital. Recall from (2.19) that the right side of this expression is equal to 1 in the steady state. If $k < k^{ss}$ so that $f_k(k) > f_k(k^{ss})$, then the right side is smaller than 1, and the marginal utility of consumption will be declining over time. It will be optimal to postpone consumption to accumulate capital and have consumption grow over time (so u_c declines over time). As long as $f_k + 1 - \delta > 1/\beta$, this process continues, but as the capital stock grows, the marginal product of capital declines until eventually $f_k(k) + 1 - \delta = 1/\beta$. The converse holds if $k > k^{ss}$. Consumption remains constant only when $f_k + 1 - \delta = 1/\beta$. If an increase in the rate of inflation were to induce households to accumulate more capital, this result would lower the marginal product of capital, leading to a situation in which $f_k + 1 - \delta < 1/\beta$. Households would then want their consumption path to decline over time, so they would immediately attempt to increase current consumption and reduce their holdings of capital. The value of k consistent with a steady state is independent of the rate of inflation.

What is affected by the rate of inflation? One thing we should expect is that the interest rate on any asset that pays off in units of money at some future date will be affected; the real value of those future units of money will be affected by expectations of inflation (and it is certainly the case in the steady state that inflation is anticipated), and this fact will be reflected in the interest rate required to induce individuals to hold the asset.

Consider the market or nominal interest rate that an asset must yield if it is to give a real return of r in terms of the consumption good. That is, consider an asset that costs 1 unit of consumption in period t and yields $(1 + r_t)$ units of consumption at $t + 1$. In units of money, this asset costs P_t units of money at time t. Since the cost of each unit of consumption at $t + 1$ is P_{t+1} in terms of money, the asset must pay off an amount equal to $(1 + r_t)P_{t+1}$. Thus, the nominal return is $[(1 + r_t)P_{t+1} - P_t]/P_t = (1 + r_t)(1 + \pi_{t+1}) - 1 \equiv i_t$, where π_{t+1} denotes the inflation rate between t and $t + 1$. In the steady state, $1 + r^{ss} = 1/\beta$, so the nominal rate of interest is given by $[(1 + \pi^{ss})/\beta] - 1$ and varies directly with the rate of inflation.

This relationship between real and nominal rates of interest is called the Fisher relationship (Fisher 1896). With r^{ss} independent of the inflation rate, the nominal rate moves (approximately) one-for-one with inflation. Because $(1 + r)(1 + \pi) - 1 \approx 1 + r + \pi - 1 = r + \pi$, the nominal rate of interest in discrete time is often written as $i = r + \pi$. Out of the steady state, the nominal rate can still be written as the sum of the expected real rate plus the expected rate of inflation; however, there is no longer any presumption that short-run variations in expected inflation will leave the real rate unaffected.

When $n = 0$, equations (2.14), (2.15), (2.17), and (2.22) imply

$$\frac{u_m(c_t, m_t)}{u_c(c_t, m_t)} = 1 - \frac{\dfrac{\beta V_\omega(\omega_{t+1})}{(1 + \pi_{t+1})}}{u_c(c_t, m_t)} = 1 - \left(\frac{1}{1 + \pi_{t+1}}\right)\frac{\beta u_c(c_{t+1}, m_{t+1})}{u_c(c_t, m_t)}$$

$$= 1 - \frac{1}{(1 + r_t)(1 + \pi_{t+1})}$$

$$= \frac{i_t}{1 + i_t} \equiv I_t \tag{2.23}$$

To interpret equation (2.23), consider a very simple choice problem in which the agent must pick x and z to maximize $u(x, z)$ subject to a budget constraint of the form $x + pz = y$ where p is the relative price of z. The first-order conditions imply $u_z/u_x = p$. Comparing this to (2.23) shows that I has the interpretation of the relative price of real money balances in terms of the consumption good. Thus, the price, or opportunity cost, of holding money is directly related to the nominal rate of interest. The household could hold one unit less of money, purchasing instead a bond yielding a nominal return of i; the real value of this payment is $\dfrac{i}{1+\pi}$, and, since it is received in period $t + 1$, its present value is $\dfrac{i}{(1+r)(1+\pi)} = \dfrac{i}{1+i}$. Since money is assumed to pay no rate of interest, the opportunity cost of holding money is affected both by the real return on capital and the rate of inflation. If the price level is constant (so $\pi = 0$), then the forgone earnings from holding money rather than capital are given by r. A rising price level ($\pi > 0$) causes the real value of money to decline, adding to the opportunity cost of holding money.

To ensure that a steady-state monetary equilibrium exists, there must exist a positive but finite level of real money balances m^{ss} that satisfies (2.23), evaluated at the steady-state level of consumption. If utility is separable in consumption and money balances, say $u(c, m) = v(c) + \phi(m)$, this condition can be written as $\phi_m(m^{ss}) = I^{ss} v_c(c^{ss})$. The right side of this expression is a positive constant; the left side approaches ∞ as $m \to 0$. If $\phi_m(m) \le 0$ for all m greater than some finite level, a steady-state equilibrium with positive real money balances is guaranteed to exist. This was the role of the earlier assumption that the marginal utility of money eventually becomes negative. Note that this assumption is not necessary; $\phi(m) = \log m$ yields a positive solution to (2.23) as long as $I^{ss} v_c(c^{ss}) > 0$. When utility is not separable, then we can still write (2.23) as $u_m = I^{ss} u_c$. If $u_{cm} < 0$, so that the marginal utility of consumption decreases with increased holdings of money, both u_m and u_c decrease with m and the solution to (2.23) may not be unique; multiple steady-state equilibria may exist.[16]

When utility is separable in c and m, $u(c, m) = v(c) + \phi(m)$, and the dynamics of real balances around the steady state can be described by multiplying both sides of (2.18) by M_t and noting that $M_{t+1} = (1 + \theta)M_t$. This yields, after rearranging,

$$B(m_{t+1}) \equiv \frac{\beta}{1+\theta}\, v_c(c_{ss})m_{t+1} = [v_c(c^{ss}) - \phi_m(m_t)]m_t \equiv A(m_t) \qquad (2.24)$$

16. For more on the conditions necessary for existence of monetary equilibria, see Brock (1974, 1975) and Bewley (1983).

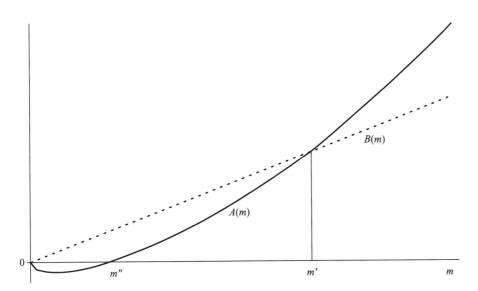

Figure 2.2
Steady-State Real Balances (Separable Utility)

which gives a difference equation in m. The properties of this equation have been examined by Brock (1974) and Obstfeld and Rogoff (1983, 1986). The functions $B(m)$ and $A(m)$ are illustrated in Figure 2.2. For the case drawn, $\lim_{m \to 0} \phi_m m = 0$ so there are two steady-state solutions to (2.24), one at m' and one at 0, so only one of these involves positive real money balances (and a positive value for money). If $\lim_{m \to 0} \phi_m m = \tilde{m} > 0$, then $\lim_{m \to 0} A(m) < 0$ and there is only one solution. Paths for m_t originating to the right of m' involve $m_{t+s} \to \infty$ as $s \to \infty$. When $\theta > 0$ (positive money growth), such explosive paths violate the transversality condition that the discounted value of asset holdings must go to zero (see Obstfeld and Rogoff 1983, 1986).[17] When $\lim_{m \to 0} A(m) < 0$, paths originating to the left of m' converge to $m < 0$; but this result is clearly not possible, since real balances cannot be negative. For the case drawn in Figure 2.2, however, some paths originating to the left of m' converge to 0 without ever involving negative real balances. For example, a path that reaches m'' at which $A(m'') = 0$ then jumps to $m = 0$. Along such an equilibrium path, the price level is growing faster than the nominal money supply (so

---

17. Obstfeld and Rogoff (1986) show that any equilibrium path with an implosive price level violates the transversality condition unless $\lim_{m \to \infty} \phi(m) = \infty$. This condition is implausible because it would require that the utility yielded by money be unbounded.

that m declines). Even if $\theta = 0$ so that the nominal money supply is constant, the equilibrium path would involve a speculative hyperinflation with the price level going to infinity.[18] Unfortunately, Obstfeld and Rogoff find that the conditions needed to ensure $\lim_{m \to 0} \phi_m m = \tilde{m} > 0$ so that speculative hyperinflations can be ruled out are restrictive. They show that $\lim_{m \to 0} \phi_m m > 0$ implies $\lim_{m \to 0} \phi(m) = -\infty$; essentially, money must be so necessary that the utility of the representative agent goes to minus infinity if her real balances fall to zero.[19]

Returning to equation (2.23), this characterizes the demand for real money balances as a function of the nominal rate of interest and real consumption. For example, if $u(c, m) = \log(c) + \gamma \log(m)$,[20] then $u_m/u_c = \gamma c/m$ and equation (2.23) can be written as

$$m = \frac{\gamma c(1 + i)}{i}$$

or, in terms of the more common specification in log form used to model empirical money demand equations (Goldfeld and Sichel 1990),

$$\log \frac{M}{pN} = \log \gamma + \log c - \log \frac{i}{1 + i} \qquad (2.25)$$

which gives the real demand for money as a negative function of the nominal rate of interest and a positive function of consumption.[21]

Before moving on to use this framework to analyze the welfare cost of inflation, we need to consider the limitations of the money-in-the-utility approach. Unlike Tobin's specification, there is a clearly defined reason for individuals to hold money—it provides direct utility. However, this essentially "solves" the problem of generating a positive demand for money by assumption; it doesn't address the reasons why money, particularly money in the form of unbacked pieces of paper, might yield utility. The money-in-the-utility-function approach has to be thought of as a

18. The hyperinflation is labeled speculative because it is not driven by fundamentals, such as the growth rate of the nominal supply of money.

19. Speculative hyperinflations are shown by Obstfeld and Rogoff to be ruled out if the government holds real resources to back a fraction of the outstanding currency. This policy ensures a positive value below which the real value of money cannot fall.

20. While this functional form is commonly used, it does violate the assumption that the marginal utility of money becomes nonpositive for a finite level of real balances.

21. The standard specification of money demand would use income in place of consumption, although see Mankiw and Summers (1986). The empirical literature on money demand is vast. See, for example, the references in Judd and Scadding (1982), Laidler (1985), or Goldfeld and Sichel (1990).

shortcut for a fully specified model of the transactions technology faced by house-holds that gives rise to a positive demand for a medium of exchange.[22]

Shortcuts are often extremely useful. But one problem with such a shortcut is that it does not provide any real understanding of, or possible restrictions on, such quantities as u_m or u_{cm} that play a role in determining equilibrium and the outcome of comparative static exercises. One possible story that can generate money in the utility function is a shopping-time story, and we will return to this idea in Chapter 3.

2.3.1.2 The Welfare Cost of Inflation   Because money holdings yield direct utility and higher inflation reduces real money balances, inflation generates a welfare loss. This fact raises two questions: (1) how large is the welfare cost of inflation? (2) Is there an optimal rate of inflation that maximizes the steady-state welfare of the representative household? The first of these questions is traditionally answered by computing the area under the money demand curve—more on this to follow.

The second question—the optimal rate of inflation—was originally addressed by Bailey (1956) and M. Friedman (1969). Their basic intuition was the following. The private opportunity cost of holding money depends on the nominal rate of interest (see equation 2.23). The social marginal cost of producing money—that is, running the printing presses—is essentially zero. The wedge that arises between the private marginal cost and the social marginal cost with a positive nominal rate of interest generates an inefficiency. This inefficiency would be eliminated if the private opportunity cost were also equal to zero, and this will be the case if the nominal rate of interest equals zero. But $i = 0$ requires that $\pi = -r/(1+r) \approx -r$. So the optimal rate of inflation is a rate of *deflation* approximately equal to the real return on capital.[23]

Since real money balances are directly related to the inflation rate in the steady state (see equation 2.23), the optimal rate of inflation is also frequently discussed under the title of the optimal quantity of money. With utility depending directly on m, one can think of the government choosing its policy instrument θ (and therefore π) to achieve the steady-state optimal value of m. Steady-state utility will be maximized when $u(c^{ss}, m^{ss})$ is maximized subject to the constraint that $c^{ss} = f(k^{ss}) - \delta k^{ss}$. But since c^{ss} is independent of θ, the first-order condition for the optimal θ is just

$$u_m \frac{\partial m}{\partial \theta} = 0, \text{ or } u_m = 0, \text{ and from (2.23), this occurs when } i = 0.[24]$$

22. For a general equilibrium analysis of asset prices in a money-in-the-utility-function framework, see LeRoy (1984a, 1984b).

23. Since $(1 + i) = (1 + r)(1 + \pi)$, $i = 0$ implies $\pi = -r/(1+r) \approx -r$.

24. Note that the earlier assumption that the marginal utility of money goes to zero at some finite level of real balances ensures that $u_m = 0$ has a solution with $m < \infty$. While we focus here on the steady state, a more appropriate perspective for addressing the optimal inflation question would not restrict attention solely to the steady state. The more general case is considered in Chapter 4.

The major criticism of this result is due to Phelps (1973), who pointed out that money growth generates revenue for the government—the inflation tax. The implicit assumption so far has been that variations in money growth are engineered via lump-sum transfers. Any effects on government revenue can be offset by a suitable adjustment in these lump-sum transfers (taxes). But if governments only have distortionary taxes available for financing expenditures, then reducing inflation tax revenues to achieve the Friedman rule for optimal inflation will require that the revenue loss be replaced through increases in other distortionary taxes. To minimize the total distortions associated with raising a given amount of revenue, it may be optimal to rely to some degree on the inflation tax. Reducing the nominal rate of interest to zero would increase the inefficiencies generated by the higher level of other taxes needed to replace lost inflation tax revenues. Recent work has examined these results in dynamic frameworks (see Chari, Christiano, and Kehoe 1991, 1996). The revenue implications of inflation are a major theme of Chapter 4.

Now let's return to the first question posed earlier—what is the welfare cost of inflation? Beginning with Bailey (1956), this welfare cost has been calculated from the area under the money demand curve (showing money demand as a function of the nominal rate of interest), since this provides a measure of the consumer surplus lost as a result of having a positive nominal rate of interest. Because nominal interest rates reflect *expected* inflation, calculating the area under the money demand curve will provide a measure of the costs of anticipated inflation and is therefore appropriate for evaluating the costs of alternative constant rates of inflation. There are other costs of inflation associated with tax distortions and with variability in the rate of inflation; these are discussed in the survey on the costs of inflation by Driffill, Mizon, and Ulph (1990).

As an example of the traditional approach, Lucas (1994) provides estimates of the welfare costs of inflation by starting with a specific specification of the instantaneous utility function:

$$u(c,m) = \frac{1}{1-\sigma}\left\{\left[c\varphi\left(\frac{m}{c}\right)\right]^{1-\sigma} - 1\right\} \tag{2.26}$$

With this utility function, equation (2.23) becomes

$$\frac{u_m}{u_c} = \frac{\varphi'(x)}{\varphi(x) - x\varphi'(x)} = \frac{i}{1+i} = I \tag{2.27}$$

where $x \equiv m/c$.[25] Normalizing so that steady-state consumption equals 1, $u(1,m)$

---

25. Lucas employs a continuous time framework in which the relevant expression is $u_m/u_c = i$.

will be maximized when $I = 0$, implying that the optimal x is defined by $\varphi'(m^*) = 0$. Lucas proposes to measure the costs of inflation by the percentage increase in steady-state consumption necessary to make the household indifferent between a nominal interest rate of i and a nominal rate of 0. If this cost is denoted $w(I)$, it is defined by

$$u[1 + w(I), m(I)] \equiv u(1, m^*) \tag{2.28}$$

where $m(I)$ denotes the solution of (2.27) for real money balances evaluated at steady-state consumption $c = 1$.

Suppose, following Lucas, that $\varphi(m) = [1 + Bm^{-1}]^{-1}$ where B is a positive constant. Solving (2.27), one obtains $m(i) = B^{0.5}I^{-0.5}$.[26] Note that $\varphi' = 0$ requires that $m^* = \infty$. But $\varphi(\infty) = 1$ and $u(1, \infty) = 0$, so $w(I)$ is the solution to $u[1 + w(I), B^{0.5}I^{-0.5}] = u(1, \infty) = 0$. Using the definition of the utility function, we obtain $1 + w(I) = 1 + \sqrt{BI}$, or

$$w(I) = \sqrt{BI} \tag{2.29}$$

Based on U.S. annual data for 1900–1985, Lucas reports an estimate of 0.0018 for B. Hence, the welfare loss arising from a nominal interest rate of 10% would be $\sqrt{(0.0018)(0.1/1.1)} = 0.013$, or just over 1% of aggregate consumption.[27]

Since U.S. government bond yields were around 10% in 1979 and 1980, we can use 1980 aggregate personal consumption expenditures of \$2,447.1 billion to get a rough estimate of the dollar welfare loss (although consumption expenditures include purchases of durables). In 1987 prices, 1.3% of \$2,447.1 billion is about \$32 billion. Since this is the annual cost in terms of steady-state consumption, we need the present discounted value of \$32 billion. Using a real rate of return of 2%, this amounts to $\$32(1.02)/0.02 = 1.632$ trillion; at 4%, the cost would be \$832 billion.

An annual welfare cost of \$32 billion seems a small number, especially when compared to the estimated costs of reducing inflation. For example, Ball (1993) reports a "sacrifice ratio" of 2.3 percentage points of output per point of inflation reduction for the United States. Since inflation was reduced from about 10% to about 3% in the early 1980s, Ball's estimate would put the costs of this disinflation as approximately 16% of GDP (2.3% times an inflation reduction of 7 percentage points).

---

26. Lucas actually starts with the assumption that money demand is equal to $m = Ai^{-0.5}$ for A equal to a constant. He then derives $\varphi(m)$ as the utility function necessary to generate such a demand function, where $B = A^2$.

27. For a recent critique of Lucas' approach and an application based on United Kingdom data, see Chadha, Haldane, and Janssen (1998).

Based on 1980 GDP of $3,776.3 billion (1987 prices), this would be $602 billion. This looks large when compared to the $32 billion annual welfare cost, but the trade-off starts looking more worthwhile if the costs of reducing inflation are compared to the present discounted value of the annual welfare cost. (See also Feldstein 1979.)

Gillman (1995) provides a useful survey of different estimates of the welfare cost of inflation. The estimates differ widely. One important reason for these differences arises from the choice of base inflation rate. Some estimates compare the area under the money demand curve between an inflation rate of zero and, say, 10%. This approach is incorrect in that a zero rate of inflation still results in a positive nominal interest rate (equal to the real rate of return) and therefore a positive opportunity cost associated with holding money. Gillman concludes, based on the empirical estimates he surveys, that a reasonable value of the welfare cost of inflation for the United States is in the range of 0.85% to 3% of real GNP for a 10% rate of inflation, a loss in 1994 dollars of $58–204 billion per year.[28]

The Sidrauski model provides a convenient framework for calculating the steady-state welfare costs of inflation, both because the lower level of real money holdings that results at higher rates of inflation has a direct effect on welfare when money enters the utility function, and because the superneutrality property of the model means that the other argument in the utility function, real consumption, is invariant across different rates of inflation. This latter property simplified the calculation because it is not necessary to account for both variation in money holdings and variations in consumption when making the welfare cost calculation. Of critical importance, however, is the ability of the money-in-the-utility-function approach to allow the costs of inflation to be calculated based on a model of money demand that is consistent with optimizing behavior on the part of economic agents.

2.3.1.3 Extensions

INTEREST ON MONEY   If the welfare costs of inflation are related to the positive private opportunity costs of holding money, an alternative to deflation as a means of eliminating these costs would be the payment of explicit interest on money. There are obvious technical difficulties in paying interest on cash, but ignoring these, assume that the government pays a nominal interest rate of i^m on nominal money balances. Assume further that these interest payments are financed by lump-sum

---

28. These estimates apply to the United States, which has experienced relatively low rates of inflation. They may not be relevant for high-inflation countries.

taxes s. The household's budget constraint, equation (2.12), now becomes (setting $n = 0$)

$$f(k_{t-1}) - s_t + \tau_t + (1 - \delta)k_{t-1} + \frac{1 + i_t^m}{1 + \pi_t} m_{t-1} = c_t + k_t + m_t \qquad (2.30)$$

and the first-order condition (2.15) becomes

$$-u_c(c_t, m_t) + u_m(c_t, m_t) + \frac{\beta(1 + i_t^m)V_\omega(\omega_{t+1})}{(1 + \pi_{t+1})} = 0 \qquad (2.31)$$

while (2.23) is now

$$\frac{u_m(c_t, m_t)}{u_c(c_t, m_t)} = \frac{i_t - i_t^m}{1 + i_t}$$

The opportunity cost of money is related to the interest-rate gap $i - i^m$, which represents the difference between the nominal return on capital and the nominal return on money. If $\theta = 0$ so that the rate of inflation in the steady state is also zero, the optimal quantity of money, the quantity such that $u_m = 0$, can be achieved if $i^m = r$.

The assumption that the interest payments are financed by the revenue from lump-sum taxes is critical for this result. One of the problems at the end of this chapter considers what happens if the government simply finances the interest payments on money by printing more money.

NONSUPERNEUTRALITY   Calculations of the steady-state welfare costs of inflation within the Sidrauski model are greatly simplified by the fact that the model exhibits superneutrality. But how robust is the result that money is superneutral? The empirical evidence of Barro (1995) suggests that high inflation has a negative effect on growth, a finding inconsistent with superneutrality.[29] For example, one channel through which inflation can have real effects in the steady state is introduced if households have a labor-supply choice. That is, suppose utility depends on consumption, real money holdings, and leisure:

$$u = u(c, m, l) \qquad (2.32)$$

The economy's production function becomes

$$y = f(k, n) = f(k, 1 - l) \qquad (2.33)$$

---

29. Of course, the empirical relationship may not be causal; both growth and inflation may be reacting to common factors. As noted in Chapter 1, McCandless and Weber (1995) find no relationship between inflation and average real growth.

where the total supply of time is normalized to equal 1 so that labor supply is just $1 - l$. The additional first-order condition implied by the optimal choice of leisure is

$$\frac{u_l(c, m, l)}{u_c(c, m, l)} = f_n(k, 1 - l) \tag{2.34}$$

Now, both steady-state labor supply and consumption may be affected by variations in the rate of inflation. Specifically, an increase in the rate of inflation reduces holdings of real money balances. If this affects the marginal utility of leisure, then (2.34) implies that labor supply will be affected, leading to a change in the steady-state per capita stock of capital, output, and consumption. But why would changes in money holdings affect the marginal utility of leisure? Because money has simply been assumed to yield utility, with no explanation why, it is difficult to answer this question. In Chapter 3 we will examine a model in which money helps to reduce the time spent in carrying out the transactions necessary to purchase consumption goods; in this case, a rise in inflation would lead to more time spent engaged in transactions and this would raise the marginal utility of leisure. But one might expect that this channel is unlikely to be important empirically, so superneutrality may remain a reasonable first approximation to the effects of inflation on steady-state real magnitudes.

Equation (2.34) suggests that if u_l/u_c were independent of m, then superneutrality would hold. This is the case because the steady-state values of k, c, and l could then be found from

$$\frac{u_l}{u_c} = f_n(k^{ss}, 1 - l^{ss})$$

$$f_k(k^{ss}, 1 - l^{ss}) = \frac{1}{\beta} - 1 + \delta$$

and

$$c^{ss} = f(k^{ss}, 1 - l^{ss}) - \delta k^{ss}$$

If u_l/u_c does not depend on m, these three equations determine the steady-state values of consumption, capital, and labor independently of inflation. So superneutrality reemerges when the utility function takes the general form $u(c, m, l) = v(c, l)g(m)$, that is, when it is separable in m. While variations in inflation will affect the agent's holdings of money, the consumption-leisure choice will not be directly affected. As McCallum (1990a) notes, Cobb-Douglas specifications, which are quite commonly used, satisfy this condition. So with a Cobb-Douglas utility function, the ratio of the marginal utility of leisure to the marginal utility of consumption will be independent of the level of real money balances, and superneutrality will hold.

Another channel through which inflation can affect the steady-state stock of capital occurs if money enters directly into the production function (S. Fischer 1974). Since steady states with different rates of inflation will have different equilibrium levels of real money balances, they will also then have different marginal products of capital if the capital-labor ratios are the same. With the steady-state marginal product of capital determined by $1/\beta - 1 + \delta$ (see equation [2.19]), the two steady states can only have the same marginal product of capital if their capital-labor ratios differ. If $\partial MPK/\partial m > 0$ (so that money and capital are complements), higher inflation, by leading to lower real money balances, also leads to a lower steady-state capital stock.[30] This is the opposite of the Tobin effect; for higher inflation to be associated with a higher steady-state capital-labor ratio requires that $\partial MPK/\partial m < 0$ (that is, higher money balances reduce the marginal product of capital; money and capital are substitutes in production).

This discussion actually has, by ignoring taxes, excluded what is probably the most important reason that superneutrality may fail in actual economies. Taxes generally are not indexed to inflation and are levied on nominal capital gains instead of real capital gains. Effective tax rates will depend on the inflation rate, generating real effects on capital accumulation and consumption as inflation varies. (See, for example, Feldstein 1978; Summers 1981; Feldstein 1996.) We will return to this issue in Chapter 4.

2.3.2   Dynamics

The analysis of the money-in-the-utility-function approach has, up to this point, focused on steady-state properties. We are also interested in understanding the implications of the model for the dynamic process the economy follows as it adjusts in response to exogenous disturbances. Even the basic Sidrauski model can exhibit nonsuperneutralities during the transition to the steady state. For example, Fischer (1979b) has shown that, for the constant-relative-risk-aversion class of utility functions, the rate of capital accumulation is positively related to the rate of money growth except for the case of log-separable utility.[31]

---

30. That is, in the steady state, $f_k(k^{ss}, m^{ss}) = \beta^{-1} - 1 + \delta$ where $f(k, m)$ is the production function and f_i denotes the partial with respect to the ith argument. It follows that $dk^{ss}/dm^{ss} = -f_{km}/f_{kk}$, so with $f_{kk} \leq 0$, $\text{sign}(dk^{ss}/dm^{ss}) = \text{sign}(f_{km})$.

31. Superneutrality holds during the transition if $u(c, m) = \ln(c) + b \ln(m)$. The general class of utility functions Fischer considers is of the form $u(c, m) = \dfrac{1}{1 - \Phi}(c^a m^b)^{1-\Phi}$; log utility obtains when $\Phi = 1$. See also Asako (1983), who shows that faster money growth can lead to slower capital accumulation under certain conditions if c and m are perfect complements. These effects of inflation on capital accumulation apply during the transition from one steady-state equilibrium to another; they differ therefore from the Tobin effect of inflation on the steady-state capital-labor ratio.

In addition, theoretical and empirical work in macroeconomics and monetary economics are closely tied, and it is important to reflect on how the theoretical models can help us understand actual observations on inflationary experiences. One way to do so is to use a theoretical model to generate artificial data by simulating the model economy; comparing the simulated data with actual data generated by real economies provides a means of validating the model. This type of approach has been popularized by the real-business-cycle literature (see Cooley 1995). Since we can vary the parameters of our theoretical models in ways that we cannot vary the characteristics of real economies, simulation methods allow us to answer a variety of "what-if" questions. For example, how does the dynamic response to a temporary change in the growth rate of the money supply depend on the degree of intertemporal substitution characterizing individual preferences?

It can also be helpful to have an analytic solution to a model; often explicit solutions help to indicate whether simulation results are likely to be sensitive to parameter values and to highlight directly the mechanisms through which changes in the processes followed by the exogenous variables lead to effects on the endogenous variables and to alterations in the equilibrium decision rules of the agents in the model. Campbell (1994) has proposed using log-linear approximation for studying a basic nonmonetary real-business-cycle model, and this approach has been further extended by Uhlig (1995). In addition, Uhlig provides easily adaptable MATLAB programs for solving log-linear dynamic stochastic models.

In this subsection, we apply these methods to the Sidrauski model. But rather than assuming that utility depends just on consumption and money holdings, we also allow utility to depend on the representative agent's consumption of leisure. This introduces a labor-supply decision into the analysis, an important and necessary extension for studying business cycle fluctuations, since employment variation is an important characteristic of cycles. By specifying functional forms for the utility function (as we did, for example, in equation [2.26]) and for the production function, we can develop approximations around the steady state that can be solved numerically. We also need to add a source, or sources, of exogenous shocks that disturb the system from its steady-state equilibrium. The two types of shocks we will consider will be productivity shocks, the driving force in real-business-cycle models, and shocks to the growth rate of the nominal stock of money.

We follow the standard specification in dynamic general equilibrium models by assuming that output is produced using capital and labor according to a Cobb-Douglas constant-returns-to-scale production function. Consistent with the real-business-cycle literature, we incorporate a stochastic disturbance to total factor productivity, so that

$$Y_t = e^{z_t} K_{t-1}^{\alpha} N_t^{1-\alpha} \tag{2.35}$$

with $0 < \alpha < 1$ and

$$z_t = \rho z_{t-1} + e_t \tag{2.36}$$

is the process followed by the productivity shock. We assume e is a serially un-correlated mean-zero process and $|\rho| < 1$. Note the timing convention in (2.35): the capital carried over from period $t - 1$, K_{t-1}, is available for use in producing output during period t.

We also need to specify the process followed by the nominal stock of money. In previous sections, we let θ denote the growth rate of the nominal money supply. As-sume then that the average growth rate is θ^{ss}, and let $u_t \equiv \theta_t - \theta^{ss}$ be the deviation in period t of the growth rate from its unconditional average value. This deviation will be treated as a stochastic process given by

$$u_t = \gamma u_{t-1} + \phi z_{t-1} + \varphi_t, \quad 0 \leq \gamma < 1 \tag{2.37}$$

where φ_t is a white-noise process. This formulation allows the growth rate to display persistence (if $\gamma > 0$), to respond to the real productivity shock z, and to be subject to random disturbances through the realizations of φ.

For the utility function, we follow Fischer (1979b) in restricting attention to pref-erences displaying constant relative risk aversion. Therefore, assume

$$u(c_t, m_t, l_t) = \frac{(c_t m_t^b)^{1-\Phi}}{1 - \Phi} + \Psi \frac{l_t^{1-\eta}}{1 - \eta} \tag{2.38}$$

with b, η, Φ, $\Psi > 0$ and $b(1 - \Phi) < 1$. In the limiting case $\Phi = 1$, preferences over consumption and money holdings are log linear. Fischer (1979b) showed that the transition paths are independent of the money supply only if $\Phi = 1$. As discussed by King, Plosser, and Rebelo (1988), preferences of the form given in (2.38) are con-sistent with steady-state growth. Normalizing the total available time for work and leisure to one, labor supply will be given by

$$n_t = 1 - l_t$$

In what follows, we will make use of the notational convention that uppercase letters denote economy-wide variables, lowercase letters denote random disturbances and variables expressed in per capita terms, and the superscript ss indicates the steady-state value of a variable. Since the focus will be of the dynamic behavior around the steady state, a "hat" ($\,\hat{}\,$) will indicate the percentage deviation of a variable from its steady-state level. The single but very important exception is that m, m^{ss}, and $\hat{m}$ will refer to *real* money balances per capita while M will represent the aggregate *nominal* stock of money.

Table 2.1
Steady-State Values

R^{ss}	$\dfrac{y^{ss}}{k^{ss}}$	$\dfrac{c^{ss}}{k^{ss}}$	$\dfrac{m^{ss}}{k^{ss}}$	$\dfrac{n^{ss}}{k^{ss}}$
$\dfrac{1}{\beta}$	$\dfrac{1}{\alpha}(\bar{R}-1+\delta)$	$\dfrac{y^{ss}}{k^{ss}}-\delta$	$\dfrac{\Theta b}{(\Theta-\beta)}\dfrac{c^{ss}}{k^{ss}}$	$\left(\dfrac{y^{ss}}{k^{ss}}\right)^{\frac{1}{1-\alpha}}$

Given these functional forms for the production function and the utility function, we need to set up the household's decision problem, find the first-order conditions, and then solve for the paths of the endogenous variables that are consistent with these first-order conditions and with the equilibrium conditions of the model. To obtain solutions, however, we will linearize the model around the steady state. The details of the derivations involved in each of these steps can be found in the chapter appendix (section 2.5).

2.3.2.1 The Steady State The appendix shows how the steady-state values can be expressed in terms of the basic parameters of the model. Letting $\Theta \equiv 1 + \theta^{ss}$ be one plus the average growth rate of the nominal supply of money, the steady-state values for the endogenous variables of the model are given in Table 2.1.

Table 2.1 reveals some of the key properties of this money-in-the-utility-function model and how variations in the steady-state rate of inflation will affect output, the capital stock, and consumption. The first thing to note is that, with the exception of real money balances relative to the capital stock, the other ratios are all independent of the steady-state growth rate of the nominal supply of money. However, the steady-state *levels* of the capital stock, output, and consumption will depend on the money growth rate through the effects of inflation on labor supply, with inflation-induced changes in n^{ss} affecting y^{ss}, c^{ss}, and k^{ss} equiproportionally.

The steady-state level of n is determined as the solution to

$$(1-n^{ss})^{-\eta}(n^{ss})^{-\upsilon} = \frac{1-\alpha}{\Psi}\left(\frac{\Theta b}{\Theta-\beta}\right)^{b(1-\Phi)}\left(\frac{c^{ss}}{k^{ss}}\right)^{\upsilon}\left(\frac{y^{ss}}{k^{ss}}\right)^{\frac{-(\alpha+\upsilon)}{1-\alpha}} \tag{2.39}$$

where $\upsilon = b(1-\Phi) - \Phi$. If $\Phi = 1$ so that utility is log separable in consumption and money holdings, then $\upsilon = -1$ and, from (2.39), $(1-n^{ss})^{-\eta}n^{ss} = \frac{1-\alpha}{\Psi}\left(\frac{c^{ss}}{k^{ss}}\right)\left(\frac{y^{ss}}{k^{ss}}\right)$, which is independent of θ^{ss}. From Table 2.1, all the real variables such as k^{ss}, y^{ss}, and c^{ss} are independent of the money growth rate θ^{ss}, and superneutrality obtains when $\Phi = 1$. Only m^{ss}/k^{ss} will depend on the growth rate of money.

But if $\Phi \neq 1$, inflation matters for the real equilibrium, and, as discussed earlier, it matters through the effect of inflation on labor supply. The independence of the various real ratios means the effect of money growth (and inflation) on the steady state operates entirely through the term $\left(\dfrac{\Theta b}{\Theta - \beta}\right)^{b(1-\Phi)}$ in (2.39). This also means we can write the steady-state condition for labor supply as

$$(1 - n^{ss})^{-\eta} (n^{ss})^{-v} = K \left(\frac{\Theta b}{\Theta - \beta}\right)^{b(1-\Phi)} = K h(\Theta) \tag{2.40}$$

where $h(\Theta) \equiv \left(\dfrac{\Theta b}{\Theta - \beta}\right)^{b(1-\Phi)}$ and $K \equiv \dfrac{1 - \alpha}{\Psi} \left(\dfrac{c^{ss}}{k^{ss}}\right)^{v} \left(\dfrac{y^{ss}}{k^{ss}}\right)^{\frac{-(\alpha + v)}{1 - \alpha}} > 0$ is independent of Θ.[32]

2.3.2.2   The Linear Approximation   The steps involved in obtaining the linear approximation around the steady state are contained in the appendix to this chapter (section 2.5) and follow the approach of Campbell (1994) and Uhlig (1995). The resulting linearized system consists of the exogenous processes for the productivity shock and the money growth rate plus the following seven equations that can be solved for the capital stock, money holdings, output, consumption, employment, the expected real rate of interest, and the inflation rate:

$$\hat{y}_t = \alpha \hat{k}_{t-1} + (1 - \alpha)\hat{n}_t + z_t \tag{2.41}$$

$$\left(\frac{y^{ss}}{k^{ss}}\right)\hat{y}_t = \left(\frac{c^{ss}}{k^{ss}}\right)\hat{c}_t + \hat{k}_t - (1 - \delta)\hat{k}_{t-1} \tag{2.42}$$

$$R^{ss}\hat{r}_t = \alpha\left(\frac{y^{ss}}{k^{ss}}\right)(E_t\hat{y}_{t+1} - \hat{k}_t) \tag{2.43}$$

$$E_t[\Phi(\hat{c}_{t+1} - \hat{c}_t) - b(1 - \Phi)(\hat{m}_{t+1} - \hat{m}_t)] - \hat{r}_t = 0 \tag{2.44}$$

$$[\hat{y}_t - \Phi\hat{c}_t + b(1 - \Phi)\hat{m}_t] = \left(1 + \eta\,\frac{n^{ss}}{1 - n^{ss}}\right)\hat{n}_t \tag{2.45}$$

$$\hat{r}_t + E_t\hat{\pi}_{t+1} = \frac{\Theta - \beta}{\beta}(\hat{c}_t - \hat{m}_t) \tag{2.46}$$

$$\hat{m}_t = \hat{m}_{t-1} - \hat{\pi}_t + u_t \tag{2.47}$$

---

32. Since $R^{ss} = 1/\beta$ and $1 + \pi^{ss} = 1 + \theta^{ss} = \Theta$, the expression $\Theta b/(\Theta - \beta)$ is equal to $b(1 + i^{ss})/i^{ss}$ where i^{ss} is the steady-state nominal rate of interest.

Equation (2.41) is the economy's production function in which output deviations from the steady state are a linear function of the percentage deviations of the capital stock and labor supply from steady state plus the productivity shock. Equation (2.42) is the resource constraint derived from the condition that output equals consumption plus investment. Deviations of the marginal product of capital are tied to deviations of the real return by equation (2.43). Equations (2.44)–(2.46) are derived from the representative household's first-order conditions for consumption, leisure, and money holdings. Finally, (2.47) relates the change in the deviation from steady state of real money balances to the inflation rate and the growth of the nominal money stock. To complete the specification, the exogenous disturbances for productivity and nominal money growth were given earlier by (2.36) and (2.37).

One conclusion follows immediately from inspecting this system. If $\Phi = 1$, then (2.44) becomes

$$0 = \mathrm{E}_t \hat{c}_{t+1} - \hat{c}_t - \hat{r}_t$$

so that, using this equation together with (2.41)–(2.43) and (2.45), we can solve for $\hat{y}$, $\hat{c}$, $\hat{r}$, $\hat{k}$, and $\hat{n}$ independently of the money-supply process and inflation. This implies that superneutrality will characterize dynamics around the steady state as well as the steady state itself. Thus, the system will exhibit superneutrality along its dynamic adjustment path. This result was first shown by Brock (1974) and S. Fischer (1979b).

While separability allows us to solve for the real equilibrium independent of money and inflation, it has more commonly been used in monetary economics to allow the study of inflation and money growth to be conducted independent of the real equilibrium. When $\Phi = 1$, equations (2.46) and (2.47) constitute a two-equation system in inflation and real money balances, with u representing an exogenous random disturbance and $\hat{c}$ and $\hat{r}$ determined by (2.41)–(2.45) and exogenous to the determination of inflation and real money balances. Letting the percentage deviation of the price level and the nominal money supply from their steady-state paths be denoted $\hat{p}$ and $\hat{\mu}$, (2.46) can be written as

$$\mathrm{E}_t \hat{\pi}_{t+1} \equiv \mathrm{E}_t \hat{p}_{t+1} - \hat{p}_t = d(\hat{\mu}_t - \hat{p}_t) + x_t$$

This is an expectational difference equation that can be solved for the equilibrium path of $\hat{p}$ for a given process for the nominal money supply and the exogenous variable $x \equiv -d\hat{c}_{t+1} - \hat{r}_t$. Models of this type have been widely employed in monetary economics, and we will return to study them in Chapter 4.

A second conclusion revealed by the dynamic system is that when $\Phi \neq 1$, only *anticipated* changes in money growth matter. To see this point, suppose $\gamma = \phi = 0$ so that the realization $u_t = \varphi_t$ is a purely unanticipated change in the growth rate of money that has no effect on anticipated future values of money growth. Now consider a positive realization of φ_t (nominal money growth is faster than average). This increases the nominal stock of money. If $\gamma = \phi = 0$, future money growth rates are unaffected by the value of φ_t. As a result, future expected inflation, $E_t \hat{\pi}_{t+1}$, is also unaffected. Therefore, a permanent jump in the price level that is proportional to the unexpected rise in the nominal money stock leaving m_t unaffected also leaves equations (2.41)–(2.46) unaffected. From (2.47), for φ_t to have no effect on m_t requires that $\hat{\pi}_t = \varphi_t$. So an unanticipated money-growth-rate disturbance has no real effects and simply leads to a one-period change in the inflation rate (and a permanent change in the price level). Unanticipated money doesn't matter.

Now consider what happens when we continue to assume $\phi = 0$ but allow γ to differ from zero. In the United States, money growth displays positive serial correlation, so assume $\gamma > 0$. A positive shock to money growth ($\varphi_t > 0$) now has implications for the future growth rate of money. With $\gamma > 0$, future money growth will be above average, so expectations of future inflation will rise. From (2.46), however, we can see that for real consumption and the expected real interest rate to remain unchanged in response to a rise in expected future inflation, current real money balances must fall. Consequently, P_t would need to rise more than in proportion to the rise in the nominal money stock. But the decline in m_t affects the first-order conditions given by (2.45) and (2.46), so the real equilibrium will not remain unchanged. Monetary disturbances have real effects by affecting the expected rate of inflation.

To actually determine how the equilibrium responds to money-growth-rate shocks and how the response depends quantitatively on γ and ϕ, we will employ numerical methods. That means we need to assign specific values to the parameters of the model, a task to which we now turn.

2.3.2.3   Calibration   Thirteen parameters appear in the equations that characterize behavior around the steady state: α, δ, ρ, σ_e^2, β, b, Ψ, η, Φ, Θ, γ, ϕ, σ_φ^2. Some of these parameters are common to standard real-business-cycle models; for example, Cooley and Prescott (1995, p. 22) report values of, in our notation, α (the share of capital income in total income), δ (the rate of depreciation of physical capital), ρ (the autoregressive coefficient in the productivity process), σ_e (the standard deviation of productivity innovations), and β (the subjective rate of time discount in the utility function). These values are based on a time period equal to three months (one quarter). We adopt these values except for the depreciation rate δ; Cooley and Prescott calibrate $\delta = 0.012$ based on a model that explicitly incorporates growth. For our purposes, we use the somewhat higher value of 0.019 given in Cooley and Hansen (1995, p. 201). For the average growth rate of the nominal money stock, an annual

Table 2.2
Baseline Parameter Values

α	δ	ρ	σ_e	β	b	η	Θ	σ_φ
0.40	0.019	0.95	0.007	0.989	0.005	1	1.0125	0.0089

Table 2.3
Steady-State Values at Baseline Parameter Values

R^{ss}	$\dfrac{y^{ss}}{k^{ss}}$	$\dfrac{c^{ss}}{k^{ss}}$	$\dfrac{m^{ss}}{k^{ss}}$	$\dfrac{n^{ss}}{k^{ss}}$
1.011	0.075	0.056	0.012	0.013

rate of 5% would imply a quarterly value of 1.0125 for Θ. Cooley and Hansen (1989) report a value of 0.0089 for σ_φ, the standard deviation of innovations to the money growth rate. We will consider various values for the autoregression coefficient for money growth, γ, and the coefficient on the productivity shock, ϕ, to see how the behavior of the model is affected by the way in which money growth evolves.

The remaining parameters are those in the utility function. The value of Ψ can be chosen so that n^{ss} is equal to 0.31 as in Cooley and Prescott. The appendix shows that the steady-state value of real money balances relative to output is equal to $b(c^{ss}/y^{ss})(1 + \pi^{ss})/(1 + \pi^{ss} - \beta)$. The benchmark parameter value $b = 0.005$ implies a value of 0.16 for m^{ss}/y^{ss}. This is approximately equal to the real value of M1 relative to GDP in the early 1990s. Both $\Phi = 1$ (log utility in c and m) and $\Phi = 2$ (so that $u_{cm} < 0$) are considered, while η is set equal to 1.

These parameter values are summarized in Table 2.2. Using the information in this table, the steady-state values for the variables reported in Table 2.1 can be evaluated. These are given in Table 2.3. The effect of money growth on the steady-state level of employment can be derived using equation (2.40). The elasticity of steady-state labor supply with respect to Θ is equal to

$$-\frac{b(1 - \Phi)\beta(1 - n^{ss})}{(\Theta - \beta)[\eta n^{ss} - v(1 - n^{ss})]} \tag{2.48}$$

Evaluating this elasticity at the benchmark values and $\Phi = 2$ yields a value of 0.07; hence a 100% change in inflation (from 5% to 10%) would increase steady-state labor supply by 7%, or from a steady-state value of 0.31 to a value of 0.33. The elasticity is zero if $\Phi = 1$, since money is superneutral when utility is log linear in c and m.

While this elasticity is positive for the basic parameter values we will use for simulation purposes, equation (2.48) indicates that the elasticity of labor supply with

Table 2.4
Implied Contemporaneous Correlations: $\eta = 1$; $\gamma = \phi = 0$

	$\Phi = 1$			$\Phi = 2$		
	S.D.	*S.D./σ_y*	*Corr.*	*S.D.*	*S.D./σ_y*	*Corr.*
$\hat{y}$	1.337	1	1	1.174	1	1
$\hat{c}$	0.354	0.26	0.89	0.283	0.24	0.94
$\hat{x}$	4.395	3.29	0.99	3.873	3.30	1.00
$\hat{r}$	0.041	0.03	0.98	0.036	0.04	0.98
$\hat{m}$	0.354	0.26	0.89	0.320	0.27	0.88
$\hat{\pi}$	0.928	0.69	−0.34	0.916	0.78	−0.31

respect to the rate of money growth will be negative if $0 < \Phi < 1$. With Φ positive but less than 1, the marginal utility of consumption is increasing in real money balances. Hence, higher inflation, along with the associated reduction in real balance holdings, decreases the marginal utility of consumption. The resulting decreased demand for consumption increases the demand for leisure and decreases labor supply (see equation [2.34]). The dependence of the elasticity of labor with respect to inflation on the partial derivatives of the utility function in a general MIU function model is discussed more fully by Wang and Yip (1992).

As discussed earlier, the value of Ψ was chosen to ensure a steady-state value of 0.31 for n^{ss}; this implied $\Psi = 1.786$ when $\Phi = 1$. The value of Ψ falls to 1.383 when $\Phi = 2$ and average inflation is 5%. Because the steady-state value of n^{ss} is held fixed at 0.31, variations in average inflation that would normally affect n^{ss} will instead cause Ψ to vary. However, this effect on Ψ is small; at an average inflation rate of 50%, Ψ rises to 1.394 and m^{ss}/y^{ss} falls from 0.16 at an average inflation rate of 5% to 0.03 at an average inflation rate of 50%.

2.3.2.4 Simulation Results Table 2.4 shows the standard deviations implied by the model for the major variables, together with the implied contemporaneous correlation with output for two different values of Φ.[33] Statistics for net investment, $\hat{x}_t = \hat{k}_t - (1 - \delta)\hat{k}_{t-1}$ are also included. Recall that the transitional dynamics exhibit superneutrality when $\Phi = 1$. When $\Phi = 2$, the marginal utility of consumption is decreasing in real money balances (see equation [2.38]).[34]

---

33. The reported correlations and standard deviations are for data first detrended using a Hodrick-Prescott filter.

34. Brock (1974) shows that multiple steady-state equilibria may exist if $u_{cm} < 0$ as is the case when $\Phi > 1$. For the utility function used here, however, the steady state is unique. As discussed later, $\Phi > 1$ is required if faster money growth is to induce a rise in output when $\gamma > 0$.

Table 2.5
Effects of Variations in the Money-Growth-Rate Process ($\Phi = 2$)

	$\gamma = 0.5, \phi = 0$		$\gamma = 0.5, \phi = 0.15$		$\gamma = 0.5, \phi = -0.15$	
	S.D.	*Corr.*	*S.D.*	*Corr.*	*S.D.*	*Corr.*
$\hat{y}$	1.174	1	1.178	1	1.171	1
$\hat{c}$	0.283	0.94	0.290	0.94	0.277	0.94
$\hat{x}$	3.873	1.00	3.865	1.00	3.881	1.00
$\hat{r}$	0.036	0.98	0.036	0.98	0.036	0.98
$\hat{m}$	0.934	0.30	3.586	-0.97	4.131	0.98
$\hat{\pi}$	1.825	-0.15	4.040	0.89	4.555	-0.92

We now want to see how the properties of the model vary as the time-series properties of the growth rate of the money stock vary. Cooley and Hansen report an estimate of approximately 0.5 for γ, the autoregressive coefficient for money growth. Table 2.5 illustrates the effects of setting $\gamma = 0.5$ combined with various values for ϕ, beginning with $\phi = 0$.[35] The table is based on $\Phi = 2$.

As Table 2.5 shows, the manner in which the growth rate of the nominal money supply responds to the real productivity shock has small but real effects on the variances of real output, consumption, and investment. Thus, the short-run dynamics can be affected by the stochastic process followed by money growth, and in particular by the way in which money growth is related to real productivity shocks. This effect implies that even within the framework of a neoclassical model, there can be a role for monetary policy to affect the evolution of real variables by the way money growth reacts to economic shocks.

But at least for plausible parameter values, the channels through which money affects the real economy in this model are very weak. That is, while monetary policy matters in this equilibrium model, it doesn't matter very much. Figure 2.3 shows how the output and labor responses to a technology shock depend on the value of ϕ. The figure plots the difference between the responses when $\phi = 0$ and when $\phi = -0.15$. When $\phi = -0.15$, employment and output are slightly lower than in the baseline case ($\phi = 0$), so the differences are negative, since a positive technology shock leads to lower expected money growth and inflation when ϕ is negative. Lower expected inflation raises real money balances, lowers the marginal utility of consumption, and lowers labor supply when, as in the case here, $\Phi > 1$ (see [2.48]). As the figure suggests, the differences are quite small.

Figure 2.4 shows how the cross correlations between output and real money bal-

---

35. Cooley and Hansen report a value of 0.89% for the variance of u_t when $M_t = \gamma M_{t-1} + (1 - \gamma)\Theta + u_t$. When ϕz_{t-1} is added to this specification of the money supply process, the variance of u is adjusted to keep the variance of $M_t - \gamma M_{t-1} - (1 - \gamma)\Theta$ equal to 0.89%.

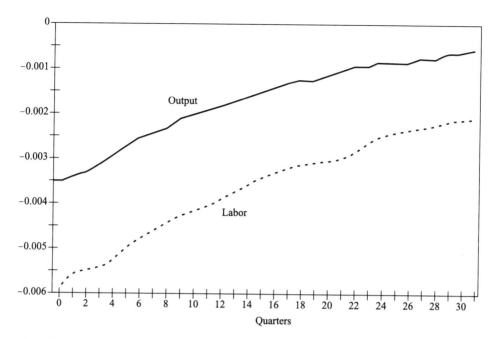

Figure 2.3
Effect of $\phi = -0.15$ versus $\phi = 0$ on Responses to a Technology Shock

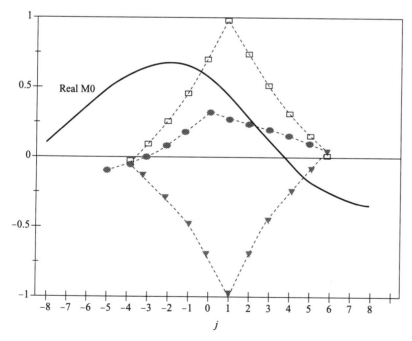

Figure 2.4
Dynamic Correlations of y_t and m_{t+j}. ● $\phi = 0$, ▼ $\phi = 0.15$, ▢ $\phi = -0.15$

ances depend on the value of ϕ. Also shown are the actual correlations based on U.S. M0 that were discussed in Chapter 1.[36] The MIU model does not capture the data correlations between lagged money and output. The correlations of real balances with lagged output clearly require a negative value of ϕ, the case in which a positive technology shock leads to a subsequent reduction in money growth. "Countercyclical" responses to productivity shocks reduce the impact of these disturbances on labor supply. As a result, the variance of output is reduced (see Table 2.5), although again, the effects are relatively small.

The nominal-interest-rate response to a technology shock is strongly affected by the choice of ϕ. This relationship is illustrated in Figure 2.5. When $\phi = 0$, money growth is not affected by a technology shock and the nominal interest rate is little affected. In contrast, when $\phi = -0.15$, a positive technology shock reduces money growth and expected inflation, leading to a fall in the nominal rate of interest.

Consistent with the earlier discussion, the monetary shock φ_t affects the labor-leisure choice only when the nominal-money-growth-rate process exhibits serial correlation ($\gamma \neq 0$) or responds to the technology shock ($\phi \neq 0$). But for the base value of 0.5 for γ, the effect of φ_t on n_t is very small. As equation (2.34) showed, variations in money holdings can affect the representative household's labor-leisure choice by affecting the ratio of the marginal utility of leisure to the marginal utility of consumption. In the calibrated model, this ratio is equal to $\Psi(1-n)^{-\eta}/c^{-\Phi}m^{b(1-\Phi)}$. With $\Phi = 2$, a positive realization of φ_t implies a rise in expected inflation when money growth is positively serially correlated ($\gamma > 0$); this reduces holdings of real money balances (m), raising the marginal utility of consumption and causing the agent to substitute away from leisure. As a consequence, labor supply (and output) rises. If $\Phi < 1$, higher expected inflation (and therefore lower real money balances) would lower the marginal utility of consumption and lead to an increase in leisure demand; labor supply and output would fall in this case.

Figure 2.6 shows that the magnitude of the effect of monetary shocks on output and labor is small, but the effects do clearly depend on the degree of persistence in the money growth process. Higher values of γ generate larger effects on labor input and output.

Finally, Figure 2.7 shows how the nominal-interest-rate response depends on γ. Notice that a positive monetary shock *increases* the nominal rate of interest. Monetary policy actions that increase the growth rate of money are usually thought to

---

36. Only the correlations for M0 are shown; M1 and M2 show similar patterns.

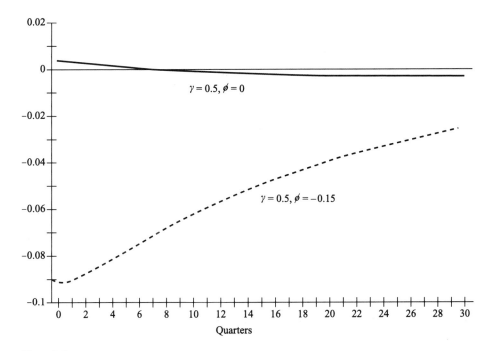

Figure 2.5
Nominal-Interest-Rate Response to a Technology Shock

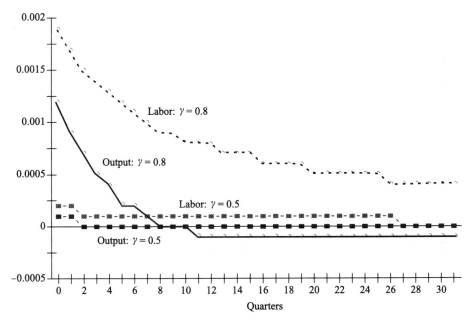

Figure 2.6
Output and Labor Responses to a Monetary Shock

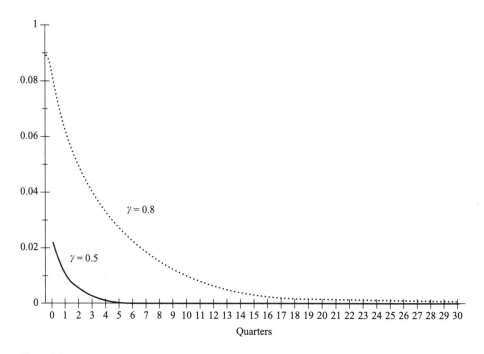

Figure 2.7
Nominal-Interest-Rate Response to a Monetary Shock

reduce nominal interest rates, at least initially. In the MIU model, the main effect of money-growth-rate shocks when $\gamma > 0$ is to increase expected inflation and raise the nominal rate.

2.4 Summary

Much of this chapter has focused on a basic money-in-the-utility-function model. Assuming that holdings of real money balances yield direct utility is a means of ensuring a positive demand for money so that, in equilibrium, money is held and has value. This assumption is clearly a shortcut; it does not address the issue of why money yields utility, nor does it address the issue of why certain pieces of paper that we call money yield utility but other pieces of paper presumably do not. And while a shortcut is often useful, we also saw in going from Tobin's framework to the Sidrauski model that important results—such as whether inflation affects the steady-state capital-labor ratio—can depend critically on the model's specification.

The Sidrauski model, because it assumed that agents act systematically to maximize utility, has the decided advantage of allowing welfare comparisons of steady states to be made. The model can be used to assess the welfare costs of inflation and to determine the optimal rate of inflation. Friedman's conclusion that the optimal inflation rate is the rate that produces a zero nominal rate of interest is one that we will see is quite robust.

Finally, by developing a linear approximation to the basic money-in-the-utility-function model (augmented to include a labor-supply choice), we were able to show how the economy responded to shocks to the growth rate of the money supply and how the short-run dynamic adjustment to real productivity shocks was affected by the feedback rule followed by money growth. For the benchmark values of the model's parameters, however, the effects of variation in the money growth process on output are quantitatively quite small.

2.5   Appendix: The MIU Approximation

The linear approximation to the MIU model that is studied in section 2.3.2 is derived in this appendix. After setting up the household's decision problem and deriving the first-order necessary conditions, the properties of the steady state are determined. Then, the first-order conditions, together with the economy's resource constraint and production function, are linearized around the steady state.

2.5.1   The Decision Problem

The household's problem is conveniently expressed using the value function. In studying a similar problem without a labor-leisure choice (see section 2.3.1), the state could be summarized by $\omega_t = y_t + \tau_t + (1 - \delta)k_{t-1} + \left(\dfrac{1}{1 + \pi_t}\right)m_{t-1}$ where y_t is per capita income, k_{t-1} is the per capita (or household) stock of capital at the start of the period, m_{t-1} is the level of real money balances at the end of the previous period, and τ_t is the real transfer payment received at the start of period t. Now, however, output y_t will depend on the household's current-period choice of labor supply, so it will prove convenient to let $a_t = \tau_t + \left(\dfrac{1}{1 + \pi_t}\right)m_{t-1}$ be the household's real money balances plus transfer at the start of period t, and define the value function $V(a_t, k_{t-1})$ as the maximum present value of utility the household can achieve if the current state is (a_t, k_{t-1}). If n_t denotes the fraction of time the household devotes to market employment, output per household y_t is given by

$$y_t = f(k_{t-1}, n_t, z_t)$$

The value function for the household's decision problem is defined by

$$V(a_t, k_{t-1}) = \max\{u(c_t, m_t, 1 - n_t) + \beta E_t V(a_{t+1}, k_t)\} \tag{2.49}$$

where the maximization is over (c_t, m_t, k_t, n_t) and is subject to

$$f(k_{t-1}, n_t, z_t) + (1 - \delta)k_{t-1} + a_t = c_t + k_t + m_t \tag{2.50}$$

$$a_{t+1} = \tau_{t+1} + \frac{m_t}{1 + \pi_{t+1}} \tag{2.51}$$

Note that the presence of uncertainty arising from the stochastic productivity and money-growth-rate shocks means that it is the expected value of $V(a_{t+1}, k_t)$ that appears in the value function (2.49). The treatment of a_t as a state variable assumes that the money growth rate shock φ_t is known at the time the household decides on c_t, k_t, and m_t, since this determines the current value of the transfer τ_t. We will also assume the productivity disturbance z_t is known at the start of period t.

Using (2.50) to eliminate k_t and (2.51) to substitute for a_{t+1}, the value function can be rewritten as

$$V(a_t, k_{t-1}) = \max \left\{ u(c_t, m_t, 1 - n_t) \right.$$
$$+ \beta E_t \left[V \left(\tau_{t+1} + \frac{m_t}{1 + \pi_{t+1}}, f(k_{t-1}, n_t, z_t) \right.\right.$$
$$\left.\left.\left. + (1 - \delta)k_{t-1} + a_t - c_t - m_t \right) \right] \right\}$$

where this is now an unconstrained maximization with respect to c_t, m_t, and n_t. The first-order conditions are

$$u_c(c_t, m_t, 1 - n_t) - \beta E_t V_k(a_{t+1}, k_t) = 0 \tag{2.52}$$

$$u_m(c_t, m_t, 1 - n_t) + \beta E_t \left[\frac{V_a(a_{t+1}, k_t)}{1 + \pi_{t+1}} \right] - \beta E_t V_k(a_{t+1}, k_t) = 0 \tag{2.53}$$

$$-u_l(c_t, m_t, 1 - n_t) + \beta E_t V_k(a_{t+1}, k_t) f_n(k_{t-1}, n_t, z_t) = 0 \tag{2.54}$$

$$V_a(a_t, k_{t-1}) = \beta E_t V_k(a_{t+1}, k_t) \tag{2.55}$$

$$V_k(a_t, k_{t-1}) = \beta E_t V_k(a_{t+1}, k_t)[f_k(k_{t-1}, n_t, z_t) + 1 - \delta] \tag{2.56}$$

Updating (2.56) one period and using (2.55), one obtains

$$V_k(a_{t+1}, k_t) = E_{t+1}\{[f_k(k_t, n_{t+1}, z_{t+1}) + 1 - \delta]V_a(a_{t+1}, k_t)\}$$

Now, using this to substitute for $V_k(a_{t+1}, k_t)$ in (2.52) yields[37]

$$u_c(c_t, m_t, 1 - n_t) - \beta E_t\{[f_k(k_t, n_{t+1}, z_{t+1}) + 1 - \delta]V_a(a_{t+1}, k_t)\} = 0 \qquad (2.57)$$

When it is recognized that $u_c(c_t, m_t, 1 - n_t) = \beta E_t V_k(a_{t+1}, k_t)$, equations (2.53), (2.57), and (2.55) take the same form as (2.15), (2.14), and (2.17), the first-order conditions for the basic Sidrauski model that did not include a labor-leisure choice. Equation (2.54) can be written, using (2.52), as

$$\frac{u_l(c_t, m_t, 1 - n_t)}{u_c(c_t, m_t, 1 - n_t)} = f_n(k_{t-1}, n_t, z_t)$$

which states that at an optimum, the marginal rate of substitution between consumption and leisure must equal the marginal product of labor.

2.5.2 Equilibrium and the Steady State

The equilibrium values of consumption, capital, money holdings, and labor supply must satisfy the conditions given in (2.52)–(2.55). These conditions can be simplified, however. Noting that (2.52) and (2.55) imply $u_c(c_t, m_t, 1 - n_t) = \beta E_t V_k(a_{t+1}, k_t) = V_a(a_t, k_{t-1})$, equations (2.53), (2.57), and (2.54) can be rewritten as

$$u_c(c_t, m_t, 1 - n_t) = u_m(c_t, m_t, 1 - n_t) + \beta E_t\left[\frac{u_c(c_{t+1}, m_{t+1}, 1 - n_{t+1})}{1 + \pi_{t+1}}\right] \qquad (2.58)$$

$$u_c(c_t, m_t, 1 - n_t) = \beta E_t R_t u_c(c_{t+1}, m_{t+1}, 1 - n_{t+1}) \qquad (2.59)$$

$$u_c(c_t, m_t, 1 - n_t)f_n(k_{t-1}, n_t, z_t) = u_l(c_t, m_t, 1 - n_t) \qquad (2.60)$$

where in (2.59),

$$R_t = f_k(k_t, n_{t+1}, z_{t+1}) + 1 - \delta \qquad (2.61)$$

is one plus the marginal product of capital net of depreciation. In addition, the economy's aggregate resource constraint, expressed in per capita terms, requires that

$$k_t = (1 - \delta)k_{t-1} + y_t - c_t \qquad (2.62)$$

---

37. This also makes use of the law of iterated expectations: $E_t(E_{t+1}x_t) = E_t x_t$.

while the production function is

$$y_t = f(k_{t-1}, n_t, z_t) \tag{2.63}$$

Finally, real money balances evolve according to

$$m_t = \left(\frac{1 + \theta_t}{1 + \pi_t}\right) m_{t-1} \tag{2.64}$$

where θ_t is the growth rate of the nominal stock of money.

To complete the model, it remains to specify the process governing the productivity disturbance z_t and the growth rate of money θ_t. Following the real-
business-cycle literature, let

$$z_t = \rho z_{t-1} + e_t \tag{2.65}$$

where e_t is a serially uncorrelated mean-zero process and $|\rho| < 1$. For money growth,
define $u_t = \theta_t - \theta^{ss}$ as the deviation of money growth around its average value θ^{ss}.
This deviation will be treated as a stochastic process given by

$$u_t = \gamma u_{t-1} + \phi z_{t-1} + \varphi_t, \quad 0 \leq \gamma < 1 \tag{2.66}$$

where φ_t is a serially uncorrelated mean-zero process.

Equations (2.58)–(2.66) represent a nonlinear system of equations to determine
the equilibrium values of the model's nine endogenous variables: y_t, c_t, k_t, m_t, n_t, R_t,
π_t, z_t, and u_t.

To analyze this system, we start by finding expressions for the steady-state values
of the endogenous variables. Evaluated at steady-state values, equation (2.59) becomes $u_c^{ss} = \beta R^{ss} u_c^{ss}$, or

$$R^{ss} = \frac{1}{\beta} \tag{2.67}$$

while (2.64) yields

$$\pi^{ss} = \theta^{ss} \tag{2.68}$$

Using these two results, equation (2.58) can be written as

$$\frac{u_m^{ss}}{u_c^{ss}} = 1 - \frac{\beta}{1 + \pi^{ss}} = 1 - \frac{1}{R^{ss}(1 + \pi^{ss})} = \frac{i^{ss}}{1 + i^{ss}} \tag{2.69}$$

where $i^{ss} = R^{ss}(1 + \pi^{ss}) - 1$ is the steady-state nominal rate of interest.

The steady-state marginal utility of leisure is, from (2.60),

$$u_l^{ss} = f_n(k^{ss}, n^{ss}, 0)u_c^{ss} \tag{2.70}$$

since from (2.65) the value of z is zero in the steady state.

From (2.61),

$$f_k(k^{ss}, n^{ss}, 0) = R^{ss} - 1 + \delta \tag{2.71}$$

while steady-state output is equal to

$$y^{ss} = f(k^{ss}, n^{ss}, 0) \tag{2.72}$$

and the resource constraint, in the steady state, takes the form

$$y^{ss} = c^{ss} + \delta k^{ss} \tag{2.73}$$

These seven conditions (2.67)–(2.73) define the steady-state values of output, consumption, capital, employment, real money balances, inflation, and the real rate of interest.

2.5.3 Functional Forms

In order to study the properties of this nonlinear system of equations, we will evaluate them using specific functional forms for the utility function and the production function. For the production function, we follow common practice in assuming a constant-returns-to-scale, Cobb-Douglas production function expressed in per capita terms:[38]

$$y_t = e^{z_t} k_{t-1}^{\alpha} n_t^{1-\alpha}$$

For the utility function, we follow Fischer (1979b) in restricting attention to preferences displaying constant relative risk aversion. Therefore, assume

$$u(c_t, m_t, l_t) = \frac{[c_t m_t^b]^{1-\Phi}}{1-\Phi} + \Psi \frac{l_t^{1-\eta}}{1-\eta}$$

with b, η, Φ, $\Psi > 0$ and $b(1-\Phi) < 1$. In the limiting case $\Phi = 1$, preferences over consumption and money holdings are log linear.

---

38. Recalling that n is the fraction of time the representative household spends in employment, aggregate output is equal to $Y = e^z(kN)^{\alpha}(nN)^{1-\alpha} = e^z(K)^{\alpha}(nN)^{1-\alpha}$ if there are N households in the economy.

Using the assumed functional forms, we can use (2.58)–(2.64) to evaluate the equilibrium conditions of the model:

$$\frac{u_m}{u_c} = \frac{bc_t}{m_t} = \frac{i_t}{1+i_t}$$

$$\frac{u_l}{u_c} = \frac{\Psi(1-n_t)^{-\eta}}{c_t^{-\Phi}m_t^{b(1-\Phi)}} = (1-\alpha)\frac{y_t}{n_t}$$

$$\alpha\frac{E_t y_{t+1}}{k_t} = R_t - 1 + \delta$$

In the steady state with $R^{ss} = \beta^{-1}$, this last condition implies that the steady-state output-capital ratio is equal to

$$\left(\frac{y^{ss}}{k^{ss}}\right) = \frac{1}{\alpha}\left(\frac{1}{\beta} - 1 + \delta\right)$$

From the production function, $(y^{ss}/k^{ss}) = (n^{ss}/k^{ss})^{1-\alpha}$, or

$$\left(\frac{n^{ss}}{k^{ss}}\right) = \left(\frac{y^{ss}}{k^{ss}}\right)^{\frac{1}{1-\alpha}} = \left[\frac{1}{\alpha}\left(\frac{1}{\beta} - 1 + \delta\right)\right]^{\frac{1}{1-\alpha}}$$

It follows from the aggregate resource constraint that

$$\left(\frac{c^{ss}}{k^{ss}}\right) = \left(\frac{y^{ss}}{k^{ss}}\right) - \delta$$

Since $R^{ss} = 1/\beta$ and $1 + \pi^{ss} = \Theta$, $i^{ss}/(1 + i^{ss}) = (\Theta - \beta)/\Theta$. Therefore, using (2.69),

$$\frac{m^{ss}}{k^{ss}} = \left(\frac{\Theta}{\Theta - \beta}\right)b\left(\frac{c^{ss}}{k^{ss}}\right) = Hb\left(\frac{c^{ss}}{k^{ss}}\right) \tag{2.74}$$

where $H \equiv \Theta/(\Theta - \beta)$. These results for the steady-state ratios are collected in Table 2.1.

To go from the steady-state ratios of Table 2.1 to the steady-state levels, it is necessary to determine the steady-state value of n, since it is through its effect on n^{ss} that inflation may affect the steady state. For this, we need to use the first-order condition given by (2.60). In the steady state, this can be written as

$$\Psi(1-n^{ss})^{-\eta} = (1-\alpha)\left(\frac{y^{ss}}{n^{ss}}\right)(m^{ss})^{b(1-\Phi)}(c^{ss})^{-\Phi}$$

Multiplying and dividing the right side by $(c^{ss})^{b(1-\Phi)}$ and recalling from (2.74) that $(m^{ss}/c^{ss}) = Hb$ yields

$$\Psi(1 - n^{ss})^{-\eta} = (1 - \alpha)\left(\frac{y^{ss}}{n^{ss}}\right)(Hb)^{b(1-\Phi)}(c^{ss})^{b(1-\Phi)-\Phi}$$

Letting $v \equiv b(1 - \Phi) - \Phi$, we can rewrite this equation in terms of the ratios c^{ss}/k^{ss} and y^{ss}/k^{ss} already found,[39]

$$
\begin{aligned}
(1 - n^{ss})^{-\eta} &= \frac{(1 - \alpha)}{\Psi}\left(\frac{y^{ss}}{k^{ss}}\right)^{\frac{-\alpha}{1-\alpha}}(Hb)^{b(1-\Phi)}\left(\frac{c^{ss}}{k^{ss}}\right)^{v}\left(\frac{k^{ss}}{n^{ss}}\right)^{v}(n^{ss})^{v} \\
&= \frac{(1 - \alpha)}{\Psi}\left(\frac{y^{ss}}{k^{ss}}\right)^{\frac{-\alpha}{1-\alpha}}(Hb)^{b(1-\Phi)}\left(\frac{c^{ss}}{k^{ss}}\right)^{v}\left(\frac{y^{ss}}{k^{ss}}\right)^{\frac{-v}{1-\alpha}}(n^{ss})^{v} \\
&= \frac{(1 - \alpha)}{\Psi}\left(\frac{y^{ss}}{k^{ss}}\right)^{\frac{-(\alpha+v)}{1-\alpha}}(Hb)^{b(1-\Phi)}\left(\frac{c^{ss}}{k^{ss}}\right)^{v}(n^{ss})^{v}
\end{aligned}
$$

Multiplying both sides of this expression by $(n^{ss})^{-v}$ results in

$$
\begin{aligned}
(n^{ss})^{-v}(1 - n^{ss})^{-\eta} &= \frac{(1 - \alpha)}{\Psi}[Hb]^{b(1-\Phi)}\left(\frac{y^{ss}}{k^{ss}}\right)^{\frac{-(\alpha+v)}{1-\alpha}}\left(\frac{c^{ss}}{k^{ss}}\right)^{v} \\
&= Kh(\Theta)
\end{aligned}
\tag{2.75}
$$

where $K = \frac{(1 - \alpha)}{\Psi}\left(\frac{y^{ss}}{k^{ss}}\right)^{\frac{-(\alpha+v)}{1-\alpha}}\left(\frac{c^{ss}}{k^{ss}}\right)^{v}$ is independent of the steady-state growth rate of the nominal money supply and $h(\Theta) = [b\Theta/(\Theta - \beta)]^{b(1-\Phi)}$ is an increasing function of the money growth rate when $\Phi > 1$.

2.5.4 The Linear Approximation

We next need to linearize the model around the steady state. Percentage deviations of a variable x will be denoted by $\hat{x}$. To obtain linear approximations around the steady state, we will set equal to zero any terms that involve the products of percentage deviations. We begin with equations (2.62) and (2.63), since they are the most straightforward.

---

39. This uses $y^{ss}/n^{ss} = (k^{ss}/n^{ss})^{\alpha}$ and $(k^{ss}/n^{ss}) = (y^{ss}/k^{ss})^{-1/(1-\alpha)}$. Combining these yields $y^{ss}/n^{ss} = (y^{ss}/k^{ss})^{-\alpha/(1-\alpha)}$.

The resource constraint (2.62) can be written in terms of percentage deviations from the steady state as

$$k^{ss}(1 + \hat{k}_t) = k^{ss}(1 - \delta)(1 + \hat{k}_{t-1}) + y^{ss}(1 + \hat{y}_t) - c^{ss}(1 + \hat{c}_t)$$

Using the fact that $y^{ss} = c^{ss} + \delta k^{ss}$, we obtain

$$k^{ss}\hat{k}_t = k^{ss}(1 - \delta)\hat{k}_{t-1} + y^{ss}\hat{y}_t - c^{ss}\hat{c}_t$$

Dividing by k^{ss},

$$\hat{k}_t = (1 - \delta)\hat{k}_{t-1} + \left(\frac{y^{ss}}{k^{ss}}\right)\hat{y}_t - \left(\frac{c^{ss}}{k^{ss}}\right)\hat{c}_t \tag{2.76}$$

The aggregate production function can be expressed in terms of percentage deviations around the steady state as

$$\hat{y}_t = \alpha\hat{k}_{t-1} + (1 - \alpha)\hat{n}_t + z_t \tag{2.77}$$

We next turn to equation (2.61), the condition linking the expected real rate of interest and the expected marginal product of capital. This can be written as

$$R^{ss}(1 + \hat{r}_t) = 1 - \delta + \alpha\left(\frac{y^{ss}}{k^{ss}}\right)E_t\left(\frac{1 + \hat{y}_{t+1}}{1 + \hat{k}_t}\right)$$

$$\approx 1 - \delta + \alpha\left(\frac{y^{ss}}{k^{ss}}\right)(1 + E_t\hat{y}_{t+1} - \hat{k}_t)$$

With $R^{ss} = \alpha\left(\frac{y^{ss}}{k^{ss}}\right) + 1 - \delta$, our approximation for the percentage deviations of the real return from its steady state is given by

$$R^{ss}\hat{r}_t = \alpha\left(\frac{y^{ss}}{k^{ss}}\right)(E_t\hat{y}_{t+1} - \hat{k}_t) \tag{2.78}$$

Equations (2.58)–(2.60) are more complicated, but we can derive approximations for them using the same methods used to obtain the other approximations. Notice that both (2.58) and (2.59) contain terms of the form $\beta E_t(u_{t+1}w_{t+1})$. Such expressions can be written as

$$\beta E_t\left[u^{ss}(1 + \hat{u}_{t+1})w^{ss}(1 + \hat{w}_{t+1})\right] \approx \beta u^{ss}w^{ss}E_t(1 + \hat{u}_{t+1} + \hat{w}_{t+1})$$

$$= \beta u^{ss}w^{ss} + \beta u^{ss}w_t^{ss}E_t(\hat{u}_{t+1} + \hat{w}_{t+1})$$

It follows that the deviation of $\beta E_t(u_{t+1} w_{t+1})$ around its steady state is $\beta u^{ss} w^{ss}(E_t \hat{u}_{t+1} + E_t \hat{w}_{t+1})$.

Now consider equation (2.59). Using the function form of the utility function, it becomes

$$c_t^{-\Phi} m_t^{b(1-\Phi)} = \beta E_t \left[R_t c_{t+1}^{-\Phi} m_{t+1}^{b(1-\Phi)} \right]$$

Since $x^a = [x^{ss}(1+\hat{x})]^a \approx (x^{ss})^a(1+a\hat{x})$, the left side of this equation can be approximated by

$$(c^{ss})^{-\Phi}(m^{ss})^{b(1-\Phi)} \{(1-\Phi\hat{c}_t)[1+b(1-\Phi)\hat{m}_t]\}$$

$$\approx (c^{ss})^{-\Phi}(m^{ss})^{b(1-\Phi)} [1 - \Phi\hat{c}_t + b(1-\Phi)\hat{m}_t]$$

For the right side, we have $u_{t+1} = R_t$ and $w_{t+1} = c_{t+1}^{-\Phi} m_{t+1}^{b(1-\Phi)}$. Hence, $u^{ss} = R^{ss}$ and $w^{ss} = (c^{ss})^{-\Phi}(m^{ss})^{b(1-\Phi)}$, implying it will be given by

$$\beta R^{ss}(c^{ss})^{-\Phi}(m^{ss})^{b(1-\Phi)} [1 + \hat{r}_t - \Phi E_t \hat{c}_{t+1} + b(1-\Phi)E_t \hat{m}_{t+1}]$$

Putting these results together, noting that $\beta R^{ss} = 1$ and dividing by $(c^{ss})^{-\Phi}(m^{ss})^{b(1-\Phi)}$, we obtain

$$E_t[\Phi(\hat{c}_{t+1} - \hat{c}_t) - b(1-\Phi)(\hat{m}_{t+1} - \hat{m}_t)] - \hat{r}_t = 0 \qquad (2.79)$$

Similarly, (2.58) becomes

$$c_t^{-\Phi} m_t^{b(1-\Phi)} = b c_t^{1-\Phi} m_t^{b(1-\Phi)-1} + \beta E_t \left[\frac{c_{t+1}^{-\Phi} m_{t+1}^{b(1-\Phi)}}{1 + \pi_{t+1}} \right]$$

or

$$1 = b c_t m_t^{-1} + \beta E_t \left[\left(\frac{1}{1 + \pi_{t+1}} \right) \frac{c_{t+1}^{-\Phi} m_{t+1}^{b(1-\Phi)}}{c_t^{-\Phi} m_t^{b(1-\Phi)}} \right]$$

which can be approximated using (2.79) as

$$1 = b \left(\frac{c^{ss}}{m^{ss}} \right) [1 + \hat{c}_t - \hat{m}_t] + \beta E_t \left[\frac{[1 - \Phi(\hat{c}_{t+1} - \hat{c}_t) + b(1-\Phi)(\hat{m}_{t+1} - \hat{m}_t)]}{(1 + \pi^{ss})(1 + \hat{\pi}_{t+1})} \right]$$

$$= b \left(\frac{c^{ss}}{m^{ss}} \right) [1 + \hat{c}_t - \hat{m}_t] + \frac{\beta}{1 + \pi^{ss}} E_t \left[\frac{1 - \hat{r}_t}{1 + \hat{\pi}_{t+1}} \right]$$

$$\approx b \left(\frac{c^{ss}}{m^{ss}} \right) [1 + \hat{c}_t - \hat{m}_t] + \frac{\beta}{1 + \pi^{ss}} E_t[1 - \hat{r}_t - \hat{\pi}_{t+1}]$$

Subtracting $1 = b\left(\dfrac{c^{ss}}{m^{ss}}\right) + \dfrac{\beta}{1 + \pi^{ss}}$ from both sides,

$$0 = b\left(\frac{c^{ss}}{m^{ss}}\right)[\hat{c}_t - \hat{m}_t] - \frac{\beta}{1 + \pi^{ss}}[\hat{r}_t + E_t\hat{\pi}_{t+1}]$$

Hence,

$$\hat{i}_t = \hat{r}_t + E_t\hat{\pi}_{t+1} = d(\hat{c}_t - \hat{m}_t)$$

where $d \equiv b\left(\dfrac{c^{ss}}{m^{ss}}\right)(1 + \pi^{ss})/\beta = (\Theta - \beta)/\beta$.

Finally, (2.60) can be approximated by first noting that it can be rewritten as $(1 - \alpha)y_t n_t^{-1} u_c = \Psi(1 - n_t)^{-\eta}$. Now $(1 - n_t)^{-\eta} = l_t^{-\eta}$, and this can be approximated by noting that $l^{ss}(1 + \hat{l}_t) = 1 - n^{ss}(1 + \hat{n}_t)$, so that $\hat{l}_t = -\left(\dfrac{n^{ss}}{l^{ss}}\right)\hat{n}_t$. Hence, $(1 - n_t)^{-\eta} = l_t^{-\eta} \approx (l^{ss})^{-\eta}(1 - \eta\hat{l}_t) \approx (l^{ss})^{-\eta}\left[1 + \eta\left(\dfrac{n^{ss}}{l^{ss}}\right)\hat{n}_t\right]$. So (2.60) is approximated by

$$\left[1 + \eta\left(\frac{n^{ss}}{l^{ss}}\right)\right]\hat{n}_t = [\hat{y}_t - \Phi\hat{c}_t + b(1 - \Phi)\hat{m}_t] \tag{2.80}$$

Equation (2.64) can be written as $m^{ss}(1 + \hat{m}_t) = \Theta(1 + u_t)m^{ss}(1 + \hat{m}_{t-1})/\Theta(1 + \hat{\pi}_t)$, or approximately,

$$\hat{m}_t = \hat{m}_{t-1} - \hat{\pi}_t + u_t \tag{2.81}$$

The equations describing the evolution of the exogenous processes z and u are straightforward, given by (2.65) and (2.66), but they are repeated here for completeness:

$$z_t = \rho z_{t-1} + e_t \tag{2.82}$$

$$u_t = \gamma u_{t-1} + \phi z_{t-1} + \varphi_t \tag{2.83}$$

Equations (2.76)–(2.83) constitute a linearized version of Sidrauski's money-in-the-utility-function model. These equations represent a linear system of difference equations involving expectational variables. The state variables are $\hat{k}$ and $\hat{m}$; the endogenous variables are $(\hat{c}, \hat{y}, \hat{\pi}, \hat{r})$; and the exogenous variables are z and u.

2.6 Problems

1. Calvo and Leiderman (1992): A commonly used specification of the demand for money, originally due to Cagan (1956), assumes $m = Ae^{-\alpha i_t}$ where A and α are parameters and i is the nominal rate of interest. In the Sidrauski (1967) model, assume that utility is separable in consumption and real money balances: $u(c_t, m_t) = w(c_t) + v(m_t)$, and further assume that $v(m_t) = m_t(B - D \ln m_t)$ where B and D are positive parameters. Show that the demand for money is given by $m_t = Ae^{-\alpha_t i_t}$ where $A = e^{(\frac{B}{D}-1)}$ and $\alpha_t = w'(c_t)/D$.

2. Suppose $u(c_t, m_t) = \sum_{i=0}^{\infty} \beta^i[\ln c_t + m_t e^{-\gamma m_t}]$, $\gamma > 0$, and $\beta = 0.95$. Assume the production function is $f(k) = k^{0.5}$ and $\delta = 0.02$. What rate of inflation maximizes steady-state welfare? How do real money balances at the welfare maximizing rate of inflation depend on γ?

3. Assume that $m_t = Ae^{-\alpha i_t}$ where A and α are constants. Calculate the welfare cost of inflation in terms of A and α, expressed as a percentage of steady-state consumption (normalized to equal 1). Does the cost increase or decrease with α? Explain why.

4. Suppose a nominal interest rate of i^m is paid on money balances. These payments are financed by a combination of lump-sum taxes and printing money. Let a be the fraction financed by lump-sum taxes. The government's budget identity is $\tau_t + v = i^m m_t$, with $\tau_t = ai^m m_t$ and $v = \theta m_t$. Using Sidrauski's model,

a. Show that the ratio of the marginal utility of money to the marginal utility of consumption will equal $r + \pi - i^m = i - i^m$. Explain why.

b. Show how $i - i^m$ is affected by the method used to finance the interest payments on money. Explain the economics behind your result.

5. Assume $u(c, m) = -c^{-a}[1 + (m^* - m)^2]$, $a > 0$. Normalize so that the steady-state value of consumption is equal to 1 ($c^{ss} = 1$). Using equation (2.23) of the text, show that there exist two steady-state equilibrium values for real money balances if $aI^{ss} < 1$. (Recall that $I = i/(1+i)$ where i is the nominal rate of interest.)

6. In Sidrauski's money-in-the-utility-function model augmented to include variable labor supply, money is superneutral if the representative agent's preferences are given by

$$\sum \beta^i u(c_{t+i}, m_{t+i}, l_{t+i}) = \sum \beta^i (c_{t+i} m_{t+i})^b l_{t+i}^d$$

but not if they are given by

$$\sum \beta^i u(c_{t+i}, m_{t+i}, l_{t+i}) = \sum \beta^i (c_{t+i} + km_{t+i})^b l_{t+i}^d$$

Discuss. (Assume that output depends on capital and labor and that the aggregate production function is Cobb-Douglas.)

7. Suppose the representative agent does not treat τ_t as a lump-sum transfer, but instead assumes her transfer will be proportional to her own holdings of money (since in equilibrium, τ is proportional to m). Solve for the agent's demand for money. What is the welfare cost of inflation?

3 Money and Transactions

3.1 Introduction

The previous chapter introduced a role for money by assuming that individuals derived direct utility from their holdings of real money balances. Models that generate a positive demand for money by assuming that real balances appear in the utility function have been criticized for solving the problem of creating positive value for money by simply assuming the problem away. Postulating that money yields direct utility guarantees that money will be valued (as long as the utility function is suitably defined). Yet we usually think of money as yielding utility through use—we value money because it is useful in facilitating transactions. As described by Clower (1967), goods buy money and money buys goods, but goods don't buy goods. And because "goods don't buy goods," a medium of exchange that serves to aid in the process of transacting will have value.

A medium of exchange that facilitates transactions yields utility indirectly by allowing certain purchases to be made, or by reducing the costs associated with transactions, and the demand for money is then generated by the nature of the economy's transactions technology. The first formal models of the demand for money that emphasized the role of transactions costs were due to Baumol (1952) and Tobin (1956).

The first model we examine in this chapter is one in which time and money are used to produce transaction services that are required in order to purchase consumption goods. The consumer must balance the opportunity cost of holding money against the value of leisure in deciding how to combine time and money to facilitate transactions. The cost of transacting influences money demand and consumption decisions. The production technology used to produce transaction services determines how much time must be spent "shopping" for given levels of consumption and money holdings. Higher levels of money holdings reduce the time needed for shopping, thereby raising the individual agent's leisure. When leisure enters the utility function of the representative agent, such shopping-time models provide a link between the money-in-the-utility-function approach of the previous chapter and models of money that focus more explicitly on transactions services and money as a medium of exchange.

Most of this chapter, however, will be devoted to the study of models that impose a rigid restriction on the nature of transactions. Rather than allowing substitutability between time and money in carrying out transactions, *cash-in-advance* (CIA) models simply require that money balances be held to finance certain types of purchases. After examining theoretical CIA frameworks, we study a stochastic simulation model that introduces a cash-in-advance constraint into a basic real-business-cycle model.

CIA models, like the MIU models of the previous chapter, assume that money is special; unlike other financial assets, it either yields direct utility, and therefore belongs in the utility function, or it has unique properties that allow it to be used to facilitate transactions. This chapter concludes with a look at some recent attempts based on search theory to explain how the nature of transactions gives rise to "money."

3.2   Shopping-Time Models

A direct means of modeling the notion that money facilitates transactions is to assume that the purchase of goods requires the input of transaction services which, in turn, are produced by money and time. Larger holdings of money allow the household to reduce the time it needs to devote to producing transaction services.[1]

Shopping-time models begin with the assumption that utility depends on consumption and leisure: $v(c, l)$. Leisure is equal to $l = 1 - n - n^s$ where n is time spent in market employment and n^s is time spent shopping. Total time available is normalized to equal 1. Suppose that purchasing consumption requires transactions services ψ, with units chosen so that consumption of c requires transaction services $\psi = c$. These transaction services are produced with inputs of real cash balances $m \equiv \dfrac{M}{P}$ and shopping time n^s:

$$\psi = c = \psi(m, n^s) \tag{3.1}$$

where $\psi_m \geq 0$, $\psi_{n^s} \geq 0$, $\psi_{mm} \leq 0$, and $\psi_{n^s n^s} \leq 0$. This specification assumes that it is the agent's holdings of *real* money balances that produce transaction services; a change in the price level requires a proportional change in nominal money holdings to generate the same level of real consumption purchases, holding shopping time n^s constant. Rewriting (3.1) in terms of the shopping time required for given levels of consumption and money holdings:

$$n^s = g(c, m); \quad g_c > 0, \quad g_m \leq 0$$

With shopping time n^s an increasing function of consumption and a decreasing function of real money holdings, time available for leisure is $1 - n - g(c, m)$. We can

---

1. See Brock (1974) for an earlier use of a shopping-time model to motivate a money-in-the-utility-function approach. The use of a shopping-time approach to the study of the demand for money is presented in McCallum and Goodfriend (1987) and Croushore (1993).

now define a function

$$u(c,m,n) \equiv v[c, 1 - n - g(c,m)]$$

that gives utility as a function of consumption, labor supply, and money holdings. Thus, a simple shopping-time model can motivate the appearance of money in the utility function, and, more importantly, can help to determine the properties of the partial derivatives of the function u with respect to m.[2] By placing restrictions on the partial derivatives of the shopping-time production function $g(c,m)$, we potentially can determine what restrictions might be placed on the properties of the utility function $u(c,m,n)$. For example, if the marginal productivity of money goes to zero for some finite level of real money balances $\bar{m}$, that is, $\lim_{m \to \bar{m}} g_m = 0$, then this property will carry over to u_m.

In a money-in-the-utility-function model, higher expected inflation lowers money holdings, but the effect on consumption will depend on the sign of u_{cm}. The shopping-time model implies $u_m = -v_l g_m \geq 0$, so

$$u_{cm} = (v_{ll} g_c - v_{cl}) g_m - v_l g_{cm} \tag{3.2}$$

The sign of u_{cm} will depend on such factors as the effect of variations in leisure time on the marginal utility of consumption (v_{cl}) and the effect of variations in consumption on the marginal productivity of money in reducing shopping time (g_{cm}). In the benchmark MIU model of the previous chapter, u_{cm} was taken to be negative.[3] Relating u_{cm} to the partials of the underlying utility function v and the transactions production function g can help to suggest whether this assumption was reasonable. From (3.2), the assumption of diminishing marginal utility of leisure ($v_{ll} \leq 0$) and $g_m \leq 0$ implies $v_{ll} g_c g_m \geq 0$. If greater consumption raises the marginal productivity of money in reducing shopping time ($g_{cm} \leq 0$), then $-v_l g_{cm} \geq 0$ as well. Wang and Yip (1992) characterize the situation in which these two dominate (so that $u_{cm} \geq 0$) as the transaction-services version of the money-in-the-utility model. In this case, the MIU model implies that a rise in expected inflation would lower m and u_c, and this effect would lower labor supply and output (see section 2.3.2.3). If consumption and leisure are strong substitutes so that $v_{cl} \leq 0$, then u_{cm} could be negative, a situation Wang and Yip describe as corresponding to an asset-substitution model and the version of the MIU model implied by the benchmark parameters used in Chapter 2.

---

2. Note that we have assumed that transaction services are needed only for the purchase of consumption goods and not for the purchase of capital goods. In the next section, we will see that alternative treatments of investment and the transactions technology have implications for the steady state.

3. This assumption corresponded to $\Phi > 1$ in the benchmark utility function used in Chapter 2.

With $u_{cm} < 0$, a monetary injection that raises expected inflation will increase consumption, labor supply, and output.

The household's problem analyzed in the appendix to Chapter 2 for the MIU model can be easily modified to incorporate a shopping-time role for money. The household's objective is to maximize

$$\sum_{i=0}^{\infty} \beta^i v[c_{t+i}, 1 - n_{t+i} - g(c_{t+i}, m_{t+i})]; \quad 0 < \beta < 1$$

subject to

$$f(k_{t-1}, n_t) + \tau_t + (1 - \delta)k_{t-1} + \frac{m_{t-1}}{1 + \pi_t} = c_t + k_t + m_t \tag{3.3}$$

Defining $a_t \equiv \tau_t + \frac{m_{t-1}}{1 + \pi_t}$, the household's decision problem can be written in terms of the value function $V(a_t, k_{t-1})$:

$$V(a_t, k_{t-1}) = \max \{v[c_t, 1 - n_t - g(c_t, m_t)] + \beta V(a_{t+1}, k_t)\}$$

where the maximization is subject to the constraints $f(k_{t-1}, n_t) + (1 - \delta)k_{t-1} + a_t = c_t + k_t + m_t$ and $a_{t+1} = \tau_{t+1} + \frac{m_t}{1 + \pi_{t+1}}$. Proceeding as in Chapter 2 by using these two constraints to eliminate k_t and a_{t+1} from the expression for the value function, the necessary first-order conditions for real money holdings, capital holdings, and labor supply are

$$u_c - u_l g_c - \beta V_k(a_{t+1}, k_t) = 0 \tag{3.4}$$

$$-u_l g_m + \beta \frac{V_a(a_{t+1}, k_t)}{1 + \pi_{t+1}} - \beta V_k(a_{t+1}, k_t) = 0 \tag{3.5}$$

$$-u_l + \beta V_k(a_{t+1}, k_t) f_n(k_{t-1}, n_t) = 0 \tag{3.6}$$

$$V_a(a_t, k_{t-1}) = \beta V_k(a_{t+1}, k_t) \tag{3.7}$$

$$V_k(a_t, k_{t-1}) = \beta V_k(a_{t+1}, k_t)[f_k(k_{t-1}, n_t) + 1 - \delta] \tag{3.8}$$

Letting w_t denote the marginal product of labor [i.e., $w_t = f_n(k_{t-1}, n_t)$], equations (3.6) and (3.7) yield $u_l = w_t V_a(a_t, k_{t-1})$. This implies that (3.4) can be written as

$$u_c(c_t, l_t) = V_a(a_t, k_{t-1})[1 + w_t g_c(c_t, m_t)]$$

The marginal utility of consumption is set equal to the marginal utility of wealth,

$V_a(a_t, k_{t-1})$, plus the cost, in utility units, of the marginal time needed to purchase consumption. The increased shopping time involved in additional consumption is g_c; its value in terms of goods is obtained by multiplying this by the real wage w; and its value in terms of utility is $V_a(a, k)wg_c$.

With $g_m \le 0$, $u_l g_m = w g_m V_a$ is the value in utility terms of the shopping-time savings that results from additional holdings of real money balances. Equation (3.5) states that money will be held to the point where the marginal net benefit, equal to the value of shopping-time savings plus the discounted value of money's wealth value next period, or $-u_l g_m + \beta \dfrac{V_a(a_{t+1}, k_t)}{1 + \pi_{t+1}}$, just equals the net marginal utility of consumption. Letting $R_t = f_k(k_t, n_{t+1}) + 1 - \delta$ denote one plus the real rate of return net of depreciation, the first-order condition for optimal money holdings, together with (3.7) and (3.8), implies

$$-u_l g_m = \beta V_k(a_{t+1}, k_t) - \beta \frac{V_a(a_{t+1}, k_t)}{1 + \pi_{t+1}}$$

$$= V_a(a_t, k_{t-1}) \left[1 - \beta \frac{V_a(a_{t+1}, k_t)/V_a(a_t, k_{t-1})}{1 + \pi_{t+1}} \right]$$

$$= V_a(a_t, k_{t-1}) \left\{ 1 - \left[\frac{1}{R_t(1 + \pi_{t+1})} \right] \right\} = V_a(a_t, k_{t-1}) \left(\frac{i_t}{1 + i_t} \right)$$

where $1 + i_t = R_t(1 + \pi_{t+1})$ is the nominal rate of interest and $\beta[V_a(a_{t+1}, k_t)/V_a(a_t, k_{t-1})] = R_t^{-1}$.

Since no social cost of producing money has been introduced, optimality would require that the private marginal product of money, g_m, be driven to zero. Private agents will hold money to a point where $g_m = 0$ if and only if $i = 0$; we thus obtain the standard result for the optimal rate of inflation as seen earlier in the MIU model.

The chief advantage of the shopping-time approach as a means of motivating the presence of money in the utility function is its use in tying the partials of the utility function with respect to money to the specification of the production function relating money, shopping time, and consumption. But this representation of the medium-of-exchange role of money is also clearly a shortcut. The transaction services production function $\psi(m, n^s)$ is simply postulated; this approach does not help to determine what constitutes money. Why, for example, does holding certain types of green paper facilitate transactions (at least in the United States) while yellow pieces of paper don't? Section 3.4.2 will review models based on search theory that attempt to derive money demand from a more primitive specification of the transactions process.

3.3 Cash-in-Advance Models

The shopping-time model allows time and money to serve as substitutes in carrying out transactions. A somewhat more direct approach, proposed by Clower (1967), captures the role of money as a medium of exchange by requiring explicitly that money be used to purchase consumption goods. Such a requirement can also be viewed as replacing the substitution possibilities between time and money highlighted in the shopping-time model with a transactions technology in which shopping time is zero if $M/P \geq c$ and infinite otherwise (McCallum 1990a). This can be represented by assuming that the individual faces, in addition to a standard budget constraint, a "cash-in-advance" constraint. The exact form the constraint takes will depend on which transactions or purchases are subject to the cash-in-advance requirements. For example, both consumption goods and investment goods might be subject to the requirement. Or only consumption might be subject to the constraint. Or only a subset of all consumption goods may require cash for their purchase. The constraint will also depend on what constitutes "cash." Can bank deposits that earn interest, for example, also be used to carry out transactions? As we will see, the exact specification of the transactions subject to the cash-in-advance constraint can be important.

To understand aspects of the basic specification of CIA models, the next subsection reviews a simplified version of a model due to Svensson (1985). The simplification we adopt involves eliminating uncertainty. Once the basic framework of a CIA model has been reviewed, however, we consider a stochastic CIA model that was developed by Cooley and Hansen (1989) as a means of studying the role of money in a stochastic dynamic general equilibrium model in which business cycles are generated by both real productivity shocks and random shocks to the money-growth-rate process. Developing a linearized version of the Cooley-Hansen model will serve to illustrate how the cash-in-advance approach differs from the money-in-the-utility-function approach that was discussed in Chapter 2.

3.3.1 The Certainty Case

To get a feel for how a cash-in-advance constraint can be incorporated into a basic neoclassical model, we start with a case that parallels the basic Sidrauski model of Chapter 2 in that we assume there is no uncertainty. In general, uncertainty can have important effects on money demand in cash-in-advance models, depending on the assumed timing of transactions in asset and goods markets. For example, if uncertainty is resolved *after* money balances are chosen, an agent may find that she is holding cash balances that are too low to finance her desired spending level. Or she may be left with more cash than she needs, thereby forgoing interest income. To understand the basic structure of such a model, however, it is useful to start with the simplest case, one in which there is no uncertainty. To do so, we incorporate capital accumulation into the model of Svensson (1985) to facilitate comparing results with the Sidrauski model.

Consider the following representative-agent model. The agent's objective is to chose a path for consumption and asset holdings to maximize

$$\sum_{t=0}^{\infty} \beta^t u(c_t) \tag{3.9}$$

for $0 < \beta < 1$, where $u(\cdot)$ is bounded, continuously differentiable, strictly increasing, and strictly concave, and the maximization is subject to a sequence of budget constraints which, in nominal terms, take the form

$$P_t \omega_t \equiv P_t f(k_{t-1}) + (1-\delta)P_t k_{t-1} + T_t + M_{t-1} + I_{t-1} B_{t-1}$$

$$\geq P_t c_t + M_t + B_t + P_t k_t \tag{3.10}$$

where P_t is the aggregate price level, ω_t is the agent's time-t real resources, B_{t-1} is the individual's $t-1$ holdings of nominal one period bonds that yield a gross nominal return of I_{t-1} from period $t-1$ to period t, T_t is a lump-sum transfer from the government, and M_t are nominal holdings of cash carried into period $t+1$. Physical capital depreciates at the rate δ. Dividing through by the time-t price level, the budget constraint can be rewritten in real terms as

$$\omega_t \equiv f(k_{t-1}) + (1-\delta)k_{t-1} + \tau_t + \frac{m_{t-1} + I_{t-1}b_{t-1}}{\Pi_t} \geq c_t + m_t + b_t + k_t \tag{3.11}$$

where m and b are real cash and bond holdings, $\tau_t = T_t/P_t$, and $\Pi_t \equiv 1 + \pi_t = P_t/P_{t-1}$ is one plus the rate of inflation. Note that real resources available to the representative agent in period $t+1$ are given by

$$\omega_{t+1} = f(k_t) + (1-\delta)k_t + \tau_{t+1} + \frac{m_t + I_t b_t}{\Pi_{t+1}} \tag{3.12}$$

The period t nominal interest factor I_t divided by Π_{t+1} is the gross real rate of return from period t to $t+1$ and can be denoted by $R_t \equiv I_t/\Pi_{t+1}$.

The second constraint faced by the representative agent is the cash-in-advance constraint:

$$c_t \leq \frac{M_{t-1}}{P_t} + \tau_t = \frac{m_{t-1}}{\Pi_t} + \tau_t \tag{3.13}$$

Real spending on consumption in period t cannot exceed the amount of real money balances carried into the period plus the transfer payment received at the start of period t. Note the timing: M_{t-1} refers to nominal money balances chosen by the agent in period $t-1$ and carried into period t. The real value of these is determined by the period-t price level P_t. Since we have assumed away any uncertainty, the agent knows P_t at the time M_{t-1} is chosen. This specification of the cash-in-advance constraint assumes that income from production during period t will not be available for consumption purchases during period t. These timing choices are arbitrary, and a number of authors have explored the implications of alternatives.

If there is any opportunity cost of holding money, the agent will only hold an amount of money that is just sufficient to finance the desired level of consumption. Since the opportunity cost of holding m is given by the nominal interest rate, (3.13) will always hold with equality as long as the nominal rate of interest is positive. This need not be the case if uncertainty is introduced. For example, if period t's income is uncertain and is realized after M_{t-1} has been chosen, a bad income realization may cause the agent to reduce consumption to a point where the constraint is no longer binding. Or a disturbance that causes an unexpected price decline might, by increasing the real value of the agent's money holdings, result in a nonbinding constraint.

The choice variables at time t are c_t, M_t, B_t, and k_t. An individual agent's state at time t can be characterized by her resources ω_t and her real cash holdings m_{t-1}; both are relevant because consumption choice is constrained by the agent's resources and by cash holdings. To analyze the agent's decision problem, we can define the value function

$$V(\omega_t, m_{t-1}) = \max\{u(c_t) + \beta V(\omega_{t+1}, m_t)\} \tag{3.14}$$

where the maximization is subject to (3.11), (3.12), and (3.13).

Equation (3.11) can be used to eliminate real bond purchases b_t from (3.12), yielding

$$\omega_{t+1} = f(k_t) + (1-\delta)k_t + \tau_{t+1} + \frac{m_t}{\Pi_{t+1}} + R_t[w_t - c_t - m_t - k_t]$$

Using this expression for ω_{t+1} in (3.14) and letting μ_t denote the Lagrangian multiplier associated with the cash-in-advance constraint (3.13), the first-order necessary conditions for the agent's choice of consumption, capital, and money holdings take the form[4]

$$u_c(c_t) - \beta R_t V_\omega(\omega_{t+1}, m_t) - \mu_t = 0 \tag{3.15}$$

$$\beta[f_k(k_t) + 1 - \delta - R_t] V_\omega(\omega_{t+1}, m_t) = 0 \tag{3.16}$$

$$\beta\left(\frac{1}{\Pi_{t+1}} - R_t\right) V_\omega(\omega_{t+1}, m_t) + \beta V_m(\omega_{t+1}, m_t) = 0 \tag{3.17}$$

From the envelope theorem,

$$V_\omega(\omega_t, m_{t-1}) = \beta R_t V_\omega(\omega_{t+1}, m_t) \tag{3.18}$$

$$V_m(\omega_t, m_{t-1}) = \mu_t \frac{1}{\Pi_t} \tag{3.19}$$

Let λ_t denote the marginal value of wealth at time t: $\lambda_t \equiv V_\omega(\omega_t, m_{t-1})$. Then by using (3.18), equation (3.15) can be written as

$$u_c(c_t) = \lambda_t + \mu_t \tag{3.20}$$

The marginal utility of consumption exceeds the marginal utility of wealth, λ_t, by the value of liquidity services μ_t (compare to equation [2.17]). The individual must hold money in order to purchase consumption, so the "cost," to which the marginal utility of consumption is set equal, is the marginal utility of wealth plus the cost of the liquidity services needed to finance the transaction.

In terms of λ, equation (3.18) becomes

$$\lambda_t = \beta R_t \lambda_{t+1} \tag{3.21}$$

which is a standard asset-pricing equation and is a familiar condition from problems involving intertemporal optimization. Along the optimal path, the marginal cost (in terms of today's utility) from reducing wealth slightly, λ_t, must equal the utility value of carrying that wealth forward one period, earning a gross return R_t, where tomorrow's utility is discounted back to today at the rate β; that is, $\lambda_t = \beta R_t \lambda_{t+1}$ along the optimal path.

The first-order condition (3.17) can be expressed using (3.18) and (3.19) as

$$\lambda_t = \beta\left(\frac{\lambda_{t+1}}{\Pi_{t+1}} + \frac{\mu_{t+1}}{\Pi_{t+1}}\right) \tag{3.22}$$

---

4. The first-order conditions also include the transversality conditions.

Equation (3.22) can also be interpreted as an asset-pricing equation for money. The price of a unit of money in terms of goods is just $\dfrac{1}{P_t}$ at time t. Now divide through by P_t to rewrite (3.22) as $\beta\left(\dfrac{\lambda'}{P'} + \dfrac{\mu'}{P'}\right) = \dfrac{\lambda}{P}$ where a prime denotes a time $t + 1$ variable. Solving forward,[5] this equation implies

$$\frac{1}{P_t} = \sum_{i=1}^{\infty} \beta^i \frac{\mu_{t+i}/P_{t+i}}{\lambda_t} \tag{3.23}$$

From (3.19), μ_{t+i}/P_{t+i} is equal to $V_m(\omega_{t+i}, m_{t+i-1})/P_{t+i-1}$. This last expression, though, is just the partial of the value function with respect to time $t + i - 1$ *nominal* money balances:

$$\partial V(\omega_{t+i}, m_{t+i-1})/\partial M_{t+i-1} = V_m(\omega_{t+i}, m_{t+i-1})(\partial m_{t+i-1}/\partial M_{t+i-1})$$

$$= V_m(\omega_{t+i}, m_{t+i-1})/P_{t+i-1}$$

$$= \mu_{t+i}/P_{t+i}.$$

This means we can rewrite (3.23) as

$$\frac{1}{P_t} = \sum_{i=1}^{\infty} \beta^i \frac{\partial V(\omega_{t+i}, m_{t+i-1})/\partial M_{t+i-1}}{\lambda_t}$$

In other words, the current value of money is equal to the present value of the marginal utility of money in all future periods. Equation (3.23) is an interesting result; it says that money is just like any other asset in the sense that we can think of its value (i.e., its price today) as equal to the present discounted value of the stream of returns generated by the asset. In the case of money, these returns take the form of liquidity services. If the cash-in-advance constraint were not binding, these liquidity services would not have value ($\mu = V_m = 0$), and neither would money. But if the constraint is binding, then money has value because it yields valued liquidity services.[6]

   The result that the price of money, $1/P$, satisfies an asset-pricing relationship is not unique to the cash-in-advance approach. For example, a similar relationship is implied by the money-in-the-utility-function approach. The model employed for our

5. For references on solving difference equations forward in the context of rational expectations models, see Blanchard and Kahn (1980) or McCallum (1989).
6. Bohn (1991b) provides an analysis of the asset-pricing implications of a cash-in-advance model.

analysis of the dynamics of the money-in-the-utility-function approach (see the appendix to Chapter 2), implied

$$\frac{\lambda}{P} = \beta\left(\frac{\lambda'}{P'}\right) + \frac{u_m}{P}$$

which can be solved forward to yield

$$\frac{1}{P_t} = \sum_{i=1}^{\infty} \beta^i \frac{u_m/P_{t+i}}{\lambda_t}$$

Here, the marginal utility of money u_m plays a role exactly analogous to that played by the Lagrangian on the cash-in-advance constraint μ. The one difference is that in the MIU approach, m_t yields utility at time t, while in the CIA approach, the value of money accumulated at time t is measured by μ_{t+1}, since the cash cannot be used to purchase consumption goods until period $t + 1$.

An expression for the gross nominal rate of interest can be obtained from (3.21) as $I_t = (1 + \pi_{t+1})R_t = \frac{(1 + \pi_{t+1})\lambda_t}{\beta\lambda_{t+1}}$. But from (3.22), $\lambda_t = \beta\frac{\lambda_{t+1} + \mu_{t+1}}{1 + \pi_{t+1}}$, or $(1 + \pi_{t+1})\lambda_t = \beta(\lambda_{t+1} + \mu_{t+1})$, so $I_t = \beta(\lambda_{t+1} + \mu_{t+1})/\beta\lambda_{t+1} = 1 + \mu_{t+1}/\lambda_{t+1}$. Hence, the nominal interest rate is given by

$$i_t = I_t - 1 = \frac{\mu_{t+1}}{\lambda_{t+1}} \tag{3.24}$$

Thus, the nominal rate of interest is positive if and only if money yields liquidity services ($\mu_{t+1} > 0$).

We can use the relationship between the nominal rate of interest and the Lagrangian multipliers to rewrite the expression for the marginal utility of consumption, given in equation (3.20), as $u_c = \lambda\left(1 + \frac{\mu}{\lambda}\right) = \lambda(1 + i) \geq \lambda$. Since λ represents the marginal value of income, the marginal utility of consumption exceeds that of income whenever the nominal interest rate is positive. Even though the economy's technology allows output to be directly transformed into consumption, the "price" of consumption is not equal to 1 but is $1 + i$ since the household must hold money to finance consumption. Thus, in this cash-in-advance model, a positive nominal interest rate functions like a tax on consumption; it raises the price of consumption above its production costs.

The cash-in-advance constraint holds with equality when the nominal rate of interest is positive, so $c_t = \frac{M_{t-1}}{P_t} + \tau_t$. Since the monetary transfer τ_t is equal to

$(M_t - M_{t-1})/P_t$, this implies that $c_t = \dfrac{M_t}{P_t} = m_t$. Consequently, the consumption velocity of money is identically equal to 1 (velocity $= P_t c_t / M_t = 1$). Since actual velocity varies over time, cash-in-advance models have been modified in ways that break this tight link between c and m implied by the model. One way to avoid this problem is to introduce uncertainty; if money balances have to be chosen prior to the resolution of uncertainty, it may turn out that the desired level of consumption is less than the amount of real money balances being held. In this case, some money balances will be unspent, and velocity can be less than one. Velocity may also vary if the cash-in-advance constraint only applies to a subset of consumption goods. Then, variations in the rate of inflation can lead to substitution between goods whose purchase requires cash and those whose purchase doesn't.

3.3.1.1 The Steady State   If we restrict ourselves to considering the steady state, (3.21) implies that $R^{ss} = \dfrac{1}{\beta}$, and, from (3.24), $i^{ss} \approx \dfrac{1}{\beta} - 1 + \pi^{ss}$. Thus, the Fisher relationship holds in which the nominal interest rate moves one-for-one with variations in the rate of inflation. In addition, equation (3.16) gives the steady-state capital stock as the solution to

$$f_k(k^{ss}) = R - 1 + \delta = \frac{1}{\beta} - 1 + \delta$$

So this CIA model, like the Sidrauski MIU model, exhibits superneutrality. The steady-state capital stock depends only on the time-preference parameter β, the rate of depreciation δ, and the production function. It is independent of the rate of inflation. Since steady-state consumption is equal to $f(k^{ss}) - \delta k^{ss}$, it too is independent of the rate of inflation.[7]

We have seen already that the marginal utility of consumption could be written as the marginal utility of wealth (λ) times one plus the nominal rate of interest, reflecting the opportunity cost of holding the money required to purchase goods for consumption. Using (3.15) and (3.17), we can derive

$$\frac{\beta V_m}{u_c} = \frac{i}{1+i}$$

---

7. The expression for steady-state consumption can be obtained from (3.11) by noting that $m_t = \tau_t + \dfrac{m_{t-1}}{\Pi_t}$ and, with all households identical, $b = 0$ in equilibrium. Then (3.11) reduces to

$$c^{ss} + k^{ss} = f(k^{ss}) + (1 - \delta)k^{ss}$$

or $c^{ss} = f(k^{ss}) - \delta k^{ss}$.

This expression is exactly parallel to our result in the MIU framework that the ratio of the marginal utility of money to the marginal utility of consumption is equal to the nominal interest rate divided by one plus the nominal rate—that is, the relative price of money in terms of consumption. Since money accumulated during period t can only be used to finance consumption at time $t + 1$, V_m is discounted by the factor β.

With the cash-in-advance constraint binding, real consumption is equal to real money balances. In the steady state, constant consumption implies that the stock of nominal money balances and the price level must be changing at the same rate. If $M_t = (1 + \theta)M_{t-1}$ (so that $T_t = \theta M_{t-1}$), then

$$\pi^{ss} = \theta^{ss}$$

The steady-state inflation rate is, as usual, determined by the rate of growth of the nominal money stock.

3.3.1.2   The Welfare Costs of Inflation   The CIA model, because it is based explicitly on behavioral relationships consistent with utility maximization, can be used to assess the welfare costs of inflation and to determine the optimal rate of inflation. The money-in-the-utility-function approach of Chapter 2 had very strong implications for the optimal inflation rate. Steady-state utility of the representative household was maximized when the nominal rate of interest was equal to zero. We have already suggested that this conclusion continues to hold when money produces transaction services.

In the basic CIA model, however, there is no optimal rate of inflation that maximizes steady-state welfare of the representative household. The reason follows directly from the specification of utility as a function only of consumption and the result that consumption is independent of the rate of inflation (superneutrality). Steady-state welfare is equal to

$$\sum_{t=0}^{\infty} \beta^t u(c^{ss}) = \frac{u(c^{ss})}{1 - \beta}$$

and is invariant to the inflation rate. Comparing across steady states, any inflation rate is as good as any other.[8]

This finding is not robust to modifications in the basic CIA model. In particular, once we extend the model to incorporate a labor-leisure choice, utility will no

---

8. By contrast, the optimal rate of inflation was well defined even in the basic Sidrauski model that exhibited superneutrality.

longer be independent of the inflation rate, and there will be a well-defined optimal rate of inflation. Because leisure can be "purchased" without the use of money (i.e., leisure is not subject to the cash-in-advance constraint), variations in the rate of inflation will affect the marginal rate of substitution between consumption and leisure. With different inflation rates then leading to different levels of steady-state consumption and leisure, steady-state utility will be a function of inflation. This type of substitution plays an important role in the model of Cooley and Hansen (1989) which will be discussed in the next section; in their model, inflation leads to an increased demand for leisure and a reduction in labor supply. But before including a labor-leisure choice, we can briefly review some other modifications of the basic CIA model, modifications that will, in general, generate a unique optimal rate of inflation.

CASH AND CREDIT GOODS   Lucas and Stokey (1983, 1987) introduced the idea that the cash-in-advance constraint may only apply to a subset of consumption goods— the "cash" goods. They model this by assuming that the representative agent's utility function is defined over her consumption of two types of consumption goods; cash goods and credit goods. In this case, paralleling equation (3.20), the marginal utility of cash goods will be equated to $\lambda + \mu = \lambda \left(1 + \frac{\mu}{\lambda} \right) \geq \lambda$ while the marginal utility of credit goods will be equated to λ. Hence, the cash-in-advance requirement for cash goods drives a wedge between the marginal utilities of the two types of goods. It is exactly as if the consumer faces a tax of μ/λ on purchases of the cash good. Higher inflation, by reducing holdings of real cash balances, serves to raise the tax on cash goods and generates a substitution away from the cash good and toward the credit good. (See also Hartley 1988.)

The obvious difficulty with this approach is that the classifications of goods into "cash" and "credit" goods is exogenous. And it is common to assume a one-good technology so that the goods are not differentiated by any technological considerations. The advantage of these models is that they can produce time variation in velocity. Recall that in the basic cash-in-advance model, any equilibrium with a positive nominal rate of interest was characterized by a binding cash-in-advance constraint, and this meant that $c = M/P$. With both cash and credit goods, M/P will equal the consumption of cash goods, allowing the ratio of total consumption to money holdings to vary with expected inflation.

CIA AND INVESTMENT GOODS   A second modification to the basic model involves extending the cash-in-advance constraint to cover investment goods. In this case, the inflation tax applies to both consumption and investment goods. Higher rates of inflation will tend to discourage capital accumulation and leave the economy in a steady state characterized by a lower capital-labor ratio. Stockman (1981) showed that higher inflation would lower the steady-state capital-labor ratio (see problem 5 at the end of the chapter). This finding runs directly counter to Tobin's model in which higher inflation raised the steady-state value of k/n (see section 2.2).[9]

IMPLICATIONS FOR OPTIMAL INFLATION   In cash-in-advance models, inflation acts as a tax on goods or activities whose purchase requires cash. This tax then introduces a distortion by creating a wedge between the marginal rates of transformation implied by the economy's technology and the marginal rates of substitution faced by consumers. Since the CIA model, like the MIU model of the previous chapter, offers no reason for such a distortion to be introduced (there is no inefficiency that calls for Pigovian taxes or subsidies on particular activities, and the government's revenue needs can be met through lump-sum taxation), optimality calls for setting the inflation tax equal to zero. The inflation tax is directly related to the nominal rate of interest; a zero inflation tax is achieved when the nominal rate of interest is equal to zero.

3.3.2   A Stochastic Cash-in-Advance Model

While the models of Svensson (1985) and Lucas and Stokey (1987) provide theoretical frameworks for assessing the role of inflation on asset prices and interest rates, they do not provide any guide to the empirical magnitude of inflation effects or the welfare costs of inflation. What one would like is a dynamic equilibrium model that one could simulate under alternative monetary policies—for example, for alternative steady-state rates of inflation—in order to assess quantitatively the effects of inflation. Such an exercise is conducted by Cooley and Hansen (1989).

Cooley and Hansen follow the basic framework of Lucas and Stokey (1987). However, important aspects of their specification include (1) the introduction of capital and, consequently, an investment decision; (2) the introduction of a labor-leisure choice; and (3) the identification of consumption as the cash good and investment and leisure as credit goods.

Inflation represents a tax on the purchases of the cash good, and therefore higher rates of inflation shift household demand away from the cash good and toward the credit good. In Cooley and Hansen's formulation, this shift implies that higher inflation increases the demand for leisure. One effect of inflation, then, is to reduce

9. Abel (1985) studies the dynamics of adjustment in a model in which the cash-in-advance constraint applies to both consumption and investment.

the supply of labor. This then reduces output, consumption, investment, and the steady-state capital stock.

Cooley and Hansen express welfare losses across steady states in terms of the consumption increase (as a percentage of output) required to yield the same utility as would arise if the cash-in-advance constraint were nonbinding.[10] For a 10% inflation rate, they report a welfare cost of inflation of 0.387 percent of output if the cash-in-advance constraint is assumed to apply at a quarterly time interval. Not surprisingly, if the constraint only binds at a monthly time interval, the cost falls to 0.112 percent of output. Again, these costs are small. For much higher rates of inflation, they do start to look significant. For example, with a monthly time period for the cash-in-advance constraint, a 400% annual rate of inflation generates a welfare loss equal to 2.137% of output.

3.3.2.1 A Basic Model To model the behavior of the representative agent faced with a cash-in-advance constraint, we assume the agent's objective is to maximize

$$\mathrm{E}_0 \sum_{i=0}^{\infty} \beta^i u(c_{t+i}, 1 - n_{t+i}) = \mathrm{E}_0 \sum_{i=0}^{\infty} \beta^i \left[\frac{c_{t+i}^{1-\Phi}}{1-\Phi} + \Psi \frac{(1 - n_{t+i})^{1-\eta}}{1-\eta} \right] \qquad (3.25)$$

$0 < \beta < 1$; c_t is real consumption while n_t is labor supplied to market activities expressed as a fraction of the total time available; $1 - n_t$ is equal to the fraction of time devoted to leisure.[11] The parameters Φ, Ψ, and η are restricted to be positive.

Households supply labor and rent capital to firms that produce goods. The household enters each period with nominal money balances M_{t-1} and receives a nominal lump-sum transfer equal to T_t.[12] In the aggregate, this transfer is related to the growth rate of the nominal supply of money. Letting the stochastic variable θ_t denote the rate of money growth $[M_t = (1 + \theta_t)M_{t-1}]$, the per capita transfer will equal $\theta_t M_{t-1}$. At the start of period t, θ_t is known to all households.

The cash-in-advance constraint is taken to apply only to the purchase of consumption goods.

10. Refer to Cooley and Hansen (1989, section II) or Hansen and Prescott (Chapter 2 in Cooley 1995) for discussions of the computational aspects of this exercise.

11. In order to allow for comparison between the money-in-the-utility-function model developed earlier and a cash-in-advance model, we have modified the preference function used earlier, equation (2.38), by setting $b = 0$ so that real balances do not yield direct utility. The resulting utility function given in (3.25) differs from Cooley and Hansen's specification; they assume that the preferences of the identical (ex ante) households are log separable in consumption and leisure.

12. Cooley and Hansen distinguish between individual specific decision variables and the corresponding aggregate per capita quantity, although in equilibrium the two will be equal. In order to simplify the notation, we will only call attention to this distinction when necessary to avoid confusion.

$$P_t c_t \leq M_{t-1} + T_t$$

where P_t is the time-t price level. Note that time-t transfers are available to be spent in period t. In real terms, the cash-in-advance constraint becomes

$$c_t \leq \frac{m_{t-1}}{\Pi_t} + \tau_t \equiv a_t \tag{3.26}$$

where $\Pi_t = P_t/P_{t-1} = 1 + \pi_t$ is equal to one plus the rate of inflation.

In addition to the cash-in-advance constraint, the household faces a flow budget constraint of the form

$$y_t + (1 - \delta)k_{t-1} + a_t \geq c_t + k_t + m_t \tag{3.27}$$

where $0 \leq \delta \leq 1$ is the depreciation rate.

The individual's decision problem is characterized by the value function

$$V(a_t, k_{t-1}) = \max\left\{ \frac{c_t^{1-\Phi}}{1-\Phi} + \Psi \frac{(1-n_t)^{1-\eta}}{1-\eta} + \beta E_t V(a_{t+1}, k_t) \right\}$$

where the maximization is with respect to $\{c_t, n_t, k_t,$ and $m_t\}$ and is subject to the constraints (3.27) and (3.26).

The economy's technology is given by a Cobb-Douglas constant-returns-to-scale production function, expressed in per capita terms as

$$y_t = e^{z_t} k_{t-1}^{\alpha} n_t^{1-\alpha} \tag{3.28}$$

where $0 \leq \alpha \leq 1$. The exogenous productivity shock z_t follows

$$z_t = \rho z_{t-1} + e_t$$

with $0 \leq \rho \leq 1$. The innovation e has mean zero and variance σ_e^2.

The final aspect is a specification for the behavior of the growth rate of the nominal money supply θ_t. Adopting the process used in Chapter 2, let u_t be equal to the deviation of money growth around the steady state: $u_t = \theta_t - \theta^{ss}$. Assume

$$u_t = \gamma u_{t-1} + \phi z_{t-1} + \varphi_t$$

where φ_t is a white-noise innovation with variance σ_φ^2.

The first-order conditions for the representative agent's decision problem are presented in the chapter appendix (section 3.6).

3.3.2.2   The Steady State   The steady-state values of the ratios that were reported in Table 2.1 of Chapter 2 for the money-in-the-utility function are also the steady-state values for the cash-in-advance model, the one exception being that for real money balances. In the steady state, the cash in advance constraint is binding as long as the nominal rate of interest is positive. Hence, $c^{ss} = \dfrac{m^{ss}}{\Pi^{ss}} + \tau^{ss} = m^{ss}$, so $m^{ss}/k^{ss} = c^{ss}/k^{ss}$. The other values reported in Table 2.1 hold for the cash-in-advance model; even though the method used to generate a demand for money has changed, the steady-state values of the output-capital, capital-labor, and consumption-labor ratios are the same. Note that none of these steady-state ratios depend on the growth rate of the nominal money supply θ.

What will depend on the money growth rate, and therefore on the rate of inflation, will be the steady-state value of labor supply. The appendix shows that n^{ss} satisfies

$$(1 - n^{ss})^{-\eta}(n^{ss})^{-v} = \frac{(1 - \alpha)}{\Psi} \left(\frac{\beta}{\Theta} \right) \left(\frac{c^{ss}}{k^{ss}} \right)^{v} \left(\frac{y^{ss}}{k^{ss}} \right)^{\frac{-(\alpha+v)}{1-\alpha}} \tag{3.29}$$

where $v = -\Phi$.[13] Since the left side of this expression is increasing in n^{ss}, a rise in Θ, which implies a rise in the steady-state inflation rate, lowers steady-state labor supply. This is the source of the welfare cost of inflation in this cash-in-advance model. The elasticity of labor supply with respect to the growth rate of money Θ is equal to

$$-\left[\Phi + \eta \frac{n^{ss}}{1 - n^{ss}} \right]^{-1} < 0.$$

It is useful to note the similarity between the expression for steady-state labor supply in the cash-in-advance model and the corresponding expression given in equation (2.39) that was obtained in the money-in-the-utility-function model.

3.3.2.3   Calibration   In order to assess the effects of money using this model, we need to assign values to the specific parameters; that is, we need to calibrate the model. The steady state depends on the values of $(\alpha, \beta, \delta, \eta, \Psi, \Phi)$. The baseline value reported in Table 2.3 for the MIU model will be employed for the CIA model as well. This implies $\alpha = 0.4$, $\beta = 0.989$, and $\delta = 0.019$. Assuming $\eta = 1$ implies that utility is log linear in leisure. The value of Ψ is then determined so that the steady-state value of n is 0.31. For the baseline parameters, this yields $\Psi = 1.34$. To maintain some comparability with the MIU model, the utility function parameter Φ will be set equal to 2 for the baseline solutions.

3.3.2.4   Dynamics   The dynamic implications of the cash-in-advance model can be explored by obtaining a log-linear approximation around the steady state. The deri-

---

13. The expression is written using v to make comparison with the results from Chapter 2 more direct. In that chapter, v was defined as $b(1 - \Phi) - \Phi$, which reduces to $-\Phi$ in the present case, since $b = 0$.

vation of the approximation is contained in the appendix. It proves convenient to use the fact that $c_t = m_t$ in equilibrium to eliminate consumption from the system and instead to include directly the marginal utility of wealth, denoted by $\hat{\lambda}_t$ (see the appendix). As in Chapter 2, a variable $\hat{x}$ denotes the percentage deviation of x around the steady state. The cash-in-advance model can then be approximated around the steady state by the following seven equations:

$$\hat{y}_t = \alpha \hat{k}_{t-1} + (1 - \alpha)\hat{n}_t + z_t \tag{3.30}$$

$$\left(\frac{y^{ss}}{k^{ss}}\right)\hat{y}_t = \left(\frac{c^{ss}}{k^{ss}}\right)\hat{m}_t + \hat{k}_t - (1 - \delta)\hat{k}_{t-1} \tag{3.31}$$

$$R^{ss}\hat{r}_t = \alpha \left(\frac{y^{ss}}{k^{ss}}\right)(E_t\hat{y}_{t+1} - \hat{k}_t) \tag{3.32}$$

$$\hat{\lambda}_t = E_t\hat{\lambda}_{t+1} + \hat{r}_t \tag{3.33}$$

$$\hat{y}_t + \hat{\lambda}_t = \left(1 + \eta \frac{n^{ss}}{1 - n^{ss}}\right)\hat{n}_t \tag{3.34}$$

$$\hat{\lambda}_t = -E_t(\Phi\hat{m}_{t+1} + \hat{\pi}_{t+1}) \tag{3.35}$$

$$\hat{m}_t = \hat{m}_{t-1} - \hat{\pi}_t + u_t \tag{3.36}$$

Note that the first three equations (the production function, the resource constraint, and the marginal product of capital equation) are identical to those found with the money-in-the-utility-function approach except that the cash-in-advance constraint allows $\hat{m}$ to replace $\hat{c}$ in the resource constraint (3.31). The critical differences between the two approaches appears in a comparison of (3.33)–(3.35) with equations (2.44)–(2.46). Recall that the MIU displayed short-run dynamics in which the real variables such as output, consumption, the capital stock, and employment were independent of the nominal-money-supply process when utility was log linear in consumption and money balances.[14] While $\hat{m}$ does not directly enter the utility function in the CIA model, note that in the case of log-linear utility (that is, when $\Phi = \eta = 1$), the short-run real dynamics in the CIA model are not independent of the process followed by $\hat{m}$ as they were in the MIU model. We can see this point by noting that (3.34), (3.35), and (3.36) imply, when $\Phi = 1$,

$$-E_t[\hat{m}_{t+1} + \hat{\pi}_{t+1}] = -\hat{m}_t - E_t u_{t+1} = \left(1 + \eta \frac{n^{ss}}{1 - n^{ss}}\right)\hat{n}_t - \hat{y}_t$$

14. This was the case in which $\Phi = 1$.

Table 3.1
Implied Contemporaneous Correlations: $\Phi = 2$; $\eta = 1$; $\gamma = \phi = 0$

	S.D.	S.D./σ_y	Corr.
$\hat{y}$	1.174	1	1
$\hat{c}$	0.277	0.24	0.94
$\hat{x}$	3.896	3.32	1.00
$\hat{r}$	0.036	0.03	0.98
$\hat{m}$	0.277	0.24	0.94
$\hat{\pi}$	0.902	0.77	−0.29

Table 3.2
Effects of the Money-Growth-Rate Process

	$\gamma = 0.5, \phi = 0$		$\gamma = 0.5, \phi = 0.15$		$\gamma = 0.5, \phi = -0.15$	
	S.D.	Corr.	S.D.	Corr.	S.D.	Corr.
$\hat{y}$	1.174	1	1.127	1	1.222	1
$\hat{c}$	0.406	0.65	0.363	0.56	0.457	0.71
$\hat{x}$	3.978	0.97	3.972	0.97	3.988	0.97
$\hat{r}$	0.036	0.98	0.035	0.97	0.037	0.98
$\hat{m}$	0.406	0.65	0.363	0.56	0.457	0.71
$\hat{\pi}$	1.247	−0.22	1.223	−0.06	1.327	−0.36

Thus, variations in the expected future growth rate of money, $E_t u_{t+1}$, force adjustment to either $\hat{y}$, $\hat{c}$, or $\hat{n}$ (or all three). In particular, for given output and consumption, higher expected money growth (and therefore higher expected inflation) produces a fall in $\hat{n}_t$. This is the effect discussed earlier by which higher inflation reduces labor supply and output.

Note that the current growth rate of the nominal money stock, u_t, and the current rate of inflation, $\hat{\pi}_t$, only appear in the form $u_t - \hat{\pi}_t$ (see equation 3.36). Hence, as we saw in the MIU model, unanticipated monetary shocks affect only current inflation and have no real effects unless they affect expectations of future money growth (i.e., unless $E_t u_{t+1}$ is affected).

Table 3.1, which should be compared with Table 2.5, shows the contemporaneous correlations implied by the cash-in-advance model. The effects of altering the money-growth-rate process are illustrated in Table 3.2. Comparing Tables 2.5 and 3.2 reveals that the money-growth-rate process has much larger real effects in the cash-in-advance framework. In particular, the variance of output declines by 4% when ϕ is increased from 0 to 0.15. When money growth is positively serially correlated ($\gamma = 0.5$), a positive money growth rate disturbance ($u_t > 0$) reduces employment, and the effect of the u disturbance is significantly larger (as well as of opposite sign) than was found with the MIU model.

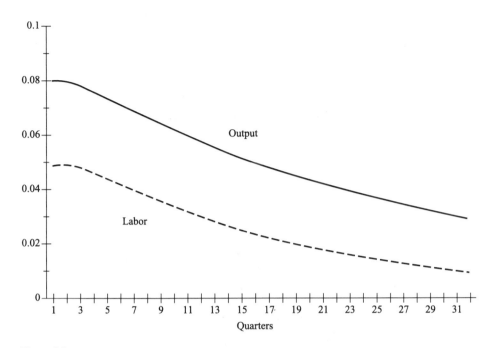

Figure 3.1
Effect of $\phi = -0.15$ versus $\phi = 0$ on Responses to a Technology Shock

The effect of variation in the endogenous monetary response to technology shocks in the CIA model is illustrated in Figure 3.1, which plots the difference between the output response when $\phi = -0.15$ and the baseline case with $\phi = 0$. The economy's response to a productivity shock is larger when $\phi = -0.15$ than when $\phi = 0$. Because a negative value of ϕ implies that money growth will decline after a positive productivity shock, expected inflation also declines. The resulting reduction in the nominal interest rate (see Figure 3.2) lowers the effective inflation tax on consumption and increases labor supply. A comparison of Figure 3.1 with Figure 2.3 of Chapter 2 shows that the impact of variation in the money-growth-rate response to the technology shock is significantly larger in the cash-in-advance model than in the money-in-the-utility-function example.

Figure 3.3, paralleling Figure 2.4 of Chapter 2, shows the implied cross correlations of real balances with output for $\phi = -0.15, 0, 0.15$. Also shown in the figure are the actual correlations from the United States. As we found with the MIU model, the simulation fails to capture the positive correlation at lags of over a year between output and lagged money.

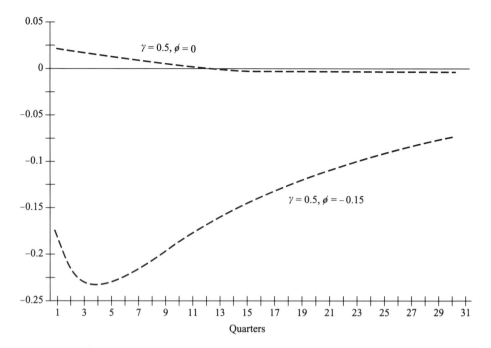

Figure 3.2
Nominal-Interest-Rate Response to a Technology Shock

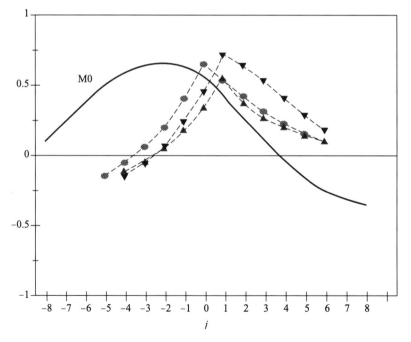

Figure 3.3
Dynamic Correlations of y_t and m_{t+j}. ● $\phi = 0$, ▲ $\phi = 0.15$, ▼ $\phi = -0.15$.

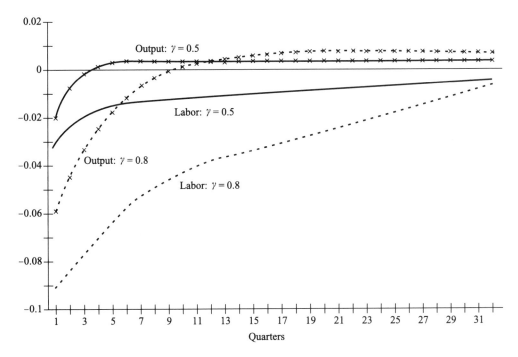

Figure 3.4
Output and Labor Responses to a Monetary Shock

The behavior of output and labor supply in response to a positive shock to the growth rate of the nominal money supply is shown in Figure 3.4 for $\gamma = 0.5$ (the baseline value) and $\gamma = 0.8$. The response of the nominal interest rate is shown in Figure 3.5. Greater persistence of the money-growth-rate process leads to larger movements in expected inflation in response to a monetary shock. This in turn produces larger adjustments of labor supply and output. As illustrated in Figure 3.4, a positive shock, by raising the expected rate of inflation and thereby increasing the inflation tax on labor supply, induces a substitution toward leisure that lowers labor supply. As was also the case with the MIU model, a positive money-growth shock, by raising expected inflation when $\gamma > 0$, raises the nominal rate of interest.

3.4   Other Approaches

3.4.1   Real Resource Costs

An alternative approach to the cash-in-advance or shopping-time models is to assume that transaction costs take the form of real resources that are used up in

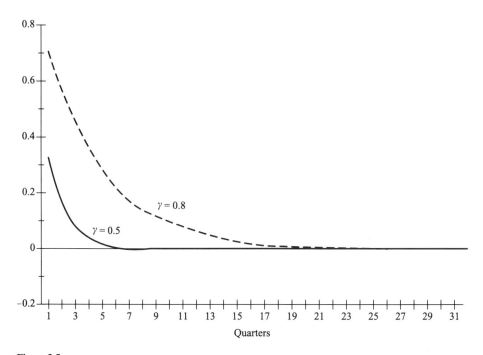

Figure 3.5
Nominal-Interest-Rate Response to a Monetary Shock

the process of exchange (Brock 1974, 1990). An increase in the volume of goods exchanged would lead to a rise in transaction costs, while higher average real money balances would, for a given volume of transactions, lower costs. In a shopping-time model, these costs are time costs and so enter the utility function indirectly by affecting the time available for leisure.

If goods must be used up in transacting, the household's budget constraint must be modified, for example by adding a transaction-cost term $\Upsilon(c, m)$ that depends on the volume of transactions (represented by c) and the level of money holdings. The budget constraint (3.11) then becomes

$$f(k_{t-1}) + (1 - \delta)k_{t-1} + \tau_t + \frac{m_{t-1}}{\Pi_t} + \frac{I_t b_{t-1}}{\Pi_t} \geq c_t + m_t + b_t + k_t + \Upsilon(c_t, m_t)$$

Feenstra (1986) considers a variety of transactions-cost formulations to show that they all lead to the presence of a function involving c and m appearing on the right side of the budget constraint. He also shows that transaction costs satisfy the

LASSELLE

following condition for all $c, m \geq 0$: Υ is twice continuously differentiable and $\Upsilon \geq 0$; $\Upsilon(0, m) = 0$; $\Upsilon_c \geq 0$; $\Upsilon_m \leq 0$; $\Upsilon_{cc}, \Upsilon_{mm} \geq 0$; $\Upsilon_{cm} \leq 0$; and $c + \Upsilon(c, m)$ is quasi-convex with expansion paths having nonnegative slope. These conditions all have intuitive meanings: $\Upsilon(0, m) = 0$ means that the consumer bears no transaction costs if consumption is zero, the sign restrictions on the partial derivatives reflect the assumption that transaction costs rise at an increasing rate as consumption increases and that money has positive but diminishing marginal productivity in reducing transaction costs. The assumption that $\Upsilon_{cm} \leq 0$ means that the marginal transaction costs of additional consumption do not increase with money holdings. Expansion paths with nonnegative slopes imply $c + \Upsilon$ increases with income. Positive money holdings can be ensured by the additional assumption that $lim_{m \to 0} \Upsilon_m(c, m) = -\infty$; that is, money is essential.

Now consider how the money-in-the-utility-function approach compares to a transactions-costs approach. Suppose we define a function $W(x, m)$ with the following properties: for all $x, m \geq 0$, W is twice continuously differentiable and satisfies $W \geq 0$; $W(0, m) = 0$; $W(x, m) \to \infty$ as $x \to \infty$ for fixed m; $W_m \geq 0$; $0 \leq W_x \leq 1$; $W_{xx} \leq 0$; $W_{mm} \leq 0$; $W_{xm} \geq 0$; W is quasi-concave with Engel curves with nonnegative slope. Consider the following two static problems representing simple transactions-costs and money-in-the-utility-fraction approaches:

$$\max \; U(c) \text{ subject to } c + \Upsilon(c, m) + b + m = y \tag{3.37}$$

and

$$\max \; V(x, m) \text{ subject to } x + b + m = y \tag{3.38}$$

where $V(x, m) = U[W(x, m)]$. These two problems are equivalent if (c^*, b^*, m^*) solves (3.37) if and only if (x^*, b^*, m^*) solves (3.38) with $x^* = c^* + \Upsilon(c^*, m^*)$. Feenstra shows that equivalence holds if the functions $\Upsilon(c, m)$ and $W(x, m)$ satisfy the stated conditions.

This "functional equivalence" (Wang and Yip 1992) between the transactions-cost and money-in-the-utility-function approaches suggests that conclusions derived within one framework will also hold under the alternative. However, this equivalence is obtained by redefining variables. So, for example, the "consumption" variable x in the utility function is equal to consumption *inclusive* of transactions costs [i.e., $x = c + \Upsilon(c, m)$] and is therefore not independent of money holdings. At the very least, the appropriate definition of the consumption variable needs to be considered if one attempts to use either framework to draw implications for actual macro time series.

3.4.2 Search

Both the money-in-the-utility-function and the cash-in-advance approaches should
be viewed as potentially useful means of introducing money into a general equilibrium framework. However, neither approach is very specific about the exact role
played by money. MIU models are motivated by a claim that the direct utility
yielded by money is proxying for the services money produces in facilitating transactions. However, the nature of these transactions and, more importantly, the resource costs they might involve and the ways in which these costs might be reduced
by holding more money are not specified. The cash-in-advance model is motivated
by appealing to the idea that some form of nominal asset is required to facilitate
transactions. Yet the constraint used is very extreme, implying that there are no
alternative means of carrying out transactions. The cash-in-advance constraint is
meant to capture the role of money as a medium of exchange, but in this case
we might also wish to start from a specification of the transactions technology in
order to understand why some commodities and assets serve as money and others
do not.

A number of papers have employed search theory to motivate the development of
media of exchange (examples include Jones 1976; Diamond 1983; Oh 1989; Kiyotaki
and Wright 1989, 1993; Trejos and Wright 1993, 1995; Shi 1995; and Ritter 1995). In
these models, individual agents must exchange the goods they produce (or with which
they are endowed) for the goods they can consume. During each period, individuals
randomly meet other agents; exchange takes place if it is mutually beneficial. In a
barter economy, exchange is only possible if an agent holding good i and wishing
to consume good j (call this an ij agent) meets an individual holding good j who
wishes to consume good i (a ji agent). This requirement is known as the "double
coincidence of wants," and limits the feasibility of direct barter exchange when production is highly specialized. Trade could occur if agent ij meets a ki agent for $k \neq j$
as long as the exchange of goods is costless and the probability of meeting a jk agent
is the same as meeting a ji agent. In this case, agent ij would be willing to exchange i
for k (thereby becoming a kj agent).

In the Kiyotaki and Wright (1993) model, direct exchange of commodities is
assumed to be costly, but there exists a fiat money that can be traded costlessly for
commodities. The assumption that there exists "money" with certain exchange
properties (costless trade with commodities) serves a role similar to putting money
directly into the utility function in the MIU approach, or specifying that money must

be used in certain types of transactions in the CIA approach.[15] Whether an agent will accept money in exchange for goods will depend on the probability the agent places on being able to later exchange money for a consumption good.

Suppose agents are endowed with a new good according to a Poisson process with arrival rate a.[16] Trading opportunities arrive at rate b. A successful trade can occur if there is a double coincidence of wants. If x is the probability that another agent located at random is willing to accept the trader's commodity, the probability of a double coincidence of wants is x^2. A successful trade can also take place if there is a single coincidence of wants (i.e., one of the agents has a good the other wants), if one agent has money and the other agent is willing to accept it. That is, a trade can take place when an ij agent meets a jk agent if the ij agent has money and the jk agent is willing to accept it. Let μ be the fraction of traders with money, and let s be the probability that a random trader accepts money.

In this simple framework, agents can be in one of three states; an agent can be waiting for a new endowment to arrive (state 0), can have a good to trade and be waiting to find a trading partner (state 1), or can be holding money and be waiting for a trading opportunity (state m). Let N_0, N_1, and N_m denote the fraction of the population in each state, and define V_i as the value function of an agent currently in state i. If β is the rate of time preference, the following conditions must hold for a representative agent j:

$$\beta V_0 = a(V_1 - V_0)$$

$$\beta V_1 = b(1 - \mu)x^2(U - \varepsilon + V_0 - V_1) + b\mu x \max_{s_j} s_j(V_m - V_1)$$

and

$$\beta V_m = b(1 - \mu)sx(U - \varepsilon + V_0 - V_m)$$

The first of these equations states that the return from waiting for a new endowment is equal to the arrival rate of goods times the value from switching from state 0 to state 1 (having a good to trade). The return to agent j from having a good, βV_1, is equal to the sum of two terms. The first is the probability $b(1 - \mu)x^2$ that agent j

---

15. In an early analysis, Alchian (1977) attempted to explain why there might exist a commodity with the type of exchange properties assumed in the new search literature. He stressed the role of information and the costs of assessing quality. Any commodity whose quality can be assessed at low cost can facilitate the acquisition of information about other goods by serving as a medium of exchange.

16. In Kiyotaki and Wright (1993), this is interpreted as a production technology.

meets another agent with a commodity to trade (rather than money) and the double coincidence of wants is satisfied, times the consumption value of the trade U minus the costs of commodity trading ε, plus the value from switching from state V_1 to state V_0 (waiting for another endowment). The second is the probability the agent j will meet a trader with money who wants j's good (a single coincidence of wants) times the probability that agent j will accept money s_j times the value of switching from state 1 to state m. Note that s_j is chosen optimally to maximize agent j's gain. Finally, the last of the three conditions requires that the return from holding money equal the arrival rate of trading opportunities (i.e., meeting someone with no money and a good j wants) times the net gain from the resulting consumption and switching to state V_0.

In a steady state, $s_j = s$ for all j, and the proportions in each of the three states must remain constant, requiring that

$$aN_0 = b(1-\mu)x^2 N_1 + b(1-\mu)sxN_m \tag{3.39}$$

and

$$b\mu sxN_1 = b(1-\mu)sxN_m \Rightarrow N_1 = \frac{1-\mu}{\mu}N_m \tag{3.40}$$

The left side of (3.39) is the flow out of state 0 (waiting for a new commodity endowment). The right side of (3.39) is the flow into state 0. The first term represents the flow into state 0 arising from successful commodity trades. With probability $b(1-\mu)x^2$, an agent meets another agent with a commodity to trade (rather than money), and the double coincidence of wants is satisfied. The last term arises from agents meeting other agents for which a single coincidence is satisfied and the trader is willing to accept money.

The second steady-state condition, (3.40), equates the flow of commodity traders who successfully trade goods for money (i.e., the flow into state m) to the flow of money holders who successfully trade for a consumption good (i.e., the flow out of state m).

Because $N_0 + N_1 + N_m = 1$, equation (3.39) can be rewritten as

$$a(1 - N_1 - N_m) = b(1-\mu)x^2 N_1 + b(1-\mu)sxN_m$$

Now using (3.40), this becomes

$$N_m = \frac{a\mu}{a + \varphi(\mu, s)}$$

where $\varphi(\mu, s) = \{a + b(1-\mu)[\mu xs + (1-\mu)x^2]\}$.

In this environment, three equilibria are possible. Suppose $s < x$, then the probability of making a trade holding money is less than the probability of making a trade holding a commodity. In this case, individuals will prefer to hold on to their good when they meet another trader (absent a double coincidence) rather than trade for money. With no one willing to trade for money, money will be valueless in equilibrium. A second equilibrium arises when $s > x$. In this case, holding money makes a successful trade more likely than continuing to hold a commodity. So every agent will be willing to hold money, and in equilibrium all agents will be willing to accept money in exchange for goods. If $s = x$, then what Kiyotaki and Wright characterize as a mixed-monetary equilibrium exists; agents accept money with probability x as long as they believe other agents will accept it with probability x.

The Kiyotaki and Wright model emphasizes the exchange process and the possibility for an intrinsically valueless "money" to be accepted in trade. It does so, however, by assuming a fixed rate of exchange—one unit of money is exchanged for one unit of goods whenever a trade takes place. The value of money in terms of goods is either zero (in a nonmonetary equilibrium) or 1. In Trejos and Wright (1995), however, the goods price of money is determined endogenously as part of the equilibrium. This price is the outcome of a bargaining process between buyers and sellers who meet through a process similar to that in Kiyotaki and Wright.

Following Trejos and Wright (1993), assume the consumption of q units yields utility $u(q)$ and can be produced at a cost (in units of utility) of $c(q)$. If agents could consume their own production, q would be determined by the condition that marginal utility equals marginal cost: $u_q(q) = c_q(q)$. Suppose, however, that agents cannot consume their own output. Instead, they must trade. To keep the example simple, assume that barter is prohibitively expensive, so consumption requires meeting someone willing to accept money for goods. Once two traders meet, they bargain over how much of the consumption good will be traded for one unit of money. Thus, money is assumed to be indivisible while goods are infinitely divisible (i.e., all trades involve $1, but the quantity of goods exchanged for that dollar may vary).

Assume that while bargaining, the buyer and seller cannot search for alternative trading opportunities.[17] Trejos and Wright analyze a situation in which the seller and buyer participate in bargaining rounds, each of which consists of one party making a take-it-or-leave-it offer. As the time between rounds goes to zero, the bargaining solution q is a Nash equilibrium that can be found as the value that

---

17. Trejos and Wright also consider the situation in which agents can look for alternative bargaining opportunities between rounds, and they examine cases in which barter is feasible. See Trejos and Wright (1993).

maximizes $[u(q) + V_s][V_b - c(q)]$ where V_s and V_b are the value functions for a seller and a buyer. For any quantity transacted Q, these must satisfy

$$\beta V_s = b\mu x[V_b - V_s - c(Q)] \tag{3.41}$$

and

$$\beta V_b = b(1 - \mu)x[u(Q) + V_s - V_b] \tag{3.42}$$

Solving these two equations,

$$V_s = \frac{b^2 x^2 \mu(1 - \mu)u(Q) - b\mu x[\beta + b(1 - \mu)x]c(Q)}{(\beta + b\mu x)[\beta + b(1 - \mu)x] - b^2 x^2 \mu(1 - \mu)}$$

$$V_b = \frac{b(1 - \mu)x(\beta + b\mu x)u(Q) - b^2 x^2 \mu(1 - \mu)c(Q)}{(\beta + b\mu x)[\beta + b(1 - \mu)x] - b^2 x^2 \mu(1 - \mu)}$$

In addition, for a buyer to accept a bargain, it must be the case that $u(q) + V_s - V_b \geq 0$, and for a seller to accept, it must be that $-c(q) + V_b - V_s \geq 0$.

In an equilibrium, q must maximize $[u(q) + V_s][V_b - c(q)]$, V_s and V_b are functions of Q given by the solutions to (3.41) and (3.42), and $q = Q$. Assuming an interior solution, the first order condition for q is

$$T(q, Q) = u_q(q)[V_b(Q) - c(q)] - c_q(q)[u(q) + V_s(Q)] = 0$$

where V_s and V_b have been written explicitly as functions of Q. Trejos and Wright (1995) prove that $T(q, q) = 0$ has a unique solution with $q > 0$.[18] By substituting the expressions for V_s and V_b into $T(q, q) = 0$, we can study the effect of changes in the primitive parameters of the model such as μ (the fraction of the population holding units of money) on the value of money as measured by q (the quantity of goods one unit of money can command). For example, Trejos and Wright (1993) discuss the effects of changes in μ on the equilibrium value of q. However, as Marshall (1993) stresses, the search-theoretic models still lack any connection between standard monetary policy instruments (even as basic as the quantity of money) and the variables in the theory. The changes in μ studied by Trejos and Wright are changes in the cross-sectional distribution of money, not changes in the quantity of money.[19]

---

18. Since $-c(q) + V_b - V_s \geq 0$ and $u(q) + V_s - V_b \geq 0$ in this equilibrium, Trejos and Wright label it as unconstrained. If barter is possible, there can exist constrained monetry equilibrium in which $c(q) = V_b - V_s$. See Shi (1995).

19. Chapter 5 will discuss a model in which policy affects the distribution of money holdings when certain restrictions on transactions are imposed (Christiano and Eichenbaum 1995).

The search-theoretic approach to monetary economics provides a natural framework for addressing a number of issues. Ritter (1995) has used it to examine the conditions necessary for fiat money to arise, linking it to the credibility of the issuer. Governments lacking in credibility would be expected to overissue the currency to gain seigniorage. In this case, agents would be unwilling to hold the fiat money. Soller and Waller (1997) use a search-theoretic approach to study the coexistence of legal and illegal currencies. By stressing the role of money in facilitating exchange, the search-theoretic approach emphasizes the role of money as a medium of exchange. The approach also emphasizes the social aspect of valued money; agents are willing to accept fiat money only in environments in which they expect others similarly to accept money.[20]

3.5 Summary

The models we have examined in this and the previous chapter are variants of Walrasian economies in which prices are perfectly flexible and adjust to ensure that market equilibrium is continuously maintained. The money-in-the-utility-function, cash-in-advance, and shopping-time models, as well as the other approaches discussed, all represent means of introducing valued money into the Walrasian equilibrium. Each approach captures some aspects of the role that money plays in facilitating transactions.

Despite the different approaches, several conclusions are common to all. First, because the price level is completely flexible, the value of money, equal to one over the price of goods, behaves like an asset price. The return money yields, however, differs in the various approaches. In the money-in-the-utility-function approach, the marginal utility of money is the direct return, while in the cash-in-advance model, this return is measured by the Lagrangian multiplier on the cash-in-advance constraint. In the shopping-time model, the return arises from the time savings provided by money in carrying out transactions, and the value of this time savings depends on the real wage.

All these models have similar implications for the optimal rate of inflation. An efficient equilibrium will be characterized by equality between social and private costs. Because the social cost of producing money is zero, the private opportunity cost of holding money must be zero in order to achieve optimality. The private opportunity cost is measured by the nominal interest rate, so the optimal rate of

---

20. Samuelson (1958) is one of the earliest modern treatments of money as a social construct.

inflation in the steady state is the rate that achieves a zero nominal rate of interest. While this result is quite general, two important considerations—the effects of inflation on government revenues and the interaction of inflation with other taxes in a nonindexed tax system—have been ignored. These will be among the topics of Chapter 4.

Finally, the class of models studied in this chapter are among the basic frameworks that monetary economists have found useful for understanding the steady-state implications of inflation and the steady-state welfare implications of alternative rates of inflation. However, the dynamics implied by these models fail to mimic the types of short-run behavior that characterize modern economies. That failure is perhaps not surprising; almost all economists believe that sluggish wage and price adjustments, absent from the models of this chapter, play critical roles in determining the short-run real effects of monetary disturbances and monetary policy. While systematic monetary policy can have real effects with flexible prices, simulations suggested these effects are small, at least at moderate rates of inflation, and, more importantly, the models produced correlations that were at variance with those observed in actual data. To understand how the observed correlations might be generated in a monetary economy, we will need to introduce price stickiness, a topic taken up in Chapter 5.

3.6 Appendix: The CIA Approximation

The method used to obtain a linear approximation around the steady state for the cash-in-advance model is discussed here. Since the approach is similar to the one followed for the MIU model of Chapter 2 (and discussed in the appendix to that chapter), some details are skipped.

3.6.1 The Basic Decision Problem

The utility function of the representative agent is given by

$$\mathrm{E}_0 \sum_{t=0}^{\infty} \beta^t u(c_t, 1 - n_t) = \mathrm{E}_0 \sum_{t=0}^{\infty} \beta^t \left[\frac{c_t^{1-\Phi}}{1-\Phi} + \Psi \frac{(1 - n_t)^{1-\eta}}{1-\eta} \right] \tag{3.43}$$

$0 < \beta < 1$; c_t is real consumption while n_t is labor supplied to market activities expressed as a fraction of the total time available; $1 - n_t$ is equal to leisure time, also as a fraction of total time. The parameters Φ, Ψ, and η are restricted to be positive.

The cash-in-advance constraint is assumed to apply only to the purchase of consumption goods, and it takes the form

$$P_t c_t \leq M_{t-1} + T_t$$

where P_t is the time-t price level. Note that time-t transfers are available to be spent in period t. Dividing by P_t, this constraint in real terms becomes

$$c_t \leq \frac{m_{t-1}}{\Pi_t} + \tau_t \equiv a_t \tag{3.44}$$

where $\Pi_t = P_t/P_{t-1} = 1 + \pi_t$ is equal to one plus the rate of inflation. From the definition of the transfer payment, $a_t = m_t$, but this is an equilibrium condition; the individual takes a_t as given while deciding on a level of real money balances to hold. In equilibrium, the demand for money by the representative agent must equal the per capita stock of money.

In addition to the cash-in-advance constraint, the household faces a flow-budget constraint of the form

$$e^{z_t} k_{t-1}^\alpha n_t^{1-\alpha} + (1 - \delta)k_{t-1} + a_t \geq c_t + k_t + m_t \tag{3.45}$$

where the depreciation rate on capital satisfies $0 \leq \delta \leq 1$. Notice that we have assumed that the production technology is Cobb-Douglas with constant returns to scale, $0 \leq \alpha \leq 1$. The exogenous productivity shock z_t follows

$$z_t = \rho z_{t-1} + e_t$$

with $0 \leq \rho \leq 1$. The innovation e has mean zero and variance σ_e^2.

The individual's decision problem is characterized by the value function

$$V(a_t, k_{t-1}) = \max \left\{ \frac{c_t^{1-\Phi}}{1-\Phi} + \Psi \frac{(1-n_t)^{1-\eta}}{1-\eta} + \beta E_t V(a_{t+1}, k_t) \right\}$$

where the maximization is with respect to c_t, n_t, k_t, and m_t and is subject to the constraints (3.26) and (3.27). Substituting $\tau_{t+1} + \dfrac{m_t}{\Pi_{t+1}}$ for a_{t+1} and using (3.27) to eliminate k_t, the value function can be written

$$V(a_t, k_{t-1}) = \max \left\{ \frac{c_t^{1-\Phi}}{1-\Phi} + \Psi \frac{(1-n_t)^{1-\eta}}{1-\eta} \right.$$

$$\left. + \beta E_t V \left[\tau_{t+1} + \frac{m_t}{\Pi_{t+1}}, e^{z_t} k_{t-1}^\alpha n_t^{1-\alpha} + (1 - \delta)k_{t-1} + a_t - c_t - m_t \right] \right\}$$

The maximization problem is now subject only to the cash-in-advance constraint.

Let μ_t be the Lagrangian associated with the cash-in-advance constraint. The first-order necessary conditions for c_t, m_t, and n_t, along with the budget constraint and the cash-in-advance constraint, are

$$c_t^{-\Phi} = \beta E_t V_k(a_{t+1}, k_t) + \mu_t \qquad (3.46)$$

$$\beta E_t \left[\frac{V_a(a_{t+1}, k_t)}{\Pi_{t+1}} \right] = \beta E_t V_k(a_{t+1}, k_t) \qquad (3.47)$$

$$-\Psi(1-n)^{-\eta} + (1-\alpha)\beta E_t V_k(a_{t+1}, k_t) e^{z_t} k_{t-1}^{\alpha} n_t^{-\alpha} = 0 \qquad (3.48)$$

$$V_a(a_t, k_{t-1}) = \mu_t + \beta E_t V_k(a_{t+1}, k_t) \qquad (3.49)$$

$$V_k(a_t, k_{t-1}) = \beta E_t V_k(a_{t+1}, k_t)[\alpha e^{z_t} k_{t-1}^{\alpha-1} n_t^{1-\alpha} + 1 - \delta] \qquad (3.50)$$

Define $\lambda_t = \beta E_t V_k(a_{t+1}, k_t)$ and let $y_t = e^{z_t} k_{t-1}^{\alpha} n_t^{1-\alpha}$. The first-order conditions (3.46)–(3.48) and (3.50) can now be rewritten as

$$c_t^{-\Phi} = \lambda_t + \mu_t \qquad (3.51)$$

$$\beta E_t \left(\frac{\lambda_{t+1} + \mu_{t+1}}{\Pi_{t+1}} \right) = \lambda_t \qquad (3.52)$$

$$-\Psi(1-n_t)^{-\eta} + \lambda_t(1-\alpha)\left(\frac{y_t}{n_t} \right) = 0$$

$$\lambda_t = \beta E_t R_t \lambda_{t+1}$$

where $R_t = \alpha e^{z_{t+1}} k_t^{\alpha-1} n_{t+1}^{1-\alpha} + 1 - \delta$.

3.6.2   The Steady State

The steady-state values of the ratios that were reported in Table 2.1 for the money-in-the-utility model also characterize the steady state for this cash-in-advance model. In a steady state, (3.50) yields the standard result that

$$\beta \left[\alpha \left(\frac{y^{ss}}{k^{ss}} \right) + 1 - \delta \right] = \beta R^{ss} = 1$$

or $R^{ss} = 1/\beta$ and

$$\left(\frac{y^{ss}}{k^{ss}}\right) = \frac{1}{\alpha}(R^{ss} - 1 + \delta)$$

From the economy's resource constraint, $y^{ss} = c^{ss} + \delta k^{ss}$, so

$$\left(\frac{c^{ss}}{k^{ss}}\right) = \left(\frac{y^{ss}}{k^{ss}}\right) - \delta$$

With a binding cash-in-advance constraint, $c^{ss} = \tau^{ss} + m^{ss}/(1 + \pi^{ss})$, but in a steady state with m constant, $\tau^{ss} + m^{ss}/(1 + \pi^{ss}) = m^{ss}$. Thus, $c^{ss} = m^{ss}$.

The production function implies $y^{ss}/k^{ss} = (n^{ss}/k^{ss})^{1-\alpha}$, or

$$\left(\frac{n^{ss}}{k^{ss}}\right) = \left(\frac{y^{ss}}{k^{ss}}\right)^{\frac{1}{1-\alpha}}$$

This leaves n^{ss} to be determined. From the first-order condition for the household's choice of n,

$$\Psi(1 - n^{ss})^{-\eta} = \lambda^{ss}(1-\alpha)\left(\frac{y^{ss}}{n^{ss}}\right) = \lambda^{ss}(1-\alpha)\left(\frac{y^{ss}}{k^{ss}}\right)\left(\frac{n^{ss}}{k^{ss}}\right)^{-1} \qquad (3.53)$$

so the only remaining value to find is λ^{ss}. From (3.51), $(c^{ss})^{-\Phi} = \lambda^{ss} + \mu^{ss}$, and (3.52) then yields $\lambda^{ss} = \frac{\beta}{\Theta}(c^{ss})^{-\Phi}$ where $\Theta \equiv 1 + \theta^{ss} = \Pi^{ss}$. Combining this with (3.53) and recalling that $\left(\frac{n^{ss}}{k^{ss}}\right) = \left(\frac{y^{ss}}{k^{ss}}\right)^{\frac{1}{1-\alpha}}$, results in

$$(1 - n^{ss})^{-\eta}(n^{ss})^{-\upsilon} = \frac{(1-\alpha)}{\Psi}\left(\frac{\beta}{\Theta}\right)\left(\frac{c^{ss}}{k^{ss}}\right)^{\upsilon}\left(\frac{y^{ss}}{k^{ss}}\right)^{\frac{-(\alpha+\upsilon)}{1-\alpha}}$$

where $\upsilon = -\Phi$.

3.6.3   The Linear Approximation

Expressions linear in the percentage deviations around the steady state can be obtained for the economy's resource constraint, the production function, the definition of the marginal product of capital, and the first-order conditions for consumption, money holdings, and labor supply, just as was done for the MIU model of Chapter 2. As in Chapter 2, $\hat{x}$ denotes the percentage deviation of a variable x around its steady-state value. The economy's resource constraint, the production function, and the definition of the expected marginal product of capital are identical to those of the MIU model,[21] so they are simply stated here:

$$\hat{k}_t = (1 - \delta)\hat{k}_{t-1} + \left(\frac{y^{ss}}{k^{ss}}\right)\hat{y}_t - \left(\frac{c^{ss}}{k^{ss}}\right)\hat{c}_t \tag{3.54}$$

$$\hat{y}_t = \alpha\hat{k}_{t-1} + (1 - \alpha)\hat{n}_t + z_t \tag{3.55}$$

$$R^{ss}\hat{r}_t = \alpha\left(\frac{y^{ss}}{k^{ss}}\right)(E_t\hat{y}_{t+1} - \hat{k}_t) \tag{3.56}$$

From the cash-in-advance constraint, $c_t = m_t$ in an equilibrium with a positive nominal rate of interest. Eliminating consumption and noting that $\lambda_{t+1} + \mu_{t+1} = c_{t+1}^{-\Phi} = m_{t+1}^{-\Phi}$ yields

$$\lambda_t = \beta E_t\left[\frac{m_{t+1}^{-\Phi}}{\Pi_{t+1}}\right]$$

$$\Psi(1 - n_t)^{-\eta} = \lambda_t(1 - \alpha)\left(\frac{y_t}{n_t}\right)$$

$$\lambda_t = \beta E_t R_t \lambda_{t+1}$$

Linearized around the steady state, these three equations become

$$\hat{\lambda}_t = -E_t[\Phi\hat{m}_{t+1} + \hat{\pi}_{t+1}] \tag{3.57}$$

$$\left(1 + \eta\frac{n^{ss}}{1 - n^{ss}}\right)\hat{n}_t = \hat{y}_t + \hat{\lambda}_t \tag{3.58}$$

and

$$\hat{\lambda}_t = E_t\hat{\lambda}_{t+1} + \hat{r}_t \tag{3.59}$$

3.7 Problems

1. Suppose the production function for shopping takes the form $\psi = c = e^x(n^s)^a m^b$, where a and b are both positive but less than 1 and x is a productivity factor. The agent's utility is given by $v(c, l) = \frac{c^{1-\Phi}}{1 - \Phi} + \frac{l^{1-\eta}}{1 - \eta}$ where $l = 1 - n - n^s$ and n is time spent in market employment.

21. See the appendix to Chapter 2.

a. Derive the transaction time function $g(c,m) = n^s$.

b. Derive the money-in-the-utility-function specification implied by the shopping-production function. How does the marginal utility of money depend on the parameters a and b? How does it depend on x?

c. Is the marginal utility of consumption increasing or decreasing in m?

2. Define superneutrality. Carefully explain whether the Cooley-Hansen cash-in-advance model exhibits superneutrality. What role does the cash-in-advance constraint play in determining whether superneutrality holds?

3. Is the steady-state equilibrium in the Cooley-Hansen cash-in-advance model affected by any of the following modifications? Explain.

a. Labor is supplied inelastically (normalize so that $n = 1$, where n is the supply of labor).

b. Purchases of capital are also subject to the cash-in-advance constraint (i.e., one needs money to purchase both consumption and investment goods).

c. The growth rate of money follows the process $u_t = \gamma u_{t-1} + \varphi_t$ where $0 < \gamma < 1$ and φ is a mean zero i.i.d. process.

4. Money-in-the-utility-function and cash-in-advance constraints are alternative means for constructing models in which money has positive value in equilibrium.

a. What strengths and weaknesses do you see with each of these approaches?

b. Suppose you wanted to study the effects of the growth of credit cards on money demand. Which approach would you adopt? Why?

5. Consider the model of section 3.3.1. Suppose that money is required to purchase both consumption and investment goods. The cash-in-advance constraint then becomes $c_t + x_t \le m_{t-1}/\Pi_t + \tau_t$ where x is investment. Assume the aggregate production function takes the form $y_t = e^{z_t} k_{t-1}^\alpha n_t^{1-\alpha}$. Show that the steady-state capital-labor ratio is affected by the rate of inflation. Does a rise in inflation raise or lower the steady-state capital-labor ratio? Explain.

6. Consider the following model:

$$\text{Preferences: } E_t \sum_{i=0}^{\infty} \beta^i (\ln c_{t+i} + b \ln d_{t+i})$$

Budget constraint: $c_t + d_t + m_t + k_t = Ak_{t-1}^a + \tau_t + \dfrac{m_{t-1}}{1+\pi_t} + (1-\delta)k_{t-1}$ (3.60)

Cash-in-advance constraint: $c_t \leq \tau_t + \dfrac{m_{t-1}}{1+\pi_t}$ (3.61)

where m denotes real money balances and π_t is the inflation rate from period $t-1$ to period t. The two consumption goods, c and d, represent cash (c) and credit (d) goods. The net transfer τ is viewed as a lump-sum payment (or tax) by the household.

a. Does this model exhibit superneutrality? Explain.

b. What is the rate of inflation that maximizes steady-state utility?

7. Consider the following model:

$$\text{Preferences: } E_t \sum_{i=0}^{\infty} \beta^i (\ln c_{t+i} + \ln d_{t+i})$$

Budget constraint: $c_t + d_t + m_t + k_t = Ak_{t-1}^a + \tau_t + \dfrac{m_{t-1}}{1+\pi_t} + (1-\delta)k_{t-1}$

where m denotes real money balances and π_t is the inflation rate from period $t-1$ to period t. Utility depends on the consumption of two types of good; c must be purchased with cash, while d can be purchased using either cash or credit. The net transfer τ is viewed as a lump-sum payment (or tax) by the household. If a fraction q of d is purchased using cash, then the household also faces a cash-in-advance constraint that takes the form

$$c_t + qd_t \leq \dfrac{m_{t-1}}{1+\pi_t} + \tau_t$$

What is the relationship between the nominal rate of interest and whether the cash-in-advance constraint is binding? Explain. Will the household ever use cash to purchase d (i.e., will the optimal q ever be greater than zero)?

8. Trejos and Wright (1993) find that if no search is allowed while bargaining takes place, output tends to be too low (the marginal utility of output exceeds the marginal production costs). Show that output is also too low in a basic cash-in-advance model. (For simplicity, assume that only labor is needed to produce output according to the production function $y = n$.) Does the same hold true in a money-in-the-utility-function model?

4 Money and Public Finance

4.1 Introduction

Inflation is a tax. And as a tax, it both generates revenue for the government and distorts private sector behavior. The previous two chapters focused on these distortions. In the Cooley-Hansen cash-in-advance model, inflation serves as an implicit tax on consumption, so a higher inflation rate generates a substitution toward leisure, leading to lower labor supply, output, and consumption. In the Sidrauski model, inflation distorts the demand for money, thereby generating welfare effects because real money holdings directly yield utility.

In our analysis of these distortions, we ignored the revenue side of the inflation tax except to note that the Friedman rule for the optimal rate of inflation may need to be modified if the government does not have lump-sum sources of revenue available. Any change in inflation that affects the revenue from the inflation tax will have budgetary implications for the government. If higher inflation allows other forms of distortionary taxation to be reduced, this fact must be incorporated into any assessment of the costs of the inflation tax. In this chapter, we introduce the government sector's budget constraint and examine the revenue implications of inflation. Doing so allows us to focus more explicitly on the role of inflation in a theory of public finance and to draw on the optimal taxation literature in analyzing the effects of inflation.

The public-finance approach yields several insights. Among the most important is the recognition that fiscal and monetary policy are linked through the government sector's budget constraint. Variations in the inflation rate can have implications for the fiscal authority's decisions about expenditures and taxes, and, conversely, decisions by the fiscal authority can have implications for money growth and inflation. When inflation is viewed as a distortionary revenue-generating tax, the degree to which it should be relied upon will depend on the set of alternative taxes available to the government and on the reasons individuals hold money. Whether the most appropriate strategy is to think of money as entering the utility function as a final good or as serving as an intermediate input into the production of transaction services can have implications for whether money should be taxed. The optimal-tax perspective also has empirical implications for inflation that can be used to test the theory.

In the next section, the consolidated government's budget identity is set out, and some of the revenue implications of inflation are examined. Section 4.3 presents a simple model of inflation in which a fixed amount of revenue must be raised from the inflation tax. Then, in section 4.4, inflation revenue (seigniorage) and other taxes are brought together to analyze the joint determination of the government's tax instruments. This theme is continued in section 4.5, which explores the implications of optimal Ramsey taxation for inflation. Despite the need to raise revenue, there are important classes of preferences and technology that imply that the Friedman rule (a zero nominal rate of interest) remains optimal. Finally, section 4.6 briefly discusses some additional effects that arise when the tax system is not fully indexed.

4.2   Budget Accounting

In order to obtain goods and services, governments in market economies need to generate revenue. And one way that they can obtain goods and services is to print money that is then used to purchase resources from the private sector. However, to understand the revenue implications of inflation (and the inflation implications of the government's revenue needs), we must start with the government's budget constraint.[1]

Consider the following identity for the fiscal branch of a government:

$$G_t + i_{t-1}B_{t-1}^T = T_t + (B_t^T - B_{t-1}^T) + RCB_t \tag{4.1}$$

where all variables are in nominal terms. The left side consists of government expenditures (on goods, services, and transfers) plus interest payments on the outstanding debt (assumed to be one period in maturity), and the right side consists of tax revenue (T_t) plus new issues of interest-bearing debt $(B_t^T - B_{t-1}^T$, the superscript T denoting total) plus any direct receipts from the central bank (RCB_t). As an example of RCB, the U.S. Federal Reserve turns over to the Treasury almost all the interest earnings on its portfolio of government debt.[2] We will refer to (4.1) as the Treasury's budget constraint.

The monetary authority, or central bank, also has a budget identity that links changes in its assets and liabilities. This takes the form

$$(B_t^M - B_{t-1}^M) + RCB_t = i_{t-1}B_{t-1}^M + (H_t - H_{t-1}) \tag{4.2}$$

where $B_t^M - B_{t-1}^M$ is equal to the central bank's purchases of government debt, $i_{t-1}B_{t-1}^M$ is the central bank's receipt of interest payments from the Treasury, and $H_t - H_{t-1}$ is the change in the central bank's own liabilities. These liabilities are called *high-powered money* or sometimes the *monetary base* since they form the stock of currency held by the nonbank public plus bank reserves, and they represent the

---

1. Bohn (1992) provides a general discussion of government deficits and accounting.

2. In 1996, the Federal Reserve turned over $20.1 billion to the Treasury (*83rd Annual Report of the Federal Reserve System* 1996, p. 268). Klein and Neumann (1990) show how the revenue generated by seigniorage and the revenue received by the fiscal branch can differ.

reserves private banks can use to back deposits under a fractional reserve system. Changes in the stock of high-powered money will lead to changes in broader measures of the money supply, measures that normally include various types of bank deposits as well as currency held by the public.

By letting $B = B^T - B^M$ be the stock of government interest-bearing debt held by the public, the budget identities of the Treasury and the central bank can be combined to produce the consolidated government-sector budget identity:

$$G_t + i_{t-1}B_{t-1} = T_t + (B_t - B_{t-1}) + (H_t - H_{t-1}) \tag{4.3}$$

From the perspective of the consolidated government sector, only debt held by the public (i.e., outside the government sector) represents an interest-bearing liability, and changes in the central bank's liabilities, $H_t - H_{t-1}$, represent an additional source of revenue.

In the United States, the sum of the last two terms on the right side of (4.3) would represent total new debt issued by the Treasury, with $B_t - B_{t-1}$ representing purchases of new debt by the public and $H_t - H_{t-1}$ representing purchases by the Federal Reserve. Since the Fed returns the interest it receives on its holdings of government debt to the Treasury (minus its operating expenses, which we have ignored), the interest payment term on the left side of (4.3) just includes interest paid on privately held government debt. According to (4.3), the dollar value of government purchases, G_t, plus its payment of interest on outstanding privately held debt, $i_t B_{t-1}$, must be funded by revenue that can be obtained from one of three alternative sources. First, T_t represents revenues generated by taxes (other than inflation). Second, the government can obtain funds by borrowing from the private sector. This borrowing is equal to the change in the debt held by the private sector, $B_t - B_{t-1}$. Finally, the government can print currency to pay for its expenditures, and this is represented by the change in the outstanding stock of noninterest-bearing debt, $H_t - H_{t-1}$.

We can divide equation (4.3) by $P_t N_t y_t$, where P_t is the price level, N_t is the population, and y_t is real per capita output, to obtain

$$\frac{G_t}{P_t N_t y_t} + i_t \frac{B_{t-1}}{P_t N_t y_t} = \frac{T_t}{P_t N_t y_t} + \frac{B_t - B_{t-1}}{P_t N_t y_t} + \frac{H_t - H_{t-1}}{P_t N_t y_t}$$

Note that terms like $B_{t-1}/P_t N_t y_t$ can be multiplied and divided by $P_{t-1}N_{t-1}y_{t-1}$, yielding $B_{t-1}/P_t N_t y_t = \left(\dfrac{B_{t-1}}{P_{t-1}N_{t-1}y_{t-1}}\right)\left(\dfrac{P_{t-1}N_{t-1}y_{t-1}}{P_t N_t y_t}\right)$. This can then be written

as $\quad b_{t-1}\left(\dfrac{P_{t-1}}{P_t}\right)\left(\dfrac{N_{t-1}}{N_t}\right)\left(\dfrac{y_{t-1}}{y_t}\right) = b_{t-1}\left(\dfrac{1}{1+\pi}\right)\left(\dfrac{1}{1+n}\right)\left(\dfrac{1}{1+\lambda}\right)\quad$ where $\quad b_{t-1} =$

$\dfrac{B_{t-1}}{P_{t-1}N_{t-1}y_{t-1}}$ represents real debt relative to income, π is the inflation rate, n is the population growth rate, and λ is the growth rate of real per capita output.

Employing the convention that lowercase letters denote variables deflated by the price level, population, and real output, the government's budget identity is

$$g_t + r_t^* b_{t-1} = t_t + (b_t - b_{t-1}) + \frac{H_t - H_{t-1}}{P_t N_t y_t} \qquad (4.4)$$

where $r^* = \dfrac{1+i}{(1+\pi)(1+n)(1+\lambda)} - 1$. It will be convenient to define R, Π, N, and Λ as 1 plus r, π, n, and λ. If r is the ex ante real rate of return and π^e is the expected rate of inflation, then $1 + i \equiv I = (1+r)(1+\pi^e) = R\Pi^e$. Adding and subtracting $b_{t-1}\dfrac{R\Pi}{\Pi N \Lambda}$ to the left side of (4.4) and rearranging, the budget constraint becomes

$$g_t + \frac{r - n - \lambda}{N\Lambda} b_{t-1} = t_t + (b_t - b_{t-1}) + \frac{R(\pi - \pi^e)}{\Pi N \Lambda} b_{t-1} + \frac{H_t - H_{t-1}}{P_t N_t y_t} \qquad (4.5)$$

The third term on the right side of this expression, involving $(\pi - \pi^e)b_{t-1}$, represents the revenue generated when unanticipated inflation reduces the real value of the government's outstanding interest-bearing nominal debt. To the extent that inflation is anticipated, it will be reflected in higher nominal interest rates that the government must pay. Inflation by itself does not reduce the burden of the government's interest-bearing debt; only unexpected inflation has such an effect.

The last term in (4.5) represents seigniorage, the revenue from money creation. If h is the real per capita value of the monetary base, seigniorage can be written as

$$s_t \equiv \frac{H_t - H_{t-1}}{P_t N_t y_t} = (h_t - h_{t-1}) + \left(\frac{\Pi N \Lambda - 1}{\Pi N \Lambda}\right) h_{t-1} \qquad (4.6)$$

Seigniorage arises from two sources. First, $h_t - h_{t-1}$ is equal to the change in real, per capita high-powered money holdings relative to income. Since the government is the monopoly issuer of high-powered money, an increase in the amount of high-powered money the private sector is willing to hold allows the government to obtain real resources in return. In a steady-state equilibrium, h is constant, so that this source of seigniorage then equals zero. The second term in (4.6) is normally the focus of analyses of seigniorage because it can be nonzero even in the steady state. To maintain a constant level of real money holdings per capita, the private sector needs to increase its nominal holdings of money at the rate $\pi + n$ (approximately) to offset the effects of inflation and population growth on per capita real holdings. In addition, if the elasticity of real money demand with respect to income is equal to one, real per capita demand for money will rise at the rate λ. Thus, the demand for nominal balances rises at the rate $\Pi N \Lambda - 1 \approx \pi + n + \lambda$ when h is constant. By supplying this demand, the government is able to obtain goods and services or reduce other taxes.

If we denote the growth rate of nominal money H by θ (and so $\Theta \equiv 1 + \theta$), the growth rate of h will equal $(\Theta - \Pi N \Lambda)/\Pi N \Lambda \approx \theta - \pi - n - \lambda$. In a steady state, h will be constant, implying that $\Pi N \Lambda = 1 + \theta$.[3] In this case, (4.6) shows that seigniorage will be equal to

$$\frac{\theta}{1+\theta} h$$

Ignoring population and real per capita income growth for the moment, the rate of inflation will equal θ, and seigniorage will equal $\frac{\pi}{1+\pi} h$. For small values of the rate of inflation, $\frac{\pi}{1+\pi}$ is approximately equal to π, so s can be thought of as the product of a tax rate of π, the rate of inflation, and a tax base of h, the real stock of base money. Since base money does not pay interest, its real value is depreciated by inflation whether the inflation is anticipated or not.

The definition of s would appear to imply that the government receives no revenue if inflation is zero. But this inference neglects the real interest savings to the government of issuing h, which is noninterest-bearing debt, as opposed to b, which is interest-bearing debt. That is, for a given level of the government's total liabilities $d_t = b_t + h_t$, interest costs will be a decreasing function of the fraction of this total that consists of h_t. A shift from interest-bearing to noninterest-bearing debt would allow the government to reduce total tax revenues or increase transfers or purchases. This observation suggests that one should consider the government's budget constraint expressed in terms of the total liabilities of the government. Using (4.5) and (4.6), we can rewrite the budget constraint as[4]

$$g_t + \frac{r-n-\lambda}{N\Lambda} d_{t-1} = t_t + (d_t - d_{t-1}) + \left[\frac{R(\pi - \pi^e)}{\Pi N \Lambda}\right] d_{t-1} + \left(\frac{i}{\Pi N \Lambda}\right) h_{t-1} \qquad (4.7)$$

---

3. Or, approximately, $\pi = \theta - n - \lambda$.
4. To obtain this, add $(r - n - \lambda)h_{t-1}/(1+\pi)(1+n)(1+\lambda)$ to both sides of (4.5).

If we ignore population and real income growth, seigniorage, defined as the last term in (4.7), becomes

$$\bar{s} = \frac{i}{1+\pi}h \tag{4.8}$$

This equation shows that the relevant tax rate on high-powered money depends directly on the nominal rate of interest. Thus, under the Friedman rule for the optimal rate of inflation, the government collects no revenue from seigniorage because the nominal rate of interest is zero. The budget constraint also illustrates that any change in seigniorage requires an offsetting adjustment in the other components of (4.7). Reducing the nominal interest rate to zero implies that the lost revenue must be replaced by an increase in other taxes, real borrowing that increases the government's net indebtedness, or reductions in expenditures.

The various forms of the government's budget identity suggest at least three alternative measures of the revenue that governments generate through money creation. First, the measure that might be viewed as appropriate from the perspective of the Treasury is simple RCB, total transfers from the central bank to the Treasury (see 4.1). For the United States, King and Plosser (1985) report that the real value of these transfers amounted to 0.02% of real GNP during the 1929–1952 period, and 0.15% of real GNP in the 1952–1982 period. Under this definition, shifts in the ownership of government debt between the private sector and the central bank would affect the measure of seigniorage even if high-powered money remained constant. That is, from (4.2), if the central bank used interest receipts to purchase debt, B^M would rise, RCB would fall, and the Treasury would, from (4.1), need to raise other taxes, reduce expenditures, or issue more debt. But this last option means the Treasury could simply issue debt equal to the increase in the central bank's debt holdings, leaving private debt holdings, government expenditures, and other taxes unaffected. Thus, changes in RCB do not represent real changes in the Treasury's finances and are therefore not the appropriate measure of seigniorage.

A second possible measure of seigniorage is given by (4.6); the real value of the change in high-powered money. King and Plosser report that s equaled 1.37% of real GNP during 1929–1952 but only 0.3% in the 1952–1982 period. This measure of seigniorage equals the revenue from money creation for a given path of interest-bearing government debt. That is, s equals the total expenditures that could be funded, holding constant other tax revenues and the total private sector holdings of interest-bearing government debt. While s, expressed as a fraction of GNP, has been quite small during the postwar period in the United States, King and Plosser report much higher values for other countries. For example, it was more than 6% of GNP in Argentina and over 2% in Italy.

Finally, equation (4.8) provides a third definition of seigniorage as the nominal interest savings from issuing noninterest-bearing as opposed to interest-bearing debt.[5] Using the 4–6-month commercial paper rate as a measure of the nominal interest rate, King and Plosser report that this measure of seigniorage equaled 0.2% of GNP from 1929 to 1952 and 0.47% from 1952 to 1982. This third definition equals the revenue from money creation for a given path of total (interest- and noninterest-bearing) government debt; it equals the total expenditures that could be funded, holding constant other tax revenues and the total private sector holdings of real government liabilities.

The difference between s and $\bar{s}$ arises from alternative definitions of fiscal policy. To understand the effects of monetary policy, we need to consider changes in monetary policy holding fiscal policy constant (and perhaps other things also). Suppose tax revenues t are simply treated as lump sum. Then, one definition of fiscal policy would be in terms of a time series for government purchases and interest-bearing debt: $\{g_{t+i}, b_{t+i}\}_{i=0}^{\infty}$. Changes in s, together with the changes in t necessary to maintain $\{g_{t+i}, b_{t+i}\}_{i=0}^{\infty}$ unchanged, would constitute monetary policy. Under this definition, monetary policy would change the total liabilities of the government (i.e., $b + h$). An open-market purchase by the central bank would, ceteris paribus, lower the stock of interest-bearing debt held by the public. The Treasury would then need to issue additional interest-bearing debt to keep the b_{t+i} sequence unchanged. Total government liabilities would rise. Under the definition $\bar{s}$, fiscal policy sets the path $\{g_{t+i}, d_{t+i}\}_{i=0}^{\infty}$, and monetary policy determines the division of d between interest- and noninterest-bearing debt.

The expressions we have obtained for the government's budget constraint can be simplified by using some approximations. If we let $\dfrac{(1+z)(1+x)}{1+w} \approx 1 + z + x - w$ for small z, x, and w,[6] the budget constraint (4.5) can be written as

$$g_t + (r - n - \lambda)b_{t-1} = t_t + (b_t - b_{t-1}) + (\pi - \pi^e)b_{t-1} + (\pi + n + \lambda)h_{t-1} + h_t - h_{t-1}$$

---

5. And these three are not the only possible definitions. See King and Plosser (1985) for an additional three.

6. This approximation involves ignoring terms such as xz, xw, and zw. To see this point, note that multiplying both sides by $(1 + w)$ yields, for the left side, $(1 + z)(1 + x) = 1 + z + x + zx \approx 1 + z + x$, while for the right side, $(1 + w)(1 + z + x - w) = 1 + z + x - w + w + wz + wx - w^2 \approx 1 + z + x$.

Adding and subtracting $rh_{t-1} \approx (i - \pi^e)h_{t-1}$ to both sides yields

$$g_t + (r - n - \lambda)d_{t-1} = t_t + (d_t - d_{t-1}) + (\pi - \pi^e)d_{t-1} + ih_{t-1} \tag{4.9}$$

Equations (4.7) and (4.9) show how the elements of the government's budget are linked. To see the restrictions that the budget identity might place on the government's choices of expenditures, taxes, and seigniorage, we need to investigate the intertemporal condition that the government must satisfy if it is to remain solvent.

4.2.1   Intertemporal Budget Balance

The budget relationships derived in the previous section link the government's choices concerning expenditures, taxes, debt, and seigniorage at each point in time. However, unless there are restrictions on the government's ability to borrow or raise revenue from seigniorage, (4.7) places no real constraint on expenditure or tax choices. In fact, governments, like individuals, are constrained in their ability to borrow. But to see exactly how this constraint limits the government's choices requires that we focus on the intertemporal budget constraint of the government.

Ignoring the effect of surprise inflation, the single-period budget identity of the government can be written as[7]

$$g_t + (r - n - \lambda)b_{t-1} = t_t + (b_t - b_{t-1}) + s_t$$

Assuming the interest factor $r - n - \lambda \equiv \rho$ is a constant (and is positive), this equation can be solved forward to obtain

$$(1 + \rho)b_{t-1} + \sum_{i=0}^{\infty} \frac{g_{t+i}}{(1+\rho)^i} = \sum_{i=0}^{\infty} \frac{t_{t+i}}{(1+\rho)^i} + \sum_{i=0}^{\infty} \frac{s_{t+i}}{(1+\rho)^i} + \lim_{i \to \infty} \frac{b_{t+i}}{(1+\rho)^i} \tag{4.10}$$

The government's expenditure and tax plans are said to satisfy the requirement of intertemporal budget balance (the "no Ponzi condition") if the last term in (4.10) equals zero:

$$\lim_{i \to \infty} \frac{b_{t+i}}{(1+\rho)^i} = 0 \tag{4.11}$$

In this case, the right side of (4.10) becomes the present discounted value of all current and future tax and seigniorage revenues, and this is equal to the left side, which is the present discounted value of all current and future expenditures plus current outstanding debt (the principal plus interest). In other words, the government

---

7. We employ the approximations discussed in the previous section.

must plan to raise sufficient revenue, in present-value terms, to repay its existing debt and finance its planned expenditures. Defining the primary deficit as $\Delta \equiv g - t - s$, intertemporal budget balance implies, from (4.10), that

$$(1 + \rho)b_{t-1} = -\sum_{i=0}^{\infty} \frac{\Delta_{t+i}}{(1 + \rho)^i}$$

Thus, if the government has outstanding debt ($b_{t-1} > 0$), then the present value of future primary deficits must be negative (i.e., it must run primary surpluses in the future). These surpluses can be generated through adjustments in expenditures, taxes, or seigniorage.

An important issue is whether the requirement of intertemporal budget balance imposes any testable restrictions on the behavior of government deficits. After all, a long sequence of primary deficits could be consistent with intertemporal budget balance as long as the government is expected to run sufficiently large primary surpluses sometime in the future. A closely related issue is whether a long sequence of primary deficits has any implications for future seigniorage. Often, concern is expressed that deficits might imply higher future inflation as seigniorage is used to generate the necessary future surpluses. Most of the empirical work in this area has focused on a narrower test: is the time-series behavior of expenditures, tax revenues, and debt consistent with intertemporal budget balance? A finding that it isn't might imply that the historical patterns are expected to change. (If they weren't expected to change, then the public would believe the government is borrowing and running a Ponzi scheme. If such is the case, why are they buying the government's debt? That is, why are they lending to the government?)

To determine the empirical restrictions that intertemporal budget balance might impose on the time-series behavior of expenditures, taxes, and debt, suppose that the first difference of the primary deficit is stationary (this is stronger than one needs; see Trehan and Walsh 1991). This supposition allows Δ_t to be integrated of order one, denoted $I(1)$. Then, intertemporal budget balance holds if Δ_t and b_{t-1} are co-integrated. In other words, if there exists a linear combination of the primary deficit and the stock of debt that is stationary, then intertemporal balance holds.

A number of authors have applied tests for intertemporal budget balance to determine if deficit processes are sustainable. Often the results have been mixed, depending on the country examined and the time period used. Trehan and Walsh (1988) fail to reject intertemporal budget balance for the United States based on data covering 1890 to 1986. Other authors have rejected budget balance using post-1960 U.S. data (see Hamilton and Flavin 1986; Hakkio and Rush 1991; Wilcox 1989).

This analysis has assumed that ρ remained constant and that $\rho > 0$. This latter condition requires that $r > n + \lambda$, a condition associated with dynamic efficiency (see Able, Mankiw, Summers, and Zeckhauser 1989). But, in fact, the safe real rate of return in the United States is less than the economy's average growth rate, a situation that can arise in a stochastic environment. Bohn (1991d, 1995) analyzes sustainability in a stochastic environment and argues that, in the absence of lump-sum taxes, even seemingly prudent fiscal policies such as running a balanced budget may be unsustainable. The problem arises if the growth rate of real income is a unit root process that can take on negative values. In this case, there is a positive probability of large income declines that can make the debt-to-income ratio become large enough to threaten sustainability. At a minimum, Bohn's results are a reminder that the simple implications of debt sustainability derived in the case of certainty may not carry over to more realistic settings.

4.2.2   Deficits and Inflation

The intertemporal budget constraint implies that any government with a current outstanding debt must run, in present-value terms, future surpluses. One way to generate a surplus is to increase revenues from seigniorage, and for that reason, economists have been interested in the implications of budget deficits for future money growth. Two questions have formed the focus of studies of deficits and money: First, do fiscal deficits necessarily imply that inflation will eventually occur? Second, if inflation is not a necessary consequence of deficits, is it in fact a historical consequence?

The literature on this first question has focused on the implications for inflation if the monetary authority must act to ensure that the government's intertemporal budget is balanced. Leeper (1991) describes such a situation as one in which there is an active fiscal policy and a passive monetary policy. It is also described as a situation of fiscal dominance. With fiscal dominance, an increase in government debt will eventually require an increase in seigniorage. A contractionary monetary policy aimed at producing lower inflation will initially lower seigniorage revenue and require that additional debt be issued; this ultimately leads to higher inflation (Sargent and Wallace 1985). The mechanism is straightforward; by lowering current inflation-tax revenues, the deficit grows and the stock of debt rises. A larger debt implies an increase in the present discounted value of future tax revenues, including revenues from seigniorage. If the fiscal authority does not adjust, the monetary authority will be forced eventually into producing higher inflation.

The literature on the second question has focused on empirically estimating the effects of budget deficits on money growth. Joines (1985) finds money growth in the

United States to be positively related to major war spending but not to non-war deficits. Grier and Neiman (1987) summarize a number of earlier studies of the relationship between deficits and money growth (and other measures of monetary policy) in the United States. That the results were generally inconclusive is perhaps not surprising, since the studies they review were all based on postwar but pre-1980 data. Thus, the samples covered periods in which there was relatively little deficit variation and in which much of the variation that there was arose from the endogenous response of deficits to the business cycle as tax revenues varied procyclically.[8] Grier and Neiman do find that the structural deficit is a determinant of money growth. This finding is consistent with that of King and Plosser (1985), who report that the fiscal deficit does help to predict future seigniorage for the United States. They interpret this finding as mixed evidence for fiscal dominance.

Demopoulos, Katsimbris, and Miller (1987) provide evidence on debt accommodation for eight OECD countries. These authors estimate a variety of central bank reaction functions (regression equations with alternative policy instruments on the left-hand side) in which the government deficit is included as an explanatory variable. For the post–Bretton Woods period, they find a range of outcomes, from no accommodation by the Federal Reserve and the Bundesbank, to significant accommodation by the Bank of Italy and the Nederlandse Bank.

One objection to this empirical literature is that simple regressions of money growth on the deficits, or unrestricted VARs used to assess Granger causality (i.e., whether deficits contain any predictive information about future money growth), ignore information about the long-run behavior of taxes, debt, and seigniorage that is implied by intertemporal budget balance. Intertemporal budget balance implies a cointegrating relationship between the primary deficit and the stock of debt. This link between the components of the deficit and the stock of debt restricts the time-series behavior of expenditures, taxes, and seigniorage, and this fact in turn implies that empirical modeling of their behavior should be carried out within the framework of a vector error correction model (VECM).[9]

Suppose $X_t' = (g_t\, T_t\, b_{t-1})$ where $T = t + s$ is defined as total government receipts from taxes and seigniorage. If the elements of X are nonstationary, intertemporal budget balance implies that the deficit inclusive of interest, or $(1\ \ -1\ \ r)X_t = \beta'X_t =$

8. For that reason, some of the studies cited by Grier and Neiman employed a measure of the high-employment surplus (i.e., the surplus estimated to occur if the economy had been at full employment). Grier and Neiman conclude, "The high employment deficit (surplus) seems to have a better 'batting average'..." (p. 204).

9. See Engle and Granger (1987).

$g_t - T_t + rb_{t-1}$, is stationary. Hence, $\beta' = (1 -1\ r)$ is a cointegrating vector for X. The appropriate specification of the time series process is then a VECM of the form

$$C(L)\Delta X_t = -\alpha\beta' X_t + e_t \tag{4.12}$$

The presence of the deficit inclusive of interest, $\beta' X_t$, ensures that the elements of X cannot drift too far apart; doing so would violate intertemporal budget balance.

Bohn (1991a) has estimated a model of the form (4.12) using U.S. data from 1800 to 1988. Unfortunately for our purposes, Bohn does not treat seigniorage separately, and thus his results are not directly relevant for determining the effects of spending or tax shocks on the adjustment of seigniorage. He does find, however, that one-half to two-thirds of a deficit initiated by a tax-revenue shock is eventually eliminated by spending adjustments, while about one-third of spending shocks are essentially permanent and result in tax changes.

4.2.3   Money and Debt

Most analyses of monetary phenomena and monetary policy assume, usually without statement, that variations in the stock of money matter but that how that variation occurs does not. The nominal money supply could change due to a shift from tax-financed government expenditures to seigniorage-financed expenditures. Or it could change as the result of an open market operation in which the central bank purchases interest-bearing debt, financing the purchase by an increase in noninterest-bearing debt, holding other taxes constant (see equation 4.2). Because these two means of increasing the money stock have differing implications for taxes and the stock of interest-bearing government debt, they may lead to different effects on prices and/or interest rates.

The government sector's budget constraint links monetary and fiscal policy in ways that can matter for determining how a change in the money stock affects the equilibrium price level.[10] The budget link also means one needs to be precise about defining monetary policy as distinct from fiscal policy. An open market purchase increases the stock of money, but by reducing the interest-bearing government debt held by the public, it has implications for the future stream of taxes needed to finance the interest cost of the government's debt. So an open market operation potentially has a fiscal side to it, and this fact can lead to ambiguity in defining what one means by a change in monetary policy, "holding fiscal policy constant."

---

10. See, for example, Sargent and Wallace (1981) and Wallace (1981). The importance of the budget constraint for the analysis of monetary topics is clearly illustrated in Sargent (1987).

In an early contribution, Metzler (1951) argued that an open market purchase, that is, an increase in the nominal quantity of money held by the public and an offsetting reduction in the nominal stock of interest-bearing debt held by the public, would raise the price level less than proportionally to the increase in M. An open market operation would, therefore, affect the real stock of money and lead to a change in the equilibrium rate of interest. Metzler assumed households' desired portfolio holdings of bonds and money would depend on the expected return on bonds. An open market operation, by altering the ratio of bonds to money, would require a change in the rate of interest to induce private agents to hold the new portfolio composition of bonds and money. A price-level change proportional to the change in the nominal money supply would not restore equilibrium because it would not restore the original ratio of nominal bonds to nominal money.

An important limitation of Metzler's analysis was its dependence on portfolio behavior that was not derived directly from the decision problem facing the agents of the model. As we saw in Chapter 2 with the Sidrauski model, embedding asset-accumulations decisions within a model of utility maximization can have important implications for the relationship between inflation, monetary policy, and the real equilibrium.

The analysis is also limited in that it ignores the consequence for future taxes of shifts in the composition of the government's debt, a point made by Patinkin (1965), who noted that Metzler had ignored the fiscal implications of changes in the stock of government debt. We have seen that the government's intertemporal budget constraint requires the government to run surpluses in present-value terms equal to its current outstanding interest-bearing debt. An open market purchase by the monetary authority reduces the stock of interest-bearing debt held by the public. This reduction will have consequences for future expected taxes in ways that critically affect the outcome of policies that affect the stock of interest-bearing debt.

Sargent and Wallace (1981) have shown that the "backing" for government debt, whether it is ultimately paid for by taxes or by printing money, is important in determining the effects of debt issuance and open market operations. This finding can be illustrated following the analysis of Aiyagari and Gertler (1985). They use a two-period overlapping-generations model that allows debt policy to affect the real intergenerational distribution of wealth. This effect is absent from the representative-agent models we have been using, but the representative-agent framework can still be used to show how the specification of fiscal policy will have important implications for conclusions about the link between the money supply and the price level.[11]

---

11. See also Woodford (1995, 1996).

In order to focus on debt, taxes, and seigniorage, set government purchases equal to zero and ignore population and real income growth, in which case the government's budget constraint takes the form

$$(1 + r)b_{t-1} = t_t + b_t + s_t \tag{4.13}$$

with s_t denoting seigniorage.

In addition to the government's budget constraint, we need to specify the budget constraint of the representative agent. Assume that this agent receives an exogenous endowment y each period, and pays (lump-sum) taxes t_t in period t. She also receives interest payments on any government debt held at the start of the period; these payments, in real terms, are given by $(1 + i_{t-1})B_{t-1}/P_t$ where i_{t-1} is the nominal interest rate in period $t - 1$, B_{t-1} is the number of bonds held at the start of the period, and P_t is the period-t price level. We can write this equivalently as $(1 + r_{t-1})b_{t-1}$, where $r_{t-1} = (1 + i_{t-1})/(1 + \pi_t) - 1$ is the ex post real rate of interest. Finally, the agent has real money balances equal to $M_{t-1}/P_t = (1 + \pi_t)^{-1}m_{t-1}$ that are carried into period t from period $t - 1$. The agent allocates these resources to consumption, real money holdings, and real bond purchases:

$$y + (1 + r_{t-1})b_{t-1} + (1 + \pi_t)^{-1}m_{t-1} - t_t = c_t + m_t + b_t \tag{4.14}$$

Aiyagari and Gertler (1985) address whether the price level will depend only on the stock of money or whether debt policy and the behavior of the stock of debt might also be relevant for price-level determination. They assume that the government sets taxes to back a fraction ψ, $0 \le \psi \le 1$, of its interest-bearing debt liabilities. If $\psi = 1$, government's interest-bearing debt is completely backed by taxes in the sense that the government commits to maintaining the present discounted value of current and future tax receipts equal to its outstanding debt liabilities. Such a fiscal policy is called Ricardian by Sargent (1982), although it is more common for Ricardo's name to be linked with debt in the form of the Ricardian equivalence theorem under which shifts between debt and tax financing of a given expenditure stream have no real effects.[12] Ricardian equivalence holds in the representative-agent framework we are using; the issue is whether debt policy as characterized by ψ matters for price-level determination.

Let T_t denote the present discounted value of taxes. Under the assumed debt policy, the government ensures that $T_t = \psi(1 + r_{t-1})b_{t-1}$, since $(1 + r_{t-1})b_{t-1}$ is the net liability of the government (including its current interest payment). Because T_t is

12. See Barro (1974) or Romer (1996).

a present value, we can also write

$$T_t = t_t + \mathrm{E}_t \frac{T_{t+1}}{(1+r_t)} = t_t + \mathrm{E}_t \frac{\psi(1+r_t)b_t}{(1+r_t)}$$

or $T_t = t_t + \psi b_t$. Now because $T_t = \psi(1+r_{t-1})b_{t-1}$, it follows that

$$t_t = \psi(R_{t-1}b_{t-1} - b_t) \tag{4.15}$$

where $R_{t-1} = 1 + r_{t-1}$.

With taxes adjusting to ensure that the fraction ψ of the government's debt liabilities are backed by taxes, the remaining fraction, $1 - \psi$, represents the portion backed by seigniorage. Given (4.15), the household's budget constraint (4.14) becomes

$$y + (1 - \psi)R_{t-1}b_{t-1} + (1 + \pi_t)^{-1}m_{t-1} = c_t + m_t + (1 - \psi)b_t$$

In the Ricardian case ($\psi = 1$), all terms involving the government's debt drop out; only the stock of money matters. If $\psi < 1$, however, debt does not drop out. We can then rewrite the budget constraint as $y + R_{t-1}w_{t-1} = c_t + w_t + \dfrac{i_{t-1}}{1 + \pi_t}m_{t-1}$ where $w \equiv m + (1 - \psi)b$, showing that the relevant measure of household income is $y + Rw_{t-1}$, and this is then used to purchase consumption, financial assets, or money balances [where the opportunity cost of money is $i/(1 + \pi)$]. With asset demand depending on ψ through w_{t-1}, the equilibrium price level and nominal rate of interest will generally depend on ψ.[13]

While we have derived the representative agent's budget constraint and shown how it is affected by the means the government uses to back its debt, to actually determine the effects on the equilibrium price level and nominal interest rate we must determine the agent's demand for money and bonds and then equate these demands to the (exogenous) supplies. To illustrate the role of debt policy, assume log-separable utility, $\ln c_t + b \ln m_t$, and consider a perfect-foresight equilibrium. The demand for money is given by $m_t = b\left(\dfrac{1 + i_t}{i_t}\right)c_t$. The Euler condition implies that $c_{t+1} = \beta(1 + r_t)c_t$. Using these in the agent's budget constraint, $c_t + w_t = y + R_{t-1}w_{t-1} - \dfrac{i_{t-1}}{1 + \pi_t}b\left(\dfrac{1 + i_{t-1}}{i_{t-1}}\right)\beta^{-1}(1 + r_{t-1})^{-1}c_t$, or

---

13. In this example, $c = y$ in equilibrium, since there is no capital good that would allow the endowment to be transferred over time.

$$\left(1 + \frac{b}{\beta}\right)c_t + w_t = y + R_{t-1}w_{t-1}$$

In equilibrium, $c_t = y$, so this becomes $w_t = -(b/\beta)y + R_{t-1}w_{t-1}$. If we now consider the steady state, $w_t = w_{t-1} = w^{ss} = by/\beta(R^{ss} - 1)$. But $w = [M + (1 - \psi)B]/P$, so the equilibrium steady-state price level is equal to

$$P^{ss} = \frac{\beta r^{ss}}{by}[M + (1 - \psi)B] \tag{4.16}$$

If government debt is entirely backed by taxes ($\psi = 1$), we get the standard result; the price level is proportional to the nominal stock of money. The stock of debt has no effect on the price-level. With $\psi < 1$, however, both the nominal money supply and the nominal stock of debt play a role in price-level determination. Proportional changes in M *and* B produce proportional changes in the price level; increases in the government's total nominal debt, $M + B$, raise P^{ss} proportionately.

Let $\lambda = M/(M + B)$ be the fraction of government liabilities that consists of noninterest-bearing debt. Since open market operations affect the relative proportions of money and bonds in government liabilities, open market operations determine λ. Equation (4.16) can then be written as

$$P^{ss} = \frac{\beta r}{by}[1 - \psi(1 - \lambda)](M + B)]$$

Open market purchases (an increase in λ) that substitute money for bonds but leave $M + B$ unchanged raise P^{ss} when $\psi > 0$. The rise in P^{ss} is not proportional to the increase in M. Shifting the composition of its liabilities away from interest-bearing debt reduces the present discounted value of the private sector's tax liabilities by less than the fall in debt holdings; a rise in the price level proportional to the rise in M would leave household wealth lower (households' bond holdings are reduced in real value, but the decline in the real value of their tax liabilities is only $\psi < 1$ times as large).

Leeper (1991) argues that even if $\psi = 1$ on average (that is, all debt is backed by taxes) the means used to finance shocks to the government's budget have important implications. He distinguishes between active and passive policies; an active monetary and passive fiscal policy would be one in which monetary policy acts to target nominal interest rates and does not respond to the government's debt while fiscal policy must then adjust taxes to ensure intertemporal budget balance. Conversely, an active fiscal policy and passive monetary policy would be one in which the monetary authority must adjust seigniorage revenues to ensure intertemporal budget balance while fiscal policy does not respond to shocks to debt. Leeper shows that the inflation and debt processes are unstable if both policy authorities follow active policies, while there is price level indeterminacy if both follow passive policies.

4.2.4 Summary

Monetary and fiscal actions are linked through the government's budget constraint. Changes in the money stock or its growth rate will require that some other variable in the budget constraint—taxes, expenditures, or borrowing—adjust. A complete analysis of monetary changes requires a specification of these other changes and how they might matter for determining the impact of the monetary action.

Nevertheless, despite the emphasis budget relationships have received in the work by Wallace and Sargent among others, much of monetary economics ignores the implications of the budget constraint. Doing so is valid in the presence of lump-sum taxes; any effects on the government's budget can simply be offset by an appropriate variation in lump-sum taxes. Traditional analyses that focus only on the stock of outside money are also valid when governments follow a Ricardian policy of fully backing interest-bearing debt with tax revenues, either now or in the future. In general, though, we should be concerned with the fiscal implications of any analysis of monetary policy, since changes in the quantity of money that alter the interest payments of the government have implications for future tax liabilities.

4.3 Equilibrium Seigniorage

Because seigniorage and other tax revenues are linked through the government's intertemporal budget constraint, a natural perspective is to think of a government jointly choosing inflation and other tax rates. Studying this decision problem requires the government's objective function to be clearly specified; the specification might be to minimize the present discounted value of tax distortions, subject to the constraint that the expected present discounted value of revenues equal the expected present discounted value of expenditures. Before considering that decision problem, insight into the implications of the inflation tax can be gained by studying the situation in which a fixed amount of revenue must be raised from seigniorage. That is, suppose, given its expenditures and other tax sources, the government has a deficit of Δ that must be financed by money creation. What will be the equilibrium rate of inflation? And when will it be feasible to raise Δ in a steady-state equilibrium?

The answer to these questions would be straightforward if there were a one-to-one relationship between the revenue generated by the inflation tax and the inflation rate.

If this were the case, the inflation rate would be uniquely determined by the amount of revenue that needs to be raised. But the inflation tax affects the base against which the tax is levied. For a given base, a higher inflation rate raises seigniorage, but a higher inflation rate raises the opportunity cost of holding money and reduces the demand for money, thereby lowering the base against which the tax is levied. This analysis raises the possibility that a given amount of revenue can be raised by more than one rate of inflation.

It will be helpful to impose additional structure so that we can say more about the demand for high-powered money h. The standard approach used in most analyses of seigniorage is to specify directly a functional form for the demand for h as a function of the nominal rate of interest. An early example of this approach, and one of the most influential, is that of Cagan (1956); a more recent example is Bruno and Fischer (1990). We will return to this approach, but we start by following Calvo and Leiderman (1992) in using a variant of the Sidrauski model of Chapter 2 to motivate a demand for money. That is, suppose the economy consists of identical individuals and the utility of the representative agent is given by

$$\sum_{t=0}^{\infty} \beta^t u(c_t, m_t) \tag{4.17}$$

where $0 < \beta < 1$, c is per capita consumption, m is per capita real money holdings, and the function $u(\cdot)$ is strictly concave and twice continuously differentiable. The representative agent chooses consumption, money balances, and holdings of interest-earning bonds to maximize the expected value of (4.17) subject to the following budget constraint:

$$c_t + b_t + m_t = y_t - \tau_t + (1+r)b_{t-1} + \frac{m_{t-1}}{\Pi_t}$$

where b is the agent's holdings of bonds, y is real income, τ is equal to the net taxes of the agent, r is the real rate of interest, assumed constant for simplicity, and $\Pi_t = P_t/P_{t-1} = 1 + \pi_t$ where π_t is the inflation rate. Thus, the last term in the budget constraint, m_{t-1}/Π_t, is equal to the period-t real value of money balances carried into period t; that is, M_{t-1}/P_t where M represents nominal balances.

If we define w_t as the agent's real wealth in period t, $w_t = b_t + m_t$, and let $R = 1 + r$, then the budget constraint can be rewritten as

$$c_t + w_t = y_t - \tau_t + Rw_{t-1} - \left(\frac{R\Pi_t - 1}{\Pi_t}\right)m_{t-1} = y_t - \tau_t + Rw_{t-1} - \left(\frac{i_{t-1}}{\Pi_t}\right)m_{t-1}$$

by using the fact that $R\Pi_{t+1} = 1 + i_t$ where i is the nominal rate of interest. Writing the budget constraint in this way, we can see that the cost of holding wealth in the form of money, as opposed to interest-earning bonds, is equal to i/Π.[14] The first-order condition for optimal money holdings sets the marginal utility of money equal to the cost of holding money times the marginal utility of wealth. Since the interest forgone by holding money in period t is a cost that is incurred in period $t+1$, this cost must be discounted back to period t using the discount factor β to compare with the marginal utility of money in period t. Thus, $u_m(c_t, m_t) = \beta\left(\dfrac{i_t}{\Pi_{t+1}}\right)u_c(c_{t+1}, m_{t+1})$.
But the standard Euler condition for optimal consumption implies $u_c(c_t, m_t) = \beta R u_c(c_{t+1}, m_{t+1})$. Combining these first-order conditions yields

$$u_m(c_t, m_t) = \left(\frac{i_t}{R\Pi_{t+1}}\right)u_c(c_t, m_t) = \left(\frac{i_t}{1 + i_t}\right)u_c(c_t, m_t) \qquad (4.18)$$

Suppose the utility function takes the form $u(c, m) = \ln c + m(B - D \ln m)$. If we use this functional form in (4.18), we obtain

$$m_t = A e^{-\omega_t/D c_t} \qquad (4.19)$$

where $A = e^{\left(\frac{B}{D} - 1\right)}$ and $\omega = \dfrac{i}{1 + i}$. Equation (4.19) provides a convenient functional representation for the demand for money.

Since Cagan's seminal contribution to the study of seigniorage and hyperinflations (Cagan 1956), economists have often followed him in specifying a money demand function of the form $m = Ke^{-\alpha\pi}$; (4.19) shows how something similar can be derived from an underlying utility function. As Calvo and Leiderman point out, the advantage is that one sees how the parameters K and α depend on more primitive parameters of the representative agent's preferences and how they may actually be time dependent. For example, α depends on c_t and, as a consequence, will be time dependent unless K varies appropriately or c itself is constant.

The reason for deriving the demand for money as a function of the rate of inflation is that, having done so, we can now express seigniorage as a function of the rate of inflation. Recall from (4.8) that seigniorage was equal to $\dfrac{i}{1 + \pi}m =$

---

14. Recall from the derivation of equation (4.9) that the term for the government's revenue from seigniorage was $ih/(1 + \pi) = (i/\Pi)h \approx ih$. Comparing this to the household's budget constraint shows that the cost of holding money is exactly equal to the revenue obtained by the government.

$(1+r)\dfrac{i}{1+i}m$. Using our expression for the demand for money, steady-state seigniorage is equal to

$$s = (1+r)\left(\frac{i}{1+i}\right) A \exp\left[-\frac{i}{Dc(1+i)}\right]$$

If we assume that superneutrality characterizes the model, then c will be constant in the steady state and independent of the rate of inflation. The same will be true of the real rate of interest.

To determine how seigniorage varies with the rate of inflation, think of choosing $\omega = i/(1+i)$ through the choice of π. Then $s = (1+r)\omega A e^{-\omega/Dc}$ and

$$\partial s/\partial \omega = (1+r)A e^{-\omega/Dc}\left(1 - \frac{\omega}{Dc}\right) = \frac{s}{\omega}\left(1 - \frac{\omega}{Dc}\right)$$

Since $\dfrac{\partial s}{\partial \pi} = \dfrac{\partial s}{\partial \omega}\dfrac{\partial \omega}{\partial i}\dfrac{\partial i}{\partial \pi} = \dfrac{\partial s}{\partial \omega}\dfrac{1+r}{(1+i)^2}$, the sign of $\partial s/\partial \pi$ will be determined by the sign

of $\dfrac{\partial s}{\partial \omega}$ and that, in turn, depends on the sign of $1 - \dfrac{\omega}{Dc}$. As illustrated in Figure 4.1, seigniorage increases with inflation initially but eventually begins to decline with further increases in π as the demand for real balances shrinks.

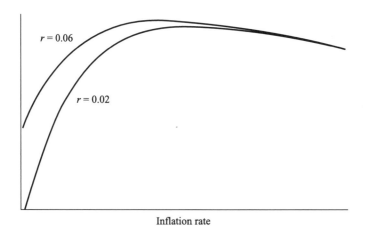

Inflation rate

Figure 4.1
Seigniorage as a Function of Inflation

To determine the inflation rate that maximizes seigniorage, note that $\partial s/\partial \pi = 0$ if and only if

$$\omega \equiv \frac{i}{1+i} = Dc, \text{ or } \pi^{\max} = \left(\frac{1}{1+r}\right)\left(\frac{1}{1-Dc}\right) - 1$$

For inflation rates less than $\pi^{\max}$, the government's revenue is increasing in the inflation rate. The effect of an increase in the tax rate dominates the effect of higher inflation in reducing the real demand for money. As inflation increases above $\pi^{\max}$, the tax base shrinks sufficiently that revenues from seigniorage decline. Consequently, governments face a seigniorage Laffer curve; raising inflation beyond a certain point results in lower real tax revenue.

4.3.1   Cagan's Model

Though the preceding discussion has been carried out in terms of the rate of inflation, the actual policy instrument of the government is the rate of growth of the nominal supply of high-powered money. Suppose the real, per capita deficit that needs to be financed is exogenously given and equal to Δ. In continuous time, the revenue from seigniorage is given by $\dot{H}/PY$, where $\dot{H}$ is the derivative of H with respect to time, so

$$\Delta = \frac{\dot{H}}{H}\frac{H}{PY} = \theta h$$

The demand for real balances will depend on the nominal interest rate and therefore the expected rate of inflation. Treating real variables such as the real rate of interest and real output as constant (an assumption that is appropriate in a steady state characterized by superneutrality and is usually taken as reasonable during hyper-inflations, since all the action really is with money and prices), let $h = \exp(-\alpha\pi^e)$ be the demand for h. Then the government's revenue requirement implies

$$\Delta = \theta e^{-\alpha\pi^e} \tag{4.20}$$

We also know that, for h to be constant in equilibrium requires that $\pi = \theta - n$, where n is the growth rate of real income. And in a steady-state equilibrium, $\pi^e = \pi$, so (4.20) becomes

$$\Delta = \theta e^{-\alpha(\theta-n)} \tag{4.21}$$

the solutions of which give the rates of money growth that are consistent with raising Δ through seigniorage. The right side of (4.21) equals zero when money growth is

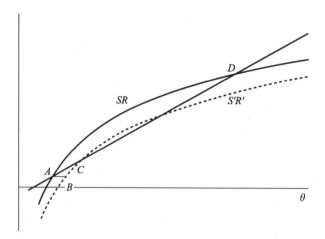

Figure 4.2
Money Growth and Revenue

equal to zero, rises to a maximum at $\theta = \dfrac{1}{\alpha}$, and then declines.[15] That is, for rates of money growth above $\dfrac{1}{\alpha}$ (and therefore inflation rates above $\dfrac{1}{\alpha} - n$), higher inflation actually leads to lower revenues because the tax base falls sufficiently to offset the rise in inflation. Thus, any deficit less than $\Delta^* = \dfrac{1}{\alpha}\exp(\alpha n - 1)$ can be financed by either a low rate of inflation or a high rate of inflation.

Figure 4.2, based on Bruno and Fischer (1990), illustrates the two inflation rates consistent with seigniorage revenues of Δ. The curve SR is derived from (4.20) and shows, for each rate of money growth, the expected rate of inflation needed to generate seigniorage revenues of Δ.[16] The 45° line gives the steady-state inflation rate as a function of the money growth rate: $\pi^e = \pi = \theta - n$. The two points of intersection labeled A and D are the two solutions to (4.21).

What determines whether, for a given deficit, the economy ends up at the high-inflation equilibrium or the low-inflation equilibrium? Which equilibrium is picked

---

15. More generally, with h a function of the nominal interest rate, and r a constant, seigniorage can be written as $s = \theta h(\theta)$. This is maximized at the point where the elasticity of real money demand with respect to θ is equal to minus one: $\theta h'(\theta)/h = -1$.

16. That is, SR shows $\pi^e = (\ln \theta - \ln \Delta)/\alpha$. A reduction in θ continues to yield Δ only if money holdings rise, and this would require a fall in expected inflation.

out depends on the stability properties of the economy. Determining these, in turn, requires a more complete specification of the dynamics of the model. Recall that the demand for money depends on expected inflation through the nominal rate of interest, while the inflation tax rate depends on actual inflation. In considering the effects of variations in the inflation rate, we need to determine how expectations will adjust. Cagan (1956) addressed this question by assuming that expectations adjust adaptively to actual inflation:

$$\frac{\partial \pi^e}{\partial t} = \dot{\pi}^e = \eta(\pi - \pi^e) \tag{4.22}$$

where η captures the "speed of adjustment" of expectations. A low η implies that expectations respond slowly to forecast errors. Since $h = \exp(-\alpha \pi^e)$, we can differentiate this expression with respect to time, obtaining

$$\frac{\dot{h}}{h} = \theta - n - \pi = -\alpha \dot{\pi}^e$$

Solving for π and using (4.22) yields $\pi = \theta - n + \alpha \dot{\pi}^e = \theta - n + \alpha \eta(\pi - \pi^e)$, or $\pi = \frac{\theta - n - \alpha \eta \pi^e}{1 - \alpha \eta}$. Substituting this back into the expectations adjustment equation (4.22) yields

$$\dot{\pi}^e = \frac{\eta(\theta - n - \pi^e)}{1 - \alpha \eta} \tag{4.23}$$

This equation implies that the low-inflation equilibrium will be stable as long as $\alpha \eta < 1$. This requires that expectations adjust sufficiently slowly ($\eta < 1/\alpha$).

If we assume that expectations adjust adaptively and sufficiently slowly, consider what happens when the deficit is increased. Since the demand for real money balances depends on expected inflation, and because the adjustment process does not allow the expected inflation rate to jump immediately, the higher deficit can be financed by an increase in the rate of inflation (assuming the new deficit is still below the maximum that can be financed, Δ^*). Since actual inflation now exceeds expected inflation, $\dot{\pi}^e > 0$ and π^e begins to rise. The economy converges into a new equilibrium at a higher rate of inflation.

In terms of Figure 4.2, an increase in the deficit shifts the SR line to the right to $S'R'$ (for a given expected rate of inflation, money growth must rise in order to generate more revenue). Assume that initially the economy is at point A, the low-inflation equilibrium. Budget balance requires that the economy be on the $S'R'$ line, so θ jumps to the rate associated with point B. But now, at point B, inflation has risen and $\pi^e < \pi = \theta - n$. Expected inflation rises (as long as $\alpha\eta < 1$, see 4.23), and the economy converges to C. The high-inflation equilibrium, in contrast, is unstable.

Adaptive expectations of the sort Cagan assumed disappeared from the literature under the onslaught of the rational-expectations revolution pioneered by Lucas and Sargent in the early 1970s. If agents are systematically attempting to forecast inflation, then their forecast will depend on the actual process governing the evolution of inflation; only rarely will this imply an adjustment process such as (4.22). Stability in the Cagan model also required that expectations not adjust too quickly $(\eta < 1/\alpha)$, and this requirement conflicts with the rational-expectations notion that expectations adjust quickly in response to new information. Bruno and Fischer (1990) show that, to some degree, assuming that agents adjust their holdings of real money balances slowly plays a role under rational expectations similar to the role that the slow adjustment of expectations plays in Cagan's model in ensuring stability under adaptive expectations.

4.3.2 Hyperinflation

Since 1970, the Consumer Price Index for the United States has risen just over fourfold; that is inflation.[17] In Hungary, the index of wholesale prices was 38,500 in January 1923 and 1,026,000 in January 1924, one year later, a 27-fold increase; that's hyperinflation (Sargent 1986, p. 64).

Why do countries find themselves in situations of hyperinflation? Most explanations of hyperinflation point to fiscal sources as the chief culprit. Governments that are forced to print money to finance real government expenditures often end up generating hyperinflations. In that sense, rapid money growth does lead to hyperinflation, consistent with the relationship between money growth and inflation implied by the models we have examined, but money growth is no longer exogenous. Instead, it is endogenously determined by the need to finance a fiscal deficit.

Two explanations for the development of a hyperinflation suggest themselves. Under adaptive expectations, suppose that $\alpha\eta < 1$ so that the low-inflation equilibrium is stable. Now suppose that a shock pushes the inflation rate above the high-inflation equilibrium (above point D in Figure 4.2). If that equilibrium is unstable, the economy continues to diverge—moving to higher and higher rates of inflation. So one explanation for hyperinflations is that they represent situations in which exogenous shocks push the economy into an unstable region.

---

17. The all-items CPI-U was 38.8 in 1970 and 159.6 in 1996 (*Economic Report of the President* 1997, page 365).

Alternatively, suppose the deficit that needs to be financed with seigniorage grows. If it rises above Δ^*, the maximum that can be financed by money creation, the government finds itself unable to obtain enough revenue, so it runs the printing presses faster, further reducing the real revenue it obtains and forcing it to print money even faster. Most hyperinflations have occurred after wars (and on the losing side). Such countries face an economy devastated by war and a tax system that no longer functions effectively. At the same time, there are enormous demands on the government for expenditures to provide the basics of food and shelter and to rebuild the economy. Revenue needs outpace the government's ability to raise tax revenues. The ends of such hyperinflations usually involve a fiscal reform that allows the government to reduce its reliance on seigniorage (see Sargent 1986).

When expected inflation falls in response to the reforms, the opportunity cost of holding money is reduced, and the demand for real money balances rises. Thus, the growth rate of the nominal money supply normally continues temporarily at a very high rate after a hyperinflation has ended. A similar, if smaller-scale, phenomenon occurred in the United States in the mid-1980s. The money supply, as measured by M1, grew very rapidly. At the time there were concerns that this growth would lead to a return of higher rates of inflation. Instead, it seemed to reflect the increased demand for money resulting from the decline in inflation from its peak levels in 1979–1980. The need for real money balances to grow as inflation is reduced often causes problems for establishing and maintaining the credibility of policies designed to reduce inflation. If a disinflation is credible, so that expected inflation falls, it may be necessary to increase the rate of growth of the nominal money supply temporarily. But when inflation and rapid money growth are so closely related, doing so may be taken as a signal that the central bank has given up on its disinflation policy.

Fiscal theories of seigniorage, inflation, and hyperinflations are theories based on fundamentals—there really is a deficit that needs to be financed and that is what leads to money creation. An alternative view of hyperinflations is that they are simply *bubbles*, similar to bubbles in financial markets. Such phenomena are based on the possibility of multiple equilibria in which expectations can be self-fulfilling.

Suppose the real demand for money is given by, in log terms,

$$m_t - p_t = -\alpha(\mathrm{E}_t p_{t+1} - p_t)$$

where $\mathrm{E}_t p_{t+1}$ denotes the expectation formed at time t of time $t+1$ prices. This money-demand function is the log version of Cagan's demand function. We can rearrange this equation to express the current price level as

$$p_t = \frac{m_t}{1+\alpha} + \frac{\alpha \mathrm{E}_t p_{t+1}}{1+\alpha} \tag{4.24}$$

Suppose that the growth rate of the nominal money supply process is given by $m_t = \theta_0 + (1 - \gamma)\theta_1 t + \gamma m_{t-1}$. Since m is the log money supply, the growth rate of the money supply is $m_t - m_{t-1} = (1 - \gamma)\theta_1 + \gamma(m_{t-1} - m_{t-2})$, and the trend (average) growth rate is θ_1. Given this process, and the assumption that agents make use of it and the equilibrium condition (4.24) in forming their expectations, one solution for the price level is given by

$$p_t = \frac{\alpha[\theta_0 + (1 - \gamma)\theta_1(1 + \alpha)]}{1 + \alpha(1 - \gamma)} + \frac{\alpha(1 - \gamma)\theta_1}{1 + \alpha(1 - \gamma)} t + \frac{1}{1 + \alpha(1 - \gamma)} m_t$$

$$= A_0 + A_1 t + A_2 m_t$$

That this is a solution can be verified by noting that it implies $E_t p_{t+1} = A_0 + A_1(t + 1) + A_2 E_t m_{t+1} = A_0 + A_1(t + 1) + A_1[\theta_0 + (1 - \gamma)\theta_1(t + 1) + \gamma m_t]$; substituting this into (4.24) yields the proposed solution. Under this solution, the inflation rate $p_t - p_{t-1}$ converges to θ_1, the average growth rate of the nominal supply of money.[18]

Consider, now, an alternative solution:

$$p_t = A_0 + A_1 t + A_2 m_t + B_t \tag{4.25}$$

where B_t is time varying. We are interested in determining whether there exists a B_t process consistent with (4.24). Substituting the new proposed solution into the equilibrium condition for the price level yields

$$A_0 + A_1 t + A_2 m_t + B_t = \frac{m_t}{1 + \alpha} + \frac{\alpha[A_0 + A_1(t + 1) + A_2 E_t m_{t+1} + E_t B_{t+1}]}{1 + \alpha}$$

which, to hold for all realizations of the nominal money supply, requires that, as before, $A_0 = \dfrac{\alpha[\theta_0 + (1 - \gamma)\theta_1(1 + \alpha)]}{1 + \alpha(1 - \gamma)}$, $A_1 = \dfrac{\alpha(1 - \gamma)\theta_1}{1 + \alpha(1 - \gamma)}$, and $A_2 = \dfrac{1}{1 + \alpha(1 - \gamma)}$. This then implies that the B process must satisfy

$$B_t = \left(\frac{\alpha}{1 + \alpha}\right) E_t B_{t+1}$$

which holds if B follows the explosive process

$$B_{t+1} = k B_t \tag{4.26}$$

18. This follows because $p_t - p_{t-1} = A_1 + A_2(m_t - m_{t-1})$ converges to $A_1 + A_2\theta_1 = \theta_1$.

for $k \equiv \dfrac{1 + \alpha}{\alpha} > 1$. In other words, (4.25) is an equilibrium solution for *any* process satisfying (4.26). Since B grows at the rate $k - 1 = \dfrac{1}{\alpha}$, and since α, the elasticity of money demand with respect to expected inflation, is normally thought to be small, its inverse would be large. The actual inflation rate along a bubble solution could greatly exceed the rate of money growth.

The methods developed to test for bubbles are similar to those that have been employed to test for intertemporal budget balance. For example, if the nominal money stock is nonstationary, then the absence of bubbles implies that the price level will be nonstationary *but cointegrated with the money supply*. This is a testable implication of the no-bubble assumption. Equation (4.26) gives the simplest example of a bubble process. Evans (1991) shows how the cointegration tests can fail to detect bubbles that follow periodically collapsing processes. For more on asset prices and bubbles, see Shiller (1981); West (1987, 1988); Mattey and Meese (1986); Diba and Grossman (1988a, 1988b); and Evans (1991).

Obstfeld and Rogoff (1983, 1986) have considered whether speculative hyper-inflations are consistent with equilibrium when agents are utility maximizing. As discussed in section 2.3.1.1, they show that speculative hyperinflation in unbacked, fiat money systems cannot generally be ruled out. Equilibrium paths may exist along which real money balances eventually converge to zero as the price level goes to $+\infty$.

4.4   Optimal Taxation and Seigniorage

If the government can raise revenue by printing money, how much should it raise from this source? If only distortionary revenue sources are available, it is generally desirable to raise some revenue from all available sources in order to minimize the overall distortions from raising a given amount of revenue. As first noted by Phelps (1973), this generalization suggests that an optimal tax package should include some seigniorage.

If the objective of the government is to raise a given amount of revenue while causing the minimum deadweight loss caused by tax-induced distortions, then the government should generally set its tax instruments so that the marginal distor-tionary cost per dollar of revenue raised is equalized across all taxes. This pre-scription links the optimal inflation tax to a more general problem of determining optimal levels of all tax instruments. If governments are actually attempting to mini-mize the distortionary costs of raising revenue, then the optimal tax literature pro-vides a positive theory of inflation.

This basic idea is developed in the next subsection and was originally used by
Mankiw (1987) to explain nominal-interest-rate setting by the Federal Reserve.
However, the implications of this approach are rejected for the industrialized economies (Poterba and Rotemberg 1990; Trehan and Walsh 1990), although this
rejection may not be too surprising because seigniorage plays a fairly small role as
a revenue source for these countries. Calvo and Leiderman (1992) have used the
optimal-tax approach to examine the experiences of some Latin American economies with more promising results. An excellent survey of optimal seigniorage that
links the topic with the issues of time inconsistency treated in Chapter 8 can be
found in Herrendorf (1997). Section 4.4.2 considers the role inflation might play as
an optimal response to the need to finance temporary expenditure shocks.

4.4.1 A Partial Equilibrium Model

In this section, we assume the government has available to it two revenue sources.
The government can also borrow. It needs to finance a constant, exogenous level of
real expenditures g, plus interest on any borrowing. To simplify the analysis, the real
rate of interest is assumed to be constant, and we specify ad hoc descriptions of both
money demand and the distortions associated with the two tax instruments.

With these assumptions, the basic real budget identity of the government can be
obtained by dividing (4.3) by the time-t price level to obtain

$$b_t = Rb_{t-1} + g - \tau_t - s_t \tag{4.27}$$

where R is the gross interest factor (i.e., one plus the rate of interest), τ is non-
seigniorage tax revenue, and s is seigniorage revenue. Seigniorage is given by

$$s_t = (M_t - M_{t-1})/P_t = m_t - \frac{m_{t-1}}{1 + \pi_t} \tag{4.28}$$

Taking expectations of (4.27) conditional on time-t information and recursively
solving forward yields the intertemporal budget constraint of the government:

$$E_t \sum_{i=0}^{\infty} R^{-i}(\tau_{t+i} + s_{t+i}) = Rb_{t-1} + \frac{R}{R-1}g \tag{4.29}$$

Note that (4.29) imposes a constraint on the government, since $E_t \lim_{i\to\infty} R^{-i}b_{t+i}$ has
been set equal to zero. Absent this constraint, the problem of choosing the optimal
time path for taxes and seigniorage becomes trivial—just set both equal to zero and
borrow continually to finance expenditures plus interest, since debt never needs to be
repaid.

The government is assumed to set τ_t and the inflation rate π_t, as well as planned paths for the future values of these taxes, in order to minimize the present discounted value of the distortions generated by these taxes, taking as given the inherited debt b_{t-1}, the path of expenditures, and the financing constraint given by (4.29). The assumption that the government can commit to a planned path for future taxes and inflation is an important one. Much of Chapter 8 will deal with outcomes when governments cannot precommit to future policies.

In order to illustrate the key implications of the joint determination of inflation and taxes, assume that the distortions arising from taxes are quadratic in the tax rate: $(\tau_t + \phi_t)^2/2$, where ϕ is a stochastic term that allows the marginal costs of taxes to vary randomly.[19] Similarly, costs associated with seigniorage are taken to equal $(s_t + \varepsilon_t)^2/2$ where ε is a stochastic shift in the cost function. Thus, the present discounted value of revenue collection costs is given by

$$\tfrac{1}{2}E_t \sum_{i=0}^{\infty} R^{-i}[(\tau_{t+i} + \phi_{t+i})^2 + (s_{t+i} + \varepsilon_{t+i})^2] \qquad (4.30)$$

The government's objective is to choose paths for the tax rate and inflation to minimize (4.30) subject to (4.29).

Letting λ represent the Lagrangian multiplier associated with the intertemporal budget constraint, the necessary first-order conditions for the government's setting of τ and s take the form

$$E_t(\tau_{t+i} + \phi_{t+i}) = \lambda, \quad i \geq 0$$

$$E_t(s_{t+i} + \varepsilon_{t+i}) = \lambda, \quad i \geq 0$$

These conditions simply state that the government will arrange its tax collections to equalize the marginal distortionary costs across tax instruments, that is, $E_t(\tau_{t+i} + \phi_{t+i}) = \lambda = E_t(s_{t+i} + \varepsilon_{t+i})$ for each $i \geq 0$ and across time, that is, $E_t(\tau_{t+i} + \phi_{t+i}) = E_t(\tau_{t+j} + \phi_{t+j})$ and $E_t(s_{t+i} + \varepsilon_{t+i}) = E_t(s_{t+j} + \varepsilon_{t+j})$ for all i and j.

The first of these conditions implies $\tau_t + \phi_t = \lambda = s_t + \varepsilon_t$ and represents an *intratemporal* optimality condition. It implies that changes in the government's revenue needs will lead the tax rate and the inflation rate to move in the same direction. The value of λ will depend on the total revenue needs of the government; increases in $\frac{R}{R-1}g + Rb_{t-1}$ will cause the government to increase the revenue raised from both

---

19. This approach follows Poterba and Rotemberg (1990), who specify tax costs directly as we are doing here, although they assume a more general functional form for which the quadratic specification is a special case. See also Trehan and Walsh (1988).

tax sources. Thus, we would expect to observe τ_t and s_t moving in similar directions (given ϕ_t and ε_t).

Intertemporal optimality requires that marginal costs be equated across time periods for each of these tax instruments:

$$E_t \tau_{t+1} = \tau_t - E_t \phi_{t+1} + \phi_t \qquad (4.31)$$

and

$$E_t s_{t+1} = s_t - E_t \varepsilon_{t+1} + \varepsilon_t \qquad (4.32)$$

These intertemporal conditions lead to standard "tax-smoothing" conclusions; for each tax instrument, the government will equate the expected marginal distortionary costs in different time periods. If the random shocks to tax distortions follow $I(1)$ processes and $E_t \Delta \phi_{t+1} = E_t \Delta \varepsilon_{t+1} = 0$, then these intertemporal optimality conditions imply that both τ and s follow Martingale processes, an implication of the tax-smoothing model originally developed by Barro (1979a). If $E_t \varepsilon_{t+1} = \varepsilon_t$, (4.32) implies that future changes in seigniorage revenues should be unpredictable based on information available at time t.

Changes in revenue sources might be predictable, and still be consistent with this model of optimal taxation, if the expected $t + 1$ values of ϕ and/or ε, conditional on period-t information, are nonzero. For example, if $E_t \varepsilon_{t+1} - \varepsilon_t > 0$, that is, if the distortionary cost of seigniorage revenue were expected to rise, it would be optimal to plan to reduce future seigniorage.

Using a form of (4.32), Mankiw (1987) argued that the near random-walk behavior of inflation (actually nominal interest rates) is consistent with U.S. monetary policy having been conducted in a manner consistent with optimal finance considerations. Poterba and Rotemberg (1990) provide some cross-country evidence on the joint movements of inflation and other tax revenues. In general, this evidence is not favorable to the hypothesis that inflation (or seigniorage) has been set on the basis of optimal finance considerations. Although Poterba and Rotemberg find the predicted positive relationship between tax rates and inflation for the United States and Japan, there is a negative relationship for France, Germany, and the United Kingdom.

The implications of the optimal finance view of seigniorage are, however, much stronger than simply that seigniorage and other tax revenues are positively correlated. Since the unit root behavior of both s and τ arises from the same source (their dependence on $\dfrac{R}{R-1} g + R b_{t-1}$ through λ), the optimizing model of tax setting has the joint implication that both tax rates and inflation should contain unit roots

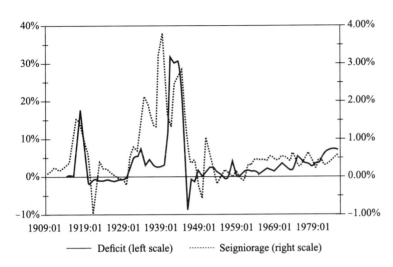

Figure 4.3
U.S. Deficits and Seigniorage 1909–1986 (as % of GNP)

(they respond to permanent shifts in government revenue needs), and they should be cointegrated.[20] Trehan and Walsh (1990) show that this implication is rejected for U.S. data.

The optimal finance view of seigniorage fails for the United States because seigniorage appears to behave more like the stock of debt than like general tax revenues. Under a tax-smoothing model, temporary variations in government expenditures should be met through debt financing. Variations in seigniorage should reflect changes in expected permanent government expenditures, or, from (4.32), stochastic shifts in the distortions associated with raising seigniorage (due to the ε realizations). In contrast, debt should rise in response to a temporary revenue need (such as a war), and then gradually decline over time. However, as Figure 4.3 shows, the behavior of seigniorage, particularly during the World War II period, mimics that of the deficit much more than it does other tax revenues.

One drawback of this analysis is that the specification of the government's objective function is ad hoc; the assumed form of the tax distortions was not related in any way to the underlying sources of the distortions in terms of the allocative effects of taxes or the welfare costs of inflation. These costs depend on the demand for money, and, therefore, the specification of the distortions should be consistent with the particular approach used to motivate the demand for money.

20. That is, if ϕ and ε are $I(0)$ processes, then τ and s are $I(1)$ but $\tau - s = \varepsilon - \phi$ is $I(0)$.

Calvo and Leiderman (1992) provide an analysis of optimal intertemporal inflation taxation that uses a money-demand specification that is consistent with utility maximization. They show that the government's optimality condition requires that the nominal rate of interest vary with the expected growth of the marginal utility of consumption. Optimal tax considerations call for high taxes when the marginal utility of consumption is low and low taxes when the marginal utility of consumption is high. Thus, models of inflation in an optimal finance setting will generally imply restrictions on the joint behavior of inflation and the marginal utility of consumption, not just on inflation alone. Calvo and Leiderman estimate their model using data from three countries that have experienced periods of high inflation, Argentina, Brazil, and Israel. While the overidentifying restrictions implied by their model are not rejected for the first two countries, they are for Israel.

4.4.2   Optimal Seigniorage and Temporary Shocks

The prescription to smooth marginal distortionary costs over time implies that tax levels are set on the basis of some estimate of permanent expenditure needs. In Barro's original formulation, temporary fluctuations in government expenditures did not lead to tax adjustments, but, instead, temporary increases in expenditures were deficit financed; periods of temporarily low expenditures were used to generate the surpluses needed to retire the previously issued debt. To allow tax rates to fluctuate in response to temporary and unanticipated fluctuations in expenditures would result in a higher total efficiency loss in present-value terms because of the distortions induced by non-lump-sum taxes. As extended to seigniorage by Mankiw (1987), the same argument implied that seigniorage should be set on the basis of permanent expenditure needs and not adjusted in response to unanticipated temporary events.

The allocative distortions induced by the inflation tax, however, were shown in Chapters 2 and 3 to be based on anticipated inflation. Consumption, labor-supply, and money-holding decisions are made by households on the basis of expected inflation, and for this reason, variations in expected inflation generate distortions. In contrast, unanticipated inflation has wealth effects but no substitution effects. It serves, therefore, as a form of lump-sum tax. Given real money holdings, which will be based on the public's expectations about inflation, a government interested in minimizing distortionary tax costs should engineer a surprise inflation. If sufficient revenue could be generated in this way, socially costly distortionary taxes could be avoided.[21]

---

21. Auernheimer (1974) provides a guide to seigniorage for an "honest" government, one that does not generate revenue by allowing the price level to jump unexpectedly, even though this would represent an efficient lump-sum tax.

Unfortunately, private agents are likely to anticipate that the government will have an incentive to attempt a surprise inflation, and the outcome in such a situation will be the major focus of Chapter 8. But suppose the government can commit itself to, on average, only inflating at a rate consistent with its revenue needs based on average expenditures. That is, average inflation (and other taxes as well) is set according to permanent expenditures as implied by the tax-smoothing model. But if there are unanticipated fluctuations in expenditures, these should be met through socially costless unanticipated inflation.

Calvo and Guidotti (1993) make this argument rigorous. They show that when the government can commit to a path for anticipated inflation, it is optimal for unanticipated inflation to respond flexibly to unexpected disturbances. Recall from Figure 4.3 that seigniorage in the United States followed a pattern that appeared to be more similar to that of the federal government deficit than to a measure of the average tax rate. During war periods, when most of the rise in expenditures could be viewed as temporary, taxes were not raised sufficiently to fund the war effort. Instead, the U.S. government borrowed heavily, just as the Barro tax-smoothing model implies. But the United States did raise the inflation tax; seigniorage revenues rose during the war, falling back to lower levels at the war's conclusion. This type of behavior is much closer to that implied by Calvo and Guidotti's theory than to the basic implications of Mankiw's.

4.5 Friedman's Rule Revisited

The preceding analysis has gone partway toward integrating the choice of inflation with the general-public-finance choice of tax rates, and the discussion was motivated by Phelps' conclusion that some revenue should be raised from the inflation tax if only distortionary tax sources are available. However, this conclusion has been questioned by Kimbrough (1986a, 1986b); Faig (1988); Chari, Christiano, and Kehoe (1991, 1996); and Correia and Teles (1996). They show that there are conditions under which Friedman's rule for the optimal inflation rate—a zero nominal rate of interest—continues to be optimal even in the absence of lump-sum taxes.

These results build on findings in the optimal tax literature that identify situations in which the structure of optimal indirect taxes calls for different final goods to be taxed at the same rate or for the tax rate on goods that serve as intermediate inputs to be zero (see Diamond and Mirrlees 1971; Atkinson and Stiglitz 1972). Using a money-in-the-utility-function approach, for example, treats money as a final good; in contrast, a shopping-time model, or a more general model in which money serves to produce transaction services, treats money as an intermediate input. Thus, it is important to examine the implications that these alternative assumptions about the role of money might have for the optimal tax approach to inflation determination, and how optimal inflation-tax results might depend on particular restrictions on preferences or on the technology for producing transaction services.

Chari, Christiano, and Kehoe (1996) and Correia and Teles (1996) have recently applied results from the optimal tax literature to the optimal inflation issue using a variety of monetary models (money-in-the-utility-function, cash-in-advance, and shopping-time models).[22] We can consider each of these cases in turn, beginning with a cash-in-advance example.

4.5.1   A Cash-in-Advance Model

Suppose that the consumer faces a cash-in-advance constraint on a subset of its purchases. Specifically, assume c_1 represents cash goods, while c_2 represents credit goods. Let l denote leisure. The household's objective is to maximize

$$E_t \sum_{i=0}^{\infty} \beta^i U(c_{1,t+i}, c_{2,t+i}, l_{t+i})$$

subject to the budget constraint

$$(1 + \tau_t^c)Q_t(c_{1,t} + c_{2,t}) + M_t + B_t = (1 - \tau_t^h)Q_t(1 - l_t) + (1 + i_{t-1})B_{t-1} + M_{t-1}$$

where M and B are nominal money and bond holdings, i_{t-1} is the nominal rate of interest from $t-1$ to t, Q is the producer price of output, and τ^c and τ^h are the tax rates on consumption (both cash and credit goods) and hours of work. In addition, we have assumed that the production function exhibits constant returns to scale and that labor hours, $1 - l$, are transformed into output according to $y = 1 - l$. Define $P \equiv (1 + \tau^c)Q$. Household real wealth is $w_t = (M_t + B_t)/P_t = m_t + b_t$, and the budget constraint can be written as

$$c_{1,t} + c_{2,t} + w_t = \frac{1 - \tau_t^h}{1 + \tau_t^c}(1 - l_t) + (1 + r_{t-1})b_{t-1} + (1 + \pi_t)^{-1}m_{t-1}$$

$$= (1 - \tau_t)(1 - l_t) + (1 + r_{t-1})w_{t-1} - i_{t-1}m_{t-1} \quad (4.33)$$

where $1 - \tau_t \equiv \dfrac{1 - \tau_t^h}{1 + \tau_t^c}$ and $(1 + r) - (1 + \pi)^{-1} = \left(\dfrac{1+i}{1+\pi} - \dfrac{1}{1+\pi}\right) = i/(1+\pi)$ has

---

22. An early example of the use of optimal tax models to study the optimal inflation rate issue is Drazen (1979). See also Walsh (1984).

been approximated by i.[23] In addition, the cash-in-advance constraint requires that

$$c_{1,t} \leq (1 + \pi_t)^{-1} m_{t-1}$$

Before considering when the optimal inflation tax might be positive, suppose we ignore the credit good c_2 for the moment so that the model is similar to the basic cash-in-advance model studied in section 3.3.1. The budget constraint becomes $c_t + w_t = (1 - \tau_t)(1 - l_t) + (1 + r_{t-1})w_{t-1} - i_{t-1}m_{t-1}$. Recall that inflation served as a tax on labor supply in that model. But according to the budget constraint, the government already has, in τ, a tax on labor supply. Thus, the inflation tax is redundant.[24] Because it is redundant, the government can achieve an optimal allocation without using the inflation tax.

In a cash-and-credit-good economy, the inflation tax is no longer redundant if the government cannot set different commodity taxes on the two types of goods. So if we return to the model with both cash and credit goods, the first-order conditions for the household's decision problem imply that cash and credit goods will be chosen such that

$$\frac{U_1(c_1, c_2, l)}{U_2(c_1, c_2, l)} = 1 + i$$

Atkinson and Stiglitz (1972) show that if the two goods are produced under conditions of constant returns to scale, a sufficient condition for uniform tax rates is that the utility function is homothetic.[25] With equal tax rates, the ratio of marginal utilities equals the ratio of producer prices. The analysis of Atkinson and Stiglitz implies that, if preferences are homothetic in c_1 and c_2, the ratio of the marginal utility of cash and credit goods should equal 1, the ratio of their production prices. This outcome occurs only if $i = 0$; hence, homothetic preferences implies that the nominal rate of interest should be set equal to zero. But this is just the Friedman rule for the optimal rate of inflation.

---

23. That is,

$$\frac{i}{1 + \pi} = \frac{1 + i - 1}{1 + \pi} = \frac{1 + i}{1 + \pi} - \frac{1}{1 + \pi} \approx (1 + i - \pi) - (1 - \pi) = i$$

24. See Chari, Christiano, and Kehoe (1996).

25. Homothetic preferences imply that $u(c_1, c_2)$ is homogeneous of degree 1 and that u_i is homogeneous of degree 0. With homothetic preferences, indifference curves are parallel to each other with constant slope along any ray; $\dfrac{u_2(c_1, c_2)}{u_1(c_1, c_2)} = f\left(\dfrac{c_2}{c_1}\right)$.

Thus, the optimal inflation tax should be zero if for all $\lambda > 0$,

$$\frac{U_1(\lambda c_1, \lambda c_2, l)}{U_2(\lambda c_1, \lambda c_2, l)} = \frac{U_1(c_1, c_2, l)}{U_2(c_1, c_2, l)} \tag{4.34}$$

in which case the utility function has the form

$$U(c_1, c_2, l) = V[\phi(c_1, c_2), l]$$

where ϕ is homogenous of degree 1. If this relation holds, the government should avoid using the inflation tax even though it must rely on distortionary taxes. Positive nominal rates of interest impose an efficiency cost by distorting the consumer's choice between cash and credit goods.

How reasonable is this condition? Recall that we have offered no explanation for why one good is a cash good and the other is a credit good. This distinction has simply been assumed, and therefore it is difficult to argue intuitively why the preferences for cash and credit goods should (or should not) satisfy the condition (4.34). In aggregate analysis, it is common to combine all goods into one composite good; this is standard in writing utility as $u(c, l)$ with c representing an aggregation over all consumption goods. Interpreting c as $\phi(c_1, c_2)$, that is, interpreting ϕ as an aggregator function, implies that preferences would satisfy the properties necessary for the optimal inflation tax to be zero. However, this is not an innocuous restriction. It requires, for example, that the ratio of the marginal utility of coffee at the local coffee cart (a cash good) to that of books at the bookstore (a credit good) remain constant if coffee and book consumption double.

4.5.2 Money in the Utility Function

Chari, Christiano, and Kehoe (1996) show that a similar conclusion arises when money itself is a final good, entering directly into the utility function. If the representative household's utility during period t is given by $U(c_t, m_t, l_t)$ and the household's objective is to maximize $E_t \sum_{i=0}^{\infty} \beta^i U(c_{t+i}, m_{t+i}, l_{t+i})$ subject to the budget constraint given by (4.33), then the first-order conditions for the household's decision problem imply that consumption, money balances, and leisure will be chosen such that (see equation 2.23)

$$\frac{U_m(c_t, m_t, l_t)}{U_c(c_t, m_t, l_t)} = \frac{i_t}{1 + i_t}$$

With the production costs of money assumed to be zero, the ratio of marginal utilities differs from the ratio of production costs unless $i = 0$. Hence, with preferences that are homothetic in c and m, the Atkinson-Stiglitz result implies it will be optimal to set the nominal rate of interest equal to zero.

As in the cash-in-advance framework, we can recover Friedman's rule for the optimal rate of inflation even in the absence of lump-sum taxes. But it is important to recognize that the restrictions on preferences necessary to restore Friedman's rule are very strong and, as discussed by Braun (1991), different assumptions about preferences will lead to different conclusions. The assumption that the ratio of the marginal utilities of consumption and money is independent of leisure can certainly be questioned. However, it is very common in the literature to assume separability between leisure, consumption, and money holdings. The standard log utility specification, for example, displays this property and so would imply that a zero nominal interest rate is optimal.[26]

4.5.3 Money as an Intermediate Input

The approach in the previous subsections motivated a demand for money by imposing a cash-in-advance constraint that applied to a subset of goods or by including real money balances as an element in the representative agent's utility function. If the role of money arises because of the services it provides in facilitating transactions, then it might be more naturally viewed as an intermediate good, a good used as an input in the production of the final goods that directly enter the utility function. The distinction between final goods and intermediate goods is important for determining the optimal structure of taxation; Diamond and Mirrlees (1971), for example, showed that under certain conditions it may be optimal to tax only final goods. In particular, when the government can levy taxes on each final good, then intermediate goods should not be taxed.

The importance of money's role as an intermediate input was first stressed by Kimbrough (1986a, 1986b) and Faig (1988).[27] Their work suggested that the Friedman rule might apply even in the presence of distortionary taxes, and conclusions to the contrary arose from the treatment of money as a final good that enters the utility function directly. Under conditions of constant returns to scale, the Diamond-Mirrlees result called for efficiency in production, implying that money

---

26. As Chari, Christiano, and Kehoe note, the preference restrictions are sufficient for the Friedman rule to be optimal but not necessary. For example, in the cash/credit model, suppose preferences are not homothetic and the optimal tax structure calls for taxing credit goods more heavily. A positive nominal interest rate taxes cash goods, and negative nominal rates are not feasible. Thus, a corner solution can arise in which the optimal nominal interest rate is zero. Note that this assumes the government cannot impose separate goods taxes on cash and credit goods.

27. See also Guidotti and Végh (1993).

and labor inputs into producing transactions should not be taxed. Since the money-in-the-utility function approach is usually motivated as a shortcut for modeling situations in which money serves as a medium of exchange by facilitating transactions, the work of Kimbrough and Faig indicates that such shortcuts can have very important implications. However, the requirement that taxes be available for every final good is not satisfied in practice, and the properties of the transactions technology of the economy are such that, until these are better understood, there is no clear case for assuming constant returns to scale.

In a recent contribution, Correia and Teles (1996) have provided further results on the applicability of the Friedman rule. They show that Friedman's result holds for any shopping-time model in which shopping-time is a homogeneous function of consumption and real money balances. To investigate this result, consider a generalized shopping-time model in which money and time are inputs into producing transaction services. Specifically, assume that the representative agent has a total time allocation normalized to 1 that can be allocated to leisure (l), market activity (n), or shopping (n^s):

$$l_t + n_t + n_t^s = 1 \tag{4.35}$$

Shopping time depends on the agent's choice of consumption and money holdings, with n_t^s increasing in c_t and decreasing in m_t according to the shopping production function

$$n_t^s = G(c_t, m_t)$$

Assume that G is homogeneous of degree η so that we can write $G(\lambda_t c_t, \lambda_t m_t) = \lambda_t^\eta G(c_t, m_t)$. Letting $\lambda_t = 1/c_t$, $G(1, m_t/c_t) = c_t^{-\eta} n_t^s$, or

$$n_t^s = c_t^\eta G\left(1, \frac{m_t}{c_t}\right) = c_t^\eta g\left(\frac{m_t}{c_t}\right)$$

In addition, assume g is a convex function, $g' \le 0$, $g'' \ge 0$, which implies that shopping time is nonincreasing in m_t/c_t but real money balances exhibit diminishing marginal productivity. Constant returns to scale corresponds to $\eta = 1$. Assume there exists a level of real balances relative to consumption $\bar{u}$ such that $g'(x) = 0$ for $x \ge \bar{u}$, corresponding to a satiation level of real balances.

The representative agent chooses paths for consumption, labor supply, money holdings, and capital holdings to maximize

$$\sum \beta^i u\left[c_{t+i}, 1 - n_{t+i} - c_{t+i}^\eta g\left(\frac{m_{t+i}}{c_{t+i}}\right)\right] \tag{4.36}$$

subject to the following budget constraint:

$$w_t \equiv \frac{1+i_{t-1}}{1+\pi_t}d_{t-1} - \frac{i_{t-1}}{1+\pi_t}m_{t-1} = c_t + d_t - (1-\tau_t)f(n_t) \qquad (4.37)$$

where $f(n_t)$ is a standard, constant-returns-to-scale, neoclassical production function, τ_t is the tax rate on income, $d_t = m_t + b_t$ is total real assets holdings, equal to government interest-bearing debt holdings (b_t) plus real money holdings, i_{t-1} is the nominal interest rate from $t-1$ to t, and π_t is the inflation rate from $t-1$ to t. Notice that we have ignored capital accumulation in this analysis. Further assume that initial conditions include $M_{t-1} = B_{t-1} = 0$ where these are the nominal levels of money and bond stocks. A final, important assumption in Correia and Teles's analysis is that $f(n) = 1 - l - n^s$.

The government's optimal tax problem is to pick time paths for τ_{t+i} and i_{t+i} to maximize (4.36) subject to the economy resource constraint $c_t + g_t \leq 1 - l_t - n_t^s$ and to the requirement that consumption and labor supply be consistent with the choices of private agents. Following Lucas and Stokey (1983), this problem can be recast by using the first-order conditions from the individual agent's decision problem to express, in terms of the government's tax instruments, the equilibrium prices that will support the paths of consumption and labor supply that solve the government's problem. This analysis leads to an additional constraint on the government's choices and can be summarized in terms of an implementability condition.

To derive this implementability condition, we start with the first order conditions for the representative agent's problem. Define the value function

$$v(w_t) = \max\left\{u\left[c_t, 1-n_t - c_t^\eta g\left(\frac{m_t}{c_t}\right)\right] + \beta v(w_{t+1})\right\}$$

where the maximization is subject to the budget constraint (4.37). Letting $\lambda_t = v_w(w_t)$ denote the marginal value of wealth, the first order conditions imply

$$u_c - u_l\left(\eta g - \frac{m_t}{c_t}g'\right)c_t^{\eta-1} = \lambda_t \qquad (4.38)$$

$$\frac{u_l}{(1-\tau_t)} = \lambda_t \qquad (4.39)$$

$$-u_l g' c^{\eta-1} = \lambda_t I_t \qquad (4.40)$$

$$\lambda_t = \beta R_t \lambda_{t+1} \qquad (4.41)$$

where $I_t = \dfrac{i_t}{1+i_t}$ and $R_t = \dfrac{1+i_t}{1+\pi_{t+1}}$.

The next step is to recast the budget constraint (4.37). This constraint can be written as

$$d_{t-1} = \sum_{i=0}^{\infty} D_i[c_{t+i} - (1 - \tau_{t+i})(1 - l_{t+i} - n_{t+i}^s) + R_{t+i-1}I_{t+i-1}m_{t+i-1}] \qquad (4.42)$$

where we have imposed a no-Ponzi condition and the discount factor D_i is defined as $D_i \equiv \Pi_{j=0}^{i} R_{t+j-1}^{-1}$. The terms involving m_{t+i-1} can be simplified by noting that $\sum_{i=0}^{\infty} D_i(R_{t+i-1}I_{t+i-1}m_{t+i-1}) = \sum_{i=0}^{\infty} D_i I_{t+i}m_{t+i}$ since we have assumed that the initial stocks of money and bonds equal zero.[28] With $d_{t-1} = 0$, equation (4.42) becomes

$$\sum_{i=0}^{\infty} D_i[c_{t+i} - (1 - \tau_{t+i})(1 - l_{t+i} - n_{t+i}^s) + I_{t+i}m_{t+i}] = 0$$

The implementability condition is obtained by replacing the prices in this budget constraint using the first-order conditions of the agent's problem to express the prices in terms of quantities.[29] Recalling that $c^{\eta}g = n^s$, first multiply and divide the intertemporal budget constraint by λ_{t+i}, then use the result from the first order conditions (4.41) that $D_i = \beta^i D_0 \lambda_{t+i}/\lambda_t$ to write

$$\frac{D_0}{\lambda_t} \sum_{i=0}^{\infty} \beta^i[\lambda_{t+i}c_{t+i} - \lambda_{t+i}(1 - \tau_{t+i})(1 - l_{t+i} - n_{t+i}^s) - \lambda_{t+i}I_{t+i}m_{t+i}] = 0$$

Now use the first order conditions (4.38)–(4.40) to obtain

$$\sum_{i=0}^{\infty} \beta^i\left[u_c c_{t+i} - u_l \eta n_{t+i}^s + u_l \frac{m}{c}g'c_{t+i}^{\eta} - u_l(1 - l_{t+i} - n_{t+i}^s) - u_l \frac{m}{c}g'c_{t+i}^{\eta}\right] = 0$$

Since the term $u_l \dfrac{m}{c}g'c_{t+i}^{\eta}$ appears twice, with opposite signs, these cancel, and this

---

28. This uses the fact that $m_{t-1} = 0$ so we can write

$$\sum_{i=0} D_i R_{t+i-1}I_{t+i-1}m_{t+i-1} = D_0 R_{t-1}I_{t-1}m_{t-1} + D_1 R_t I_t m_t + \cdots$$

$$= D_1 R_t I_t m_t + D_2 R_{t+1}I_{t+1}m_{t+1} + \cdots$$

$$= D_0 I_t m_t + D_1 I_{t+1}m_{t+1} + \cdots$$

$$= \sum_{i=0} D_i I_{t+i}m_{t+i}$$

29. The price of consumption is 1, the price of leisure is $1 - \tau$, and the price of real balances is I.

condition becomes

$$\sum_{i=0}^{\infty} \beta^i [u_c c_{t+i} - u_l(1 - l_{t+i}) + u_l(1 - \eta)n_{t+i}^s)] = 0 \tag{4.43}$$

The government's problem is now to choose c_{t+i}, m_{t+i} and l_{t+i} to maximize the utility of the representative agent, subject to the economy's resource constraint, the production function for shopping time, and equation (4.43). That is, $\max \sum \beta^i u(c_{t+i}, l_{t+i})$ subject to (4.43) and $c_t + g_t \leq (1 - l_t - n_t^s)$ where $n_t^s = c_t^\eta g(m_t/c_t)$.

Since m appears in this problem only in the production function for shopping time, the first-order condition for the optimal choice of m_t is

$$[\beta^i \psi u_l(1 - \eta) - \mu_{t+i}]g' = 0 \tag{4.44}$$

where $\psi \geq 0$ is the multiplier on the implementability constraint (4.43), and $\mu \geq 0$ is the multiplier on the resource constraint. Correia and Teles show that $\beta^i \psi u_l(1 - \eta) - \mu_{t+i} = 0$ cannot characterize the optimum, so for (4.44) to be satisfied requires that $g' = 0$. From the first-order conditions for the representative agent's problem, $-u_l g' c^{\eta-1} = \lambda_t I_t$; this implies that $g' = 0$ requires $I = 0$. That is, the nominal rate of interest should equal zero, and the optimal tax on money is zero.

The critical property of money, according to Correia and Teles, is its status as a free primary good. Free in this context means that it can be produced at zero variable cost. The costless production assumption is standard in monetary economics, and it provided the intuition for Friedman's original result. With a zero social cost of production, optimality requires that the private cost also be zero. This occurs only if the nominal rate of interest is zero.

We have now seen that there are quite general cases in which Phelps' conclusion no longer holds. Even in the absence of lump-sum taxation, optimal tax policy should not distort the relative price of cash and credit goods or distort money holdings. But it is important to recognize that the restrictions on preferences and technology necessary to restore Friedman's rule are not trivial, and, as discussed by Braun (1991), different assumptions can lead to different conclusions.

4.6 Nonindexed Tax Systems

Up to this point, our discussion has assumed that the tax system is indexed so that taxes are levied on real income; a one-time change in all nominal quantities, and the price level would leave the real equilibrium unchanged. This assumption requires that a pure price change have no effect on the government's real tax revenues or the tax rates faced by individuals and firms in the private sector. Most actual tax systems, however, are not completely indexed to ensure that pure price-level changes leave real tax rates and real tax revenue unchanged. Inflation-induced distortions generated by the interaction of inflation and the tax system have the potential to be much larger than the revenue-related effects on which most of the seigniorage and optimal inflation literature has focused. Feldstein (1996) provides a recent analysis of the net benefits of reducing inflation from 2% to zero,[30] and he concludes that for his preferred parameter values the effects due to reducing distortions related to the tax system are roughly twice those associated with the change in government revenue.

One important distortion arises when nominal interest income and not real interest income is taxed. After-tax real rates of return will be relevant for individual agents in making savings and portfolio decisions, and if nominal income is subject to a tax rate of τ, the real after-tax return will be

$$r_a = (1 - \tau)i - \pi$$
$$= (1 - \tau)r - \tau\pi$$

where $i = r + \pi$ is the before tax nominal return and r is the before-tax real return. Thus, for a given pretax real return r, the after-tax real return is decreasing in the rate of inflation.

To see how this distortion will affect the steady-state capital-labor ratio, consider the basic money-in-the-utility-function model of Chapter 2 with an income tax of τ on total nominal income. Nominal income is assumed to include any nominal capital gain on capital holdings:

$$Y_t \equiv [P_t f(k_{t-1}) + i_{t-1}B_{t-1} + P_t T_t + (P_t - P_{t-1})(1 - \delta)k_{t-1}]$$

and the representative agent's budget constraint becomes

$$(1 - \tau)Y_t = P_t c_t + P_t k_t - P_t(1 - \delta)k_{t-1} + (B_t - B_{t-1}) + (M_t - M_{t-1}) \qquad (4.45)$$

where M is the agent's nominal money holdings, B his bond holdings, and $P_t T_t$ a nominal transfer payment.[31] In real terms, the budget constraint becomes[32]

30. Feldstein allows for an upward bias in the inflation rate as measured by the *CPI* so that his estimates apply to reducing *CPI* inflation from 4% to 2%.

31. For simplicity, assume T is adjusted in a lump-sum fashion to ensure that variations in inflation and the tax rate on income leave the government's budget balanced. Obviously, if lump-sum taxes actually were available, the optimal policy would involve setting $\tau = 0$ and following Friedman's rule for the optimal rate of inflation. The purpose here is to examine the effects of a nonindexed tax system on the steady-state capital stock in the easiest possible manner.

32. This formulation asumes that real economic depreciation is tax deductible. If depreciation allowances are based on historical nominal cost, a further inflation-induced distortion would be introduced.

$$(1 - \tau)\left[f(k_{t-1}) + \frac{i_{t-1}b_{t-1}}{1 + \pi_t} + T_t \right] - \tau \frac{\pi_t}{1 + \pi_t}(1 - \delta)k_{t-1}$$

$$= c_t + k_t - (1 - \delta)k_{t-1} + \left(b_t - \frac{b_{t-1}}{1 + \pi_t} \right) + \left(m_t - \frac{m_{t-1}}{1 + \pi_t} \right)$$

Assuming the agent's objective is to maximize the present discounted value of expected utility that depends on consumption and money holdings, the first-order conditions for capital and bonds imply, in the steady state,

$$(1 - \tau)f_k(k) + \frac{1 + (1 - \tau)\pi}{1 + \pi}(1 - \delta) = \frac{1}{\beta} \tag{4.46}$$

and

$$(1 - \tau)\left(\frac{1 + i}{1 + \pi} \right) + \frac{\tau}{1 + \pi} = \frac{1}{\beta} \tag{4.47}$$

The steady-state capital-labor ratio is determined by

$$f_k(k^{ss}) = \left(\frac{1}{1 - \tau} \right)\left[\frac{1}{\beta} - \left(\frac{1 + (1 - \tau)\pi}{(1 + \pi)} \right)(1 - \delta) \right]$$

Since $[1 + (1 - \tau)\pi]/(1 + \pi)$ is decreasing in π, k^{ss} is decreasing in the inflation rate; higher inflation leads to larger nominal capital gains on existing holdings of capital, and, since these are taxed, increases the effective tax rate on capital.

Equation (4.47) can be solved for the steady-state nominal rate of interest to yield

$$1 + i^{ss} = \frac{1}{\beta}\left(\frac{1 + \pi}{1 - \tau} \right) - \frac{\tau}{1 - \tau}$$

Thus, the pretax real return on bonds, $(1 + i)/(1 + \pi)$ increases with the rate of inflation, implying that nominal rates rise more than proportionately with an increase in inflation.

It is important to recognize that we have examined only one aspect of the effects of inflation and the tax system.[33] Because of the taxation of nominal returns, higher inflation distorts individuals' decisions, but it also generates revenue for the government that, with a constant level of expenditures (in present-value terms), would allow other taxes to be reduced. Thus, the distortions associated with the higher inflation

---

33. Feldstein, Green, and Sheshinski (1978) employed a version of Tobin's money and growth model to explore the implications of a nonindexed tax system when firms use both debt and equity to finance capital.

are potentially offset by the reduction in the distortions caused by other tax sources. As noted earlier, however, Feldstein (1996) argues that the offset is only partial, leaving a large net annual cost of positive rates of inflation. Feldstein identifies the increased effective tax rate on capital that occurs because of the treatment of depreciation and the increased subsidy on housing associated with the deductibility of nominal mortgage interest in the United States as important distortions generated by higher inflation interacting with a nonindexed tax system. Including these effects with an analysis of the implications for government revenues and, consequently, possible adjustments in other distortionary taxes, Feldstein estimates that a two-percentage-point reduction in inflation (from 2% to zero) increases net welfare by between 0.63% and 1.01% of GDP annually. These figures assume an elasticity of savings with respect to the after-tax real return of 0.4 and a deadweight loss of taxes of between 40 cents for every dollar of revenue (leading to the 0.63% figure) and $1.50 per dollar of revenue (leading to the 1.01% figure). Since these are annual gains, the present discounted value of permanently reducing inflation would be quite large.

4.7 Problems

1. Consider the version of the Sidrauski (1967) model studied in problem 1 of Chapter 2. Utility was given by $u(c_t, m_t) = w(c_t) + v(m_t)$, with $w(c_t) = \ln c_t$ and $v(m_t) = m_t(B - D \ln m_t)$ where B and D are positive parameters. Steady-state revenue from seigniorage is given by θm, where θ is the growth rate of the money supply.

a. Is there a "Laffer curve" for seigniorage (i.e., are revenues increasing in θ for all $\theta \le \theta^*$ and decreasing in θ for all $\theta > \theta^*$ for some θ^*?

b. What rate of money growth maximizes steady-state revenues from seigniorage?

c. Assume now that the economy's rate of population growth is n, and reinterpret m as real money balances per capita. What *rate of inflation* maximizes seigniorage? How does it depend on n?

2. Suppose that government faces the following budget identity:

$$b_t = Rb_{t-1} + g_t - \tau_t y_t - s_t$$

where the terms are one-period debt, gross interest payments, government purchases, income tax receipts, and seigniorage. Assume seigniorage is given by $f(\pi_t)$ where π is the rate of inflation. The interest factor R is constant and the expenditure process $\{g_{t+i}\}_{i=0}^{\infty}$ is exogenous. The government sets time paths for the income tax rate and for inflation to minimize

$$E_t \sum_{i=0}^{\infty} \beta^i [h(\tau_{t+i}) + k(\pi_{t+i})]$$

where the functions h and k represent the distortionary costs of the two tax sources. Assume the functions h and k imply positive and increasing marginal costs of both revenue sources.

a. What is the *intratemporal* optimality condition linking the choices of τ and π at each point in time?

b. What is the *intertemporal* optimality condition linking the choice π at different points in time?

c. Suppose $y = 1$, $f(\pi) = a\pi$, $h(\tau) = b\tau^2$, and $k(\pi) = c\pi^2$. Evaluate the inter- and intratemporal conditions. Find the optimal settings for τ_t and π_t in terms of b_{t-1} and $\sum R^{-i} g_{t+i}$.

d. Using your results from part c, when will optimal financing imply constant planned tax rates and inflation over time?

3. Mankiw (1987) suggested that the nominal interest rate should evolve as a random walk under an optimal tax policy. Suppose the real rate of interest is constant and that the equilibrium price level is given by equation (4.24). Suppose the nominal money supply is given by $m_t = m_t^p + v_t$ where m_t^p is the central bank's planned money supply and v_t is a white-noise control error. Let θ be the optimal rate of inflation. There are different processes for m^p that lead to the same average inflation rate but different time series behavior of the nominal interest rate. For each of the processes for m_t^p given in a and b, show that average inflation is equal to θ; also show whether the nominal interest rate is a random walk.

a. $m_t^p = \theta(1 - \gamma)t + \gamma m_{t-1}$

b. $m_t^p = m_{t-1} + \theta$

4. Suppose the Correia-Teles model of section 4.5.3 is modified so that output is equal to $f(n)$ where f is a standard neoclassical production function exhibiting positive but diminishing marginal productivity of n. If $f(n) = n^a$ for $0 < a < 1$ does the optimality condition given by (4.44) continue to hold?

5 Money and Output in the Short Run

5.1 Introduction

Chapter 1 provided evidence that monetary policy actions have effects on real output that persist for appreciable periods of time. The empirical evidence from the United States is consistent with the notion that positive monetary shocks lead to a hump-shaped response of output, and Sims (1992) finds similar patterns for other OECD economies. We have not yet addressed why such a response is produced. Certainly the models of Chapters 2–4 did not seem capable of producing such an effect. So why does money matter?[1] Is it only through the tax effects that arise from inflation? Or are there other channels through which monetary actions have real effects? This question is critical for any normative analysis of monetary policy, since designing good policy requires an understanding of how monetary policy affects the real economy and of how changes in the way policy is conducted might affect economic behavior.

In the models examined in earlier chapters, monetary disturbances did cause output movements, but these movements arose from substitution effects induced by expected inflation. The simulation exercises suggested that such effects were too small to account for the empirical evidence on the output responses to monetary shocks. In addition, the evidence in many countries is that inflation responds only slowly to monetary shocks.[2] If actual inflation responds gradually, so should expectations. Thus, the evidence does not appear supportive of theories that require monetary shocks to affect labor-supply decisions and output by causing shifts in expected inflation.

In this chapter, the focus shifts away from the role of inflation as a tax and toward the effects of policy-induced changes in real interest rates that affect aggregate spending decisions. In making this shift, we move from the general equilibrium models built on the joint foundations of individual optimization and flexible prices to the class of models used in most discussions of short-run economic fluctuations and monetary policy analysis.

We begin this chapter with a discussion of models that maintain the assumption that nominal wages and prices are flexible, exploring channels for money to have real effects that were missing in Chapters 2–4. These channels involve informational or distributional effects. As we will see, these attempts to account for the empirical

---

1. For a survey on this topic, see Blanchard (1990). See also Romer (1996, Chapters 5 and 6).

2. The impulse responses reported by Sims (1992), for example, or the models fitted to international data by Taylor (1993b) indicate this slow response.

evidence on the short-run effects of monetary policy have so far had mixed success. We then turn to models in which monetary policy and monetary disturbances can have important short-run effects on real economic activity because of nominal wage and price rigidities.

It is easy to see why nominal price stickiness is important. As we have seen in the previous chapters, the nominal quantity of money affects equilibrium in two ways. First, its rate of change affects the rate of inflation. Changes in expected inflation affect the opportunity cost of holding money, leading to real effects on labor-leisure choices and the choice between cash and credit goods. However, these substitution effects seem small empirically. Second, money appears in household budget constraints, cash-in-advance constraints, and utility functions in the form of real money balances. If prices are perfectly flexible, changes in the nominal quantity of money via monetary policy actions will not necessarily affect the real supply of money. When prices are sticky, however, changing the nominal stock of money will directly alter the real stock of money. These changes will then affect the economy's real equilibrium. Short-run price and wage stickiness implies a much more important role for monetary disturbances and monetary policy.

Our focus will not be on the microeconomic theories that account for nominal rigidities but will instead concentrate on the implications for monetary policy. In doing so, some attempt will be made to show how the basic structure of commonly used short-run models can be viewed as an approximation to the general equilibrium models of Chapters 2–4. Once this basic framework has been discussed, it can be used to highlight the transmission process through which monetary policy affects real economic activity.

5.2 Flexible Prices

In Chapters 2–4 the emphasis was on the importance of anticipated money growth that affected expectations of inflation, and it was through substitution effects induced by expected inflation that money mattered. In contrast, an unanticipated change in money that did not affect expectations about future money growth had no real effects and simply resulted in a proportionate change in the price level; money was neutral even in the short run.

Monetary models that maintain the assumption of price flexibility need to introduce new channels through which money can affect the real equilibrium to account for the empirical evidence. In this section we review two attempts to resolve the tension between the long-run neutrality of money and the short-run real effects of money while still maintaining the assumption that wages and prices are flexible. The first approach focuses on misperceptions about aggregate economic conditions; the second focuses on trading restrictions in financial markets.

5.2.1 Imperfect Information

How can the long-run neutrality of money be reconciled with the apparent short-run nonneutrality of money? During the 1960s the need to reconcile these two was not considered a major research issue in macroeconomics. Models used for policy analysis incorporated a Phillips curve relationship between wage (or price) inflation and unemployment that allowed for a long-run trade-off between the two. In 1968, Milton Friedman and Edmund Phelps (M. Friedman 1968; Phelps 1968) independently argued on theoretical grounds that the inflation-unemployment trade-off was only a short-run trade-off at best; attempts to exploit the trade-off by engineering higher inflation to generate lower unemployment would ultimately result only in higher inflation.

Milton Friedman (1968, 1977) reconciled the apparent short-run trade-off with the neutrality of money by distinguishing between actual real wages and perceived real wages.[3] The former were relevant for firms making hiring decisions; the latter were relevant for workers making labor-supply choices. In a long-run equilibrium, the two would coincide; the real wage would adjust to clear the labor market. Since economic decisions would depend on real wages, the same labor-market equilibrium would be consistent with any level of nominal wages and prices or any rate of change of wages and prices that left the real wage equal to its equilibrium level.

An unexpected increase in inflation would disturb this real equilibrium. As nominal wages and prices rose more rapidly than previously expected, workers would see their nominal wages rising but would initially not realize that the prices of all the goods and services they consumed were also rising more rapidly. They would misperceive the nominal wage increase as a rise in their real wage. Labor supply would increase, shifting labor-market equilibrium to a point of higher employment and lower actual real wages. As workers then engaged in shopping activities, they would discover that not only the nominal price of their labor services had risen unexpectedly, but all prices had risen. Real wages had actually fallen, not risen. Labor supply would shift back, and the initial equilibrium would be restored eventually.

The critical insight is that changes in wages and prices that are unanticipated generate misperceptions about relative prices (the real wage in Friedman's version).

---

3. A nice exposition of Friedman's model is provided by Rasche (1973).

Economic agents, faced with what they perceive to be changes in relative prices, alter their real economic decisions, and the economy's real equilibrium is affected. Once expectations adjust, however, the economy's natural equilibrium is reestablished. Expectations, and the information on which they are based, become central to understanding the effects of money.

5.2.1.1 The Lucas Model Friedman's insight was given an explicit theoretical foundation by Lucas (1972). Lucas showed how unanticipated changes in the money supply could generate short-run, transitory movements in real economic activity. He did so by analyzing the impact of monetary fluctuations in an overlapping-generations environment with two physically separate markets. The demand for money in each location was made random by assuming that the allocation of the population to each location was stochastic.[4] The key features of this environment can be illustrated by employing the analogy of an economy consisting of a large number of individual islands. Agents are randomly reallocated among islands after each period, so individuals care both about prices on the island they currently are on and prices on other islands to which they may be reassigned. Individuals on each island are assumed to have imperfect information about aggregate economic variables such as the nominal money supply and price level. Thus, when individuals observe changes in the prices on their island, they must decide whether they reflect purely nominal changes in aggregate variables or island-specific relative price changes.

Lucas's basic results can be derived by employing a variant of the MIU model developed in Chapter 2. We will simplify the model in three ways, however. First, we will ignore capital. This choice implies that only labor is used to produce output and, with no investment, equilibrium requires that output equal consumption. Second, we will assume money is the only available asset. Third, assume the monetary transfers associated with changes in the nominal quantity of money are viewed by agents as being proportional to their own holdings of cash. This change has substantive implications and is not done just to simplify the model. It implies that the transfers will appear to money holders just like interest payments on cash holdings. This approach eliminates inflation-tax effects so that we can concentrate on the role of imperfect information.[5]

---

4. In Lucas's formulation, agents had two-period lives; young agents were distributed randomly to each location.

5. Recall that in Chapter 2 transfers were viewed as lump sum. With higher inflation, the transfers rose (as the seigniorage revenues were returned to private agents), but each individual viewed these transfers as unrelated to his or her own money holdings. If the transfers are viewed as interest payments, higher inflation does not raise the opportunity cost of holding money, since the interest payment on cash also rises. In this case, money is superneutral.

Suppose the aggregate economy consists of several islands, indexed by i; thus, x^i will denote the value of variable x on island i, while x will denote its economy-wide average value. Using the model from the appendix to Chapter 2, we can express equilibrium deviations from steady state on each island by the following four conditions:[6]

$$y_t^i = (1 - \alpha)n_t^i \tag{5.1}$$

$$y_t^i = c_t^i \tag{5.2}$$

$$d_1 n_t^i = y_t^i - \Phi c_t^i + b(1 - \Phi)(m_t^i - p_t^i) \tag{5.3}$$

$$d_0(c_t^i - m_t^i + p_t^i) = E^i(p_{t+1} - p_t^i) - E^i \tau_{t+1}$$
$$- E^i[d_1(n_{t+1} - n_t^i) - (y_{t+1} - y_t^i)] \tag{5.4}$$

where, in contrast to Chapters 2–4, m^i denotes the *nominal* supply of money on island i. Equation (5.1) is the production function linking labor input (n_t^i) to output.[7] Equation (5.2) is the goods equilibrium condition requiring that consumption equal output (no trade between islands). Equation (5.3) comes from the first-order condition linking the marginal utility of leisure, the marginal utility of consumption, and the real wage (see the appendix to Chapter 2).[8] Assume $0 < \Phi < 1$ so an increase in real money balances acts to increase labor supply and output.[9] Finally, equation

---

6. All variables are expressed as natural log deviations around steady-state values. Since all values will be in terms of deviations, the "hat" notation of Chapters 2–4 will be dropped for convenience.

7. Note that any productivity disturbance has been eliminated, since the focus will be on monetary disturbances.

8. With the instantaneous utility function in levels given by

$$\frac{\left[C\left(\frac{M}{P}\right)^b\right]^{1-\Phi}}{1-\Phi} + \frac{(1-N)^{1-\eta}}{1-\eta}$$

and the marginal product of labor equal to $(1-\alpha)Y/N$, equation (5.3) arises from the requirement that the marginal utility of leisure $\left(\eta \frac{n^{ss}}{1-n^{ss}} n_t \text{ in percentage deviation around the steady state}\right)$ equal the real wage times the marginal utility of consumption $[y_t - n_t - \Phi c_t + b(1-\Phi)(m_t - p_t)]$. So in (5.3), $d_1 = \left(1 + \eta \frac{n^{ss}}{1-n^{ss}}\right)$.

9. With $\Phi < 1$, $u_{cm} = b(1-\Phi)c^{-\Phi}\left(\frac{M}{P}\right)^{b(1-\Phi)-1} > 0$. An increase in M/P increases the marginal utility of consumption, leading to a decline in leisure demand, a rise in labor supply, and an increase in output. Recall from section 2.3.2 that a rise in expected inflation that reduces real money balances leads to a fall in output when $\Phi < 1$.

(5.4) is derived from the first-order condition for the individual agent's holdings of real money balances. This first-order condition requires that reducing consumption at time t slightly, thereby carrying higher money balances into period $t+1$ and then consuming them, must, at the margin, have no effect on total utility over the two periods. In the present context, the cost of reducing consumption in period t is the marginal utility of consumption; the additional money balances yield the marginal utility of money in period t and yield a gross return of T/Π in period $t+1$ where T is the gross nominal transfer per dollar on money holdings and Π is one plus the inflation rate from t to $t+1$. This return can be consumed at $t+1$, yielding in terms of period t utility, $\beta(T/\Pi)$ times the marginal utility of consumption, where β is the representative household's discount factor. Linearizing the result around the steady state leads to equation (5.4); details can be found in the appendix (section 5.7.1).[10] In this money-demand condition, equation (5.3) has been used to express the expected marginal utility of consumption in terms of employment and output.

If agents are reallocated randomly across islands each period, then the relevant period $t+1$ variables in (5.4) are aggregate per capita real money balances, $m_{t+1} - p_{t+1}$; consumption, c_{t+1}; and the nominal transfer, τ_{t+1}. However, information, and therefore expectations, will differ across islands, so the expectations operator has a superscript i.

The final component of the model is the specification of the nominal money supply process. Assume that on island i,

$$m_t^i = \gamma m_{t-1} + v_t + u_t + u_t^i$$

with u^i being an island-specific money shock that averages to zero across all islands and has variance σ_i^2. Hence, the aggregate average nominal money supply evolves as[11]

$$m_t = \gamma m_{t-1} + v_t + u_t \tag{5.5}$$

The aggregate supply is assumed to depend on two shocks v and u assumed to have zero means and variances σ_v^2 and σ_u^2. The difference between the two is that we will assume v is public information while u is not. Including both will help to illustrate how imperfect information (in this case about u) will influence the real effects of

---

10. In (5.4), $d_0 = (1-\beta)/\beta$. The marginal utility of consumption, $-\Phi c_t^i + b(1-\Phi)(m_t^i - p_t^i)$, has been replaced in (5.4) by $d_1 n_t^i - y_t^i$ using (5.3).

11. With money-supply changes engineered via transfers,

$$\tau_t = m_t - m_{t-1} = (\gamma - 1)m_{t-1} + v_t + u_t$$

money shocks. If the aggregate money stock at time $t-1$, as well as v, is public information, then observing the island-specific nominal money stock m_t^i allows individuals on island i to infer $u_t + u_t^i$ but not u and u^i separately. This point is important because only u affects the aggregate money stock (see equation [5.5]), and, as long as $\gamma \neq 0$, knowledge about u would be useful in forecasting m_{t+1}.

Since $m_{t+1} = \gamma m_t + v_{t+1} + u_{t+1} = \gamma(\gamma m_{t-1} + v_t + u_t) + v_{t+1} + u_{t+1}$, the expectation of the time $t+1$ money supply, conditional on the information available on island i, will be $\mathrm{E}^i m_{t+1} = \gamma^2 m_{t-1} + \gamma v_t + \gamma \mathrm{E}^i u_t$. But what will $\mathrm{E}^i u_t$ equal? Agents on island i can infer $u_t + u_t^i$, so if expectations are equated with linear least squares projections,

$$\mathrm{E}^i u_t = \kappa(u_t + u_t^i)$$

where $\kappa = \sigma_u^2/(\sigma_u^2 + \sigma_i^2)$, $0 \leq \kappa \leq 1$. If aggregate money shocks tend to be large relative to island-specific shocks (i.e., σ_u is large relative to σ_i), κ will be close to one as movements in $u + u^i$ are interpreted as predominantly reflecting movements in the aggregate shock u. In contrast, if the variance of the island-specific shocks is large, κ will be close to zero as movements in $u + u^i$ are interpreted as predominantly reflecting island-specific shocks.

Using (5.1) and (5.2) in (5.3) and (5.4) yields a two-equation system for the price level and aggregate employment. Section 5.7.1 of the appendix shows that the solution to this system is given by

$$p_t = \gamma m_{t-1} + v_t + \left(\frac{\kappa + K}{1 + K}\right)u_t \tag{5.6}$$

and

$$n_t = A(m_t - p_t) = A\left(\frac{1 - \kappa}{1 + K}\right)u_t \tag{5.7}$$

where A and K depend on the underlying parameters of the model.[12]

Equation (5.7) reveals Lucas's basic result; aggregate monetary shocks, represented by u, have real effects on employment (and therefore output) if and only if there is imperfect information ($\kappa < 1$). Publicly announced changes in the money supply, represented by the v shocks, have no real effects on output (v does not appear in equation 5.7) but simply move the price level one-for-one (v has a coefficient equal to 1 in equation 5.6). But the u shocks will affect employment and output if private agents are unable to determine whether the money stock movements they observe on

---

12. The expressions for A and K are given in the appendix.

island i (m^i) reflect aggregate or island-specific movements. Predictable movements in money (captured here by γm_{t-1}) or announced changes (captured by v) have no real effects. Unanticipated changes in the money supply, represented by the error agents make in inferring u [given by $(1 - \kappa)u$] will have real effects.

Equation (5.7) can be rewritten in a form that emphasizes the role of "money surprises" in producing employment and output effects. From (5.5), we can write $u_t = m_t - E(m_t|\Omega_{t-1}, v_t)$ where $E(m_t|\Omega_{t-1}, v_t)$ denotes the expectation of m_t conditional on aggregate information on variables dated $t - 1$ or earlier, summarized by the information set Ω_{t-1}, and the announced money injection v_t. Thus,

$$n_t = A\left(\frac{1 - \kappa}{1 + K}\right)[m_t - E(m_t|\Omega_{t-1}, v_t)]$$

Equations of this form provided the basis for the empirical work of Barro (1977) and others in testing whether unanticipated or anticipated changes in money matter for real output.

In writing employment as a function of money surprises, it is critically important to specify correctly the information set on which agents base their expectations. In empirical work, this is often simply lagged values of relevant variables. But in our example, $E(m_t|\Omega_{t-1}) = \gamma m_{t-1}$ and $m_t - E(m_t|\Omega_{t-1}) = u_t + v_t \neq u_t$. Misspecifying the information set can create difficulties in testing models that imply that only surprises matter.

Because we have derived (5.7) directly from a model consistent with optimizing behavior, we are able to relate the effects of an unanticipated money-supply shock on employment to the basic underlying parameters of the production and utility functions.[13] Using the basic parameter values given in Table 2.2, we can evaluate the coefficient on money surprises implied by the model. For $\Phi = 0.5, A/[1 + K] = 0.002$; for $\Phi = 0.25, A/[1 + K] = 0.004$; for $\Phi = 0, A/[1 + K] = 0.005$. These results imply that even if κ is close to zero, the elasticity of employment with respect to a money surprise is less than 0.01; a 10 percent surprise increase in the money supply would raise employment by less than 0.1% and output by less than $(1 - \alpha) \times 0.1\% = 0.6 \times 0.1\% = 0.06\%$.[14] The effect, though small, is increasing as $\Phi \to 0$.

The impact of money surprises in this example works through labor-supply decisions. An increase in real money balances raises the marginal utility of consumption

---

13. McCallum (1984a) presents a linearized approximation to Lucas's model within an overlapping-generations framework. See also Romer (1996). However, both simply postulate some of the basic behavioral relationships of the model.

14. This calculation uses the baseline value of 0.4 for α.

and induces agents to increase consumption and labor supply (since $0 < \Phi < 1$). This effect is larger as agents are more willing to substitute consumption over time. Thus, when $\Phi = 0$ and utility is linear in $(c_t m_t^b)$, the impact of a money surprise is larger than when the degree of intertemporal substitution is smaller.[15] The effect of a money surprise on output is increasing in the wage elasticity of labor supply.[16]

While other variants of Lucas's island model emphasize other channels, the basic idea is that unpredicted variations in money generate price movements that agents may misinterpret as relative price movements. If a general price rise is misperceived to be a rise in the relative price of what the individual or firm sells, the price rise will induce an increase in employment and output. Once individuals and firms correctly perceive that the price rise was part of an increase in all prices, output returns to its former equilibrium level.

5.2.1.2 Implications Lucas's model makes clear the important distinction between expected and unexpected variations in money. Economic agents face a signal-extraction problem because they have imperfect information about the current money supply. If all changes in the nominal supply of money were perfectly predictable, money would have no real effects. Short-run fluctuations in money are likely to be at least partially unpredictable, so they will cause output and employment movements. In this way, Lucas was able to reconcile the neutrality of money in the long run with important real effects in the short run. Sargent and Wallace (1975) and Barro (1976) provide important early contributions that employed the general approach pioneered by Lucas to examine its implications for monetary policy issues.

Lucas's model has several important testable implications, and these were the focus of a great deal of empirical work in the late 1970s and early 1980s. A first implication is that the distinction between anticipated and unanticipated money matters. Barro (1977, 1978) was the first to directly examine whether output was related to anticipated or unanticipated money. He concluded the evidence supported Lucas's model, but subsequent empirical work by Mishkin (1982) and others showed that both anticipated and unanticipated money appear to influence real economic activity. A survey of the general approach motivated by Lucas's work and of the empirical literature can be found in Chapter 2 of Barro (1981).

A second implication is that the short-run relationship between output and inflation will depend on the relative variance of real and nominal disturbances. The

---

15. See Barro and King (1984).

16. In the Federal Reserve's FRB/US structural econometric model, the wage elasticity of labor supply is assumed to be zero (Brayton and Tinsley 1996) so that this channel for misperceptions of money disturbances to have real effects is absent.

parameter κ in (5.7) depends on the predictability of aggregate changes in the money supply, and this can vary across time and across countries. Lucas (1973) examined the slopes of short-run Phillips curves in a cross-country study and showed that, as predicted by his model, there was a positive correlation between the slope of the Phillips curve and the relative variance of nominal aggregate volatility. A rise in aggregate volatility (an increase in σ_u^2 in the version of Lucas's model developed in the previous section) implies that an observed increase in prices is more likely to be interpreted as resulting from an aggregate price increase. A smaller real response occurs as a result, and aggregate money surprises have smaller real effects.

A third influential implication of Lucas's model was demonstrated by Sargent and Wallace (1975) and became known as the *policy irrelevance hypothesis*. If changes in money have real effects only when they are unanticipated, then any policy that generates systematic, predictable variations in the money supply will have no real effect. For example, equation (5.7) shows that employment, and therefore output, is independent of the degree of serial correlation in m as measured by γ. Because the effects of lagged money on the current aggregate money stock are completely predictable, no informational confusion is created and the aggregate price level simply adjusts, leaving real money balances unaffected (see equation 5.6). A similar conclusion would hold if policy responded to lagged values of u (or to lagged values of anything else), as long as private agents knew the rule being followed by the policy maker.

The empirical evidence that both anticipated and unanticipated money affect output implies, however, that the policy irrelevance hypothesis does not hold. Systematic responses to lagged variables seem to matter, and therefore the choice of policy rule is not irrelevant for the behavior of real economic activity.

The misperceptions model in the original form developed by Lucas, and popularized by Sargent and Wallace (1975) and Barro (1976), who employed tractable log-linear models based on Lucas's theory, is no longer viewed as an adequate explanation for the short-run real effects of monetary policy. It has had, and continues to have, however, an enormous influence on modern monetary economics. For example, the finding that announced changes in money (the v term in our example) have no real effects implies that inflation could be reduced at no output cost simply by announcing a reduction in money growth. But such announcements must be credible so that expectations are actually reduced as money growth falls; disinflations will be costly if announcements are not credible. This point has produced a large literature on the role of credibility, a literature that will be discussed in Chapter 8.

5.2.2 Limited Participation and Liquidity Effects

Nominal interest rates can be expressed as the sum of an expected real return and the expected rate of inflation. The impact of a monetary disturbance on market rates can also be decomposed into its effect on the expected real rate of return and its effect on the expected inflation rate. If money growth is positively serially correlated, an increase in money growth will be associated with higher future inflation, and therefore, higher *expected* inflation. As we saw in Chapters 2 and 3, the flexible price MIU and CIA models implied that faster money growth immediately increases nominal interest rates.

Most economists, and certainly monetary policy makers, believe that central banks can reduce short-term market (nominal) interest rates and can do so by engaging in policies that will lead to faster growth in the money supply. This belief is often interpreted to mean that faster money growth will produce lower nominal interest rates, an impact called the liquidity effect. This effect is usually viewed as an important channel through which a monetary expansion affects real consumption, investment, and output.[17]

A number of authors have explored flexible-price models in which monetary injections reduce nominal interest rates (Lucas 1990; Fuerst 1992; Christiano 1991; Christiano and Eichenbaum 1992a, 1995; Dotsey and Ireland 1995; King and Watson 1996). These models generate real effects of monetary shocks on real interest rates by imposing restrictions on the ability of agents to engage in certain types of financial transactions.[18] For example, Lucas modifies a basic cash-in-advance framework in a way that allows him to study effects that arise when monetary injections are not distributed equally across a population of otherwise representative agents. If a monetary injection affects agents differentially, a price-level increase proportional to the aggregate change in the money stock will not restore the initial real equilibrium. Some agents will be left with higher real money holdings, others with lower real balances.

Fuerst (1992) and Christiano and Eichenbaum (1992a) introduce a liquidity effect by modifying a basic cash-in-advance model to distinguish between households, firms, and financial intermediaries. Households can allocate resources between bank

---

17. A thorough discussion of possible explanations of liquidity effects is provided by Ohanian and Stockman (1995) and Hoover (1995).

18. The first limited-participation models were due to Grossman and Weiss (1983) and Rotemberg (1984). Models that restrict financial transactions can be viewed as variants of the original Baumol-Tobin models with infinite costs for certain types of transactions, rather than the finite costs of exchanging money and interest-earning assets assumed by Baumol (1952) and Tobin (1956).

deposits and money balances that are then used to finance consumption. Intermediaries lend out their deposits to firms who borrow to finance purchases of labor services from households. After households have made their choice between money and bank deposits, financial intermediaries receive lump-sum monetary injections. Only firms and intermediaries interact in financial markets after the monetary injection; the model limits the ability of households to participate in financial markets.[19]

In a standard representative-agent cash-in-advance model, monetary injections are distributed proportionately to all agents. Thus, a proportional rise in the price level leaves all agents with the same level of real money balances as previously. In contrast, if the injections initially affect only the balance sheets of the financial intermediaries, a new channel is introduced by which employment and output will be affected. As long as the nominal interest rate is positive, intermediaries will wish to increase their lending in response to a positive monetary injection. To induce firms to borrow the additional funds, the interest rate on loans must fall. Hence, a liquidity effect is generated; interest rates decline in response to a positive monetary injection.[20] Because of the restrictions on trading, cash injections create a wedge between the value of cash in the hands of households shopping in the goods market and the value of cash in the financial market.[21] Because Fuerst and Christiano and Eichenbaum assume firms must borrow to fund their wage bill, the appropriate marginal cost of labor to firms is the real wage times the gross rate of interest on loans. The interest-rate decline generated by the liquidity effect lowers the marginal cost of labor; at each real wage, labor demand rises. As a result, equilibrium employment and output increase.

Models that generate real effects of money by restricting financial transactions can account for nominal (and real) interest-rate declines in response to monetary policy shocks. But as Dotsey and Ireland (1995) show, this class of models does not

19. Allowing for heterogeneity greatly complicates the analysis, but these limited-participation models overcome this problem by following the modeling strategy introduced by Lucas (1990) in which each representative "family" consists of a household supplying labor and purchasing goods; a firm hiring labor, producing goods, and borrowing from the intermediary; and an intermediary. At the end of each period, the various units of the family are reunited and pool resources. As a result, there can be heterogeneity within periods as the new injections of money affect only firms and intermediaries, but between periods all families are identical, so the advantages of the representative-agent formulation are preserved.

20. Expected inflation effects will also be at work, so the net impact on nominal interest rates will depend on, among other things, the degree of positive serial correlation in the growth rate of the money supply.

21. In Fuerst (1992), this wedge is measured by the difference between the Lagrangian multiplier on the household's cash-in-advance constraint and that on the firm's cash-in-advance constraint. A cash injection lowers the value of cash in the financial market and lowers the nominal rate of interest.

account for interest-rate effects of the magnitude actually observed in the data. Similarly, King and Watson (1996) find that monetary shocks do not produce significant business-cycle fluctuations in their version of a limited-participation model (which they call a liquidity-effect model). Christiano, Eichenbaum, and Evans (1996) show that their limited-participation model is able to match evidence on the effects of monetary shocks on prices, output, real wages, and profits only if the labor-supply wage elasticity is assumed to be very high. They argue that this outcome is due, in part, to the absence of labor-market frictions in the current generation of limited-participation models.

Because limited-participation models were developed to account for the observation that monetary injections lower market interest rates, the real test of whether they have isolated an important channel through which monetary policy operates must come from comparing their other implications with the data. Christiano, Eichenbaum, and Evans (1996) examine real wage and profit movements to test their models. They argue that limited-participation models are able to account for the increase in profits that follow a monetary expansion. A further implication of such models relates to the manner in which the impact of monetary injections will change over time as financial sectors evolve and the cost of transactions falls. Financial markets today are very different than they were 25 years ago, and these differences should show up in the way money affects interest rates now as compared to 25 years ago.[22] While financial market frictions are likely to be important in understanding the impact effects of monetary policy actions on short-term market interest rates, the relevance of the channels emphasized in limited-participation models for understanding the broader effects of monetary policy on the aggregate economy remains an open debate.

5.3   Sticky Prices and Wages

Whereas flexible-price, imperfect-information models enjoyed popularity during the 1970s and flexible-price, limited-participation models have attracted attention only recently, most macroeconomic models attribute the short-run real effects of monetary disturbances to the presence of wage and/or price rigidities. These rigidities lead nominal wages and prices to adjust incompletely to changes in the nominal quantity of money. In the next subsection, we introduce one-period wage stickiness into the

---

22. Cole and Ohanian (1997) argue that the impact of money shocks in the United States has declined with the ratio of M_1 to nominal GDP, a finding they cite as consistent with the implications of limited-participation models.

basic MIU model. This modification increases the impact that monetary disturbances have on real output. The effects, however, are short-lived, and fail to replicate the hump-shaped response of output spread out over many quarters that characterizes actual responses to monetary policy disturbances. Section 5.3.2 introduces a model of overlapping price adjustment that can generate the type of persistent output responses observed in the data. This model, based on monopolistic competition, leads to a dynamic adjustment of prices that is similar to that proposed by Taylor (1979, 1980, 1993b).[23]

5.3.1 Wage Rigidity in an MIU Model

In Chapter 2 a linear approximation was used to examine the time-series implications of a money-in-the-utility-function model. Wages and prices were assumed to adjust to ensure market equilibrium, and, as a consequence, the behavior of the money supply mattered only to the extent that anticipated inflation was affected. A positive disturbance to the growth rate of money would, assuming the growth rate of money was positively serially correlated, raise the expected rate of inflation, leading to a rise in the nominal rate of interest and effects on labor supply and output. These last effects depended on the form of the utility function; if utility was separable in money, changes in expected inflation had no effect on labor supply or real output. Introducing wage stickiness into this model will serve to illustrate the effect such a modification has on the impact of monetary disturbances.

Suppose we use the linear approximation to the Sidrauski money-in-the-utility-function model employed in Chapter 2. The equations characterizing equilibrium in this model were as follows:[24]

$$y_t = \alpha k_{t-1} + (1 - \alpha)n_t + z_t \tag{5.8}$$

$$\left(\frac{y^{ss}}{k^{ss}}\right)y_t = \left(\frac{c^{ss}}{k^{ss}}\right)c_t + k_t - (1 - \delta)k_{t-1} \tag{5.9}$$

$$R^{ss}r_t = \alpha\left(\frac{y^{ss}}{k^{ss}}\right)(E_t y_{t+1} - k_t) \tag{5.10}$$

$$E_t c_{t+1} - c_t - r_t = 0 \tag{5.11}$$

---

23. Section 5.5 contains a discussion of some alternative price-adjustment specifications. Coverage of a variety of price-adjustment models can be found in Romer (1996, Chapter 6).

24. As before, $d_1 \equiv \left(1 + \eta\frac{n^{ss}}{1 - n^{ss}}\right)$, and $d_2 \equiv (\Theta - \beta)/\beta$.

$$d_1 n_t = y_t - c_t \tag{5.12}$$

$$i_t \equiv r_t + \mathrm{E}_t[p_{t+1} - p_t] = d_2(c_t - m_t + p_t) \tag{5.13}$$

$$m_t = \gamma m_{t-1} + u_t \tag{5.14}$$

The system is written in terms of the price level p rather than the inflation rate, and, in contrast to the notation of Chapter 2, m now represents the nominal stock of money. To briefly review these equations, (5.8) is the economy's production function in which output deviations from the steady state are a linear function of the deviations of the capital stock and labor supply from steady state and a productivity disturbance z_t. Equation (5.9) is the resource constraint derived from the condition that output equals consumption plus investment, where δ is the rate of depreciation. Deviations of the marginal product of capital are tied to deviations of the expected real rate of return by equation (5.10). Equations (5.11)–(5.13) are derived from the representative household's first-order conditions for consumption, leisure, and money holdings. Equation (5.14) gives the exogenous process for the nominal money supply.[25]

This version of the model assumes separability ($\Phi = 1$ in terms of the parameters of the model used in Chapter 2) so money and monetary shocks have no effect on the real variables when prices are perfectly flexible.[26] Equations (5.8)–(5.12) form a system of five equations that can be solved for the equilibrium time paths of output, capital, labor, consumption, and the real rate of interest. Equations (5.13) and (5.14) then determine the evolution of real money balances and the price level. Thus, realizations of the monetary disturbance u_t have no effect on output. This version of the MIU model displays the *classical dichotomy* (Modigilani 1963; Patinkin 1965); real variables such as output, consumption, and the real interest rate are determined independently of both the money-supply process and money-demand factors.[27]

Now suppose the nominal wage rate is set prior to the start of the period, and that it is set equal to the level *expected* to produce the *real* wage that equates labor supply and labor demand. Since workers and firms are assumed to have a real wage target

25. Alternatively, the nominal interest rate i_t could be taken as the instrument of monetary policy, with equation (5.13) then determining m_t.

26. From (5.7), money surprises also have no effect on employment and output when $\Phi = 1$ in the imperfect-information model.

27. This independence is stronger than the property of monetary superneutrality in which the real variables are independent of the money-supply process. For example, Lucas's model given by (5.1)–(5.4) does not display the classical dichotomy as long as $\Phi \neq 1$, since the production function, the resource constraint, and the labor-supply condition cannot be solved for output, consumption, and employment without knowing the real demand for money, since real balances enter equation (5.3).

in mind, the nominal wage will adjust fully to reflect expectations of price-level changes held at the time the nominal wage is set. As a result, the information available at the time the wage is set and on which expectations will be based will be important. In the standard formulation, firms are assumed to determine employment on the basis of the actual, realized real wage. If unanticipated changes in prices occur, the actual real wage and employment will differ from their expected values. For example, if prices are unexpectedly low, the actual real wage will exceed the level expected to clear the labor market, and firms will reduce employment.[28]

While labor supply is given by equation (5.12), labor demand is derived from the condition that labor is employed up to the point where the marginal product of labor equals the real wage. With the Cobb-Douglas production function underlying (5.8), this condition, expressed in terms of percentage deviations from the steady state, can be written as[29]

$$w_t - p_t = y_t - n_t$$

The contract nominal wage w^c satisfies

$$w_t^c = \mathrm{E}_{t-1}p_t + \mathrm{E}_{t-1}y_t - \mathrm{E}_{t-1}n_t \tag{5.15}$$

where E_{t-1} denotes the expectation conditional on information available at the end of period $t - 1$.

With firms equating the marginal product of labor to the actual real wage, employment will equal

$$n_t = y_t - (w_t^c - p_t)$$
$$= (y_t - \mathrm{E}_{t-1}y_t) + (p_t - \mathrm{E}_{t-1}p_t) + \mathrm{E}_{t-1}n_t \tag{5.16}$$

where expected employment is, from equation (5.12), given by

$$\mathrm{E}_{t-1}n_t = d_1^{-1}(\mathrm{E}_{t-1}y_t - \mathrm{E}_{t-1}c_t)$$

Equation (5.16) shows that employment deviates from its expected value in the face of unexpected movements in output or prices. An unanticipated rise in output in-

---

28. This analysis implies that the real wage falls in response to a money shock that raises the price level unexpectedly. Using a VAR approach based on U.S. data, Christiano, Eichenbaum, and Evans (1996) find that an expansionary monetary policy shock actually leads to a slight increase in real wages.

29. If $Y = K^\alpha N^{1-\alpha}$, then the marginal product of labor is $(1 - \alpha)\dfrac{Y}{N}$. In log terms, the real wage is then equal to $\ln W - \ln P = \ln(1 - \alpha) + \ln Y - \ln N$, or, in terms of deviations from steady state, $w - p = y - n$.

creases the marginal product of labor and increases employment, while an un-anticipated increase in prices reduces the real value of the contract wage and leads firms to expand employment.

By substituting (5.16) into the production function, equation (5.8) becomes

$$y_t = \alpha k_{t-1} + (1 - \alpha)[(y_t - E_{t-1}y_t) + (p_t - E_{t-1}p_t) + E_{t-1}n_t] + z_t \qquad (5.17)$$

which implies that

$$y_t - E_{t-1}y_t = a(p_t - E_{t-1}p_t) + \varepsilon_t \qquad (5.18)$$

where $a = (1 - \alpha)/\alpha$ and $\varepsilon_t \equiv (z_t - E_{t-1}z_t)/\alpha$. Innovations to output are positively related to price innovations. Thus, monetary shocks that produce unanticipated price movements will now directly affect real output.[30]

Because of the endogenous dynamics associated with consumption decisions and capital accumulation, any initial innovation will cause output to trace out a dynamic response over time. In fact, the appendix shows that $E_{t-1}y_t$ will depend on the lagged capital stock, lagged consumption, and the expected productivity disturbance, so output can be expressed as

$$y_t = a(p_t - E_{t-1}p_t) + \phi_k k_{t-1} - \phi_c c_{t-1} + \phi_z E_{t-1}z_t + \varepsilon_t$$

where ϕ_k, ϕ_c, and ϕ_z are nonnegative parameters whose values are given in the appendix. Output persistence occurs through three channels in this model. First, be-cause of consumption-smoothing behavior by households, a transitory shock to out-put leads to movements in investment that alter the capital stock available in the following period. Second, changes in consumption affect the expected marginal util-ity of consumption, which alters labor supply and expected employment. Ceteris paribus, higher consumption at time $t - 1$ implies higher expected consumption at time t (see equation 5.11). This, in turn, implies a lower marginal utility of time-t consumption, an increased demand for leisure, and a lower supply of labor (see equation 5.12). Hence, expected time-t output is decreasing in c_{t-1}. Third, persistence in the productivity disturbance z_t generates output persistence.

Benassy (1995) shows how one-period wage contracts affect the time-series be-havior of output in a model similar to the one used here. However, the dynamics

---

30. According to (5.18), a 1% deviation of p from its expected value will cause a $\dfrac{1 - \alpha}{\alpha} \approx 1.5\%$ deviation of output if the benchmark value of 0.4 is used for α. Notice that in (5.18), the coefficient a on price sur-prises depends on parameters of the production function, in contrast to Lucas's misperceptions model in which the impact on output of a price surprise depends on the variances of shocks (see 5.7). Lucas (1973) presents some cross-country evidence that the output-inflation relationship varies with the variance of inflation.

associated with consumption smoothing and capital accumulation are inadequate on their own to produce anything like the output persistence that is revealed by the data.[31] It was for that reason that real-business-cycle models assumed that the productivity disturbance itself is highly serially correlated. Since we have assumed that nominal wages are fixed for only one period, the estimated effects of a monetary shock on output die out almost completely after one period.[32] This would continue to be the case even if the money shock were serially correlated. While serial correlation in the u_t shock would affect the behavior of the price level, this will be incorporated into expectations, and the nominal wage set at the start of $t + 1$ will adjust fully to make the expected real wage (and therefore employment and output) independent of the predictable movement in the price level. Just adding one-period sticky nominal wages will not capture the persistent effects of monetary shocks, but it will significantly influence the impact effect of a money shock on the economy.

Figure 5.1 shows the impulse response of output to a u shock to the nominal supply of money. Recall that in the basic flexible-price MIU model of Chapter 2, Figure 2.5 showed that the impact effect of a money shock on output was only 0.002.[33] Adding one-period wage rigidity increases the impact of a money shock tenfold. A positive money shock causes prices to rise, and this has a direct effect on the actual real wage, since the nominal wage is unable to adjust. With real wages reduced by the unanticipated price rise, firms find it profitable to expand employment and output.

While one-period nominal wage rigidity leads to larger real effects of money shocks, the shocks produce almost none of the output persistence observed in the data. Taylor (1979, 1980) has shown how much more complicated, and realistic, the dynamics can become if nominal wages are adjusted in a pattern of overlapping, multiperiod contracts. The resulting staggered adjustment process can lead to an output response to a serially uncorrelated money shock that looks similar to the estimated response patterns discussed in Chapter 1.

We will return to the model of this section in section 5.4.1 and revisit the issue of persistence in section 5.5. The linear approximation to the MIU model, augmented with one-period nominal wage contracts, can be shown to reduce to a four-equation system in output, the price level, and the real and nominal interest rates. This will provide a benchmark for analyzing a simple model of aggregate supply and

31. Cogley and Nason (1995) demonstrate this point for standard real-business-cycle models.

32. In Benassy's model with parameters $\alpha = 0.40$ and rate of depreciation $\delta = 0.019$, equilibrium output (expressed as a deviation from trend) is given by $y_t \approx 0.6 \times (1 + 0.006L - 0.002L^2 \cdots)(m_t - m_t^e)$, so that the effects of a money surprise die out almost immediately (Benassy 1995, equation 51, p. 313).

33. This value occurred when the money-supply process exhibited high serial correlation ($\gamma = 0.8$).

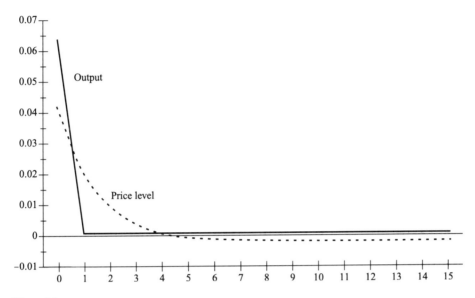

Figure 5.1
Money Shock in an MIU Model with One-Period Wage Contracts

aggregate demand in section 5.4.2 that is one of the basic frameworks used for addressing policy issues. First, however, we turn to a model of monopolistic competition; discussions of sticky wages or prices need to be placed within the context of a model in which firms are actually setting prices.

5.3.2   Money, Imperfect Competition, and Price Stickiness

The previous section illustrated how wage inflexibility had quite dramatic effects on the impact of monetary disturbances. Except for the assumption that the nominal wage was set one period in advance, the model was identical to an equilibrium model of an economy characterized by perfect competition. A problem with simply introducing nominal wage rigidity into an otherwise competitive model is that any sort of price rigidity naturally raises the question of who is setting wages and prices, a question the perfectly competitive model begs. Once we need to address the issue of price setting, we must examine models that incorporate some aspect of imperfect competition, such as monopolistic competition.

5.3.2.1   A Basic Model   In this subsection, we set out a basic model that incorporates monopolistic competition among intermediate-goods producers. Examples of similar models include Blanchard and Kiyotaki (1987), Ball and Romer (1991), Beaudry and Devereux (1993), and King and Watson (1996). Imperfect competition can lead to aggregate-demand externalities (Blanchard and Kiyotaki 1987), equilibria in which output is inefficiently low, and multiple equilibria (Ball and Romer 1991; Rotemberg and Woodford 1995), but imperfect competition alone does not lead to monetary nonneutrality. If prices are free to adjust, one-time, permanent changes in the level of the money supply will induce proportional changes in all prices, leaving the real equilibrium unaffected. Price stickiness remains critical to generating significant real effects of money. Our example follows Chari, Kehoe, and McGrattan (1996), and, in the following subsection, we add price stickiness by assuming that producers engage in multiperiod, staggered price setting.

Let Y_t be the output of the final good; it is produced using inputs supplied by a continuum of intermediate-goods-producing firms indexed by $i \in [0, 1]$. The production function for final output is given by

$$Y_t = \left[\int_0^1 Y_t(i)^q \, di \right]^{\frac{1}{q}}, \quad 0 < q \leq 1 \tag{5.19}$$

where $Y_t(i)$ is the input of intermediate good i. Firms producing final goods operate in competitive output markets and maximize profits given by $P_t Y_t - \int P_t(i) Y_t(i) \, di$ where P is the price of final output and $P(i)$ is the price of input i. The first-order conditions for profit maximization by final-goods producers yield the following input demand functions:

$$Y_t^d(i) = \left[\frac{P_t}{P_t(i)} \right]^{\frac{1}{1-q}} Y_t \tag{5.20}$$

Final-goods firms earn zero profit as long as

$$P_t = \left[\int P_t(i)^{\frac{q}{q-1}} \, di \right]^{\frac{q-1}{q}}$$

Each intermediate good is produced according to a constant-returns-to-scale, Cobb-Douglas production function:

$$Y_t(i) = K_t(i)^\alpha L_t(i)^{1-\alpha} \tag{5.21}$$

where K and L denote capital and labor inputs, purchased in competitive factor markets at prices r and W, respectively. The producer of good $Y(i)$ chooses $P(i)$,

$K(i)$, and $L(i)$ to maximize profits subject to the demand function (5.20) and the production function (5.21). Intermediate profits are equal to

$$\pi_t(i) = P_t(i)\, Y_t(i) - r_t K_t(i) - W_t L_t(i)$$

$$= [P_t(i) - P_t V_t]\left[\frac{P_t}{P_t(i)}\right]^{\frac{1}{1-q}} Y_t \tag{5.22}$$

where V_t is equal to minimized unit costs of production (so $P_t V_t$ is the nominal unit cost). The first-order condition for the value of $P_t(i)$ that maximizes profits for the intermediate-goods-producing firm is

$$\left[\frac{P_t}{P_t(i)}\right]^{\frac{1}{1-q}} Y_t - \frac{1}{1-q}[P_t(i) - P_t V_t]\left[\frac{P_t}{P_t(i)}\right]^{\frac{1}{1-q}}\left(\frac{1}{P_t(i)}\right) Y_t = 0$$

After some rearranging, this equation yields

$$P_t(i) = \frac{1}{q}\, P_t V_t \tag{5.23}$$

Thus, the price of intermediate good i is set as a constant markup $\dfrac{1}{q}$ over nominal unit costs PV.

For the intermediate-goods producers, labor demand will involve setting

$$\frac{W_t}{P_t(i)} = q\left[\frac{(1-\alpha)\, Y_t(i)}{L_t(i)}\right] \tag{5.24}$$

where W_t is the nominal wage rate and $\dfrac{(1-\alpha)\, Y_t(i)}{L_t(i)}$ is the marginal product of labor. In a symmetric equilibrium, all intermediate firms charge the same relative price, employ the same labor and capital inputs, and produce at the same level, so $P_t(i) = P_t(j) = P_t$, and (5.24) implies that employment is equal to

$$L_t = \frac{q(1-\alpha)\, Y_t}{W_t/P_t} \tag{5.25}$$

Firms will be concerned with their relative price, not the absolute price level, so money remains neutral. As equations (5.24) and (5.25) show, proportional changes in all nominal prices [i.e., $P(i)$, P, and W] leave firm i's optimal relative price and aggregate labor demand unaffected. If we do not alter the household's decision problem from our earlier analysis, neither consumption, labor-supply, nor investment decisions would be altered by proportional changes in all nominal prices and the nominal stock of money.[34]

To complete the specification of the model, the aggregate demand for labor given by (5.25) must be equated to the aggregate labor supply derived from the outcome of household choices. Previously, the resulting expression for labor-market equilibrium took the form of (5.12), which was obtained from the condition that the marginal utility of leisure equals the real wage times the marginal utility of consumption. The real wage was then replaced by the marginal product of labor under the assumption of competitive factor markets. With imperfect competition, this last substitution is no longer valid; as (5.25) shows, the factor q drives a wedge between the real wage and the marginal product of labor.[35] Thus, labor-market equilibrium requires that

$$\frac{U_l}{U_c} = \frac{W}{P} = qMPL \leq MPL \qquad (5.26)$$

If we now linearize the model in terms of percentage deviations around the steady state, q drops out of the labor-market equilibrium condition because of the way in which it enters multiplicatively. This result does not mean the short-run dynamics are independent of q; the marginal product of capital condition (equation 5.10) is modified to become $R^{ss}r_t = q\alpha\left(\frac{Y^{ss}}{K^{ss}}\right)(E_t y_{t+1} - k_t)$ where lowercase letters denote percentage deviations from steady-state values.

5.3.2.2 Adding Price Stickiness

Several authors have argued that nominal rigidities arise because of small "menu costs," essentially fixed costs, associated with changing prices. As economic conditions change, a firm's "optimal" price will also change, but if there are fixed costs of changing prices, it may not be optimal for the firm to continuously adjust its price to economic changes. Only if the firm's actual price diverges sufficiently from the equilibrium price will it be worthwhile to bear the fixed cost and adjust prices. The macroeconomic implications of menu cost models were first explored by Akerlof and Yellen (1985) and Mankiw (1985) and are surveyed by Romer (1996, Chapter 6). Ball and Romer (1991) show how small menu costs can interact with imperfect competition in either goods or labor markets to

34. The household's budget constraint is altered because real profits of the intermediate goods producers must be paid out to households. However, as (5.22) shows, nominal profits are homogeneous of degree 1 in prices, so their real value will be homogeneous of degree 0. Thus, proportional changes in the nominal money stock and all prices leave the household's budget constraint unaffected.

35. In their calibrations, Chari, Kehoe, and McGrattan use a value of 0.9 for q.

amplify the impact of monetary disturbances, create strategic complementaries, and lead, potentially, to multiple equilibria.

As we saw earlier, simply introducing wage stickiness that lasts for one period significantly changes the impact effects of monetary shocks but does little to account for persistence. Taylor (1979, 1980) argued that the presence of multiperiod nominal contracts, with only a fraction of wages or prices negotiated each period, could generate the type of persistence present in the data. When setting a price during period t that will remain in effect for several periods, a firm will base its decisions on its expectations of conditions in future periods. But the aggregate price level will also depend on prices set in earlier periods that are still in effect. These considerations impart both forward-looking and backward-looking aspects to the aggregate price level and, as Taylor showed, provide a framework capable of replicating aggregate dynamics.

To develop a simple example, suppose that each intermediate-goods-producing firm sets its price $P(i)$ for two periods, with half of all firms adjusting each period.[36] Thus, if $i \in [0, 0.5)$, assume $P(i)$ is set in period $t, t+2, t+4$, etc. If $i \in [0.5, 1)$, the firm sets prices in periods $t+1, t+3, \ldots$. Since we will only consider symmetric equilibria in which all firms setting prices at time t pick the same price, we can drop the index i and let $\bar{P}_{t+j}$ denote the intermediate-goods price set in period $t+j$ for periods $t+j$ and $t+j+1$.

Consider a firm i setting its price in period t. This price will be in effect for periods t and $t+1$. Thus, $\bar{P}_t$ will be chosen to maximize

$$
E_t\left\{ [\bar{P}_t - P_t V_t]\left[\frac{P_t}{\bar{P}_t}\right]^{\frac{1}{1-q}} Y_t + R_{t+1}^{-1}[\bar{P}_t - P_{t+1} V_{t+1}]\left[\frac{P_{t+1}}{\bar{P}_t}\right]^{\frac{1}{1-q}} Y_{t+1} \right\}
$$

which represents the expected discounted profits over periods t and $t+1$ if firm i sets a price $\bar{P}_t$ for the two periods.[37] After some manipulation of the first-order condition, one obtains

---

36. This is a form of nonstate-contingent pricing; prices are set for a fixed length of time regardless of economic conditions. An alternative means of formulating sluggish price adjustment is due to Calvo (1983), who assumed that each period there was a constant probability that an individual firm would adjust its price. In the aggregate, this probability determines the fraction of all firms who actually adjust in a given period. Roberts (1995) provides a brief discussion of various models of price adjustment. See also section 5.5.

37. Chari, Kehoe, and McGrattan (1996) consider situations in which a fraction $1/N$ of all firms set prices each period for N periods. They can then vary N to examine its role in affecting aggregate dynamics. They alter the interpretation of the time period so that N always corresponds to one year; thus, varying N alters the degree of staggering. They conclude that N has little effect.

$$\bar{P}_t = \frac{E_t[P_t^\theta V_t Y_t + R_{t+1}^{-1} P_{t+1}^\theta V_{t+1} Y_{t+1}]}{qE_t\left[P_t^{\frac{1}{1-q}} Y_t + R_{t+1}^{-1} P_{t+1}^{\frac{1}{1-q}} Y_{t+1}\right]} \tag{5.27}$$

where $\theta = (2-q)/(1-q)$. If prices are set for only one period, the terms involving $t+1$ drop out, and one obtains the earlier pricing equation (5.23).

What does (5.27) imply about aggregate price adjustment? Let $\bar{p}, p$, and v denote percentage deviations of $\bar{P}, P$, and V around the steady state. If we ignore discounting for simplicity, equation (5.27) can be approximated in terms of percentage deviations from steady state as

$$\bar{p}_t = \tfrac{1}{2}[p_t + E_t p_{t+1}] + \tfrac{1}{2}[v_t + E_t v_{t+1}] \tag{5.28}$$

The average price of the final good, expressed in terms of deviations from the steady state, is $p_t = \tfrac{1}{2}[\bar{p}_{t-1} + \bar{p}_t]$ where $\bar{p}_{t-1}$ is the price of intermediate goods set at time $t-1$ and $\bar{p}_t$ is the price set in period t. Similarly, $E_t p_{t+1} = \tfrac{1}{2}[\bar{p}_t + E_t\bar{p}_{t+1}]$. Substituting these expressions into equation (5.28) yields

$$\bar{p}_t = \tfrac{1}{2}\bar{p}_{t-1} + \tfrac{1}{2}E_t\bar{p}_{t+1} + [v_t + E_t v_{t+1}]$$

This reveals the backward-looking (via the presence of $\bar{p}_{t-1}$) and forward-looking (via the presence of $E_t\bar{p}_{t+1}$ and $E_t v_{t+1}$) nature of price adjustment.

The variable v_t is the percentage deviation of minimized unit costs from its steady state. Suppose this is proportional to output: $v_t = \gamma y_t$.[38] If we further assume a simple money-demand equation of the form $m_t - p_t = y_t$, we obtain

$$\bar{p}_t = \tfrac{1}{2}\bar{p}_{t-1} + \tfrac{1}{2}E_t\bar{p}_{t+1} + [\gamma y_t + \gamma E_t y_{t+1}]$$
$$= \tfrac{1}{2}\bar{p}_{t-1} + \tfrac{1}{2}E_t\bar{p}_{t+1} + \gamma[m_t - p_t + E_t m_{t+1} - E_t p_{t+1}]$$
$$= \tfrac{1}{2}\left(\frac{1-\gamma}{1+\gamma}\right)[\bar{p}_{t-1} + E_t\bar{p}_{t+1}] + \left(\frac{\gamma}{1+\gamma}\right)[m_t + E_t m_{t+1}] \tag{5.29}$$

This is a difference equation in $\bar{p}$. It implies that the behavior of prices set during period t will depend on prices set during the previous period, on prices expected to be set next period, and on the path of the nominal money supply over the two periods during which $\bar{p}_t$ will be in effect. For the case in which m_t follows a random walk (so that $E_t m_{t+1} = m_t$), the solution for $\bar{p}_t$ is

---

38. The coefficient γ will depend on both the markup and the elasticity of labor supply with respect to the real wage. See Chari, Kehoe, and McGrattan (1996).

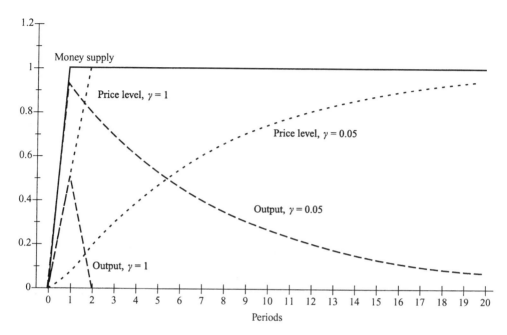

Figure 5.2
Staggered Price Adjustment

$$\bar{p}_t = a\bar{p}_{t-1} + (1-a)m_t \tag{5.30}$$

where $a = \dfrac{1 - \sqrt{\gamma}}{1 + \sqrt{\gamma}}$ is the root less than 1 of $a^2 - \dfrac{2(1+\gamma)}{1-\gamma}a + 1 = 0$.[39] Since the aggregate price level is an average of prices set at t and $t-1$,

$$p_t = ap_{t-1} + \tfrac{1}{2}(1-a)[m_t + m_{t-1}] \tag{5.31}$$

Taylor (1979, 1980) demonstrated a price adjustment equation of the form given by (5.31) that was capable of mimicking the dynamic response of U.S. prices.[40] The response, however, depends critically on the value of a (which in turn depends on γ). Figure 5.2 shows the response of the price level and output for $\gamma = 1$ $(a = 0)$ and $\gamma = 0.05$ $(a = 0.87)$. This latter value is the one Taylor finds matches U.S. data, and, as the figure shows, an unexpected, permanent increase in the nominal money supply

39. See problem 2 at the end of the chapter.
40. Taylor's actual model was based on nominal wage adjustment rather than price adjustment as presented here.

produces a rise in output with a slow adjustment back to the baseline, mirrored by a gradual rise in the price level. Though the model assumed prices were set for only two periods, the money shock leads to persistent, long-lasting effects on output with this value of γ.

Chari, Kehoe, and McGrattan assume employment must be consistent with household labor-supply choices, and they show that γ is a function of the parameters of the utility function. They argue that a very high labor-supply elasticity is required to obtain values of γ of the order of 0.05. With a low labor-supply elasticity, as seems more plausible, γ will be greater than or equal to 1. If this is the case, the Taylor-staggered price adjustment is not capable of capturing realistic adjustment to monetary shocks. However, rather than drawing the implication that staggered price (or wage) adjustment is unimportant for price dynamics, the assumption that observed employment is consistent with the labor-supply behavior implied by the model of the household should be questioned; models that interpret observed employment as tracing out a labor-supply function typically have difficulty matching other aspects of labor-market behavior (Christiano and Eichenbaum 1992b).

While menu costs rationalize sluggish price-setting behavior, such costs may seem implausible as the reason monetary disturbances have significant real effects. After all, adjusting production is also costly, and it is difficult to see why shutting down an assembly line is less costly than reprinting price catalogs. And computers have lowered the cost of changing prices for most retail establishments, though it seems unlikely that this fact has had an important effect on the ability of monetary authorities to have short-run real effects on the economy. Money seems to matter in important ways because of price rigidities, but we still do not have a satisfactory integration of microeconomic models of price adjustment with monetary models of macroeconomic equilibrium.

5.4 A Framework for Monetary Analysis

The standard approach to monetary policy analysis involves an assumption that nominal wages and prices are set in advance so that unanticipated price movements cause real output movements. This is then combined with a simple structure linking the quantity of money to aggregate spending, usually directly through a quantity-theory equation in which nominal demand is equal to the nominal money supply, perhaps plus a random error, or through a traditional textbook IS-LM model. This approach has proven remarkably useful in addressing a wide range of monetary-policy topics. During the 1970s and 1980s, attention was focused mainly on the role of expectations, and how expectations altered conclusions drawn from 1960s-vintage IS-LM models. More recently, attention has been placed on ensuring that the model structure is consistent with the underlying behavior of optimizing economic agents. This section will show how the MIU model can form the basis for a simple linear model that resembles commonly used aggregate-supply, IS-LM models (AS-IS-LM). This will provide a benchmark for considering aspects of economic behavior that are typically missing from the models used to address policy issues.

Three key modifications of the MIU model will be made. First, endogenous variations in the capital stock will be ignored. This approach follows McCallum and Nelson (1997), who argue that little is lost for the purposes of short-run business-cycle analysis by assuming an exogenous process for the capital stock. They show that, at least for the United States, there is little relationship between the capital stock and output at business-cycle frequencies.

Endogenous capital-stock dynamics play a key role in equilibrium business-cycle models in the real-business-cycle tradition, but as Cogley and Nason (1995) show, the response of investment and the capital stock to productivity shocks actually contributes little to the dynamics implied by such models. For simplicity, then, the capital stock will be ignored, leaving money and nominal one-period bonds as the only assets in the model.

The second modification will be to assume an inelastic labor-supply curve.[41] This simplifies the exposition by eliminating any dynamics associated with variation over time in expected employment; in each period, expected employment will be the same.

The third key modification will be to incorporate one-period nominal-wage rigidity into the MIU model. With nominal wages set in advance, as in the Lucas misperceptions model of section 5.2.1 and the sticky wage MIU model of section 5.3.1, unanticipated changes in the price level alter the ex post real wage, employment, and output. The nominal wage is assumed to be set to achieve, in expectation, a constant employment level. Firms determine actual employment by equating the marginal product of labor to the realized real wage.

These modifications yield a framework consistent with optimizing behavior yet usable to explore a number of policy issues. The objective is to move from fully specified general equilibrium models, in which behavioral relationships are derived from the underlying optimization problems faced by individual agents, to the type of simple theoretical models that have typically been found useful for monetary-policy analysis. The resulting version of the MIU model can be linked directly to the

---

41. In terms of the underlying utility function employed in Chapters 2 and 3, this corresponds to letting $\eta \to \infty$ so that $d_1 \to \infty$.

standard AS-IS-LM model that has long served as one of the workhorses for
monetary-policy analysis. McCallum and Nelson (1997) also provide a version of an
AS-IS-LM model derived as an approximation to a dynamic stochastic general
equilibrium model. The most important omission from the simple framework will be
a mechanism for generating the output and inflation persistence that seems to follow
monetary disturbances. The issue of inflation persistence will be discussed in section
5.5.[42]

5.4.1 A Model Consistent with Optimizing Agents

Section 5.3.1 demonstrated how an MIU framework consisting of equations (5.8)–
(5.13) could be modified to incorporate one-period nominal wage rigidity. Building
on that model, this section shows how equilibrium can be characterized in terms of
a four-equation dynamic system in output, the real rate of return, the nominal rate
of interest, and the price level. The four equations correspond to the traditional
aggregate-supply, aggregate-demand, and money-demand equations common in
intermediate macroeconomics textbooks, plus a Fisher equation linking real and
nominal interest rates.

With capital eliminated from the model, the aggregate production function (5.8) is
replaced with one that depends only on employment and a productivity disturbance:
$y_t = (1 - \alpha)n_t + z_t$. Since aggregate labor supply is normally viewed as quite inelastic
with respect to the real wage (i.e., d_1 is large), a second simplification is to let
$d_1 \to \infty$.

With wages set one period in advance based on expectations of the price level,
deviations of the actual level of prices from what had been expected will result in
real output movements. From equation (5.18),

$$y_t = E_{t-1}y_t + a(p_t - E_{t-1}p_t) + \varepsilon_t$$

where $\varepsilon_t \equiv (z_t - E_{t-1}z_t)/\alpha$ is proportional to the innovation to aggregate productivity. As noted earlier, expected output will in general depend on the lagged capital
stock and lagged consumption—the former because period $t - 1$'s capital stock is
used to produce period-t output, the latter because labor supply depends on the
marginal utility of consumption, and expected period-t consumption depends on
time-$t - 1$ consumption. However, if output is produced only with labor and labor
supply is inelastic, $E_{t-1}y_t = E_{t-1}z_t$ where z_t is the time-t productivity disturbance.[43]

---

42. Issues of persistence will also be discussed in Chapter 10.

43. With the aggregate production function, expressed in terms of deviations from steady state, given
by $y_t = (1 - \alpha)n_t + z_t$, $E_{t-1}y_t = E_{t-1}z_t$, since the expected deviation of employment from steady state is
$E_{t-1}n_t = 0$.

With no capital, and therefore no investment, the economy's aggregate resource constraint is simply

$$y_t = c_t \tag{5.32}$$

Now using the optimality condition (5.11) for consumption, $c_t = E_t c_{t+1} - r_t$, one obtains

$$y_t = E_t c_{t+1} - r_t = E_t y_{t+1} - r_t \tag{5.33}$$

Aggregate demand depends positively on expected future output and negatively on the real rate of return.

The last component of the model is the money-demand relationship (5.13). This can be written as

$$m_t - p_t = c_t - d_2^{-1} i_t$$
$$= y_t - d_2^{-1} i_t$$

We can now collect the equations of the model:

Aggregate supply: $y_t = E_{t-1} y_t + a(p_t - E_{t-1} p_t) + \varepsilon_t \tag{5.34}$

Aggregate demand: $y_t = E_t y_{t+1} - r_t + u_t \tag{5.35}$

Money demand: $m_t - p_t = y_t - d_2^{-1} i_t + v_t \tag{5.36}$

Fisher equation: $i_t = r_t + E_t p_{t+1} - p_t = r_t + E_t \pi_{t+1} \tag{5.37}$

The random disturbances u_t and v_t have been added to the aggregate-demand and money-demand relationship to represent other factors influencing the demands for goods and money that are not captured by the model.[44] These four equations determine equilibrium values of output, real and nominal interest rates, and the price level.

The framework given by (5.34)–(5.37) differs from a familiar AS-IS-LM model only by the presence of expected future output in the aggregate-demand relationship. This forward-looking expectation affects current demand because households choose consumption optimally, implying that current consumption will respond to expectations of future income. However, under the simplifying assumptions we have made (no capital and a constant expected level of employment each period), $E_t y_{t+1}$ is

---

44. For example, the appendix shows that when capital is reintroduced into the model, u_t would include the term $E_t x_{t+1} - x_t$ where x_t is investment.

equal to $E_t z_{t+1}$. If the productivity disturbance is serially uncorrelated, $E_t y_{t+1} = 0$. Thus, the aggregate demand condition reduces, in this case, to $y_t = -r_t + u_t$.[45] In the more general case, predictable movements in productivity will influence the level of current demand. For example, if the productivity disturbance follows the process $z_t = \rho z_{t-1} + e_t$, then $E_t y_{t+1} = \rho z_t$.[46]

The reason for going through this derivation is to show how the types of models commonly used for policy analysis are related to the theoretical models employed in earlier chapters. The three key modifications used to go from the MIU model to the AS-IS-LM framework involved ignoring the role of the capital stock, assuming that employment fluctuates around a fixed level due to an inelastic labor supply, and imposing one-period nominal wage contracts. The AS-IS-LM framework is often criticized as "starting from curves" rather than starting from the primitive tastes and technology from which behavioral relationships can be derived, given maximizing behavior and a market structure (Sargent 1982). Instead, the framework simply assumes certain behavioral relationships. For many questions, however, such an approach is extremely useful. But it is important to recognize that some thought experiments that we might like to conduct may change the economic environment facing decision makers in ways that would render invalid the "curves" we have assumed. That is, demand and supply relationships might change.

Various versions of equations (5.34)–(5.37) have played an important role in advancing our understanding of the role of monetary policy. For example, a simplified version of the model can be obtained if the interest elasticity of money demand is set equal to zero (i.e., $d_2 = \infty$), in which case equations (5.34) and (5.36) form a two-equation system that can be solved for output and the price level, given the process followed by the nominal money supply.[47] This particular version forms the basis of much of the work on the time inconsistency of optimal monetary policy that is examined in Chapter 8.

45. When output displays persistence, Kerr and King (1996) show how including expected future output as a determinant of aggregate demand can have important implications for the analysis of interest-rate monetary-policy rules.

46. In this case, $y_t = \rho z_t - r_t + u_t = -r_t + u_t'$, where $u_t' = u_t + \rho z_t$. The disturbance in the aggregate-demand condition contains the aggregate productivity disturbance, so the standard practice of treating disturbances in the aggregate supply and demand equations as orthogonal would be inappropriate.

47. Central banks often employ a short-term nominal interest rate as their policy instrument. If i_t is the policy instrument, equations (5.34), (5.35), and (5.37) constitute a three-equation system to determine output, the real return, and the price level. Equation (5.36) then determines the nominal money supply consistent with equilibrium. Important issues of price-level determinacy arise under interest-rate-setting policies, and these will be discussed in Chapter 10.

5.4.2   Solving the Model

A key property of the system (5.34)–(5.37) is that changes in the nominal money supply that can be predicted at the time when nominal wages are set have no real effects. Under the assumption of rational expectations, the effect on the price level of any predicted change in m will be fully reflected in $\mathrm{E}_{t-1}p_t$. Consequently, $p_t - \mathrm{E}_{t-1}p_t$ is not affected by the change in m_t. With no price-level forecast error, output is equal to z_t. From (5.35), this outcome implies that the expected real rate of return is also unaffected by predictable movements in m_t. With y_t and r_t unaffected, equations (5.36) and (5.37) can be combined to yield

$$m_t - p_t = -\phi(\mathrm{E}_t p_{t+1} - p_t) + \varphi_t$$

where $\phi = d_2^{-1}$ and $\varphi_t = (1 + \phi)\varepsilon_t - \phi u_t + v_t$.[48] This equation can be solved forward for p_t to show how the equilibrium price level will depend on both the current and the expected future money supply:

$$p_t = \frac{1}{1+\phi} \sum_{i=0}^{\infty} \left(\frac{\phi}{1+\phi}\right)^i \mathrm{E}_t m_{t+i} - \frac{1}{1+\phi}\,\varphi_t$$

If the anticipated change in m_t is expected to be temporary, affecting only m_t with no effect on m_{t+i} for $i > 0$, then the change in p_t is equal to $\dfrac{1}{1+\phi}$ times the change in m_t. A temporary change in m alters the current price level relative to future expected price levels. This change affects expected inflation and the nominal interest rate. If, for example, m is anticipated to increase temporarily, p_t rises relative to $\mathrm{E}_t p_{t+1}$; the resulting expected deflation lowers the nominal rate of interest, and the lower interest rate increases real money demand by ϕ times the fall in expected inflation. So p rises by less than $m\left(\dfrac{1}{1+\phi} < 1\right)$ to ensure that the real supply of money rises.

In contrast, if the expected change in the nominal money supply is anticipated to be permanent, so that m_t, m_{t+1}, $m_{t+2}, \ldots$ are all expected to change by the same amount, then the change in p_t is equal to $\dfrac{1}{1+\phi}\sum\left(\dfrac{\phi}{1+\phi}\right)^i = 1$ times the change in m_t. If the effect on the money supply is permanent, p jumps in proportion to the

---

48. A similar model in which the real effects of money on output and interest rates were ignored in order to study the behavior of the price level was used in the discussion of hyperinflations in Chapter 4. The solution for p_t assumes that the productivity shock z_t is white noise; otherwise, $\varphi_t = (1 + \phi)(\mathrm{E}_{t-1}z_t + \varepsilon_t) - \phi(\mathrm{E}_t z_{t+1} + u_t) + v_t$.

change in m, leaving real money balances, expected inflation, and the nominal interest rate unchanged.

If the change in m_t is not completely anticipated, the effects on p_t will not be fully incorporated in $E_{t-1}p_t$; unexpected changes in m_t can cause price surprises that affect output according to (5.34). An unanticipated rise in m_t will, for a given initial price level, raise the real money supply, requiring a fall in the nominal interest rate to re-store money-market equilibrium. Unless expected inflation has also fallen, the fall in i_t is associated with a decline in the expected real rate. From (5.35), this increases aggregate demand. Equilibrium requires a rise in p that induces an increase in output by lowering the real value of the nominal wage. The new equilibrium involves higher output and prices and lower nominal and real interest rates. These effects last only one period in this model because any effect of the change in m_t on the future path of the money supply will now be incorporated into future nominal wage levels. This is the basic transmission mechanism of the standard aggregate-supply, aggregate-demand model.

To obtain the general solution to equations (5.34)–(5.37), begin by substituting the Fisher equation into (5.36) and then eliminating the real rate of interest r_t using (5.35). This process yields

$$y_t = \frac{d_2(m_t - p_t) + E_t\pi_{t+1} + E_t y_{t+1} - d_2 v_t + u_t}{1 + d_2} \tag{5.38}$$

where $E_t\pi_{t+1} = E_t p_{t+1} - p_t$ is the expected rate of inflation. This equation, which corresponds to a textbook aggregate-demand curve, relates real income negatively to the price level for a given level of the nominal money supply and positively to expectations of future inflation and output. The aggregate-demand curve, together with the aggregate-supply curve (5.34), can be solved for equilibrium output and the price level as functions of the money supply and expectations. For the remainder of this section, assume aggregate productivity is serially uncorrelated; $z_t = e_t$ where e is a mean-zero, white-noise process. This assumption implies $E_t y_{t+1} = 0$. Problem 8 at the end of the chapter deals with the case in which $z_t = \rho z_{t-1} + e_t$ so that $E_t y_{t+1} = \rho z_t$ with $\rho \neq 0$.

Equating aggregate demand from (5.38) and aggregate supply from (5.34) and solving for p_t yields

$$p_t = \frac{d_2 m_t + a(1 + d_2)E_{t-1}p_t + E_t\pi_{t+1} - d_2 v_t + u_t - (1 + d_2)\varepsilon_t}{d_2 + a(1 + d_2)} \tag{5.39}$$

Taking expectations as of time $t - 1$ to obtain an expression for $E_{t-1}p_t$ and then subtracting the result from the expression for p_t gives

$$p_t - E_{t-1}p_t = \frac{d_2(m_t - E_{t-1}m_t) + (E_t\pi_{t+1} - E_{t-1}\pi_{t+1}) - d_2v_t + u_t - (1+d_2)\varepsilon_t}{d_2 + a(1+d_2)} \quad (5.40)$$

Now substituting this into the aggregate-supply equation (5.34) shows that output depends only on unexpected changes in the nominal supply of money, the disturbance terms, and changes in expectations of future inflation:

$$y_t = \frac{a[d_2(m_t - E_{t-1}m_t) + (E_t\pi_{t+1} - E_{t-1}\pi_{t+1}) - d_2v_t + u_t] + d_2\varepsilon_t}{d_2 + a(1+d_2)} \quad (5.41)$$

The transmission mechanism from a change in m to prices and output is that of the familiar AS-IS-LM model. A change in m that is unexpected is nonneutral; if p were to increase in proportion (to leave $m - p$ unchanged), output would rise, since the unexpected price increase lowers real wages and increases employment. The rise in output can occur in equilibrium only if demand also rises, and increased demand requires a fall in the expected real interest rate. With expected inflation assumed unchanged, the fall in the nominal interest rate and the rise in income both act to increase real money demand. Hence, the increase in p must be less than the rise in m so that $m - p$ rises. An unexpected rise in the nominal money supply is predicted to increase output, employment, and prices, and to lower real wages and real and nominal interest rates.

One problem with this analysis is that we are unable to link changes in the money supply with their effects in causing the public to revise expectations about future inflation. The change in m may cause inflation expectations to adjust, so holding expectations about future inflation constant while analyzing a change in m is potentially misleading. If the unexpected rise in m is associated with a rise in expected future inflation, the price and output effects of the increase in m will be larger (see equations [5.40] and [5.41]). A rise in expected inflation means that the nominal interest rate falls by less than the real interest rate, and, since money demand depends on the nominal interest rate, money demand rises by less than in the previous case. Thus, p must rise by more, inducing a larger increase in output.

Using (5.39) and replacing expected inflation with $E_t p_{t+1} - p_t$ yields a single equilibrium condition in the price level and expectations of the price level:

$$p_t = \frac{d_2 m_t + a(1+d_2)E_{t-1}p_t + E_t p_{t+1} - d_2 v_t + u_t - (1+d_2)\varepsilon_t}{(1+a)(1+d_2)} \quad (5.42)$$

Because p_t will depend on m_t, expectations of p_t formed in period $t - 1$ will depend on expectations of m_t, and $E_t p_{t+1}$ will depend on expectations of the future behavior of the money supply. To determine how an unexpected change in the money supply might affect expectations requires that we assume a specific process for the money supply; this provides a basis for determining rational expectations of future price movements.

Suppose, then, that the monetary policy authority sets m_t according to the following rule:

$$m_t = \mu + m_{t-1} + a_1 u_t + a_2 \varepsilon_t + a_3 v_t + \omega_t \qquad (5.43)$$

where μ is the average growth rate of the money supply and ω_t is a disturbance reflecting the policy maker's imperfect control over the nominal money supply. This policy rule specifies that the policy maker is able to respond contemporaneously to the supply shock ε_t, the aggregate-demand shock u_t, and the money-demand shock v_t. Since these responses will generate movements in m_t that could not have been predicted when $E_{t-1} p_t$ was formed, they will introduce a role for policy, interpreted as the choice of a_1, a_2, and a_3, to affect real output.

Equation (5.42) can be solved using the method of undetermined coefficients; the details are presented in section 5.7.3 of the appendix. The equilibrium price and output equations are

$$
\begin{aligned}
p_t &= \frac{\mu(1 + d_2)}{d_2} + m_{t-1} + \frac{[1 + a_1(1 + d_2)]u_t + [a_3(1 + d_2) - d_2]v_t}{(1 + a)(1 + d_2)} \\
&\quad + \frac{(a_2 - 1)\varepsilon_t + \omega_t}{1 + a} \\
&\equiv \frac{\mu(1 + d_2)}{d_2} + m_{t-1} + b_1 u_t + b_2 \varepsilon_t + b_3 v_t + b_4 \omega_t
\end{aligned}
$$

and

$$
\begin{aligned}
y_t &= a\left\{ \frac{[1 + a_1(1 + d_2)]u_t + [a_3(1 + d_2) - d_2]v_t + (1 + d_2)\omega_t}{(1 + a)(1 + d_2)} \right\} \\
&\quad + \frac{(aa_2 + 1)\varepsilon_t}{1 + a}
\end{aligned}
$$

These expressions show how the equilibrium is affected by the manner in which the nominal money supply is adjusted in response to the underlying disturbances as well as by predicted movements in m_t. The way in which m_t responds to shocks affects the impact of such shocks on the price level and on output.

For general values of the policy parameters, the expected rate of inflation is given by

$$E_t \pi_{t+1} = \mu + (a_1 - b_1)u_t + (a_2 - b_2)\varepsilon_t + (a_3 - b_3)v_t + (1 - b_4)\omega_t$$

which shows that, on average, expected inflation equals the average rate of growth of the nominal money supply (μ) and that the response of expected inflation to economic disturbances depends on both the policy response induced by shocks (the a_i's) and the "structural" parameters of the model (d_2 and a, together with the a_i's, determine the b_i's).

Finally, from (5.36), the equilibrium nominal rate of interest is equal to

$$i_t = d_2(y_t - m_t + p_t + v_t)$$

$$= \mu + \frac{d_2}{1 + d_2}[u_t - d_2 v_t]$$

5.4.3 Implications

Several important conclusions are implied by this solution. First, output does not depend on m_{t-1} or μ; output does, however, depend on the parameters a_i's of the policy rule governing the evolution of the money supply. Because we have assumed that the policy maker can adjust m in light of the current realizations of the shocks to aggregate supply and demand, while aggregate supply depends on expectations formed prior to the realizations of the shocks, systematic policy responses matter. If a_1 is negative, for example, a positive demand shock reduces the nominal supply of money; this reduction in money lowers output and offsets the positive effect of the shock. If $a_2 = -1/a < 0$, output is completely stabilized in the face of supply shocks, while the impact of supply shocks on the price level can be eliminated if $a_2 = 1 > 0$. Offsetting more of the price effect of ε increases its impact on real output, while offsetting the real output effects of ε increases its impact on the price level. In this simple model, setting $a_1 = -(1 + d_2)^{-1} < 0$, $a_2 = 1 > 0$, and $a_3 = d_2(1 + d_2)^{-1} > 0$ would completely insulate the price level from all three disturbances. By preventing demand and money-demand shocks from causing price-level movements, this policy would also insulate output from u_t and v_t realizations. However, aggregate-supply shocks will still affect output. Preventing supply shocks from affecting prices causes output to fully absorb ε shocks.

The expression for the nominal rate of interest reveals that ω shocks do not affect i. Since ω represents money-supply disturbances of the sort a VAR would identify as monetary policy shocks, it may seem strange that they have no impact on the nominal interest rate. The absence of a liquidity effect arises because of the process assumed for the nominal money supply and the particular parameter values of the model. According to (5.43), shocks to the nominal money supply are permanent; m is a random walk with drift μ and innovation $a_1 u + a_2 e + a_3 v + \omega$. Innovations to m are permanent and are eventually fully translated into permanent changes to the price level. This result occurs after two periods, since wage contracts have been assumed to last only one period. During the period of a positive ω innovation, p rises by $\omega/(1 + a)$; it rises by $a\omega/(1 + a)$ in the following period. Expected inflation is initially μ, jumps to $\mu + a\omega/(1 + a)$, and then returns to μ. By itself, this process would act to raise the nominal rate of interest. However, from (5.34), the unexpected price increase causes aggregate supply to expand by $a\omega/(1 + a)$. To induce an equal rise in aggregate demand, the real rate of interest must fall by this same amount (r has a coefficient of -1 in equation 5.35). Combining the effects of the fall in the real rate and rise in expected inflation, the change in the nominal interest rate is $-a\omega/(1 + a) + a\omega/(1 + a) = 0$.

The nominal rate of interest moves one-for-one with changes in μ, reflecting that average inflation is determined by μ. Real money balances can be shown to be decreasing in the average rate of inflation μ. An increase in average inflation raises the nominal interest rate and the opportunity cost of holding money. These changes lower the real demand for money.

There are several major criticisms of the transmission process captured in this model. First, the sticky-wage model implies that real wages should move countercyclically; a monetary expansion raises the price level, and the resulting decline in real wages induces firms to increase employment and output. The empirical evidence for the United States suggests real wages are procyclical, although not strongly so. This is not necessarily inconsistent with the basic monetary transmission mechanism because cycles are presumably caused by nonmonetary forces (that may cause wages to move procyclically) as well as monetary disturbances, so the observed correlations will reflect the net balance of several types of disturbances.

Second, the model emphasizes changes in the nominal money supply, but many authors have argued that it is credit, not money, that matters for real economic activity. Since most measures of the money supply consist largely of bank liabilities, measures of m and measures of bank credit tend to move together. They represent different sides of the banking sector's balance sheet. Chapter 7 discusses the role of credit channels in the monetary transmission process.

Third, it is argued that changes in the money supply have direct effects on aggregate demand that are independent of the interest-rate channels that operate on consumption and investment. Real money holdings represent part of household wealth; an increase in real balances should induce an increase in consumption spending through a wealth effect. This channel is often called the Pigou effect and was viewed as generating a channel through which price-level declines during a depression would eventually increase real balances and household wealth sufficiently to restore consumption spending. During the Keynesian/monetarist debates of the 1960s and early 1970s, some monetarists argued for a direct wealth effect that linked changes in the money supply directly to aggregate demand (Patinkin 1965). The effect of money on aggregate demand operating through interest-rate effects was viewed as a Keynesian interpretation of the transmission mechanism. However, since wealth effects are likely to be small at business-cycle frequencies, most simple models used for policy analysis ignore them.[49]

5.4.4   Interest Rate Policies

The discussion to this point has assumed that the nominal supply of money can be treated as the instrument of monetary policy. Most central banks in the major industrialized economies actually implement monetary policy by controlling a short-term nominal rate of interest. The reasons why policy is implemented in this manner are discussed in Chapter 9, while the implications of interest rate policies are covered in Chapter 10. It is useful at this point, however, to illustrate how the basic structure of the model is altered when i_t, rather than m_t, is viewed as the policy instrument.

Rewriting the aggregate supply relationship (5.34) in terms of inflation rather than the price level, and using the Fisher equation (5.37) to eliminate the real rate of interest from the aggregate demand relationship (5.35), the model can be written as a two equation system consisting of an aggregate supply function and an aggregate demand function

$$y_t = E_{t-1}y_t + a(\pi_t - E_{t-1}\pi_t) + \varepsilon_t$$

$$y_t = E_t y_{t+1} - (i_t - E_t \pi_{t+1}) + u_t$$

where $E_{t-1}y_t = E_{t-1}z_t$ and $E_t y_{t+1} = E_t z_{t+1}$ if z_t is the aggregate productivity disturbance. These two equations can be solved for output and inflation. However, a key implication to make note of is the absence of the price level from either equation. This means that interest rate policies may leave the price level indeterminate, an

49. Wealth effects could be incorporated by including $m_t - p_t$ as a determinate of aggregate demand in equation (5.35). Empirical models used for policy analysis by agencies such as the Federal Reserve usually incorporate wealth effects, although these include much broader definitions of wealth than simply real money balances. Wealth effects then arise from the impact of interest rates on asset prices.

issue taken up in section 10.2.1. A second aspect of this system to note is that the money demand, or LM, relationship given by equation (5.36) is no longer needed in order to solve for output and inflation. Given y_t and i_t (and the disturbance v_t), the LM equation simply determines the real demand for money. To control the nominal interest rate, the central bank must allow the nominal supply of money to adjust endogenously to ensure the real demand for money is equal to the real supply.

Because output and inflation are determined independently of money demand and supply factors when the central bank controls the nominal interest rate, some of the current large scale econometric models employed by central banks no longer even include a role for the quantity of money. For example, the FRB/US model of the Federal Reserve Board has this characteristic [Brayton and Tinsley (1996)]. In fact, many recent models designed for monetary policy analysis have a basic structure that consists of three components. First, there is an aggregate supply function, more commonly recast as a Phillips curve. Second, there is an aggregate demand function. And third, there is an equation to explain the central bank's setting of the nominal interest rate. We will examine models of this type in Chapter 10.

To illustrate how a policy rule for i_t can be used with the aggregate supply and demand equations to determine equilibrium output and inflation, suppose the central bank sets i_t according to

$$i_t = b_y y_t + b_\pi \pi_t$$

Equations of this type are called Taylor rules, after John Taylor, who showed that a simple equation of this form (with $b_y = 0.5$ and $b_\pi = 1.5$) does a surprisingly good job of capturing Fed policy during the last 15 years (Taylor 1993a). Clarida, Galí, and Gertler (1997) estimate interest rate rules for the United States, the United Kingdom, France, Germany, and Italy that are variants of this basic Taylor rule. They also provide references to the recent literature estimating interest rate policy reaction functions.

Using the Taylor rule to eliminate i_t from the aggregate demand function, the model becomes

$$y_t = E_{t-1}y_t + a(\pi_t - E_{t-1}\pi_t) + \varepsilon_t$$

$$y_t = \frac{E_t y_{t+1} - (b_\pi \pi_t - E_t \pi_{t+1}) + u_t}{1 + b_y}$$

If we simplify by assuming the aggregate productivity shock z_t is serially uncorrelated, $E_{t-1}y_t$ and $E_t y_{t+1}$ will both equal zero. In this case, the equilibrium rate of inflation must satisfy

$$[a(1 + b_y) - b_\pi]\pi_t + a(1 + b_y)E_{t-1}\pi_t - E_t\pi_{t+1} = u_t - (1 + b_y)\varepsilon_t$$

Employing McCallum's minimum state variable solution approach [McCallum (1983a)], the equilibrium inflation rate is given by

$$\pi_t = \frac{u_t - (1 + b_y)\varepsilon_t}{a(1 + b_y) + b_\pi}$$

which depends on the supply and demand shocks and the parameters of the policy rule. With this solution, output is equal to

$$y_t = \left[\frac{au_t + b_\pi\varepsilon_t}{a(1 + b_y) + b_\pi} \right]$$

Models in which the nominal interest rate is the instrument of monetary policy are important because they better represent the manner in which many central banks actually implement policy. The example here illustrates the structure of the basic model when i_t is the policy instrument. As was mentioned previously, however, interest rate policies raise additional important issues, and discussion of these will be postponed until Chapter 10.

5.5 Inflation Persistence

The assumption of one-period nominal wage contracts was employed in the previous section to demonstrate how a general equilibrium MIU model could be viewed as providing the underlying theoretical basis for an AS-IS-LM system. One-period contracts can help to account for the impact effects of monetary disturbances, but the economy was predicted to return to its steady-state equilibrium after one period. Thus, this framework can help to provide insight into the channels through which monetary disturbances have real effects on the economy, but it cannot mimic the persistence of these effects.

Before preceding, it is important to distinguish between two sources of persistence in observed inflation. Inflation can display persistence if money growth rates display persistence. If this were the only sense in which inflation appears to exhibit persistence, it could easily be explained within the context of flexible price models. The behavior of inflation would simply reflect the behavior of the money growth rate; if the way policy is conducted introduces a high degree of serial correlation into the money growth process, then this will be reflected in the behavior of the inflation rate.

The second source of inflation persistence is the one of focus here. In response to serially uncorrelated monetary policy shocks (measured either by money growth rates or interest rate movements), the response of inflation appears to follow a highly serially correlated pattern. This is the sense of persistence with which we are concerned here.

In this section, we follow Roberts (1995) and discuss models of price-level adjustment that attempt to capture the dynamic aspects of inflation adjustment. Models due to Taylor (1979, 1980), Calvo (1983), McCallum (1994c), and Fuhrer and Moore (1995a), are developed. An important distinction turns out to be whether it is the price level or the inflation rate that is sticky.

5.5.1   Taylor's Model

Taylor (1979, 1980) originally developed his model in terms of nominal-wage-setting behavior, so we follow that approach here. With prices assumed to be a constant markup over wage costs, the adjustment of wages translates directly into an adjustment equation for prices.

Assume wages are set for two periods, with x_t equal to the log contract wage set at time t. The average wage faced by the firm is equal to $w_t = (x_t + x_{t-1})/2$, since in period t contracts set in the previous period (x_{t-1}) are still in effect. Assuming a constant markup, the log price level is given by

$$p_t = w_t + q$$

where q is the log markup. For convenience, normalize so that $q = 0$.

For workers covered by the contract set in period t, the average expected real wage over the life of the contract is $\frac{1}{2}[x_t - p_t + (x_t - E_t p_{t+1})] = x_t - \frac{1}{2}(p_t + E_t p_{t+1})$.[50] In Taylor (1980) the expected average real contract wage is assumed to be increasing in the level of economic activity, represented by log output:

$$x_t = \tfrac{1}{2}(p_t + E_t p_{t+1}) + ky_t \tag{5.44}$$

With $p_t = \frac{1}{2}(x_t + x_{t-1})$,

$$p_t = \tfrac{1}{2}\left[\tfrac{1}{2}(p_t + E_t p_{t+1}) + ky_t + \tfrac{1}{2}(p_{t-1} + E_{t-1}p_t) + ky_{t-1}\right]$$

$$= \tfrac{1}{4}(2p_t + E_t p_{t+1} + p_{t-1} + \eta_t) + \frac{k}{2}(y_t + y_{t-1})$$

---

50. It would be more appropriate to assume that workers care about the present discounted value of the real wage over the life of the contract. This assumption would lead to a specification of the form $0.5(1 + \beta)x_t - 0.5(p_t + \beta E_t p_{t+1})$ for $0 < \beta < 1$, where β is a discount factor.

where $\eta_t \equiv E_{t-1}p_t - p_t$ is an expectational error term. Rearranging,

$$p_t = \tfrac{1}{2}p_{t-1} + \tfrac{1}{2}E_t p_{t+1} + k(y_t + y_{t-1}) + \tfrac{1}{2}\eta_t$$

The basic Taylor specification leads to inertia in the aggregate price level. The value of p_t is influenced both by expectations of future prices and by the price level in the previous period.

Expressed in terms of the rate of inflation $\pi_t = p_t - p_{t-1}$,

$$\pi_t = E_t\pi_{t+1} + 2k(y_t + y_{t-1}) + \eta_t \tag{5.45}$$

The key aspect of this specification is that while prices display inertia, there is no inertia in the rate of inflation. This is important, as can be seen by considering the implications of (5.45) for a policy of disinflation. Suppose that the economy is in an initial equilibrium with a constant inflation rate π_1. This rate is expected to continue, so $E_t\pi_{t+1} = \pi_1$, and equation (5.45) reduces to $y_t = -y_{t-1} - \dfrac{\eta_t}{2k}$. Now suppose at the beginning of period t, the policy maker announces a policy that will change the inflation rate to π_2 and maintain it at this new level. As long as expected future inflation changes to π_2, (5.45) becomes

$$\pi_2 = \pi_2 + 2k(y_t + y_{t-1}) + \eta_t$$

or $y_t = -y_{t-1} - \dfrac{\eta_t}{2k}$. The change in the level of inflation has no impact on the behavior of real output. Inflation can be costlessly reduced. The price level is sticky in Taylor's specification, but the rate at which it changes, the rate of inflation, is not. The backward-looking aspect of price behavior causes unanticipated reductions in the *level* of the money supply to cause real output declines. Prices set previously are "too" high relative to the new path for the money supply; only as contracts expire can their real value be reduced to levels consistent with the new, lower money supply. However, as Ball (1994a) has shown, price rigidities based on such backward-looking behavior need not imply that policies to reduce inflation by reducing the *growth rate* of money will cause a recession. Since m continues to grow, just at a slower rate, the real value of preset prices continues to be eroded, unlike the case of a level reduction in m.[51]

51. Ball (1994a) shows that the announcement of a disinflation can actually generate an economic expansion if Taylor's specification is correct. The nominal wage in new contracts is equal to the average of the current and expected future money supply. Since the growth rate of the money supply has decreased, the path of money is concave, so the average contract wage falls below m; the resulting temporary rise in m relative to p is expansionary.

5.5.2 Calvo's Model

An alternative model of staggered price adjustment is due to Calvo (1983). He assumed that firms adjust their prices infrequently, and that opportunities to adjust arrived as an exogenous Poisson process. Each period, there is a constant probability q that the firm will be able to adjust its price; the expected time between price adjustments is $1/q$. Because these adjustment opportunities occur randomly, the interval between price changes for an individual firm will be a random variable.

Following Rotemberg (1987), suppose the representative firm i sets its price to minimize a quadratic loss function that depends on the difference between the firm's actual price in period t, p_{it}, and its optimal price p_t^*.[52] This latter might denote the profit-maximizing price for firm i in the absence of any restrictions or costs associated with price adjustment. If the firm can adjust at time t, then it will set its price to minimize

$$\tfrac{1}{2}\mathrm{E}_t \sum_{j=0}^{\infty} \beta^j (p_{it+j} - p_{t+j}^*)^2 \tag{5.46}$$

subject to the assumed process for determining when the firm will next be able to adjust. If the terms in (5.46) involving the price set at time t are written out, they are

$$(p_{it} - p_t^*)^2 + (1-q)\beta \mathrm{E}_t(p_{it} - p_{t+1}^*)^2 + (1-q)^2\beta^2 \mathrm{E}_t(p_{it} - p_{t+2}^*)^2 + \cdots$$

or

$$\sum_{j=0}^{\infty}(1-q)^j \beta^j \mathrm{E}_t(p_{it} - p_{t+j}^*)^2$$

since $1-q$ is the probability that the firm cannot adjust so that the price set at t still holds in $t+1$. Thus, the first-order condition for the optimal choice of p_{it} requires that

$$p_{it}\sum_{j=0}^{\infty}(1-q)^j \beta^j - \sum_{j=0}^{\infty}(1-q)^j \beta^j \mathrm{E}_t p_{t+j}^* = 0$$

Rearranging, and letting x_t denote the price set at t by all firms adjusting their price,

---

52. Since all firms are assumed to be identical (except for the timing of their price adjustments), the subscript i on p^* is dropped.

$$x_t = [1 - (1 - q)\beta] \sum_{j=0}^{\infty} (1 - q)^j \beta^j E_t p_{t+j}^* \qquad (5.47)$$

The price set by the firm at time t is a weighted average of current and expected future values of the target price p^*. If q is large, the expected time until the firm can next adjust its price is small. In this case, less weight is placed on future p^*'s.

Equation (5.47) can be rewritten as

$$x_t = [1 - (1 - q)\beta] p_t^* + (1 - q)\beta E_t x_{t+1}$$

If the price target p^* is assumed to depend on the aggregate price level and output, as would be the case if the firm faces a downward-sloping demand curve, we can replace p_t^* with $p_t + \gamma y_t + \omega_t$ where ω is a random disturbance to capture other determinants of p^*.[53] With a large number of firms, a fraction q will actually adjust their price each period, and the aggregate price level can be expressed as $p_t = q x_t + (1 - q) p_{t-1}$.

We then have the following two equations to describe the evolution of x_t and p_t:

$$x_t = [1 - (1 - q)\beta](p_t + \gamma y_t + \omega_t) + (1 - q)\beta E_t x_{t+1} \qquad (5.48)$$

$$p_t = q x_t + (1 - q) p_{t-1} \qquad (5.49)$$

In order to obtain an expression for aggregate inflation, update (5.49) by one period and take expectations to obtain $E_t p_{t+1} = q E_t x_{t+1} + (1 - q) p_t$. This can be rewritten as $q E_t x_{t+1} = E_t \pi_{t+1} + q p_t$. Use this to eliminate $E_t x_{t+1}$ from (5.48), and then use the resulting expression to eliminate x_t from (5.49), yielding

$$p_t = q[1 - (1 - q)\beta](p_t + \gamma y_t + \omega_t) + (1 - q)\beta(E_t \pi_{t+1} + q p_t) + (1 - q) p_{t-1}$$

Collecting terms,

$$\pi_t = \beta E_t \pi_{t+1} + q \frac{[1 - (1 - q)\beta]}{1 - q}(\gamma y_t + \omega_t)$$

$$= \beta E_t \pi_{t+1} + \gamma' y_t + \omega_t' \qquad (5.50)$$

where $\gamma' = \gamma q[1 - (1 - q)\beta]/(1 - q)$ and $\omega_t' = \omega_t q[1 - (1 - q)\beta]/(1 - q)$.

---

53. In levels, assume the firm faces the demand curve $Y = a(P_i/P)^{-\gamma} e^{\phi}$ where P_i is the firm's price and P is the aggregate price level. In log terms, $y = \ln a - \gamma(p_i - p) + \phi$ so that if y is the firm's output level, $p_i^* = p - \gamma^{-1}(y - \ln a - \phi)$.

Comparing this expression to the inflation equation from Taylor's model, equation (5.45), shows them to be quite similar. Current inflation depends on expectations of future inflation and on current output. One difference is that in deriving an inflation equation based on Calvo's specification, ·expected future inflation has a coefficient equal to the discount factor $\beta < 1$. In deriving an expression for inflation using Taylor's specification, however, we ignored discounting in equation (5.44), the equation giving the value of the contract wage.

One attractive aspect of Calvo's model is that it shows how the coefficient on output in the inflation equation will depend on the frequency with which prices are adjusted. A fall in q, which means that the average time between prices changes for an individual firm increases, causes γ' in (5.50) to decrease. Output movements have a smaller impact on current inflation, holding expected future inflation constant. Because opportunities to adjust prices occur less often, current demand conditions are less important.

5.5.3   The *p*-Bar Model

McCallum (1994c) has criticized inflation equations of the form (5.45) and (5.50) as violating the natural-rate hypothesis. This hypothesis states that the unconditional mean of y_t cannot be affected by any aspect of monetary policy. Recall that y is the log deviation of output around its steady state. The natural-rate hypothesis implies that monetary policy cannot be used to keep output permanently about the value it would assume if all prices and wages were perfectly flexible. As McCallum notes, specifications of inflation, such as equation (5.45) from the Taylor formulation and equation (5.50) from Calvo's, violate this natural-rate hypothesis. To see this point using the Taylor version, rewrite (5.45) as $(y_t + y_{t-1}) = \frac{1}{2k}[\pi_t - E_t\pi_{t+1}] - \frac{1}{2k}\eta_t$.

Taking unconditional expectations, average output over periods t and $t-1$ is

$$\tfrac{1}{2}E[y_t + y_{t-1}] = \frac{1}{4k}[E\pi_t - E\pi_{t+1}]$$

For any constant rate of inflation, the right side of this equation equals zero, so monetary policy cannot affect average output by its choice of average inflation. However, a falling inflation rate can keep $\tfrac{1}{2}E[y_t + y_{t-1}] > 0$. Fuhrer (1994b) characterizes the Taylor specification as satisfying the first-order natural-rate hypothesis (average output is independent of the average level of inflation) but not the second-order version (average output does depend on the rate of change of inflation). He concludes, though, that since we do not observe periods in which policy has generated differences in the average rate of change of the inflation rate, we do not have the evidence that would be necessary to determine whether the second-order natural-rate hypothesis is likely to hold.[54]

McCallum (1994c) has studied a price-level adjustment specification that he calls the p-bar model, based on Mussa (1981a, 1981b). Define $\bar{y}_t$ as the economy's natural rate of output (since we have defined y as a deviation around the steady state, $\bar{y}$ will equal 0, but it will be convenient to have some notation for the natural rate). Define $\bar{p}_t$ as the price level that would be consistent with $y_t = \bar{y}_t = 0$. The actual price level is then assumed to adjust according to

$$p_t - p_{t-1} = \gamma(y_{t-1} - \bar{y}_{t-1}) + E_{t-1}[\bar{p}_t - \bar{p}_{t-1}] \qquad (5.51)$$

The adjustment parameter γ is assumed to be positive. The actual price level increases if output exceeded its natural rate in the previous period or if p-bar itself is expected to increase. The p-bar adjustment equation can be written as

$$p_t - E_{t-1}\bar{p}_t = \gamma(y_{t-1} - \bar{y}_{t-1}) + p_{t-1} - E_{t-1}\bar{p}_{t-1} \qquad (5.52)$$

to show that deviations of the actual level from the expected value of p-bar reflect output deviations from $\bar{y}$ and lagged price deviations from p-bar. Since all variables other than p_t in the p-bar model are determined prior to the start of period t, p_t is also a predetermined variable.

A model of aggregate demand is now needed to determine the factors that affect $\bar{p}_t$. If we use equations (5.35)–(5.37), and assume the productivity disturbance is serially uncorrelated, these three equations can be solved to express the aggregate demand for output as

$$y_t = \frac{d_2 m_t - (1 + d_2)p_t + E_t p_{t+1} - d_2 v_t + u_t}{1 + d_2}$$

Solving for p_t,

$$p_t = \frac{d_2 m_t + E_t p_{t+1} - d_2 v_t + u_t}{1 + d_2} - y_t \qquad (5.53)$$

and p-bar is then equal to

$$\bar{p}_t = \frac{d_2 m_t + E_t p_{t+1} - d_2 v_t + u_t}{1 + d_2} - \bar{y}_t$$

$$= \frac{d_2 m_t + E_t p_{t+1} - d_2 v_t + u_t}{1 + d_2} \qquad (5.54)$$

---

54. This is similar to the point made by Fisher and Seater (1993) about testing for monetary neutrality.

since $\bar{y}_t = 0$. Thus subtracting (5.54) from (5.53), $p_t - \bar{p}_t = -y_t$, and

$$p_t - E_{t-1}\bar{p}_t = \frac{d_2(m_t - E_{t-1}m_t) + E_t p_{t+1} - E_{t-1}p_{t+1} - d_2 v_t + u_t}{1 + d_2} - y_t$$

Using this equation, together with the fact that $p_{t-1} - E_{t-1}\bar{p}_{t-1} = p_{t-1} - \bar{p}_{t-1} = -y_{t-1}$, equation (5.52) implies

$$y_t = \frac{d_2(m_t - E_{t-1}m_t) + E_t p_{t+1} - E_{t-1}p_{t+1} - d_2 v_t + u_t}{1 + d_2} + (1 - \gamma)y_{t-1}$$

The unconditional mean of y_t then satisfies

$$Ey_t = (1 - \gamma)Ey_{t-1} \tag{5.55}$$

which is independent of money and prices. Thus, the unconditional mean of the output deviation is invariant to the money-supply process; a natural-rate hypothesis of any order holds when prices adjust according to the p-bar model.

Monetary policy can affect the variance of output, though, if it responds to the time-t realizations of any of the underlying shocks. If m_t responds predictably to, say, u_t, this response may affect the expectations-revision term $E_t p_{t+1} - E_{t-1}p_{t+1}$. To illustrate this point, suppose $m_t = m_{t-1} + au_t$. Then, if we simplify by eliminating the effect of lagged output for the purposes of this example by setting $\gamma = 1$, the equilibrium price level (see problem 7) is given by

$$p_t = m_{t-1}$$

and output is equal to

$$y_t = \frac{d_2 a u_t + [m_{t-1} + au_t] - [m_{t-1}] - d_2 v_t + u_t}{1 + d_2}$$

$$= \frac{[1 + a(d_2 + 1)]u_t - d_2 v_t}{1 + d_2}$$

which depends on the parameter a of the money-supply process.

The p-bar model can be manipulated to yield an expression for inflation that is directly comparable to those obtained from the Taylor and Calvo models. Using the first difference operator Δ, equation (5.54) implies

$$E_{t-1}\Delta\bar{p}_t = \frac{1}{1 + d_2}[d_2 E_{t-1}\Delta m_t + E_{t-1}\Delta p_{t+1} - u_{t-1} + d_2 v_{t-1}]$$

The inflation rate is just $\Delta p_t = \pi_t$, so we can now rewrite the price-adjustment equation (5.51) as

$$\pi_t = \kappa E_{t-1}\pi_{t+1} + (1-\kappa)E_{t-1}\Delta m_t + \gamma y_{t-1} - \varphi_{t-1} \qquad (5.56)$$

where $\kappa = 1/(1+d_2)$ and $\varphi_{t-1} = \kappa[u_t - d_2 v_{t-1}]$. While this looks quite similar to the inflation equations obtained from the Taylor and Calvo specifications (see equations [5.45] and [5.50]), the presence of the expected rate of money growth makes a significant difference. For example, set $\varphi \equiv u \equiv v \equiv 0$ consider the effects of a constantly increasing, deterministic, money growth rate; $\Delta m_t = m_0 + gt$. Inflation will then be given by $\pi_t = \pi_0 + gt$. Substituting these into (5.56) gives, after some rearranging,

$$d_2\pi_0 = d_2 m_0 + g + (1+d_2)\gamma y_{t-1} \qquad (5.57)$$

But if the money demand relationship (5.36) is first differenced, $\Delta m_t - \Delta p_t = \Delta y_t - d_2^{-1}[\Delta r_t + E_t p_{t+1} - E_{t-1}p_t - \Delta p_t]$, which, since $y_t = -r_t$, can be written as

$$d_2(\Delta m_t - \pi_t) = (1+d_2)\Delta y_t - [E_t\pi_{t+1} - E_{t-1}\pi_t]$$

or

$$d_2(m_0 - \pi_0) = (1+d_2)\Delta y_t - g \qquad (5.58)$$

Adding (5.57) and (5.58),

$$\Delta y_t = -\gamma y_{t-1}$$

so that the process for output is independent of g.[55]

In contrast, from the Taylor specification, equation (5.45) implies $\pi_0 + gt = \pi_0 + g(t+1) + 2k(y_t + y_{t-1})$ or

$$\tfrac{1}{2}E(y_t + y_{t-1}) = \frac{-g}{4k} < 0$$

The p-bar adjustment model is designed to ensure that the natural-rate hypothesis holds by giving an important role to the theoretical entity $\bar{p}$, the price level that would support $y = 0$ as an equilibrium. As long as the actual price level differs from $\bar{p}$, actual prices adjust toward $\bar{p}$. The natural-rate hypothesis is enforced by the additional assumption that actual prices adjust one-for-one with expected changes in $\bar{p}$. The p-bar specification, like that of Taylor and Calvo, makes prices, but not the inflation rate, sticky (see 5.56).

---

55. Note that taking unconditional expectations of this expression yields (5.52).

5.5.4   Fuhrer and Moore's Specification

Disinflations are costly; they have normally been accompanied by below-trend growth and higher-than-average unemployment.[56] This fact suggests that it may be the inflation rate and not just the price level that exhibits some degree of stickiness. This view has been adopted by Fuhrer and Moore (1995a) in modeling the inflation process. Fuhrer and Moore assume that wage negotiations are conducted in terms of the wage relative to an average of real contract wages in effect over the life of a contract. Specifically, define the real value of contracts negotiated at time t as $x_t - p_t \equiv \psi_t$. Define the index of average "real" contract wages in contracts still in effect at time t as

$$v_t \equiv \tfrac{1}{2}(\psi_t + \psi_{t-1}) \tag{5.59}$$

Fuhrer and Moore (1995a) assume that in setting x_t, agents take two factors into account. First, they attempt to achieve a current real contract price equal to the expected average of the real contract index over the two-period life of the contract, $\tfrac{1}{2}(v_t + E_t v_{t+1})$. Second, the contracted real price can deviate from this average expected index to reflect the current state of the business cycle, $k y_t$.[57] Combining these assumptions with (5.59) yields

$$\psi_t = \tfrac{1}{2}(v_t + E_t v_{t+1}) + k y_t$$
$$= \tfrac{1}{4}(\psi_{t-1} + 2\psi_t + E_t \psi_{t+1}) + k y_t$$
$$= \tfrac{1}{2}(\psi_{t-1} + E_t \psi_{t+1}) + 2 k y_t$$

Recalling that $\psi_t = x_t - p_t$, this can be rewritten as

$$x_t - p_t = \tfrac{1}{2}(x_{t-1} - p_{t-1} + E_t[x_{t+1} - p_{t+1}]) + 2 k y_t \tag{5.60}$$

which highlights the difference between the Taylor specification in (5.44) and the Fuhrer-Moore specification in (5.60). After some rearranging, (5.60) can be written in terms of the rate of change in the contract wage as

$$\Delta x_t = \tfrac{1}{2}(\pi_t + E_t \pi_{t+1}) + 2 k y_t \tag{5.61}$$

---

56. Ball (1993, 1994b) provides some evidence on the costs of disinflations. As noted in Chapter 1, Sargent (1986) has argued that hyperinflations have often ended with relatively little output cost.

57. Fuhrer and Moore also allow the real contract wage to respond to the expected state of the business cycle by including $E_t y_{t+1}$ in the equation for ψ_t. We follow Roberts (1997) in excluding this factor in order to focus on the main differences between the Taylor specification and that of Fuhrer and Moore.

With the price level equal to $0.5(x_t + x_{t-1})$, inflation is given by $\pi_t = 0.5(\Delta x_t + \Delta x_{t-1})$, implying

$$\pi_t = \tfrac{1}{2}(\pi_{t-1} + E_t\pi_{t+1}) + 2k(y_t + y_{t-1}) + \tfrac{1}{2}\eta_t \qquad (5.62)$$

where $\eta_t = -[\pi_t - E_{t-1}\pi_t]$.[58] Contrasting this with the inflation equation (5.45) shows that the Fuhrer-Moore specification imparts a sluggishness to inflation adjustment; new information about current or future monetary policy that becomes available at the start of period t can be reflected in $E_t\pi_{t+1}$ but not, by definition, in π_{t-1}. Therefore, the flexibility of current inflation to jump in response to new information is limited. An announced disinflation will not leave output unaffected. In the Fuhrer-Moore specification, the backward-looking nature of the *inflation* process implies that reductions in the growth rate of money will be costly in terms of output.

Whether price stickiness or inflation stickiness best characterizes actual inflation processes is an open empirical issue. Fuhrer and Moore (1995a) argue that their specification fits U.S. data better than the Taylor model does. Roberts (1997) provides some evidence favoring the sticky-price version. However, he also shows that equation (5.62) could arise under the sticky-price model if expectations are not rational. Recall that η_t in (5.45) was equal to $-(p_t - E_{t-1}p_t) = -(\pi_t - E_{t-1}\pi_t)$. Under the assumption of rational expectations, this expectational error will be uncorrelated with information available at time $t - 1$, the date at which the expectation is formed. Suppose instead that expectations are actually better proxied as an average of rational expectations and a simple extrapolation of current inflation. In this case, the expectation of future inflation in (5.45) would be replaced by $0.5(E_t\pi_{t+1} + \pi_t)$, while the previous period's expectation of π_t would equal $0.5(E_{t-1}\pi_t + \pi_{t-1})$. With these substitutions, the Taylor model can be written

$$\pi_t = \tfrac{1}{2}(\pi_{t-1} + E_t\pi_{t+1}) + 2k(y_t + y_{t-1}) + \tfrac{1}{2}\eta_t$$

which is of exactly the same form as (5.62). Based on an analysis of survey measures

---

58. Using (5.61),

$$\pi_t = 0.5(\Delta x_t + \Delta x_{t-1})$$

$$= \frac{1}{4}(\pi_t + E_t\pi_{t+1}) + ky_t + \frac{1}{4}(\pi_{t-1} + E_{t-1}\pi_t) + ky_{t-1}$$

$$= \frac{1}{4}(\pi_t + E_t\pi_{t+1}) + ky_t + \frac{1}{4}(\pi_{t-1} + \pi_t) + ky_{t-1} + \frac{1}{4}\eta_t$$

Rearranging yields equation (5.62).

of inflation expectations for the United States, Roberts concludes that the evidence supports the view that inflation-rate stickiness actually arises from the presence of less than perfectly rational expectations.[59]

Is it the inflation process that is sticky? Or is it just that expectations are sticky? The distinction is important for understanding the costs of policies to lower inflation and the role of credibility. Disinflations must inevitably create recessions if inflation is sticky; they need do so under price-level stickiness only if the policy lacks full credibility. In evaluating the eventual behavior of inflation after the adjustment to a change in policy, the assumption of rational expectations is likely to be appropriate. Otherwise, one is left with the unsatisfactory presumption that the public never fully learns about the policy. During transitional periods, as the way in which policy is conducted changes, the assumption of fully rational expectations may be inappropriate; backward-looking expectational behavior may play an important role in expectations formation. Predicting the effects of a change in policy may require that both types of behavior be recognized.[60]

5.6 Summary

Three major issues in monetary economics have been addressed in this chapter. First, we have examined how the models of Chapters 2–4, models that were useful for examining issues such as the welfare cost of inflation and the optimal inflation tax, need to be modified to account for the short-run effects of monetary factors on the economy. The necessary modification requires recognition that most wages and prices are not adjusted instantaneously in response to changes in economic conditions. Second, we have made a transition from the fully specified general equilibrium models in which equilibrium conditions are based on agents' decision rules and resource constraints to the type of models commonly employed to study policy issues. Finally, we have examined some standard models of price adjustment.

In subsequent chapters, the framework of section 5.4 will be used to study a variety of monetary-policy issues. However, an important omission must first be addressed: the analysis has so far dealt only with a closed economy. Monetary policy can affect the economy through additional channels once the linkages between economies are

---

59. The dependence of expected inflation on lagged actual inflation need not reflect less than fully rational expectations. For example, suppose the public is uncertain as to the central bank's target rate of inflation. The public may base its beliefs about this target value on observed inflation under Bayesian updating.

60. Taylor (1975) provided an early analysis of monetary policy during the transition to rational expectations. In his model, the monetary authority could influence the rate at which the public learned about policy by following a randomized rule for inflation.

recognized. Domestic output and prices will depend on exchange rates, which in turn may depend on monetary policy. In the next chapter, the policy framework of section 5.4 will be modified to incorporate open-economy factors.

5.7 Appendix

5.7.1 An Imperfect-Information Model

Lucas's imperfect-information model generated real output effects of monetary surprises because individual agents faced a signal-extraction problem; if prices in local markets rose, agents needed to estimate to what extent these increases represented an economy-wide general rise in the price level versus a rise in local prices relative to the economy-wide average.

The equilibrium in local market i, or island i, could be represented by the following four equations:

$$y_t^i = (1 - \alpha)n_t^i \tag{5.63}$$

$$y_t^i = c_t^i \tag{5.64}$$

$$d_1 n_t^i = y_t^i - \Phi c_t^i + b(1 - \Phi)(m_t^i - p_t^i) \tag{5.65}$$

$$d_0(c_t^i - m_t^i + p_t^i) = E^i(p_{t+1} - p_t^i) - E^i \tau_{t+1}$$
$$+ E^i\{\Phi(c_{t+1} - c_t^i) - b(1 - \Phi)(m_{t+1} - p_{t+1} - m_t^i + p_t^i)\} \tag{5.66}$$

where m^i denotes the *nominal* supply of money on island i, $d_1 = \left(1 + \eta \dfrac{n^{ss}}{1 - n^{ss}}\right)$, and $d_0 = (1 - \beta)/\beta$. In addition, E^i denotes the expectation conditional on island i information. Both η and Φ are nonnegative parameters from the utility function of the representative agent $\left\{ u(C^i, M^i/P^i) = \dfrac{1}{1 - \Phi}[C^i(M^i/P^i)^b]^{1-\Phi} + \Psi \dfrac{1}{1 - \eta}(1 - N^i)^{1-\eta} \right.$ where the uppercase letters denote the levels of the relevant variables $\left. \right\}$. The appendix to Chapter 2 contains a more complete derivation of the basic MIU model. Equation (5.65) is derived from the condition that the marginal utility of leisure divided by the marginal utility of consumption must equal the marginal product of labor. Equation (5.66) is derived from the first-order condition that, for an agent on island i,

$$u_c^i(t) = u_m^i(t) + \beta E^i\left(\frac{T}{\Pi}\right)u_c(t + 1) \tag{5.67}$$

where the left side is the cost in terms of utility of reducing consumption marginally in order to hold more money, and the right side is the return from higher money holdings. This return consists of the direct utility yield $u_m(t)$, plus the utility from using the real balances to increase consumption in period $t+1$. With transfers viewed as proportional to money holdings, the individual treats money as if it yielded a real return of T/Π. This is valued using $E^i u_c(t+1)$ rather than $E^i u_c^i(t+1)$ since agents are randomly relocated across islands. Given the assumed utility function, both sides of (5.67) can be divided by $u_c^i(t)$ and written as

$$
1 = \frac{b(C_t^i)^{1-\Phi}\left(\dfrac{M_t^i}{P_t^i}\right)^{b(1-\Phi)-1}}{(C_t^i)^{-\Phi}\left(\dfrac{M_t^i}{P_t^i}\right)^{b(1-\Phi)}} + \frac{\beta E^i\left(\dfrac{T}{\Pi}\right)C_{t+1}^{-\Phi}\left(\dfrac{M_{t+1}}{P_{t+1}}\right)^{b(1-\Phi)}}{(C_t^i)^{-\Phi}\left(\dfrac{M_t^i}{P_t^i}\right)^{b(1-\Phi)}}
$$

$$
= \frac{bC_t^i}{\left(\dfrac{M_t^i}{P_t^i}\right)} + \frac{\beta E^i\left(\dfrac{T}{\Pi}\right)C_{t+1}^{-\Phi}\left(\dfrac{M_{t+1}}{P_{t+1}}\right)^{b(1-\Phi)}}{(C_t^i)^{-\Phi}\left(\dfrac{M_t^i}{P_t^i}\right)^{b(1-\Phi)}}
$$

Expressed in terms of percentage deviations around the steady state (denoted by lowercase letters), the two terms on the right side become

$$
\frac{bC_t^i}{\left(\dfrac{M_t^i}{P_t^i}\right)} = b\,\frac{C^{ss}}{\left(\dfrac{M^{ss}}{P^{ss}}\right)}[1 + c_t^i - m_t^i + p_t^i]
$$

and

$$
\frac{\beta E^i\left(\dfrac{T}{\Pi}\right)C_{t+1}^{-\Phi}\left(\dfrac{M_{t+1}}{P_{t+1}}\right)^{b(1-\Phi)}}{C_t^{-\Phi}\left(\dfrac{M_t^i}{P_t^i}\right)^{b(1-\Phi)}} = \beta E^i\left(\dfrac{T^{ss}}{\Pi^{ss}}\right)(1 + \tau_{t+1} - \pi_{t+1}^i)
$$

$$
\times [1 - \Phi\Delta c_{t+1} + b(1-\Phi)(\Delta m_{t+1} - \Delta p_{t+1})]
$$

$$
\approx \beta E^i[1 + \tau_{t+1} - \pi_{t+1}^i - \Phi\Delta c_{t+1}
$$

$$
+ b(1-\Phi)(\Delta m_{t+1} - \Delta p_{t+1})]
$$

where Δ is the first difference operator ($\Delta c_{t+1} = c_{t+1} - c_t^i$) and we have used the fact that in the steady state, $T^{ss} = \Pi^{ss}$. This also implies

$$1 = b \frac{C^{ss}}{\left(\frac{M^{ss}}{P^{ss}}\right)} + \beta E^i \left(\frac{T^{ss}}{\Pi^{ss}}\right) = b \frac{C^{ss}}{\left(\frac{M^{ss}}{P^{ss}}\right)} + \beta \tag{5.68}$$

and the first-order condition becomes

$$0 = b \frac{C^{ss}}{\left(\frac{M^{ss}}{P^{ss}}\right)} [c_t^i - m_t^i + p_t^i]$$

$$+ \beta E^i [\tau_{t+1} - \pi_{t+1}^i - \Phi \Delta c_{t+1} + b(1 - \Phi)(\Delta m_{t+1} - \Delta p_{t+1})]$$

Finally, since $d_1 n_t^i - y_t^i = -\Phi c_t^i + b(1 - \Phi)(m_t^i - p_t^i)$ from (5.65),

$$\frac{bC^{ss}}{\beta \left(\frac{M^{ss}}{P^{ss}}\right)} [c_t^i - m_t^i + p_t^i] = -E^i \tau_{t+1} + E^i \pi_{t+1}^i - d_1 E^i \Delta n_{t+1} + E^i \Delta y_{t+1}$$

which is equation (5.4) of the text, where $d_0 = bC^{ss}/\beta \left(\frac{M^{ss}}{P^{ss}}\right) = (1 - \beta)/\beta$ from (5.68).

The nominal money supply on island i is assumed to evolve according to

$$m_t^i = \gamma m_{t-1} + v_t + u_t + u_t^i$$

with u^i equal to an island-specific money shock that averages to zero across all islands and has variance σ_i^2. Both v and u are aggregate disturbances (common across all islands), each assumed to have zero mean and variances σ_v^2 and σ_u^2. The value of v is announced (or observed) at the start of period t. The aggregate average nominal money supply evolves as

$$m_t = \gamma m_{t-1} + v_t + u_t$$

Therefore, the aggregate transfer τ_t is given by

$$\tau_t = m_t - m_{t-1} = (\gamma - 1)m_{t-1} + v_t + u_t$$

Individuals on island i observe the island-specific nominal money stock m_t^i. Observing m_t^i allows them to infer $u_t + u_t^i$ but not u and u^i separately. The expectation of the time $t + 1$ money supply, conditional on the information available on island i, will be $E^i m_{t+1} = \gamma^2 m_{t-1} + \gamma v_t + \gamma E^i u_t$. Equating expectations with linear least squares projections,

$$E^i u_t = \kappa(u_t + u_t^i)$$

where $\kappa = \sigma_u^2/(\sigma_u^2 + \sigma_i^2)$.   Hence, $E_t\tau_{t+1} = E_tm_{t+1} - E^im_t = (\gamma - 1)E^im_t + E^i[v_{t+1} + u_{t+1}] = (\gamma - 1)E^im_t = (\gamma - 1)[\gamma m_{t-1} + v_t + \kappa(u_t + u_t^i)]$.

Eliminating output, consumption, and the expected transfer from (5.63)–(5.66), these equations yield the following two-equation system for employment and prices:

$$n_t^i = A(m_t^i - p_t^i) \tag{5.69}$$

$$E^i\{b(1 - \Phi)(m_{t+1} - p_{t+1} - m_t^i + p_t^i) - \Phi(1 - \alpha)(n_{t+1} - n_t^i)\}$$

$$- E^i(p_{t+1} - p_t^i) + (\gamma - 1)E^im_t$$

$$= d_0[m_t^i - p_t^i - (1 - \alpha)n_t^i] \tag{5.70}$$

where $A = b(1 - \Phi)/[d_1 - (1 - \alpha)(1 - \Phi)] > 0$, since $d_1 = 1 + \eta n^{ss}/(1 - n^{ss}) > 1$ and we have assumed $0 < \Phi < 1$.

By substituting (5.69) into (5.70), we can obtain a single equation that involves the price process and the exogenous nominal money supply process:

$$[b(1 - \Phi) - \Phi(1 - \alpha)A]E^i[m_{t+1} - p_{t+1} - m_t^i + p_t^i]$$

$$- (E^i[p_{t+1}] - p_t^i) + (\gamma - 1)E^i[m_t]$$

$$= d_0[1 - (1 - \alpha)A](m_t^i - p_t^i) \tag{5.71}$$

Equation (5.71) can be solved using the method of undetermined coefficients (see McCallum 1989; Attfield, Demery, and Duck 1991). This method involves guessing a solution for p_t^i and then verifying that the solution is consistent with (5.71). Since m_t depends on m_{t-1}, v_t, u_t, and u_t^i, our guess for the minimum state-variable solution (McCallum 1983a) for the equilibrium price level takes the following form:

$$p_t^i = a_1 m_{t-1} + a_2 v_t + a_3 u_t + a_4 u_t^i \tag{5.72}$$

where the a_j's are yet-to-be determined parameters. Equation (5.72) implies that the aggregate price level is $p_t = a_1 m_{t-1} + a_2 v_t + a_3 u_t$, so

$$E^i p_{t+1} = a_1 E^i m_t$$

$$= a_1(\gamma m_{t-1} + v_t + E^i u_t)$$

$$= a_1[\gamma m_{t-1} + v_t + \kappa(u_t + u_t^i)]$$

We are now in a position to evaluate all the terms in (5.71). The left-hand side of (5.71) is equal to

$$[b(1 - \Phi) - \Phi(1 - \alpha)A]\{\gamma^2 m_{t-1} + \gamma v_t + \gamma\kappa(u_t + u_t^i) - a_1[\gamma m_{t-1} + v_t + \kappa(u_t + u_t^i)]$$

$$- \gamma m_{t-1} - v_t - u_t - u_t^i + a_1 m_{t-1} + a_2 v_t + a_3 u_t + a_4 u_t^i\}$$

$$- \{a_1[\gamma m_{t-1} + v_t + \kappa(u_t + u_t^i)] - a_1 m_{t-1} - a_2 v_t - a_3 u_t - a_4 u_t^i\}$$

$$+ (\gamma - 1)[\gamma m_{t-1} + v_t + \kappa(u_t + u_t^i)]$$

while the right-hand side will equal

$$d_0[1 - (1 - \alpha)A](\gamma m_{t-1} + v_t + u_t + u_t^i - a_1 m_{t-1} - a_2 v_t - a_3 u_t - a_4 u_t^i)$$

For these two to be equal for all possible realizations of m_{t-1}, v_t, u_t, and u_t^i requires that the following hold: the coefficient on m_{t-1} on the right side must be equal to the coefficient on the left side, or

$$[b(1 - \Phi) - \Phi(1 - \alpha)A](\gamma - 1)(\gamma - a_1) + (\gamma - 1)(\gamma - a_1)$$

$$= d_0[1 - (1 - \alpha)A](\gamma - a_1)$$

which requires that $a_1 = \gamma$; the coefficient on v_t on the right side must be equal to the coefficient on the left side, or

$$-[b(1 - \Phi) - \Phi(1 - \alpha)A](1 - a_2) - (1 - a_2) = d_0[1 - (1 - \alpha)A](1 - a_2)$$

or $a_2 = 1$; the coefficient on u_t on the right side must be equal to the coefficient on the left side, or

$$[b(1 - \Phi) - \Phi(1 - \alpha)A](a_3 - 1) + a_3 - \kappa$$

$$= d_0[1 - (1 - \alpha)A](1 - a_3)$$

or $a_3 = (\kappa + K)/(1 + K) < 1$ where $K = d_0[1 - (1 - \alpha)A] + b(1 - \Phi) - \Phi(1 - \alpha)A$; and, finally, the coefficient on u_t^i on the right side must be equal to the coefficient on the left side, or

$$[b(1 - \Phi) - \Phi(1 - \alpha)A](a_4 - 1) + a_4 - \kappa$$

$$= d_0[1 - (1 - \alpha)A](1 - a_4)$$

or $a_4 = a_3$.

Combining these results, we have the expressions for the equilibrium economy-wide price level and employment given by equations (5.6) and (5.7) of the text.

5.7.2   A Sticky-Price MIU Model

In this section, an MIU model is modified to include one-period nominal wage contracts. The equations characterizing equilibrium in the flexible-price MIU model are:

$$y_t = \alpha k_{t-1} + (1 - \alpha)n_t + z_t \tag{5.73}$$

$$\left(\frac{y^{ss}}{k^{ss}}\right)y_t = \left(\frac{c^{ss}}{k^{ss}}\right)c_t + k_t - (1 - \delta)k_{t-1} \tag{5.74}$$

$$r_t = d_3(E_t y_{t+1} - k_t) \tag{5.75}$$

$$E_t[c_{t+1}] - c_t - r_t = 0 \tag{5.76}$$

$$n_t = \frac{w_t - p_t - c_t}{d_1 - 1} \tag{5.77}$$

$$i_t \equiv r_t + E_t[p_{t+1} - p_t] = d_2(c_t - m_t + p_t) \tag{5.78}$$

where, as earlier, $d_1 \equiv \left(1 + \eta \dfrac{n^{ss}}{1 - n^{ss}}\right)$, $d_2 \equiv (\Theta - \beta)/\beta$, and equation (5.75) is now written more conveniently in terms of $d_3 \equiv \dfrac{\alpha}{R^{ss}}\left(\dfrac{y^{ss}}{k^{ss}}\right)$.[61]

If firms equate the real wage to the marginal product of labor, employment will be given by

$$n_t = y_t - (w_t^c - p_t)$$

where w^c is the contract wage. Assume the nominal contract wage is set to equate expected labor demand to expected labor supply. From (5.77), expected labor supply is equal to $E_{t-1}[w_t^c - p_t - c_t]/(d_1 - 1)$, so the contract nominal wage w^c that equates expected labor supply and demand will be

$$w_t^c = E_{t-1}p_t + (1 - d_1^{-1})E_{t-1}y_t + d_1^{-1}E_{t-1}c_t$$

The nominal contract wage adjusts fully to changes in price expectations; such adjustments reflect the dependence of both labor demand and labor supply on the real wage.

---

61. Equation (5.77) was earlier written as $d_1 n_t = y_t - c_t$. To write this in a form that expresses labor supply as a function of the real wage, in log form, it has been transformed as $(d_1 - 1)n_t = (y_t - n_t) - c_t = (w_t - p_t) - c_t$, where $y_t - n_t$ is the marginal product of labor (in terms of percentage deviations from the steady state), given the assumption of a Cobb-Douglas production function.

From the production function, actual output is

$$y_t = \alpha k_{t-1} + (1 - \alpha)(y_t - w_t^c + p_t) + z_t$$

$$= k_{t-1} + a(p_t - E_{t-1}p_t) - a(1 - d_1^{-1})E_{t-1}y_t - ad_1^{-1}E_{t-1}c_t + \alpha^{-1}z_t \qquad (5.79)$$

where $a = (1 - \alpha)/\alpha$. Taking expectations as of $t - 1$ and using (5.76) to replace $E_{t-1}c_t$ with $c_{t-1} + r_{t-1}$ while using (5.75) to replace r_{t-1} with $d_3(E_{t-1}y_t - k_{t-1})$ results in

$$E_{t-1}y_t = k_{t-1} - a(1 - d_1^{-1})E_{t-1}y_t - ad_1^{-1}c_{t-1} - ad_1^{-1}d_3(E_{t-1}y_t - k_{t-1}) + \alpha^{-1}E_{t-1}z_t$$

$$= \phi_k k_{t-1} - \phi_c c_{t-1} + \phi_z E_{t-1}z_t \qquad (5.80)$$

where

$$\phi_k = \frac{1 + ad_1^{-1}d_3}{1 + a(1 - d_1^{-1}) + ad_1^{-1}d_3} > 0$$

and

$$\phi_c = \frac{ad_1^{-1}}{1 + a(1 - d_1^{-1}) + ad_1^{-1}d_3} > 0$$

and

$$\phi_z = \frac{\alpha^{-1}}{1 + a(1 - \alpha_1^{-1}) + ad_1^{-1}d_3} > 0$$

The role of c_{t-1} arises because labor supply depends on the real wage and the marginal utility of consumption (see, for example, equation [5.12]). Ceteris paribus, higher consumption at time $t - 1$ implies higher expected consumption at time t (see equation [5.11]). This, in turn, implies a lower marginal utility of time-t consumption, an increased demand for leisure, and a lower expected supply of labor. Hence, expected time-t output is decreasing in c_{t-1}. Combining (5.79) and (5.80),

$$y_t = a[p_t - E_{t-1}p_t] + \phi_k k_{t-1} - \phi_c c_{t-1} + \phi_z E_{t-1}z_t + \varepsilon_t$$

where $\varepsilon_t = (z_t - E_{t-1}z_t)/\alpha$.

Assuming the nominal money supply follows a first-order autoregressive process of the form $m_t = \gamma m_{t-1} + u_t$, the same simulation method as employed in Chapters 2 and 3 can be used to determine the dynamic impact of a shock to the nominal money supply. Recall that this system was derived from the basic MIU model of

Chapter 2 under the assumption of log-separable utility: $\Phi = 1$. As was shown in Chapter 2, this specification implied that monetary shocks had no real effects. So any real effects of a realization of u arise solely from the presence of nominal wage contracts.

The aggregate-demand side of the model incorporates equations (5.76) and (5.75) to determine optimal consumption and investment. Making use of these, the economy's resource constraint can be written as

$$y_t = \left(\frac{c^{ss}}{y^{ss}}\right)c_t + \left(\frac{k^{ss}}{y^{ss}}\right)x_t$$

$$= \left(\frac{c^{ss}}{y^{ss}}\right)[E_t c_{t+1} - r_t] + \left(\frac{k^{ss}}{y^{ss}}\right)x_t$$

where x_t is investment. Using the resource constraint once again, $E_t c_{t+1}$ can be eliminated, yielding

$$y_t = E_t y_{t+1} - \left(\frac{c^{ss}}{y^{ss}}\right)r_t - \left(\frac{k^{ss}}{y^{ss}}\right)[E_t x_{t+1} - x_t]$$

The last term in this equation, $E_t x_{t+1} - x_t$, is the expected change in the capital stock. McCallum and Nelson (1997) have argued that, for most monetary-policy and business-cycle analyses, fluctuations in the stock of capital do not play a major role. In their log-linear approximation for aggregate demand, they ignore this final term, setting it equal to a constant. Following their lead, we are left with aggregate demand as a function of expected future income and the real rate of interest.[62] Expected future income matters for demand in the current period because consumption is determined by forward-looking, optimizing households. A rise in expected future income immediately raises current real consumption demand. The importance of incorporating a role for future income has been emphasized by Kerr and King (1996).

The last component of the model is equation (5.78). Using (5.74) and (5.75), consumption is equal to $\left(\frac{y^{ss}}{c^{ss}}\right)y_t - \left(\frac{k^{ss}}{c^{ss}}\right)[E_t y_{t+1} - d_3^{-1} r_t - (1-\delta)k_{t-1}]$. Equation (5.78) can then be written in the form of a money-demand equation as

$$m_t - p_t = \left(\frac{y^{ss}}{c^{ss}}\right)y_t - \left(\frac{k^{ss}}{c^{ss}}\right)[E_t y_{t+1} - d_3^{-1} r_t - (1-\delta)k_{t-1}] - d_2^{-1} i_t$$

---

62. In the text, capital is ignored completely so that $c^{ss} = y^{ss}$ and the coefficient on r becomes equal to -1.

Notice that expected future income affects the demand for money. Higher expected income raises investment; for a given level of current output, this increase implies lower consumption and therefore lower money demand, since money demand depends on the level of consumption.[63]

We can now collect the equations of the model:

Aggregate supply: $y_t = a(p_t - E_{t-1}p_t) - \phi_k k_{t-1} + \phi_c c_{t-1} + \phi_z E_{t-1}z_t + \varepsilon_t$

Aggregate demand: $y_t = E_t y_{t+1} - \left(\dfrac{c^{ss}}{y^{ss}}\right) r_t + u_t$

Money demand: $m_t - p_t = \left(\dfrac{y^{ss}}{c^{ss}}\right) y_t - \left(\dfrac{k^{ss}}{c^{ss}}\right)[E_t y_{t+1} - d_3^{-1}r_t - (1-\delta)k_{t-1}] - d_2^{-1}i_t$

Fisher equation: $i_t = r_t + E_t p_{t+1} - p_t$

where $u_t \equiv -\left(\dfrac{k^{ss}}{y^{ss}}\right)[E_t x_{t+1} - x_t]$.

The version of this model discussed in the text is further simplified by setting $\delta = 1$ (which implies $d_3 = 1$), eliminating the capital stock, and letting $\eta \to \infty$ (which implies $d_1 \to \infty$). Under these assumptions, $\phi_k = \phi_c = 0$, $\phi_z = 1$, $\left(\dfrac{c^{ss}}{y^{ss}}\right) = 1$, and $\left(\dfrac{k^{ss}}{y^{ss}}\right) = 0$.

5.7.3   A Simple AS-IS-LM Model

This section discusses the derivation of the rational-expectations solution to (5.34)–(5.37) when m_t follows the policy rule given by (5.43). The basic equations of the model when $E_{t-1}z_t = 0$ are repeated here:

$$y_t = a(p_t - E_{t-1}p_t) + \varepsilon_t \tag{5.81}$$

$$y_t = -r_t + u_t \tag{5.82}$$

$$m_t - p_t = y_t - d_2^{-1}i_t + v_t \tag{5.83}$$

$$i_t = r_t + E_t p_{t+1} - p_t \tag{5.84}$$

---

63. It may be useful to review why consumption is the scale variable for money demand. In the money-in-the-utility-function model, the ratio of the marginal utility of money to the marginal utility of consumption is set equal to the opportunity cost of holding money. It is because the marginal utility of consumption depends on the level of consumption that c_t appears in (5.78).

Using the Fisher relationship and the aggregate-demand equation, (5.83) can be written as

$$d_2(m_t - p_t) = d_2 y_t + (y_t - u_t) - E_t p_{t+1} + p_t + d_2 v_t$$

Now use the aggregate-supply function (5.81) to eliminate output:

$$d_2(m_t - p_t) = (1 + d_2)[a(p_t - E_{t-1}p_t) + \varepsilon_t] - u_t - E_t p_{t+1} + p_t + d_2 v_t$$

Solving for p_t yields

$$p_t = \frac{d_2 m_t + a(1 + d_2)E_{t-1}p_t + E_t p_{t+1} - d_2 v_t + u_t - (1 + d_2)\varepsilon_t}{(1 + a)(1 + d_2)} \tag{5.85}$$

In order to solve for the equilibrium-price process, assume the money supply is given by equation (5.43), repeated here as

$$m_t = \mu + m_{t-1} + a_1 u_t + a_2 \varepsilon_t + a_3 v_t + \omega_t \tag{5.86}$$

Since the state at time t is characterized by m_{t-1} and the current realizations of the disturbances, assume that the equilibrium price level is given by

$$p_t = b_0 + m_{t-1} + b_1 u_t + b_2 \varepsilon_t + b_3 v_t + b_4 \omega_t \tag{5.87}$$

where the b_i's are unknown coefficients. Notice that we have already imposed the condition that the coefficient on m_{t-1} is equal to 1. This follows from the neutrality of anticipated money; the value of m_{t-1} is fully reflected in prices in period t. This result could be derived directly by attaching a coefficient to m_{t-1} and proceeding to derive its equilibrium value; doing so would confirm that it equals 1.

This proposed solution implies that

$$E_{t-1}p_t = b_0 + m_{t-1}$$

and

$$E_t p_{t+1} = b_0 + m_t$$
$$= b_0 + (\mu + m_{t-1} + a_1 u_t + a_2 \varepsilon_t + a_3 v_t + \omega_t)$$

Now use these results in (5.85):

$$p_t = h d_2(\mu + m_{t-1} + a_1 u_t + a_2 \varepsilon_t + a_3 v_t + \omega_t) + ha(1 + d_2)(b_0 + m_{t-1})$$
$$+ h(b_0 + \mu + m_{t-1} + a_1 u_t + a_2 \varepsilon_t + a_3 v_t + \omega_t)$$
$$- h[d_2 v_t - u_t + (1 + d_2)\varepsilon_t] \tag{5.88}$$

where

$$h = \frac{1}{(1+a)(1+d_2)}$$

We now have, in (5.87) and (5.88), two expressions for p_t. Setting them equal to each other, the resulting equation will hold for all realizations of m_{t-1} and the random disturbances if the following conditions on the coefficients hold:

$$b_1 = hd_2a_1 + ha_1 + h \Leftrightarrow b_1 = \frac{a_1(1+d_2)+1}{(1+a)(1+d_2)}$$

$$b_2 = hd_2a_2 + ha_2 - h(1+d_2) \Leftrightarrow b_2 = \frac{(a_2-1)}{(1+a)}$$

$$b_3 = h(d_2a_3 + a_3 - d_2) \Leftrightarrow b_3 = \frac{a_3(1+d_2)-d_2}{(1+a)(1+d_2)}$$

$$b_4 = hd_2 + h \Leftrightarrow b_4 = \frac{(1+d_2)}{(1+a)(1+d_2)} = \frac{1}{1+a}$$

$$b_0 = hd_2\mu + ha(1+d_2)b_0 + hb_0 + h\mu \Leftrightarrow b_0 = \frac{\mu(1+d_2)}{d_2}$$

Given that we now have the solution for the price level, (5.34) can be used to obtain equilibrium output, while (5.35) and (5.37) will yield expressions for the equilibrium real and nominal interest rates.

5.8 Problems

1. Assume household preferences are given by $U = \dfrac{\left[c\left(\dfrac{M^b}{P}\right)\right]^{1-\Phi}}{1-\Phi} + \Psi\dfrac{(1-N)^{1-\eta}}{1-\eta}$
and aggregate output is given by $Y = K^\alpha N^{1-\alpha}$. Linearize around the steady state the labor-market equilibrium condition equation (5.26) from the monopolistic competition model. How does the result depend on q? Explain.

2. The Chari, Kehoe, and McGratten (1996) model of price adjustment led to equation (5.30). Using equation (5.29), show that the parameter a in (5.30) equals $(1-\sqrt{\gamma})/(1+\sqrt{\gamma})$.

3. Equation (5.28) was obtained from equation (5.27) by assuming $R = 1$. Show that, in general,

$$\bar{p}_t = \left(\frac{R^{ss}}{1 + R^{ss}}\right)\left[p_t + \frac{1}{R^{ss}}E_t p_{t+1}\right] + \left(\frac{R^{ss}}{1 + R^{ss}}\right)\left[v_t + \frac{1}{R^{ss}}E_t v_{t+1}\right]$$

4. Using the equilibrium condition (5.42) for the price level, show that equilibrium output is independent of any policy response to ε_{t-1} or v_{t-1}.

5. Assume nominal wages are set for one period but that they can be indexed to the price level:

$$w_t^c = w_t^0 + b(p_t - E_{t-1}p_t)$$

where w^0 is a base wage and b is the indexation parameter ($0 \le b \le 1$).

a. How does this change modify the aggregate-supply equation given by (5.18)?

b. Assume the indexation parameter is set to minimize $E_{t-1}(n_t - \bar{n})^2$. Using your modified aggregate-supply equation, together with (5.35)–(5.37) and a money-supply process $m_t = \omega_t$, show that the optimal degree of wage indexation is increasing in the variance of ω and decreasing in the variance of ε (Gray 1978).

6. The basic Taylor model of price-level adjustment was derived under the assumption that the nominal wage set in period t remained unchanged for periods t and $t+1$. Suppose instead that each period-t contract specifies a nominal wage x_t^1 for period t and x_t^2 for period $t+1$. Assume these are given by $x_t^1 = p_t + \kappa y_t$ and $x_t^2 = E_t p_{t+1} + \kappa E_t y_{t+1}$. The aggregate price level at time t is equal to $p_t = \frac{1}{2}(x_t^1 + x_{t-1}^2)$. If aggregate demand is given by $y_t = m_t - p_t$ and $m_t = m_0 + \omega_t$, what is the effect of a money shock ω_t on p_t and y_t? Explain why output shows no persistence after a money shock.

7. The p-bar model led to the following two equations for p_t and y_t:

$$p_t = \frac{d_2 m_t + E_t p_{t+1} - d_2 v_t + u_t}{1 + d_2} - y_t$$

$$y_t = \frac{d_2(m_t - E_{t-1}m_t) + E_t p_{t+1} - E_{t-1}p_{t+1} - d_2 v_t + u_t}{1 + d_2} + (1 - \gamma)y_{t-1}$$

Assume $\gamma = 1$ and

$$m_t = m_{t-1} + a u_t$$

Show that the variance of y_t depends on the parameter a. What value of a would minimize the impact of IS shocks (u) on output?

8. Derive the equilibrium expression for p_t and y_t corresponding to equations (5.39) and (5.41) for the case in which the aggregate productivity disturbance is given by $z_t = \rho z_{t-1} + e_t$, $-1 < \rho < 1$.

9. Suppose that the nominal money supply evolves according to $m_t = \mu + \gamma m_{t-1} + \omega_t$ for $0 < \gamma < 1$ and ω_t a white-noise control error. If the rest of the economy is characterized by equations (5.34)–(5.37), solve for the equilibrium expressions for the price level, output, and nominal rate of interest. What is the effect of a positive money shock ($\omega_t > 0$) on the nominal rate? How does this result compare to the $\gamma = 1$ case discussed in the text? Explain.

10. An increase in average inflation lowers the real demand for money. Demonstrate this relationship by using the model given by equations (5.34)–(5.37) and assuming the nominal money supply grows at a constant trend rate μ so that $m_t = \mu t$ and show that real money balances $m_t - p_t$ are decreasing in μ.

6 Money and the Open Economy

6.1 Introduction

The analysis in Chapters 2–5 was conducted within the context of a closed economy. Many useful insights into monetary phenomena can be obtained while still abstracting from the linkages that tie different economies together, but clearly many issues do require an open-economy framework if they are to be adequately addressed. New channels through which monetary factors can influence the economy arise in open economies. Exchange-rate movements, for example, play an important role in the transmission process that links monetary disturbances to output and inflation movements.[1] Open economies face the possibility of economic disturbances that originate in other countries, and this raises questions of monetary-policy design that are absent in a closed-economy environment: Should policy respond to exchange-rate movements? Should monetary policy be used to stabilize exchange rates? Should national monetary policies be coordinated?

In this chapter, we begin section 6.2 by studying a two-country model based on Obstfeld and Rogoff (1995, 1996). The two-country model has the advantage of capturing some of the important linkages between economies while still maintaining a degree of simplicity and tractability. It can be used to examine monetary-policy interactions that are absent from the closed-economy models utilized in previous chapters. Because an open economy is linked to other economies, policy actions in one economy have the potential to affect equilibrium in other economies. Spillovers can occur. Policy actions in one country will depend on the response of monetary policy in the other. Often, because of these spillovers, countries attempt to coordinate their policy actions. The role of policy coordination is examined in section 6.3 within the context of a simple two-country model.

Section 6.4 considers the case of a "small open economy." In the open-economy literature, a small open economy denotes an economy that is too small to affect world prices, interest rates, or economic activity. Since many countries really are "small" relative to the world economy, the small-open-economy model provides a framework that is relevant for studying many policy issues.

The analyses of policy coordination and the small open economy are conducted using models that are similar to those we employed in section 5.4. In these models, behavioral relationships are specified directly rather than derived from underlying assumptions about the behavior of individuals and firms. As a result, the frameworks are of limited use for conducting normative analysis, since they are not able to make predictions about the welfare of the agents in the model. This is one reason for

---

1. For empirical evidence on international business cycles, see Backus and Kehoe (1992).

beginning the discussion of the open economy with the Obstfeld-Rogoff model; it is based explicitly on the assumption of optimizing agents and therefore offers a natural metric—in the form of the utility of the representative agent—for addressing normative policy questions.

6.2 The Obstfeld-Rogoff Two-Country Model

Obstfeld and Rogoff (1995, 1996) examine the linkages between two economies within a framework that combines three fundamental building blocks we have already seen. The first is an emphasis on intertemporal decisions by individual agents; foreign trade and asset exchange open up avenues for transferring resources over time that are not available in a closed economy. A temporary positive productivity shock that raises current output relative to future output induces individuals to increase consumption both now and in the future as they try to smooth the path of consumption. Since domestic consumption rises less than domestic output, the economy increases its net exports, thereby accumulating claims against future foreign output. These claims can be used to maintain higher consumption in the future after the temporary productivity increase has ended. The trade balance therefore plays an important role in facilitating the intertemporal transfer of resources.

Monopolistic competition in the goods market is the second building block of the Obstfeld-Rogoff model. As we saw in Chapter 5, this by itself has no implications for the effects of monetary disturbances, but it does set the stage for the third aspect of their model—sticky prices. Since we have already discussed these basic building blocks, we will focus on the new aspects introduced by open-economy considerations. Detailed derivations of the various components of the model are provided in section 6.6.1 of the appendix to this chapter. It will simplify the exposition to deal with a nonstochastic model in order to highlight the new considerations that arise in the open-economy context.

Each of the two countries is populated by a continuum of agents, indexed by $z \in [0,1]$, who are monopolistic producers of differentiated goods. Agents $z \in [0,n]$ reside in the home country, while agents $z \in (n,1]$ reside in the foreign country. Thus, n provides an index of the relative sizes of the two countries. If the countries are of equal size, $n = \frac{1}{2}$. Foreign variables will be denoted by a superscript asterisk (*).

The present discounted value of lifetime utility of a domestic resident j is

$$U^j = \sum_{t=0}^{\infty} \beta^t \left[\log C_t^j + b \log \frac{M_t^j}{P_t} - \frac{k}{2} y_t(j)^2 \right] \tag{6.1}$$

where C_t^j is agent j's period-t consumption of the composite consumption good, defined by

$$C^j = \left[\int_0^1 c^j(z)^q \, dz \right]^{\frac{1}{q}}, \qquad 0 < q < 1 \tag{6.2}$$

where consumption by agent j of good z is $c^j(z)$, $z \in [0, 1]$. The aggregate domestic price deflator P is defined as

$$P = \left[\int_0^1 p(z)^{\frac{q}{q-1}} \, dz \right]^{\frac{q-1}{q}} \tag{6.3}$$

This price index P depends on the prices of all goods consumed by domestic residents (the limits of integration run from 0 to 1). It incorporates prices of both domestically produced goods $\{p(z) \text{ for } z \in [0, n]\}$ and foreign-produced goods $\{p(z) \text{ for } z \in (n, 1]\}$. Thus, P corresponds to a consumer-price-index concept of the price level, not a GDP price deflator that would include only the prices of domestically produced goods.

Utility also depends on the agent's holdings of real money balances. Agents are assumed to hold only their domestic currency, so M_t^j / P_t appears in the utility function (6.1). Since agent j is the producer of good j, the effort of producing output $y(j)$ generates disutility. Thus, we have a money-in-the-utility-function motive for holding money (domestic currency only), and the utility of leisure is implicitly incorporated through the disutility of production. A similar utility function is assumed for residents of the foreign country:

$$U^{*j} = \sum_{t=0}^{\infty} \beta^t \left[\log C_t^{*j} + b \log \frac{M_t^{*j}}{P_t^*} - \frac{k}{2} y_t^*(j)^2 \right]$$

where C^{*j} and P^* are defined analogously to C^j and P.

Agent j will pick consumption, money holdings, holdings of international traded bonds, and output of good j (or alternatively, the price of good j) to maximize utility subject to the budget constraint

$$P_t C_t^j + M_t^j + P_t T_t + P_t B_t^j \leq p_t(j) y_t(j) + R_{t-1} P_t B_{t-1}^j + M_{t-1}^j$$

The gross real rate of interest is denoted R, and T represents real taxes minus transfers. Bonds purchased at time $t - 1$, B_{t-1}^j, yield gross real return R_{t-1}. As in our analysis of Chapter 2, the role of T will be to allow for variations in the nominal supply of money, with $P_t T_t = (M_t - M_{t-1})$. Dividing the budget constraint by P_t, one obtains

$$C_t^j + \frac{M_t^j}{P_t} + T_t + B_t^j \le \frac{p_t(j)}{P_t} y_t(j) + R_{t-1} B_{t-1}^j + \frac{1}{1+\pi_t} \frac{M_{t-1}^j}{P_{t-1}} \tag{6.4}$$

where π_t is the inflation rate from $t-1$ to t. To complete the description of the agent's decision problem, we need to specify the demand for the good the agent produces. This specification is provided in the appendix (section 6.6.1.1). Section 6.6.1.2 then shows that the following necessary first-order conditions can be derived from the individual consumer/producer's decision problem:

$$C_{t+1}^j = \beta R_{t+1} C_t^j \tag{6.5}$$

$$k y_t^j = q \left(\frac{1}{C_t^j}\right) \left(\frac{y_t^j}{C_t^w}\right)^{q-1} \tag{6.6}$$

$$\frac{M_t^j}{P_t} = b C_t^j \left(\frac{1+i_t}{i_t}\right) \tag{6.7}$$

together with the budget constraint (6.4) and the transversality condition

$$\lim_{i\to\infty} \prod_{s=0}^{i} R_{t+s-1}^{-1} \left(B_{t+i}^j + \frac{M_{t+i}^j}{P_{t+i}}\right) = 0$$

In these expressions, i_t is the nominal rate of interest, defined as $R_t(1+\pi_{t+1}) - 1$.

In (6.6), $C^w \equiv nC_t + (1-n)C_t^*$ is world consumption, where $C_t = \int_0^n C_t^j \, dj$ and $C_t^* = \int_n^1 C_t^j \, dj$ equal total home and foreign consumption. Equation (6.5) is a standard Euler condition for the optimal consumption path. Equation (6.6) states that the ratio of the marginal disutility of work to the marginal utility of consumption must equal the marginal product of work.[2] Equation (6.7) is the familiar condition for the demand for real balances of the domestic currency, requiring that the ratio of the marginal utility of money to the marginal utility of consumption equal $i_t/(1+i_t)$. Similar expressions hold for the foreign consumer/producer.

We have yet to introduce the exchange rate and the link between prices for similar goods in the two countries. Let S_t denote the nominal exchange rate, defined as the price of foreign currency in terms of domestic currency. A rise in S_t means that the price of foreign currency has risen in terms of domestic currency, and consequently, a unit of domestic currency buys fewer units of foreign currency. So a rise in S_t corresponds to a fall in the value of the domestic currency.

---

2. See equation (6.72) in the appendix.

While S_t is the exchange rate between the two currencies, the exchange rate between goods produced domestically and goods produced in the foreign economy will play an important role. The law of one price requires that good z sell for the same price in both the home and the foreign countries when expressed in a common currency.[3] This requires

$$p(z) = Sp^*(z)$$

It follows from the definitions of the home and foreign price levels that

$$P_t = S_t P_t^* \tag{6.8}$$

Any equilibrium must satisfy the first-order conditions for the agents' decision problem, the law-of-one-price condition, and the following additional market-clearing conditions:

Goods-market clearing: $C_t^w = n \dfrac{p_t(h)}{P_t} y_t(h) + (1 - n) \dfrac{p_t^*(f)}{P_t^*} y_t^*(f) \equiv Y_t^w$

where $p(h)$ and $y(h)$ are price and output of the representative home good [and similarly for $p^*(f)$ and $y^*(f)$]; and

Bond-market clearing: $nB_t + (1 - n)B_t^* = 0$

From the structure of the model, it should be clear that one-time proportional changes in the nominal home money supply, all domestic prices, and the nominal exchange rate leave the equilibrium for all real variables unaffected—the model displays monetary neutrality. An increase in M accompanied by a proportional decline in the value of home money in terms of goods [i.e., a proportional rise in all $p(j)$] and a decline in the value of M in terms of M^* (i.e., a proportional rise in S) leaves equilibrium consumption and output in both countries, together with prices in the foreign country, unchanged.

If we consider the model's steady state, the budget constraint (6.4) becomes

$$C = \frac{p(h)}{P} y(h) + (R - 1)B \tag{6.9}$$

---

3. While the law of one price is intuitively appealing and provides a convenient means of linking the prices $p(j)$ and $p^*(j)$ to the nominal exchange rate, it may be a poor empirical approximation. In a study of prices in different U.S. cities, Parsley and Wei (1996) find rates of price convergence to be faster than in cross-country comparisons, and they conclude that tradable-goods prices converge quickly. Even so, the half-life of a price difference among U.S. cities for tradables is estimated to be on the order of 12–15 months.

where B is the steady-state real stock of bonds held by the home country. For the foreign country,

$$C^* = \frac{p^*(f)}{P^*} y^*(f) - (R-1)\left(\frac{n}{1-n}\right)B \qquad (6.10)$$

These imply that real consumption equals real income (the real value of output plus income from net asset holdings) in the steady state.

6.2.1 The Linear Approximation

It will be helpful to develop a linear approximation to the basic Obstfeld-Rogoff model in terms of percentage deviations around the steady state. This serves to make the underlying structure of the linkages between the two economies clearer and will provide a base of comparison when, in the following section, we employ a more traditional open-economy model that is not directly derived from the assumption of optimizing agents. Using lowercase letters to denote percentage deviations around the steady state, the equilibrium conditions can be expressed as[4]

$$p_t = np_t(h) + (1-n)[s_t + p_t^*(f)] \qquad (6.11)$$

$$p_t^* = n[p_t(h) - s_t] + (1-n)p_t^*(f) \qquad (6.12)$$

$$y_t = \frac{1}{1-q}[p_t - p_t(h)] + c_t^w \qquad (6.13)$$

$$y_t^* = \frac{1}{1-q}[p_t^* - p_t^*(f)] + c_t^w \qquad (6.14)$$

$$nc_t + (1-n)c_t^* = c_t^w \qquad (6.15)$$

$$c_{t+1} = c_t + r_t \qquad (6.16)$$

$$c_{t+1}^* = c_t^* + r_t \qquad (6.17)$$

$$(2-q)y_t = (1-q)c_t^w - c_t \qquad (6.18)$$

$$(2-q)y_t^* = (1-q)c_t^w - c_t^* \qquad (6.19)$$

$$m_t - p_t = c_t - \delta(r_t + \pi_{t+1}) \qquad (6.20)$$

$$m_t^* - p_t^* = c_t^* - \delta(r_t + \pi_{t+1}^*) \qquad (6.21)$$

---

4. In Chapters 2–4, percentage deviations around the steady state were denoted by $\hat{x}$.

where $\delta = \beta/(\overline{\Pi} - \beta)$ and $\overline{\Pi}$ is one plus the steady-state rate of inflation (assumed to be equal in both economies). Equations (6.11) and (6.12) express the domestic and foreign price levels as weighted averages of the prices of home- and foreign-produced goods expressed in common currencies. The weights depend on the relative sizes of the two countries as measured by n. Equations (6.13) and (6.14) are derived from equation (6.64) of the appendix and give the demand for each country's output as a function of world consumption and relative price. Increases in world consumption (c^w) increase the demand for the output of both countries, while demand also depends on a relative-price variable. Home-country demand, for example, falls as the price of home production $p(h)$ rises relative to the home price level. Equation (6.15) defines world consumption as the weighted average of consumption in the two countries.

Equations (6.16) through (6.21) are from the individual agents' first-order conditions (6.5), (6.6), and (6.7). The first two of these equations are simply the Euler conditions for the optimal intertemporal allocation of consumption; the change in consumption is equal to the real rate of return. Equations (6.18) and (6.19) are implied by optimal production decisions. Finally, equations (6.20) and (6.21) give the real demand for home and foreign money as functions of consumption and nominal interest rates. While both countries face the same real interest rate r_t, nominal interest rates may differ if expected inflation rates differ between the two countries.

The equilibrium path of home and foreign production (y_t, y_t^*); home, domestic, and world consumption (c_t, c_t^*, c_t^w); prices and the nominal exchange rate $[p_t(h), p_t, p_t^*(f), p_t^*, s_t]$; and the real interest rate (r_t) must be consistent with these equilibrium conditions.[5] Note that subtracting equation (6.12) from (6.11) implies

$$s_t = p_t - p_t^* \qquad (6.22)$$

while the addition of n times (6.13) and $1 - n$ times (6.14) yields the goods-market-clearing relationship equating world production to world consumption: $ny_t + (1 - n)y_t^* = c_t^w$.

6.2.2   Equilibrium with Flexible Prices

The linear version of the two-country model serves to highlight the channels that link open economies. Using this framework, we first discuss the role of money when prices are perfectly flexible. As in the closed-economy case, the real equilibrium is

---

5. Equations (6.20)–(6.21) differ somewhat from Obstfeld and Rogoff's specification because of differences in the methods used to obtain linear approximations. See Obstfeld and Rogoff (1996, Chapter 10).

independent of monetary phenomena when prices can move to offset the effects of changes in the nominal supply of money.[6] Prices and the nominal exchange rate will depend on the behavior of the money supplies in the two countries, and the adjustment of the nominal exchange rate becomes part of the equilibrating mechanism that insulates real output and consumption from monetary effects.

The assumption of a common capital market, implying that consumers in both countries face the same real interest rate, means from the Euler conditions (6.16) and (6.17) that $c_{t+1} - c_{t+1}^* = c_t - c_t^*$; any difference in relative consumption is permanent. And world consumption c^w is the relevant scale variable for demand facing both home and domestic producers.

6.2.2.1 Real-Monetary Dichotomy With prices and the nominal exchange rate free to adjust immediately in the face of changes in either the home or foreign money supply, the model displays the classical dichotomy discussed in section 5.3.1, under which the equilibrium values of all real variables can be determined independently of money-supply and money-demand factors. To see this point, define the two relative price variables $\chi_t \equiv p_t(h) - p_t$ and $\chi_t^* \equiv p_t^*(f) - p_t^*$. Equations (6.11)–(6.12) imply

$$n\chi_t + (1 - n)\chi_t^* = 0$$

while (6.13)–(6.14) can be rewritten as

$$y_t = -\frac{\chi_t}{1 - q} + c_t^w$$

$$y_t^* = -\frac{\chi_t^*}{1 - q} + c_t^w$$

These three equations, together with (6.15)–(6.19), suffice to determine the real equilibrium. The money-demand equations (6.20) and (6.21) determine the price paths, while (6.22) determines the equilibrium nominal exchange rate, given these price paths. Thus, an important implication of this model is that monetary policy (defined as changes in nominal money supplies) has no short-run effects on the real interest rate, output, or consumption in either country. Rather, only nominal interest rates, prices, and the nominal exchange rate are affected by variations in the nominal money stock. One-time changes in m produce proportional changes in $p, p(h)$, and s.

---

6. Recall from the discussion in Chapter 2 that the dynamic adjustment outside the steady state is independent of money when utility is log separable as assumed in equation (6.1). This result would also characterize this open-economy model if it were modified to incorporate stochastic uncertainty due to productivity and money-growth-rate disturbances.

Changes in the growth rate of m will affect inflation and nominal interest rates. Equation (6.20) shows that inflation affects the real demand for money, so different rates of inflation are associated with different levels of real-money balances. Changes in nominal-money growth rates produce changes in the inflation rate and nominal interest rates, thereby affecting the opportunity cost of holding money and, in equilibrium, the real stock of money. The price level and nominal exchange rate jump to ensure that the real supply of money is equal to the new real demand for money.

Equation (6.21) can be subtracted from equation (6.20), yielding

$$m_t - m_t^* - (p_t - p_t^*) = (c_t - c_t^*) - \delta(\pi_{t+1} - \pi_{t+1}^*)$$

which, using (6.22), implies[7]

$$m_t - m_t^* - s_t = (c_t - c_t^*) - \delta(s_{t+1} - s_t) \tag{6.23}$$

Solving this equation forward for the nominal exchange rate, the no-bubbles solution is

$$s_t = \frac{1}{1+\delta} \sum_{i=0}^{\infty} \left(\frac{\delta}{1+\delta}\right)^i [(m_{t+i} - m_{t+i}^*) - (c_{t+i} - c_{t+i}^*)] \tag{6.24}$$

Since equations (6.16) and (6.17) imply $c_{t+i} - c_{t+i}^* = c_t - c_t^*$, the expression for the nominal exchange rate can be rewritten as

$$s_t = -(c_t - c_t^*) + \frac{1}{1+\delta} \sum_{i=0}^{\infty} \left(\frac{\delta}{1+\delta}\right)^i (m_{t+i} - m_{t+i}^*)$$

The current nominal exchange rate depends on the current and future path of the nominal money supplies in the two countries and on consumption differentials. The exchange rate measures the price of one money in terms of the other, and, as (6.24) shows, this depends on the relative supplies of the two monies. An increase in one country's money supply relative to the other's depreciates that country's exchange rate. From the standard steady-state condition that $\beta R^{ss} = 1$ and the definition of δ as $\beta/(\overline{\Pi} - \beta)$, the discount factor in (6.24), $\delta/(1+\delta)$, is equal to $\beta/\overline{\Pi} = 1/R^{ss}\overline{\Pi} = 1/(1+i^{ss})$. Future nominal money supply differentials are discounted by the steady-state nominal rate of interest. Because agents are forward looking in their decision making, it is only the present discounted value of the relative money supplies that matters. In other words, the nominal exchange rate depends on a measure of the

---

7. This derivation uses the fact that $\pi_{t+1} - \pi_{t+1}^* = (p_{t+1} - p_{t+1}^*) - (p_t - p_t^*) = s_{t+1} - s_t$.

permanent money-supply differential. Letting $x_{t+i} \equiv (m_{t+i} - m_{t+i}^*) - (c_{t+i} - c_{t+i}^*)$, the equilibrium condition for the nominal exchange rate can be written as

$$s_t = \frac{1}{1+\delta} \sum_{i=0}^{\infty} \left(\frac{\delta}{1+\delta}\right)^i x_{t+i} = \frac{1}{1+\delta} x_t + \frac{\delta}{1+\delta} \sum_{i=0}^{\infty} \left(\frac{\delta}{1+\delta}\right)^i x_{t+1+i} = \frac{1}{1+\delta} x_t + \frac{\delta}{1+\delta} s_{t+1}.$$

Rearranging and using (6.24) yields

$$s_{t+1} - s_t = -\frac{1}{\delta}(x_t - s_t)$$

$$= -\frac{1}{\delta} \left[(m_t - m_t^*) - \frac{1}{1+\delta} \sum_{i=0}^{\infty} \left(\frac{\delta}{1+\delta}\right)^i (m_{t+1+i} - m_{t+1+i}^*) \right]$$

Analogously to Friedman's permanent-income concept, the term

$$\frac{1}{1+\delta} \sum_{i=0}^{\infty} \left(\frac{\delta}{1+\delta}\right)^i (m_{t+1+i} - m_{t+1+i}^*)$$

can be interpreted as the permanent money-supply differential. If the current value of $m - m^*$ is high relative to the permanent value of this differential, the nominal exchange rate will fall (the home currency will appreciate). If s_t reflects the permanent money-supply differential at time t, and m_t is temporarily high relative to m_t^*, then the permanent differential will be lower beginning in period $t + 1$. As a result, the home currency appreciates.

An explicit solution for the nominal exchange rate in the flexible price case can be obtained if specific processes for the nominal money supplies are assumed. To take a very simple case, suppose m and m^* each follow constant, deterministic growth paths given by

$$m_t = m_0 + \mu t$$

and

$$m_t^* = m_0^* + \mu^* t$$

Strictly speaking, equation (6.24) applies only to deviations around the steady state and not to money-supply processes that include deterministic trends. However, it is very common to specify equations (6.20) and (6.21), which were used to derive (6.24), in terms of the log levels of the variables, perhaps adding a constant to represent steady-state levels. The advantage of interpreting (6.24) as holding for the log levels of the variables is that we can then use it to analyze shifts in the trend growth paths of the nominal money supplies, rather than just deviations around the trend. It is important to keep in mind, however, that the underlying representative-agent model implied that the interest rate coefficients in the money-demand equations were functions of the steady-state rate of inflation. We assumed this was the same in both countries, implying that the δ parameter was the same as well. The assumption of common coefficients in two country models is common, and we will maintain it in the following examples. The limitations of doing so should be kept in mind.

If the assumed money-supply processes are substituted into (6.24), then

$$s_t = -(c_t - c_t^*) + \frac{1}{1+\delta} \sum_{i=0}^{\infty} \left(\frac{\delta}{1+\delta} \right)^i [m_0 - m_0^* + (\mu - \mu^*)(t+i)]$$

$$= s_0 + (\mu - \mu^*)t - (c_t - c_t^*)$$

where $s_0 = m_0 - m_0^* + \delta(\mu - \mu^*)$.[8] In this case, the nominal exchange rate has a deterministic trend equal to the difference in the trend-money-growth rates in the two economies (also equal to the inflation-rate differentials, since $\pi = \mu$ and $\pi^* = \mu^*$). If domestic money growth exceeds foreign money growth ($\mu > \mu^*$), s will rise over time to reflect the falling value of the home currency relative to the foreign currency.

6.2.2.2   Uncovered Interest Parity   Real rates of return in the two countries have been assumed to be equal, so the Euler conditions for the optimal consumption paths (equations [6.16] and [6.17] imply the same expected consumption growth in each economy. It follows from the equality of real returns that nominal interest rates must satisfy $i_t - \pi_{t+1} = r_t = i_t^* - \pi_{t+1}^*$, and therefore, using (6.22),

$$i_t - i_t^* = \pi_{t+1} - \pi_{t+1}^*$$

$$= s_{t+1} - s_t$$

The nominal-interest-rate differential is equal to the actual change in the exchange rate in a perfect-foresight equilibrium. This statement would not be so in the presence of uncertainty, since then variables dated $t+1$ would need to be replaced with their expected values, conditional on the information available at time t. In this case,

$$E_t s_{t+1} - s_t = i_t - i_t^* \tag{6.25}$$

and nominal-interest-rate differentials would reflect expected exchange-rate changes. If the home country has a higher nominal interest rate in equilibrium, its currency

---

8. This uses the fact that $\sum_{i=0}^{\infty} ib^i = 1/(1-b)^2$ for $|b| < 1$.

must be expected to depreciate (s must be expected to rise) to equalize real returns across the two countries.

This condition, known as uncovered nominal-interest parity, links interest rates and exchange-rate expectations in different economies if their financial markets are integrated. Under rational expectations, we can write the actual exchange rate at $t + 1$ as equal to the expectation of the future exchange rate plus a forecast error φ_t uncorrelated with $E_t s_{t+1}$: $s_{t+1} = E_t s_{t+1} + \varphi_t$. Uncovered interest parity then implies

$$s_{t+1} - s_t = i_t - i_t^* + \varphi_{t+1}$$

The ex post observed change in the exchange rate between times t and $t + 1$ is equal to the interest rate differential at time t plus a random, mean-zero forecast error. Since this forecast error will, under rational expectations, be uncorrelated with information, such as i_t and i_t^*, that is known at time t, we can recast uncovered interest parity in the form of a regression equation:

$$s_{t+1} - s_t = a + b(i_t - i_t^*) + \varphi_{t+1} \tag{6.26}$$

with the null hypothesis of uncovered interest parity implying $a = 0$ and $b = 1$. Unfortunately, the evidence rejects this hypothesis.[9] In fact, estimated values of b are often negative.

One interpretation of these rejections is that the error term in an equation such as (6.26) is not simply due to forecast errors. Suppose, more realistically, that (6.25) does not hold exactly:

$$E_t s_{t+1} - s_t = i_t - i_t^* + v_t$$

where v_t captures factors such as risk premia that would lead to divergences between real returns in the two countries. In this case, the error term in the regression of $s_{t+1} - s_t$ on $i_t - i_t^*$ becomes $v_t + \varphi_{t+1}$. If v_t and $i_t - i_t^*$ are correlated, ordinary least squares estimates of the parameter b in (6.26) will be biased and inconsistent.

Correlation between v and $i - i^*$ might arise if monetary policies are implemented in a manner that leads the nominal-interest-rate differential to respond to the current exchange rate. For example, suppose that the monetary authority in each country tends to tighten policy whenever its currency depreciates. This type of behavior could occur if the monetary authorities are concerned with inflation; a depreciation raises the domestic currency price of foreign goods and raises the domestic price

---

9. For a summary of the evidence, see Froot and Thaler (1990). See also McCallum (1994a), Eichenbaum and Evans (1995), and Schlagenhauf and Wrase (1995).

level. To keep the example simple for illustrative purposes, suppose that as a result of such a policy, the nominal interest rate differential is given by

$$i_t - i_t^* = \mu s_t + u_t, \qquad \mu > 0$$

where u_t captures any other factors affecting the interest-rate differential.[10] Assume u is an exogenous, white-noise process. Substituting this into the uncovered-interest-parity condition yields

$$E_t s_{t+1} = (1 + \mu) s_t + u_t + v_t \tag{6.27}$$

the solution to which is[11]

$$s_t = -\frac{1}{1+\mu}(u_t + v_t)$$

Since this solution implies $E_t s_{t+1} = -\frac{1}{1+\mu} E_t(u_{t+1} + v_{t+1}) = 0$, the interest-parity condition is given by

$$E_t s_{t+1} - s_t = \frac{1}{1+\mu}(u_t + v_t) = i_t - i_t^* + v_t$$

or

$$i_t - i_t^* = \frac{1}{1+\mu}(u_t - \mu v_t).$$

Now what does this imply for tests of uncovered interest parity? From the solution for s_t, $s_{t+1} - s_t = -\frac{1}{1+\mu}(u_{t+1} - u_t + v_{t+1} - v_t)$. The probability limit of the interest-rate coefficient in the regression of $s_{t+1} - s_t$ on $i_t - i_t^*$ is equal to

$$\frac{\text{cov}(s_{t+1} - s_t, i_t - i_t^*)}{\text{var}(i_t - i_t^*)} = \frac{\frac{1}{(1+\mu)^2}(\sigma_u^2 - \mu\sigma_v^2)}{\frac{1}{(1+\mu)^2}(\sigma_u^2 + \mu^2\sigma_v^2)} = \frac{\sigma_u^2 - \mu\sigma_v^2}{\sigma_u^2 + \mu^2\sigma_v^2}$$

10. The rationale for such a policy is clearly not motivated within the context of a model with perfectly flexible prices in which monetary policy has no real effects. And notice that we are treating nominal interest rates, rather than the nominal money supply, as the policy instrument, an issue that will be addressed in Chapters 9 and 10. The general point is to illustrate how empirical relationships such as (6.26) can depend on the conduct of policy.

11. From (6.27), the equilibrium-exchange-rate process must satisfy $E_t s_{t+1} = (1+\mu)s_t + u_t + v_t$ so that the state variables are u_t and v_t. Following McCallum (1983a), the minimal state solution takes the form $s_t = b_0 + b_1(u_t + v_t)$. This implies $E_t s_{t+1} = b_0$. So the interest-parity condition becomes $b_0 = (1+\mu) \times [b_0 + b_1(u_t + v_t)] + u_t + v_t$, which will hold for all realizations of u and v if $b_0 = 0$ and $b_1 = -1/(1+\mu)$.

which will not generally equal 1, the standard null in tests of interest parity. If $u \equiv 0$, the probability limit of the regression coefficient is $-1/\mu$. That is, the regression estimate uncovers the policy parameter μ. Not only would a regression of the change in the exchange rate on the interest differential not yield the value of 1 predicted by the uncovered-interest-parity condition, but the estimate would be negative.

McCallum (1994a) develops more fully the argument that rejections of uncovered interest parity may arise because standard tests compound the parity condition with the manner in which monetary policy is conducted. While uncovered interest parity was implied by the model independently of the manner in which policy is conducted, the outcomes of statistical tests may in fact be dependent on the behavior of monetary policy, since policy may influence the time-series properties of the nominal-interest-rate differential.

As noted earlier, tests of interest parity often report negative regression coefficients on the interest rate differential in (6.26). This finding is also consistent with the empirical evidence reported by Eichenbaum and Evans (1995). They estimate the impact of monetary shocks on nominal and real exchange rates and interest-rate differentials between the United States and France, Germany, Italy, Japan, and the United Kingdom. A contractionary U.S. monetary-policy shock leads to a persistent nominal and real appreciation of the dollar and a fall in $i_t^* - i_t + s_{t+1} - s_t$ where i is the U.S. interest rate and i^* is the foreign rate. Uncovered interest parity implies that this expression should have expected value equal to zero, yet it remains predictably low for several months. Rather than leading to an expected depreciation that offsets the rise in i, excess returns on U.S. dollar securities remain high for several months following a contractionary U.S. monetary-policy shock.[12]

This example illustrates an important point: the empirical correlations among economic variables may depend critically on the manner in which policy is being conducted. Such situations arise frequently in monetary economies. Interest rates, exchange rates, and asset prices are forward-looking variables. They depend, therefore, on private agents' expectations about the future path of monetary policy. The contemporaneous correlations between forward-looking variables and policy variables will be affected by the information that current observations on policy provide about the future course of policy. Anticipated future policy actions can affect current

---

12. Eichenbaum and Evans measure monetary-policy shocks in a variety of ways (VAR innovations to nonborrowed reserves relative to total reserves, VAR innovations to the federal funds rate, and Romer and Romer [1989] measures of policy shifts). However, the identification scheme used in their VARs assumes that policy does not respond contemporaneously to the real exchange rate. As a result, the specific illustrative policy response to the exchange rate that led to (6.27) is ruled out by their framework.

exchange rates; this fact makes it difficult to test structural hypotheses and to isolate the effects due to systematic policy feedback.

6.2.3   Sticky Prices

Just as was the case with the closed economy, flexible-price models of the open economy appear unable to replicate the size and persistence of monetary shocks on real variables. And just as with closed-economy models, this inability can be remedied by the introduction of nominal rigidities. Obstfeld and Rogoff (1996, Chapter 10) provide an analysis of their basic two-country model under the assumption that prices are set one period in advance.[13] The presence of nominal rigidities leads to real effects of monetary disturbances through the channels discussed in Chapter 5, but new channels through which monetary disturbances have real effects are now also present.

Suppose $p(h)$, the domestic-currency price of domestically produced goods, is set one period in advance and fixed for one period. A similar assumption is made for the foreign-currency price of foreign-produced goods, $p^*(f)$. Although $p(h)$ and $p^*(f)$ are preset, the aggregate price indices in each country will fluctuate with the nominal exchange rate according to (6.11) and (6.12). A nominal depreciation, for example, raises the domestic price index p by increasing the domestic-currency price of foreign-produced goods. This process introduces a new channel, one absent in a closed economy, through which monetary disturbances can have an immediate impact on the price level. Recall that in the closed economy, there was no distinction between the price of domestic output and the general price level. Nominal price rigidities implied that the price level could not adjust immediately to monetary disturbances. Exchange-rate movements alter the domestic currency price of foreign goods, allowing the consumer price index to move in response to such disturbances, even in the presence of nominal rigidities.

Now suppose in period t the home country's money supply rises unexpectedly relative to that of the foreign country.[14] Under Obstfeld and Rogoff's simplifying assumption that prices adjust completely after one period, both economies return to their steady state one period after the change in m. But during the one period in which product prices are set, real output and consumption levels will be affected.[15]

---

13. They also consider the case in which nominal wages are preset.

14. An unexpected change is inconsistent with the assumption of perfect foresight implicit in the non-stochastic version of the model derived earlier. However, the linear approximation will continue to hold under uncertainty if future variables are replaced with their mathematical expectation.

15. By considering a situation in which the economies are initially in a steady state, the preset values for $p(h)$ and $p^*(f)$ will equal zero.

And these real effects mean that the home country may run a current-account surplus or deficit in response to the change in m. Such a result alters the net asset position of the two economies and can affect the new steady-state equilibrium.

Interpreting the model consisting of (6.11)–(6.21) as applied to deviations around the initial steady state, the Euler conditions (6.16) and (6.17) imply $c_{t+1} - c_{t+1}^* = c_t - c_t^*$. Since the economies are in the new steady state after one period (i.e., in $t + 1$), $c_{t+1} - c_{t+1}^* \equiv \mathscr{C}$ is the steady-state consumption differential between the two countries. But since we also have that $c_t - c_t^* = c_{t+1} - c_{t+1}^* = \mathscr{C}$, this relationship implies that relative consumption in the two economies immediately jumps in period t to the new steady-state value. Equation (6.23), which expressed relative money demands in the two economies, can then be written $m_t - m_t^* - s_t = \mathscr{C} - \delta(s_{t+1} - s_t)$. Solving this equation forward for the nominal exchange rate (assuming no bubbles),

$$s_t = -\mathscr{C} + \frac{1}{1+\delta} \sum_{i=0}^{\infty} \left(\frac{\delta}{1+\delta}\right)^i (m_{t+i} - m_{t+i}^*)$$

If the change in $m_t - m_t^*$ is a permanent one-time change, we can let $\Omega \equiv m - m^*$ without time subscripts denote this permanent change. The equilibrium exchange rate is then equal to

$$s_t = -\mathscr{C} + \frac{1}{1+\delta} \sum_{i=0}^{\infty} \left(\frac{\delta}{1+\delta}\right)^i \Omega = \Omega - \mathscr{C} \qquad (6.28)$$

Since $\Omega - C$ is a constant, (6.28) implies that the exchange rate jumps immediately to its new steady state following a permanent change in relative nominal money supplies. If relative consumption levels did not adjust (i.e., if $\mathscr{C} = 0$), then the permanent change in s is just equal to the relative change in nominal money supplies Ω. An increase in m relative to m^* (i.e., $\Omega > 0$) produces a depreciation of the home-country currency. If $\mathscr{C} \neq 0$, then changes in relative consumption affect the relative demand for money from (6.20) and (6.21). For example, if $\mathscr{C} > 0$, consumption, as well as money demand, in the home country is higher than initially. Equilibrium between home money supply and home money demand can be restored with a smaller increase in the home price level. Since $p(h)$ and $p^*(f)$ are fixed for one period, the increase in p necessary to maintain real money demand and real money supply equally is generated by a depreciation (a rise in s). The larger is the rise in home consumption, the larger is the rise in real money demand, and the smaller is the necessary rise in s. This is just what (6.28) says.

While we have determined the impact of a change in $m - m^*$ on the exchange rate, given $\mathscr{C}$, the real consumption differential is itself endogenous. To determine $\mathscr{C}$ requires that we work through several steps. First, the linear approximation to the current account relates the home country's accumulation of net assets to the excess of its real income over its consumption: $b = y_t + [p_t(h) - p_t] - c_t = y_t - (1 - n)s_t - c_t$ where $[p_t(h) - p_t] = -(1 - n)s_t$ follows from (6.11) and the fact that $p_t(h)$ is fixed (and equal to zero) during period t. Similarly, for the foreign economy, $-\left(\dfrac{n}{1 - n}\right)b = y_t^* + ns_t - c_t^*$. Together, these imply

$$\frac{b}{1 - n} = (y_t - y_t^*) - (c_t - c_t^*) - s_t \tag{6.29}$$

From (6.13) and (6.14), we have that $y_t - y_t^* = \dfrac{1}{1 - q}\, s_t$, so (6.29) becomes

$$\frac{b}{1 - n} = \left(\frac{q}{1 - q}\right)s_t - (c_t - c_t^*)$$

$$= \left(\frac{q}{1 - q}\right)s_t - \mathscr{C} \tag{6.30}$$

where we have made use of the definition of $\mathscr{C}$ as the consumption differential.

The last step is to use the steady-state relationship between consumption, income, and asset holdings given by (6.9) and (6.10) to eliminate b in (6.30) by expressing it in terms of the exchange rate and consumption differences. In the steady state, b is constant and current accounts are zero, so consumption equals real income inclusive of asset income. In terms of the linear approximation, (6.9) and (6.10) become

$$c = rb + y + [p(h) - p] = rb + y - (1 - n)[s + p^*(f) - p(h)] \tag{6.31}$$

and

$$c^* = -\left(\frac{n}{1 - n}\right)rb + y^* + n[s + p^*(f) - p(h)] \tag{6.32}$$

From the steady-state labor-leisure choice linking output and consumption given in equations (6.18) and (6.19), $(2 - q)(y - y^*) = -(c - c^*)$, and from the link between relative prices and demand from equations (6.13) and (6.14), $y - y^* = \dfrac{1}{1 - q} \times [s + p^*(f) - p(h)]$. Using these relationships, we can now subtract (6.32) from (6.31), yielding

$$\mathscr{C} = \left(\frac{1}{1-n}\right)rb + (y - y^*) - [s + p^*(f) - p(h)]$$

$$= \left(\frac{1}{1-n}\right)rb + q(y - y^*)$$

$$= \left(\frac{1}{1-n}\right)rb + \left(\frac{q}{q-2}\right)\mathscr{C}$$

Finally, this yields

$$b = \frac{1-n}{r}\left(\frac{2}{2-q}\right)\mathscr{C} \tag{6.33}$$

Substituting (6.33) into (6.30), $\frac{1}{r}\left(\frac{2}{2-q}\right)\mathscr{C} = \left(\frac{q}{1-q}\right)s_t - \mathscr{C}$. Solving for s in terms of $\mathscr{C}$,

$$s_t = \psi\mathscr{C} \tag{6.34}$$

where $\psi = \frac{1-q}{q}\left[1 + \frac{2}{r(2-q)}\right] > 0$. But from (6.28), we have already seen that $s_t = \Omega - \mathscr{C}$, so $\psi\mathscr{C} = \Omega - \mathscr{C}$. It follows that the consumption differential is $\mathscr{C} = \frac{1}{1+\psi}\Omega$. The equilibrium nominal-exchange-rate adjustment to a permanent change in the home country's nominal money supply is then given by

$$s_t = \left(\frac{\psi}{1+\psi}\right)\Omega < \Omega$$

With $\psi > 0$, the domestic monetary expansion leads to a depreciation that is less than proportional to the increase in m. This induces an expansion in domestic production and consumption. Consumption rises by less than income, so the home country runs a current account surplus and accumulates assets that represent claims against the future income of the foreign country. This allows the home country to maintain higher consumption forever. As we have seen, consumption levels jump immediately to their new steady-state levels with $\mathscr{C} = \left(\frac{1}{1+\psi}\right)\Omega > 0$. To provide a rough magnitude for ψ, if $q = 0.9$ and $r = 0.05$, $\psi \approx 4$, so $s_t = 0.8\Omega$ while $C = 0.2\Omega$.

The two-country model employed in this section has the advantage of being based on the clearly specified decision problems faced by agents in the model. As a consequence, the responses of consumption, output, interest rates, and the exchange rate are consistent with optimizing behavior. Unanticipated monetary disturbances can have a permanent impact on real consumption levels and welfare when prices are preset. These effects arise because the output effects of a monetary surprise alter each country's current account, thereby altering their relative asset positions. A monetary expansion in the home country, for instance, produces a currency depreciation and a rise in the domestic price level p. This in turn induces a temporary expansion in output in the home country [see (6.13)]. With consumption determined on the basis of permanent income, consumption rises less than output, leading the home country to run a trade surplus as the excess of output over domestic consumption is exported. As payment for these exports, the home country receives claims against the future output of the foreign country. Home consumption does rise, even though the increase in output lasts only one period, as the home country's permanent income has risen by the annuity value of its claim on future foreign output.

A domestic monetary expansion leads to permanently higher real consumption for domestic residents; welfare is increased. This observation suggests that each country has an incentive to engage in a monetary expansion. However, a joint proportionate expansion of each country's money supply leaves $m - m^*$ unchanged. There are then no exchange-rate effects, and relative consumption levels do not change. After one period, when prices fully adjust, a proportional change in $p(h)$ and $p^*(f)$ returns both economies to the initial equilibrium. But since output is inefficiently low because monopolistic competition is present, the one-period rise in output does increase welfare in both countries. Both countries have an incentive to expand their money supplies, either individually or in a coordinated fashion. But the analysis we have carried out has involved changes in money supplies that were unexpected. If they had been anticipated, the level at which price setters would set individual goods prices would have incorporated expectations of money-supply changes. As we have seen in Chapter 5, fully anticipated changes in the nominal money supply will not have the real effects that unexpected changes do when there is some degree of nominal wage or price rigidity. As we will see in Chapter 8, the incentive to create surprise expansions can, in equilibrium, lead to steady inflation without the welfare gains an unanticipated expansion would bring.

6.3   Policy Coordination

An important issue facing economies linked by trade and capital flows is the role to be played by policy coordination. Monetary policy actions by one country will affect other countries, leading to spillover effects that open the possibility of gains from policy coordination. As demonstrated in the previous section, the real effects of an unanticipated change in the nominal money supply in the two-country model depend on how $m - m^*$ is affected. A rise in m, holding m^* unchanged, will produce a home-country depreciation, shifting world demand toward the home country's output. With preset prices and output demand determined, the exchange-rate movement represents an important channel through which a monetary expansion affects domestic output. If both monetary authorities attempt to generate output expansions by increasing their money supplies, this exchange-rate channel will not operate, since the exchange rate depends on the relative money supplies. Thus, the impact of an unanticipated change in m depends critically on the behavior of m^*.

This dependence raises the issue of whether there are gains from coordinating monetary policy. Hamada (1976) is closely identified with the basic approach that has been used to analyze policy coordination, and in this section, we develop a version of his framework. Canzoneri and Henderson (1989) provide an extensive discussion of monetary-policy coordination issues; a survey is provided by Currie and Levine (1991).

Suppose we consider a model with two economies. We will assume each economy's policy authority can choose its inflation rate, and, because of nominal rigidities, monetary policy can have real effects in the short run. In this context, a complete specification of policy behavior is more complicated than in a closed-economy setting; we need to specify how each national policy authority interacts strategically with the other policy authority. We will examine two possibilities. First, we consider coordinated policy, meaning that inflation rates in the two economies are chosen jointly to maximize a weighted sum of the objective functions of the two policy authorities. Second, we consider noncoordinated policy with the policy authorities interacting in a Nash equilibrium. In this setting, each policy authority sets its own inflation rate to maximize its objective function, taking as given the inflation rate in the other economy. These clearly are not the only possibilities. One economy may act as a Stackelberg leader, recognizing the impact its choice has on the inflation rate set by the other economy. Reputational considerations along the lines we will study in Chapter 8 can also be incorporated into the analysis (see Canzoneri and Henderson 1989).

6.3.1 The Basic Model

The two-country model is specified as a linear system in log deviations around a steady state and represents an extension to the open-economy environment of the

AS-IS model of Chapter 5. The LM relationship is dispensed with by assuming that the monetary-policy authorities in the two countries set the inflation rate directly. An asterisk will denote the foreign economy, and ρ will be the real exchange rate, defined as the relative price of home and foreign output, expressed in terms of the home currency; a rise in ρ represents a real depreciation for the home economy. If s is the nominal exchange rate and $p(h)$ and $p^*(f)$ are the prices of home and foreign output, then $\rho = s + p^*(f) - p(h)$. The model should be viewed as an approximation that is appropriate when nominal wages are set in advance so that unanticipated movements in inflation affect real output. In addition to aggregate supply and demand relationships for each economy, an interest-parity condition links the real interest-rate differential to anticipated changes in the real exchange rate:

$$y_t = -b_1\rho_t + b_2(\pi_t - \mathrm{E}_{t-1}\pi_t) + e_t \tag{6.35}$$

$$y_t^* = b_1\rho_t + b_2(\pi_t^* - \mathrm{E}_{t-1}\pi_t^*) + e_t^* \tag{6.36}$$

$$y_t = a_1\rho_t - a_2r_t + a_3y_t^* + u_t \tag{6.37}$$

$$y_t^* = -a_1\rho_t - a_2r_t^* + a_3y_t + u_t^* \tag{6.38}$$

$$\rho_t = r_t^* - r_t + \mathrm{E}_t\rho_{t+1} \tag{6.39}$$

Equations (6.35) and (6.36) relate output supply to inflation surprises and the real exchange rate. A real-exchange-rate depreciation reduces home aggregate supply by raising the price of imported materials and by raising consumer prices relative to producer prices. This latter effect increases the real wage in terms of producer prices. Equations (6.37) and (6.38) make demand in each country an increasing function of output in the other to reflect spillover effects that arise as an increase in output in one country increases demand for the goods produced by the other. A rise in ρ_t (a real domestic depreciation) makes domestically produced goods less expensive relative to foreign goods and shifts demand away from foreign output and toward home output.

To simplify the analysis, the inflation rate is treated as the choice variable of the policy maker. An alternative to treating inflation as the policy variable would be to specify money-demand relationships for each country and then take the nominal money supply as the policy instrument. This would complicate the analysis without offering any new insights.

A third approach would be to replace r_t with $i_t - \mathrm{E}_t\pi_{t+1}$, where i_t is the nominal interest rate, and treat i_t as the policy instrument. An advantage of this approach is that it more closely reflects the way most central banks actually implement policy.

Because a number of new issues arise under nominal interest rate policies (see Chapters 9 and 10), we will simply interpret policy as choosing the rate of inflation in order to focus, in this section, on the role of policy coordination. Finally, a further simplification is reflected in the assumption that the parameters (the a_i's and b_i's) are the same in the two countries.

Demand (u_t, u_t^*) and supply (e_t, e_t^*) shocks are included to introduce a role for stabilization policy. These disturbances are assumed to be mean-zero, serially uncorrelated processes, but we will allow them to be correlated so that it will be possible to distinguish between common shocks that affect both economies and asymmetric shocks that originate in a single economy.

Equation (6.39) is an uncovered-interest-rate-parity condition. Rewritten in the form $r_t = r_t^* + E_t \rho_{t+1} - \rho_t$, it implies the home-country real interest rate will exceed the foreign real rate if the home country is expected to experience a real depreciation.

Evaluating outcomes under coordinated and noncoordinated policies requires some assumption about the objective functions of the policy makers. In models built more explicitly on the behavior of optimizing agents, alternative policies could be ranked according to their implications for the utility of the agents in the economies. In Chapter 5, it was shown how the AS-IS-LM could be viewed as an approximation to a model consistent with optimizing agents, but this analogy will not be pursued here. Instead, we follow a common approach in which polices are evaluated on the basis of loss functions that depend on output variability and inflation variability:

$$V_t = E_t \sum_{i=0}^{\infty} \beta^i [\lambda y_{t+i}^2 + \pi_{t+i}^2] \qquad (6.40)$$

$$V_t^* = E_t \sum_{i=0}^{\infty} \beta^i [\lambda (y_{t+i}^*)^2 + (\pi_{t+i}^*)^2] \qquad (6.41)$$

The parameter β is a discount factor between zero and one. The weight attached to output fluctuations relative to inflation fluctuations is λ. While these objective functions are ad hoc, they capture the idea that policy makers prefer to minimize output fluctuations around the steady state and fluctuations of inflation.[16] Objective func-

---

16. The steady-state values of y and y^* are zero by definition. The assumption that the policy loss functions depend on the variance of output around its steady-state level, and not some higher output target, is critical for the determination of average inflation. Chapter 8 deals extensively with the time-inconsistency issues that arise when policy makers target a level of output that exceeds the economy's equilibrium level.

tions of this basic form have played a major role in the analysis of policy, and we will make extensive use of them in Chapter 8. Equations (6.40) and (6.41) reflect the assumption that steady-state output will be independent of monetary policy, so policy should focus on minimizing fluctuations around the steady state, not on the level of output.

The model can be solved to yield expressions for equilibrium output in each economy and for the real exchange rate. To obtain the real exchange rate, first subtract foreign aggregate demand (6.38) from domestic aggregate demand (6.37), using the interest parity condition (6.39) to eliminate $r_t - r_t^*$. This process yields an expression for $y_t - y_t^*$. Next, subtract foreign aggregate supply (6.36) from domestic aggregate supply (6.35) to yield a second expression for $y_t - y_t^*$. Equating these two expressions and solving for the equilibrium real exchange rate leads to the following:

$$\rho_t = \frac{1}{B}\{b_2(1 + a_3)[(\pi_t - \mathrm{E}_{t-1}\pi_t) - (\pi_t^* - \mathrm{E}_{t-1}\pi_t^*)]$$

$$+ (1 + a_3)(e_t - e_t^*) - (u_t - u_t^*) + a_2\mathrm{E}_t\rho_{t+1}\} \tag{6.42}$$

where $B \equiv 2a_1 + a_2 + 2b_1(1 + a_3) > 0$. An unanticipated rise in domestic inflation relative to unanticipated foreign inflation or in e_t relative to e_t^* will increase domestic output supply relative to foreign output. Equilibrium requires a decline in the relative price of domestic output; the real exchange rate rises (depreciates), shifting demand toward domestic output. If the domestic aggregate demand shock exceeds the foreign shock, $u_t - u_t^* > 0$, the relative price of domestic output must rise (ρ must fall) to shift demand toward foreign output. A rise in the expected future exchange rate also leads to a rise in the current equilibrium ρ. If ρ_t were to increase by the same amount as the rise in $\mathrm{E}_t\rho_{t+1}$, the interest differential $r_t - r_t^*$ would be left unchanged, but the higher ρ_t would, from (6.35) and (6.36), lower domestic supply relative to foreign supply. So ρ_t rises by less than the increase in $\mathrm{E}_t\rho_{t+1}$ to maintain goods-market equilibrium.[17]

Notice that equation (6.42) can be written as $\rho_t = A\mathrm{E}_t\rho_{t+1} + v_t$ where $0 < A < 1$ and v_t is white noise, since the disturbances are assumed to be serially uncorrelated and the same will be true of the inflation forecast errors under rational expectations. It follows that $\mathrm{E}_t\rho_{t+1} = 0$ in any no-bubbles solution. This would not be the case, however, if either the aggregate-demand or aggregate-supply shocks were serially correlated.

---

17. The coefficient on $\mathrm{E}_t\rho_{t+1}$, a_2/B, is less than one in absolute value.

Having obtained an expression for the equilibrium real exchange rate, this can be substituted into the aggregate-supply relationships (6.35) and (6.36) to yield

$$y_t = b_2 A_1 (\pi_t - E_{t-1}\pi_t) + b_2 A_2 (\pi_t^* - E_{t-1}\pi_t^*)$$

$$- a_2 A_3 E_t \rho_{t+1} + A_1 e_t + A_2 e_t^* + A_3 (u_t - u_t^*) \qquad (6.43)$$

$$y_t^* = b_2 A_2 (\pi_t - E_{t-1}\pi_t) + b_2 A_1 (\pi_t^* - E_{t-1}\pi_t^*)$$

$$+ a_2 A_3 E_t \rho_{t+1} + A_2 e_t + A_1 e_t^* - A_3 (u_t - u_t^*) \qquad (6.44)$$

The A_i parameters are given by

$$A_1 \equiv \frac{2a_1 + a_2 + b_1(1 + a_3)}{B} > 0$$

$$A_2 \equiv \frac{b_1(1 + a_3)}{B} > 0$$

$$A_3 \equiv \frac{b_1}{B} > 0$$

Equations (6.43) and (6.44) reveal the spillover effects through which the inflation choice of one economy affects the other economy when $b_2 A_2 \neq 0$. An increase in inflation in the home economy (assuming it is unanticipated) leads to a real depreciation. This occurs since unanticipated inflation leads to a home output expansion (see 6.35). Equilibrium requires a rise in demand for home-country production. In the closed economy, this occurs through a fall in the real interest rate. In the open economy, an additional channel of adjustment arises from the role of the real exchange rate. If $E_t \rho_{t+1} = 0$, the interest parity condition (6.39) becomes $\rho_t = r_t^* - r_t$ so, for given r_t^*, the fall in r_t requires a rise in ρ_t (a real depreciation), which also serves to raise home demand.

The rise in ρ_t represents a real appreciation for the foreign economy, and this raises consumer-price wages relative to producer-price wages and increases aggregate output in the foreign economy (see 6.36). As a result, an inflation surprise in the home country produces an economic expansion in the foreign country. But as (6.42) shows, a surprise inflation by both countries leaves the real exchange rate unaffected. It is this link that opens the possibility that outcomes will depend on the extent to which the two countries coordinate their policies.

6.3.2 Equilibrium with Coordination

In order to focus on the implications of coordination for monetary policy, we will restrict attention to the case of a common aggregate supply shock, common in the sense that it affects both countries. That is, suppose $e_t = e_t^* \equiv \varepsilon_t$ where ε_t is the common disturbance. For the rest of this section, we will assume $u \equiv u^* \equiv 0$ so that ε represents the only disturbance.

In solving for equilibrium outcomes under alternative policy interactions, the objective functions (6.40) and (6.41) simplify to a sequence of one-period problems (the problem is a static one with no link between periods). Assuming that the policy authority is able to set inflation rates after observing the supply shock ε_t, the decision problem in period t under a coordinated policy is

$$\min_{\pi, \pi^*}\{\tfrac{1}{2}(\lambda y_t^2 + \pi_t^2) + \tfrac{1}{2}[\lambda(y_t^*)^2 + (\pi_t^*)^2]\}$$

subject to (6.43) and (6.44).[18] The first-order conditions are

$$0 = \lambda b_2 A_1 y_t + \pi_t + \lambda b_2 A_2 y_t^*$$
$$= (1 + \lambda b_2^2 A_1^2 + \lambda b_2^2 A_2^2)\pi_t + 2\lambda b_2^2 A_1 A_2 \pi_t^* + \lambda b_2 \varepsilon_t$$
$$0 = \lambda b_2 A_2 y_t + \lambda b_2 A_1 y_t^* + \pi_t^*$$
$$= (1 + \lambda b_2^2 A_1^2 + \lambda b_2^2 A_2^2)\pi_t^* + 2\lambda b_2^2 A_1 A_2 \pi_t + \lambda b_2 \varepsilon_t$$

where we have used the fact that $A_1 + A_2 = 1$ and the result that the first-order conditions imply $E_{t-1}\pi_t = E_{t-1}\pi_t^* = 0$.[19] Solving these two equations yields the equilibrium inflation rates under coordination:

$$\pi_{c,t} = \pi_{c,t}^* = -\left(\frac{\lambda b_2}{1 + \lambda b_2^2}\right)\varepsilon_t \equiv -\theta_c \varepsilon_t \qquad (6.45)$$

Both countries maintain equal inflation rates. In response to an adverse supply shock ($\varepsilon < 0$), inflation in both countries rises to offset partially the decline in output. Substituting (6.45) into the expressions for output and the equilibrium real exchange rate,

$$y_{c,t} = y_{c,t}^* = \left(\frac{1}{1 + \lambda b_2^2}\right)\varepsilon_t < \varepsilon_t$$

and

$$\rho_t = 0$$

18. In defining the objective function under coordinated policy, we have assumed that each country's utility receives equal weight.

19. Writing out the first-order condition for π_t in full, $0 = \pi_t + \lambda b_2^2(A_1^2 + A_2^2)(\pi_t - E_{t-1}\pi_t) + 2\lambda b_2^2 A_1 A_2(\pi_t^* - E_{t-1}\pi_t^*) + \lambda b_2 \varepsilon_t$. Taking expectations conditional on time $t-1$ information (i.e., prior to the realization of ε_t), we obtain $E_{t-1}\pi_t = 0$.

The policy response acts to partially offset the output effects of the supply shock. The larger is the weight placed on output in the loss function (λ), the larger is the inflation response and the more output is stabilized. Because both economies respond symmetrically, the real exchange rate is left unaffected.[20]

6.3.3 Equilibrium without Coordination

When policy is not coordinated, some assumption must be made about the nature of the strategic interaction between the two separate policy authorities. One natural case to consider corresponds to a Nash equilibrium; the policy authorities choose inflation to minimize loss, taking as given the inflation rate in the other economy. An alternative case corresponds to a situation in which one country behaves as a Stackelberg leader, taking into account how the other policy authority will respond to the leader's choice of inflation. We will analyze the Nash case, leaving the Stackelberg case to be studied as a problem at the end of the chapter.

The home policy authority picks inflation to minimize $\lambda y_t^2 + \pi_t^2$, taking π_t^* as given. The first-order condition is

$$0 = \lambda b_2 A_1 y_t + \pi_t$$

$$= (1 + \lambda b_2^2 A_1^2)\pi_t + \lambda b_2^2 A_1 A_2 \pi_t^* + \lambda b_2 A_1 \varepsilon_t$$

so that the home country's reaction function is

$$\pi_t = -\left(\frac{\lambda b_2^2 A_1 A_2}{1 + \lambda b_2^2 A_1^2}\right)\pi_t^* - \left(\frac{\lambda b_2 A_1}{1 + b_2^2 A_1^2}\right)\varepsilon_t \tag{6.46}$$

A rise in the foreign country's inflation rate is expansionary for the domestic economy (see equation 6.43). The domestic policy authority lowers domestic inflation to partially stabilize domestic output. A parallel treatment of the foreign-country policy authority's decision problem leads to the reaction function

$$\pi_t^* = -\left(\frac{\lambda b_2^2 A_1 A_2}{1 + \lambda b_2^2 A_1^2}\right)\pi_t - \left(\frac{\lambda b_2 A_1}{1 + \lambda b_2^2 A_1^2}\right)\varepsilon_t \tag{6.47}$$

Jointly solving these two reaction functions for the Nash-equilibrium inflation rates yields

$$\pi_{N,t} = \pi_{N,t}^* = -\left(\frac{\lambda b_2 A_1}{1 + \lambda b_2^2 A_1}\right)\varepsilon_t \equiv -\theta_N \varepsilon_t \tag{6.48}$$

---

20. This would not be the case in response to an asymmetric supply shock. See problem 4.

How does stabilization policy with noncoordinated policies compare with the coordinated policy response given in (6.45)? Since $0 < A_1 < 1$,

$$|\theta_N| < |\theta_c|$$

Policy responds less to the aggregate supply shock in the absence of coordination, and, as a result, output fluctuates more:

$$y_{N,t} = y^*_{N,t} = \left(\frac{1}{1 + \lambda b_2^2 A_1}\right)\varepsilon_t > \left(\frac{1}{1 + \lambda b_2^2}\right)\varepsilon_t$$

Because the output and inflation responses are symmetric in the Nash equilibrium, the real exchange rate does not respond to ε_t.

Why does policy respond less in the absence of coordination? For each individual policy maker, the perceived marginal output gain from more inflation when there is an adverse realization of ε reflects the two channels through which inflation affects output. First, surprise inflation directly increases real output because of the assumption of nominal rigidities. This direct effect is given by the term $b_2(\pi_t - \mathrm{E}_{t-1}\pi_t)$ in (6.35). Second, for given foreign inflation, a rise in home inflation leads to a real depreciation [see (6.42)] and, again from (6.35), the rise in ρ_t acts to lower output, reducing the net impact of inflation on output. With π^*_t treated as given, the exchange-rate channel implies that a larger inflation increase is necessary to offset the output effects of an adverse supply shock. Since inflation is costly, the optimal policy response involves a smaller inflation response and less output stabilization. With a coordinated policy, the decision problem faced by the policy authority recognizes that a symmetric increase in inflation in both countries leaves the real exchange rate unaffected. With inflation perceived to have a larger marginal impact on output, the optimal response is to stabilize more.

The loss functions of the two countries can be evaluated under the alternative policy regimes (coordination and noncoordination). Because the two countries have been specified symmetrically, the value of the loss function will be the same for each. For the domestic economy, the loss function when policies are coordinated is equal to

$$L^c = \tfrac{1}{2}\left(\frac{1}{1 + \lambda b_2^2}\right)\lambda\sigma_\varepsilon^2$$

When policies are determined in a Nash noncooperative equilibrium,

$$L^N = \tfrac{1}{2}\left[\frac{1 + \lambda b_2^2 A_1^2}{(1 + \lambda b_2^2 A_1)^2}\right]\lambda\sigma_\varepsilon^2$$

Because $0 < A_1 < 1$, it follows that $L^c < L^N$; coordination achieves a better outcome than occurs in the Nash equilibrium.

This example appears to imply that coordination will always dominate non-coordination. It is important to recall that we considered the case in which the only source of disturbance was a common aggregate-supply shock. The case of asymmetric shocks is addressed in problem 4. But even when there are only common shocks, coordination need not always be superior. Rogoff (1985a) provides a counter-example. His argument is based on a model in which optimal policy is time incon-sistent, a topic we will cover in Chapter 8, but we can briefly describe the intuition behind Rogoff's results. A coordinated monetary expansion leads to a larger short-run real-output expansion because it avoids changes in the real exchange rate. But this fact increases the incentive to engineer a surprise monetary expansion if the policy makers believe the natural rate of output is too low. Wage and price setters will anticipate this tactic, together with the associated higher inflation. Equilibrium involves higher inflation, but because it has been anticipated, output (which depends on inflation surprises) does not increase. Consequently, coordination leads to better stabilization but higher average inflation. If the costs of the latter are high enough, noncoordination can dominate coordination.

The discussion of policy coordination serves to illustrate several important aspects of open-economy monetary economics. First, the simple framework introduced in this section provides a two-country model that closely corresponds to the type of closed-economy aggregate-supply, aggregate-demand model discussed in Chapter 5. This framework is commonly used to analyze many policy topics. Second, the model incorporated several channels through which monetary policy can affect the real economy that are absent when the analysis is limited to a closed economy. The real exchange rate is the relative price of output in the two countries, so it plays an important role in equilibrating relative demand and supply in the two countries. Third, foreign shocks matter for the domestic economy; both aggregate-supply and aggregate-demand shocks originating in the foreign economy affect output in the domestic economy. As equations (6.43) and (6.44) show, however, the model implies that common demand shocks that leave $u - u^*$ unaffected have no effect on output levels or the real exchange rate. Since these shocks do affect demand in each country, a common demand shock raises real interest rates in each country. Fourth, policy coordination can matter.

While the two-country model of this section is useful, it has several omissions that may limit the insights that can be gained from its use. First, the aggregate demand and supply relationships are not derived explicitly within an optimizing framework.

As we saw in Chapter 5 and in the Obstfeld-Rogoff model, expectations of future income will play a role when consumption is determined by forward-looking, rational economic agents. Second, there is no role for current-account imbalances to affect equilibrium through their effects on foreign asset holdings. Third, no distinction has been drawn between the price of domestic output and the price index relevant for domestic residents. The loss function for the policy maker may depend on CPI inflation. Fourth, the inflation rate was treated as the instrument of policy, directly controllable by the central bank. This is an obvious simplification, one that abstracts from the linkages (and slippages) between the actual instruments of policy and the realized rate of inflation. Although such simplifications are useful for addressing many policy issues, Chapters 9 and 10 will examine these linkages in more detail. Finally, the model, like the Obstfeld-Rogoff example, assumed one-period nominal contracts. Such a formulation will fail to capture the persistence that generally characterizes actual inflation and the lags between changes in policy and the resulting changes in output and inflation.

6.4   The Small Open Economy

A two-country model provides a useful framework for examining policy interactions in an environment in which developments in one economy affect the other. For many economies, however, domestic developments have little or no impact on other economies. Decisions about policy can, in this case, treat foreign interest rates, output levels, and inflation as exogenous because the domestic economy is "small" relative to the rest of the world. The small open economy is a useful construct for analyzing issues when developments in the country of interest are unlikely to influence other economies.

In this case, the model used in the previous section to study policy coordination simplifies to become

$$y_t = -b_1\rho_t + b_2(p_t - \mathrm{E}_{t-1}p_t) + e_t \qquad (6.49)$$

$$y_t = a_1\rho_t - a_2r_t + u_t \qquad (6.50)$$

$$\rho_t = r_t^* - r_t + \mathrm{E}_t\rho_{t+1} \qquad (6.51)$$

The real exchange rate ρ is equal to $s + p^* - p$, where s is the nominal exchange and p^* and p are the prices of foreign and domestic output, all expressed in log terms. The aggregate-supply relationship has been written in terms of the unanticipated price level rather than unanticipated inflation.[21] The dependence of output on price surprises arises from the presence of nominal wage and price rigidities. With foreign income and consumption exogenous, the impact of world consumption on the domestic economy can be viewed as one of the factors giving rise to the disturbance term u_t.

Consumer prices in the domestic economy are defined as

$$q_t = hp_t + (1 - h)(s_t + p_t^*) \tag{6.52}$$

where h is the share of domestic output in the consumer price index, while the Fisher relationship links the real rate of interest appearing in (6.50) and (6.51) with the nominal interest rate,

$$r_t = i_t - E_t p_{t+1} + p_t \tag{6.53}$$

Uncovered interest parity links nominal interest rates. Since i^* will be exogenous from the perspective of the small open economy, we can rewrite (6.51) as

$$i_t = E_t s_{t+1} - s_t + i_t^* \tag{6.54}$$

where $i^* = r^* + E_t p_{t+1}^* - p_t^*$. Finally, real money demand is assumed to be given by

$$m_t - q_t = y_t - ci_t + v_t \tag{6.55}$$

Notice that the basic structure of the model, like the closed-economy models of Chapter 5 based on wage and price rigidity, displays the classical dichotomy between the real and monetary sectors if wages are flexible. That is, if nominal wages adjust completely to equate labor demand and labor supply, the price-surprise term in (6.49) disappears.[22] In this case, equations (6.49)–(6.51) constitute a three-equation system for real output, the real interest rate, and the real exchange rate. Using the interest parity condition to eliminate r_t from the aggregate-demand relationship and setting the resulting expression for output equal to aggregate supply yields the following equation for the equilibrium real exchange rate when wages and prices are flexible:

$$(a_1 + a_2 + b_1)\rho_t = a_2[r_t^* + E_t p_{t+1}] + e_t - u_t$$

---

21. Since $p_t - E_{t-1} p_t = p_t - p_{t-1} - (E_{t-1} p_t - p_{t-1}) = \pi_t - E_{t-1}\pi_t$, the two formulations are equivalent.
22. Recall from Chapter 5 that the assumption behind an aggregate-supply function such as (6.49) is that nominal wages are set in advance on the basis of expectations of the price level while actual employment is determined by firms on the basis of realized real wages (and therefore on the actual price level).

This can be solved forward for p_t:

$$p_t = \sum_{i=0}^{\infty} d^i \mathrm{E}_t \left[\frac{a_2 r_{t+i}^* + e_{t+i} - u_{t+i}}{a_1 + a_2 + b_1} \right]$$

$$= d \sum_{i=0}^{\infty} d^i \mathrm{E}_t r_{t+i}^* + \frac{e_t - u_t}{a_1 + a_2 + b_1}$$

where $d \equiv a_2/(a_1 + a_2 + b_1) < 1$ and the second equals sign follows from the assumption that e and u are serially uncorrelated processes. The real exchange rate responds to excess supply for domestic output; if $e_t - u_t > 0$, a real depreciation increases aggregate demand and lowers aggregate supply to restore goods-market equilibrium.

The monetary sector consists of equations (6.52)–(6.53) and (6.55), plus the definition of the nominal exchange rate as $s_t = \rho_t - p_t^* + p_t$. When wages and prices are flexible, these determine the nominal exchange rate, the nominal interest rate, and the two price levels p (the price of domestic output) and q (the consumer price index). From the Fisher equation, the money-demand equation, and the definition of q_t,

$$m_t - p_t = y_t + (1 - h)\rho_t - c[r_t + \mathrm{E}_t p_{t+1} - p_t] + v_t$$

Because the real variables are exogenous with respect to the monetary sector when prices are flexible, this equation can be solved for the equilibrium value of p:

$$p_t = \frac{1}{1+c} \sum_{i=0}^{\infty} \left(\frac{c}{1+c}\right)^i \mathrm{E}_t[m_{t+i} - z_{t+i} - v_{t+i}]$$

where $z_{t+i} \equiv y_{t+i} + (1 - h)\rho_{t+i} - cr_{t+i}$. The equilibrium p_t depends not just on the current money supply but on the expected future path of m. Since (6.52) implies $p_t = q_t - (1 - h)\rho_t$, the equilibrium behavior of the domestic consumer price index q follows from the solutions for p and ρ.

When nominal wages are set in advance, the classical dichotomy no longer holds. With $p_t - \mathrm{E}_{t-1} p_t$ affecting the real wage, employment, and output, any disturbance in the monetary sector that was unanticipated will affect output, the real interest rate, and the real exchange rate. Since the model does not incorporate any mechanism to generate real persistence, these effects last only for one period.

With nominal wage rigidity, monetary policy affects real aggregate demand through both interest-rate and exchange-rate channels. As can be seen from equation (6.50), these two variables appear in the combination $a_1\rho_t - a_2 r_t$. For this reason, the interest rate and exchange rate are often combined to create a monetary-conditions index; in the context of the present model, this index would be equal to

$r_t - a_1 p_t / a_2$. Variations in the real interest rate and real exchange rates that leave this linear combination unchanged would be neutral in their impact on aggregate demand, since the reduction in domestic aggregate demand caused by a higher real interest rate could be offset by a depreciation in the real exchange rate.

6.4.1   Flexible Exchange Rates

Suppose that nominal wages are set in advance, but the nominal exchange rate is free to adjust flexibly in the face of economic disturbances, and monetary policy is implemented through control of the nominal money supply. In this case, the model consisting of (6.49)–(6.55) can be reduced to two equations involving the price level, the nominal exchange rate, and the nominal money supply (see the appendix, section 6.6.2, for details). Equilibrium will depend on expectations of the period $t+1$ exchange rate, and the response of the economy to current policy actions may depend on how these expectations are affected.

To determine how the exchange rate and the price level respond to monetary shocks, we will assume a specific process for the nominal money supply. To allow for a distinction between transitory and permanent monetary shocks, assume

$$m_t = \mu + m_{t-1} + \varphi_t - \gamma \varphi_{t-1}, \qquad 0 \le \gamma \le 1 \tag{6.56}$$

where φ is a serially uncorrelated white-noise process. If $\gamma = 0$, m_t follows a random walk with drift μ; innovations φ have a permanent impact on the level of m. If $\gamma = 1$, the money supply is white noise around a deterministic trend. If $0 < \gamma < 1$, a fraction $(1 - \gamma)$ of the innovation has a permanent effect on the level of the money supply.

In order to analyze the impact of foreign price shocks on the home country, let

$$p_t^* = \pi^* + p_{t-1}^* + \phi_t \tag{6.57}$$

where ϕ is a random, white-noise disturbance. This equation allows for a constant average foreign inflation rate of π^* with permanent shifts in the price path due to the realizations of ϕ.

Using the method of undetermined coefficients, the appendix shows that the following solutions for p and s are consistent with (6.49)–(6.55), and with rational expectations:

$$p_t = k_0 + m_{t-1} + \frac{B_2[1 + c(1 - \gamma)]}{K} \varphi_t - \gamma \varphi_{t-1}$$

$$+ \frac{[(A_2 - B_2)u_t - A_2 e_t - B_2 v_t]}{K} \tag{6.58}$$

$$s_t = d_0 + m_{t-1} - p_{t-1}^* - \phi_t - \frac{B_1[1 + c(1 - \gamma)]}{K} \varphi_t$$

$$- \gamma\varphi_{t-1} + \frac{[(B_1 - A_1)u_t + A_1 e_t + B_1 v_t]}{K} \tag{6.59}$$

where $A_1 = h - a_1 - a_2$, $A_2 = 1 + c - A_1 > 0$, $B_1 = -(a_1 + a_2 + b_1 + b_2) < 0$, $B_2 = a_1 + a_2 + b_1 > 0$, and

$$K = -[(1 + c)B_1 + b_2 A_1]$$

The constants k_0 and d_0 are given by

$$k_0 = (1 + c)\mu + \left[c - \frac{a_2(1 - h - b_1)}{a_1 + b_1}\right] r^*$$

and

$$d_0 = (1 + c)\mu + \left[c - \frac{a_2(1 - h - b_1)}{a_1 + b_1}\right] r^* - \pi^*$$

Of particular note is the way a flexible exchange rate insulates the domestic economy from the foreign price shock ϕ. Neither p_{t-1}^* nor ϕ_t affects the domestic price level under a flexible-exchange-rate system (see 6.58). Instead, (6.59) shows how they move the nominal exchange rate to maintain the domestic currency price of foreign goods, $s + p^*$, unchanged. This insulates the real exchange rate and domestic output from fluctuations in the foreign price level.

With $\frac{B_2[1 + c(1 - \gamma)]}{K} > 0$ and $-\frac{B_1[1 + c(1 - \gamma)]}{K} > 0$, a positive monetary shock increases the equilibrium price level and the nominal exchange rate. That is, the domestic currency depreciates in response to a positive money shock. The effect is offset partially the following period if $\gamma > 0$. The shape of the exchange rate response to a monetary shock is shown in Figure 6.1 for different values of γ.

The $\gamma < 1$ cases in Figure 6.1 illustrate Dornbusch's overshooting result (Dornbusch 1976). To the extent that the rise in m is permanent (i.e., $\gamma < 1$), the price level and the nominal exchange rate will eventually rise proportionately. With one-period nominal rigidities, this outcome occurs in period 2. A rise in the nominal money supply that increases the real supply of money also reduces the nominal interest rate to restore money-market equilibrium. From the interest-parity condition, the domestic nominal rate can fall only if the exchange rate is expected to fall. Yet the exchange rate will be higher than its initial value in period 2, so to generate an expectation of a

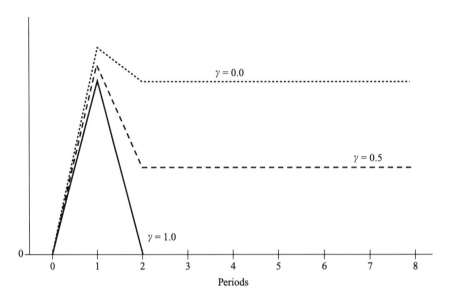

Figure 6.1
Nominal-Exchange-Rate Response to a Monetary Shock

fall, s must rise more than proportionately to the permanent rise in m so that it is then expected to fall from period 1 to period 2. The nominal rate overshoots its new long-run value.

The Dornbusch overshooting result stands in contrast to Obstfeld and Rogoff's conclusion, derived in section 6.2.3, that a permanent change in the nominal money supply does not lead to overshooting. Instead, the nominal exchange rate jumps immediately to its new long-run level. This difference results from the ad hoc nature of aggregate demand in the model of this section. In the Obstfeld and Rogoff model, consumption is derived from the decision problem of the representative agent. As we saw in section 6.2, the Euler condition for consumption linked consumption choices over time. The desire to smooth consumption implies that consumption immediately jumps to its new equilibrium level. As a result, exchange-rate overshooting is eliminated in the basic Obstfeld-Rogoff model.

One implication of the overshooting hypothesis is that exchange-rate movements should follow a predictable or forecastable pattern in response to monetary shocks. A positive monetary shock leads to an immediate depreciation, followed by an appreciation. The path of adjustment will depend on the extent of nominal rigidities in the economy, since these influence the speed with which the economy adjusts in response to shocks. Such a predictable pattern is not clearly evident in the data. In fact, nominal exchange rates display close to random-walk behavior over short time periods (Meese and Rogoff 1983). In a VAR-based study of exchange-rate responses to U.S. monetary shocks, Eichenbaum and Evans (1995) do not find evidence of overshooting, but they do find sustained and predictable exchange-rate movements following monetary-policy shocks. A monetary contraction produces a small initial appreciation, with the effect growing so that the dollar appreciates for some time. However, in a study based on more direct measurement of policy changes, Bonser-Neal, Roley, and Sellon (1997) find general support for the overshooting hypothesis. Bonser-Neal, Roley, and Sellon measure policy changes by using data on changes in the Federal Reserve's target for the federal funds rate, rather than the actual funds rate, and restrict attention to time periods during which the funds rate was the Fed's policy instrument.

6.4.2 Fixed Exchange Rates

Under a system of fixed exchange rates, the monetary authority is committed to using its policy instrument to maintain a constant nominal exchange rate. This commitment requires that the monetary authority stand ready to buy or sell domestic currency for foreign exchange to maintain the fixed exchange rate. When it is necessary to sell foreign exchange, such a policy will be unsustainable if the domestic central bank's reserves of foreign exchange are expected to go to zero. Such expectations can produce speculative attacks on the currency.[23] In our analysis here, we will deal only with the case of a sustainable fixed rate. And to draw the sharpest contrast with the flexible-exchange-rate regime, we will assume the exchange rate is pegged. In practice, most fixed-exchange-rate regimes allow rates to fluctuate within narrow bands.[24]

Normalizing the fixed rate at $s_t = 0$ for all t, the real exchange rate equals $p_t^* - p_t$. Assuming that the foreign price level follows (6.57), the basic model becomes

$$y_t = -b_1(p_t^* - p_t) + b_2(p_t - \mathrm{E}_{t-1}p_t) + e_t$$

$$y_t = a_1(p_t^* - p_t) - a_2 r_t + u_t$$

$$r_t = r^* + \pi^* - (\mathrm{E}_t p_{t+1} - p_t)$$

The nominal interest rate has been eliminated, since the interest-parity condition and

---

23. See Krugman (1979), Garber and Svensson (1995).
24. Exchange rate behavior under a target-zone system was first analyzed by Krugman (1991).

the fixed-exchange-rate assumption imply $i = r^* + \pi^*$. These three equations can be solved for the price level, output, and the domestic real interest rate. The money demand condition plays no role because m must endogenously adjust to maintain the fixed exchange rate.

Solving for p_t,

$$p_t = \frac{(a_1 + b_1)p_t^* - a_2(r^* + \pi^*) + a_2 \mathrm{E}_t p_{t+1} + b_2 \mathrm{E}_{t-1} p_t + u_t - e_t}{a_1 + a_2 + b_1 + b_2}$$

Using the method of undetermined coefficients, one obtains

$$p_t = p_t^* - \frac{a_2 r^*}{a_1 + b_1} + \frac{u_t - e_t - b_2 \phi_t}{a_1 + a_2 + b_1 + b_2} \tag{6.60}$$

Comparing (6.60) to (6.58) reveals some of the major differences between the fixed and flexible exchange-rate systems. Under fixed exchange rates, the average domestic rate of inflation must equal the foreign inflation rate: $\mathrm{E}(p_{t+1} - p_t) = \mathrm{E}(p_{t+1}^* - p_t^*) = \pi^*$. The foreign price level and foreign price shocks (ϕ) affect domestic prices and output under the fixed-rate system. But domestic disturbances to money demand or supply (φ and v) have no price level or output effects. This situation is in contrast to the case under flexible exchange rates and is one reason why high-inflation economies often attempt to fix their exchange rates with low-inflation countries. But when world inflation is high, a country can maintain lower domestic inflation only by allowing its nominal exchange rate to adjust.

The effects on real output of aggregate demand and supply disturbances also depend on the nature of the exchange rate system. Under flexible exchange rates, a positive aggregate-demand shock increases prices and real output. Goods-market equilibrium requires a rise in the real interest rate and a real appreciation. By serving to equilibrate the goods market and partially offset the rise in aggregate demand following a positive realization of u, the exchange-rate movement helps stabilize aggregate output. As a result, the effect of u on y is smaller under flexible exchange rates than under fixed exchange rates.[25]

The choice of exchange-rate regime influences the manner in which economic disturbances affect the small open economy. While the model examined here does not provide an internal welfare criterion (such as the utility of the representative agent in the economy), such models have often been supplemented with loss functions depending on output or inflation volatility (such as we used in section 6.3.2 to study

---

25. This result is consistent with the estimates for Japan reported in Hutchison and Walsh (1992). Obstfeld (1985) discusses the insulation proportion of exchange rate regimes.

policy coordination), which are then used to rank alternative exchange-rate regimes. Based on such measures, the choice of an exchange-rate regime should depend on the relative importance of various disturbances. If volatility of foreign prices is of major concern, a flexible exchange rate will serve to insulate the domestic economy from real exchange-rate fluctuations that would otherwise affect domestic output and prices. If domestic monetary instability is a source of economic fluctuations, a fixed-exchange-rate system provides an automatic monetary response to offset such disturbances.

The role of economic disturbances in the choice of a policy regime is an important topic of study in monetary-policy analysis. It figures most prominently in discussion of the choice between using an interest rate or a monetary aggregate as the instrument of monetary policy. This topic forms the major focus of Chapter 9.

6.5 Summary

This chapter has reviewed various models that are useful for studying aspects of open-economy monetary economics. A two-country model whose equilibrium conditions were consistent with optimizing agents was presented. This model, based on the work of Obstfeld and Rogoff, preserved the classical dichotomy between real and monetary factors when prices and wages were assumed to be perfectly flexible. In this case, the price level and the nominal exchange rate could be expressed simply in terms of the current and expected future path of the nominal money supplies in the two countries.

Two primary lessons are that new channels by which monetary factors affect the economy are present in an open economy, and the choice of exchange-rate regime has important implications for the role of monetary policy. With sticky nominal wages, monetary factors have important short-run effects on the real exchange rate. Exchange-rate movements alter the relative price of domestic and foreign goods, leading to impacts on aggregate demand and supply. In addition, consumer prices, because they are indices of domestic currency prices of domestically produced and foreign-produced goods, will respond to exchange-rate movements.[26] While the models of this chapter have not addressed the issue of inflation persistence, the impact of exchange-rate movements on consumer price inflation suggests that monetary policy may have a quicker effect on inflation in more open economies.

Unlike the analysis of the closed economy, the Obstfeld-Rogoff model implied that monetary-induced output movements would have persistent real effects by altering

---

26. Duguay (1994) provides evidence on these channels in the case of Canada.

the distribution of wealth between economies. In general, standard open-economy frameworks used for policy analysis assume that the real effects of monetary policy arise only in the short run and are due to nominal rigidities. Over time, as wages and prices adjust, real output, real interest rates, and the real exchange rate return to equilibrium levels that are independent of monetary policy. This long-run neutrality means that these models, like their closed-economy counterparts, imply that the long-run effects of monetary policy fall on prices, inflation, nominal interest rates, and the nominal exchange rate. One implication is that the rate of inflation is an appropriate long-run objective for monetary policy while the growth rate of real output and the level of the real exchange rate are not. In the short run, however, monetary policy can have important effects on the manner in which real output and the real exchange rate fluctuate around their longer-run equilibrium values.

6.6   Appendix

6.6.1   The Obstfeld-Rogoff Model

This appendix provides the derivation of some of the components of the Obstfeld-Rogoff (1995, 1996) model.

6.6.1.1   Individual Product Demand   The demand functions faced by individual producers are obtained as the solution to the following problem:

$$\max \left[\int_0^1 c(z)^q \, dz \right]^{\frac{1}{q}} \quad \text{subject to} \quad \int_0^1 p(z)c(z) \, dz = Z$$

for given total expenditure Z. Letting λ denote the Lagrangian multiplier associated with the budget constraint, the first-order conditions imply, for all z,

$$c(z)^{q-1} \left[\int_0^1 c(z)^q \, dz \right]^{\frac{1}{q}-1} = \lambda p(z)$$

For any two goods z and z', therefore, $[c(z)/c(z')]^{q-1} = p(z)/p(z')$, or

$$c(z) = c(z') \left[\frac{p(z')}{p(z)} \right]^{\frac{1}{1-q}}$$

If this expression is substituted into the budget constraint, we obtain

$$\int_0^1 p(z)c(z') \left[\frac{p(z')}{p(z)} \right]^{\frac{1}{1-q}} dz = c(z')p(z')^{\frac{1}{1-q}} \left[\int_0^1 p(z)^{\frac{q}{q-1}} \, dz \right] = Z \qquad (6.61)$$

Using the definition of P given in (6.3), both sides of equation (6.61) can be divided by P to yield

$$\frac{c(z')p(z')^{\frac{1}{1-q}}\left[\int_0^1 p(z)^{\frac{q}{q-1}}\,dz\right]}{\left[\int_0^1 p(z)^{\frac{q}{q-1}}\right]^{\frac{q-1}{q}}} = \frac{Z}{P}$$

This expression can be simplified to

$$c(z')\left[\frac{p(z')}{P}\right]^{\frac{1}{1-q}} = \frac{Z}{P} \quad \text{or} \quad c(z') = \left[\frac{p(z')}{P}\right]^{\frac{1}{q-1}}C \qquad (6.62)$$

where $C = \dfrac{Z}{P}$ is total real consumption of the composite good. Equation (6.62) implies the demand for good z by agent j is equal to $c^j(z) = \left[\dfrac{p(z)}{P}\right]^{1/(q-1)}C^j$, so the world demand for product z will be equal to

$$y_t^d(z) \equiv n\left[\frac{p_t(z)}{P_t}\right]^{\frac{1}{q-1}}C_t + (1-n)\left[\frac{p_t^*(z)}{P_t^*}\right]^{\frac{1}{q-1}}C_t^*$$

$$= \left[\frac{p_t(z)}{P_t}\right]^{\frac{1}{q-1}}C_t^w \qquad (6.63)$$

where $C^w = nC + (1-n)C^*$ is world real consumption. Notice that we have used the law of one price here, since it implies that the relative prices for good z are the same for home and foreign consumers: $\dfrac{p(z)}{P} = \dfrac{Sp^*(z)}{SP^*} = \dfrac{p^*(z)}{P^*}$. Finally, note that (6.63) implies

$$p_t(z) = P_t\left[\frac{y_t^d(z)}{C_t^w}\right]^{q-1} \qquad (6.64)$$

6.6.1.2 The Individual's Decision Problem Each individual begins period t with existing asset holdings B_{t-1}^j and M_{t-1}^j and chooses how much of good j to produce (subject to the world demand function for good j), how much to consume, and what levels of real bonds and money to hold. These choices are made to maximize utility given by (6.1) and subject to the following budget constraint:

$$C_t^j + B_t^j + \frac{M_t^j}{P_t} \leq \frac{p_t(j)}{P_t}y_t(j) + R_{t-1}B_{t-1}^j + \frac{M_{t-1}^j}{P_t} + \tau_t$$

where τ_t is the real net transfer from the government and R_t is the real gross rate of return. From equation (6.64), agent j's real income from producing $y(j)$ will be equal to $y(j)^q (C_t^w)^{1-q}$, so the budget constraint can be written as

$$C_t^j + B_t^j + \frac{M_t^j}{P_t} = y_t(j)^q (C_t^w)^{1-q} + R_{t-1} B_{t-1}^j + \frac{M_{t-1}^j}{P_t} + \tau_t \qquad (6.65)$$

The value function for the individual's decision problem is

$$V(B_{t-1}^j, M_{t-1}^j) = \max \left\{ \log C_t^j + b \log \frac{M_t^j}{P_t} - \frac{k}{2} y_t(j)^2 + \beta V(B_t^j, M_t^j) \right\}$$

where the maximization is subject to (6.65). Letting λ denote the Lagrangian multiplier associated with the budget constraint, first-order conditions are

$$\frac{1}{C_t^j} - \lambda_t = 0 \qquad (6.66)$$

$$\frac{b}{M_t^j} + \beta V_2(B_t^j, M_t^j) - \frac{\lambda_t}{P_t} = 0 \qquad (6.67)$$

$$-k y_t(j) + \lambda_t q y_t(j)^{q-1} (C_t^w)^{1-q} = 0 \qquad (6.68)$$

$$\beta V_1(B_t^j, M_t^j) - \lambda_t = 0 \qquad (6.69)$$

$$V_1(B_{t-1}^j, M_{t-1}^j) = \lambda_t R_{t-1} \qquad (6.70)$$

$$V_2(B_{t-1}^j, M_{t-1}^j) = \frac{\lambda_t}{P_t} \qquad (6.71)$$

We also have the transversality condition $\lim_{i \to \infty} \prod_{k=0}^{i} R_{t+k-1}^{-1} \left(B_{t+i}^j + \frac{M_{t+i}^j}{P_{t+i}} \right) = 0$.

These first-order conditions lead to the standard Euler condition for consumption

$$C_{t+1}^j = \beta R_t C_t^j$$

which is obtained using (6.66), (6.69), and (6.70). Equations (6.68) and (6.66) imply that the optimal production level the individual chooses satisfies

$$y_t(j)^{2-q} = \frac{q}{k} \frac{(C_t^w)^{1-q}}{C_t^j} \qquad (6.72)$$

Equation (6.67) yields an expression for the real demand for money,

$$\frac{M_t^j}{P_t} = bC_t^j \left(\frac{1+i_t}{i_t} \right)$$

where $(1 + i_t) = R_t P_{t+1}/P_t$ is the gross nominal rate of interest from period t to $t + 1$. This expression should look familiar from Chapter 2.

6.6.2 The Small-Open-Economy Model

This appendix employs the method of undetermined coefficients to obtain the equilibrium exchange-rate and price-level processes consistent with (6.49)–(6.57). The equations of the model are repeated here, where the real exchange rate ρ_t has been replaced by $s_t + p_t^* - p_t$, r_t by $r^* - (s_t + p_t^* - p_t) + \mathrm{E}_t(s_{t+1} + p_{t+1}^* - p_{t+1})$, i_t by $i_t^* + \mathrm{E}_t s_{t+1} - s_t$, and q_t by $p_t + (1 - h)(s_t + p_t^* - p_t)$:

$$y_t = -b_1(s_t + p_t^* - p_t) + b_2(p_t - \mathrm{E}_{t-1}p_t) + e_t \tag{6.73}$$

$$y_t = a_1(s_t + p_t^* - p_t) - a_2[r^* - (s_t + p_t^* - p_t) + \mathrm{E}_t(s_{t+1} + p_{t+1}^* - p_{t+1})] + u_t \tag{6.74}$$

$$m_t - [p_t + (1 - h)(s_t + p_t^* - p_t)] = y_t - c(i_t^* + \mathrm{E}_t s_{t+1} - s_t) + v_t \tag{6.75}$$

$$m_t = \mu + m_{t-1} + \varphi_t - \gamma\varphi_{t-1}, \quad 0 \le \gamma \le 1 \tag{6.76}$$

$$p_t^* = \pi^* + p_{t-1}^* + \phi_t \tag{6.77}$$

Substituting the aggregate-demand relationship (6.74), the money-supply process (6.76), and the foreign price process (6.77) into the money demand equation (6.75) yields, after some rearrangement,

$$A_1 p_t + A_2 s_t = C_0 + \mu + m_{t-1} + \varphi_t - \gamma\varphi_{t-1}$$

$$- (1 - h + a_1)(p_{t-1}^* + \phi_t) - a_2 \mathrm{E}_t p_{t+1}$$

$$+ (a_2 + c)\mathrm{E}_t s_{t+1} - u_t - v_t \tag{6.78}$$

where $A_1 = h - a_1 - a_2$, $A_2 = 1 - h + a_1 + a_2 + c > 0$ and $C_0 = (c + a_2)r^* - (1 - h + a_1 - a_2 - c)\pi^*$. In deriving equation (6.78), two additional results have been used: from (6.77), $\mathrm{E}_t p_{t+1}^* = 2\pi^* + p_{t-1} + \phi_t$, and $i_t^* = r^* + \mathrm{E}_t p_{t+1}^* - p_t^* = r^* + \pi^*$.

Using the aggregate-supply and -demand relationships (6.73) and (6.74),

$$B_1 p_t + B_2 s_t = -b_2 \mathrm{E}_{t-1}p_t + a_2(\mathrm{E}_t s_{t+1} - \mathrm{E}_t p_{t+1}) - (a_1 + b_1)\pi^*$$

$$+ a_2(r^* + \pi^*) + e_t - u_t - (a_1 + b_1)(p_{t-1}^* + \phi_t) \tag{6.79}$$

where $B_1 = -(a_1 + a_2 + b_1 + b_2) < 0$, and $B_2 = a_1 + a_2 + b_1 > 0$.

The state variables at time t are m_{t-1}, p_{t-1}^*, and the various random disturbances. To rule out possible bubble solutions, we follow McCallum (1983a) and hypothesize minimum state-variable solutions of the form:[27]

$$p_t = k_0 + m_{t-1} + k_1 p_{t-1}^* + k_2 \varphi_t + k_3 \varphi_{t-1} + k_4 u_t + k_5 e_t + k_6 v_t + k_7 \phi_t$$
$$s_t = d_0 + m_{t-1} + d_1 p_{t-1}^* + d_2 \varphi_t + d_3 \varphi_{t-1} + d_4 u_t + d_5 e_t + d_6 v_t + d_7 \phi_t$$

These imply

$$E_{t-1} p_t = k_0 + m_{t-1} + k_1 p_{t-1}^* + k_3 \varphi_{t-1}$$

$$E_t p_{t+1} = k_0 + m_t + k_1 p_t^* + k_3 \varphi_t$$

$$= k_0 + \mu + m_{t-1} + (1+k_3)\varphi_t - \gamma\varphi_{t-1} + k_1(\pi^* + p_{t-1}^* + \phi_t)$$

and

$$E_t s_{t+1} = d_0 + \mu + m_{t-1} + (1+d_3)\varphi_t - \gamma\varphi_{t-1} + d_1(\pi^* + p_{t-1}^* + \phi_t)$$

These expressions for p_t and s_t, together with those for the various expectations of p and s, can be substituted into (6.78) and (6.79). These then yield a pair of equations that must be satisfied by each pair (k_i, d_i). For example, the coefficients on p_{t-1}^* in (6.78) and (6.79) must satisfy

$$A_1 k_1 + A_2 d_1 = -(1 - h + a_1) - a_2 k_1 + (a_2 + c) d_1$$

and

$$B_1 k_1 + B_2 d_1 = a_2(d_1 - k_1) - b_2 k_1 - (a_1 + b_1)$$

Using the definitions of A_i and B_i to cancel terms, the second equation implies $d_1 = k_1 - 1$. Substituting this back into the first equation yields $k_1 = 0$. Therefore, the solution pair is $(k_1, d_1) = (0, -1)$. Repeating this process yields the values for (k_i, d_i) reported in equations (6.58) and (6.59).

6.7   Problems

1. Suppose $m_t = m_0 + \gamma m_{t-1}$ and $m_t^* = m_0^* + \gamma^* m_{t-1}^*$. Use equation (6.24) to show how the behavior of the nominal exchange rate under flexible prices depends on the degree of serial correlation exhibited by the home and foreign money supplies.

---

27. We have set the coefficient on m_{t-1} equal to 1 in these trial solutions. It is easy to verify that this assumption is in fact correct.

2. In the model of section 6.3 used to study policy coordination, aggregate-demand shocks were set equal to zero in order to focus on a common aggregate-supply shock. Suppose instead that the aggregate-supply shocks are zero, and the demand shocks are given by $u \equiv x + \phi$ and $u^* \equiv x + \phi^*$ so that x represents a common demand shock and ϕ and ϕ^* are uncorrelated country-specific demand shocks. Derive policy outcomes under coordinated and (Nash) noncoordinated policy settings. Is there a role for policy coordination in the face of demand shocks? Explain.

3. Continuing with the same model as in the previous question, how are real interest rates affected by a common aggregate-demand shock?

4. Policy coordination with asymmetric supply shocks: Continuing with the same model as in the previous two questions, assume that there are no demand shocks but that the supply shocks e and e^* are uncorrelated. Derive policy outcomes under co-ordinated and uncoordinated policy settings. Does coordination or noncoordination lead to a greater inflation response to supply shocks? Explain.

5. Assume the home-country policy maker acts as a Stackelberg leader and recog-nizes that foreign inflation will be given by equation (6.47). How does this change in the nature of the strategic interaction affect the home country's response to disturbances?

6. In a small open economy with perfectly flexible nominal wages, the text showed that the real exchange rate and domestic price level were given by

$$p_t = \sum_{i=0}^{\infty} d^i E_t \left[\frac{a_2 r^*_{t+i} + e_{t+i} - u_{t+i}}{a_1 + a_2 + b_1} \right]$$

and

$$p_t = \frac{1}{1+c} \sum_{i=0}^{\infty} \left(\frac{c}{1+c} \right)^i E_t [m_{t+i} - z_{t+i} - v_{t+i}]$$

where $z_{t+i} \equiv y_{t+i} + (1 - h)p_{t+i} - cr_{t+i}$. Assume $r^* = 0$ for all t and that e, u, and $z + v$ all follow first-order autoregressive processes (e.g., $e_t = \rho_e e_{t-1} + x_{et}$ for x_e white noise). Let the nominal money supply be given by

$$m_t = g_1 e_{t-1} + g_2 u_{t-1} + g_3 (z_{t-1} + v_{t-1})$$

Find equilibrium expressions for the real exchange rate, the nominal exchange rate, and the consumer price index. What values of the parameters g_1, g_2, and g_3 minimize fluctuations in s_t? in q_t? in p_t? Are there any conflicts between stabilizing the exchange rate (real or nominal) and stabilizing the consumer price index?

7. Equation (6.42) for the equilibrium real exchange rate in the two-country model of section 6.3.1 takes the form $p_t = AE_t p_{t+1} + v_t$. Suppose $v_t = \gamma v_{t-1} + \psi_t$, where ψ_t is a mean-zero, white-noise process. Suppose the solution for p_t is of the form $p_t = bv_t$. Find the value of b. How does it depend on γ?

7 The Credit Channel of Monetary Policy

7.1 Introduction

The previous chapters have illustrated several channels through which monetary factors and monetary policy may affect the real economy. When prices are flexible, anticipated inflation affects the opportunity cost of holding money. This effect taxes money holdings, reducing utility directly if real balances enter agents' utility functions or indirectly in cash-in-advance models by raising the total cost of goods whose purchase requires cash. When prices or nominal wages are sticky, changes in the current and expected future path of the money supply affect real aggregate demand and output. These effects operated, in the closed economy, through interest rates and the impact interest rates have on real aggregate demand.

In the open economy, exchange-rate channels operate. The exchange rate affects the domestic price level directly by influencing the domestic currency price of imports. A depreciation raises the domestic consumer price index. Because exchange rates respond quickly to interest-rate changes, this exchange-rate-to-inflation channel speeds up the impact of monetary policy on domestic inflation. Exchange-rate movements also alter relative prices when nominal wages or prices are sticky, and these real-exchange-rate effects induce substitution effects between domestic and foreign goods, thereby influencing aggregate demand and supply.

Many economists, however, have argued that monetary policy has direct effects on aggregate spending that do not operate through traditional interest-rate or exchange-rate channels, and a large literature in recent years has focused on credit markets as playing a critical role in the transmission of monetary policy actions to the real economy. Money has traditionally played a special role in macroeconomics and monetary theory because of the relationship between the nominal stock of money and the aggregate price level. The importance of money for understanding the determination of the general level of prices and average inflation rates, however, does not necessarily imply that the stock of money is the key variable that links the real and financial sectors or the most appropriate indicator of the short-run influence of financial factors on the economy.

The credit view stresses the distinct role played by financial assets and liabilities. Rather than aggregate all nonmoney financial assets into a single category called bonds, the credit view argues that macroeconomic models need to distinguish between different nonmonetary assets, either along the dimension of bank versus nonbank sources of funds or along the more general dimension of internal versus external financing. The credit view also highlights heterogeneity among borrowers, stressing that some borrowers may be more vulnerable to changes in credit conditions than others. Finally, investment may be sensitive to variables such as net worth or cash flow if agency costs associated with imperfect information or costly monitoring create a wedge between the cost of internal and external finance. A rise in interest rates may have a much stronger contractionary impact on the economy if balance sheets are already weak, introducing the possibility that nonlinearities in the impact of monetary policy may be important.

Discussions of the credit channel often distinguish between a bank lending channel and a broader financial-accelerator mechanism.[1] The bank lending channel emphasizes the special nature of bank credit and the role of banks in the economy's financial structure. In the bank lending view, banks play a particularly critical role in the transmission of monetary-policy actions to the real economy. Policy actions that affect the reserve positions of banks will generate adjustments in interest rates and in the components of the banking sector's balance sheet. Traditional models of the monetary transmission mechanism focus on the impact of these interest-rate changes on money demand and on consumption and investment decisions by households and firms. The ultimate effects on bank deposits and the supply of money are reflected in adjustments to the liability side of the banking sector's balance sheet.

The effects on banking-sector reserves and interest rates also influence the supply of bank credit, the asset side of the balance sheet. If banks cannot offset a decline in reserves by adjusting securities holdings or raising funds through issuing nonreservable liabilities (such as CDs in the United States), bank lending must contract. If banking lending is "special" in the sense that bank borrowers do not have close substitutes for obtaining funds, variation in the availability of bank lending may have an independent impact on aggregate spending. Key then to the bank lending channel is the lack of close substitutes for deposit liabilities on the liability side of the banking sector's balance sheet and the lack of close substitutes for bank credit on the part of borrowers.

Imperfect information plays an important role in credit markets, and bank credit may be "special," that is, have no close substitutes, because of information advantages banks have in providing both transactions services and credit to businesses. Small firms in particular may have difficulty obtaining funding from nonbank sources, so a contraction in bank lending will force these firms to contract their activities.

The broad credit channel is not restricted to the bank lending channel. Credit-market imperfections may characterize all credit markets, influencing the nature of financial contracts, raising the possibility of equilibria with rationing, and creating a wedge between the costs of internal and external financing. This wedge arises be-

---

1. A variety of excellent surveys and overviews of the credit channel are available. These include Gertler (1988), Bernanke (1993), Ramey (1993), Gertler and Gilchrist (1993), Kashyap and Stein (1993), Bernanke and Gertler (1995), Cecchetti (1995), Hubbard (1995), and Bernanke, Gertler, and Gilchrist (1996).

cause of agency costs associated with information asymmetries and the inability of lenders to monitor borrowers costlessly. As a result, cash flow and net worth become important in affecting the cost and availability of finance and the level of investment spending. A recession that weakens a firm's sources of internal finance can generate a "financial-accelerator" effect; the firm is forced to rely more on higher-cost external funds just at the time the decline in internal finance drives up the relative cost of external funds. Contractionary monetary policy that produces an economic slowdown will reduce firm cash flow and profits. If this policy increases the external finance premium, there will be further contractionary effects on spending. In this way, the credit channel can serve to propagate and amplify an initial monetary contraction.

Financial-accelerator effects can arise from the adjustment of asset prices to contractionary monetary policy. Borrowers may be limited in the amount they can borrow by the value of their assets that can serve as collateral. A rise in interest rates that lowers asset prices reduces the market value of borrowers' collateral. This reduction in value may then force some firms to reduce investment spending as their ability to borrow declines.

The credit channel also operates when shifts in monetary policy alter either the efficiency of financial markets in matching borrowers and lenders or the extent to which borrowers face rationing in credit markets so that aggregate spending is influenced by liquidity constraints. There are several definitions of nonprice credit rationing. Jaffee and Russell (1976) define credit rationing as existing when, at the quoted interest rate, the lender supplies a smaller loan than the borrower demands. Jaffee and Stiglitz (1990), however, point out that this practice represents standard price rationing; larger loans will normally be accompanied by a higher default rate and therefore carry a higher interest rate. Instead, Jaffee and Stiglitz characterize "pure credit rationing" as occurring when, among a group of agents (firms or individuals) who appear to be identical, some receive loans and others do not. Stiglitz and Weiss define equilibrium credit rationing as present whenever "either (a) among loan applicants who appear to be identical some receive a loan and others do not, and the rejected applicants would not receive a loan even if they offered to pay a higher interest rate; or (b) there are identifiable groups of individuals in the population who, with a given supply of credit, are unable to obtain loans at any interest rate, even though with a larger supply of credit, they would" (Stiglitz and Weiss 1981, pp. 394–395). The critical aspect of this definition is that at the market equilibrium interest rate, there is an unsatisfied demand for loans that cannot be eliminated through higher interest rates. Rejected loan applicants cannot succeed in getting a loan by offering to pay a higher interest rate.

It is important to recognize that credit rationing is sufficient but not necessary for a credit channel to exist. A theme of Gertler (1988), Bernanke (1993), and Bernanke and Gertler (1989) is that agency costs in credit markets will vary countercyclically; a monetary tightening that raises interest rates and generates a real economic slowdown will cause firm balance sheets to deteriorate, raising agency costs and lowering the efficiency of credit allocation. Changes in credit conditions are not reflected solely in interest-rate levels. Thus, the general issue is to understand how credit-market imperfections affect macroeconomic equilibrium and the channels through which monetary policy actions are transmitted to the real economy.

Critical to the presence of a distinct credit channel is the presence of market imperfections in financial markets. This first task then, is to review theories of credit-market imperfections based on adverse selection, moral hazard, and monitoring costs; this is done in section 7.2. These theories help to explain many of the distinctive features of financial markets, from collateral to debt contracts to the possibility of credit rationing. This material provides the microfoundations for the macroeconomic analysis of credit channels in section 7.3. Section 7.4 reviews the empirical evidence on the role played by credit channels in the transmission of monetary-policy actions. The main focus of the chapter will be on credit markets for firms undertaking investment projects. This approach is chosen primarily for convenience; the theoretical models may also be applied to the consumer loan market, and there is evidence that a significant fraction of households behave as if they face liquidity constraints that link consumption spending more closely to current income than would be predicted by forward-looking models of consumption.[2]

7.2   Imperfect Information in Credit Markets

The role of credit effects in the transmission of monetary policy arises as a result of imperfect information between parties in credit relationships. The information that each party to a credit transaction brings to the exchange will have important implications for the nature of credit contracts, the ability of credit markets to efficiently match borrowers and lenders, and the role played by the rate of interest in allocating credit among borrowers. The nature of credit markets can lead to distinct roles for different types of lenders (for example, bank versus nonbank) and different types of borrowers (e.g., small firms versus large firms).

2. Empirical evidence on consumption and liquidity constraints can be found in Campbell and Mankiw (1989, 1991), who provide estimates of the fraction of liquidity-constrained households for a number of OECD countries.

Whereas the early large-scale econometric models such as the MPS model did incorporate credit-rationing channels, the modern analysis of credit markets from the perspective of imperfect-information theory dates from Jaffee and Russell (1976), Keeton (1979), and Stiglitz and Weiss (1981). These models of credit rationing rely on imperfect information, although the exact mechanisms emphasized by different authors—adverse selection, moral hazard, or monitoring costs—have varied. These models generally imply that in some circumstances the lender's expected profits will decline with an increase in the interest rate charged to borrowers. Lenders will not raise interest rates on loans past the point at which expected profits start to decline even if there are borrowers who would be willing to borrow at higher interest rates. Equilibrium may then be characterized by an excess demand for loans and rationing.

7.2.1   Adverse Selection

Jaffee and Russell (1976) analyze a credit-market model in which there are two types of borrowers, "honest" ones who always repay and "dishonest" ones who only repay if it is in their interest to do so. Ex ante, the two types appear identical to lenders. Default is assumed to impose a cost on the defaulter, and dishonest borrowers default whenever the loan repayment amount exceeds the cost of default. By assuming a distribution of default costs across the population of borrowers, Jaffee and Russell show that the fraction of borrowers who default is increasing in the loan amount.[3] In a pooling equilibrium, lenders offer the same loan contract (interest rate and amount) to all borrowers, since they are unable to distinguish between the two types.[4] If lenders operate with constant returns to scale, if there is free entry, and if funds are available to lenders at an exogenously given opportunity cost, then the equilibrium loan rate must satisfy a zero-profit condition for lenders. Since the expected return on a loan is less than or equal to the interest rate charged, the actual interest rate on loans must equal or exceed the opportunity cost of funds to the lenders.[5]

The effect of borrower heterogeneity and imperfect information on credit-market equilibria can be illustrated following Stiglitz and Weiss (1981). The lender's ex-

---

3. See Smith (1983) for a general equilibrium version of Jaffee and Russell's model using an overlapping-generations framework.

4. This model ignores the possibility of separating equilibrium in which the lender offers two contracts and the borrowers (truthfully) signal their type by the contract they choose.

5. If the probability of default were zero, the constant-returns-to-scale assumption with free entry would ensure that lenders charge an interest rate on loans equal to the opportunity cost of funds. If default rates are positive, then the expected return on a loan is less than the actual interest rate charged, and the loan interest rate must be greater than the opportunity cost of funds.

pected return on a loan is a function of the interest rate charged and the probability the loan is repaid, but individual borrowers differ in their probabilities of repayment. Suppose borrowers come in two types. Type G repays with probability q_g; type B repays with probability $q_b < q_g$. If lenders can observe borrower type, each type will be charged a different interest rate to reflect the differing repayment probabilities. If the supply of credit is perfectly elastic at the opportunity cost of r, and if lenders are risk neutral and able to lend to a large number of borrowers so that the law of large numbers holds, then all type G's can borrow at an interest rate of r/q_g, while type B's borrow at $r/q_b > r/q_g$. At these interest rates, the lender's expected return from lending to either type of borrower is equal to her opportunity cost of r. No credit rationing occurs; riskier borrowers are simply charged higher interest rates.

Now suppose the lender cannot observe the borrower's type. It may be the case that changes in the terms of a loan (interest rate, collateral, amount) affect the mix of borrower types the lender attracts. If increases in the loan interest rate shift the mix of borrowers, raising the fraction of type B's, the expected return to the lender might actually decline with higher loan rates because of adverse selection. In this case, further increases in the loan rate would lower lender-expected profits, even if an excess demand for loans remains. The intuition is similar to Akerlof's market for lemons (Akerlof 1970). Assume that a fraction g of all borrowers are of type G. Suppose the lender charges an interest rate of r_l such that $g q_g r_l + (1 - g) q_b r_l = r$, or $r_l = r/[g q_g + (1 - g) q_b]$. At this loan rate, the lender earns her required return of r if borrowers are drawn randomly from the population. But at this rate, the pool of borrowers is no longer the same as in the population at large. Since $r/q_g < r_l < r/q_b$, the lender is more likely to attract type B borrowers, and the lender's expected return would be less than r.

Loans are, however, characterized by more than just their interest rate. For example, suppose a loan is characterized by its interest rate r_l, the loan amount L, and the collateral the lender requires C. The borrower repayment probability depends on the (risky) return yielded by the borrower's project. If the project return is R, then the lender is repaid if

$$L(1 + r_l) \leq R + C$$

If $L(1 + r_l) > R + C$, the borrower defaults and the lender receives $R + C$.

Suppose the return R is $R' + x$ with probability $\frac{1}{2}$ and $R' - x$ with probability $\frac{1}{2}$. The expected return is R' while the variance is x^2. An increase in x represents a mean-preserving spread in the return distribution and corresponds to an increase in the project risk. Assume that $R' - x < (1 + r_l)L - C$ so that the borrower must default when the bad outcome occurs. If the project pays off $R' + x$, the borrower receives $R' + x - (1 + r_l)L$; if the bad outcome occurs, the borrower receives $-C$, that is, any collateral is lost. The expected profit to the borrower is

$$\mathrm{E}\pi^B = \tfrac{1}{2}[R' + x - (1 + r_l)]L - \tfrac{1}{2}C$$

Define

$$x^*(r_l, L, C) \equiv (1 + r_l)L + C - R' \tag{7.1}$$

Expected profits for the borrower are positive for all $x > x^*$. This critical cutoff value of x is increasing in r_l. Recall that increases in x imply an increase in the project risk as measured by the variance of returns. An increase in the loan rate r_l increases x^*, and this implies that some borrowers with less risky projects will find it unprofitable to borrow if the loan rate rises, while borrowers with riskier projects will still find it worthwhile to borrow. Because the borrower can lose no more than her collateral in the bad state, expected profits are a convex function of the project return and therefore increase with an increase in risk (for a constant-mean return).

While the expected return to the firm is increasing in risk as measured by x, the lender's return is decreasing in x. To see this point, note that the lender's expected return is

$$\mathrm{E}\pi^L = \tfrac{1}{2}[(1 + r_l)L] + \tfrac{1}{2}[C + R' - x]$$

which decreases with x. Because the lender receives a fixed amount in the good state, the lender's expected return is a concave function of the project's return and therefore decreases with an increase in risk.

Now suppose there are two groups of borrowers, those with $x = x_g$ and those with $x = x_b$, with $x_g < x_b$. Type x_g's have lower risk projects. From (7.1), if the loan rate r_l is low enough such that $x_b > x_g \geq x^*(r_l, B, C)$, then both types will find it profitable to borrow. If each type is equally likely, the lender's expected return is

$$\mathrm{E}\pi^L = \tfrac{1}{4}[(1 + r_l)L + C + R' - x_g] + \tfrac{1}{4}[(1 + r_l)L + C + R' - x_b]$$

$$= \tfrac{1}{2}[(1 + r_l)L + C + R'] - \tfrac{1}{4}(x_g + x_b), \qquad x^*(r_l, L, C) \leq x_g$$

which is increasing in r_l. But as soon as r_l increases to the point where $x^*(r_l, B, C) = x_g$, any further increase causes all x_g types to stop borrowing. Only type x_b's will still find it profitable to borrow, and the lender's expected profit falls to

$$\mathrm{E}\pi^L = \tfrac{1}{2}[(1 + r_l)L + C + R'] - \tfrac{1}{2}x_b, \qquad x_g \leq x^*(r_l, L, C) \leq x_b$$

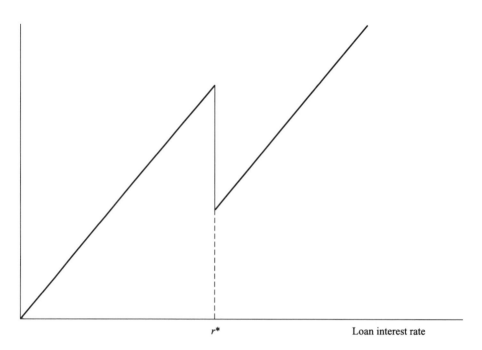

Figure 7.1
Expected Loan Profit with Adverse Selection

As a result, the lender's expected profit as a function of the loan rate is increasing for $x^*(r_l, L, C) \leq x_g$ and then falls discretely at $1 + r_l = (x_g - C + R')/L$ as all low-risk types exit the market. This situation is illustrated in Figure 7.1, where r^* denotes the loan rate that tips the composition of the pool of borrowers.

The existence of a local maximum in the lender's profit function at r^* introduces the possibility that credit rationing will occur in equilibrium. Suppose at r^* there remains an excess demand for loans. Type x_g's would not be willing to borrow at a rate above r^*, but type x_b's would. If the lender responds to the excess demand by raising the loan rate, expected profits decline. Equilibrium may involve a loan rate of r^* with some potential borrowers being rationed.[6] Thus, adverse selection provides one rationale for a lender's profit function that is not monotonic in the loan rate. Equilibrium credit rationing may exist because lenders find it unprofitable to raise the interest rate on loans even in the face of an excess demand for loans.

6. As Figure 7.1 suggests, if the demand for loans is strong enough, the lender may be able to raise the loan rate sufficiently so that expected profits do rise.

7.2.2   Moral Hazard

Moral hazard can arise in credit markets when the borrower's behavior is influenced by the terms of the loan contract. In the model of the previous section, the borrower decided whether to borrow, but the project return was exogenous. Borrowers differed in terms of the underlying riskiness of their projects, and adverse selection occurred as loan rate changes affected the pool of borrowers. Suppose instead that each borrower can choose between several projects of differing risk. If the lender cannot monitor this choice, a moral-hazard problem arises. The lender's expected return may not be monotonic in the interest rate charged on the loans. Higher loan rates lead the borrower to invest in riskier projects, lowering the expected return to the lender.

To illustrate this situation, again following Stiglitz and Weiss (1981), suppose the borrower can invest in either project A, which pays off R^a in the good state and 0 in the bad state, or in project B, which pays off $R^b > R^a$ in the good state and 0 in the bad state. Suppose the probability of success is p^a for project A and p^b for project B, with $p^a > p^b$. Project B is the riskier project. Further, assume the expected payoff from A is higher: $p^a R^a > p^b R^b$. By investing in A, the borrower's expected return is

$$\mathrm{E}\pi^A = p^a[R^a - (1 + r_l)L] - (1 - p^a)C$$

where the borrower loses collateral C if the project fails. The expected return from project B is

$$\mathrm{E}\pi^B = p^b[R^b - (1 + r_l)L] - (1 - p^b)C$$

The expected returns on the two projects depend on the interest rate on the loan r_l. It is straightforward to show that

$$\mathrm{E}\pi^A > \mathrm{E}\pi^B$$

if and only if

$$\frac{p^a R^a - p^b R^b}{p^a - p^b} > (1 + r_l)L - C$$

The left side of this condition is independent of the loan rate, but the right side is increasing in r_l. Define r_l^* as the loan rate at which the expected returns to the borrower from the two projects are equal. This outcome occurs when

$$(1 + r_l^*)L - C = \frac{p^a R^a - p^b R^b}{p^a - p^b} > 0$$

For a loan rate less than r_l^*, the borrower will prefer to invest in project A; for a loan rate above r_l^*, the riskier project B is preferred. The expected return to the lender, therefore, will be $p^a(1 + r_l)L + (1 - p^a)C$ if $r_l < r_l^*$, and $p^b(1 + r_l)L + (1 - p^b)C$ for $r_l > r_l^*$. Since

$$p^a(1 + r_l^*)L + (1 - p^a)C > p^b(1 + r_l^*)L + (1 - p^b)C \qquad (7.2)$$

lender profits are not monotonic in the loan rate.[7] Just as in the example of the previous section, this conclusion leads to the possibility that credit rationing may characterize the loan-market equilibrium.

7.2.3 Monitoring Costs

The previous analysis illustrated how debt contracts in the presence of adverse selection or moral hazard could lead to credit rationing as an equilibrium phenomena. One limitation of the discussion, however, was the treatment of the nature of the loan contract—repayment equal to a fixed interest rate times the loan amount in some states of nature, zero or a predetermined collateral amount in others—as exogenous. Williamson (1986, 1987a, 1987b) has illustrated how debt contracts and credit rationing can arise, even in the absence of adverse-selection or moral-hazard problems, if lenders must incur costs to monitor borrowers.[8] The intuition behind his result is straightforward. Suppose the lender can observe the borrower's project outcome only at some positive cost. Any repayment schedule that ties the borrower's payment to the project outcome would require that the monitoring cost be incurred; otherwise, the borrower always has an incentive to underreport the success of the project. Expected monitoring costs can be reduced if the borrower is monitored only in some states of nature. If the borrower reports a low project outcome and defaults on the loan, the lender incurs the monitoring cost to verify the truth of the report. If the borrower reports a good project outcome and repays the loan, the lender does not need to incur the monitoring cost.

Following Williamson (1987a), assume there are two types of agents, borrowers and lenders. Lenders are risk neutral and have access to funds at an opportunity cost

---

7. To see this point, note that using the definition of r_l^* implies that after subtracting C from both sides of (7.2) the left side is equal to $p^a[(1 + r_l^*)L - C] = p^a\left(\dfrac{p^a R^a - p^b R^b}{p^a - p^b}\right)$ while the right side is equal to $p^b[(1 + r_l^*)L - C] = p^b\left(\dfrac{p^a R^a - p^b R^b}{p^a - p^b}\right)$. The direction of the inequality follows since $p^a > p^b$.

8. Townsend (1979) provided the first analysis of optimal contracts when it is costly to verify the state.

of r. Each lender takes r as given and offers contracts to borrowers that yield, to the lender, an expected return of r. Assume there are two periods. In period 1, lenders offer contracts to borrowers who have access to a risky investment project that yields a payoff in period 2 of $x \in [0, \bar{x}]$. The return x is a random variable, drawn from a distribution known to both borrowers and lenders. The actual realization is observed costlessly by the borrower; the lender can observe it by first paying a cost of c. This assumption captures the idea that borrowers are likely to have better information about their own projects than do lenders. Lenders can obtain this information by monitoring the project, but such monitoring is costly.

In period 2, after observing x, the borrower reports the project outcome to the lender. Let this report be x^s. While x^s must be in $[0, \bar{x}]$, it need not equal the true x, since the borrower will have an incentive to misreport if doing so is in the borrower's own interest. By choice of normalization, projects require an initial resource investment of 1 unit. Although borrowers have access to an investment project, we assume they have no resources of their own, so to invest they must obtain resources from lenders.

Suppose that monitoring occurs whenever $x^s \in S \subset [0, \bar{x}]$. Otherwise, the lender does not monitor. Denote by $R(x)$ the payment from the borrower to the lender if $x^s \in S$ and monitoring takes place. Because the lender monitors and therefore observes x, the repayment can be made directly a function of the actual x. The return to the lender net of monitoring costs is $R(x) - c$. If the reported value $x^s \notin S$, then no monitoring occurs and the borrower pays $K(x^s)$ to the lender. This payment can only depend on the signal, not the true realization of x, since the lender cannot verify the latter. In this case, the return to the lender is simply $K(x^s)$. Whatever the actual value of $x^s \notin S$, the borrower will report the value that results in the smallest payment to the lender; hence, if monitoring does not occur, the payment to the lender must be equal to a constant, $\bar{K}$.[9] Since all loans are for 1 unit, $\bar{K} - 1$ is the interest rate on the loan when $x^s \notin S$.

If the reported signal is in S, then monitoring occurs so that the lender can learn the true value of x. The borrower will only report an x^s in S if it is in her best interest—that is, reporting $x^s \in S$ must be incentive compatible. For this to be the case requires that the net return to the borrower when $x^s \in S$, equal to $x - R(x)$,

9. That is, suppose x_1 and x_2 are project-return realizations such that the borrower would report x_1^s and $x_2^s \notin S$. If reporting x_1^s results in a larger payment to the lender, the borrower would always report x_2^s.

must exceed the return from reporting a signal not in S, $x - \bar{K}$. That is, incentive compatibility requires that

$$x - R(x) > x - \bar{K} \quad \text{or} \quad \bar{K} > R(x) \quad \text{for all } x^s \in S$$

The borrower will only report a signal that leads to monitoring if $R(x) < \bar{K}$ and will report a signal not in S (so that no monitoring occurs) if $R(x) \geq \bar{K}$.

The optimal contract is a payment schedule $R(x)$ and a value $\bar{K}$ that maximize the borrower's expected return, subject to the constraint that the lender's expected return be at least equal to her opportunity cost r. Let $\Pr[x < y]$ denote the probability that x is less than y. The expected return to the borrower can be written as the expected return conditional on monitoring occurring, $\mathrm{E}[x - R(x) | R(x) < \bar{K}]$ times the probability that $R(x) < \bar{K}$, plus the expected return conditional on $R(x) \geq \bar{K}$ so that no monitoring occurs, times the probability that $R(x) \geq \bar{K}$:

$$\mathrm{E}[R^b] = \mathrm{E}[x - R(x) | R(x) < \bar{K}] \Pr[R(x) < \bar{K}]$$
$$+ \mathrm{E}[x - K | R(x) \geq \bar{K}] \Pr[R(x) \geq \bar{K}] \tag{7.3}$$

The optimal loan contract maximizes this expected return subject to the constraint that the lender's expected return be at least r:

$$\mathrm{E}[R(x) - c | R(x) < \bar{K}] \Pr[R(x) < \bar{K}] + \bar{K} \Pr[R(x) \geq K] \geq r \tag{7.4}$$

The solution to this problem, and therefore the optimal loan contract, has $R(x) = x$. In other words, if the borrower reports a signal that leads the lender to monitor, then the lender takes the entire actual project return. This result corresponds to a loan default in which the lender takes over the project, incurs the monitoring cost c (which in this case we could think of as a liquidation cost), and ends up with $x - c$. If the project earns a sufficient return—that is, $R(x) = x \geq \bar{K}$—then the borrower pays the lender the fixed amount $\bar{K}$. Since $\bar{K}$ is independent of the realization of x, no monitoring is necessary. The presence of monitoring costs and imperfect information leads to the endogenous determination of the optimal loan contract.

The proof that $R(x) = x$ whenever monitoring takes place is straightforward. In equilibrium, the constraint given by (7.4) will be satisfied with equality. Otherwise, the payment to the lender could be reduced in some states, which would increase the expected return to the borrower. Hence,

$$\mathrm{E}[R(x) - c | R(x) < \bar{K}] \Pr[R(x) < \bar{K}] + \bar{K} \Pr[R(x) \geq \bar{K}] = r$$

Any contract that called for $R(x) < x$ for some realizations of x could be replaced by another contract that increases repayment slightly when monitoring occurs but lowers $\bar{K}$ to decrease the range of x for which monitoring actually takes place. This can be done such that the lender's expected profit is unchanged.[10] Using the constraint for the lender's expected return, the expected return to the borrower can be written as

$$\mathrm{E}[R^b] = \mathrm{E}[x - R(x)|R(x) < \bar{K}]\Pr[R(x) < \bar{K}] + \{\mathrm{E}[x|R(x) \geq \bar{K}] - \bar{K}\}\Pr[R(x) \geq \bar{K}]$$

$$= \mathrm{E}[x - R(x)|R(x) < \bar{K}]\Pr[R(x) < \bar{K}] + \mathrm{E}[x|R(x) \geq \bar{K}]\Pr[R(x) \geq \bar{K}]$$

$$\quad - \{r - \mathrm{E}[R(x) - c|R(x) < \bar{K}]\Pr[R(x) < \bar{K}]\}$$

$$= \mathrm{E}[x - c|R(x) < \bar{K}]\Pr[R(x) < \bar{K}] + \mathrm{E}[x|R(x) \geq \bar{K}]\Pr[R(x) \geq \bar{K}] - r$$

$$= \mathrm{E}[x] - c\Pr[R(x) < \bar{K}] - r \tag{7.5}$$

where $\Pr[R(x) < \bar{K}]$ is the probability that monitoring occurs. Equation (7.5) shows that the expected return to the borrower is decreasing in $\bar{K}$. Any contract that lowers $\bar{K}$ and reduces the probability of monitoring while leaving the lender with an expected return of r will be strictly preferred by the borrower. Such a contract can be constructed if $R(x) < x$.[11]

To make the example more specific, suppose x is uniformly distributed on $[0, \bar{x}]$. The expected return to the lender is equal to

$$\int_0^{\bar{K}} (x - c)\frac{1}{x}\,dx + \int_{\bar{K}}^{\bar{x}} \bar{K}\frac{1}{x}\,dx$$

The first term is the expected return to the lender if the borrower defaults, an outcome that occurs whenever $x < \bar{K}$; the probability of this outcome is $\bar{K}/\bar{x}$. The second term is the fixed payment received by the lender whenever $x \geq \bar{K}$, an outcome that occurs with probability $[\bar{x} - \bar{K}]/\bar{x}$. Evaluating the expected return and equating it to r yields the following condition to determine $\bar{K}$:

$$\left(\frac{1}{2}\frac{\bar{K}^2}{\bar{x}} - c\frac{\bar{K}}{\bar{x}}\right) + \bar{K}\left(1 - \frac{\bar{K}}{\bar{x}}\right) = r$$

---

10. $R(x) > x$ is ruled out by the assumption that the borrower has no other resources. If $R(x) < x$ for some x for which monitoring occurs, then the new contract that increases $R(x)$ in those states increases $R(x) - c$ when monitoring does occur. For a given $\bar{K}$, this increases $\mathrm{E}[R(x) - c|R(x) < \bar{K}]$, making the lender's expected profit greater than r. By then lowering $\bar{K}$, monitoring occurs in fewer states, thereby reducing the lender's expected profit so that it again equals r.

11. One implication of (7.5) is that the borrower bears the cost of monitoring; the expected return to the borrower is equal to the total expected project return net of the opportunity cost of funds (r) and expected monitoring costs ($c\Pr[R(x) < \bar{K}]$).

If $(\bar{x} - c)^2 > 2\bar{x}r$, this quadratic has two real solutions, one less than $\bar{x} - c$ and one greater than $\bar{x} - c$.[12] However, the effect of $\bar{K}$ on the lender's expected return is

$$\frac{\bar{K}}{\bar{x}} - \frac{c}{\bar{x}} + \left(1 - \frac{2\bar{K}}{\bar{x}}\right) = 1 - \frac{c + \bar{K}}{\bar{x}}$$

which becomes negative for $\bar{K} > \bar{x} - c$. This means that when the loan repayment amount is large, further increases in the contracted repayment would actually lower the lender's expected return; loan contracts with less monitoring (a lower $\bar{K}$) would be preferred by both borrower and lender, so $\bar{K} > \bar{x} - c$ cannot be in equilibrium.

When the lender's expected profits are no longer monotonic in the loan interest rate but can actually decrease at higher interest rates, the possibility exists of an equilibrium in which some borrowers face credit rationing. In a nonrationing equilibrium, all borrowers receive loans.[13] The expected rate of return r is determined by the condition that loan demand equal loan supply, and the gross interest rate on loans, $\bar{K}$, is less than $\bar{x} - c$. In a credit-rationing equilibrium, $\bar{K} = \bar{x} - c$, and not all potential borrowers receive loans. Even though there are unsatisfied potential borrowers, the interest rate on loans will not rise because the lenders' expected profits are decreasing in the loan rate when $\bar{K} > \bar{x} - c$. Even though all potential borrowers were assumed to be identical ex ante, some receive loans, others do not. The ones that do not get loans would be willing to borrow at an interest rate above the market rate, yet no lenders are willing to lend.

Williamson's model illustrates that neither adverse selection nor moral hazard is necessary for rationing to characterize credit markets. The presence of monitoring costs can account for both the general form of loan contracts in which monitoring occurs only when the borrower defaults—in which case the lender takes over the entire project return—and for rationing to arise in some equilibria.

7.2.4 Agency Costs

Adverse selection, moral hazard, and monitoring costs can all arise as important factors in any relationship in which a principal delegates decision-making authority to an agent. In credit markets, the lender delegates control over resources to a bor-

---

12. These are given by

$$\bar{x} - c \pm \sqrt{(\bar{x} - c)^2 - 2\bar{x}r}$$

13. A complete specification of the model requires assumptions on the number of (potential) borrowers and lenders that ensure an upward-sloping supply curve of funds. See Williamson (1987a) for details on one such specfication.

rower. The inability to monitor the borrower's actions or to share in the borrower's information gives rise to agency costs. Bernanke and Gertler (1989) and Gertler (1988) have emphasized that agency costs make external funding sources more expensive for firms than internal sources. As a consequence, a firm's balance sheet can play a role in affecting the cost of finance. In recessions, internal sources of funds decline, forcing firms to turn to external sources. But the deterioration of the firm's balance sheet worsens the agency problems and increases the cost of external funds, thereby further contracting investment spending and contributing to the recession. Thus, credit conditions can play a role in amplifying the impact of other shocks to the economy and affecting their propagation throughout the economy and through time.

In the model of the previous section, borrowers relied entirely on external funds to finance their project. The role of internal funds in the presence of monitoring costs has been studied by Bernanke and Gertler (1989). In their model, firms are assumed to be able to costlessly observe the outcome of their own investment projects; others must incur a monitoring cost to observe project outcomes. Firms and lenders are assumed to be risk neutral. Firms are indexed by efficiency type ω, distributed uniformly on $[0, 1]$. More efficient types (ones with low ω's) need to invest fewer inputs into a given project. Projects themselves require inputs of $x(\omega)$, yielding gross payoff κ_1 with probability π_1 and $\kappa_2 > \kappa_1$ with probability $\pi_2 = 1 - \pi_1$. The function $x(.)$ is increasing in ω. The expected project return, $\pi_1\kappa_1 + \pi_2\kappa_2$, will be denoted κ. The realized outcome of a particular project can be observed costlessly by the firm undertaking the project and at cost c by others. Firms are assumed to have internal sources of financing equal to S; S is assumed to be less than $x(0)$, so that even the most efficient firm must borrow to undertake a project. Finally, let r denote the opportunity cost of funds to lenders; firms who do not undertake a project also receive this rate on their funds.[14]

If lenders could costlessly observe project outcomes, equilibrium would involve lenders financing all projects whose expected payoff exceeds their opportunity cost of rx. Thus, all firms whose ω is less than a critical value ω^* defined by

$$\kappa - rx(\omega^*) = 0$$

would receive loans. Firms with $\omega < \omega^*$ borrow $B \equiv x(\omega) - S$.

With imperfect information, the firm clearly has an incentive to always announce that the bad outcome, κ_1, occurred, and it will never pay for the lender to incur the

---

14. Bernanke and Gertler develop a general equilibrium model; we describe a partial equilibrium version to focus here on the role played by credit-market imperfections in investment decisions.

monitoring cost if the firm announces κ_2. Let p be the probability that the firm is audited (i.e., the lender pays the monitoring cost to observe the true outcome) when the firm announces κ_1. Let P_1^a be the payment to the firm when κ_1 is announced and auditing takes place, P_1 the payment when κ_1 is announced and no auditing occurs, and P_2 the payment if κ_2 is announced. The optimal lending contract must maximize the expected payoff to the firm, subject to several constraints. First, the lender's expected return must be at least as great as her opportunity cost rB. Second, the firm must have no incentive to report the bad state when in fact the good state occurred. Third, even in the bad state, limited liability requires that the P_1^a and P_1 be non-negative. This means the optimal contract is characterized by the values of $\{p, P_1^a, P_1, P_2\}$ that solve

$$\max \pi_1 [pP_1^a + (1-p)P_1] + \pi_2 P_2$$

subject to

$$\pi_1 [\kappa_1 - p(P_1^a + c) - (1-p)P_1] + \pi_2 [\kappa_2 - P_2] \geq rB \tag{7.6}$$

$$P_2 \geq (1-p)(\kappa_2 - \kappa_1 + P_1) \tag{7.7}$$

$$P_1^a \geq 0 \tag{7.8}$$

$$P_1 \geq 0 \tag{7.9}$$

and $0 \leq p \leq 1$.

Constraint (7.6) ensures that the lender's expected return is at least rB. The constraint given by equation (7.7) may require more comment. The left side is the firm's payment in the good state. The right side gives the firm's expected payment if the good state occurs but the firm reports the bad state. After reporting the bad state, the firm is audited with probability p. So with probability $1 - p$ the firm is not audited, turns over κ_1 to the lender, and receives P_1. But the firm now gets to keep the amount $\kappa_2 - \kappa_1$, since, by assumption, the good state has actually occurred. If the firm is audited and found to have misreported the amount, we assume it receives nothing. If (7.7) is satisfied, the firm has no incentive to conceal the truth in announcing the project outcome.

Assuming an interior solution, the first-order necessary conditions for this problem are

$$\pi_1 [(P_1^a - P_1) + \mu_1(P_1 - P_1^a - c)] + \mu_2(\kappa_2 - \kappa_1 + P_1) = 0 \tag{7.10}$$

$$\pi_1 p(1 - \mu_1) + \mu_3 = 0 \tag{7.11}$$

$$\pi_1(1-p)(1-\mu_1) - \mu_2(1-p) + \mu_4 = 0 \qquad (7.12)$$

$$\pi_2(1-\mu_1) + \mu_2 = 0 \qquad (7.13)$$

where the μ_i's are the (nonnegative) Lagrangian multipliers associated with constraints (7.6)–(7.9).

Since $\mu_3 \geq 0$, equation (7.11) implies $\mu_1 \geq 1$. As a result, the constraint on the lender's return (7.6) must hold with equality. With $\pi_1[\kappa_1 - p(P_1^a + c) - (1-p)P_1] + \pi_2(\kappa_2 - P_2) - rB = 0$, this can be added to the objective function, yielding an equivalent problem that the optimal contract solves given by $\max[\pi_1(\kappa_1 - pc) + \pi_2\kappa_2]$, subject to (7.7) and the nonnegative constraints on P_1^a and P_1. However, $\pi_1(\kappa_1 - pc) + \pi_2\kappa_2 = \kappa - \pi_1 pc$, and with κ an exogenous parameter, this new problem becomes equivalent to minimizing expected auditing costs $\pi_1 pc$.

If the project return exceeds the lender's required return rB even in the bad state κ_1, then no auditing is ever necessary and $p = 0$. Agency costs are zero, therefore, whenever $\kappa_1 \geq rB$. Recall that the amount borrowed, B, was equal to $x(\omega) - S$, where S represented the firm's internal funds invested in the project, so the no-agency cost condition can be written

$$S \geq x(\omega) - \frac{\kappa_1}{r} \equiv S^*(\omega)$$

Any type ω with internal funds greater than or equal to $S^*(\omega)$ can always repay the lender, so no auditing on the project is required. When $S < S^*(\omega)$, a situation Bernanke and Gertler label as one of incomplete collateralization, constraints (7.6)–(7.9) all hold with equality. Since auditing is costly, the optimal auditing probability is just high enough to ensure that the firm truthfully reports the good state when it occurs. From the incentive constraint (7.7), $P_2 = (1-p)(\kappa_2 - \kappa_1)$, since $P_1 = P_1^a = 0$ when (5.8) and (5.9) are binding (the firm keeps nothing in the bad state). Substituting this into the lender's required return condition (7.6),

$$p = \frac{r[x(\omega) - S] - \kappa_1}{\pi_2(\kappa_2 - \kappa_1) - \pi_1 c}$$

The auditing probability is decreasing in the return in the bad state (κ_1) and the firm's own contribution S. If the firm invests little in the project and borrows more, then the firm receives less of the project's return in the good state, increasing its incentive to falsely claim the bad state occurred. To remove this incentive, the probability of auditing must rise.

Bernanke and Gertler characterize the expected costs of project auditing, $\pi_1 pc$, as the agency costs due to asymmetric information. As they show, some firms with intermediate values of ω (i.e., not the most nor least efficient), will find that the investment project is not worth undertaking if they have only low levels of internal funds to invest. The probability of auditing that lenders would require makes agency costs too high to justify investment. If the firm had a higher level of internal funds, it would undertake the project. Even though the opportunity cost of funds r and the project inputs x and returns (κ_1 and κ_2) have not changed, variations in S can alter the number of projects undertaken. This fact illustrates how investment levels may depend on the firm's internal sources of financing. Agency costs drive a wedge between the costs of internal and external funds so that investment decisions will depend on variables such as cash flow that would not play a role if information were perfect. Since a recession will worsen firms' balance sheets, reducing the availability of internal funds, the resulting rise in agency costs and reduction in investment may serve to amplify the initial cause of a recession.

7.2.5 Summary

In this section, a number of microeconomic models of credit-market imperfection have been present. All emphasize the key role of imperfect information in relationships between borrowers and lenders. Adverse selection, moral hazard, and costly monitoring affect the nature of credit contracts and may lead to the presence of equilibrium rationing. While the various models build on different foundations, emphasizing the role of different mechanisms, they all highlight the importance of information in the market for credit.

7.3 Macroeconomic Implications

The presence of credit-market imperfections can play a role in determining how the economy responds to economic disturbances and how these disturbances are propagated throughout the economy and over time. Various partial equilibrium models have provided insights into how imperfect information and costly state verification affect the nature of credit-market equilibria. The next step is to embed these partial equilibrium models of the credit market within a general equilibrium macro model so that the qualitative and quantitative importance of credit channels can be assessed. As Bernanke, Gertler, and Gilchrist (1996) discuss, there are difficulties in taking this step. For one, distributional issues are critical. Private-sector borrowing and lending do not occur in a representative-agent world, so agents must differ in ways that give rise to borrowers and lenders. And both the source of credit and the characteristics of the borrower matter, so not all borrowers and not all lenders are alike. Changes in the distribution of wealth or the distribution of cash flow can affect the ability of agents to obtain credit. In this section, two simple models that help highlight the macro implication of credit are discussed.

7.3.1 A Simple Model with Bank Loans

Bernanke and Blinder (1988) provide a modified version of a traditional IS-LM framework into which they incorporate a bank lending channel. The standard IS-LM model distinguishes between money and bonds as the only two financial assets. Money is assumed to pay a zero nominal interest rate, so the nominal rate determined in the IS-LM analysis is the return on bonds. Bernanke and Blinder modify this framework by distinguishing between money, bonds, and bank loans. With three financial assets, the model will determine the interest rates on bonds and loans and the level of output consistent, for a given price level, with equilibrium in the money market, the market for bank loans, and the equality of output and aggregate demand. Since the focus here is on how monetary policy affects aggregate demand, we can ignore the supply side of the model and simply treat the price level as given.

The bank lending channel can be illustrated by adding a stylized banking sector to an otherwise standard IS-LM model. Banks are assumed to hold bonds (B), loans (L), and reserves (R) as assets; their liabilities are deposits (D). The representative bank's balance sheet is

$$B + L + R = D$$

Assume reserves are held only to meet a legal reserve requirement:

$$R^d = \sigma D$$

where σ is the required reserve ratio on deposits. Loans and bond holdings must then sum to $(1 - \sigma)D$. Bernanke and Blinder specify directly the banking sector's portfolio demands for bonds and loans as functions of total available assets after meeting reserve requirements and the returns on bonds I_b and loans I_l.

$$\frac{B}{(1 - \sigma)D} = b(I_b, I_l), \qquad b_b \geq 0, b_l \leq 0$$

where b_j is the partial derivative with respect to I_j. The fraction of the bank's net-of-required-reserves assets held in loans is assumed to be decreasing in I_b and increasing in I_l:

$$\frac{L}{(1 - \sigma)D} = 1 - b(I_b, I_l) \equiv l^s(I_b, I_l), \qquad l_b^s \leq 0, l_l^s \geq 0$$

This equation gives loan supply.

In equilibrium, bank reserve demand must equal the reserve supply determined by the central bank, and the level of deposits supported by the supply of reserves must equal the demand for deposits by the nonbank public. Let R^s denote reserve supply, and let deposit demand depend on output (positively) and the interest rate on bonds (negatively). Then, equating reserve supply and demand, we can approximate the deviations around steady state as

$$r^s = y_t - ci_b + v \tag{7.14}$$

where lowercase letters denote percentage deviations around the steady state, so r^s, y, and i_b are the percentage deviations of R^s, output, and I_b around their steady-state values. To allow for money-demand shocks (actually deposit-demand shocks), the random error v is included in (7.14).

Loan demand is assumed to depend on the interest rate on loans and the level of economic activity:

$$L^d = l^d(I_l, Y), \qquad l_l^d \le 0, l_y^d \ge 0$$

Assuming no credit rationing, equilibrium in the market for loans requires

$$l^d(I_l, Y) = l^s(I_b, I_l)(1-\sigma)D = l^s(I_b, I_l)\left(\frac{1-\sigma}{\sigma}\right)R^s$$

which can be approximated around the steady state as

$$l_l^d i_l + l_y^d y = l_b^s i_b + l_l^s i_l + r^s + \omega'$$

or

$$i_l = h_1 i_b + h_2 y - h_3 r^s + \omega \tag{7.15}$$

where $h_1 = l_b^s/(l_l^d - l_l^s)$, $h_2 = -l_y^d/(l_l^d - l_l^s)$, and $h_3 = -1/(l_l^d - l_l^s)$ are all positive, and $\omega = \omega'/(l_l^d - l_l^s)$ is a random disturbance that could incorporate both credit-supply and credit-demand shocks. An adverse credit-supply shock would correspond to a positive realization of ω that increases the loan interest rate for given levels of reserve, output, and the bond rate. A positive credit-demand shock would also correspond to a positive realization of ω.

The final component of this simple model is an IS relationship that links output demand to the interest rates on loans and bonds and a random disturbance:

$$y = -c_1 i_l - c_2 i_b + u \tag{7.16}$$

Equations (7.14), (7.15), and (7.16) constitute a three-equation system to determine aggregate demand and the two interest rates as a function of reserve supply. Substituting the loan market condition (7.15) into the IS function (7.16), the loan rate can be eliminated, yielding

$$y = \frac{c_1 h_3 r^s - (c_2 + c_1 h_1) i_b + u - c_1 \omega}{1 + c_1 h_2} \tag{7.17}$$

This modified IS curve reveals the key difference between the standard IS-LM model and a model that distinguishes between bonds and loans: the quantity of reserves appears in the IS curve as long as $c_1 h_3 \neq 0$. Changes in monetary policy influence aggregate demand by affecting the bond rate (this is the traditional interest rate channel), but changes in the policy variable r^s also have a direct impact that shifts the IS curve by altering the equilibrium interest rate on bank loans. A rise in r^s allows banks to expand deposits and increase the supply of loans. This causes i_l to fall, increasing aggregate demand.

The framework suggested by Bernanke and Blinder attempts to capture in a simple way the additional linkages that arise through the bank lending version of the credit view. The approach, based on direct specification of behavioral relationships, is more in keeping with an older tradition in monetary economics as exemplified by the work of Tobin and Brainard (1963), Tobin (1969), or Brunner and Meltzer (1988, 1972).[15] It does, however, provide a simple means of highlighting the critical factors in the bank lending channel. First, bank loans must be essential for spending ($c_1 \neq 0$). Suppose firms could substitute away from bank loans to other forms of intermediated credit with little cost. In this case, a rise in i_l might have a large impact on the quantity of bank loans outstanding, but c_1 would be small and there would be little impact on aggregate spending. Second, the bank lending channel requires that $h_3 = -1/(l_l^d - l_l^s) \neq 0$. If loan supply or demand are perfectly elastic, then $h_3 = 0$, and the bank lending channel would not operate. Loan demand will be very elastic if alternative credit sources are available that serve as close substitutes for bank lending.

To investigate the conditions under which loan supply might be perfectly elastic, it is useful to be more explicit about the representative bank's portfolio decisions. Assume, in contrast to the preceding discussion, that deposit liabilities come in two

---

15. The Tobin-Brainard approach, with its emphasis on asset substitutability and the role of money substitutes, was labeled the "New View." This label was meant to differentiate it from an older approach that built on money-multiplier analysis. In principle, there is no conflict between these approaches, but in practice, the money-multiplier view was characterized as ignoring the behavioral determinants of the ratios in the multiplier expressions. See Walsh (1992).

forms: demand deposits D_d that for simplicity will be assumed to pay a zero rate of interest but are subject to a reserve requirement ratio of σ, and D_{od}, other non-reservable deposits on which the bank pays an interest rate of i_d. The representative bank maximizes profits given by

$$i_b B + i_l L - i_d D_{od} - C(L, D_d, D_{od}) \qquad (7.18)$$

subject to the balance sheet constraint

$$B + L = (1 - \sigma)D_d + D_{od} \qquad (7.19)$$

where $C(L, D_d, D_{od})$ is the bank's cost function.[16] Assume the return on loans is a decreasing function of the quantity of loans: $i_l(L)$, $i_l' \leq 0$. Assume also that the bank faced an upward-sloping supply-of-deposits function $D_{od}(i_d)$, $D_{od}'(i_d) \geq 0$. This latter function might arise from the types of credit-market imperfections discussed previously, since D_{od} represents a liability of the bank. The first-order conditions for the bank's decision problem imply that i_l and i_d satisfy

$$i_l = i_b + C_1 - i_l' L$$

which implies the marginal loan return $(i_l + i_l' L - C_1)$ is equated to the opportunity cost of funds i_b, and

$$i_d = i_b - \frac{C_3 D_{od}' + D_{od}}{D_{od}'} \qquad (7.20)$$

which implies the marginal cost of funds $[i_d + (C_3 D_{od}' + D_{od})/D_{od}']$ is also equated with the opportunity cost of funds i_b. If the cost function is separable in demand deposits, then these two equations determine the interest rate on nondemand-deposit liabilities and loan supply $[L^s = b(i_l - i_b - C_1)$, where $b = -1/i_l' > 0$ independent of reserves and demand deposits]. In the situation in which banks face a perfectly elastic supply of nondemand-deposits, $D_{od}' \to \infty$ and (7.20) implies $i_d = i_b$.

Equating loan supply and loan demand,

$$i_l = i_b + C_1 - i_l' l^d(i_l, y) \qquad (7.21)$$

Equations (7.20) and (7.21) determine i_l and i_d as functions of i_b.[17] Bond holdings are residually determined by the bank's balance sheet and are equal to

16. It is assumed that there are no significant costs associated with holding bonds.

17. The loan-demand function and the other deposit-supply functions must be used to eliminate L and D from the cost function.

$$B = \left(\frac{1-\sigma}{\sigma}\right) R^s + D_{od}(i_d) - L$$

A change in reserves that changes demand deposits is entirely reflected in security holdings. In the aggregate, an increase in reserves will lower i_b and stimulate loan supply, but this effect operates through traditional interest-rate channels. With banks holding securities and having access to managed liabilities, such as certificates of deposits, the marginal return on loans will be set equal to the marginal opportunity cost of funds. Variations in reserve supply will affect the quantity of bank loans, but they will do so through banking-sector response to changes in market interest rates (see Romer and Romer 1990).

If the cost function is not separable in demand deposits, then D_d affects C_1 and C_3, the marginal costs of servicing loans and other deposits. This might be the case if the provision of transactions accounts lowers the costs to banks of monitoring borrowers. If loans and demand deposits are complements in the bank's cost function, then a change in reserves that lowers deposits may directly raise the cost of loans, leading to a shift in the loan-supply function. This shift would then represent a distinct bank lending channel leading to a drop in loans in addition to the reduction that results from the impact of a rise in i_b on the loan interest rate.

Bank lending channels were likely to have been more important during periods in which financial markets were more heavily regulated. In the United States, Regulation Q imposed limits on the deposit interest rates that banks and other financial institutions could offer and limited the ability of banks to offset declines in banking-sector reserves. In an environment in which interest rates are free to adjust, the bank lending channel of monetary policy is likely to be of lesser importance. Such a conclusion is still consistent with the notion that banks cater to a particular clientele, and for that reason, most recent discussions of the credit channel focus on the characteristics of borrowers and not on those of the lenders. This "broad" credit channel (Oliner and Rudebusch 1995) does not give a prominent role to banks but instead stresses the general implications of credit-market imperfections for different types of borrowers.

7.3.2 General Equilibrium Models

The micro literature on imperfect information provides insights into the structure of credit markets. Embedding these insights into a macroeconomic framework to determine how credit markets affect the nature of the equilibrium and the manner in which the economy responds to macro disturbances is much more difficult. In representative-agent models, no lending actually takes place. And with all agents identical, the distinctive features of credit markets that have been emphasized in the literature on credit channels are absent. Incorporating heterogeneity among agents in a tractable general equilibrium model is difficult, particularly when the nature of debt and financial contracts in the model economy should be derived from the characteristics of the basic technology and informational assumptions of the model environment.

Two early examples of general equilibrium models designed to highlight the role of credit factors were due to Williamson (1987b) and Bernanke and Gertler (1989). In these models, credit markets play an important role in determining how the economy responds to a real productivity shock. Williamson embeds his model of financial intermediation with costly monitoring (discussed in section 7.2.3) in a dynamic general equilibrium model. In response to shocks to the riskiness of investment, credit rationing increases, loans from intermediaries fall, and investment declines. The decline in investment reduces future output and contributes to the propagation of the initial shock. Bernanke and Gertler (1989) incorporate the model of costly state verification reviewed in section 7.2.4 into a general equilibrium framework in which shocks to productivity drive the business-cycle dynamics. A positive productivity shock increases the income of the owners of the production technology; this rise in their net worth lowers agency costs associated with external financing of investment projects, allowing for increased investment. This effect serves to propagate the shock through time. Fuerst (1995) develops a general equilibrium model that attempts to capture the role of internal finance emphasized by Bernanke and Gertler (1989). Fuerst's model can be simulated to assess the quantitative significance of agency costs in affecting the dynamic response of the economy to shocks. He finds that financial factors make only a small contribution to the propagation mechanism, although Gertler (1995) shows that this contribution can be significantly increased by allowing internal funds to fluctuate more in response to output movements, by assuming investment projects are lumpy, and by incorporating a variable labor supply.

Recently, Kiyotaki and Moore (1997) have developed a model that illustrates the role of net worth and credit constraints on equilibrium output. In their model economy, there are two types of agents. One group, called farmers, can combine their own labor with land to produce output. They can borrow to purchase additional land, but face credit constraints in so doing. These arise because a farmer's labor input is assumed to be critical to production—once a farmer starts producing, no one else can replace her—and the farmer is assumed to be unable to precommit to work. Thus, if any creditor attempts to extract too much from a farmer, the farmer can simply walk away from the land, leaving the creditor with only the value of the land; all current production is lost. The inability to precommit to work plays a role similar to the assumption of cost-state verification; in this case, the creditor is unable to monitor the farmer to ensure that she continues to work. As a result, the farmer's ability to borrow will be limited by the collateral value of her land.

Letting k_t denote the quantity of land cultivated by farmers, output by farmers is produced according to a linear technology:

$$y^f_{t+1} = (a + c)k_t$$

where ck_t is nonmarketable output ("bruised fruit" in the farmer analogy) that can be consumed by the farmer.

The creditors in Kiyotaki and Moore's model are called gatherers—they too can use land to produce output, employing a technology characterized by decreasing returns to scale. Output of gatherers is

$$y^g_{t+1} = G(\bar{k} - k_t), \qquad G' \geq 0, G'' \leq 0$$

where $\bar{k}$ is the total, fixed stock of land, so $\bar{k} - k_t$ is the amount cultivated by gatherers.

Utility of both farmers and gatherers is assumed to be linear in consumption, although farmers are assumed to discount the future more. Because of the linear utility, along with the assumption that labor generates no disutility, the socially efficient allocation of the fixed stock of land between the two types of agents would ensure that the marginal product of land is equalized between the two production technologies, or

$$G'(\bar{k} - k^*) = a + c \tag{7.22}$$

where k^* is the efficient amount of land allocated to farmers.

We can now consider the market equilibrium. Taking the gatherers first, given that they are not credit constrained and have linear utility, the real rate of interest will simply equal the inverse of their subjective rate of time preference: $R = 1/\beta$.[18] Again exploiting the unconstrained nature of the gatherers' decision, the value of a unit of land, q_t, must satisfy

$$q_t = \beta[G'(\bar{k} - k_t) + q_{t+1}]$$

The present value of a unit of land is just equal to the discounted marginal return G'

---

18. The standard Euler condition for optimal consumption requires that $u_c(t) = \beta R u_c(t+1)$ where $u_c(s)$ is the marginal utility of consumption at date s. With linear utility, $u_c(t) = u_c(t+1) = h$ for some constant h. Hence, $h = \beta R h$ or $R = 1/\beta$.

plus its resale value at time $t + 1$. Since $\beta = R^{-1}$, this condition can be rewritten as

$$\frac{1}{R} G'(\bar{k} - k_t) = q_t - \frac{q_{t+1}}{R} \equiv u_t \tag{7.23}$$

The variable u_t will play an important role in the farmers' decision problem. To interpret it, q_{t+1}/R is the present value of land in period $t + 1$. This represents the collateralized value of a unit of land; a creditor who lends q_{t+1}/R or less against a piece of land is ensured of being repaid. The price of a unit of land at time t is q_t, so u_t is the difference between the cost of land and the amount that can be borrowed against the land. It thus represents the down payment a farmer will need to make in order to purchase more land.

Kiyotaki and Moore construct the basic parameters of the model to ensure that farmers will wish to consume only their nonmarketable output (ck_{t-1}). Farmers then use the proceeds of their marketable output plus new loans minus repayment of old loans (inclusive of interest) to purchase more land. However, the maximum a farmer can borrow will be the collateralized value of the land, equal to $q_{t+1}k_t/R$. Hence, if b_t is the farmer's debt,

$$b_t \leq \frac{q_{t+1}k_t}{R} \tag{7.24}$$

This can be shown to be a binding constraint in equilibrium, and land purchases by farmers will satisfy

$$q_t(k_t - k_{t-1}) = ak_{t-1} + \frac{q_{t+1}k_t}{R} - Rb_{t-1}$$

where b_{t-1} is debt incurred in the previous period. Rearranging,

$$k_t = \frac{(a + q_t)k_{t-1} - Rb_{t-1}}{u_t} \tag{7.25}$$

The numerator of this expression represents the farmer's net worth—current output plus land holdings minus existing debt. With u_t equal to the required down payment per unit of land, the farmer invests her entire net worth in purchasing new land.

To verify that the borrowing constraint is binding, it is necessary to show that the farmer always finds it optimal to use all marketable output to purchase additional land (after repaying outstanding loans). Suppose instead that the farmer consumes a unit of output over and above ck_{t-1}. This unit yields marginal utility u_c (a constant by the assumption of linear utility), but by reducing the farmer's land in period t by $1/u_t$, this additional consumption costs

$$u_c\left[\beta_f\frac{c}{u_t}+\beta_f^2\left(\frac{a}{u_t}\left(\frac{c}{u_{t+1}}+\beta_f\left(\frac{a}{u_{t+1}}\left(\frac{c}{u_{t+2}}+\cdots\right)\cdots\right)\cdots\right)\cdots\right)\right]$$

since the $1/u_t$ units of land purchased at time t would have yielded additional consumption c/u_t plus marketable output a/u_t that could have been used to purchase more land that would have yielded c/u_{t+1} in consumption and so on. Each of these future consumption additions must be discounted back to time t using the farmer's discount rate β_f. As will be demonstrated, the steady-state value of u will be a. Making this substitution, the farmer will always prefer to use marketable output to purchase land if

$$1<\left[\beta_f\frac{c}{a}+\beta_f^2\left(\frac{a}{a}\left(\frac{c}{a}+\beta_f\left(\frac{a}{a}\left(\frac{c}{a}+\cdots\right)\cdots\right)\cdots\right)\cdots\right)\right]=\frac{\beta_f}{1-\beta_f}\frac{c}{a}$$

or

$$\frac{a+c}{a}>\frac{1}{\beta_f}>\frac{1}{\beta}=R \tag{7.26}$$

since $\beta_f<\beta$ by assumption. Kiyotaki and Moore assume that c is large enough to ensure that (7.26) holds. This assumption means that farmers would always like to postpone consumption and will borrow as much as possible to purchase land. Hence, the borrowing constraint will bind.

Equation (7.25) can be written as $u_t k_t = (a+q_t)k_{t-1} - Rb_{t-1}$. But $Rb_{t-1} = q_t k_{t-1}$ from (7.24), so $u_t k_t = ak_{t-1}$. Now using (7.23) to eliminate u_t, the capital stock held by farmers satisfies the following difference equation:

$$\frac{1}{R}G'(\bar{k}-k_t)k_t=ak_{t-1} \tag{7.27}$$

Assuming standard restrictions on the gatherers' production function, (7.27) defines a convergent path for the land held by farmers.[19] The steady-state value of k is then given as the solution k^{ss} to

$$\frac{1}{R}G'(\bar{k}-k^{ss})=a \tag{7.28}$$

Multiplying through by R, $G'(\bar{k}-k^{ss})=Ra$. From (7.23), this implies

$$u^{ss}=a$$

19. As long as $G'(\bar{k}-k)$ is monotonically increasing in k, $G'(\bar{k})<a$, and $G'(0)>a$, there will be a single stable equilibirum.

Equation (7.28) can be compared with equation (7.22), which gives the condition for an efficient allocation of land between farmers and gatherers. The efficient allocation of land to farmers, k^*, was such that $G'(\bar{k} - k^*) = a + c > Ra = G'(\bar{k} - k^{ss})$ where the inequality sign is implied by equation (7.26). Since the marginal product of gatherers' output is positive but declines with the amount of land held by gatherers, it follows that $k^{ss} < k^*$. The market equilibrium is characterized by too little land in the hands of farmers. As a consequence, aggregate output is too low.

Using the definition of u, the steady-state price of land is equal to $q^{ss} = Ra/(R-1)$, and steady-state debt is equal to $b^{ss} = q^{ss}k^{ss}/R = ak^{ss}/(R-1)$. The farmer's debt repayments each period are then equal to $Rb^{ss} = [R/(R-1)]ak^{ss} > ak^{ss}$.

Kiyotaki and Moore extend this basic model to allow for reproducible capital and are able to study the dynamics of the more general model. The simple version, though, allows the key channels through which credit affects the economy's equilibrium to be highlighted. First, output is inefficiently low due to borrowing restrictions; even though farmers have access to a technology that, at the steady state, is more productive than that of gatherers, they cannot obtain the credit necessary to purchase additional land. Second, the ability of farmers to obtain credit is limited by their net worth. Equation (7.25) shows how the borrowing constraint makes land holdings at time t dependent on net worth (marketable output plus the value of existing land holdings minus debt). Third, land purchases by farmers will depend on asset prices. A fall in the value of land that is expected to persist (so q_t and q_{t+1} both fall) reduces the farmer's net worth and demand for land. This follows from (7.25), which can be written as $k_t = \dfrac{q_t k_{t-1}}{u_t} + \dfrac{ak_{t-1} - Rb_{t-1}}{u_t}$. A proportional fall in q_t and q_{t+1} leaves the first term, $q_t k_{t-1}/u_t$, unchanged. The second term increases in absolute value, but at the steady state, $Rb > ak$, so this term is negative. Thus, farmers' ability to purchase land declines with a fall in land prices.

These mechanisms capture the financial accelerator effect as can be seen by considering the impact of an unexpected but transitory productivity shock. Suppose output of both farmers and gatherers increases unexpectedly at time t. Assume the economy was initially at the steady state, and let Δ be the productivity increase for farmers. Then equation (7.25) implies

$$u(k_t)k_t = (a + \Delta a + q_t - q^{ss})k^{ss} \tag{7.29}$$

since $q^{ss}k^{ss} = Rb^{ss}$ from the borrowing constraint and we have written the required down payment u as a function of k.[20] Two factors are at work in determining the

---

20. Recall that $u_t = G'(\bar{k} - k_t)/R$ from equation (7.23).

impact of the productivity shock on the farmers' demand for land. First, because
marketable output rises by $\Delta a k^{ss}$, this directly increases farmers' demand for land.
Second, the term $(q_t - q^{ss})k^{ss}$ represents a capital gain on existing holdings of land.
Both factors act to increase farmers' net worth and their demand for land.

One way to highlight the dynamics induced by a productivity shock is to examine
a linear approximation to (7.29) around the steady state. Letting e denote the elasticity of the user costs of land $u(k)$ with respect to k, the left side of (7.29) can be
approximated by

$$ak^{ss}[1 + (1+e)\hat{k}]$$

where we have used the fact that $u(k^{ss}) = a$ and have adopted the notation that $\hat{x}$
denotes the percentage deviation of a variable x around its steady state.[21] The right
side of (7.29) can be written

$$(a + \Delta a + q^{ss}\hat{q}_t)k^{ss}$$

Equating these two and using the steady-state result that $q^{ss} = Ra/(R-1)$ yields

$$(1 + e)\hat{k} = \Delta + \frac{R}{R-1}\hat{q}_t \tag{7.30}$$

The capital-gain effect on farmers' land purchases is, as Kiyotaki and Moore
emphasize, scaled up by $R/(R-1) > 1$ because farmers are able to leverage their
net worth. This factor can be quite large; if $R = 1.05$, the coefficient on $\hat{q}_t$ is 21.

Consistent with the notion of the financial accelerator, the asset price effects of the
temporary productivity shock reinforce the original disturbance. These effects also
generate a channel for persistence. If more land is purchased in period t, the initial
rise in aggregate output persists.[22]

7.4 Does Credit Matter?

The theoretical work incorporating imperfect information into models of credit provides important insights into the nature of credit transactions, the characteristics of
financial contracts, and the properties of credit-market equilibria. A separate set
of issues revolve around whether these aspects of credit markets are important for

21. The elasticity e is equal to $[u'(k^{ss})k^{ss}]/u(k^{ss}) = u'(k^{ss})k^{ss}/a$ where u' denotes the derivative of u with respect to k. Since u was increasing in $\bar{k} - k$, $u' < 0$.

22. Recall that at the margin, farmers are more productive than gatherers; a shift of land from gatherers to farmers raises total output.

determining the impact of monetary policy on the economy or play an independent role as a source of economic disturbances. If credit channels are important for the monetary transmission process, then evolution in financial markets, whether due to changes in regulations or to financial innovations, may change the manner in which monetary policy affects the real economy. It also implies that the level of real interest rates may not provide a sufficient indicator of the stance of monetary policy. And credit shocks may have played an independent role in creating economic fluctuations. In this section, the empirical evidence on the credit channel is reviewed. The coverage will be selective, as a number of recent surveys exist that discuss (and extend) the empirical work in the area (Gertler 1988; Gertler and Gilchrist 1993; Ramey 1993; Kashyap and Stein 1993; Hubbard 1995; Bernanke, Gertler, and Gilchrist 1996).

In an influential article, Bernanke (1983) provided evidence consistent with an important role for nonmonetary financial factors in accounting for the severity of the Great Depression in the United States. After controlling for unexpected money growth, he found that proxies for the financial crises of the early 1930s contributed significantly in regressions for the growth rate of industrial production.[23] If pure monetary causes were responsible for the decline in output during the depression, the other measures of financial disruptions should not have added explanatory power to the regression.

As Bernanke notes, his evidence is "not inconsistent" with the proposition that the financial crisis in the United States represented a distinct, nonmonetary channel through which real output was affected during the depression. The evidence is not conclusive, however, since an alternative hypothesis is simply that the depression itself was the result of nonmonetary factors (or at least factors not captured by unanticipated money growth), and that these caused output to decline, business to fail, and banks to close. By controlling only for unanticipated money growth, Bernanke's measures of financial crisis may only be picking up the effects of the underlying nonmonetary causes of the depression. Still, Bernanke's results offered support for the notion that the massive bank failures of the 1930s in the United States were not simply a sideshow but were at least partially responsible for the output declines.

Attempts to isolate a special role for credit in more normal business-cycle periods have been plagued by identification problems that are essentially similar. Are movements in credit aggregates a reflection of shifts in demand resulting from effects operating through the traditional money channel, or do they reflect supply factors

23. Bernanke employed the real change in the deposits at failing banks and the real change in the liabilities of failing businesses as his measures of the financial crises.

that constitute a distinct credit channel? Most macroeconomic variables behave similarly under either a money view or a credit view, so distinguishing between the two views based on time-series evidence is difficult. For example, under the traditional money-channel view, a contractionary shift in monetary policy raises interest rates and reduces investment spending. The decline in investment is associated with a decline in credit demand, so quantity measures of both bank and nonbank financing should fall. The competing theories are not sufficiently powerful to draw sharp predictions about the timing of interest-rate, money, credit, and output movements that would allow the alternative views to be tested. As a consequence, much of the empirical work has focused on compositional effects, seeking to see whether there are differential impacts of interest-rate and credit movements that might distinguish between the alternative views. After considering some of the evidence on the bank lending channel, the evidence on the broad credit channel is discussed.

7.4.1   The Bank Lending Channel

Banks play an important role in discussions of the monetary transmission mechanism, but the traditional approach stresses the role of bank liabilities as part of the money supply. Part of the reason for the continued focus on the liabilities side is the lack of convincing empirical evidence that bank lending plays a distinct role in the transmission process through which monetary policy affects the real economy. As Romer and Romer state,

A large body of recent theoretical work argues that the Federal Reserve's leverage over the economy may stem as much from the distinctive properties of the loans that banks make as from the unique characteristics of the transaction deposits that they receive.... Examining the behavior of financial variables and real output in a series of episodes of restrictive monetary policy, we are unable to find any support for this view. (Romer and Romer 1990, pp. 196–197)

One of the first attempts to test for a distinct bank lending channel was that of S. King (1986). He found that monetary aggregates were better predictors of future output than were bank loans. More recently, Romer and Romer (1990) and Ramey (1993) reach similar conclusions. Unfortunately, our theories are usually not rich enough to provide sharp predictions about the timing patterns that are critical for drawing conclusions from evidence on the predictive content of macro variables. This is particularly true when behavior depends on forward-looking expectations. Anticipations of future output movements can lead to portfolio and financing readjustments that will affect the lead-lag relationship between credit measures and output. Because a decline in output may be associated with inventory buildups, the demand for short-term credit can initially rise, and the existence of loan commitments will limit the ability of banks to alter their loan portfolios quickly. These factors make money-credit-output timing patterns difficult to interpret.

In part, Romer and Romer's negative assessment of the bank lending channel reflects the difficult identification problem mentioned earlier. A policy-induced contraction of bank reserves will lead to a fall in both bank liabilities (deposits) and bank assets (loans and securities). With both sides of the banking sector's balance sheet shrinking, it is clearly difficult to know whether to attribute a subsequent decline in output to the money channel, the credit channel, or both.[24] Kashyap, Stein, and Wilcox (1993) address this problem by examining the composition of credit between bank and nonbank sources. Under the money view, a contractionary policy raises interest rates, lowering aggregate demand and the total demand for credit. Consequently, all measures of outstanding credit should decline. Under the bank lending view, the contractionary policy has a distinct effect in reducing the supply of bank credit. With bank credit less available, borrowers will attempt to substitute other sources of credit, and the relative demand for nonbank credit should rise. Thus, the composition of credit should change if the bank lending view is valid, with bank credit falling more in response to contractionary monetary policy than other forms of credit.

Kashyap, Stein, and Wilcox do find evidence for the bank lending channel when they examine aggregate U.S. data on bank versus nonbank sources of finance, the latter measured by the stock of outstanding commercial paper. Using the Romer and Romer (1989) dates to identify contractionary shifts in monetary policy,[25] Kashyap, Stein, and Wilcox find that the financing mix shifts away from bank loans following a monetary contraction. However, this shift occurs primarily because of a rise in commercial paper issuance, not a contraction in bank lending.

Evidence based on aggregate-credit measures can be problematic, however, if borrowers are heterogeneous in their sensitivity to the business cycle and in the types of credit they use. For example, the sales of small firms fluctuate more over the business cycle than those of large firms, and small firms are more reliant on bank credit than large firms, which have greater access to the commercial paper market. Contractionary monetary policy that causes both small and large firms to reduce their demand for credit will cause aggregate bank lending to fall relative to nonbank

24. The identification problems are not quite so severe in attempting to estimate the role of credit-supply versus credit-demand shocks on the economy. A contractionary bank-credit-supply shock would generally lower loan quantity and raise loan interest rates; a contraction in loan quantity caused by a demand shock would lower loan interest rates.

25. Romer and Romer (1989) base their dating of monetary policy shifts on a reading of FOMC documents. See Chapter 1.

financing as small firms contract more than large firms. This effect could account for the behavior of the debt mix even in the absence of any bank lending channel. Oliner and Rudebusch (1995, 1996b) argue that this is exactly what happens. They use disaggregate data on large and small firms and show that, in response to a monetary contraction, there is no significant effect on the mix of bank/nonbank credit used by either small or large firms. Instead, the movement in the aggregate debt mix arises because of a general shift of short-term debt away from small firms and toward large firms. They conclude that the evidence does not support the bank lending channel as an important part of the transmission process of monetary policy. Similar conclusions are reached by Gertler and Gilchrist (1994) in an analysis also based on disaggregated data.

While the bank lending channel as part of the monetary-policy transmission process may not be operative, it might still be the case that shifts in bank loan supply are a cause of economic fluctuations. In the United States, the 1989–1992 period generated a renewed interest in credit channels and monetary policy.[26] An unusually large decline in bank lending, as well as stories, particularly from New England, of firms facing difficulty borrowing, led many to seek evidence that credit markets played an independent role in contributing to the 1990–1991 recession. One difficulty facing attempts to isolate the impact of credit-supply disturbances is the need to separate movements caused by a shift in credit supply from movements that result from changes in credit demand.

Walsh and Wilcox (1995) estimate a monthly VAR in which bank-loan supply shocks are identified with innovations in the prime lending rate. They show that their estimated loan supply innovations are related to changes in bank capital ratios, changes in required reserves, and the imposition of credit controls. This finding provides some evidence that the innovations are actually picking up factors that affect the supply of bank loans. While prime rate shocks are estimated to lower loan quantity and output, they were not found to play a major causal role in U.S. business cycles, although their role was somewhat atypically large during the 1990–1991 recession.

7.4.2 The Broad Credit Channel

The broad credit channel for the transmission of monetary policy is based on the view that credit-market imperfections are not limited to the market for bank loans

---

26. See, for example, Bernanke and Lown (1992), the papers collected in Federal Reserve Bank of New York (1994), and Peek and Rosengren (1995). Mosser (1994) discusses the empirical evidence of credit effects on aggregate demand and focuses on the 1990–1991 recession.

but instead are important for understanding all credit markets. If agency costs create a wedge between internal and external finance, measures of cash flow, net worth, and the value of collateral should affect investment spending in ways not captured by traditional interest-rate channels. The evidence in support of a broad credit channel has recently been surveyed by Bernanke, Gertler, and Gilchrist (1996), who conclude: "We now have fairly strong evidence—at least for the case of firms—that downturns differentially affect both the access to credit and the real economic activity of high-agency-cost borrowers" (p. 14).

Hubbard (1995) and Bernanke, Gertler, and Gilchrist (1996) list three empirical implications of the broad credit channel. First, external finance is more expensive for borrowers than internal finance. This greater expense should apply particularly to uncollateralized external finance. Second, because the cost differential between internal and external finance arises from agency costs, the gap should depend inversely on the borrower's net worth. A fall in net worth raises the cost of external finance. Third, adverse shocks to net worth should reduce borrowers' access to finance, thereby reducing their investment, employment, and production levels.

If, as emphasized under the broad credit channel, agency costs worsen during recessions and in response to contractionary monetary policy, then the share of credit going to low-agency-cost borrowers should rise. Bernanke, Gertler, and Gilchrist characterize this response as the flight to quality. Aggregate data are likely to be of limited usefulness in testing such a hypothesis, since most data on credit stocks and flows are not constructed based on the characteristics of the borrowers. Because small firms presumably are subject to greater agency costs than are large firms, much of the evidence for a broad credit channel has been sought by looking for differences in the behavior of large and small firms in the face of monetary contractions.

Gertler and Gilchrist (1994) document that small firms do behave differently than large firms over the business cycle, with small firms being much more sensitive to cyclical fluctuations. Kashyap, Lamont, and Stein (1994) find that inventory investment by firms without access to public bond markets appeared to be affected by liquidity constraints.[27] Oliner and Rudebusch (1996a) assess the role of financial factors by examining the behavior of small and large firms around changes in monetary policy. Interest-rate increases in response to a monetary contraction lower asset values and the value of collateral, increasing the cost of external funds relative to internal funds. Since agency problems are likely to be more severe for small firms than large firms, the linkage between internal sources of funds and investment

---

27. They focus on the 1981–1982 recession in the United States, a recession typically attributed to tight monetary policy.

spending should be particularly strong for small firms after a monetary contraction. Oliner and Rudebusch do find that the impact of cash flow on investment increases for small firms, but not for large firms, when monetary policy tightens.

7.5 Summary

The economics of imperfect information has provided numerous insights into the structure of credit markets. Adverse selection and moral hazard account for many of the distinctive features of credit contracts when monitoring is costly. Credit-market imperfections commonly lead to situations in which the lender's expected profits are not monotonic in the interest rate charged on a loan; expected profits initially rise with the loan rate but can then reach a maximum before declining. As a result, it is possible for equilibrium to be characterized by credit rationing; excess demand fails to induce lenders to raise the loan rate because doing so lowers their expected profits. Perhaps more importantly, balance sheets matter. Variations in borrowers' net worth affect their ability to gain credit. A recession that lowers cash flows or a decline in asset prices that lowers net worth will reduce credit availability and increase the wedge between the costs of external and internal finance. The resulting impact on aggregate demand can generate a financial accelerator effect.

Kashyap and Stein (1993) summarize the general state of the credit view among monetary economists:

Still, the failure of the lending view to be widely embraced cannot be completely ascribed to theoretical discomfort—it has also suffered until recently from a lack of clear-cut, direct empirical support. (p. 7)

Despite Kashyap and Stein's conclusion that such direct empirical support now exists, skepticism still surrounds the existence, and importance, of the credit channel. Certainly the evidence on the empirical importance of a distinct bank lending channel for monetary policy is mixed. While periods of monetary contraction are followed by a fall in bank credit relative to open-market credit, this relationship may reflect simple composition effects and not a bank lending channel. The access to managed liabilities also suggests that variations in banking-sector reserves caused by changes in monetary policy will affect bank lending mainly through traditional interest-rate channels.

The evidence for a broad credit channel or for financial accelerator effects is more favorable. Recessions are associated with flights to quality. Small firms, a group likely to face large agency costs in obtaining external financing, are affected more severely during recessions. Net worth and cash flow do seem to affect investment, inventory, and production decisions.

For the analysis of monetary policy, it is important to know whether the general level of interest rates adequately captures the effects operating through credit channels. If so, then the traditional approach that focuses on interest rates as the key linkage between monetary policy and the real economy may prove sufficient for the analysis of many issues. The distinction between the credit and money views of the transmission process becomes more important if the nonlinearities suggested by the financial accelerator are quantitatively important. If they are, then the impact of monetary policy will depend on the initial condition of firm and household balance sheets.

8 Discretionary Policy and Time Inconsistency

8.1 Introduction

Macroeconomic equilibrium depends on both the current and the expected future behavior of monetary policy. Illustrations of this dependence were seen most clearly in the equilibrium expressions for the price level in the money-in-the-utility-function model, the cash-in-advance model, the models of hyperinflation, and the equilibrium expression for the nominal exchange rate. If policy behaves according to a systematic rule, the rule can be used to determine rational expectations of future policy actions under the assumption that the central bank continues to behave according to the policy rule. In the simulations used to study the cash-in-advance model, for example, the growth rate of the money supply followed an autoregressive process that included a response to productivity shocks. The equilibrium response to such shocks depended on how money growth reacted to productivity movements. In principle, one could derive an "optimal" policy rule by specifying an objective function for the central bank and then determining the values of the parameters in the policy rule that maximized the expected value of the objective function.

But what ensures that the central bank will find it desirable to behave according to such a policy rule? Absent enforcement, it may be optimal to deviate from the rule once private agents have made commitments based on the expectation that the rule will be followed. Firms and workers may agree to set nominal wages or prices based on the expectation that monetary policy will be conducted in a particular manner, yet once these wage and price decisions have been made, the central bank may have an incentive to deviate from actions called for under the rule. The rule may not be incentive compatible. If deviations from a strict rule are possible—that is, if the policy makers can exercise discretion—then agents will need to consider the policy makers' incentive to deviate; they can no longer simply base their expectations on the policy rule that the policy makers say they will follow.

Much of the modern analysis of monetary policy has focused on the incentives central banks face when actually setting their policy instrument. Following the seminal contribution of Kydland and Prescott (1977), attention has been directed to issues of central bank credibility and the ability to precommit to policies. Absent some means of committing in advance to take specific policy actions, central banks may find they face incentives to act in ways that are inconsistent with their earlier plans and announcements.

A policy is *time consistent* if an action planned at time t for time $t + i$ remains optimal to implement when time $t + i$ actually arrives. The policy can be state contingent; that is, it can depend on the realizations of events that are unknown at time t when the policy is originally planned. But a time-consistent policy is one in which the planned response to new information remains the optimal response once the new information arrives. A policy is *time inconsistent* if at time $t + i$ it will not be optimal to respond as originally planned.

The analysis of time inconsistency in monetary policy is important for two reasons. First, it forces one to examine the incentives faced by the central bank. The impact of current policy is often dependent upon the public's expectations, either about current policy or about future policy actions. To predict how policy affects the economy, we need to understand how expectations will respond, and this under-standing can only be achieved if policy behaves in a systematic manner. Just as with a study of private-sector behavior, an understanding of systematic behavior by the central bank requires an examination of the incentives the policy maker faces. And by focusing on the incentives faced by central banks, models of time inconsistency have had an important influence as *positive* theories of observed rates of inflation. These models provide the natural starting point for attempts to explain the actual behavior of central banks and actual policy outcomes.

Second, if time inconsistency is important, then models that help us to understand the incentives faced by policy makers and the nature of the decision problems they face are important for the normative task of designing policy-making institutions. Recent years have seen the reform and redesign of the central banks of many nations. In order to influence these reform efforts, monetary economists need models that help in understanding how institutional structures affect policy outcomes.

In the next section, we develop a framework, originally due to Barro and Gordon (1983a), that has served, despite its simplicity, as the workhorse for studying prob-lems of time inconsistency in monetary policy. The discretionary conduct of policy, meaning that the central bank is free at any time to alter its instrument setting, is shown to produce an average inflationary bias. That is, equilibrium involves a rate of inflation that exceeds the socially desired rate. This bias arises from a desire for economic expansions above the economy's equilibrium (or for unemployment rates below the economy's natural rate) and the inability of the central bank to credibly commit to a low rate of inflation. Section 8.3 examines some of the solutions that have been proposed for overcoming this inflationary bias. Central banks very often seem to be concerned with their reputations, and subsection 8.3.1 examines how such a concern might reduce or even eliminate the inflation bias. Subsection 8.3.2 consid-ers the possibility that society, or the government, might wish to delegate responsi-bility for monetary policy to a central banker with preferences between employment and inflation fluctuations that differ from those of society as a whole. Since the inflation bias can be viewed as arising because the central bank faces the wrong incentives, a third approach to solving the inflation bias is to design mechanisms for creating the right incentives. This approach is discussed in subsection 8.3.3. Subsection 8.3.4 considers the role of institutional structures in solving the inflation bias arising from discretion. Finally, the role of explicit targeting rules is studied in subsection 8.3.5.

Though the models of sections 8.2 and 8.3, with their focus on the inflationary bias that can arise under discretion, have played a major role in the academic literature on inflation, their success as positive theories of inflation—that is, as explanations for the actual historical variations of inflation both over time and across countries—is open to debate. Section 8.4 discusses the empirical importance of the inflation bias in accounting for episodes of inflation.

Differences in institutional structures, differences that presumably affect the incentives faced by central bankers in different countries, seem to influence macroeconomic outcomes. Specifically, the degree of independence from political influence enjoyed by central banks seems to show, at least for the developed economies, a significant correlation with average rates of inflation; increased central bank independence is associated with lower average inflation. Section 8.5 examines this empirical evidence and discusses its implications for central bank design and the role of institutions. Lessons we can draw from the issues covered in this chapter are summarized in section 8.6.

8.2   Inflation under Discretionary Policy

If inflation is costly (even a little), and if there is no real benefit to having 5% inflation on average as opposed to 1% inflation or 0% inflation, why do we observe average rates of inflation that are consistently positive? In recent years, most explanations of positive average rates of inflation have built on the time-inconsistency analysis of Kydland and Prescott (1977) and Calvo (1978).[1] The basic insight is that, while it may be optimal to achieve a low average inflation rate, such a policy is not time consistent. If the public were to expect low inflation, the central bank would face an incentive to inflate at a higher rate. Understanding this incentive and believing that the policy maker will succumb to it, the public correctly anticipates a higher inflation rate.

---

1. For a survey dealing with time-inconsistency problems in the design of both monetary and fiscal policies, see Persson and Tabellini (1990). Cukierman (1992) also provides an extensive discussion of the theoretical issues related to the analysis of inflation in models in which time inconsistency plays a critical role. Persson and Tabellini's survey of political economy covers many of the issues discussed in this chapter (Persson and Tabellini 1997). See also Driffill (1988).

8.2.1 Policy Objectives

To determine the central bank's policy choice, we need to specify the preferences of the central bank. It is standard to assume that the central bank's objective function involves output (or employment) and inflation, although the exact manner in which output has been assumed to enter the objective function has taken two different forms. In the formulation of Barro and Gordon (1983b), the central bank's objective is to maximize the expected value of

$$U = \lambda(y - y_n) - \tfrac{1}{2}\pi^2 \tag{8.1}$$

where y is output, y_n is the economy's natural rate of output, and π is the inflation rate. More output is preferred to less output with constant marginal utility, so output enters linearly, while inflation is assumed to generate increasing marginal disutility and so enters quadratically. The parameter λ governs the relative weight that the central bank places on output expansions relative to inflation stabilization. Often the desire for greater output is motivated by an appeal to political pressure on monetary policy that is due to the effects of economic expansions on the reelection prospects of incumbent politicians.[2] Alternatively, distortions due to taxes, monopoly unions, or monopolistic competition may lead y_n to be inefficiently low. The exact motivation for the output term in (8.1) will not be particularly important. What will be critical is that the central bank would like to expand output, but, because of the standard specification of aggregate-supply (see, for example, equation 5.34), it can do so only by generating surprises. For discussions of alternative motivations for this type of loss function, see Cukierman (1992).

The other standard specification for preferences assumes that the central bank desires to minimize the expected value of a loss function that depends on output and inflation fluctuations. Thus, the loss function is quadratic in both output and inflation and takes the form

$$V = \tfrac{1}{2}\lambda(y - y_n - k)^2 + \tfrac{1}{2}\pi^2 \tag{8.2}$$

The key aspect of this loss function is the parameter k. The assumption is that the central bank desires to stabilize both output and inflation, inflation around zero but output around $y_n + k$, which exceeds the economy's equilibrium output of y_n by the

2. The influence of reelections on the central bank's policy choices is studied by Fratianni, von Hagen, and Waller (1997) and Herrendorf and Neumann (1997).

constant k.[3] Because (8.2) involves the variance of output, the loss function (8.2) will generate a role for stabilization policy that is absent when the central bank cares only about the level of output as in (8.1).

There are several common interpretations for the assumption that $k > 0$, and these parallel the arguments for the output term in the linear preference function (8.1). Most often, some appeal is made to the presence of labor-market distortions (a wage tax, for example) that lead the economy's equilibrium rate of output to be inefficiently low. A rationale can also be provided by the presence of monopolistic competitive sectors that lead equilibrium output to be inefficiently low. Attempting to use monetary policy to stabilize output around $y_n + k$ then represents a second-best solution (the first-best would involve eliminating the original distortion). An alternative interpretation is that k arises from political pressure on the central bank. Here the notion is that elected officials have a bias for economic expansions because expansions tend to increase their probability of reelection. Since, as we will see, the presence of k leads to a third-best outcome, this second interpretation motivates institutional reforms designed to minimize political pressures on the central bank.

The two alternative objective functions (8.1) and (8.2) are clearly closely related. Expanding the term involving output in the quadratic loss function, (8.2) can be written as

$$V = -\lambda k(y - y_n) + \tfrac{1}{2}\pi^2 + \tfrac{1}{2}\lambda(y - y_n)^2 + \tfrac{1}{2}k^2$$

The first two terms are the same as the linear utility function (with signs reversed since V is a loss function), showing that the assumption of a positive k is equivalent to the presence of a utility gain from output expansions above y_n. In addition, V includes a loss arising from deviations of output around y_n [the $\lambda(y - y_n)^2$ term]. This introduces a role for stabilization policies that is absent when the central bank's preferences are assumed to be strictly linear in output. The final term involving k^2 is simply a constant and so has no effect on the central bank's decisions.

If the aggregate-supply equation depends on inflation surprises, both (8.1) and (8.2) can be written in the form $\overline{U}(\pi - \pi^e, \pi, e)$. Thus, the general framework is one in which the central bank's objective function depends on both surprise inflation and actual inflation. In addition to the employment motives already mentioned, one could emphasize the desire for seigniorage as leading to a similar objective function, since surprise inflation, by depreciating the real value of both interest-bearing and

---

3. See equation (8.3). Note that the inflation term in (8.1) and (8.2) could be replaced by $\tfrac{1}{2}(\pi - \pi^*)^2$ if the monetary authority has a target inflation rate π^* that differs from zero.

noninterest-bearing liabilities of the government, produces larger revenue gains for the government than does anticipated inflation (which only erodes noninterest-bearing liabilities).[4]

The alternative formulations reflected in (8.1) and (8.2) produce many of the same insights. Following Barro and Gordon (1983b), we will work initially with the function that is linear in output (8.1). The equilibrium concept in the basic Barro-Gordon model is noncooperative Nash. Given the public's expectations, the central bank's policy choice maximizes its objective function (or, equivalently, minimizes its loss function), given the public's expectations. The assumption of rational expectations implicitly defines the loss function for private agents as $L^P = \mathrm{E}(\pi - \pi^e)^2$; given the public's understanding of the central bank's decision problem, their choice of π^e is optimal.

Before turning to the determination of equilibrium output and inflation, it is worth noting that the assumption in both the linear and the quadratic versions of the central bank's objective function is that inflation stabilization, and not price-level stabilization, is the appropriate objective of monetary policy. Even in countries with legislative price-stability objectives, such as New Zealand, the operational conduct of policy has focused on achieving a desired inflation target. Under a price-level objective, fluctuations that cause the price level to deviate from target must be offset; a price rise then requires a deflation to reduce the price level. Under a policy that cares only about the inflation rate, such a price rise is permanent; policy ensures that the inflation rate returns to target, but no attempt is made to restore the initial price level. The general presumption is that the costs of a policy of maintaining a stable price level would be greater inflation-rate and output variability; the gain would be in lower long-term price-level uncertainty. For discussions of this issue, see S. Fischer (1994), Goodhart and Viñals (1994), the papers in Bank of Canada (1993), and Svensson (1996).

A final point to note is that the tax distortions of inflation analyzed in Chapter 4 were a function of anticipated inflation. Fluctuations in unanticipated inflation caused neutral price-level movements, while expected inflation altered nominal interest rates and the opportunity cost of money, leading to tax effects on money holdings, the consumption of cash goods, and labor supply. As we will see, equilibrium inflation will depend on the central bank's evaluation of the marginal costs and benefits of

---

4. See Cukierman (1992) for more detailed discussions of alternative motivations that might lead to objective functions of the forms given by either (8.1) or (8.2). In an open-economy framework, Bohn (1991c) shows how the incentives for inflation will depend on foreign-held debt denominated in the domestic currency.

inflation. If the costs of inflation arise purely from expected inflation, while surprise inflation generates economic expansions, then a central bank would perceive only benefits from attempting to produce unexpected inflation. Altering the specification of the central bank's objective function in (8.2) or (8.1) to depend only on output and expected inflation would then imply that the equilibrium inflation rate could be infinite (see Auernheimer [1974], Calvo [1978], and problem 5 at the end of this chapter).

8.2.2   The Economy

The specification of the economy is quite simple and follows the analysis of Barro and Gordon (1983a, 1983b). Aggregate output is given by a Lucas-type aggregate-supply function of the form

$$y = y_n + a(\pi - \pi^e) + e \tag{8.3}$$

This can be motivated as arising from the presence of one-period nominal wage contracts set at the beginning of each period based on the public's expectation of the rate of inflation. If actual inflation exceeds the expected rate, real wages will be eroded and firms will expand employment. If actual inflation is less than the rate expected, realized real wages will exceed the level expected and employment will be reduced. One can derive equation (8.3) from the assumption that output is produced according to a Cobb-Douglas production function in which output is a function of labor input, the nominal wage is set at the start of the period at a level consistent with labor-market equilibrium (given expectations of inflation), and firms base actual employment levels on the realized real wage.[5] A critical discussion of this basic aggregate-supply relationship can be found in Cukierman (1992, Chapter 3).

The rest of the model is a simple link between inflation and the policy authority's actual policy instrument.

$$\pi = \Delta m + v \tag{8.4}$$

where Δm is the growth rate of the money supply (the first difference of the log nominal money supply), assumed to be the central bank's policy instrument, and v is a velocity disturbance. The private sector's expectations are assumed to be determined prior to the central bank's choice of a growth rate for the nominal money

---

5. If, in levels, $Y = AL^{\alpha}$, firms equate the ex post real wage to the marginal product of labor, the supply of labor is fixed, the nominal wage is set to yield the expected market-clearing real wage, and A is a mean-1 random productivity shock, then in equation (8.3), $a = \dfrac{\alpha}{1-\alpha}$ and $e = \dfrac{1}{1-\alpha} \ln A$.

supply. Thus, in setting Δm, the central bank will take π^e as given. We will also assume that the central bank can observe e (but not v) prior to setting Δm; this assumption will generate a role for stabilization policy. Finally, assume that e and v are uncorrelated.[6]

The sequence of events is important. First, the private sector sets nominal wages based on their expectations of inflation. Thus, in the first stage, π^e is set. Then the supply shock e is realized. Because expectations have already been determined, they do not respond to the realization of e. Policy can respond, however, and the policy instrument Δm is set after the central bank has observed e. The velocity shock v is then realized, and actual inflation and output are determined.

Several important assumptions have been made here. First, as with most models involving expectations, the exact specification of the information structure is important. Most critically, we have assumed that private agents must commit to nominal wage contracts before the central bank has to set the rate of growth of the nominal money supply. This means that the central bank has the opportunity to surprise the private sector by acting in a manner that differs from what private agents had expected when they locked themselves into nominal contracts. We have also assumed that the money growth rate, rather than an interest rate, is the policy instrument. In fact, central banks have more often employed a short-term interest rate as the instrument of policy (see Chapters 9 and 10). If the main objective is to explain the determinants of average inflation rates, the distinction between money and interest rates as the policy instrument is probably not critical. However, the models we will be examining are often used to account for stabilization issues as well, and here the appropriate modeling of the choice of the policy instrument is more important. In keeping with the literature, we will assume the central bank sets money growth as its policy instrument. Given the focus on inflation, it will also be convenient at times simply to treat the inflation rate as the policy instrument. The basic model also incorporates the assumption that the central bank can react to the realization of the supply shock e while the public commits to wage contracts prior to observing this shock. This informational advantage on the part of the central bank introduces a role for stabilization policy and is meant to capture the fact that policy decisions can be made more frequently than can most wage and price decisions. As a result, the central bank can respond to economic disturbances before private agents have had the chance to revise all nominal contracts.

Finally, the assumption that v is observed after Δm is set is not critical. It is easy to show that the central bank will always adjust Δm to offset any observed or fore-

---

6. This basic framework can be viewed as a special case of the one employed in parts of Chapter 5.

castable component of the velocity shock, and this is why the rate of inflation itself is often treated as the policy instrument. Output and inflation will only be affected by the component of the velocity disturbance that was unpredictable at the time policy was set. This is modeled by assuming v is realized after the central bank chooses its policy.

8.2.3   Equilibrium Inflation

Since we are assuming that the central bank acts before observing the disturbance v, its objective will be to maximize the expected value of U, where the central bank's expectation is defined over the distribution of v. Substituting (8.3) and (8.4) into the central bank's objective function yields

$$U = \lambda[a(\Delta m + v - \pi^e) + e] - \tfrac{1}{2}(\Delta m + v)^2$$

The first-order condition for the optimal choice of Δm, conditional on e and taking π^e as given, is

$$a\lambda - \Delta m = 0$$

or

$$\Delta m = a\lambda > 0 \tag{8.5}$$

Given this policy, actual inflation will equal $a\lambda + v$. Because private agents are assumed to understand the incentives facing the central bank—that is, they are rational—they use (8.5) in forming their expectations about inflation. With private agents forming expectations prior to observing the velocity shock v, (8.4) and (8.5) imply

$$\pi^e = \mathrm{E}[\Delta m] = a\lambda$$

Thus, average inflation is fully anticipated. As a result, inflation produces no output gain, and output is given by $y = y_n + av + e$.

The equilibrium when the central bank acts with discretion in setting Δm produces a positive average rate of inflation equal to $a\lambda$. This has no effect on output, since the private sector completely anticipates inflation at this rate ($\pi^e = a\lambda$), so the economy suffers from positive average inflation to no benefit. The size of the bias is increasing in the effect of a money surprise on output, a, since this parameter governs the marginal benefit in the form of extra output that can be obtained from an inflation surprise. The larger is a, the greater is the central bank's incentive to inflate. Recognizing this fact, private agents anticipate a higher rate of inflation. The inflation bias

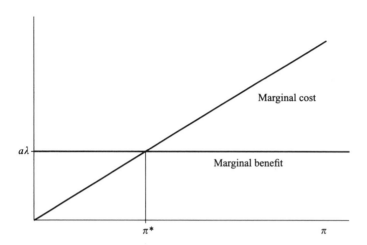

Figure 8.1
Equilibrium Inflation under Discretion (Linear Objective Function)

is also increasing in the weight the central bank places on its output objective, λ. A small λ implies that the gains from economic expansion are low relative to achieving inflation objectives, so the central bank has less of an incentive to generate inflation.

Why does the economy end up with positive average inflation even though it confers no benefits and the central bank dislikes inflation? The central bank is acting systematically to maximize the expected value of its objective function, so it weighs the costs and benefits of inflation in setting its policy. At a zero rate of inflation, the marginal benefit of generating a little inflation is positive, since, with wages set, the effect of an incremental rise in inflation on output is equal to $a > 0$. The value of this output gain is $a\lambda$. This is illustrated in Figure 8.1 by the horizontal line at height equal to $a\lambda$. The marginal cost of inflation is equal to π. At an inflation rate of zero, this marginal cost is zero, and so the marginal benefit of inflation exceeds the marginal cost. But the marginal cost rises (linearly) with inflation, as illustrated in Figure 8.1. At an expected inflation rate of $a\lambda$, the marginal cost equals the marginal benefit.

Under this discretionary policy outcome, the unconditional expected utility of the central bank is equal to

$$\mathrm{E}[U^d] = \mathrm{E}[\lambda(av + e) - \tfrac{1}{2}(a\lambda + v)^2]$$
$$= -\tfrac{1}{2}[a^2\lambda^2 + \sigma_v^2]$$

where $E[v] = E[e] = 0$ and σ_v^2 is the variance of the random inflation-control error v. Expected utility is decreasing in the variance of the random control error v and decreasing in the weight placed on output relative to inflation objectives (λ) since a larger λ increases the average rate of inflation. While the control error is unavoidable, the loss due to the inflation bias only arises from the monetary authority's fruitless attempt to stimulate output.

This outcome under discretion can be contrasted with the situation in which, for some as yet unexplained reason, the monetary authority is able to commit to setting money growth always equal to zero: $\Delta m = 0$. In this case, $\pi = v$ and expected utility would equal

$$E[U^c] = E[\lambda(av + e) - \tfrac{1}{2}v^2] = -\tfrac{1}{2}\sigma_v^2 > E[U^d]$$

So the central bank (and society if the central bank's utility is interpreted as a social welfare function) would be better off if it were possible to commit to a zero-money-growth-rate policy. Discretion, in this case, generates a cost.

As noted earlier, an alternative specification of the central bank's objectives focuses on the loss associated with output and inflation fluctuations around desired levels. This alternative formulation, given by the loss function (8.2), leads to the same basic conclusions. Discretion will lead to an average inflation bias and lower expected utility. In addition, though, specifying the loss function so that the central bank cares about output fluctuations means that there will be a potential role for policy to reduce output fluctuations caused by the supply shock e.

Substituting (8.3) and (8.4) into the quadratic loss function (8.2) yields

$$V = \tfrac{1}{2}\lambda[a(\Delta m + v - \pi^e) + e - k]^2 + \tfrac{1}{2}(\Delta m + v)^2$$

If Δm is chosen after observing the supply shock e, but before observing the velocity shock v, to minimize the expected value of the loss function, then the first-order condition for the optimal choice of Δm, conditional on e and taking π^e as given, is

$$a\lambda[a(\Delta m - \pi^e) + e - k] + \Delta m = 0$$

or

$$\Delta m = \frac{a^2\lambda\pi^e + a\lambda(k - e)}{1 + a^2\lambda} \tag{8.6}$$

There are two important differences to note in comparing (8.5), the optimal setting for money growth from the model with a linear objective function, to (8.6). First, the aggregate-supply shock appears in (8.6); because the central bank wants to minimize the variance of output around its target level, it will make policy conditional on the realization of the supply shock. Thus, an explicit role for stabilization policies arises that will involve trading off some inflation volatility for reduced output volatility. Second, the optimal policy depends on private-sector expectations about inflation.

Private agents are assumed to understand the incentives facing the central bank, so they use (8.6) in forming their expectations about inflation. However, private agents are atomistic; they do not take into account the effect their choice of expected inflation might have on the central bank's decision.[7] With expectations formed prior to observing the aggregate-supply shock e, (8.4) and (8.6) imply

$$\pi^e = \text{E}[\Delta m] = \frac{a^2 \lambda \pi^e + a\lambda k}{1 + a^2 \lambda}$$

Solving for π^e yields $\pi^e = a\lambda k > 0$. Substituting this back into (8.6) and using (8.4) gives an expression for the equilibrium rate of inflation:

$$\pi^d = \Delta m + v = a\lambda k - \left(\frac{a\lambda}{1 + a^2 \lambda}\right) e + v \tag{8.7}$$

where the superscript d stands for discretion. Note that the equilibrium when the central bank acts with discretion implies a positive average rate of inflation equal to $a\lambda k$. This has no effect on output, since the private sector completely anticipates this rate ($\pi^e = a\lambda k$). The size of this inflation bias is increasing in the distortion (k), the effect of a money surprise on output (a), and the weight the central bank places on its output objective (λ).

If, for the moment, we ignore the random disturbances e and v, the equilibrium with the quadratic loss function can be illustrated using Figure 8.2. Equation (8.6) is shown, for $e = 0$, as the straight line OP (for optimal policy), giving the central bank's reaction function for its optimal inflation rate as a function of the public's expected rate of inflation. The slope of this line is $a^2 \lambda / (1 + a^2 \lambda) < 1$, with intercept $a\lambda k / (1 + a^2 \lambda) > 0$. An increase in the expected rate of inflation requires that the central bank increase actual inflation by the same amount in order to achieve the same output effect, but because this action raises the cost associated with inflation, the central bank finds it optimal to raise π by less than the increase in π^e. Hence the

---

7. This assumption is natural in the context of individual firms and workers determining wages and prices. If nominal wages are set in a national bargaining framework, for example by a monopoly union and employer representatives, then it may be more appropriate to assume wages are set strategically, taking into account the impact of the wage decision on the incentives faced by the central bank. The case of a monoploy union has been analyzed by Tabellini (1988) and Cubitt (1992).

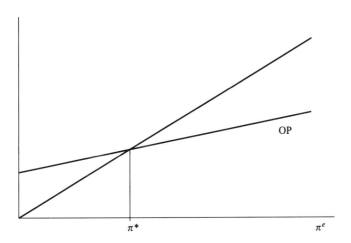

Figure 8.2
Equilibrium Inflation under Discretion (Quadratic Loss Function)

slope is less than 1. The positive intercept reflects the fact that, if $\pi^e = 0$, the central bank's optimal policy is to set a positive rate of inflation.

In equilibrium, expectations of private agents must be consistent with the behavior of the central bank. In the absence of any random disturbances, this requires that $\pi^e = \pi$. Thus, equilibrium must lie along the 45° line in Figure 8.2.

An increase in k, the measure of the output distortion, shifts the OP line upward and leads to a higher rate of inflation in equilibrium. An increase in a, the impact of an inflation surprise on real output, has two effects. First, it increases the slope of the OP line; by increasing the output effects of an inflation surprise, it raises the marginal benefit to the central bank of more inflation. By increasing the impact of an inflation surprise on output, however, a rise in a reduces the inflation surprise needed to move output to $y_n + k$, and, if λ is large, the intercept of OP could actually fall; the net effect of a rise in a, however, is to raise the equilibrium inflation rate (see equation [8.7], which shows that the equilibrium inflation rate when $e = 0$ is $a\lambda k$, which is increasing in a).

The coefficient on e in equation (8.7) is negative; a positive supply shock leads to a reduction in money growth and inflation. This response acts to reduce the impact of e on output [the coefficient on e in the output equation becomes $1/(1 + a^2\lambda)$, which is less than 1]. The larger the weight on output objectives (λ), the smaller the impact of e on output. In contrast, a central bank that places a larger relative weight on inflation objectives (a small λ) will tend to engage in less output stabilization.

Using (8.7), the loss function under discretion is

$$V^d = \frac{1}{2}\lambda\left[\left(\frac{1}{1+a^2\lambda}\right)e + av - k\right]^2 + \frac{1}{2}\left[a\lambda k - \left(\frac{a\lambda}{1+a^2\lambda}\right)e + v\right]^2 \qquad (8.8)$$

The unconditional expectation of this loss is

$$E[V^d] = \frac{1}{2}\lambda(1 + a^2\lambda)k^2 + \frac{1}{2}\left[\left(\frac{\lambda}{1+a^2\lambda}\right)\sigma_e^2 + (1+a^2\lambda)\sigma_v^2\right] \qquad (8.9)$$

where σ_x^2 denotes the variance of x.

Now suppose that the central bank had been able to precommit to a policy rule prior to the formation of private expectations. Because there is a role for stabilization policy in the present case (i.e., the monetary authority would like to respond to the supply shock e), the policy rule will not simply be a fixed growth rate for Δm as it was in the previous case with welfare a linear function of output. Instead, suppose the central bank is able to commit to a policy rule of the form

$$\Delta m^c = b_o + b_1 e$$

In the present linear-quadratic framework, a linear rule such as this will be optimal. Given this rule, $\pi^e = b_o$. Now substituting this into the loss function gives

$$V^c = \frac{1}{2}\lambda[a(b_1 e + v) + e - k]^2 + \frac{1}{2}[b_o + b_1 e + v]^2 \qquad (8.10)$$

Under a commitment policy, the central bank commits itself to particular values of the parameters b_o and b_1 *prior* to the public forming its expectations of inflation and *prior* to observing the particular realization of the shock e. Thus, b_o and b_1 are chosen to minimize the unconditional expectation of the loss function. Solving this minimization problem gives the optimal policy under precommitment as

$$\Delta m^c = -\frac{a\lambda}{1+a^2\lambda}e \qquad (8.11)$$

Note that average inflation under precommitment will be zero ($b_o = 0$), but the response to the aggregate-supply shock is the same as under discretion. The unconditional expectation of the loss function under precommitment is

$$E[V^d] = \frac{1}{2}\lambda k^2 + \frac{1}{2}\left[\left(\frac{\lambda}{1+a^2\lambda}\right)\sigma_e^2 + (1+a^2\lambda)\sigma_v^2\right] \qquad (8.12)$$

which is strictly less than the loss under discretion. Comparing (8.9) and (8.12), the "cost" of discretion is equal to $(a\lambda k)^2/2$ which is simply the loss attributable to the nonzero rate of inflation.

The inflation bias that arises under discretion occurs for two reasons; first, the central bank has an incentive to inflate once private-sector expectations are set, and second, the central bank is unable to precommit to a zero average inflation rate. To see why it cannot commit, suppose the central bank announces that it will deliver zero inflation. If the public believes the announced policy, and therefore $\pi^e = 0$, it is clear from (8.5) or (8.6) that the optimal policy for the central bank to follow would involve setting $\Delta m > 0$, and the average inflation rate would be positive. So the central bank's announcement would not be believed in the first place. The central bank cannot believably commit to a zero-inflation policy because under such a policy (i.e., if $\pi = \pi^e = 0$) the marginal cost of a little inflation is $\partial \frac{1}{2}\pi^2/\partial \pi = \pi = 0$, while the marginal benefit is $a\lambda > 0$ under the linear-objective-function formulation, or $-a^2\lambda(\pi - \pi^e) + a\lambda k = a\lambda k > 0$ under the quadratic formulation. Because the marginal benefit exceeds the marginal cost, the central bank has an incentive to break its commitment.

Society is clearly worse off under the discretionary policy outcome because it experiences a positive average inflation with no systematic improvement in output performance. This result fundamentally alters the long-running debate in economics over rules versus discretion in the conduct of policy. Prior to Kydland and Prescott's analysis of time inconsistency, economists had debated whether monetary policy should be conducted according to a simple rule, such as Milton Friedman's $k\%$-growth-rate rule for the nominal supply of money, or whether central banks should have the flexibility to respond with discretion. When the question is posed in this form, the answer is clearly that discretion is better. After all, if following a simple rule is optimal, under discretion one could always choose to follow such a rule. Thus, one could do no worse under discretion, and one might do better. But as the Barro-Gordon model illustrates, one might actually do worse under discretion; restricting the flexibility of monetary policy may result in a superior outcome. To see this, suppose the central bank is forced (somehow) to set $\Delta m = 0$. This avoids any inflation bias, but it also prevents the central bank from engaging in any stabilization policy. With the loss function given by (8.2), the unconditional expected loss under such a policy rule is $\frac{1}{2}\lambda(\sigma_e^2 + k^2) + \frac{1}{2}(1 + a^2\lambda)\sigma_v^2$. If this is compared to the unconditional expected loss under discretion, $E[V^d]$ given in equation (8.9), the zero money growth rule will be preferred if

$$\left(\frac{a^2\lambda^2}{1 + a^2\lambda}\right)\sigma_e^2 < a^2\lambda^2 k^2$$

The left side measures the gains from stabilization policy under discretion; the right side measures the cost of the inflation bias that arises under discretion. If the latter is greater, expected loss is lower if the central bank is forced to follow a fixed growth rate rule. Whether following a simple rule, thereby limiting the central bank's ability to respond to new circumstances, or allowing discretion, thereby generating an average inflation bias, will result in better policy outcomes becomes an open question.

By focusing on the strategic interaction of the central bank's actions and the public's formation of expectations, the Barro-Gordon model provides a simple but rich game-theoretical framework for studying monetary-policy outcomes. The approach emphasizes the importance of understanding the incentives faced by the central bank in order to understand policy outcomes. It also helps to highlight the role of credibility, illustrating why central bank's promises to reduce inflation may not be believed. The viewpoint provided by models of time inconsistency contrasts sharply with the traditional analysis of policy outcomes as either exogenous or as determined by a rule that implicitly assumes an ability to precommit.

8.3 Solutions to the Inflation Bias

A large literature has adopted the basic framework we have just set out to examine alternative solutions to the inflationary bias that arises under discretion.[8] Because the central bank is assumed to set the inflation rate so that the marginal cost of inflation (given expectations) is equal to the marginal benefit, most solutions alter the basic model to raise the marginal cost of inflation as perceived by the central bank. For example, the first class of solutions we will examine incorporates notions of reputation into a repeated-game version of the basic framework. Succumbing to the temptation to inflate today worsens the central bank's reputation for delivering low inflation; as a consequence, the public expects more inflation in the future, and this response lowers the expected value of the central bank's objective function. By "punishing" the central bank, the loss of reputation raises the marginal cost of inflation.

The second class of solutions we will examine can also be interpreted in terms of the marginal cost of inflation. Rather than viewing inflation as imposing a reputational cost on the central bank, one could allow the central bank to have preferences that differ from those of society at large so that the marginal cost of inflation as

---

8. See Persson and Tabellini (1990) for an in-depth discussion of much of this literature. Many of the most important papers are collected in Persson and Tabellini (1994).

perceived by the central bank is higher. One way to do so is simply to select as the policy maker an individual who places a larger than normal weight on achieving low inflation, and then give that individual the independence to conduct policy. Another way involves thinking of the policy maker as an executive whose compensation package is structured so as to raise the marginal cost of inflation. Or, if the inflation bias arises from political pressures on the central bank, institutions might be designed to reduce the effect of the current government on the conduct of monetary policy.

Finally, a third class of solutions involves imposing limitations on the central bank's flexibility. The most common such restriction is a targeting rule that requires the central bank to achieve a preset rate of inflation or imposes a cost related to deviations from this target. An analysis of inflation targeting is important because many central banks have recently adopted inflation targeting as a framework for the conduct of policy.[9]

Before proceeding to consider these solutions, however, it is important to note that the tradition in the monetary policy literature has been to assume that the underlying cause of the bias, the desire for economic expansions captured either by the presence of output in the case of the linear objective function (8.1) or the parameter k in the quadratic loss function (8.2), is given. Clearly, policies that might eliminate the factors that create a wedge between the economy's equilibrium output and the central bank's desired level would lead to the first-best outcome.

8.3.1 Reputation

One potential solution to an inflationary bias is to force the central bank to bear some cost if it deviates from its announced policy of low inflation, thereby raising the marginal cost of inflation as perceived by the central bank. One form such a cost might take is a lost reputation. The central bank might, perhaps through its past behavior, demonstrate that it will deliver zero inflation despite the apparent incentive to inflate. If the central bank then deviates from the low-inflation solution, credibility is lost and the public expects high inflation in the future. That is, the public employs a trigger strategy. The folk theorem for infinite-horizon repeated games (Fudenburg and Maskin 1986) suggests that equilibria exist in which inflation remains below the discretionary equilibrium level as long as the central bank's discount rate is not too high. Hence, as long as the central bank cares enough about the future, a low-inflation equilibrium can be supported. This idea is developed in the next subsection.

---

9. Australia, Canada, Finland, New Zealand, Sweden, and the United Kingdom are among the countries in which inflation targeting plays an important role in the formulation of monetary policy.

An alternative approach to reputation is to consider situations in which the public may be uncertain about the true preferences of the central bank. In the resulting imperfect-information game, the public's expectations about inflation must be based on their beliefs about the central bank's preferences or "type." Based on observed outcomes, these beliefs evolve over time, and central banks may have incentives to affect these beliefs through their actions; a central bank willing to accept some inflation in return for an economic expansion may still find it optimal initially to build a reputation as an anti-inflation central bank.

8.3.1.1 A Repeated Game The basic Barro-Gordon model is a one-shot game; even if the central bank's objective is to maximize $E_t \sum_{i=0}^{\infty} \beta^i U_{t+i}$ where U_t is defined by (8.1) and β is a discount factor $(0 < \beta < 1)$, nothing links time-t decisions with future periods.[10] Thus, the inflation rate in each period $t+s$ is chosen to maximize the expected value of U_{t+s} and the discretionary equilibrium of the one-shot game is a noncooperative Nash equilibrium of the repeated game. Barro and Gordon (1983b) evaluate the role of reputation by considering a repeated game in which the choice of inflation at time t can affect expectations during future periods. The public bases its expectations on the most recent rate of inflation, and Barro and Gordon examine whether inflation rates below the one-shot discretionary equilibrium rate can be sustained in a trigger-strategy equilibrium.

To illustrate their approach, suppose that the central bank's objective is to maximize the expected present discounted value of (8.1) and that the public behaves in the following manner: If in period $t-1$ the central bank delivered an inflation rate equal to what the public had expected (i.e., the central bank did not fool them in the previous period), the public expects an inflation rate in period t of $\bar{\pi} < a\lambda$. But if the central bank did fool them, the public expects the inflation rate that would arise under pure discretion, $a\lambda$. The hypothesized behavior of the public is summarized by

$$\pi_t^e = \bar{\pi} < a\lambda \quad \text{if} \quad \pi_{t-1} = \pi_{t-1}^e$$

$$\pi_t^e = a\lambda \quad \text{otherwise}$$

It is important to note that this trigger strategy involves a one-period punishment. If, after deviating and inflating at a rate that differs from $\bar{\pi}$, the central bank delivers an inflation rate of $a\lambda$ for one period, the public again expects the lower rate $\bar{\pi}$.[11]

10. The same clearly applies to the case of a quadratic objective function of the form (8.2).

11. This type of one-period punishment strategy has little to commend itself in terms of plausibility. It does, however, provide a useful starting point for analyzing a situation in which the central bank might refrain from inflating at the discretionary rate because it recognizes that the public will subsequently expect higher inflation.

The central bank's objective is to maximize the expected present value of its period-by-period utility function:

$$\sum_{i=0}^{\infty} \beta^i E_t[U_{t+i}]$$

where U_t is given by (8.1). Previously, the central bank's actions at time t had no effects in any other period. Consequently, the problem simplified to a sequence of one-period problems. This statement is no longer true in this repeated game with reputation; inflation at time t affects expectations at time $t+1$ and therefore the expected value of U_{t+1}. The question is whether equilibria exist for inflation rates $\bar{\pi}$ that are less then the outcome under pure discretion.

Suppose, then, that the central bank has set $\pi_s = \bar{\pi}$ for all $s < t$. Under the hypothesis about the public's expectations, $\pi_t^e = \bar{\pi}$. What can the central bank gain by deviating from the $\bar{\pi}$ equilibrium? If we ignore any aggregate supply shocks (i.e., $e \equiv 0$) and assume the central bank controls inflation directly, then setting inflation a little above $\bar{\pi}$, say $\pi_t = \varepsilon > \bar{\pi}$, increases the time-$t$ value of the central bank's objective function by

$$\left[a\lambda(\varepsilon - \bar{\pi}) - \tfrac{1}{2}\varepsilon^2\right] - (-\tfrac{1}{2}\bar{\pi}^2) = a\lambda(\varepsilon - \bar{\pi}) - \tfrac{1}{2}(\varepsilon^2 - \bar{\pi}^2)$$

This is maximized for $\varepsilon = a\lambda$, the inflation rate under discretion. So if the central bank deviates, it will set inflation equal to $a\lambda$ and gain

$$G(\bar{\pi}) \equiv a\lambda(a\lambda - \bar{\pi}) - \tfrac{1}{2}[(a\lambda)^2 - \bar{\pi}^2] = \tfrac{1}{2}(a\lambda - \bar{\pi})^2 \geq 0$$

Barro and Gordon refer to this as the "temptation" to cheat. The function $G(\bar{\pi})$ is shown as the dashed line in Figure 8.3. It is positive for all $\bar{\pi}$ and reaches a minimum at $\bar{\pi} = a\lambda$.

Cheating carries a cost because in the period following a deviation the public will punish the central bank by expecting an inflation rate of $a\lambda$. Since $a\lambda$ maximizes the central bank's one-period objective function for any expected rate of inflation, the central bank sets $\pi_{t+1} = a\lambda$. The subsequent loss, relative to the $\bar{\pi}$ inflation path, is given by

$$C(\bar{\pi}) \equiv \beta\left(-\frac{1}{2}\bar{\pi}^2\right) - \beta\left(-\frac{1}{2}a^2\lambda^2\right) = \frac{\beta}{2}[(a\lambda)^2 - \bar{\pi}^2] \qquad (8.13)$$

Since the loss occurs in period $t + 1$, we multiply it by the central bank's discount factor β. Barro and Gordon refer to this as the enforcement. The function $C(\bar{\pi})$ is positive and decreasing for $\bar{\pi} > 0$ and is shown as the solid line in Figure 8.3.

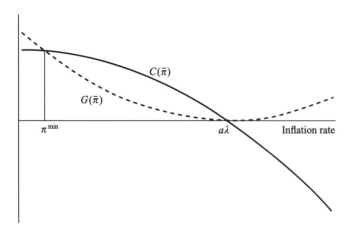

Figure 8.3
Temptation and Enforcement

The central bank will deviate from the proposed equilibrium if the gain (the temptation) exceeds the loss (the enforcement). Any $\bar{\pi}$ such that $C(\bar{\pi}) \geq G(\bar{\pi})$ can be supported as an equilibrium; with the loss exceeding the gain, the central bank has no incentive to deviate. As shown in the figure, $C(\bar{\pi}) < G(\bar{\pi})$ for inflation rates less than $\pi^{\min} \equiv \dfrac{1-\beta}{1+\beta}\, a\lambda < a\lambda$; since $\pi^{\min} > 0$, the trigger strategy cannot support the socially optimal, zero-inflation outcome. However, any inflation rate in the interval $[\pi^{\min}, a\lambda]$ is sustainable. The minimum sustainable inflation rate $\pi^{\min}$ is decreasing in β; the greater is the weight the central bank places on the future, the greater is the enforcement mechanism provided by the public's expectations and the lower is the inflation rate that can be sustained.[12]

This example is a simple illustration of a trigger strategy. The public expects one rate of inflation ($\bar{\pi}$ in this example) as long as the central bank "behaves"; and it expects a different, higher rate of inflation if the central bank misbehaves. But how does the public coordinate on this trigger strategy? If the public is atomistic, each member would take the expectations of others as given in forming her own expectations, and the notion of public coordination makes little sense. This problem is

12. With the central bank's objective given by (8.2), a zero inflation rate can be supported with a one-period punishment trigger strategy of the type considered as long as the central bank places sufficient weight on the future. In particular, zero inflation is an equilibrium if $\beta(1 + a^2\lambda) > 1$. See problem 6 at the end of this chapter.

even more severe when multiperiod punishment periods are considered in which the public expects high inflation for some fixed number of periods greater than one. Again, how is this expectation determined?

One way to solve the coordination problem is to assume that the central bank plays a game against a monopoly union.[13] With only one agent in the private sector (the union), the issue of atomistic agents coordinating on a trigger strategy no longer arises. Of course, the coordination problem has, in some sense, been solved by simply assuming it away, but it is also the case that many countries do have labor markets that are dominated by national unions and business organizations that negotiate over wages.[14]

The general point, though, is that the reputational solution works because the loss of reputation represents a cost to the central bank. Raising the marginal cost of inflation lowers the equilibrium rate of inflation. If $C(\bar{\pi}) > G(\bar{\pi})$, the central bank will not have an incentive to cheat, and inflation at the rate $\bar{\pi}$ can be supported. But can it really? Suppose the central bank does cheat. Will it be in the interests of a private sector that has somehow coordinated on a trigger strategy to actually punish the central bank? If by punishing the central bank the private sector also punishes itself, the threat to punish may not be credible. If punishment is not credible, the central bank is not deterred from cheating in the first place.

The credibility of trigger strategies in the context of the Barro-Gordon model (with the utility function 8.1) has been examined by al-Nowaihi and Levine (1994). They consider the case of a single monopoly union and show that if one requires that the punishment hurt the central bank but not the private sector (that is, consider only equilibria that are renegotiation-proof), then the only equilibrium is the high-inflation discretionary equilibrium. Thus, it would appear that trigger strategies will not support a low-inflation equilibrium.

Requiring that the punishment hurt only the central bank imposes strong restrictions on the possible equilibria. Adopting a weaker notion of renegotiation, al-Nowaihi and Levine introduce the concept of "chisel-proof credibility"[15] by asking, if the central bank cheats just a little, will the public be better off simply acquiescing, or will it be better off punishing? They show that the lowest inflation rate that can be

---

13. Tabellini (1988) studies the case of a monopoly union in the Barro-Gordon framework, although he focuses on imperfect information about the central bank's type, a topic we will discuss. See also Cubitt (1992).

14. al-Nowaihi and Levine (1994) provide an interpretation in terms of a game involving successive governments rather than a monopoly union and the government (or the central bank). See also Herrendorf and Lockwood (1996).

15. See also Herrendorf (1995a).

supported in a chisel-proof equilibrium is positive but less than the discretionary rate.

This discussion of trigger-strategy equilibria assumed the trigger was pulled whenever inflation deviated from its optimal value. If inflation differed from zero, this fact revealed to the public that the central bank had cheated. But for such strategies to work, the public must be able to determine whether the central bank cheated. If inflation depends not just on the central bank's policy setting but also on the outcome of a random disturbance as in (8.4), then the trigger strategy must be based directly on the central bank's policy instrument rather than the realized rate of inflation. Simply observing the actual rate of inflation may only reveal the net effects of both the central bank's policy actions and the realizations of a variety of random effects that influence the inflation rate.

This consequence raises a difficulty, one first analyzed by Canzoneri (1985). Suppose inflation is given by $\pi = \Delta m + v$. In addition, suppose that the central bank has a private, unverifiable forecast of v, call it v^f, and that Δm can be set conditional on v^f. Reputational equilibria will now be harder to sustain. Recall that the trigger-strategy equilibrium required that the public punish the central bank whenever the central bank deviated from the low-inflation policy. In the absence of private information, the public can always determine whether the central bank deviated by simply looking at the value of Δm. When the central bank has private information on the velocity shock, it should adjust Δm to offset v^f. So if the central bank forecasts a negative v, it should raise Δm. Simply observing, ex post, a high value of Δm, therefore, will not allow the public to determine if the central bank cheated; the central bank can always claim that v^f was negative and that it had not cheated.[16]

Canzoneri shows that a trigger-strategy equilibrium can be constructed in which the public assumes that the central bank cheated whenever the implicit forecast error of the central bank is too large. That is, a policy designed to achieve a zero rate of inflation would call for setting $\Delta m = -v^f$, and this might involve positive rates of money growth. Whenever money growth is too high, that is, whenever $\Delta m > -\bar{v}$ for some $\bar{v}$, the public assumes the central bank has cheated. The public then expects high inflation in the subsequent period; this result punishes the central bank. The constant $\bar{v}$ is chosen to ensure that the central bank has no incentive to deviate from the zero-inflation policy. This policy leads to a situation in which there are occa-

---

16. Herrendorf (1995b) considers situations in which v has a bounded support $[\underline{v}, \bar{v}]$. If the optimal commitment policy is $\Delta m = 0$, then as long as $\underline{v} \leq \pi \leq \bar{v}$, the public cannot tell whether the central bank cheated. However, if $\pi > \bar{v}$, the public knows the central bank cheated. Thus, the probability of detection is $\text{Prob}(v > \bar{v} - m)$.

sional periods of inflation; whenever the random variable v takes on a value such that $\Delta m = -v^f > -\bar{v}$, expected inflation (as well as actual inflation) rises. One solution to this problem may involve making policy more transparent by establishing targets that allow deviations to be clearly observed by the public. Herrendorf (1995b), for example, argues that a fixed-exchange-rate policy may contribute to credibility, since any deviation is immediately apparent. This solves the Canzoneri problem; the public does not need to verify the central bank's private information about velocity. If the central bank has private information on the economy that would call, under the optimal commitment policy, for a change in the exchange rate, a fixed-exchange-rate regime will limit the flexibility of the central bank to act on this information. Changing the exchange rate would signal to the public that the central bank was attempting to cheat. As a result, a trade-off between credibility and flexibility in conducting stabilization policy can arise.

8.3.1.2 Central Bank "Types"

In Canzoneri (1985), the central bank has private information about the economy in the form of an unverifiable forecast of an economic disturbance. The public doesn't know what the central bank knows about the economy, and, more importantly, the public cannot, ex post, verify the central bank's information. An alternative aspect of asymmetric information involves situations in which the public is uncertain about the central bank's true preferences. Backus and Driffill (1985), Barro (1986), Vickers (1986), Tabellini (1988), Cukierman and Liviatan (1991), Cukierman and Meltzer (1986), Andersen (1989), Ball (1995), Drazen and Masson (1994), García de Paso (1993), al-Nowaihi and Levine (1996), Herrendorf (1995b), Nolan and Schaling (1996), and Briault, Haldane, and King (1997), among others, study models in which the public is uncertain about the central bank's "type," usually identified either as its preference between output and inflation stabilization or its ability to commit. In these models, the public must attempt to infer the central bank's type from its policy actions, and equilibria in which central banks may deviate from one-shot optimal policies in order to develop reputations have been studied (for a survey, see Rogoff 1989). In choosing its actions, a central bank must take into account the uncertainty faced by the public, and it may be advantageous for one type of bank to mimic the other type to conceal (possibly only temporarily) its true type from the public.

In one sense, the discussion of models with uncertainty over the central bank type is out of place here, since our focus is on solutions to the inflationary bias that arises under policy discretion. Such models do not offer solutions unless one were to propose solving the inflation bias by concealing the identity of the central banker. Instead, these models are more appropriately viewed as offering positive theories of inflation, and so we will return to them again in discussing the ability of models that emphasize time-inconsistency problems to explain actual inflation experiences. But it is useful to discuss these models here, as well, because they correspond to game-theoretic notions of reputation, and reputational effects are widely viewed as relevant for explaining how low-inflation equilibria might be sustained. That is, they do explain how the inflation bias that can arise under discretion might be solved by the central bank's decision to preserve its reputation.

In one of the earliest reputational models of monetary policy, Backus and Driffill (1985) assumed that governments (or central banks) come in two types: optimizers who always act to maximize the expected present discounted value of a utility function of the form (8.1) and single-minded inflation fighters who always pursue a policy of zero inflation.[17] Alternatively, the inflation-fighter types can be described as having access to a precommitment technology. The government in office knows which type it is, but this information is unverifiable by the public. Simply announcing that it is a zero-inflation government would not be credible, since the public realizes that an optimizing central bank would also announce that it is a strict inflation fighter to induce the public to expect low inflation.[18]

Initially, the public is assumed to have prior beliefs about the current government's type (where these beliefs come from is unspecified, and therefore there will be multiple equilibria, one for each set of initial beliefs). If the government is actually an optimizer and ever chooses to inflate, its identity is revealed, and from then on the public expects the equilibrium inflation rate under discretion. To avoid this outcome, the optimizing government may have an incentive to conceal its true identity by mimicking the zero-inflation type, at least for a while. Equilibrium may involve pooling in which both types behave in the same way. In a finite-period game, the optimizer will always inflate in the last period because there is no future gain from further attempts at concealment.

Backus and Driffill solve for the equilibrium in their model by employing the concept of a sequential equilibrium (Kreps and Wilson 1982) for a finitely repeated game. Let π_t^d equal the inflation rate for period t set by the zero-inflation ("dry") government, and let π_t^w be the rate set by an optimizing ("wet") government. We

---

17. Ball (1995) provides a more recent model of inflation that is based on the same assumption concerning types.

18. Vickers (1986) assumes the types differ with respect to the weight placed on inflation in the loss function. Thus, a "dry" central bank places greater weight on achieving its inflation objectives than does a "wet" central bank. In Tabellini (1988), the "tough" type has $\lambda = 0$ (i.e., no weight on output), while the "weak" type is characterized by a $\lambda > 0$. Cukierman and Leviatan (1991) assume the types differ in their ability to commit; that is, the dry type is commited, whereas the wet one has discretion.

start in the final period T. The zero-inflation type always sets $\pi_T^d = 0$, while an optimizing government will always inflate in the last period at the discretionary rate $\pi_T^w = a\lambda$. With no further value in investing in a reputation, a wet government just plays the optimal inflation rate derived from the one-period Barro-Gordon model analyzed earlier.

In periods prior to T, however, the government's policy choice affects its future reputation, and it may therefore benefit a wet government to choose a zero rate of inflation in order to build a reputation as a dry. Thus, equilibrium may consist of an initial series of periods in which the wet government mimics the dry government, and inflation is zero. For suitable values of the parameters, the sequential equilibrium concept that Backus and Driffill employ also leads to mixed strategies in which the wet government inflates with some probability. So the wet government randomizes; if the outcome calls for it to inflate, the wet government is revealed as wet and, from then on, inflation is equal to $a\lambda$. If it doesn't inflate, the public updates its beliefs about the government's type using Bayes' rule.

Ball (1995) develops a model of inflation persistence based on the same notion of central bank types used by Backus and Driffill (1985) and Barro (1986). That is, one type, type D, always sets inflation equal to zero, while type W acts opportunistically to minimize the expected discounted value of a quadratic loss function of the form:

$$L^W = \sum_{i=0}^{\infty} \beta^i [\lambda(y_{t+i} - y_n - k)^2 + \pi_{t+i}^2] \tag{8.14}$$

where $0 < \beta < 1$. To account for shifts in policy, Ball assumes that the central bank type follows a Markov process. If the central bank is of type D in period t, then the probability the central bank is still type D in period $t+1$ is d; the probability the type switches to type W in $t+1$ is $1 - d$. Similarly, if the period-t central bank is type W, then the $t+1$ central bank is type W with probability w and type D with probability $1 - w$.

The specification of the economy is standard, with output a function of inflation surprises and an aggregate supply shock:

$$y_t = y_n + a(\pi_t - \pi_t^e) + e_t \tag{8.15}$$

To capture the idea that economies are subject to occasional discrete supply shocks, Ball assumes that e takes on only two possible values: 0 with probability $1 - q$ and $\bar{e}$ with probability q. If shifts in policy and supply shocks are infrequent, then $1 - d$, $1 - w$, and q are all small.

The timing in this game has the public forming expectations of inflation; then the supply shock and the central bank type are determined. It is assumed that the realization of e but not the central bank type is observable. Finally, the central bank sets π. In this game, there are many possible equilibria depending on how the public is assumed to form its expectations about the central bank type. Ball considers a perfect Nash equilibrium concept in which actions depend only on variables that directly affect current payoffs. Such equilibria are Markov perfect equilibria (Maskin and Tirole 1988) and rule out the type of trigger-strategy equilibria considered, for example, by Barro (1986).[19] Ball then shows that such an equilibrium exists and involves the W type setting $\pi = 0$ as long as $e = 0$; if $e = \bar{e}$, the type W inflates at the discretionary rate. Since this action reveals the identify of the central bank (i.e., as a type W), inflation remains at the discretionary rate until such time as a type D central bank takes over. At this point, inflation drops to zero, remaining there until a bad supply shock is again realized.[20]

This outcome predicts periodic and persistent bouts of inflation in response to adverse economic disturbances. This prediction for inflation appears to provide a good representation of actual inflation experiences, at least in the developed economies over the last 30 years.

One undesirable aspect of the Backus and Driffill framework is its assumption that one government, the dry government, is simply an automaton, always playing zero inflation. While serving a useful purpose in allowing one to characterize how beliefs about type might affect reputation and the behavior of a government that would otherwise like to inflate, the myopic behavior of the dry government is unsatisfactory; such a government might also wish to signal its type to the public or otherwise attempt to differentiate itself from a wet type.

One way a dry government might distinguish itself would be to announce a planned or target rate of inflation and then build credibility by actually delivering on its promises. In the Backus and Driffill model, the dry government could be thought of as always announcing a zero target for inflation, but as Cukierman and Liviatan (1991) note, even central banks that seem committed to low inflation often set positive inflation targets, and they do so in part because low inflation is not perfectly credible. That is, if the public expects a positive rate of inflation because the central bank's true intentions are unknown, then even a dry central bank may feel the need

---

19. In the trigger-strategy equilibria, current actions depend on π_{t-1} even though payoffs do not depend directly on lagged inflation.

20. For this to be an equilibrium, the discount factor must be large, but not too large. As in standard reputational models, the type W central bank must place enough weight on the future that it is willing to mimic the type D in order to develop a reputation for low inflation. However, if the future receives too much weight, the type W will be unwilling to separate, that is, inflate, when the bad shock occurs. See Ball (1995).

to partially accommodate these expectations. Doing otherwise would produce a recession.

To model this, Cukierman and Liviatan assume that there are two potential government or central bank types, D and W, who differ in their ability to commit. Type D commits to its announced policy; type W cannot precommit. In contrast to Backus and Driffill, Cukierman and Liviatan allow their central banks to make announcements, and the D type is not simply constrained to always maintain a zero rate of inflation. If the public assigns some prior probability to the central bank being a type W, the type D's announcement will not be fully credible. As a result, a type D central bank may find it optimal to announce a positive rate of inflation.

To show the effect on inflation of the public's uncertainty about the type of central bank in office, the basic points can be illustrated within the context of a two-period model. To determine the equilibrium behavior of inflation, we need to solve the model backward by first considering the equilibrium during the last period.

Assume that both central bank types share a utility function that is linear in output and quadratic in inflation as given by (8.1). With utility linear in output, stabilization will not play a role, so, let output be given by (8.3) with $e \equiv 0$. In the second period, reputation has no further value, so the type W central bank will simply set inflation at the optimal discretionary rate $a\lambda$. To determine D's strategy, however, we need to consider whether the equilibrium will be a separating, pooling, or mixed-strategy equilibrium. In a separating equilibrium, the behavior of the central bank during the first period reveals its identity; in a pooling equilibrium, both types behave in the same way during the first period, so the public will remain uncertain as to the true identity of the bank. A mixed-strategy equilibrium would involve the type W mimicking the type D with positive probability less than one.

Since a separating equilibrium is a bit simpler to construct, let us start with that case. With first-period behavior revealing its type, the public, in period 2, now knows the identity of the central bank. Since type D is able to commit, its optimal policy is to announce a zero rate of inflation for period 2. The public, knowing a type D is truthful, expects a zero inflation rate, and in equilibrium $\pi_2^D = 0$.

In the first period of a separating equilibrium, the public is uncertain about the type of central bank actually in power. Suppose the public assigns an initial probability q that the central bank is of type D. Since we are, by hypothesis, considering a separating equilibrium in which the W type reveals its type by inflating at a rate that differs from the announced rate, a type W will choose to inflate at the rate $a\lambda$ because this values maximizes its utility function.[21] So if the type D announces π^a,

---

21. Recall that with the utility function (8.1), the central bank's optimal period-1 inflation rate is independent of the expected rate of inflation.

then the public will expect an inflation rate of $\pi_1^e = q\pi^a + (1-q)a\lambda$.[22] Our last step to fully characterize the separating equilibrium is to determine the optimal announcement (since the D type actually inflates at the announced rate and the W type inflates at the rate $a\lambda$).

If future utility is discounted at the rate β, the utility of the type D central bank is given by

$$U_{sep}^D = \lambda(y_1 - y_n) - \tfrac{1}{2}\pi_1^2 + \beta[\lambda(y_2 - y_n) - \tfrac{1}{2}\pi_2^2]$$

$$= a\lambda(\pi_1 - \pi_1^e) - \tfrac{1}{2}\pi_1^2$$

since, in period 2, $y_2 = y_n$ and $\pi_2^D = 0$. The type D picks first-period inflation subject to $\pi_1 = \pi^a$ and $\pi_1^e = q\pi^a + (1-q)a\lambda$. This yields

$$\pi_1^D = (1-q)a\lambda \le a\lambda$$

The role of credibility is clearly illustrated in this result. If the central bank were known to be of type D, that is, if $q = 1$, it could announce and deliver a zero rate of inflation. The possibility that the central bank might be of type W, however, forces the D type to announce, and deliver, a positive rate of inflation. The public's uncertainty leads them to expect a positive rate of inflation; the type D central banker could announce and deliver a zero rate of inflation, but doing so would create a recession whose cost outweighs the gain from a lower inflation rate.

To summarize, in a separating equilibrium, the type W inflates at the rate $a\lambda$ in each period, while the type D inflates at the rate $(1-q)a\lambda$ during the first period and 0 during the second period. Since expected inflation in the first period is $q(1-q)a\lambda + (1-q)a\lambda = (1-q^2)a\lambda$, which is less than $a\lambda$ but greater than $(1-q)a\lambda$, output is above y_n if the central banker is actually a type W and below y_n if a type D.

What happens in a pooling equilibrium? A pooling equilibrium requires that the W type not only make the same first-period announcement as the D type, but it must also pick the same actual inflation rate in period 1 (otherwise it would reveal itself). In this case, the D type faces period-2 expectations $\pi_2^e = q\pi_2^a + (1-q)a\lambda$.[23] Since

---

22. The W type will also announce the same inflation rate as the type D, since doing otherwise would immediately raise the public's expectations about first-period inflation and lower type W's utility.

23. In the pooling equilibrium, first-period outcomes do not reveal any information about the identity of the central bank type, so the public continues to assess the probability of a type D as equal to q. This would not be the case if the equilibrium involved the W type following a mixed strategy in which it inflates in period one with probability $p < 1$. In a sequential Bayesian equilibrium, the public updates the probability of a D type on the basis of the period-one outcomes using Bayes' rule.

this is just like the problem we analyzed for the first period of the separating equilibrium, $\pi_2^D = \pi_2^a = (1-q)a\lambda > 0$. The type D inflates at a positive rate in period 2, since her announcement lacks complete credibility. In the first period of a pooling equilibrium, however, things are different. In a pooling equilibrium the D type knows that the W type will mimic whatever the D type does. And the public knows the same thing, so both types will inflate at the announced rate of inflation and $\pi_1^e = \pi_1^a$. In this case, with the announcement fully credible, the D type will announce and deliver $\pi_1 = 0$.

To summarize, in the pooling equilibrium, inflation will equal 0 in period 1 and either $(1-q)a\lambda$ or $a\lambda$ in period 2 depending on which type is actually in office. In the separating equilibrium, inflation will equal $(1-q)a\lambda$ in period 1 and 0 in period 2 if the central bank is of type D, and $a\lambda$ in both periods if the central bank is of type W.

Which equilibrium will occur? If the type W separates by inflating at the rate $a\lambda$ during period 1, its utility will be $a\lambda[a\lambda - (1-q^2)a\lambda] - \frac{1}{2}(a\lambda)^2 - \beta\frac{1}{2}(a\lambda)^2$, or

$$U_{sep}^W = (a\lambda)^2[q^2 - \tfrac{1}{2}(1+\beta)]$$

If type W deviates from the separating equilibrium and mimics type D instead by only inflating at the rate $(1-q)a\lambda$ during period 1, it would achieve a utility payoff of $a\lambda[(1-q)a\lambda - (1-q^2)a\lambda] - \frac{1}{2}[(1-q)a\lambda]^2 + \beta a\lambda(a\lambda - 0) - \beta\frac{1}{2}(a\lambda)^2$, or

$$U_m^W = \tfrac{1}{2}(a\lambda)^2(q^2 - 1 + \beta)$$

since mimicking fools the public into expecting zero inflation in period 2. Type W will separate if and only if $U_{sep}^W > U_m^W$, which occurs when

$$\beta < q^2/2 \equiv \underline{\beta} \tag{8.16}$$

Thus, the separating equilibrium occurs if the public places a high initial probability on the central bank being of type D (q is large). In this case, type D is able to set a low first-period rate of inflation, and the W type does not find it worth while to mimic. Only if the W type places a large weight on being able to engineer a surprise inflation in period 2 (i.e., β is large), would deviating from the separating equilibrium be profitable.

Suppose $\beta \geq \underline{\beta}$; will pooling emerge? Not necessarily. If the type W pools, her utility payoff will be

$$a\lambda[0] - \tfrac{1}{2}[0]^2 + \beta a\lambda[a\lambda - \pi_2^e] - \beta\tfrac{1}{2}(a\lambda)^2$$

or, since $\pi_2^e = q\pi_2^a + (1-q)a\lambda = (1-q^2)a\lambda,$

$$U_p^W = \beta(a\lambda)^2(q^2 - \tfrac{1}{2})$$

If the type W deviates from the pooling equilibrium, she will generate an output expansion in period 1, but because this reveals her identity, period 2 inflation is fully anticipated, and output equals y_n. Thus, deviating gives type W a payoff of $a\lambda[a\lambda] - \tfrac{1}{2}[a\lambda]^2 + \beta a\lambda[0] - \beta\tfrac{1}{2}[a\lambda]^2$ or

$$U_{dev}^W = \tfrac{1}{2}(a\lambda)^2(1-\beta)$$

By comparing the incentive for W to deviate from a pooling equilibrium, the pooling outcome is an equilibrium whenever

$$\beta > \frac{1}{2q^2} \equiv \bar{\beta} \tag{8.17}$$

since in this case $U_p^W > U_{dev}^W$. If β is large enough, meaning $\beta > 1/(2q^2)$, a type W places enough weight on the future that she is willing to forgo the temptation to immediately inflate, and zero inflation is the equilibrium in period 1. Of course in period 2, there is no further value in maintaining a reputation, so the type W inflates. Equation (8.17) shows that the critical cutoff value for β depends on q, the prior probability the public assigns to a type D setting policy. A larger q makes pooling an equilibrium for more values of β, so that even less patient type W's will find it advantageous to not deviate from the pooling equilibrium. If q is large, then the public thinks it likely that the central bank is a type D. This belief leads them to expect low inflation in period 2, so the output gains of inflating at the rate $a\lambda$ will be large. By pooling during period 1 a type W can then benefit from causing a large expansion in period 2. If the type W deviates and reveals her type during period 1, the first-period output gain is independent of q.[24] So a rise in q leaves the period 1 advantage of deviating unchanged while increasing the gain from waiting until period 2 to inflate.

Comparing (8.16) and (8.17) shows that $\beta < \bar{\beta}$, so there will be a range of values for the discount factor for which neither the separating nor the pooling outcomes will be an equilibrium. For β in this range, there will be mixed-strategy equilibria (see Cukierman and Liviatan for details).

This model reveals how public uncertainty about the intentions of the central bank affect the equilibrium inflation rate. In both the separating equilibrium and the mixed-strategy equilibrium, the type D central bank inflates in the first period even

---

24. This result occurs because expected inflation equals zero during the first period of a pooling equilibrium. Consequently, the output expansion of inflating at the rate $a\lambda$ is $a[a\lambda - 0] = a^2\lambda$ which is independent of q.

though it is (by assumption) capable of commitment and always delivers on its announcements.

The formulation of Cukierman and Liviatan also provides a nice illustration of the role that announcements can play in influencing the conduct of policy. It also illustrates why central banks might be required to make announcements about their inflation plans. The type D central bank is clearly better off making announcements; as long as $q > 0$, making an announcement allows the D type to influence expectations and reduce the first-period inflation rate (this situation occurs in the separating and pooling equilibria as we have shown, but it also occurs in mixed-strategy equilibria). Even when there may exist incentives to manipulating announcements, they can serve to constrain the subsequent conduct of policy. They may also convey information about the economy if the central bank has private and unverifiable information such as its own internal forecast of economic conditions.[25]

8.3.2 Preferences

An alternative approach to solving the inflationary bias of discretion focuses directly on the preferences of the central bank. This branch of the literature has closer connections with the extensive empirical work that has found, at least for the industrialized economies, that average inflation rates across countries are negatively correlated with measures of the degree to which a central bank is independent from the political authorities.[26] If the central bank is independent, then one can begin to think of the preferences of the central bank as differing from those of the elected government. And if they can differ, then one can ask how they might differ and how the government, through its appointment process, might influence the preferences of the central bank(er).

Rogoff (1985b) was the first to analyze explicitly the issue of the optimal preferences of the central banker.[27] He did so in terms of the relative weight the central banker places on its inflation objective. In the objective function (8.2), λ measures the weight on output relative to a weight normalized to 1 on inflation objectives. Rogoff concluded that the government should appoint as central banker someone who places greater relative weight on the inflation objective than does society (the government) as a whole. That is, the central banker should have preferences that are

---

25. See Persson and Tabellini (1993), Walsh (1996), and Muscatelli (In press).

26. This empirical work will be discussed in section 8.5.

27. Interestingly, Barro and Gordon recognized that outcomes could be improved under discretion by distorting the central banker's preferences so that "there is a divergence in preferences between the principal (society) and its agent (the policymaker)" (Barro and Gordon 1983a, p. 607, footnote 19). This insight is also relevant for the contracting approach to be discussed in section 8.3.3.

of the form given by (8.2) but with a weight on inflation of $1 + \delta > 1$. Rogoff characterized such a central banker as more "conservative" than society as a whole. This is usefully described as "weight" conservatism (Svensson 1997b), since there are other interpretations of conservatism; for example, the central bank might have a target inflation rate that is lower than that of the government. In most of the literature, however, "conservative" is interpreted in terms of the weight placed on inflation objectives relative to output objectives.

The intuition behind Rogoff's result is easily understood by referring back to equation (8.7), which showed the inflation rate under discretion for the quadratic loss function (8.2). If the central banker conducting monetary policy has a loss function that differs from (8.2) only by placing weight $1 + \delta$ on inflation rather than 1, then inflation under discretion will equal

$$\pi^d(\delta) = \Delta m + v = \frac{a\lambda k}{1 + \delta} - \frac{a\lambda}{1 + \delta + a^2\lambda} e + v \qquad (8.18)$$

The equilibrium inflation rate is a function δ. Two effects are at work. First, the inflation bias is reduced, since $1 + \delta > 1$. This tends to reduce the social loss function (the loss function with weight 1 on inflation and λ on output). But the coefficient on the aggregate-supply shock is also reduced; stabilization policy is distorted and the central bank responds too little to e. As a consequence, output fluctuates more than is socially optimal in response to supply shocks. The first effect (lower average inflation) makes it optimal to appoint a central banker who places more weight on inflation than does society; this rule is usually interpreted to mean that society should appoint a "conservative" to head the central bank. But the second effect (less output stabilization) limits how conservative the central banker should be.

Using (8.18), we can evaluate the government's loss function V as a function of δ. By then minimizing the government's expected loss function with respect to δ, we can find the "optimal preferences" for a central banker. The expected value of the government's objective function is

$$E[V] = \tfrac{1}{2} E(\lambda\{a[\pi^d(\delta) - \pi^e] + e - k\}^2 + [\pi^d(\delta)]^2)$$

$$= \frac{1}{2}\left[\lambda k^2 + \lambda\left(\frac{1+\delta}{1+\delta+a^2\lambda}\right)^2 \sigma_e^2 + a^2\lambda\sigma_v^2\right]$$

$$+ \frac{1}{2}\left[\left(\frac{a\lambda k}{1+\delta}\right)^2 + \left(\frac{a\lambda}{1+\delta+a^2\lambda}\right)^2 \sigma_e^2 + \sigma_v^2\right]$$

where we have used (8.18) to replace π^e with $a\lambda k/(1 + \delta)$ under the assumption that

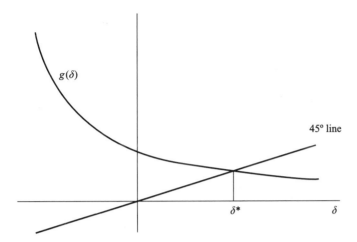

Figure 8.4
Optimal Degree of "Conservatism"

the public knows δ when forming its expectations. Minimizing this expression with respect to δ yields, after some manipulation, the following condition that must be satisfied by the optimal value of δ:

$$\delta = \frac{k^2}{\sigma_e^2} \left(\frac{1+\delta+a^2\lambda}{1+\delta} \right)^3 \equiv g(\delta) \tag{8.19}$$

The function $g(\delta)$ is shown in Figure 8.4.[28] Equation (8.19) is satisfied where $g(\delta)$ crosses the 45° line. Since $\lim_{\delta \to \infty} g(\delta) = \frac{k^2}{\sigma_e^2} > 0$, the intersection always occurs in the range $\delta \in (0, \infty]$; given the trade-off between distorting the response of policy to aggregate-supply shocks and reducing the average inflation bias, it is always optimal to appoint a central banker who places more weight $(\delta > 0)$ on inflation objectives than the government itself does.

Rogoff's solution is often characterized as involving the appointment of a conservative to head an independent central bank. The concept of independence means that, once appointed, the central banker is able to set policy without interference or restriction, and she will do so to minimize her own assessment of social costs. Thus, the inflation bias problem is solved partially through delegation; the government

---

28. See Eijffinger, Hoeberichts, and Schaling (1995) for a discussion of this graphical representation of the determinants of the optimal degree of conservatism. Eijffinger and Schaling (1995) extend the framework to an open-economy context.

delegates responsibility for monetary policy to an independent central bank. The benefit of this independence is lower average inflation; the cost depends on the realization of the aggregate-supply shock. If shocks are small, the gain in terms of low inflation clearly dominates the distortion in stabilization policy; if shocks take large values, the costs associated with the stabilization distortion can dominate the gain from low inflation.[29]

Lohmann (1992) shows that the government can do even better if it appoints a weight-conservative central banker but limits the central bank's independence. If the aggregate-supply shock turns out to be too large, the government overrides the central banker, where the critical size determining what is too large is determined endogenously as a function of the costs of overriding. The knowledge that she can be overridden also affects the way the central banker responds to shocks that are less than the threshold level that triggers an override. By responding more actively to large shocks, the central banker is able to extend the range of shocks over which she maintains independence.

This type of outcome—a relatively independent and conservative central bank whose independence may be overruled in the face of large economic disturbances—provides an appealing model of the structure of monetary policy in a country such as Germany. There, the Bundesbank is perceived to place a large weight on achieving low inflation and to enjoy a high degree of political independence. Yet, at the time of the unification of East and West Germany, the Bundesbank recommended against exchanging East for West marks at a one-for-one exchange rate but was overruled by the government of Helmut Kohl. While exchange-rate policy in Germany, as in other countries, is generally under the government's control and not the central bank's, this example illustrates how even independent central banks do not operate in a political vacuum.

Rogoff's solution highlights a trade-off—one can reduce the bias but only at the cost of distorting stabilization policy. One implication is that countries with central banks that place a high weight on inflation objectives should have, on average, lower inflation, but they should also experience greater output variance. The variance of output is equal to

$$\left(\frac{1+\delta}{1+\delta+a^2\lambda}\right)^2 \sigma_e^2 + a^2\sigma_v^2$$

and this is increasing in δ. Highly independent central banks are presumed to place

---

29. Since society is better off appointing a conservative, the expected gain from low inflation exceeds the expected stabilization cost, however.

more weight on achieving low inflation, and a large literature has investigated the finding that measures of central bank independence are negatively correlated with average inflation, at least for the industrialized economies (see Cukierman 1992; Eijffinger and de Haan 1996). Alesina and Summers (1993) have shown, however, that such measures do not appear to be correlated with the variance of real output. This finding runs counter to the implications of the Rogoff model.

Solving the inflationary bias of discretionary policy through the appointment of a conservative raises several issues. First, how does the government identify the preference parameter δ? Second, how does it commit to a δ? Once expectations are set, the government has an incentive to fire the conservative central banker and replace her with one sharing the government's preferences. Third, what prevents further delegation? If a government finds it optimal to delegate monetary policy to a central banker with preference parameter $1 + \delta > 1$, the same argument implies it will be optimal for the conservative central bank to delegate policy to an even more conservative staff member with preference parameter $1 + \delta' > 1 + \delta > 1$. Finally, the focus on preferences, as opposed to incentives, clouds the model's implications for institutional structure and design. Should institutions be designed to generate appropriate incentives for policy makers? Or does good policy simply require putting the right people in charge?

8.3.3   Contracts

The problems that can occur under discretion arise because central banks are responding optimally to the incentive structure they face, but the incentives are wrong. This statement suggests that, rather than relying on central bankers having the right preferences, one might try to affect the incentives central banks face. But this task requires first determining what incentives central banks *should* face.

The appropriate perspective for addressing such issues is provided by the principal-agent literature.[30] A key insight that has motivated the large literature expanding on the analysis of the time inconsistency of optimal plans is the recognition that central banks respond to the incentives they face. These incentives may be shaped by the institutional structure within which policy is conducted. For example, as we have already seen, Lohmann shows how policy is affected when the central banker knows she will be overridden by the government if the economy is subject to a disturbance that is "too" big. Rogoff (1985b, p. 1180) argues that targeting rules might be enforced by making the monetary authority's budget depend on adherence to the rule,

---

30. This section draws heavily on Walsh (1995a). See also Persson and Tabellini (1993) and Waller (1995).

and in a similar vein, Garfinkel and Oh (1993) suggest that a targeting rule might be enforced by legislation punishing the monetary authority if it fails to achieve the target. Such institutional aspects of the central bank's structure and its relationship with the government can be thought of as representing a "contract" between the government and the monetary authority. The conduct of monetary policy is then affected by the contract the government offers to the central bank.

The government's (or perhaps society's) problem can be viewed as that of designing an optimal incentive structure for the central bank. Following Walsh (1995a), the most convenient way to determine an optimal incentive structure is to assume that the government can offer the head of the central bank a state-contingent wage contract. Such a contract allows one to derive explicitly the manner in which the bank's incentives should be dependent on the state of the economy. While there are numerous reasons to question the effectiveness and implementability of such employment contracts in the context of monetary-policy determination, a (possibly) state-contingent wage contract for the central banker represents a useful fiction for deriving the optimal incentive structure with which the central bank should be faced and provides a convenient starting point for the analysis of optimal central bank incentives.[31]

The basic structure of the model is identical to that used earlier, consisting of an aggregate-supply relationship given by (8.3), a link between money growth and inflation given by (8.4), and an objective function that depends on output fluctuations and inflation variability as in (8.2). The private sector's expectations are assumed to be determined prior to the central bank's choice of a growth rate for the nominal money supply. Thus, in setting Δm, the central bank will take π^e as given. We will also assume that the central bank can observe the supply shock e prior to setting Δm, since this assumption will generate a role for stabilization policy. The disturbance v in the link between money growth and inflation is realized after the central bank sets Δm. Finally, assume e and v are uncorrelated.

Monetary policy is conducted by an independent central bank, one which shares the government's preferences, V, but which also receives a monetary transfer payment from the government. This payment could be thought of either as the direct income of the central banker or as the budget of the central bank. Or the transfer payment can be viewed more broadly as reflecting legislated performance objectives for the central bank. Let t represent the transfer to the central bank, and assume that the central bank's utility is given by

$$\mathbf{U} = t - V$$

31. Walsh (1994, 1995c) demonstrates that a dismissal rule can, in some circumstances, substitute for a state-contingent wage contract in affecting the central bank's incentives.

That is, the central bank cares about both the transfer it receives and the social loss generated by inflation and output fluctuations. The central bank sets Δm to maximize the expected value of $\mathbf{U}$, conditional on the realization of e. The problem faced by the government (the principal) is to design a transfer function t that induces the central bank to choose $\Delta m = \Delta m^c(e)$, where Δm^c is the socially optimal commitment policy. As we have already seen, the optimal commitment policy in this framework is

$\Delta m^c(e) = -\dfrac{a\lambda}{1+a^2\lambda}e$ (see equation 8.11).

If the government can verify e ex post, there are clearly many contracts that would achieve the desired result. For example, any contract that imposes a large penalty on the central bank if Δm deviates from Δm^c will ensure that Δm^c is chosen. However, the difficulty of determining both the possible states of nature ex ante and the actual realization of shocks ex post makes such contracts infeasible. This task is particularly difficult if the central bank must respond to a forecast of e, since its internal forecast might be difficult to verify ex post, leading to the problems of private information highlighted by Canzoneri's analysis (Canzoneri 1985). Therefore, consider a transfer function $t(\pi)$ that makes the government's payment to the central bank contingent only on the observed rate of inflation. The transfer function implements the optimal policy $\pi^c(e) = \Delta m^c(e) + v$ if π^c maximizes $\mathrm{E}^{cb}[t(\pi) - V]$ for all e where $\mathrm{E}^{cb}[\ ]$ denotes the central bank's expectation conditional on e.

The first-order condition for the central banker's problem can be solved for $\Delta m^{cb}(e)$, the optimal discretionary policy:

$$\Delta m^{cb}(e) = \frac{a\lambda k}{1+a^2\lambda} + \frac{a^2\lambda}{1+a^2\lambda}\pi^e + \frac{\mathrm{E}^{cb}(t')}{1+a^2\lambda} - \frac{a\lambda}{1+a^2\lambda}e \qquad (8.20)$$

where $t' = \partial t(\pi)/\partial \pi$. The last term in (8.20) shows that the optimal discretionary policy response to the supply shock is equal to the response under the optimal commitment policy Δm^c. This is important because it implies that the government's objective will be to design a contract that eliminates the inflationary bias while leaving the central bank free to respond with discretion to e. Taking expectations of (8.20) and letting $\mathrm{E}[\ ]$ denote the public's expectation, we obtain

$$\mathrm{E}[\Delta m^{cb}(e)] = \pi^e = a\lambda k + \mathrm{E}[t'(\pi)]$$

When this is substituted back into (8.20), we obtain

$$\Delta m^{cb}(e) = a\lambda k + \mathrm{E}[t'(\pi)] - \frac{\mathrm{E}[t'] - \mathrm{E}^{cb}[t']}{1+a^2\lambda} - \frac{a\lambda}{1+a^2\lambda}e$$

Setting $\Delta m^{cb}(e)$ equal to the optimal commitment policy $\Delta m^c(e)$ for all e requires that the first three terms vanish. They do vanish if $t(\pi)$ satisfies

$$t' = \frac{\partial t}{\partial \pi} = -a\lambda k$$

The optimal commitment policy can be implemented, therefore, by the linear transfer function

$$t(\pi) = t_0 - a\lambda k\pi$$

The constant t_0 is set to ensure that the expected return to the central banker is sufficient to ensure her participation.[32] Presenting the central banker with this incentive contract achieves the dual objectives of eliminating the inflationary bias while still ensuring optimal stabilization policy in response to the central bank's information about the aggregate-supply shock.

Why does the transfer function take such a simple linear form? Recall that the time-consistent policy under discretion resulted in an inflationary bias of $a\lambda k$. The key insight is that this is constant; it does not vary with the realization of the aggregate-supply shock. Therefore, the incentive structure for the central bank just needs to raise the marginal cost of inflation (from the perspective of the central banker) by a constant amount; that is what the linear transfer function does. Because the bias is independent of the realization of the underlying state of nature, it is not necessary for the government to actually verify the state, and so the presence of private information about the state of the economy on the part of the central bank does not affect the ability of the linear contract to support the optimal policy. This case contrasts sharply with the one in which reputation is relied upon to achieve low average inflation (Canzoneri 1985).

One interpretation of the linear-inflation-contract result is that it simply points out that the Barro-Gordon framework is too simple to adequately capture important aspects of monetary-policy design. In this view, there really is a trade-off between credibility and flexibility, and the fact that this trade-off can be made to disappear so easily represents a methodological criticism of the Barro-Gordon model.[33] Several authors have explored modifications to the Barro-Gordon model that allow this trade-off to be reintroduced. They do so by making the inflation bias state depen-

---

32. This is known as the individual rationality constraint. Since $\frac{\partial \pi}{\partial m} = 1$, a contract of the form $t_0 - akm$ based on the observed rate of money growth would also work.

33. This argument is made by Canzoneri, Nolan, and Yates (1997).

dent. In this way, the linear contract, which raises the marginal cost of inflation by a constant amount for all state realizations, cannot achieve the socially optimal commitment policy. If the penalty cannot be made state contingent, then average inflation can be eliminated, but inflation will remain too volatile. For example, Walsh (1995c), Canzoneri, Nolan, and Yates (1997), and Herrendorf and Lockwood (1996) introduce a state-contingent bias by modifying the basic model structure. Walsh assumes there exists a flexible wage sector in addition to a nominal-wage-contract sector. Herrendorf and Lockwood assume labor-market participants can observe a signal that reveals information about aggregate-supply shocks prior to forming nominal wage contracts. Canzoneri, Nolan, and Yates assume the central bank has an interest-rate-smoothing objective. As Herrendorf and Lockwood show, once a linear inflation contract has eliminated the average inflation bias, a role for a conservative central bank reemerges in order to reduce excessive inflation volatility.

The contracting approach has been developed further in Persson and Tabellini (1993). Walsh (1994) shows how the properties of a linear inflation contract can be mimicked by a dismissal rule under which the central banker is fired if inflation ever rises above a critical level. Lockwood (1997), Jonsson (1995), and Svensson (1997b) have shown how linear inflation contracts are affected when the inflation bias is time dependent because of persistence in the unemployment process. Persistence means that a surprise expansion in period t reduces unemployment (increases output) in period t, but it also leads to lower expected unemployment in periods $t + 1$, $t + 2$, and so on. Thus, the benefits of a surprise inflation are larger, leading to a higher average inflation rate under discretionary policy. The bias at time t, though, will depend on the unemployment rate at $t - 1$, since, with persistence, unemployment at $t - 1$ affects the average unemployment rate expected for period t. Therefore, the inflation bias will be time varying. The simple linear contract with a fixed weight on inflation will no longer be optimal if the inflation bias is state dependent. However, a state-contingent contract can support the optimal commitment policy.

Like the Rogoff conservative-central-banker solution, the contracting solution *relocates* the commitment problem that gives rise to the inflation bias in the first place.[34] In the case of the conservative central banker, the proposed solution assumes that the government cannot commit to a specific inflation policy but can commit to the appointment of an agent with specific preferences. In the contracting case, the government is assumed to be able to commit to a specific contract. Both of these assumptions are plausible; relocating the commitment problem is often a

---

34. McCallum (1995, 1997a) has emphasized the relocation issue with respect to the contracting approach. A similar criticism applies to the conservative-central-banker solution as well.

means of solving commitment problems. Confirmation processes, together with long terms of office, can reveal the appointee's preferences and ensure that policy is actually conducted by the appointed agent. Incentives called for in the contracting approach can similarly be thought of as aspects of the institutional structure and may therefore be more difficult to change than are actual policy instrument settings.

As al-Nowaihi and Levine (1996) argue, relocation can allow the government to commit credibly to a contract or to a particular appointee if the process is public. If contract renegotiations or the firing of the central banker are publicly observable, then it may be in the interest of the government to forgo any short-term incentive to renegotiate in order to develop a reputation as a government that can commit. Thus, the transparency of any renegotiation serves to support a low-inflation equilibrium; relocating the time-inconsistency problem can solve it.[35]

The type of policy transparency emphasized by al-Nowaihi and Levine characterizes the policy process established under the 1989 central banking reform in New Zealand. There, the government and the Reserve Bank establish short-run inflation targets under a Policy Targets Agreement (PTA). The PTA can be renegotiated, and once current economic disturbances have been observed, both the government and the Reserve Bank have incentives to renegotiate the target (Walsh 1995c). Because this renegotiation must be public, however, reputational considerations may sustain an equilibrium in which the targets are not renegotiated. When we turn to an analysis of inflation-targeting rules, we will see that inflation targeting may also replicate the optimal incentives called for under the linear-inflation contract (Svensson 1997b).

8.3.4 Institutions

One interpretation of the contracting approach is that the incentive structures might be embedded in the institutional structure of the central bank. If institutions are costly to change, then institutional reforms designed to raise the costs of inflation can serve as commitment devices. Incorporating a price-stability objective directly in the central bank's charter legislation, for example, might raise the implicit penalty (in terms of institutional embarrassment) that the central bank would suffer if it failed to control inflation. Most discussions of the role of institutional structure and inflation have, however, focused on the effects alternative structures have on the extent to which political pressures affect the conduct of monetary policy.

A starting point for such a focus is Alesina's model of policy in a two-party system (Alesina 1987; Alesina and Sachs 1988; Alesina and Roubini 1992). Suppose there is

---

35. See also Herrendorf (1995a), who develops a similar point using inflation targeting.

uncertainty about the outcome of an approaching election, and suppose that the parties differ in their economic policies so that inflation in the postelection period will depend on which party wins the election. Let the parties be denoted A and B. The inflation rate expected if party A is elected is π^A; inflation under party B will be π^B. Assume $\pi^A > \pi^B$. If the probability party A wins the election is q, then expected inflation prior to the election will be $\pi^e = q\pi^A + (1-q)\pi^B$. Since q is between 0 and 1, expected inflation falls in the interval $[\pi^B, \pi^A]$. If postelection output is equal to $y = a[\pi - \pi^e]$, where π is actual inflation, then the election of party A will generate an economic expansion [since $\pi^A - \pi^e = (1-q)(\pi^A - \pi^B) > 0$], while the election of party B will lead to an output contraction [$\pi^B - \pi^e = q(\pi^B - \pi^A) < 0$].

This very simple framework provides an explanation for a political business cycle that arises because of policy differences between parties and electoral uncertainty. Because parties are assumed to exploit monetary policy to get their desired inflation rate, and because election outcomes cannot be predicted with certainty, inflation surprises will occur after an election. Alesina and Sachs (1988) provide evidence for this theory based on U.S. data, while Alesina and Roubini (1992) examine OECD countries. Faust and Irons (1996), however, conclude that there is little evidence from the United States to support the hypothesis that political effects generate monetary policy surprises.

Waller (1989, 1992) shows how the process used to appoint members of the central bank policy board can influence the degree to which partisan political factors are translated into monetary-policy outcomes. If policy is set by a board whose members serve overlapping but noncoincident terms, the effect of policy shifts resulting from changes in governments is reduced. In a two-party system in which nominees forwarded by the party in power are subject to confirmation by the out-of-power party, the party in power will nominate increasingly moderate candidates as elections near. Increasing the length of terms of office for central bank board members also reduces the role of partisanship in monetary policy making.[36] Waller and Walsh (1996) consider a partisan model of monetary policy. They focus on the implications for output of the degree of partisanship in the appointment process and the term length of the central banker. Similarly, Alesina and Gatti (1995) show that electorally induced business cycles can be reduced if political parties jointly appoint the central banker.

While most work has focused on the appointment of political nominees to the policy board, the Federal Reserve's policy board (the FOMC) includes both political appointees (the governors) and nonappointed members (the regional bank

36. See also García de Paso (1994).

presidents).[37] Faust (1996) provides an explanation for this structure by developing an overlapping-generations model in which inflation has distributional effects. If monetary policy is set by majority vote, excessive inflation results as the (larger) young generation attempts to transfer wealth from the old generation. If policy is delegated to a board consisting of one representative from the young generation and one from the old, the inflationary bias is eliminated. Faust argues that the structure of the FOMC takes the shape it does because of the advantages of delegating to a board in which the relative balance of different political constituencies differs from that of the voting public as a whole.

Who makes policy and who appoints the policy makers can affect policy outcomes, but institutional design also includes mechanisms for accountability, and these can affect policy as well. Minford (1995), in fact, argues that democratic elections can enforce low-inflation outcomes if voters punish governments that succumb to the temptation to inflate, while Lippi (1996) develops a model in which rational voters choose a weight-conservative central banker. O'Flaherty (1990) shows how finite term lengths can ensure accountability, while Walsh (1995c) shows that the type of dismissal rule incorporated into New Zealand's Reserve Bank Act of 1989 can partially mimic an optimal contract.

8.3.5   Targeting Rules

The contracting approach focuses on the incentive structure faced by the central bank; once the incentives are correct, complete flexibility in the actual conduct of policy is allowed. This allows the central bank to respond to new and possibly unverifiable information. An alternative approach acts to reduce the problems arising from discretion by *restricting* policy flexibility. The gold standard or a fixed-exchange-rate regime provide examples of situations in which policy flexibility is deliberately limited; Milton Friedman's proposal that the Fed be required to maintain a constant growth rate of the money supply is another famous example. A wide variety of rules designed to restrict the flexibility of the central bank have been proposed and analyzed. The cost of reduced flexibility will depend on the nature of the economic disturbances affecting the economy and the original scope for stabilization policies in the first place, while the gain from reducing flexibility takes the form of a lower average inflation rate.

In this section, we examine targeting rules, that is, rules under which the central bank is judged in part on its ability to achieve a prespecified value for some macro

---

37. Havrilesky and Gildea (1991, 1995) argue that the voting behavior of regional bank presidents and board governors differs, with regional bank presidents tending to be tougher on inflation; this conclusion is disputed by Tootell (1991), however.

variable. Inflation targeting is currently the most commonly discussed form of targeting, and some form of inflation targeting has been adopted in Canada, Sweden, Finland, the United Kingdom, and New Zealand. The mandate of the European Central Bank to pursue price stability as its sole objective can also be viewed as representing a form of inflation targeting.[38] Fixed or target-zone exchange-rate systems also can be interpreted as targeting regimes. The central bank's ability to respond to economic disturbances, or to succumb to the temptation to inflate, is limited by the need to maintain an exchange-rate target. When the lack of credibility is a problem for the central bank, commiting to maintaining a fixed nominal exchange rate against a low-inflation country can serve to import credibility. Giavazzi and Pagano (1988) provide an analysis of the advantages of "tying one's hands" by committing to a fixed exchange rate.

8.3.5.1 Flexible Targeting Rules

Suppose the central bank cares about output and inflation stabilization but is, in addition, penalized for deviations of actual inflation from a target level.[39] In other word, the central bank's objective is to minimize

$$V^{cb} = \tfrac{1}{2}\lambda E_t(y_t - y_n - k)^2 + \tfrac{1}{2}E_t(\pi_t - \pi^*)^2 + \tfrac{1}{2}hE_t(\pi_t - \pi^T)^2 \qquad (8.21)$$

where this differs from (8.2) in that π^* now denotes the socially optimal inflation rate (which may differ from zero), and the last term represents the penalty related to deviations from the target inflation rate π^T. The parameter h measures the weight placed on deviations from the target inflation rate. We will refer to targeting rules of this form as "flexible targeting rules." They do not require that the central bank hit its target exactly; instead, one can view the last term as representing a penalty suffered by the central bank based on how large the deviation from target turns out to be. This type of targeting rule allows the central bank to trade off achieving its target for achieving more desired values of its other goals.

The rest of the model consists of an aggregate-supply function and a link between the policy instrument, the growth rate of money, and inflation:

$$y_t = y_n + a(\pi_t - \pi^e) + e_t$$

---

38. For recent discussions of inflation-targeting experiences, see Ammer and Freeman (1995), Fischer (1995), McCallum (1996), Mishkin and Posen (1997), and the papers in Leiderman and Svensson (1995), Haldane (1995) and Lowe (1997).

39. The central bank might be required to report on its success or failure in achieving the target, with target misses punished by public censure and embarrassment or by some more formal dismissal procedure.

and

$$\pi_t = \Delta m_t + v_t$$

where v is a velocity disturbance. It will be assumed the public's expectations are formed prior to observing either e or v, but the central bank can observe e (but not v) before setting Δm.

Before deriving the policy followed by the central banker, note that the socially optimal commitment policy is given by[40]

$$\Delta m_t^S = \pi^* - \frac{a\lambda}{1 + a^2\lambda} e_t \tag{8.22}$$

Now consider policy under discretion. Using the aggregate-supply curve and the link between inflation and money growth, the loss function (8.21) can be written as

$$V^{cb} = \tfrac{1}{2}\lambda E[a(\Delta m + v - \pi^e) + e - k]^2 + \tfrac{1}{2}E(\Delta m + v - \pi^*)^2 + \tfrac{1}{2}hE(\Delta m + v - \pi^T)^2$$

The first-order condition for the optimal choice of Δm, taking expectations as given, is

$$a^2\lambda(\Delta m - \pi^e) + a\lambda(e - k) + (\Delta m - \pi^*) + h(\Delta m - \pi^T) = 0$$

Solving yields

$$\Delta m = \frac{1}{1 + h + a^2\lambda}(a^2\lambda\pi^e - a\lambda e + a\lambda k + \pi^* + h\pi^T) \tag{8.23}$$

Assuming rational expectations, $\pi^e = \Delta m^e = \dfrac{1}{1 + h}(a\lambda k + \pi^* + h\pi^T)$, since the public forms expectations prior to knowing e. Substituting this result into (8.23) yields the time-consistent money-growth rate:

$$\begin{aligned}
\Delta m^T &= \frac{a\lambda k + \pi^* + h\pi^T}{1 + h} - \frac{a\lambda}{1 + h + a^2\lambda} e \\
&= \pi^* + \frac{a\lambda k}{1 + h} + \frac{h(\pi^T - \pi^*)}{1 + h} - \frac{a\lambda}{1 + h + a^2\lambda} e \tag{8.24}
\end{aligned}$$

---

40. This is obtained by substituting the commitment policy $\Delta m = a + be$ into the social objective function $0.5E(y - y_n - k)^2 + 0.5\beta E(\pi - \pi^*)^2$ and minimizing the unconditional expectation with respect to a and b.

If the target inflation rate is equal to the socially optimal inflation rate ($\pi^T = \pi^*$), (8.24) reduces to

$$\Delta m^T = \pi^* + \frac{a\lambda k}{1+h} - \frac{a\lambda}{1+h+a^2\lambda}e \qquad (8.25)$$

Setting $h = 0$ yields the time-consistent discretionary solution *without* targeting:

$$\Delta m^{NT} = \pi^* + a\lambda k - \frac{a\lambda}{1+a^2\lambda}e \qquad (8.26)$$

with the inflation bias equal to $a\lambda k$.

Comparing (8.22), (8.25), and (8.26) reveals that the targeting penalty reduces the inflation bias from $a\lambda k$ to $a\lambda k/(1+h)$. The targeting requirement imposes an additional cost on the central bank if it allows inflation to deviate too much from π^T; this raises the marginal cost of inflation and reduces the time-consistent inflation rate. The cost of this reduction in the average inflation bias is the distortion that targeting introduces into the central bank's response to the aggregate-supply shock e. Under pure discretion, the central bank responds optimally to e (note the coefficient on the supply shock is the same in [8.26] as in [8.22]), but the presence of a targeting rule distorts the response to e. Comparing (8.25) with (8.22) shows that the central bank will respond too little to the supply shock [the coefficient on e falls from $a\lambda/(1+a^2\lambda)$ to $a\lambda/(1+h+a^2\lambda)$].

This trade-off between bias reduction and stabilization response is one we have seen earlier in discussing Rogoff's model.[41] Note that if $\pi^T = \pi^*$, the central bank's objective function can be written as

$$V^{cb} = \tfrac{1}{2}\lambda E(y_t - y_n - k)^2 + \tfrac{1}{2}(1+h)E(\pi - \pi^*)^2 \qquad (8.27)$$

So the parameter h plays exactly the same role as Rogoff's degree of conservatism played. From the analysis of Rogoff's model, we know that the optimal value of h will be positive, so that the total weight placed on the inflation objective exceeds society's weight which is equal to 1. A flexible inflation target, interpreted here as a value for h that is positive, leads to an outcome that dominates pure discretion.[42]

While we have just highlighted the connection between an inflation-targeting rule and Rogoff's conservative-central-banker approach, Svensson (1997b) has recently

---

41. Canzoneri (1985), Garfinkel and Oh (1993), and García de Paso (1993, 1994) consider multiperiod targeting rules as solutions to this trade-off between stabilization and inflation bias. Defining money growth or inflation targets as averages over several periods restricts average inflation while allowing the central bank more flexibility in each period to respond to shocks.

42. That is, of course, unless h is too large.

shown that a similar connection exists between inflation targeting and the linear inflation contract. Svensson demonstrates that the optimal linear inflation contract can be implemented if the central bank is required to target an inflation rate π^T that is actually less than the socially optimal rate of inflation. To see how this result is obtained, let $H = 1 + h$, replace π^* with π^T in (8.27) and expand the resulting second term so that the expression becomes

$$V^{cb} = \tfrac{1}{2}\lambda \mathrm{E}(y_t - y_n - k)^2 + \tfrac{1}{2}H\mathrm{E}(\pi - \pi^* + \pi^* - \pi^T)^2$$
$$= \tfrac{1}{2}\lambda \mathrm{E}(y_t - y_n - k)^2 + \tfrac{1}{2}H\mathrm{E}(\pi - \pi^*)^2 + D\mathrm{E}(\pi - \pi^*) + C$$

where $D = H(\pi^* - \pi^T)$ and $C = \tfrac{1}{2}H(\pi^* - \pi^T)^2$. Since C is a constant, it does not affect the central bank's behavior. Notice that V^{cb} is equal to $V + \tfrac{1}{2}h\mathrm{E}(\pi - \pi^*)^2 + D\mathrm{E}(\pi - \pi^*) + C$. This is exactly equivalent to the incentive structure established under the optimal linear inflation contract if and only if $h = 0$ and $D = -a\lambda k$. The condition $h = 0$ is achieved if the central banker is not a weight conservative but instead shares society's preferences (so $H = 1$); the condition $D = -a\lambda k$ is then achieved if

$$\pi^T = \pi^* - a\lambda k < \pi^*$$

Thus, the optimal linear contract can be implemented by assigning to the central bank an inflation target that is actually below the rate that is socially preferred. But at the same time, policy should be assigned to an agent who shares the same preferences between inflation and output stabilization as society more generally does.

Muscatelli (1998), Schaling, Hoebrichts, and Eijffinger (1998), and Beetsma and Jensen (In press) examine the role of inflation contracts and inflation targets in the presence of uncertainty about the central bank's preferences between output stabilization and stabilizing inflation around a target rate. In general, preference uncertainty introduces stochastic fluctuations in the inflation bias and distorts the stabilization policy that arises under pure discretion. Assigning the central bank a linear inflation contract, as in Walsh (1995a), leads to a better policy outcome than is obtained by assigning the central bank an inflation target. However, an even better outcome results when both an inflation target and a linear contract are used. Interestingly, since Svensson's result indicates the inflation target can be set to eliminate the average inflation bias, the role of the inflation contract is to improve stabilization policy; this contrasts with the role of the contract in Walsh (1995a) where it was designed solely to eliminate the average inflation bias and leave stabilization unaffected. Beetsma and Jensen (1998) and Schaling, Hoebrichts, and Eijffinger (1998) show that uncertainty about the central bank's preferences implies an optimal incentive contract that includes both linear and quadratic terms. Because a quadratic penalty for inflation target misses was shown to be equivalent to appointing a Rogoff weight-conservative central banker, this result is similar to that of Herrendorf and Lockwood (1997), who found that a linear inflation contract and a conservative central banker were needed in the presence of a stochastic inflation bias.

8.3.5.2 Strict Targeting Rules The preceding analysis considered a flexible targeting rule. The central bank was penalized for deviations of π around a targeted level but was not required to achieve the target precisely. This rule allowed the central bank to trade off the objective of meeting the target against achieving its other objectives. Often, however, targeting is analyzed in terms of strict targets; the central bank is required to achieve a specific target outcome, regardless of the implications for its other objectives.

As an example, consider a strict money-growth-rate target under which the central bank is required to set the growth rate of the money supply equal to some constant:[43]

$$\Delta m = \Delta m^T$$

Since the desired rate of inflation is π^*, it makes sense to set $\Delta m^T = \pi^*$, and the public will set $\pi^e = \pi^*$. With this rule in place, we can now evaluate the social loss function. If social loss is given by

$$V = \tfrac{1}{2}\lambda E_t(y_t - y_n - k)^2 + \tfrac{1}{2}E_t(\pi_t - \pi^*)^2$$

then under a strict money-growth-rate target it takes the value

$$V(\Delta m^T) = \tfrac{1}{2}[\lambda k^2 + \lambda \sigma_e^2 + (1 + a^2\lambda)\sigma_v^2]$$

Recall that under pure discretion, the expected value of the loss function was, from (8.9),

$$V^d = \tfrac{1}{2}\lambda(1 + a^2\lambda)k^2 + \tfrac{1}{2}\left[\left(\frac{\lambda}{1 + a^2\lambda}\right)\sigma_e^2 + (1 + a^2\lambda)\sigma_v^2\right]$$

Comparing these two, we have

$$V(\Delta m^T) - V^d = -\tfrac{1}{2}(a\lambda k)^2 + \tfrac{1}{2}\frac{a^2\lambda^2}{(1 + a^2\lambda)}\sigma_e^2$$

---

43. Alternatively, the targeting rule could require the central bank to minimize $E(m - m^T)^2$. However, this expression is minimized if the central bank sets policy such that $E(m) = m^T$. If m is controlled exactly, this expression is equivalent to $m = m^T$.

Notice that this expression can be either positive or negative. It is more likely to be negative (implying that the strict money growth rate target is superior to discretion) if the underlying inflationary bias of discretion, $a\lambda k$, is large. Since the strict targeting rule ensures that average inflation is π^*, it eliminates any inflationary bias, so the gain is larger, the larger is the bias that arises under discretion. However, discretion is more likely to be preferred to the strict rule when σ_e^2 is large. The strict targeting rule eliminates any stabilization role for monetary policy. The cost of doing so will depend on the variance of supply shocks. Eliminating the central bank's flexibility to respond to economic disturbances increases welfare if

$$ k > \sigma_e \sqrt{\frac{1}{1 + a^2 \lambda}} $$

If σ_e^2 is large, pure discretion, even with its inflationary bias, may still be the preferred policy (Flood and Isard 1988).

Another alternative targeting rule that has often been proposed focuses on nominal income (see, for example, Hall and Mankiw 1994). If we interpret $y - y_n$ as the percentage output deviation from trend, we can approximate a nominal income rule as requiring that

$$ (y - y_n) + \pi = g^* $$

where g^* is the target growth rate for nominal income. Since the equilibrium growth rate of $y - y_n$ is zero (because it is a deviation from trend), and the desired rate of inflation is π^*, we should set $g^* = 0 + \pi^* = \pi^*$. Under this rule, expected inflation is $\pi^e = g^* - \mathrm{E}(y - y_n) = g^* - 0 = g^* = \pi^*$. Aggregate output is given by

$$ y = y_n + a(\pi - \pi^e) + e = y_n + a(y_n - y) + e \Rightarrow y - y_n = \frac{1}{1 + a} e $$

since $\pi = g^* - (y - y_n) = \pi^e - (y - y_n)$ under the proposed rule. A positive supply shock that causes output to rise will induce a contraction designed to reduce the inflation rate to maintain a constant rate of nominal income growth. The decline in inflation (which is unanticipated because it was induced by the shock e), acts to reduce output and partially offset the initial rise. With the specification used here, exactly $a/(1 + a)$ of the effect of e is offset. Substituting this result back into the policy rule implies that $\pi = \pi^* - \frac{1}{1 + a} e$.

Using these results, the expected value of the social loss function is

$$ V(g^*) = \tfrac{1}{2} \lambda k^2 + \tfrac{1}{2} \frac{(1 + \lambda)}{(1 + a)^2} \sigma_e^2 $$

In the present model, nominal income targeting stabilizes real output more than pure discretion (and the optimal commitment policy) if $a\lambda < 1$.[44]

Nominal income targeting imposes a particular trade-off between real income growth and inflation in response to aggregate-supply disturbances. The social loss function does not weigh output fluctuations and inflation fluctuations equally (unless $\lambda = 1$), but nominal income targeting does. Nevertheless, nominal income targeting is often proposed as a "reasonably good rule for the conduct of monetary policy" (Hall and Mankiw 1994). For analyzes of nominal income targeting, see Bean (1983), West (1984), Taylor (1985), McCallum (1988), and Frankel and Chinn (1995).

The analysis of targeting rules has much in common with the analysis of monetary-policy operating procedures, the topic of Chapter 9. Targeting rules limit the flexibility of the central bank to respond as economic conditions change. Thus, the manner in which disturbances will affect real output and inflation will be affected by the choice of targeting rule. For example, a strict inflation or price-level rule forces real output to absorb all the effects of an aggregate-productivity disturbance. Under a nominal income rule, such disturbances are allowed to affect both real output and the price level. As with operating procedures, the relative desirability of alternative rules will depend both on the objective function and on the relative variances of different types of disturbances.

8.4   Is the Inflation Bias Important?

During the past dozen years, a large literature has focused on issues related to the inflationary bias that might arise when monetary policy is conducted with discretion. Despite this academic interest, some have questioned whether this whole approach has anything to do with explaining actual episodes of inflation. Do these models provide useful frameworks for positive theories of inflation?

Surprisingly, there has been little attempt to test directly for the inflation bias. Since monetary models imply that the behavior of real output should be the same whether average inflation is 0% or 10%, the very fact that most economies have consistently experienced average inflation rates well above zero for extended periods of time might be taken as evidence for the existence of an inflation bias. However, in earlier chapters we examined theories of inflation based on optimal tax considerations that might imply nonzero average rates of inflation, although few argue that

---

44. Note that σ_v^2 does not appear, since the central bank was assumed able to control nominal income growth exactly. If, as is more realistic, this is not the case, a term like σ_v^2 due to control errors will also appear in the expected value of the loss function.

tax considerations alone could account for the level of inflation observed during the 1970s in most industrialized economies (or for the observed variations in inflation).

One relevant piece of evidence is provided by Romer (1993). He argues that the average inflation bias should depend on the degree to which an economy is open. If a large fraction of goods is imported, then an economic expansion at home tends to reduce the price of domestic goods relative to foreign goods. This real depreciation reduces the benefits from an expansion. In terms of our basic model, this could be interpreted as lowering the benefits of expansion relative to the costs of inflation. Consequently, the weight λ on output should be smaller (or the weight on inflation larger) in more open economies. Since the inflation bias is increasing in λ (see, for example, equation 8.7), the average inflation rate should be lower in more open economies.

A second relationship between openness and the inflation bias arises because the relevant price index for the aggregate-supply relationship is based on the prices of domestic output while the relevant price index for the inflation rate in the social loss function is more likely to be a consumer price index that incorporates the prices of both domestic and foreign goods. Thus, the real depreciation associated with a monetary expansion raises CPI inflation more than it does inflation measured by domestic output prices.[45] As a result, a given output expansion caused by an un-anticipated rise in the domestic price level brings with it a larger inflation cost in terms of the increase in CPI inflation. This should act to reduce the average inflation bias under discretion.

Romer tests these implications using data on 114 countries for the post-1973 period. Using the import share as a measure of openness, he finds the predicted negative association between openness and average inflation. The empirical results, however, do not hold for the OECD economies. For the highly industrialized, high-income countries, openness is unrelated to average inflation.

Romer's test focuses on one of the factors (openness) that might affect the in-centive to inflate. If central banks respond systematically to the costs and benefits of inflation, variations in the incentive to inflate across countries should be reflected,

---

45. That is, output depends on domestic price inflation π_d and is given by

$$y = y_n + a(\pi_d - \pi_d^e)$$

while CPI inflation is equal to

$$\pi_{cpi} = \theta \pi_d + (1 - \theta)s$$

where s is the rate of change of the nominal exchange rate and θ is the share of domestic output in the CPI.

ceteris paribus, in variations in actual inflation rates. In the next section, we will examine some empirical evidence that focuses more directly on the role of institutional structure and policy outcomes. In testing for the role of the biases arising under time inconsistency on actual inflation, however, it is important to keep in mind that observed inflation is an equilibrium outcome, and a low observed inflation rate need not imply the absence of time-inconsistency problems. As we saw in our examination of reputational models, for example, equilibrium may involve pooling in which even an opportunistic central bank delivers low inflation, at least for a while.

There are, in fact, several reasons for questioning the empirical relevance of time inconsistency as a factor in monetary policy. Some economists have argued that time inconsistency just isn't a problem. For example, Taylor (1983) points out that society finds solutions to these sorts of problems in many other areas (patent law, for example), and there is no reason to suppose that the problem is particularly severe in the monetary-policy arena.[46] Institutional solutions, such as separating responsibility for monetary policy from the direct control of elected political officials, may reduce or even eliminate the underlying bias toward expansions that leads to excessively high average inflation under discretion.[47]

One of the hallmarks of the time-inconsistency literature is its attempt to think seriously about the incentives facing policy makers. As such, it contrasts sharply with the older tradition in monetary policy in which the policy maker was simply assumed to follow an arbitrary (or perhaps optimal) rule. The newer view stresses that policy makers may face incentives to deviate from such rules. McCallum (1995, 1997a), however, has argued that central banks can be trusted not to succumb to the incentive to inflate, since they know that succumbing leads to a bad equilibrium. But such a view ignores the basic problem; even central banks who want to do the right thing may face the choice of either inflating or causing a recession. In such circumstances, the best policy may not be to cause a recession. For example, consider Cukierman and Liviatan's type D policy maker. Such a policy maker is capable of committing to and delivering on a zero-inflation policy, but if the public assigns some probability to the possibility that a type W might be in office, even the type D ends up inflating. If central banks were to define their objectives in terms of stabilizing output around

46. As Taylor puts it, "In the Barro-Gordon inflation-unemployment model, the superiority of the zero inflation policy is just as obvious to people as the well-recognized patent problem is in the real world. It is therefore difficult to see why the zero inflation policy would not be adopted in such a world" (1983, p. 125).

47. In the following section, some empirical evidence on the role of central bank independence that supports this hypothesis is reviewed.

the economy's natural rate (i.e., $k \equiv 0$), then there would be no inflationary bias; central banks would deliver the socially optimal policy. However, this corresponds to a situation in which there is no bias, not to one in which an incentive to inflate exists but the central bank resists it.

An alternative criticism of the time-inconsistency literature questions the underlying assumption that the central bank cannot commit. Blinder (1995), for example, argues that the inherent lags between a policy action and its effect on inflation and output serve as a commitment technology. Inflation in period t is determined by policy actions taken in earlier periods, so if the public knows past policy actions, the central bank can never produce a surprise inflation. More formally, assume a one-period lag between money growth Δm and inflation:

$$\pi_t = \Delta m_{t-1} \tag{8.28}$$

Now consider the discretionary outcome of the one-shot repeated game considered earlier. The central bank's choice of Δm_t only affects its loss function in period $t+1$. Since (8.28) implies that $\pi_{t+1}^e = \Delta m_t$, the loss function (8.2) becomes

$$\begin{aligned} V_{t+1} &= \tfrac{1}{2}\lambda[a(\pi_{t+1} - \pi_{t+1}^e) + e_{t+1} - k]^2 + \tfrac{1}{2}\pi_{t+1}^2 \\ &= \tfrac{1}{2}\lambda[a(\Delta m_t - \Delta m_t) + e_{t+1} - k]^2 + \tfrac{1}{2}\Delta m_t^2 \\ &= \tfrac{1}{2}\lambda(e_{t+1} - k)^2 + \tfrac{1}{2}\Delta m_t^2 \end{aligned}$$

Expected loss is minimized when $\Delta m_t = 0$. No inflationary bias arises.

The presence of lags does serve as a commitment device. If outcomes today are entirely determined by actions taken earlier, the central banker is clearly committed; nothing she can do will affect today's outcome. And few would disagree that monetary policy acts with a (long) lag. But appealing to lags solves the time-inconsistency problem by eliminating *any* real effects of monetary policy. That is, there is no incentive to inflate because expansionary monetary policy does not affect real output or unemployment. If this were the case, central banks could costlessly disinflate; seeing a shift in policy, private agents could all revise nominal wages and prices before any real effects occurred. If monetary policy does have real effects, even if these occur with a lag, the inflationary bias under discretion will reappear.

To see this, suppose we follow S. Fischer (1977) in assuming two-period overlapping nominal-wage contracts, giving rise to an aggregate-supply curve of the form

$$y_t = y_n + \tfrac{1}{2}a(\pi_t - E_{t-1}\pi_t) + \tfrac{1}{2}a(\pi_t - E_{t-2}\pi_t)$$

where $E_s\pi_t$, $s < t$, denotes the expectation of inflation during period t formed at the end of period s. If $\pi_t = \Delta m_{t-1}$, this becomes

$$y_t = y_n + \tfrac{1}{2}a(\Delta m_{t-1} - \Delta m_{t-1}) + \tfrac{1}{2}a(\Delta m_{t-1} - E_{t-2}\Delta m_{t-1})$$

$$= y_n + \tfrac{1}{2}a(\Delta m_{t-1} - E_{t-2}\Delta m_{t-1})$$

where $E_{t-2}\Delta m_{t-1}$ is the public's expectation of money growth for period $t-1$ formed at the end of $t-2$. Monetary policy actions taken in period $t-1$ affect real output in period t because wage contracts negotiated at the start of period $t-1$ (i.e., at the end of period $t-2$) are still in effect. In setting Δm_t, the central bank's objective is to minimize the expected value of the loss function for period $t+1$, taking $E_{t-1}\Delta m_t$ as given. The loss function becomes

$$V_{t+1} = \tfrac{1}{2}[\lambda(y_{t+1} - y_n - k)^2 + \pi_{t+1}^2]$$

$$= \tfrac{1}{2}\{\lambda[\tfrac{1}{2}a(\Delta m_t - E_{t-1}\Delta m_t) - k]^2 + \Delta m_t^2\}$$

The first order condition implies $\Delta m_t = (1 + \tfrac{1}{4}a^2\lambda)^{-1}(\tfrac{1}{4}a^2\lambda E_{t-1}\Delta m_t + \tfrac{1}{2}a\lambda k)$. Expected money growth is then equal to $\tfrac{1}{2}a\lambda k$, and the time-consistent equilibrium under discretion leads to an inflation rate of $\tfrac{1}{2}a\lambda k > 0$. The presence of a lag between money growth and inflation reduces the inflation bias from $a\lambda k$ to $\tfrac{1}{2}a\lambda k$, but the bias is still positive. Thus, if monetary policy has real effects, lags between the setting of policy instruments and the effects on real output and inflation do not serve to eliminate the inflation bias completely.

   In the models that have been used in the time-inconsistency literature, monetary policy affects real output through its effect on inflation—more specifically, by creating inflation surprises. The empirical evidence from most countries, however, indicates that policy actions affect output before inflation is affected.[48] Policy actions can be observed long before the effects on inflation occur. But for this to represent a commitment technology that can overcome the time-inconsistency problem requires that the observability of policy eliminate its ability to affect real output. It is the ability of monetary policy to generate real output effects that leads to the inflationary bias under discretion, and the incentive toward expansionary policies exists as long as monetary policy can influence real output. The fact that the costs of an expansion in terms of higher inflation only occur later actually increases the incentive for expansion if the central bank discounts the future.

   A serious criticism of explanations of actual inflation episodes based on the Barro-Gordon approach relates to the assumption that the central bank and the public

---

48. Kiley (1996) presents evidence for the United States, Canada, Great Britain, France, and Germany.

understand that there is no long-run trade-off between inflation and unemployment. The standard aggregate-supply curve, relating output movements to inflation surprises, implies that the behavior of real output (and unemployment) will be independent of the average rate of inflation. However, many central banks in the 1960s and into the 1970s did not accept this as an accurate description of the economy. Phillips curves were viewed as offering a menu of inflation-unemployment combinations from which policy makers could choose. Actual inflation may have reflected policy makers' misconceptions about the economy rather than their attempts to engineer surprise inflations that would not be anticipated by the public.

These criticisms, while suggesting that the simple models of time inconsistency may not account for all observed inflation, do not mean that time-inconsistency issues are unimportant. Explaining actual inflationary experiences will certainly involve consideration of the incentives faced by policy makers and the interaction of the factors such as uncertainty over policy preferences, responses to shocks, and a bias toward expansions that play a key role in models of discretionary policy.[49] So the issues that are central to the time-inconsistency literature do seem relevant for understanding the conduct of monetary policy. At the same time, important considerations faced by central banks are absent from the basic models generally used in the literature. For example, the models have implications for average inflation rates but usually do not explain variations in average inflation over longer time periods.[50] Yet one of the most important characteristics of inflation during the last 40 years in the developed economies is that it varies; it was low in the 1950s and early 1960s, much higher in the 1970s, and lower again in the mid-1980s and 1990s. Thus, average inflation changes, but it also displays a high degree of persistence.

This persistence does not arise in the models we have examined so far. Reputational models can display a type of inflation persistence; inflation may remain low in a pooling equilibrium, then, once the high-inflation central bank reveals itself, the inflation rate jumps and remains at a higher level. But this description does not seem to capture the manner in which a high degree of persistence is displayed in the response of actual inflation to economic shocks that, in principle, should cause only

49. And in reputational solutions, observed inflation may remain low for extended periods of time even though the factors highlighted in the time-inconsistency literature play an important role in determining the equilibrium.

50. Potential sources of shifts in the discretionary average rate of inflation would be changes in labor-market structure that affect the output effects of inflation (the a parameter in the basic model), shifts in the relative importance of output expansions or output stabilization in policy makers' objective functions (the λ parameter), or changes in the percentage gap between the economy's natural rate of output (unemployment) and the socially desired level (the parameter k).

one-time price-level effects. For example, consider a negative supply shock. When the central bank is concerned with stabilizing real output, such a shock leads to a rise in the inflation rate. This reaction seems consistent with the early 1970s when the worldwide oil price shock is generally viewed as being responsible for the rise in inflation. In the models of the previous sections, the rise in inflation lasts only one period. The shock may have a permanent effect on the price level, but it cannot account for persistence in the inflation rate. Ball (1991, 1995) has argued, however, that inflation results from an adverse shock and that once inflation increases, it remains high for some time. Eventually, policy shifts do bring inflation back down. Models of unemployment persistence based on labor-market hysteresis, such as those developed by Lockwood and Philippopoulos (1994), Lockwood (1997), Jonsson (1995), and Svensson (1997b), also imply some inflation persistence. A shock that raises unemployment now also raises expected unemployment in the future. This increases the incentive to generate an expansion and so leads to a rise in inflation both now and in the future. But these models imply that inflation gradually returns to its long-run average and so cannot account for the shifts in policy that often seem to characterize disinflations.

One model that does display such shifts was discussed earlier. Ball (1995) accounts for shifts in policy by assuming that the central bank type can change between a zero-inflation type and an optimizing type according to a Markov process. With imperfect information, the public must attempt to infer the current central bank's type from inflation outcomes. The wet type mimics the zero-inflation type until an adverse disturbance occurs. If such a shock occurs, and the central bank is a wet, inflation rises. This increase reveals the central bank's type, so the public expects positive inflation, and, in equilibrium, inflation remains high until a dry type takes over. As a result, the model predicts the type of periodic and persistent bouts of inflation that seem to have characterized inflation in many developed economies.

8.5   Do Central Banking Institutions Matter?

Both the academic literature on discretionary policy and the policy discussions surrounding the design of new policy-making institutions for the European Union and the emerging nations of Eastern Europe have generated increased interest in the role institutional structures play in affecting both policy and macroeconomic outcomes. While Olson (1996) argues strongly that policies and institutions are critical in accounting for cross-country differences in real economic growth, the focus in the

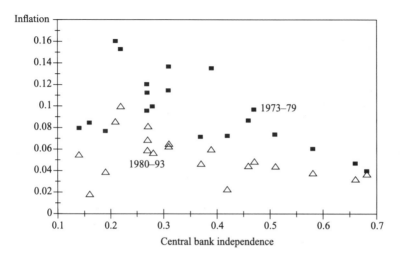

Figure 8.5
Average Inflation versus Central Bank Independence

monetary literature has predominately been on the implications of alternative institutional structures for the conduct of monetary policy and for inflation.

By far the greatest attention has been focused on the relationship between the
political independence of central banks and the resulting average inflation rates in
different countries. If political pressures lie behind the bias toward economic expansions that the Barro-Gordon model shows leads to an inflationary bias, then
central banks that are less subject to political influences should be able to deliver
consistently lower inflation.

This proposition has been intensively investigated. Beginning with Bade and
Parkin (1984), various authors have constructed measures of central bank independence and examined the relationship across countries between independence and
average inflation or measures of real economic performance.[51] Much of this literature is surveyed by Cukierman (1992) and Eijffinger and de Haan (1996). The general conclusion is that central bank independence among the industrial economies
is negatively correlated with average inflation; greater independence is associated
with lower average inflation. Using a measure of independence, denoted by LVAU,
that was constructed by Cukierman, Webb, and Neyapti (1992) based on the legal
charters of central banks, Figure 8.5 shows the relationship between independence

---

51. See Alesina (1988), Grilli, Masciandaro, and Tabellini (1991), and Eijffinger and Schaling (1993).

Table 8.1
Central Bank Independence and Inflation

	Const.	*LVAU*	R^2
1973–79	0.140[a]	−0.122[a]	0.35
1980–93	0.073[a]	−0.054[b]	0.18

[a] Significant at the 1% level.
[b] Significant at the 5% level.

and average inflation during 1973–1979 and 1980–1993 for a sample of 20 OECD countries.[52] This same information is summarized in Table 8.1 showing simple regressions of average inflation on central bank independence.

In addition to being statistically significant, the estimated effect of central bank independence on inflation is of an economically significant magnitude as well. For example, the 1973–1979 regression predicts that changing the degree of independence from that of the Bank of England (with a value of *LVAU* equal to 0.31 as measured prior to recent changes in the relationship between the Bank of England and the Treasury) to that of the Bundesbank (an *LVAU* of 0.66) would be associated with a reduction of 4 percentage points in average annual inflation.

One difficulty in interpreting this empirical literature in terms of the time-inconsistency literature arises because the link between central bank independence as measured by the various indices and the inflation bias under discretion is ambiguous. Delegating monetary policy to an independent central bank that shares the same objective function as the government would not reduce the time-consistent inflation rate.[53] However, independence is often interpreted in terms of the weight placed on inflation objectives; thus, independence may imply greater "conservativeness" in the sense used by Rogoff (1985b). Such an interpretation is consistent with greater independence being negatively correlated with average inflation (see equation [8.18]), but under this interpretation, greater independence should also be associated with less-activist stabilization policies and, as a result, higher output variance. The relationship between the volatility of real output and other measures of real economic

52. The countries included in the sample are Australia, Austria, Belgium, Canada, Denmark, Finland, France, Germany, Ireland, Italy, Japan, Luxembourg, Norway, Netherlands, New Zealand, Spain, Sweden, Switzerland, the United Kingdom, and the United States. The index of central bank independence employed is that due to Cukierman, Webb, and Neyapti (1992) and reported in Table 19.4 of Cukierman (1992).

53. Herrendorf and Neumann (1997) argue that a politically independent central bank is less likely to care about the government's reelection chances and is therefore less likely to use monetary policy in an attempt to create surprise inflation.

activity has been examined by Alesina and Summers (1993), Eijffinger and Schaling (1993), Cukierman, Kalaitzidakis, Summers, and Webb (1993), and Pollard (1993). These authors find no relationship between central bank independence and real economic volatility. This finding is inconsistent with the notion that independence is associated with a greater weight on inflation objectives. However, these findings have been interpreted to mean that granting greater central bank independence is a free lunch; average inflation is reduced with no cost in terms of greater output instability. Note that this interpretation requires that the empirical correlations be given a causal interpretation, but the empirical findings are also consistent with the implications from the contracting approach that there need be no inherent trade-off between reducing the inflation bias and achieving optimal stabilization.

Debelle and Fischer (1994), Walsh (1995d), Froyen and Waud (1995), and Fischer (1996) report that greater central bank independence is associated with greater short-run costs of disinflations. If causality runs from central bank independence to greater nominal rigidities that raise the sacrifice ratio associated with disinflations, then moves by high inflation countries to grant their central banks more independence may not lower the costs of reducing inflation. Causality could, however, run the other way. Disinflations will tend to be costly when the effects of surprise inflation on output are large. This occurs when the parameter a in our basic model is large. But a large value for a also implies that the inflation bias under discretion will be large, so countries with large a's (and high sacrifice ratios) may be more likely to have established independence central banks to avoid the inflation bias.

In support of the hypothesis that central bank independence can affect the slope of the short-run Phillips curve (i.e., the value of a), Walsh (1995d) shows that an increased focus on inflation objectives by the central bank can raise the degree of nominal wage rigidity by leading to less nominal wage indexation. Hutchison and Walsh (in press) do find that the short-run Phillips curve in New Zealand has become flatter (i.e., a has increased) since the 1989 reform of the Reserve Bank of New Zealand.

The appropriate interpretation of the empirical evidence on independence and inflation will also depend on the meaning of independence and the benefits independence confers. Suppose independence enhances the central bank's reputation in a way that reduces the inflation bias.[54] This reduction in the inflation bias lowers the optimal degree of conservativeness, since the stabilization costs of a conservative now become relatively larger. So independence may shift the relationship between average inflation and output variability, influencing the cross-country evidence on

54. Herrendorf and Lockwood (1996).

central bank independence and inflation. Or, if independence and conservatism are interpreted to be associated with a lower target for inflation, rather than a greater weight on inflation objectives, increased independence will lower average inflation but will not lead to an increase in the variability of output (Svensson 1997b).

An alternative interpretation is that the inflation bias arises from political pressures, perhaps related to electoral considerations, and that central bank independence reduces this bias by reducing direct political pressures on the central bank. That is, it is the greater autonomy associated with independence, and not a change in preferences, that accounts for the lower average inflation. By limiting the underlying source of the bias toward expansion, independence would act to reduce average inflation but would still allow the central bank to respond to economic disturbances. Independence need not imply a rise in output volatility. Waller and Walsh (1996) parameterize independence in terms of the political partisanship in the appointment process for the central banker and in the length of the term of office. They show that greater independence—a smaller role for partisan politics in the appointment process or a longer term of office—can reduce output volatility as well as average inflation.[55]

The type of independence might also matter. Debelle and Fischer (1994) draw a distinction between *instrument independence* and *goal independence*. The former refers to the ability of a central bank to sets its policy instruments without interference in the pursuit of its policy goals. The latter refers to the ability of the central bank to set policy goals. The Federal Reserve, for example, has both instrument and goal independence, while the Reserve Bank of New Zealand has instrument independence, but the goals of policy are set by the Reserve Bank Act of 1989, which specifies price stability as the sole objective of monetary policy. Prior to May 6, 1997, the Bank of England had neither instrument nor goal independence.[56] Debelle and Fischer report some (weak) empirical evidence that the presence of a formal goal of price stability (that is, a lack of goal independence) and instrument independence are related to low-inflation outcomes. Other aspects of the political linkages between the central bank and the government, such as appointment procedures, do not seem to matter.

The critical issue is the extent to which these correlations between inflation and measures of independence represent causal relationships. Will increasing the political insulation of a country's central bank actually successfully result in lower average inflation without producing any detrimental effects on real economic performance?

---

55. Alesnia and Gatti (1995) make a similar point by considering a two-party model in which the central banker is chosen jointly by the two political parties prior to an election. They show that electorally induced political business cycles are reduced.

56. The Bank of England was granted instrument independence by the Labour government elected on May 3, 1997. Some other recent central bank reforms are discussed in Walsh (1995b).

Posen (1993, 1995) has argued strongly that both average inflation and the degree of central bank independence are jointly determined by the strength of political constituencies opposed to inflation; in the absence of these constituencies, simply increasing central bank independence will not cause inflation to be lower. Cargill (1995b) has also questioned the causal significance of the statistical correlations between measures of central bank independence based on descriptions of the legal structure of the bank. In particular, Cargill emphasizes the case of Japan, where low inflation has coexisted with a very dependent central bank. McKinnon and Ohno (1997) argue that U.S. pressure on Japan over trade disputes accounts for deflationary pressures in Japan and explains Japan's low inflation despite a politically dependent central bank. In this case, the political pressures on a dependent central bank supported a low-inflation policy, in contrast to the general presumption that political pressures are always in favor of inflationary policies.

One problem with regressions of the form reported in Table 8.1 is that they fail to correct for country-specific factors that may affect inflation and may also be correlated with the measure of central bank independence. If countries with independent central banks differ systematically from countries with dependent central banks in ways that are associated with lower inflation, the Table 8.1 regressions will attribute the low inflation to central bank independence. One approach to correcting for potential bias is to include other determinants of inflation in the empirical analysis. Campillo and Miron (1997) have shown recently that central bank independence has no explanatory power for cross-country variation in average inflation once other potential determinants of inflation are included in the analysis. They argue instead that the degree of openness is an important factor in explaining inflation, a result consistent with Romer (1993) and Jonsson (1995). Campillo and Miron also find a significant effect of the debt-to-GDP ratio in accounting for cross-country inflation variation, higher values of this ratio being associated with higher average inflation. In a different approach, Johnson and Siklos (1994) find little relationship between the measured responses of short-term interest rates (the policy instrument) to political influences and measures of independence based on central banking laws.[57]

While the more recent empirical work has cast doubt on the causal role played by central bank independence in determining inflation, the earlier findings have played an important role in shaping central banking reforms around the world as countries

---

57. The discussion here applies only to developed economies. There is no statistical relationship between measures of central bank independence and average inflation among the developing economies. Cukierman (1992) has argued for the use of a measure of central-bank-governor turnover as a proxy for independence. Among the developing economies, high turnover is associated with high inflation.

attempt to design institutional structures that will support desirable policy outcomes. However, a complete understanding of the relationship between average inflation and central bank independence, even if the correlation is not causal, will require a better understanding of the factors that have, historically, led to variations in central bank independence across countries. What determines central bank independence? If independence has been employed as a means of reducing the inflation bias that might arise from political pressures on the central bank, then those countries facing the greatest bias would have had the most incentive to establish independent central banks. De Haan and van't Hag (1995) develop some implications of the hypothesis that the delegation of monetary policy to an independent central bank has been used as a commitment device and test these using data from OECD economies. Eijffinger and de Haan (1996) show how central bank independence, interpreted in terms of the degree of conservativeness, is related to factors such as the natural rate of un-employment (assumed to be related to the incentive for expansions) that are sug-gested by the basic Rogoff model.

8.6   Lessons and Conclusions

Many countries experience, for long periods of time, average inflation rates that clearly exceed what would seem to be reasonable estimates of the socially desired inflation rate. The time-inconsistency literature originated as a positive attempt to explain this observation. In the process, the approach has made important meth-odological contributions to monetary-policy analysis by emphasizing the need to treat central banks as responding to the incentives they face.

As positive theories of actual inflations, the evidence for this approach is pro-mising but mixed. In assessing the ability of this approach to account for actual inflation, one can distinguish between attempts to explain the time-series experience of a single country and the cross-sectional evidence on inflation differences among countries. The factors emphasized in this literature—central bank preferences, the short-run real effects of surprise inflation, the rate at which the central bank dis-counts the future, the effects of political influences on the central bank—are quite different from the factors that receive prominence in the optimal taxation models of inflation of Chapter 4.[58] While a large number of empirical studies of the industrial-ized economies have found that indices of central bank political independence are negatively related to average inflation, evidence also suggests the importance of financing considerations.

---

58. These two literatures are linked, however, by Herrendorf (1997) in his survey on theories of seigniorage.

Perhaps the most important contribution of the literature on time inconsistency, however, has been to provide theoretical frameworks for thinking formally about credibility issues, on the one hand, and the role of institutions and political factors, on the other, in influencing policy choices. By emphasizing the interactions of the incentives faced by the policy makers, the structure of information about the economy and about the central bank's preferences, and the public's beliefs, the models examined in this chapter provide a critical set of insights that have influenced the recent debates over rules, discretion, and the design of monetary-policy institutions.

8.7 Problems

1. Assume that firms maximize profits in competitive factor markets with labor the only variable factor of production. Output is produced according to the production function $Y = AL^{\alpha}$, $0 < \alpha < 1$. Labor is supplied inelasticly. Nominal wages are set at the start of the period at a level consistent with market clearing, given expectations of the price level. Actual employment is determined by firms once the actual price level is observed. Show that, in log terms, output is given by $y = \alpha l^* + \dfrac{\alpha}{1-\alpha}(p - p^e) + \dfrac{1}{1-\alpha} \ln A$, where l^* is the log labor supply.

2. Suppose an economy is characterized by the following three equations:

$$\pi = \pi^e + ay + e$$

$$y = -br + u$$

$$\Delta m - \pi = -di + y + v$$

where the first equation is an aggregate-supply function written in the form of an expectations-augmented Phillips curve, the second is an "IS" or aggregate-demand relationship, and the third is a money-demand equation where Δm denotes the growth rate of the nominal money supply. The real interest rate is denoted by r and the nominal rate by i, with $i = r + \pi^e$. Let the monetary authority implement policy by setting i to minimize the expected value of $\frac{1}{2}[\lambda(y - y^*)^2 + \pi^2]$ where $y^* > 0$. Assume the policy authority has forecasts e^f, u^f, and v^f of the shocks, but the public forms its expectations prior to the setting of i and without any information on the shocks.

a. Assume the monetary authority can commit to a policy of the form $i = c_0 + c_1 e^f + c_2 u^f + c_3 v^f$ prior to knowing any of the realizations of the shocks. Derive the optimal commitment policy (i.e., the optimal values of c_0, c_1, c_2, and c_3).

b. Derive the time-consistent equilibrium under discretion. How does the nominal interest rate compare to the case under commitment? What is the average inflation rate?

3. Verify that the optimal commitment rule that minimizes the unconditional expected value of the loss function given by (8.10) is $\Delta m^c = -\dfrac{a\lambda}{1+a^2\lambda}e.$

4. Suppose the central bank acts under discretion to minimize the expected value of equation (8.2). The central bank can observe e prior to setting Δm, but v is observed only after policy is set. Assume, however, that e and v are correlated, and that the expected value of v, conditional on e, is $E[v|e] = qe$ where $q = \sigma_{v,e}/\sigma_e^2$ and $\sigma_{v,e}$ is the covariance between e and v.

a. Find the optimal policy under discretion. Explain how policy depends on q.

b. What is the equilibrium rate of inflation? Does it depend on q?

5. Since the tax distortions of inflation are related to expected inflation, suppose the loss function (8.2) is replaced by

$$L = \lambda(y - y_n - k)^2 + (\pi^e)^2$$

where $y = y_n + a(\pi - \pi^e)$. How is Figure 8.2 modified by this change in the central bank's loss function? Is there an equilibrium inflation rate? Explain.

6. Based on Jonsson (1995) and Svensson (1997b): Suppose equation (8.3) is modified to incorporate persistence in the output process:

$$y_t = (1 - \theta)y_n + \theta y_{t-1} + a(\pi_t - \pi_t^e) + e_t, \qquad 0 < \theta < 1$$

Suppose the policy maker has a two-period horizon with objective function given by

$$L = \min E[L_t + \delta L_{t+1}]$$

where $L_i = \frac{1}{2}[\lambda(y_i - y_n - k)^2 + \pi_i^2]$.

a. Derive the optimal commitment policy.

b. Derive the optimal policy under discretion without commitment.

c. How does the presence of persistence ($\theta > 0$) affect the inflation bias?

7. Show that π^d given by (8.18) is equal to inflation under discretion when the weight on inflation in (8.2) becomes $1 + \delta$ and the economy is characterized by (8.3) and (8.4).

8. Suppose that the private sector forms expectations according to

$$\pi_t^e = \pi^* \qquad \text{if} \qquad \pi_{t-1} = \pi_{t-1}^e$$

$$\pi_t^e = a\lambda k \qquad \text{otherwise}$$

If the central bank's objective function is given by (8.2) and its discount rate is β, what is the minimum value of π^* that can be sustained in equilibrium?

9. Assume that nominal wages are set at the start of each period but that wages are partially indexed against inflation. If w^c is the contract base nominal wage, the actual nominal wage is $w = w^c + \kappa(p_t - p_{t-1})$ where κ is the indexation parameter. Show how indexation affects the equilibrium rate of inflation under pure discretion. What is the effect on average inflation of an increase in κ? Explain why.

10. Suppose the central bank's loss function is given by

$$V^{cb} = \tfrac{1}{2}[\lambda(y - y_n - k)^2 + (1 + \delta)\pi^2]$$

If $y = y_n + a(\pi - \pi^e) + e$ and $\pi = \Delta m + v$, verify that the inflation rate under discretion is given by equation (8.18).

11. (Based on Beetsma and Jensen 1998): Suppose the social loss function is equal to

$$V^s = \tfrac{1}{2}\mathrm{E}[\lambda(y - y_n - k)^2 + \pi^2]$$

and the central bank's loss function is given by

$$V^{cb} = \tfrac{1}{2}[(\lambda - \theta)(y - y_n - k)^2 + (1 + \theta)(\pi - \pi^T)^2] + t\pi$$

where θ is a mean zero stochastic shock to the central bank's preferences, π^T is an inflation target assigned by the government, and $t\pi$ is a linear inflation contract with t a parameter chosen by the government. Assume that private sector forms expectation before observing θ. Let $y = y_n + a(\pi - \pi^e) + e$ and $\pi = \Delta m + v$. Finally, assume θ and the supply shock e are uncorrelated.

a. Suppose the government only assigns an inflation target (so $t = 0$). What is the optimal value for π^T?

b. Now suppose the government only assigns a linear inflation contract (so $\pi^T = 0$). What is the optimal value for t?

c. Is the expected social loss lower under the inflation target arrangement or the inflation contract arrangement?

9 Monetary-Policy Operating Procedures

9.1 Introduction

Previous chapters treated the nominal money supply or even inflation as the variable directly controlled by the monetary policy maker. While this approach does allow for an analysis of many important issues, it ignores the actual problems surrounding policy implementation. Central banks do not directly control the nominal money supply, inflation, or long-term interest rates likely to be most relevant for aggregate spending. Instead, narrow reserve aggregates, such as the monetary base, or very short-term interest rates, such as the federal funds rate in the United States, are the variables over which the central bank can exercise close control. Chapter 1 claimed that a short-term interest rate typically provides a better measure of monetary-policy actions than measures of the money supply do, but no explanation was given for why this might be the case. For much of the last 30 years, shifts in U.S. monetary policy have been better captured by movements in the federal funds rate than by any monetary aggregate. Many other central banks also employ a short-term interest rate as their policy instrument. But we have not yet discussed the specific relationship between these short-term interest rates, other reserve aggregates such as non-borrowed reserves or the monetary base, and the broader monetary aggregates such as M1 or M2. And there has been no discussion of the factors that might explain why many central banks choose to use a short-term interest rate rather than a monetary aggregate as their instrument for implementing monetary policy. These issues will be addressed in this chapter.

The actual implementation of monetary policy involves a variety of rules, traditions, and practices, and these collectively are called operating procedures. Operating procedures differ according to the actual instrument the monetary authority uses in its daily conduct of policy, the operating target whose control is achieved over short horizons (a short-term interest rate versus a reserve aggregate, for example), the conditions under which the instruments and operating targets are automatically adjusted in light of economic developments, the information about policy and the type of announcements the monetary authority might make, its choice of variables for which it establishes targets (e.g., for money-supply growth or the inflation rate), and whether these targets are formal or informal.

The objective in examining monetary-policy operating procedures is to understand what instruments are actually under the control of the monetary authority, the factors that determine the optimal instrument choice, and how the choice of instrument affects the manner in which short-term interest rates, reserve aggregates, or the money stock might reflect policy actions and nonpolicy disturbances. We first examine the factors that determine the optimal choice of an operating procedure. Then we will focus on the relationship between the choice of operating procedure, the response of the market for bank reserves to various economic disturbances, and the way policy should be measured.

9.2   From Instruments to Goals

There are many interesting insights that can be obtained by ignoring the linkages between the actual tools controlled by the central bank and instead simply assuming that money growth, or even the inflation rate, can be controlled directly. But central banks don't directly control inflation, nor do their policy actions have effects on real economic activity that are always easy to determine. At best, policy actions taken today affect these variables several months in the future. The lags in the effects of policy, together with the infrequency with which observations on aggregate price indices and output become available, greatly complicate the implementation of monetary policy, even when there is agreement on the objectives. How should the central bank adjust its actual policy tools in response to economic developments? Should it focus only on its ultimate goals such as the inflation rate? Should it attempt to maintain some measure of the money supply on a target path? Should it keep a short-term nominal interest rate constant?

Discussions of monetary-policy implementation focus on instruments, operating targets, intermediate targets, and policy goals. Instruments are the variables that are directly controlled by the central bank. These typically include an interest rate charged on reserves borrowed from the central bank, the reserve requirement ratios that determine the level of reserves banks must hold against their deposit liabilities, and the composition of the central bank's own balance sheet (its holdings of government securities, for example). The instruments of policy are usually manipulated to achieve a prespecified value of an operating target, typically some measure of bank reserves (total reserves, borrowed reserves, or nonborrowed reserves—the difference between total and borrowed reserves), a very short-term rate of interest, usually an overnight interbank rate (the federal funds rate in the case of the United States), or a monetary-conditions index that combines an interest rate and the exchange rate.

Goals, such as inflation or deviations of unemployment from the natural rate, are the ultimate variables of interest to policy makers; instruments are the actual variables under their direct control. Intermediate-target variables fall between operating targets and goals in the sequence of links that run from policy instruments to real economic activity and inflation. Because observations on some or all of the goal variables are usually obtained less frequently than are data on interest rates, exchange rates, or monetary aggregates, the behavior of these latter variables can often provide the central bank with information about economic developments that will affect the goal variables. For example, faster than expected money growth may signal that real output is expanding more rapidly than previously thought. The central bank might change its operating target (in this case, raise the interbank rate or contract reserves) to keep the money growth rate on a path believed to be consistent with achieving its policy goals. In this case, money growth is serving as an intermediate-target variable.

Instruments, operating targets, intermediate targets, and goals have been described in a sequence running from the instruments directly controlled by the central bank to goals, the ultimate objectives of policy. Actually policy design operates in the reverse fashion: from the goals of policy, to the values of the intermediate targets consistent with the goals, to the values of the operating targets needed to achieve the inter-mediate targets, and finally to the instrument settings that yield the desired values of the operating targets. In earlier chapters, inflation and the money supply were treated as policy instruments, ignoring the linkages from reserve markets to interest rates to banking-sector behavior to aggregate demand. Similarly, it is often useful to ignore reserve-market behavior and treat an operating target variable, such as the overnight interbank interest rate or a reserve aggregate, as the policy instrument. Since these variables can be controlled closely over short time horizons, they are often also described as policy instruments.

A related point to note is that the definition of a policy instrument is often model dependent. Many of the models discussed in chapter 8, for example, treated the inflation rate as the direct instrument of monetary policy. The assumption was not that the central bank directly set prices in the economy; rather it was that the central bank, through its actual policy tools, could exercise sufficiently close control over the inflation rate that errors in the control process could be ignored for the purpose of the particular model. Similarly, in Chapter 10, a short-term rate of interest will be treated as the instrument of monetary policy. Again, this should be interpreted to mean that the central bank, by engaging in open-market operations (its actual instrument) can control the interest rate so that for many purposes we can simply ignore the reserve market and treat the short-term interest rate as if it were set directly by the central bank.

9.3 The Instrument-Choice Problem

If the monetary-policy authority can choose between employing an interest rate or a monetary aggregate as its policy tool, which should it choose? The classic analysis of this question is due to Poole (1970). He showed how the stochastic structure of the economy—the nature and relative importance of different types of disturbances—

would determine the optimal instrument. The analysis of the instrument-choice problem also provides a framework for discussing the role of policy targets, intermediate targets, and information in the conduct of policy.

9.3.1 Poole's Analysis

Suppose the central bank must set policy before observing the current disturbances to the goods and money markets and that information on interest rates, but not output, is immediately available. This informational assumption reflects a situation in which the central bank can observe market interest rates essentially continuously, but data on inflation and output might be available only monthly or quarterly. In such an environment, the central bank will be unable to determine from a movement in market interest rates the exact source of any economic disturbances that might be affecting the economy. To make a simple parallel with a model of supply and demand, observing a rise in price does not indicate whether there has been a positive shock to the demand curve or a negative shock to the supply curve. Only by observing both price and quantity can these two alternatives be distinguished, since a demand shift would be associated with a price and quantity rise, while a supply shift would be associated with a rise in price and a decline in quantity. At the macro level, an increase in the interest rate could be due to expanding aggregate demand (which might call for contractionary monetary policy to stabilize output) or an exogenous shift in money demand (which might call for letting the money supply expand). With imperfect information about economic developments, it will be impossible to determine the source of shocks that have caused interest rates to move.

In this environment, Poole asked whether the central bank should try to hold market interest rates constant or should hold a monetary quantity constant while allowing interest rates to move. And he assumed that the objective of policy was to stabilize real output, so that he answered his question by comparing the variance of output implied by the two alternative policies.

Poole treated the price level as fixed, and to highlight his basic results, we will do so as well. Since the instrument-choice problem primarily relates to the decision to hold either a market rate or a monetary quantity constant over a fairly short period of time (say the time between policy board meetings), ignoring price-level effects is not unreasonable as a starting point for the analysis. A simple variant of the basic IS-LM model in log terms that can be used to derive Poole's results is given by

$$y_t = -\alpha i_t + u_t \tag{9.1}$$

$$m_t = -c i_t + y_t + v_t \tag{9.2}$$

Equation (9.1) represents an aggregate-demand relationship in which output is a decreasing function of the interest rate; demand also depends on an exogenous disturbance u_t. Equation (9.2) gives the demand for money as a decreasing function of the interest rate and an increasing function of output. Money demand is subject to a random shock v_t. Equilibrium requires that the demand for money equal the supply of money m_t. For simplicity, u and v will be treated as mean-zero, serially and mutually uncorrelated processes. All other variables should be interpreted as deviations from trend values; thus, y is a measure of the output gap. These two equations represent a simple IS-LM model of output determination, given a fixed price level.[1]

The final aspect of the model is a specification of the policy maker's objective, assumed to be the minimization of the variance of output deviations:

$$E[y_t]^2 \tag{9.3}$$

where the economy's equilibrium level of the output gap in the absence of shocks is $y = 0$. Because the central bank's loss function is quadratic in output around the true steady state value of zero, the problem of time inconsistency that was the focus of Chapter 8 will not arise.

The timing is as follows: the central bank sets either i or m at the start of the period; the stochastic shocks u and v occur, determining the values of the endogenous variables (either y and i if m is the policy instrument, or y and m if i is the policy instrument).

When the money stock is the policy instrument, (9.1) and (9.2) can be solved jointly for equilibrium output:

$$y = \frac{\alpha m + cu - \alpha v}{\alpha + c}$$

Then setting m such that $E[y] = 0$,[2] we obtain $y = (cu - \alpha v)/(\alpha + c)$. Hence, the value of the objective function under a money-supply procedure is

$$E_m[y_t]^2 = \frac{c^2 \sigma_u^2 + \alpha^2 \sigma_v^2}{(\alpha + c)^2} \tag{9.4}$$

where the assumption that u and v are uncorrelated has been used.

---

1. Note that the price level has been normalized to equal 1 so that the log of the price level is zero; $p = 0$. The income elasticity of money demand has also been set equal to 1.

2. This just requires $m = 0$ because of our normalizations.

Under the alternative policy, i is the policy instrument, and (9.1) can be solved directly for output. That is, the money-market condition is no longer needed, although it will determine the level of m necessary to ensure money-market equilibrium. By fixing the rate of interest, the central bank lets the money stock adjust endogenously to equal the level of money demand given by the interest rate and the level of income. Setting i such that $E[y] = 0$,

$$E_i[y_t]^2 = \sigma_u^2 \tag{9.5}$$

The two alternative policy choices can be evaluated by comparing the variance of output implied by each. The interest-rate operating procedure is preferred to the money-supply operating procedure if and only if

$$E_i[y_t]^2 < E_m[y_t]^2$$

and, from (9.4) and (9.5), this condition is satisfied if and only if

$$\sigma_v^2 > \left(1 + \frac{2c}{\alpha}\right)\sigma_u^2 \tag{9.6}$$

Thus, an interest-rate procedure is more likely to be preferred when the variance of money-demand disturbances is larger, the LM curve is steeper (the slope of the LM curve is $\frac{1}{c}$), and the IS curve is flatter (the slope of the IS curve is $-\frac{1}{\alpha}$). Conversely, the money-supply procedure will be preferred if the variance of aggregate-demand shocks (σ_u^2) is large, the LM curve is flat, or the IS curve is steep.[3]

If only aggregate-demand shocks are present (i.e., $\sigma_v^2 = 0$), a money rule leads to a smaller variance for output. Under a money rule, a positive IS shock leads to an increase in the interest rate, and this acts to reduce aggregate spending, thereby partially offsetting the original shock. Since the adjustment of i acts to automatically stabilize output, preventing this interest-rate adjustment by fixing i leads to larger output fluctuations. If only money-demand shocks are present, (i.e., $\sigma_u^2 = 0$), output can be stabilized perfectly under an interest-rate rule. Under a money rule, money-demand shocks cause the interest rate to move to maintain money-market equilibrium; these interest-rate movements then lead to output fluctuations. With both

---

3. In the context of an open economy in which the IS relationship is $y_t = -\alpha_1 i_t + \alpha_2 s_t + u_t$ where s_t is the exchange rate, Poole's conclusions go through if the central bank's choice is expressed not in terms of i but in terms of the monetary conditions index $i - \frac{\alpha_2}{\alpha_1} s$.

types of shocks occurring, the comparison of the two types of policy rules will depend on the relative variances of u and v, as well as the respective slopes of the IS and LM curves as shown by equation (9.6).

This framework is quite simple and ignores many important factors. To take just one example, no central bank has direct control over the money supply. Instead, control can be exercised over a narrow monetary aggregate such as the monetary base, and variations in this aggregate are then associated with variations in broader measures of the money supply. To see how the basic framework can be modified to distinguish between the base as a policy instrument and the money supply, suppose the two are linked by

$$m_t = b_t + hi_t + \omega_t \tag{9.7}$$

where b is the (log) monetary base, and the money multiplier ($m - b$ in log terms) is assumed to be an increasing function of the rate of interest (i.e., $h > 0$). In addition, ω is a random money-multiplier disturbance. Equation (9.7) could arise under a fractional reserve system in which excess reserves are a decreasing function of the rate of interest.[4] Under an interest rate procedure, (9.7) is irrelevant for output determination, so $E_i[y_t]^2 = \sigma_u^2$ as before. But now, under a monetary-base operating procedure with $b_t = 0$,

$$y_t = \frac{(c + h)u_t - \alpha v_t + \alpha \omega_t}{\alpha + c + h}$$

and

$$E_b[y_t]^2 = \left(\frac{1}{\alpha + c + h}\right)^2 [(c + h)^2 \sigma_u^2 + \alpha^2 (\sigma_v^2 + \sigma_\omega^2)]$$

The interest-rate procedure is preferred over the base procedure if and only if

$$\sigma_v^2 + \sigma_\omega^2 > \left[1 + \frac{2(c + h)}{\alpha}\right] \sigma_u^2$$

Because ω shocks do not affect output under an interest-rate procedure, the presence of money-multiplier disturbances makes a base rule less attractive and makes it more likely that an interest-rate procedure will lead to a smaller output variance. This simple extension reinforces the basic message of Poole's analysis; increased financial sector volatility (money-demand or money-multiplier shocks in the model

---

4. See for example, Modigliani, Rasche, and Cooper (1970) or McCallum and Hoehn (1983).

used here) increases the desirability of an interest-rate-oriented policy procedure over a monetary-aggregate procedure. If money demand is viewed as highly unstable and difficult to predict over short-time horizons, greater output stability can be achieved by stabilizing interest rates, letting monetary aggregates fluctuate. If, however, the main source of short-run instability arises from aggregate spending, a policy that stabilizes a monetary aggregate will lead to greater output stability.

This analysis is based on the realistic assumption that policy is unable to identify and respond to underlying disturbances. Instead, policy is implemented by fixing, at least over some short time interval, the value of an operating target or policy instrument. As additional information about the economy is obtained, the appropriate level at which to fix the policy instrument changes. So the critical issue is not so much which variable is used as a policy instrument, but how that instrument should be adjusted in light of new but imperfect information about economic developments.

The basic Poole analysis ignores such factors as inflation, expectations, and aggregate-supply disturbances. These factors, and many others, have been incorporated into models to examine the choice between interest-rate- and monetary-aggregate-oriented operating procedures. B. Friedman (1990) contains a useful and comprehensive survey. In addition, as Friedman stresses, the appropriate definition of the policy maker's objective function is unlikely to be simply the variance of output once inflation is included in the model. Poole's approach provides a means of determining the optimal instrument choice, given a particular objective function. In the case examined here, the objective was the minimization of the variance of output. While it is often useful to analyze policy under the assumption that policy is implemented using a specific instrument, it is also important to recognize that the choice of instrument is an endogenous decision of the policy maker and is therefore dependent on the objectives of monetary policy.

9.3.2 Policy Rules and Information

The basic Poole analysis focuses on the major factors that determine the choice between alternatives that can be viewed as special cases of the following policy rule:[5]

$$b = \mu i \tag{9.8}$$

According to (9.8), the monetary authority adjusts the base, its actual instrument, in response to interest-rate movements. The parameter μ, both its sign and its magni-

---

5. Recall that we have normalized constants in equations such as (9.8) to be zero. More generally, we might have a rule of the form $b = b_0 + \mu(i - \mathrm{E}i)$ where b_0 is a constant and $\mathrm{E}i$ is the expected value of i. As we will see in Chapter 10, issues of price-level indeterminacy can arise if the average value of b is not tied down (as it is in this case by b_0).

tude, determine how the base is varied by the central bank as interest rates vary. If $\mu = 0$, then $b = 0$ and we have the case of a monetary-base operating procedure in which b is fixed (at zero by our normalization) and is not adjusted in response to interest-rate movements. If $\mu = -h$, then equation (9.7) implies $m = \omega$ and we have the case of a money-supply operating procedure in which the base is automatically adjusted to keep m equal to zero on average; the actual value of m varies as a result of the control error ω. In this case, b is the policy instrument, while m is the operating target. As we will see, an interest-rate operating target involves letting $\mu \to \infty$. Equation (9.8) is called a policy rule in that it provides a description of how the policy instrument, in this case, the monetary base b, is set.

By combining (9.8) with (9.1), (9.2), and (9.7) we obtain

$$i = \frac{v - \omega + u}{\alpha + c + \mu + h} \tag{9.9}$$

so that large values of μ reduce the variance of the interest rate. As $\mu \to \infty$ we approximate the interest-rate operating procedure in which i is set equal to a fixed value (zero due to the normalization). By representing policy in terms of the policy rule and then characterizing policy in terms of the choice of a value for μ, we can consider intermediate cases to the extreme alternatives considered in section 9.3.1.

Substituting (9.9) into (9.1), output is given by

$$y = \frac{(c + \mu + h)u - \alpha(v - \omega)}{\alpha + c + \mu + h}$$

From this expression, we can calculate the variance of output:

$$\sigma_y^2 = \frac{(c + \mu + h)^2\sigma_u^2 + \alpha^2(\sigma_v^2 + \sigma_\omega^2)}{(\alpha + c + \mu + h)^2}$$

If we minimize this with respect to μ, the optimal policy rule (in the sense of minimizing the variance of output) is given by

$$\mu^* = -(c + h) + \frac{\alpha(\sigma_v^2 + \sigma_\omega^2)}{\sigma_u^2} \tag{9.10}$$

In general, neither the interest-rate ($\mu \to \infty$), nor the base ($\mu = 0$), nor the money-supply ($\mu = -h$) operating procedure will be optimal. Instead, Poole demonstrated that the way policy (in the form of the setting for b) should respond to interest-rate movements will depend on the relative variances of the underlying economic disturbances.

To understand the role these variances play, suppose first that $v \equiv \omega \equiv 0$ so that $\sigma_v^2 = \sigma_\omega^2 = 0$; there are no shifts in money demand or money supply, given the base. In this environment, the earlier analysis concluded that a base rule dominates an interest-rate rule. Equation (9.10) shows that one can do even better than fixing the money supply if b is actually reduced when the interest rate rises [i.e., $b = -(c + h)i$]. With interest-rate movements signaling aggregate-demand shifts (since u is the only source of disturbance), a rise in the interest rate indicates $u > 0$; a policy designed to stabilize output should reduce m; this reduction can be done by reducing the base. Rather than "leaning against the wind" to offset the interest-rate rise, the central bank should engage in a contractionary policy that pushes i up even further.

When σ_v^2 and σ_ω^2 are positive, interest-rate increases may now be the result of an increase in money demand or a decrease in money supply. Since the appropriate response to a positive money-demand shock or a negative money-supply shock is to increase the monetary base and offset the interest-rate rise (i.e., it *is* appropriate to lean against the wind), $\mu^* > -(c + h)$; it will become optimal to actually increase the base in response to an interest-rate rise as $\sigma_v^2 + \sigma_\omega^2$ becomes sufficiently large.

The value for the policy-rule parameter in (9.10) can also be interpreted in terms of a signal-extraction problem faced by the policy authority. Recall that the basic assumption in the Poole analysis was that the policy maker could observe, and react to, the interest rate, but perhaps because of information lags, the current values of output and the underlying disturbances could not be observed. Suppose instead that the shocks u, v, and ω are observed and the central bank can respond to them. That is, suppose the policy rule could take the form $b = \mu_u u + \mu_v v + \mu_\omega \omega$ for some parameters μ_u, μ_v, and μ_ω. If we substitute this policy rule into (9.1) and (9.2), we obtain

$$y = \frac{(c + h + \alpha \mu_u)u - \alpha(1 - \mu_v)v + \alpha(1 + \mu_\omega)\omega}{\alpha + c + h}$$

In this case, which corresponds to a situation of perfect information about the basic shocks, it is clear that the variance of output can be minimized if $\mu_u = -(c + h)/\alpha$, $\mu_v = 1$, and $\mu_\omega = -1$.

If the policy maker cannot observe the underlying shocks, then policy will need to be set on the basis of forecasts of these disturbances. Given the linear structure of the model, the optimal policy can be written $b = \mu_u \hat{u} + \mu_v \hat{v} + \mu_\omega \hat{\omega} = -\dfrac{(c + h)}{\alpha} \hat{u} + \hat{v} - \hat{\omega}$

where $\hat{u}$, $\hat{v}$, and $\hat{\omega}$ are the forecasts of the shocks. In the Poole framework, the central bank observes the interest rate and can set policy conditional on i. Thus, the forecasts of u and v will depend on i and will take the form $\hat{u} = \delta_u i$, $\hat{v} = \delta_v i$, and $\hat{\omega} = \delta_\omega i$.

The policy rule can then be written as

$$b = -\frac{c+h}{\alpha}\,\hat{u} + \hat{v} - \hat{\omega} = \left(-\frac{c+h}{\alpha}\delta_u + \delta_v - \delta_\omega\right)i \tag{9.11}$$

Using this policy rule to solve for the equilibrium interest rate, determining the δ_i's from the assumption that forecasts are equal to the projections of the shocks on i, it is straightforward to verify that the coefficient on i in the policy rule (9.11) is equal to the value μ^* given in equation (9.10). Thus, the optimal policy response to interest-rate movements represents an optimal response to the central bank's forecasts of the underlying economic disturbances, where these forecasts are based on the observed interest rate.

9.3.3 Intermediate Targets

The previous subsection showed how the optimal response coefficients in the policy rule could be related to the central bank's forecast of the underlying disturbances. This interpretation of the policy-rule parameter is important, since it captures a very general way of thinking about policy. When the central bank faces imperfect information about the shocks to the economy, it should respond based on its best forecasts of these shocks.[6] In our example, the only information variable available was the interest rate, so forecasts of the underlying shocks were based on i. In more general settings, information on other variables may be available on a frequent basis, and this should also be used in forecasting the sources of economic disturbances. Examples of such information variables include—besides market interest rates— exchange rates, commodity prices, and asset prices.[7]

Policy design needs to recognize that the central bank must respond to partial and incomplete information about the true state of the economy. Given such circumstances, monetary policy is often formulated in practice in terms of intermediate targets. Intermediate targets are variables whose behavior provides information useful in forecasting the goal variables.[8] Deviations in the intermediate targets from

6. Brainard (1967) showed that this statement is no longer true when there is uncertainty about the model parameters in addition to the additive uncertainty considered here. Parameter uncertainty makes it optimal to adjust less than completely.

7. As discussed in Chapter 1, commodity prices eliminate the price puzzle in VAR estimates of monetary-policy effects because of the informational role they appear to play.

8. See Kareken, Muench, and Wallace (1973) and B. Friedman (1975, 1977b, 1990) for early treatments of the informational role of intermediate targets. More recently, Svensson (1997a, 1997c) has stressed the role of inflation forecasts as an intermediate target. Bernanke and Woodford (1997) show, however, how multiple equilibria may arise if policy is based on private sector forecasts which are, in turn, based on expectations of future policy.

their expected paths indicate a likely deviation of a goal variable from its target and signal the need for a policy adjustment. For example, if money growth, which is observed weekly, is closely related to subsequent inflation, which is observed only monthly, then faster than expected money growth signals the need to tighten policy. By acting to keep the intermediate-target variable equal to its target, the hope is that policy will be adjusted automatically to keep the goal variables close to their targets as well.[9]

To see the role of intermediate targets in a very simple framework, consider the following aggregate-supply, aggregate-demand, and money-demand system, expressed in terms of the rate of inflation.

$$y_t = a(\pi_t - E_{t-1}\pi_t) + z_t \tag{9.12}$$

$$y_t = -\alpha(i_t - E_t\pi_{t+1}) + u_t \tag{9.13}$$

$$m_t - p_t = m_t - \pi_t - p_{t-1} = y_t - ci_t + v_t \tag{9.14}$$

Equation (9.12) is standard Lucas supply curve, (9.13) gives aggregate demand as a decreasing function of the expected real interest rate, and equation (9.14) is a simple money-demand relationship. Assume that each of the three disturbances z, u, and v follows first-order autoregressive processes:

$$z_t = \rho_z z_{t-1} + e_t$$

$$u_t = \rho_u u_{t-1} + \varphi_t$$

$$v_t = \rho_v v_{t-1} + \psi_t$$

where $0 < \rho_i < 1$ for $i = z, u, v$. The innovations e, φ, and ψ are assumed to be mean-zero, serially and mutually uncorrelated processes. The interest rate i is taken to be the policy instrument of the monetary authority.

Suppose that the monetary authority's objective is to minimize expected squared deviations of the inflation rate around a target level π^*. Hence, i_t is chosen to minimize[10]

$$V = E[\pi_t - \pi^*]^2 \tag{9.15}$$

9. B. Friedman (1990) and McCallum (1990b) provide discussions of the intermediate-target problem.

10. Note that for this example we have replaced the loss function in output deviations with one involving only inflation-stabilization objectives. As is clear from (9.12), stabilizing inflation to minimize unexpected movments in π is consistent with minimizing output variability if there are no supply disturbances ($z \equiv 0$). If the loss function depends on output and inflation variability and there are supply shocks, the optimal policy will depend on the relative weight placed on these two objectives.

To complete the model, we need to specify the information structure. Suppose that i_t must be set before observing e_t, φ_t, or ψ_t but that y_{t-1}, π_{t-1}, and m_{t-1} (and therefore p_{t-1}, z_{t-1}, u_{t-1}, and v_{t-1}) are known when i_t is set. The optimal setting for the policy instrument can be found by solving for the equilibrium inflation rate in terms of the policy instrument, and then evaluating the loss function given by (9.15).

Solving the model is simplified by recognizing that i_t will always be set to ensure that the expected value of inflation equals the target value π^*. Actual inflation will differ from π^* because policy cannot respond to offset the effects of the shocks to aggregate supply, aggregate demand, or money demand, but policy will offset any expected effects of lagged disturbances to ensure that $E_{t-1}\pi_t = E_t\pi_{t+1} = \pi^*$. Using this result, (9.12) can be used to eliminate y_t from (9.13) to yield

$$\pi_t = \frac{(a+\alpha)\pi^* - \alpha i_t + u_t - z_t}{a} \tag{9.16}$$

If the policy maker had full information on u_t and z_t, the optimal policy would be to set the interest rate equal to $i_t^* = \pi^* + \frac{1}{\alpha}(u_t - z_t)$, since this would yield $\pi_t = \pi^*$. If policy must be set prior to observing the realizations of the shocks at time t, the optimal policy can be obtained by taking expectations of (9.16), conditional on time $t - 1$ information, yielding the optimal setting for i_t:

$$\hat{\imath} = \pi^* + \frac{1}{\alpha}(\rho_u u_{t-1} - \rho_z z_{t-1}) \tag{9.17}$$

Substituting (9.17) into (9.16) shows that the actual inflation rate under this policy is equal to[11]

$$\pi_t(\hat{\imath}) = \pi^* + \frac{\varphi_t - e_t}{a} \tag{9.18}$$

and the value of the loss function is equal to

$$V(\hat{\imath}) = \left(\frac{1}{a}\right)^2 (\sigma_\varphi^2 + \sigma_e^2)$$

where σ_x^2 denotes the variance of a random variable x, and, for simplicity, the shocks are assumed to be uncorrelated.

An alternative approach to setting policy in this example would be to derive the money supply consistent with achieving the target inflation π^* and then setting the

---

11. Note that under this policy, $E_{t-1}\pi_t = \pi^*$ as we assumed.

interest rate to achieve this level of m_t. Using (9.14) to eliminate i_t from (9.13),

$$y_t = \frac{\alpha}{\alpha + c}(m_t - \pi_t - p_{t-1} - v_t) + \frac{c}{\alpha + c}(u_t + \alpha \pi^*)$$

Using the aggregate-supply relationship (9.12), the equilibrium inflation rate is

$$\pi_t = \pi^* + \frac{1}{a}\left[\frac{\alpha}{\alpha + c}(m_t - \pi_t - p_{t-1} - v_t) + \frac{c}{\alpha + c}(u_t + \alpha \pi^*) - z_t\right]$$

$$= \frac{[a(\alpha + c) + \alpha c]\pi^* + \alpha(m_t - p_{t-1} - v_t) + cu_t - (\alpha + c)z_t}{a(\alpha + c) + \alpha}$$

The value of m_t consistent with $\pi_t = \pi^*$ is therefore

$$m_t^* = (1 - c)\pi^* + p_{t-1} - \frac{c}{\alpha}u_t + \left(1 + \frac{c}{\alpha}\right)z_t + v_t$$

If the money supply must be set before observing the time-t shocks, the optimal target for m is

$$\hat{m} = (1 - c)\pi^* + p_{t-1} - \frac{c}{\alpha}\rho_u u_{t-1} + \left(1 + \frac{c}{\alpha}\right)\rho_z z_{t-1} + \rho_v v_{t-1} \tag{9.19}$$

As can be easily verified, the interest rate consistent with achieving the targeted money supply $\hat{m}$ is just $\hat{\imath}$ given by (9.17). Thus, an equivalent procedure for deriving the policy that minimizes the loss function is to first calculate the value of the money supply consistent with the target for π and then set i equal to the value that achieves the targeted money supply.

Now suppose the policy maker can observe the actual realization of m_t and respond to it. Under the policy that sets i_t equal to $\hat{\imath}$, equation (9.14) implies that the actual money supply will equal $m_t = \pi_t(\hat{\imath}) + p_{t-1} + y_t(\hat{\imath}) - c\hat{\imath} + v_t$, which can be written as[12]

$$m_t(\hat{\imath}) = \hat{m} - \frac{1}{a}e_t + \left(1 + \frac{1}{a}\right)\varphi_t + \psi_t \tag{9.20}$$

12. Substituting the solution (9.18) into the aggregate supply function (9.12) yields $y(\hat{\imath}_t) = \varphi_t - e_t + z_t = \varphi_t + \rho_z z_{t-1}$. Using this result, together with (9.17) and (9.18) in (9.14),

$$m_t = \pi^* + \frac{\varphi_t - e_t}{a} + p_{t-1} + \varphi_t + \rho_z z_{t-1} - c\hat{\imath} + v_t$$

$$= \pi^* + \frac{\varphi_t - e_t}{a} + p_{t-1} + \varphi_t + \rho_z z_{t-1} - c\left[\pi^* + \frac{\rho_u u_{t-1} - \rho_z z_{t-1}}{\alpha}\right] + v_t$$

Collecting terms and using (9.19) yields (9.20).

Observing how m_t deviates from $\hat{m}$ reveals information about the shocks, and this information can be used to adjust the interest rate to keep inflation closer to target. For example, suppose aggregate-demand shocks (φ) are the only source of uncertainty (i.e., $e \equiv \psi \equiv 0$). A positive aggregate-demand shock ($\varphi > 0$) will, for a given nominal interest rate, increase output and inflation, both of which contribute to an increase in nominal money demand. Under a policy of keeping i fixed, the policy maker automatically allows reserves to increase, allowing m to rise in response to the increased demand for money. Thus, an increase in m_t above $\hat{m}$ would signal that the nominal interest rate should be increased to offset the demand shock. Responding to the money supply to keep m_t equal to the targeted value $\hat{m}$ would achieve the ultimate goal of keeping the inflation rate equal to π^*. This is an example of an intermediate targeting policy; the nominal money supply serves as an intermediate target, and by adjusting policy to achieve the intermediate target, policy is also better able to achieve the target for the goal variable π_t.

Problems arise, however, when there are several potential sources of economic disturbances. Then, it can be the case that the impact on the goal variable of a disturbance would be exacerbated by attempts to keep the intermediate-target variable on target. For example, a positive realization of the money-demand shock ψ_t does not require a change in i_t to maintain inflation on target.[13] But equation (9.20) shows that a positive money-demand shock causes m_t to rise above the target value $\hat{m}$. Under a policy of adjusting i to keep m close to its target, the nominal interest rate would be raised, causing π to deviate from π^*. In this case, responding to keep m on target will not produce the appropriate policy for keeping π on target.

Automatically adjusting the nominal interest rate to ensure that m_t always equals its target $\hat{m}$ requires that the nominal interest rate equal[14]

$$i_t^T = \hat{\imath} + \frac{(1+a)\varphi_t - e_t + a\psi_t}{ac + \alpha(1+a)} \tag{9.21}$$

In this case, inflation is equal to

$$\pi_t(i_t^T) = \pi^* + \left(\frac{1}{a}\right)[-\alpha(i_t^T - \hat{\imath}) + \varphi_t - e_t]$$

$$= \pi^* + \frac{c\varphi_t - (\alpha + c)e_t - \alpha\psi_t}{ac + \alpha(1+a)}$$

13. Equation (9.18) shows that inflation is independent of v_t.

14. Note that this discussion does not assume that the realizations of the individual disturbances can be observed by the policy maker; as long as m is observed, i can be adjusted to ensure $m = \hat{m}$, resulting in i being given by (9.21). Equation (9.21) is obtained by solving (9.12)–(9.14) for m_t as a function of i_t and the various disturbances. Setting this expression equal to $\hat{m}$ yields the required value of i_t^T.

Comparing this expression for inflation to $\pi(\hat{\imath})$ from (9.18), the value obtained when information on the money supply is not used, we can see that the impact of an aggregate-demand shock, φ, on the price level is reduced $\left[\dfrac{c}{ac + \alpha(1 + a)} < \dfrac{1}{a} \right]$; because a positive φ shock tends to raise money demand, the interest rate must be increased to offset the effects on the money supply to keep m on target. This interest-rate increase acts to offset partially the impact of a demand-shock on inflation. The impact of an aggregate-supply shock (e) under an intermediate money-targeting policy is also decreased. However, money-demand shocks, ψ_t, now affect inflation, something they did not do under a policy of keeping i equal to $\hat{\imath}$; a positive ψ_t tends to increase m above target. If i is increased to offset this shock, inflation will fall below target.

The value of the loss function under the intermediate money-targeting procedure is

$$V(i_t^T) = \left[\frac{1}{ac + \alpha(1 + a)} \right]^2 [c^2 \sigma_\varphi^2 + (\alpha + c)^2 \sigma_e^2 + \alpha^2 \sigma_\psi^2]$$

Comparing this to $V(\hat{\imath})$, the improvement from employing an intermediate targeting procedure in which the policy instrument is adjusted to keep the money supply on target will be decreasing in the variance of money-demand shocks, σ_ψ^2. As long as this variance is not too large, the intermediate targeting procedure will do better than a policy of simply keeping the nominal rate equal to $\hat{\imath}$. If this variance is too large, the intermediate targeting procedure will do worse.

An intermediate targeting procedure represents a rule for adjusting the policy instrument to a specific linear combination of the new information contained in movements of the intermediate target. Using (9.20) and (9.21), the policy adjustment can be written as

$$i_t^T - \hat{\imath} = \left[\frac{a}{ac + \alpha(1 + a)} \right] [m_t(\hat{\imath}) - \hat{m}]$$

$$= \mu^T [m_t(\hat{\imath}) - \hat{m}]$$

In other words, if the money supply realized under the initial policy setting $[m_t(\hat{\imath})]$ deviates from its expected level ($\hat{m}$), the policy instrument is adjusted. Because the money supply will deviate from target due to φ and e shocks, which do call for a policy adjustment, as well as ψ shocks, which do not call for any change in policy, an *optimal* adjustment to the new information in money-supply movements would depend on the relative likelihood that movements in m are caused by the various possible shocks. An intermediate targeting rule, by adjusting to deviations of money from target in a manner that does not take into account whether fluctuations in m are more likely to be due to φ or e or ψ shocks, represents an inefficient use of the information in m.

To derive the optimal policy response to fluctuations in the nominal money supply, let

$$i_t - \hat{i} = \mu x_t \tag{9.22}$$

where $x_t = \left(1 + \dfrac{1}{a}\right)\varphi_t - \left(\dfrac{1}{a}\right)e_t + \psi_t$ is the new information obtained from observing m_t.[15] Under an intermediate targeting rule, the monetary authority would adjust its policy instrument to minimize deviations of the intermediate target from the value consistent with achieving the ultimate policy target, in this case, an inflation rate equal to π^*. But under a policy that optimally uses the information in the intermediate-target variable, μ will be chosen to minimize $\mathrm{E}(\pi_t - \pi^*)$, not $\mathrm{E}(m_t - \hat{m})$. Using (9.22) in (9.16), one finds that the value of μ that minimizes the loss function is

$$\mu^* = \frac{1}{\alpha}\left[\frac{a(1+a)\sigma_\varphi^2 + a\sigma_e^2}{(1+a)^2\sigma_\varphi^2 + \sigma_e^2 + a^2\sigma_\psi^2}\right]$$

This is a messy expression, but some intuition for it can be gained by recognizing that, if the policy maker could observe the underlying shocks, equation (9.16) implies that the optimal policy involves setting the nominal interest rate i equal to $\hat{i} + \dfrac{1}{\alpha}(\varphi_t - e_t)$. The policy maker cannot observe φ_t or e_t, but information that can be used to estimate them is available from observing the deviation of money from its

---

15. The expression for x_t can be obtained by using the equation for m_t given in footnote 12. Taking expectations conditional on information available at the start of period t,

$$\mathrm{E}_{t-1}m_t = \pi^* + p_{t-1} + \rho_z z_{t-1} - c\left[\pi^* + \frac{\rho_u u_{t-1} - \rho_z z_{t-1}}{\alpha}\right] + \rho_v v_{t-1}$$

Subtracting this from m_t yields

$$m_t - \mathrm{E}_{t-1}m_t = \left(1 + \frac{1}{a}\right)\varphi_t - \frac{1}{a}e_t + \psi_t$$

target. As already shown, observing m_t provides information on the linear combination of the underlying shocks given by x_t. Letting $E^x[\ ]$ denote expectations conditional on x, the policy instrument should be adjusted according to

$$i(x_t) = \hat{\imath} + \frac{1}{\alpha}(E^x\varphi_t - E^x e_t) \qquad (9.23)$$

Evaluating the expectations in (9.23) gives

$$E^x\varphi_t = \left[\frac{a(1+a)\sigma_\varphi^2}{(1+a)^2\sigma_\varphi^2 + \sigma_e^2 + a^2\sigma_\psi^2}\right]x_t$$

and

$$E^x e_t = \left[\frac{-a\sigma_e^2}{(1+a)^2\sigma_\varphi^2 + \sigma_e^2 + a^2\sigma_\psi^2}\right]x_t$$

Substituting these expressions into (9.23) yields

$$i(z_t) = \hat{\imath} + \frac{1}{\alpha}\left[\frac{a(1+a)\sigma_\varphi^2 + a\sigma_e^2}{(1+a)^2\sigma_\varphi^2 + \sigma_e^2 + a^2\sigma_\psi^2}\right]x_t$$

$$= \hat{\imath} + \mu^* x_t$$

Under this policy, the information in the intermediate target is used optimally. As a result, the loss function is reduced relative to a policy that adjusts i to keep the money supply always equal to its target.

$$V^* \le V(i^T)$$

where V^* is the loss function under the policy that adjusts i according to $\mu^* x_t$.

As long as money-demand shocks are not too large, an intermediate targeting procedure does better than following a policy rule that fails to respond at all to new information. The intermediate targeting rule does worse, however, than a rule that optimally responds to the new information. This point was first made by Kareken, Muench, and Wallace (1973) and B. Friedman (1975).

Despite the general inefficiency of intermediate targeting procedures, central banks often implement policy as if they were following an intermediate targeting procedure, adjusting their policy instrument in order to keep some intermediate target on track. During the 1970s there was strong support in the United States for using money growth as an intermediate target. Support faded in the 1980s when money demand became significantly more difficult to predict.[16] The Bundesbank and the Swiss National Bank continue to formulate policy in terms of money growth rates that can be interpreted as intermediate targets.[17] Other central banks seem to use the nominal exchange rate as an intermediate target. Recently, many central banks have shifted to using inflation itself as an intermediate target.

Intermediate targets do provide a simple framework for responding automatically to economic disturbances. The model of this section can be used to evaluate desirable properties that characterize good intermediate targets. The critical condition in our example is that σ_ψ^2 be small. Since ψ_t represents the innovation or shock to the money-demand equation, intermediate monetary targeting will work best if money demand is relatively predictable. Often this has not been the case. The unpredictability of money demand is an important reason that most central banks moved away from using monetary targeting during the 1980s. The shock ψ can also be interpreted as arising from control errors. For example, if we had assumed that the monetary base was the policy instrument, unpredictable fluctuations in the link between the base and the monetary aggregate being targeted (corresponding to the ω disturbance in [9.7]) would reduce the value of an intermediate targeting procedure. Controllability is therefore a desirable property of an intermediate target.

Lags in the relationship between the policy instrument, the intermediate target, and the final goal variable represent an additional important consideration that we have not dealt with explicitly. The presence of lags introduces no new fundamental issues; as our simple framework shows, targeting an intermediate variable allows policy to respond to new information, either because the intermediate target variable is observed contemporaneously (as in the example) or because it helps to forecast future values of the goal variable. In either case, adjusting policy to achieve the intermediate target forces policy to respond to new information in a manner that is generally suboptimal. But this inefficiency will be smaller if the intermediate target is relatively easily controllable (i.e., σ_ψ^2 is small) yet is highly correlated with the variable of ultimate interest (i.e., σ_φ^2 and σ_e^2 are large) so that a deviation of the intermediate variable from its target provides a clear signal that the goal variable has deviated from its target.

---

16. B. Friedman and Kuttner (1996) examine the behavior of the Fed during the era of monetary targeting.

17. Laubach and Posen (1997) argue the targets are used to signal policy intentions rather than serving as strict intermediate targets.

9.4 Operating Procedures and Policy Measures

Understanding a central bank's operating procedures for implementing policy is important for two reasons. First, it is important in empirical work to distinguish between endogenous responses to developments in the economy and exogenous shifts in policy. But whether movements in a monetary aggregate or a short-term interest rate are predominantly endogenous responses to disturbances unrelated to policy shifts or are exogenous shifts in policy will depend on the nature of the procedures used to implement policy. Thus, some understanding of operating procedures is required for empirical investigations of the impact of monetary policy. We have already seen in Chapter 1 that estimates of the effects of monetary policy can be sensitive to the way policy is measured.

Second, operating procedures, by affecting the automatic adjustment of interest rates and monetary aggregates to economic disturbances, can have implications for the macro equilibrium. For example, operating procedures that lead the monetary authority to smooth interest-rate movements can introduce a unit root into the price level,[18] and in the models examined in Chapters 2 and 3 the economy's response to productivity shocks depended on how the money supply was adjusted (although the effects were small).

Analyses of operating procedures are based on the market for bank reserves. In the United States, this is the federal funds market. While the focus of the discussion is on the United States and the behavior of the Federal Reserve, similar issues arise in the analysis of monetary policy in other countries, although institutional details can vary considerably. Discussions of operating procedures in major OECD countries can be found in Batten et al. (1990), Borio (1997), Morton and Wood (1993), Kasman (1993), and Bernanke and Mishkin (1992).

9.4.1 Money Multipliers

Theoretical models of monetary economies often provide little guidance to how the quantity of money appearing in the theory should be related to empirical measures of the money supply. If "m" is viewed as the quantity of the means of payment used in the conduct of exchange, then cash, demand deposits, and other checkable deposits should be included in the empirical correspondence.[19] If "m" is viewed as a

---

18. See Goodfriend (1987). Interest-rate smoothing is discussed in Chapter 10.

19. Whether these different components of money should simply be added together, as they are in monetary aggregates such as M1 and M2, or whether the components should be weighted to reflect their differing degree of liquidity is a separate issue. Barnett (1980) has argued for the use of divisia indices of monetary aggregates. See also Spindt (1985).

variable set by the policy authority, then an aggregate such as the monetary base, which represents the liabilities of the central bank and so can be directly controlled, would be more appropriate. Most policy discussions focus on broader monetary aggregates, but these are not the direct instruments of monetary policy. A traditional approach to understanding the linkages between a potential instrument such as the monetary base and the various measures of the money supply is to express broader measures of money as the product of the base and a money multiplier. Changes in the money supply can then be decomposed into those resulting from changes in the base and those resulting from changes in the multiplier. The multiplier is developed using definitional relationships, combined with some simple behavioral assumptions.

The *monetary base* is equal to the sum of the reserve holdings of the banking sector and the currency held by the nonbank public.[20] These are liabilities of the central bank that can be affected through open-market operations. By purchasing securities, the central bank can increase the supply of reserves and the base. Securities sales reduce the base.[21] Denoting total reserves by TR and currency by C, the monetary base is given by

$$MB = TR + C$$

In the United States, currency represents close to 90% of the base. Aggregates such as the monetary base and total reserves are of interest because of their close connection to the actual instruments central banks can control and because of their relationship to broader measures of the money supply.

In the United States, the monetary aggregate M1 is equal to currency in the hands of the public plus demand deposits and other checkable deposits. If the deposit component is denoted D and there is a reserve requirement ratio of rr against all such deposits, we can write

$$MB = RR + ER + C = (rr + ex + c)D$$

where total reserves have been divided into required reserves (RR) and excess reserves (ER), and where $ex = ER/D$ is the ratio of excess reserves to deposits that banks choose to hold and $c = C/D$ is the currency-to-deposit ratio. This relationship allows us to write

20. There are two commonly used data series on the U.S. monetary base—one produced by the Board of Governors of the Federal Reserve System and one by the Federal Reserve Bank of St. Louis. The two series treat vault cash and the adjustments for changes in reserve requirements differently.

21. Daily Fed interventions are chiefly designed to smooth temporary fluctuations and are conducted mainly through repurchase and sale-purchase agreements rather than outright purchases or sales.

$$\text{M1} = D + C = (1+c)D = \frac{1+c}{rr + ex + c}MB \qquad (9.24)$$

Equation (9.24) is a very simple example of money-multiplier analysis; a broad monetary aggregate such as M1 is expressed as a multiplier, in this case $\frac{1+c}{rr + ex + c}$, times the monetary base. Changes in the monetary base translate into changes in broader measures of the money supply, given the ratios rr, ex, and c. Of course the ratios rr, ex, and c need not remain constant as MB changes. The ratio ex is determined by bank decisions and the Fed's policies on discount lending, while c is determined by the decisions of the public concerning the level of cash they wish to hold relative to deposits. The usefulness of this money-multiplier framework was illustrated by M. Friedman and Schwartz (1963b), who employed it to organize their study of the causes of changes in the money supply.

In terms of an analysis of the reserve market and operating procedures, the most important of the ratios appearing in (9.24) is ex, the excess reserve ratio. Since reserves earn no interest,[22] banks face an opportunity cost in holding excess reserves. As market rates rise, banks will tend to hold a lower average level of excess reserves. This drop in ex will work to increase M1. This analysis implies that, holding the base constant, fluctuations in market interest rates will induce movements in the money supply.

9.4.2   The Reserve Market

In the United States, the Federal Reserve engages in open-market operations that affect the supply of reserves in the banking system and the federal funds rate, the interest rate banks in need of reserves pay to borrow reserves from banks with surplus reserves. Variations in the total quantity of bank reserves are associated with movements in broader monetary aggregates such as measures of the money supply (M1, M2, etc.). Similarly, movements in the funds rate influence other market interest rates. It is by intervening in the reserve market that the Fed attempts to affect the money supply, market interest rates, and, ultimately, economic activity and inflation.[23] The way reserve market variables (various reserve aggregates and the funds rate) respond to disturbances depends on the operating procedure being followed by the Fed. One objective in developing a model of the reserve market is to

22. This statement is not true of all countries. For example, in New Zealand, reserves earn an interest rate set 300 basis points below the 7-day market rate.

23. In the United States, the development of the modern reserves market dates from the mid-1960s. See Meulendyke (1989).

disentangle movements in reserves and the funds rate that are due to nonpolicy sources from those caused by exogenous policy actions.

Models of the reserve market generally have a very simple structure; reserve demand and reserve supply interact to determine the funds rate. Reserve demand arises primarily from the requirement that banks hold reserves equal to a specified fraction of their deposit liabilities; consequently, variations in the public's demand for bank liabilities will alter the banking sector's demand for reserves.

In the United States, banks are required to maintain an average reserve level equal to a fraction of their deposit liabilities, where the fraction is set by the Federal Reserve.[24] These *required reserves* represent the bulk of reserve holdings, but the banking system does hold, on average, a level of reserves slightly greater than its level of required reserves. These *excess reserves* holdings are needed to meet the daily unpredictable net inflow or outflow of funds that each individual bank faces.[25] Excess reserves, when added to required reserves, yield total reserve holdings. To give some sense of the magnitudes involved, in December 1997, seasonally adjusted total reserves of U.S. depository institutions averaged $47.2 billion, of which $45.5 billion were required reserves. By way of contrast, M1 averaged $1.1 trillion in December 1997 and M2 averaged $4 trillion. An economic expansion that increases the demand for money on the part of the public will lead to an increase in the banking sector's demand for reserves as required reserves rise with the growth of deposits.

The demand for reserves will also depend on the costs of reserves and any factors that influence money demand—aggregate income, for example. In order to focus on the very short-run determination of reserve aggregates and the funds rate, factors such as aggregate income and prices are simply treated as part of the error term in the total reserve demand relationship, allowing us to write

$$TR^d = -ai^f + v^d \qquad (9.25)$$

where TR^d represents total reserve demand, i^f is the funds rate, and v^d is a demand disturbance. This disturbance will reflect variations in income or other factors that produce fluctuations in deposit demand. One interpretation of (9.25) is that it represents a relationship between the innovations in total reserve demand and the funds

---

24. The actual precedure in the United States involves maintaining an average reserve level over a two-week maintainence period based on the average level of deposit balances two weeks earlier. For a recent discussion of these points, see Hamilton (1996).

25. Models of excess reserve holdings are generally based on inventory-theoretic models. Banks hold an inventory of reserves to balance stochastic payment flows. There is a cost associated with holding excess reserve balances that are too large (reserves don't pay interest) and with holding balances that are too low (the cost of borrowing reserves to offset a deficit position).

rate after the lagged effects of all other factors have been removed. For example, Bernanke and Mihov (1996) attempt to identify policy shocks by focusing on the relationships among the innovations to reserve demand, reserve supply, and the funds rate obtained as the residuals from a VAR model of reserve-market variables. They characterize alternative operating procedures in terms of the parameters linking these innovations.[26]

The total supply of reserves held by the banking system can be expressed as equal to the quantity of reserves that banks have borrowed from the Federal Reserve System plus nonborrowed reserves:

$$TR_t^s = BR_t + NBR_t$$

The Federal Reserve can control the stock of nonborrowed reserves through open-market operations; by buying or selling government securities, the Fed affects the stock of nonborrowed reserves. For example, a purchase of government debt by the Fed raises the stock of nonborrowed reserves when the Fed pays for its purchase by crediting the reserve account of the seller's bank with the amount of the purchase. Open-market sales of government debt by the Fed reduce the stock of nonborrowed reserves. So the Fed can, even over relatively short time horizons, exercise close control over the stock of nonborrowed reserves.

The stock of borrowed reserves depends on the behavior of private banks and on their decisions about borrowing from the Fed (borrowing from the discount window). Bank demand for borrowed reserves will depend on the opportunity cost of borrowing from the Fed (the discount rate) and the cost of borrowing reserves in the federal funds market (the federal funds rate). An increase in the funds rate relative to the discount rate makes borrowing from the Fed more attractive and leads to an increase in bank borrowing. The elasticity of borrowing with respect to the spread between the funds rate and the discount rate will depend on the Fed's management of the discount window. By using nonprice methods to ration bank borrowing, the Fed affects the degree to which banks turn to the discount window to borrow as the incentive to do so, the spread between the funds rate and the discount rate, widens. Banks must weight the benefits of borrowing reserves in a particular week against the possible cost in terms of reduced future access to the discount window. Banks will reduce their current borrowing if they expect the funds rate to be higher in the future because they will prefer to preserve their future access to the discount window,

26. Kasa and Popper (1995) employ a similar approach to study monetary policy in Japan. Leeper, Sims, and Zha (1996) develop a more general formulation of the links between reserve-market variables in an identified VAR framework.

timing their borrowing for periods when the funds rate is high. Therefore, borrowing decisions will depend on the expected future funds rate as well as the current funds rate:

$$BR_t = b_1(i_t^f - i_t^d) - b_2 E_t[i_{t+1}^f - i_{t+1}^d] + v_t^b \tag{9.26}$$

where i^d is the discount rate (a policy variable) and v^b is a borrowing disturbance.

The simplest versions of a reserve-market model often postulate a borrowing function of the form

$$BR_t = b(i_t^f - i_t^d) + v_t^b \tag{9.27}$$

The manner in which an innovation in the funds rate affects borrowings, given by the coefficient b in (9.27), will vary depending on how such a funds-rate innovation affects expectations of future funds rate levels. Suppose, for example, that borrowings are actually given by equation (9.26) and that policy results in the funds rate following the process: $i_t^f = \rho i_{t-1}^f + \xi_t$. Then $E_t i_{t+1}^f = \rho i_t^f$ and, from (9.26), $BR_t = b i_t^f$ where $b = b_1 - \rho b_2$.[27] A change in operating procedures that leads the funds rate to be more highly serially correlated (increases ρ) will reduce the response of borrowings to the funds-rate–discount-rate spread.[28] While relationships such as (9.27) can help us to understand the linkages that affect the correlations among reserve-market variables for a given operating procedure, we should not expect the parameter values to remain constant across operating procedures.

To complete the reserve-market model, we need to specify the Fed's behavior in setting nonborrowed reserves. To consider a variety of different operating procedures, assume the Fed can respond contemporaneously to the various disturbances to the reserve market, so that nonborrowed reserves are given by

$$NBR_t = \phi^d v_t^d + \phi^b v_t^b + v_t^s \tag{9.28}$$

where v^s is a "monetary policy shock." Different operating procedures will be characterized by alternative values of the parameters ϕ^d and ϕ^b.[29]

27. For simplicity, this discussion ignores the discount rate i^d for the moment.

28. Goodfriend (1983) provides a formal model of borrowed reserves; see also Waller (1990). For a discussion of how alternative operating procedures affect the the relationship between the funds rate and reserve aggregates, see Walsh (1982b). Recent attempts to estimate the borrowings function can be found in Peristiani (1991) and Pearce (1993).

29. Note that ϕ^d and ϕ^b correspond to ϕ in equation (1.9), since they reflect the impact of nonpolicy-originating disturbances on the policy variable NBR.

Equilibrium in the reserve market requires that total reserve demand equal total reserve supply. This condition is stated as

$$TR^d = BR + NBR \tag{9.29}$$

If a month is the unit of observation, reserve-market disturbances are likely to have no contemporaneous effect on real output or the aggregate price level.[30] Using this identifying restriction, Bernanke and Mihov (1996) obtained estimates of the innovations to TR, BR, i^f, and NBR from a VAR system that also included GDP, the GDP deflator, and an index of commodity prices but in which the reserve market variables are ordered last.[31] Whether any of these VAR residuals can be interpreted directly as a measure of the policy shock v^s will depend on the particular operating procedure being used. For example, if $\phi^d = \phi^b = 0$, equation (9.28) implies that $NBR = v^s$; this corresponds to a situation in which the Fed does not allow non-borrowed reserves to be affected by disturbances to total reserve demand or to borrowed reserves, so the innovation to nonborrowed reserves can be interpreted directly as a policy shock. Under such an operating procedure, using nonborrowed reserve innovations (i.e., NBR) as the measure of monetary policy as Christiano and Eichenbaum (1992a) do, is correct. However, if either ϕ^d or ϕ^b differs from zero, NBR will reflect nonpolicy shocks as well as policy shocks.

Substituting (9.25), (9.27), and (9.28) into the equilibrium condition (9.29) and solving for the innovation in the funds rate yields

$$i^f = \frac{b}{a+b}i^d - \frac{1}{a+b}[v^s + (1+\phi^b)v^b - (1-\phi^d)v^d] \tag{9.30}$$

The reduced-form expressions for the innovations to borrowed and total reserves are then found to be

$$BR = -\frac{ab}{a+b}i^d - \frac{1}{a+b}[bv^s - (a-b\phi^b)v^b - b(1-\phi^d)v^d] \tag{9.31}$$

30. Referring back to the discussion in section 1.3.4, this corresponds to the assumption that $\theta = 0$ used to identify VAR innovations.

31. The commodity price index is included to eliminate the price puzzle discussed in Chapter 1. This creates a potential problem for Bernanke and Mihov's identification scheme, since forward-looking variables such as asset prices, interest rates, and commodity prices may respond immediately to policy shocks. See the discussion of this issue in Leeper, Sims, and Zha (1996), who distinguish between policy, banking-sector, production, and information variables.

$$TR = -\frac{ab}{a+b}i^d + \frac{1}{a+b}[av^s + a(1+\phi^b)v^b + (b+a\phi^d)v^d] \tag{9.32}$$

How does the Fed's operating procedure affect the interpretation of movements in nonborrowed reserves, borrowed reserves, and the fed funds rate as measures of monetary policy shocks? Under a federal-funds-rate operating procedure, the Fed offsets total reserve demand and borrowing demand disturbances so that they do not affect the funds rate. According to (9.30), this policy requires that $\phi^b = -1$ and $\phi^d = 1$. In other words, a shock to borrowed reserves leads to an equal but opposite movement in nonborrowed reserves to keep the funds rate (and total reserves) unchanged (see 9.32), while a shock to total reserve demand leads to an equal change in reserve supply through the adjustment of nonborrowed reserves. The innovation in nonborrowed reserves is equal to $v^s - v^b + v^d$ and so does not reflect solely exogenous policy shocks.

Under a nonborrowed-reserves procedure, $\phi^b = 0$ and $\phi^d = 0$ as innovations to nonborrowed reserves reflect only policy shocks. In this case, (9.30) becomes

$$i^f = \frac{b}{a+b}i^d - \frac{1}{a+b}(v^s + v^b - v^d) \tag{9.33}$$

so innovations in the funds rate reflect both policy changes and disturbances to reserve demand and the demand for borrowed reserves. In fact, if v^d arises from shocks to money demand that lead to increases in measured monetary aggregates, innovations to the funds rate can be positively correlated with innovations to broader monetary aggregates. Positive innovations in an aggregate such as M1 would then appear to increase the funds rate, a phenomena consistent with the VAR evidence of Eichenbaum (1992) that was discussed in Chapter 1.

From (9.31), a borrowed-reserves policy corresponds to $\phi^d = 1$ and $\phi^b = a/b$, since adjusting nonborrowed reserves in this manner insulates borrowed reserves from nonpolicy shocks. That is, nonborrowed reserves are fully adjusted to accommodate fluctuations in total reserve demand. Under a borrowed reserves procedure, innovations to the funds rate are, from (9.30),

$$i^f = \frac{b}{a+b}i^d - \frac{1}{a+b}\left[v^s + \left(1+\frac{a}{b}\right)v^b\right]$$

so the funds rate reflects both policy and borrowing disturbances.

Table 9.1 summarizes the values of ϕ^d and ϕ^b that correspond to different operating procedures.

Table 9.1
Parameters under Alternative Operating Procedures

| | Operating Procedure | | | |
	Funds Rate	Nonborrowed	Borrowed	Total
ϕ^d	1	0	1	$-\dfrac{b}{a}$
ϕ^b	-1	0	$\dfrac{a}{b}$	-1

In general, the innovations in the observed variables can be written (ignoring discount-rate innovations) as

$$\begin{bmatrix} i^f \\ BR \\ NBR \end{bmatrix} \equiv u = \begin{bmatrix} -\dfrac{1}{a+b} & -\dfrac{(1+\phi^b)}{a+b} & \dfrac{1-\phi^d}{a+b} \\ -\dfrac{b}{a+b} & \dfrac{a-b\phi^b}{a+b} & \dfrac{b(1-\phi^d)}{a+b} \\ 1 & \phi^b & \phi^d \end{bmatrix} \begin{bmatrix} v^s \\ v^b \\ v^d \end{bmatrix} \equiv \mathbf{A}v \qquad (9.34)$$

By inverting the matrix $\mathbf{A}$, we can solve for the underlying shocks, the vector v, in terms of the observed innovations $u : v = \mathbf{A}^{-1}u$. This operation produces

$$\begin{bmatrix} v^s \\ v^b \\ v^d \end{bmatrix} = \begin{bmatrix} b\phi^b - a\phi^d & -(\phi^d + \phi^b) & 1 - \phi^d \\ -b & 1 & 0 \\ a & 1 & 1 \end{bmatrix} \begin{bmatrix} i^f \\ BR \\ NBR \end{bmatrix}$$

Hence,

$$v^s = (b\phi^b - a\phi^d)i^f - (\phi^d + \phi^b)BR + (1 - \phi^d)NBR \qquad (9.35)$$

so that the policy shock can be recovered as a specific linear combination of the innovations to the funds rate, borrowed reserves, and nonborrowed reserves. From the parameter values in Table 9.1, we have the following relationship between the policy shock and the VAR residuals:

$$\text{Funds-rate procedure: } v^s = -(b+a)i^f$$

$$\text{Nonborrowed-reserves procedure: } v^s = NBR$$

$$\text{Borrowed-reserves procedure: } v^s = -\left(1 + \frac{a}{b}\right)BR$$

$$\text{Total-reserves procedure: } v^s = \left(1 + \frac{b}{a}\right)TR$$

Policy shocks cannot generally be identified with innovations in any one of the reserve-market variables. Only for specific values of the parameters ϕ^d and ϕ^b, that is, for specific operating procedures, might the policy shock be recoverable from the innovation to just a single one of the reserve-market variables.

9.4.3   Reserve-Market Responses

This section will use the basic reserve-market model to discuss how various disturbances affect reserve quantities and the funds rate under alternative operating procedures. Figure 9.1 illustrates reserve-market equilibrium between total reserve demand and supply. For values of the funds rate less than the discount rate reserve supply is vertical and equal to nonborrowed reserves. With the discount rate serving as a penalty rate, borrowed reserves fall to zero in this range so that total reserve supply is just *NBR*. As the funds rate increases above the discount rate, borrowings become positive (see 9.27) and the total supply of reserves increases. Total reserve demand is decreasing in the funds rate according to (9.25).

Consider first a positive realization of the policy shock v^s. The effects on i^f, *BR*, and *NBR* can be found from the first column of the matrix **A** in equation (9.34). The policy shock increases nonborrowed reserves (we could think of it as initiating an

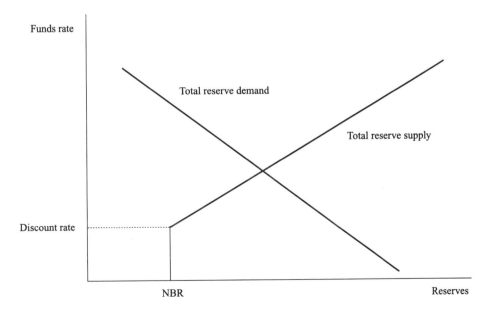

Figure 9.1
The Reserves Market

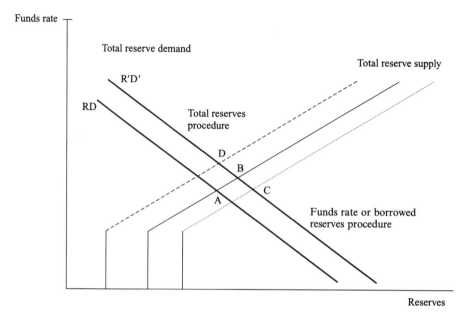

Figure 9.2
The Reserves Market Response to a Reserve Demand Increase

open-market purchase that increases banking-sector reserve assets). In Figure 9.1, the reserve supply curve shifts to the right horizontally by the amount of the increase in *NBR*. Given the borrowed-reserves and total-reserve-demand functions, this increase in reserve supply causes the funds rate to fall. Bank borrowing from the Fed decreases because the relative cost of borrowed reserves $(i^d - i^f)$ has risen, partially offsetting some of the increase in total reserve supply.[32] A policy shock is associated with an increase in total reserves, a fall in the funds rate, and a fall in borrowed reserves.

It is the response to nonpolicy disturbances that will differ depending on the operating procedures (see the second and third columns of **A**; the elements of these columns depend on the ϕ^j parameters). Suppose there is a positive disturbance to total reserve demand, $v^d > 0$. This shifts total reserve demand to the right from RD to R'D' as shown in Figure 9.2. In the absence of any policy response (i.e., if $\phi^d = 0$), the funds rate increases (shown as the move from point **A** to **B** in Figure 9.2). This

---

32. This analysis assumes that the discount rate has not changed; the Fed could, for example, change the discount rate to keep $i^f - i^d$ constant and keep borrowed reserves unchanged. Since the total supply of reserves has increased, the funds rate must fall, so this would require a cut in the discount rate.

increase tends to reduce total reserve demand (if $a > 0$), offsetting to some degree the initial increase in reserve demand. The rise in the funds rate induces an increase in reserve supply as banks increase their borrowing from the Fed. Under a funds-rate operating procedure, however, $\phi^d = 1$; the Fed lets nonborrowed reserves rise by the full amount of the rise in reserve demand to prevent the funds rate from rising. Both reserve demand and reserve supply shift to the right by the amount of the disturbance to reserve demand, and the new equilibrium is at point C. Thus, total reserve-demand shocks are completely accommodated under a funds-rate procedure. If the positive reserve-demand shock originated from an increase in the demand for bank deposits as a result of an economic expansion, a funds-rate procedure automatically accommodates the increase in money demand and has the potential to produce procyclical movements of money and output.[33]

In contrast, under a total-reserves operating procedure, the Fed would adjust nonborrowed reserves to prevent v^d from affecting total reserves. From equation (9.32), this requires that $\phi^d = -b/a$; nonborrowed reserves must be reduced in response to a positive realization of v^d. It is not sufficient to just hold nonborrowed reserves constant; the rise in the funds rate caused by the rise in total reserve demand will induce an endogenous rise in reserve supply as banks increase their borrowing from the Fed. To offset this, nonborrowed reserves are reduced. Equilibrium under a total-reserves procedure is at point D in Figure 9.2. Thus, while a funds-rate procedure offsets none of the impact of a reserve-demand shock on total reserves, a total-reserves procedure offsets all of it.

Under a nonborrowed-reserves procedure, $\phi^d = 0$; hence, a positive shock to reserve demand raises the funds rate and borrowed reserves. Total reserves rise by

$$-ai^f + v^d = \frac{b}{a+b} v^d < v^d.$$ So reserves do rise (in contrast to the case under a total-reserves procedure) but by less than under a funds-rate procedure.

Finally, under a borrowed-reserves procedure, a positive shock to total reserve demand will, by increasing the funds rate, also tend to increase bank borrowing. To hold borrowed reserves constant, the Fed must prevent the funds rate from rising (i.e., it must keep $i^f = 0$; see equation 9.27). This objective requires letting nonborrowed reserves rise. So in the face of shocks to total reserve demand, a funds-rate operating procedure and a borrowed-reserves procedure lead to the same response. In terms of Figure 9.2, both a funds-rate procedure and a borrowed-reserves

---

33. Since we have defined operating procedures in terms of the innovations to reserves and the funds rate, we have not said anything about the extent to which the funds rate might be adjusted in subsequent periods to offset output-induced movements in reserve demand.

Table 9.2
Response to a Positive Reserve-Demand Shock

	Operating Procedure			
	FF	BR	NBR	TR
Funds rate	0	0	+	+
Total reserves	+	+	+	0
Nonborrowed reserves	+	+	0	−
Borrowed reserves	0	0	+	+

Table 9.3
Response to a Positive Shock to Borrowed Reserves

	Operating Procedure			
	FF	BR	NBR	TR
Funds rate	0	−	−	0
Total reserves	0	+	+	0
Nonborrowed reserves	−	+	0	−
Borrowed reserves	+	0	+	+

procedure result in a new equilibrium at point C. As equation (9.33) shows, however, a borrowed-reserves operating procedure is an inefficient procedure for controlling the funds rate in that it allows disturbances to the borrowings function (i.e., v^b shocks) to affect the funds rate. These results are summarized in Table 9.2.

Now suppose there is a positive shock to bank borrowing; $v^b > 0$. The increase in borrowed reserves, by increasing total reserves, will lower the funds rate. Under a funds-rate procedure, the Fed prevents this outcome by reducing nonborrowed reserves ($\phi^b = -1$) to fully neutralize the effect of v^b on total reserve supply. The same response would occur under a total-reserves operating procedure. In contrast, under a nonborrowed-reserves procedure, $\phi^b = 0$, so the increase in borrowed reserves also increases total reserve supply and the funds rate must decline to clear the reserve market. These results are summarized in Table 9.3

While the focus has been on the reserve market, it is important to keep in mind that the purpose of reserve-market intervention by the Fed is not to affect the funds rate or reserve measures themselves. The Fed's objective is to influence its policy-goal variables such as the rate of inflation. The simple money-multiplier framework that was discussed earlier provides a link between the reserve market and other factors affecting the supply of money. The observed quantities of the broader monetary aggregates then reflect the interaction of the supply and demand for money.

Movements in the funds rate are linked to longer-term interest rates through the term structure, a topic discussed in Chapter 10.

9.4.4 A Brief History of Fed Operating Procedures

The model of the reserve market provides a very simple framework for analyzing how observable variables such as the funds rate and reserve aggregates respond to disturbances under alternative operating procedures. In the United States, the operating procedure employed by the Fed has changed over time. This fact, in turn, implies that the manner in which the reserve market has responded to disturbances has varied and that the appropriate measure of policy shocks has also changed.

Fed operating procedures have been discussed by various authors,[34] and major studies of operating procedures have been undertaken by the Federal Reserve (Federal Reserve 1981; Goodfriend and Small 1993). Over the last 20 years in the United States, most monetary economists have identified three different regimes, each defined according to the basic operating procedure the Fed followed. These correspond to periods of funds-rate, nonborrowed-reserves, and borrowed-reserves operating procedures, although in no case did the Fed's behavior reflect pure examples of any one type.[35]

9.4.4.1 1972–1979 The first period dates from the end of the Bretton Woods exchange-rate system in the early 1970s to October 6, 1979. The Fed is usually described as having followed a federal-funds-rate operating procedure during this period. Under such a policy, the Fed allowed nonborrowed reserves to adjust automatically to stabilize the funds rate within a narrow band around its target level.[36] Thus, a shock to total reserve demand that, in the absence of a policy response, would have led to an increase in both the funds rate and borrowed reserves, was offset by open-market purchases that expanded nonborrowed reserves sufficiently to prevent the funds rate from rising (i.e., $\phi^d = 1$). As a result, expansions in reserve demand were fully accommodated by increases in reserve supply.[37]

---

34. Examples include Meulendyke (1989), Walsh (1990), Goodfriend (1991, 1993), Strongin (1995), and the references they cite.

35. Since 1975 the Fed has also announced targets for various monetary aggregates, and these played a role as intermediate targets during some periods; see B. Friedman and Kuttner (1996).

36. Data on the Fed's funds rate target from September 1974 to August 1995 can be found in Table A1 of Roley and Sellon (1996).

37. While the discussion here focuses on reserve-market adjustments, changes in the funds-rate target then lead to changes in market interest rates. For evidence, see Cook and Hahn (1989), Rudebusch (1995), or Roley and Sellon (1996). International evidence on the response of market interest rates to changes in the short-run interest rate used to implement policy can be found in Buttiglione, Del Giovane, and Tristani (1996).

A funds-rate operating procedure only implies that shocks to the funds rate are offset initially; the targeted funds rate could, in principle, respond strongly beginning in "period $t + 1$." However, the funds-rate operating procedure came under intense criticism during the 1970s because of the Fed's tendency to stabilize interest rates for longer periods of time. Such interest-rate-smoothing behavior can have important implications for price-level behavior (see Chapter 10). Because a rise in the price level will increase the nominal demand for bank deposits as private agents attempt to maintain their real money holdings, periods of inflation will lead to increases in the nominal demand for bank reserves. If the central bank holds nonborrowed reserves fixed, the rising demand for reserves pushes up interest rates, thereby moderating the rise in money demand and real economic activity. If the central bank instead attempts to prevent interest rates from rising, it must allow the reserve supply to expand to accommodate the rising demand for reserves. Thus, interest-rate-stabilizing policies can automatically accommodate increases in the price level, contributing to ongoing inflation. Under some circumstances, an interest-rate policy can even render the price level indeterminate; an arbitrary change in the price level produces a proportionate change in nominal money demand, which the central bank automatically accommodates to keep interest rates from changing.[38] Since market interest rates incorporate a premium for expected inflation, an increase in expected inflation would, under a policy of stabilizing market interest rates, also be automatically accommodated.

Recall from our reserve-market model that under a funds-rate procedure, non-borrowed reserves are automatically adjusted to offset the impact on the funds rate of shocks to total reserve demand and to borrowed reserves. In terms of the model parameters, this adjustment required that $\phi^d = 1$ and $\phi^b = -1$. Bernanke and Mihov (1996), using both monthly and biweekly data, report that these restrictions are not rejected for the period 1972:11 to 1979:09.[39] Thus, innovations in the funds rate provide an appropriate measure of monetary policy during this period.

9.4.4.2 1979–1982 In October 1979, as part of a policy shift to lower inflation, the Fed moved to a nonborrowed-reserves operating procedure. An operating procedure that focused on a reserve quantity was viewed as more consistent with reducing money growth rates to bring down inflation.

The Fed had, in fact, begun announcing target growth rates for several monetary aggregates in 1975. Under the Humphrey-Hawkins Act, the Fed was required to

---

38. The compatibility of interest rate rules for monetary policy and price-level determinacy will be discussed in detail in Chapter 10.

39. See the test statistics reported for 1972:11–1979:09 in their Tables 1 and 2.

establish monetary targets and report these to Congress.[40] Because growth-rate target ranges were set for several measures of the money supply (there were targets for M1, M2, M3, and debt), the extent to which these targets actually influenced policy was never clear. The move to a nonborrowed-reserves operating procedure was thought by many economists to provide a closer link between the policy instrument (nonborrowed reserves) and the intermediate target of policy (the monetary growth targets). B. Friedman and Kuttner (1996) provide an evaluation of the actual effects of these targets on the conduct of policy.

Under a nonborrowed-reserves procedure, an increase in expected inflation would no longer automatically lead to an accommodative increase in bank reserves. Instead, interest rates would be allowed to rise, reducing nominal asset demand and restraining money growth. Similarly, if money growth rose above the Fed's target growth rate, reserve demand would rise, pushing up the funds rate. The resulting rise in the funds rate would tend automatically to reduce money demand.

Whether the Fed actually followed a nonborrowed-reserves procedure after October 1979 has often been questioned. Figure 9.3 plots the federal funds rate from 1965 to 1995, demarcating October 1979 by the first vertical line. The funds rate was clearly both higher and more volatile after the switch in policy procedures than before.[41] Many commentators felt that the policy shift in late 1979 was designed to allow the Fed to increase interest rates substantially while reducing the political pressures on the Fed to prevent rates from rising. Under the former funds-rate procedure, changes in short-term interest rates were (correctly) perceived as reflecting Fed decisions. By adopting a nonborrowed-reserves operating procedure and focusing more on achieving its targeted growth rates for the money supply, the Fed could argue that the high interest rates were due to market forces and not Fed policy. Cook (1989) estimates, however, that fully two-thirds of all funds-rate changes during this period were the result of "judgmental" Fed actions; only one-third represented automatic responses to nonpolicy disturbances.

The 1979–1982 period was characterized by increased attention by the Fed to its monetary targets. In principle, nonborrowed reserves were adjusted to achieve a

40. The targets for M1 for the period 1975–1986 and for M2 and M3 for the period 1975–1991 are reported in Bernanke and Mishkin (1992, Table 1, pp. 190–191). Preliminary targets for the following calendar year were set each July and confirmed in January. Discussions of the targets can be found in the various issues of the Federal Reserve's "Monetary Report to Congress." The Fed stopped setting growth-rate targets for M1 after 1986 because of the apparent breakdown in the relationship between M1 and nominal income.

41. Much of the increased volatility in early 1980 was caused by the imposition and then removal of credit controls.

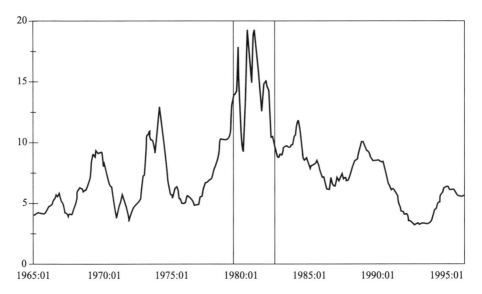

Figure 9.3
Federal Funds Rate, 1965–1995

targeted growth rate for the money stock. If the money stock was growing faster than desired, the nonborrowed reserve target would be adjusted downward to place upward pressure on the funds rate. This in turn would reduce money demand and tend to bring the money stock back on target. As a result, market interest rates responded sharply to each week's new information on the money supply. If the money supply exceeded the market's expectation, market interest rates rose in anticipation of future policy tightening (Roley and Walsh 1985 and the references listed there).

The actual practice under the nonborrowed-reserves procedure was complicated by several factors. First, the Fed established and announced targets for several different definitions of the money stock.[42] This policy reduced the transparency of the procedure, since often one monetary aggregate might be above its target while another would be below, making the appropriate adjustment to the nonborrowed-reserves path unclear. Second, because of the system of lagged reserve accounting

42. The Fed established target cones for each aggregate. For example, the target cone for M1 set in January 1980 was 4.0% to 6.5% from a base of the actual level of M1 in the fourth quarter of 1979. The use of actual levels as the base for new target cones resulted in base drift; past target misses were automatically incorporated into the new base. See Broaddus and Goodfriend (1984). For a discussion of the optimal degree of base drift, see Walsh (1986).

then in effect, required reserves were predetermined each week. The level of reserves a bank was required to hold during week t was based on its average deposit liabilities during week $t - 2$. With reserve demand essentially predetermined each week, variations in the funds rate had little contemporaneous effect on reserve demand. Changes in reserve supply would require large swings in the funds rate to equilibrate the reserve market. A rise in interest rates had no immediate effect on the banking sector's reserve demand, leading to a delay in the impact of a policy tightening on money growth. This system was criticized as reducing the ability of the Fed to control the growth rate of the monetary aggregates. See McCallum and Hoehn (1983).[43]

Referring back to our earlier reserve market model, with $\phi^d = \phi^b = 0$ under a nonborrowed-reserves operating procedure, (9.30) implies that

$$i^f_{NBR} = \frac{b}{a+b}i^d - \frac{1}{a+b}(v^s + v^b - v^d) \qquad (9.36)$$

so that, ignoring discount-rate changes, the variance of funds-rate innovations rises from $\sigma_s^2/(a+b)^2$ under a pure funds-rate operating procedure to $(\sigma_s^2 + \sigma_d^2 + \sigma_b^2)/(a+b)^2$ under a pure nonborowed-reserves operating procedure, where σ_i^2 is the variance of v^i for $i = s, d, b$. The variance of funds-rate innovations is decreasing in a, and with lagged reserve accounting, $a = 0$, further increasing the variance of the funds rate. Changes in reserve supply would require large swings in the funds rate to equilibrate the reserve market.

In practice, it was argued that the Fed actually set its nonborrowed-reserves target so as to achieve the level of the funds rate it desired. That is, the Fed started with a desired path for the money stock; since equilibrium required that money demand equal money supply, it used an estimated money-demand function to determine the level of the funds rate consistent with the targeted level of money demand. Then, based on total reserve demand (predetermined under lagged reserve accounting) and an estimated borrowed reserve function, it determined the level of nonborrowed reserves required to achieve the desired funds rate. A nonborrowed-reserves operating procedure designed to achieve a desired funds rate is simply an inefficient funds-rate procedure. However, by shifting the focus of policy away from a concern for stabilizing interest rates, the 1979 policy shift did reflect a substantive policy shift consistent with reducing the rate of inflation.

Using biweekly data for the period October 1979 to October 1982, Bernanke and Mihov (1996) report estimates of ϕ^d and ϕ^b; neither estimate is statistically

---

43. Lagged reserve accounting was replaced by the current system of contemporaneous reserve accounting in 1984. See Hamilton (1996) for a detailed discussion of the reserve accounting system.

significantly different from zero. These estimates are consistent, then, with the actual use of a nonborrowed-reserves operating procedure during this period.

Key to a nonborrowed-reserves operating procedure is the need to predict the relationship between changes in nonborrowed reserves and the resulting impact on broader monetary aggregates, inflation, and real economic activity. During the late 1970s and early 1980s, there seemed to be a fairly stable relationship between monetary aggregates such as M1 and nominal income. This relationship could be used to work backward from a desired path of nominal income growth to a growth path for M1 to a growth path for nonborrowed reserves. Unfortunately, this relationship appeared to break down in the early and mid-1980s (see, for example, B. Friedman and Kuttner 1996). In the absence of a reliable link between reserve measures and nominal income, the Fed eventually moved away from a nonborrowed-reserves operating procedure.

9.4.4.3 1982– Since 1982, the Fed has generally followed a borrowed-reserves operating procedure. As noted earlier, such a procedure is, in practice, similar to a funds-rate operating procedure, at least in the face of reserve demand shocks (see Table 9.2). The basic Poole analysis implied that an interest-rate-oriented operating procedure will tend to dominate a monetary-aggregates-oriented one as the variance of money-demand shocks rises relative to aggregate-demand shocks. B. Friedman and Kuttner (1996) provide a plot of the ratio of the variance of money-demand shocks to the variance of aggregate-demand shocks, based on an estimated VAR. The plot shows this ratio reaching a minimum during 1981 and then steadily increasing. The shift back to an interest-rate operating procedure after 1982 is consistent with the normative recommendations of Poole's model. The second vertical line in Figure 9.3 marks the shift away from the previous nonborrowed-reserves procedure.

From our earlier discussion, a borrowed-reserves operating procedure implies values of 1 and a/b for ϕ^d and ϕ^b. Bernanke and Mihov obtain point estimates for ϕ^d and ϕ^b for February 1984–October 1988 that are more consistent with a funds-rate procedure ($\phi^d = 1$; $\phi^b = -1$) than with a borrowed-reserves procedure. However, for biweekly data during the post-1988 period, Bernanke and Mihov find estimates consistent with a borrowed-reserves procedure with $a = 0$. This last parameter restriction is in agreement with the characterization of policy provided by Strongin (1995).

Cosimano and Sheehan (1994) estimate a biweekly reserve-market model using data from 1984 to 1990. Their results are consistent with a borrowed-reserves procedure over this period and not with a funds-rate procedure, although they note that actual policy under this procedure was similar to what would occur under a funds-rate procedure. The evidence also suggests that the Fed's behavior since the October 1987 stock market crash has moved more toward a funds-rate procedure.

While we have followed Bernanke and Mihov in using ϕ^d and ϕ^b to characterize different operating procedures, the parameters a and b in the total reserves demand (9.25) and the borrowed reserves (9.27) relationships may also vary under different operating procedures. Figures 9.4a–c and 9.5a–c plot total reserves versus the funds rate and borrowed reserves versus the spread between the funds rate and the discount rate, respectively.[44] Observations for the periods of funds-rate, nonborrowed-reserves, and borrowed-reserves operating procedures are distinguished. While the figures show reserve levels, not the innovations in terms of which the model was specified, Figure 9.4 suggests that Strongin's assumption of $a = 0$ appears reasonable for the pre-1982 period (i.e., under the funds-rate and nonborrowed-reserve procedures) but not under the post-1982 borrowed-reserve procedure.

Figures 9.5a–c reveal that the negative relationship between borrowed reserves and the funds-rate–discount-rate spread has a flatter slope (a smaller b) in the post-1982 period (Figure 9.5c). Models of bank borrowing from the discount window (e.g., Goodfriend 1983) imply that the slope of the borrowings function should depend on the operating procedure being employed.[45] Evidence supporting this hypothesis is reported by Pearce (1993). As noted in section 9.4.2, the coefficient b should depend on the time-series process that characterizes the funds rate. If changes in the funds rate are very persistent, b will tend to be smaller than under a procedure that leads to more transitory changes in the funds rate.

9.4.5   Other Countries

The preceding discussion focused on the United States. If measuring monetary policy requires an understanding of operating procedures, then the appropriate measure of policy in the United States will not necessarily be appropriate for other countries. Operating procedures generally depend on the specific institutional structure of a country's financial sector, and the means used to implement monetary policy have varied over time in most countries as financial markets have evolved, as the result of either deregulation or financial innovations. Borio (1997) provides a survey of policy implementation in the industrial economies. Detailed discussions of the operating procedures in France, Germany, Japan, the United Kingdom, and the United States can be found in Batten et al. (1990). Bernanke and Mishkin (1992) provide

---

44. Data are monthly; extended credit is included in nonborrowed reserves.
45. See equation (9.26) and the discussion after (9.27).

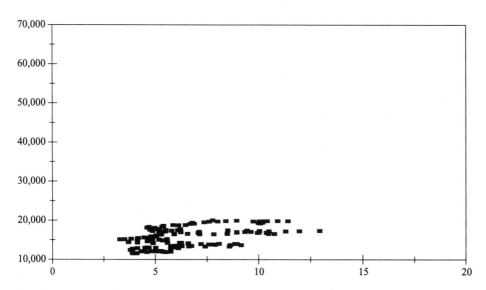

Figure 9.4a
Total Reserves and the Funds Rate, January 1959–September 1979 (millions of dollars)

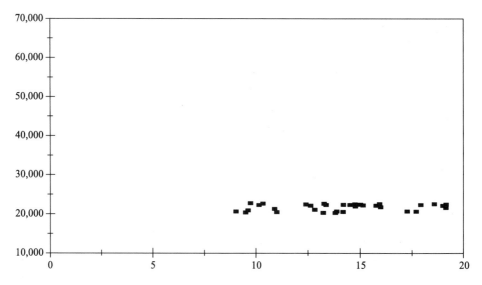

Figure 9.4b
Total Reserves and the Funds Rate, October 1979–October 1982 (millions of dollars)

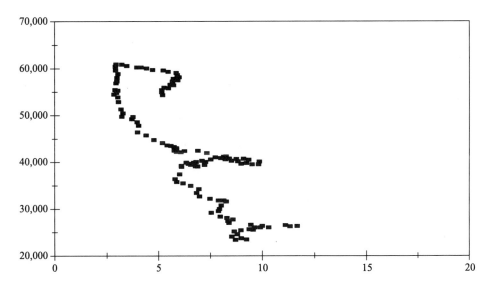

Figure 9.4c
Total Reserves and the Funds Rate, November 1982–December 1996 (millions of dollars)

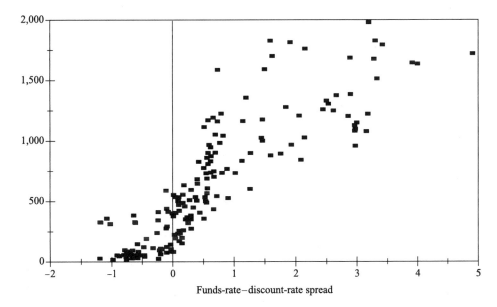

Funds-rate–discount-rate spread

Figure 9.5a
Borrowed Reserves, January 1959–September 1979 (millions of dollars)

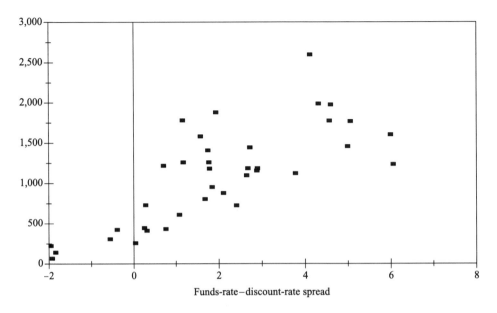

Figure 9.5b
Borrowed Reserves, October 1979–October 1982 (millions of dollars)

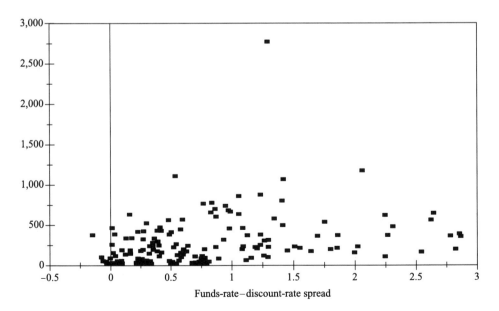

Figure 9.5c
Borrowed Reserves, November 1982–December 1996 (millions of dollars)

case studies of monetary policy strategies in the United States, the United Kingdom, Canada, Germany, Switzerland, and Japan. These countries, plus France, are discussed in Morton and Wood (1993) and Kasman (1993). The behavior of the Bundesbank is examined by Clarida and Gertler (1997). Cargill, Hutchison, and Ito (1997) provide a discussion of Japan. Goodhart and Viñals (1994) discuss policy behavior in a number of European and antipodian countries.

The experiences with monetary-policy operating procedures in all these countries have been broadly similar over the past 20 years. Beginning in the mid-1970s, many countries publicly established monetary targets. Since 1975, the U.S. Federal Reserve has been required by Congress to set targets for monetary aggregates. Germany, Canada, and Switzerland have announced money targets since 1975, the United Kingdom since 1976, and France since 1977. The weight placed on these targets has, however, varied greatly over time. In general, the financial innovations that occurred in the 1980s, together with significant deregulation of financial markets that took place after 1985, reduced reliance on monetary targets. This finding is consistent with the implications of Poole's model, which suggested that increased financial-market instability that makes money demand less predictable would lessen the advantages of any monetary-aggregates-oriented operating procedure. The last 10 years have seen a shift toward interest-rate operating procedures in all these countries except Switzerland.

Morton and Wood (1993) argue that a common theme among the six industrial countries they examine has been the move to more flexible interest-rate policies. Rather than rely on officially established interest rates, often combined with direct credit controls, central banks have moved toward more market-oriented interest-rate policies.[46] These involve control over a reserve aggregate (such as nonborrowed reserves in the United States) through which the central bank influences liquidity in the money market. This provides the central bank with control over a short-term money-market rate that balances reserve supply and demand. Typically, central banks do not intervene in the market continuously; instead they usually will estimate reserve demand and then add or subtract bank reserves to achieve the targeted interbank interest rate. Because these operations are based on reserve projections and because actual reserve demand may differ from projections, the actual value of the interest rate can differ from the central bank's target. However, by intervening daily, the central bank can keep target deviations quite small.[47]

---

46. Similarly, Kasman (1993) notes that innovation and liberalization in financial markets have made the institutional setting in which policy is conducted increasingly similar among the industrial countries.

47. In an interesting variation, the Reserve Bank of New Zealand appears to implement policy by simply making announcements—so called "open-mouth operations" (Guthrie and Wright 1998).

Finally, it is worth emphasizing that the choice of operating procedure is, in principle, distinct from the choice of ultimate goals and objectives of monetary policy. For example, a policy under which price stability is the sole objective of monetary policy could be implemented through either an interest-rate procedure or a reserve-aggregate procedure. A policy that incorporates output-stabilization or exchange-rate considerations can similarly be implemented through different procedures. The choice of operating procedure is significant, however, for interpreting the short-term response of financial markets to economic disturbances. And inefficient procedures can introduce unnecessary volatility into financial markets.

9.5 Problems

1. Suppose equations (9.1) and (9.2) are modified as follows:

$$y_t = -\alpha i_t + u_t$$

$$m_t = -c i_t + y_t + v_t$$

where $u_t = \rho_u u_{t-1} + \varphi_t$, $v_t = \rho_v v_{t-1} + \psi_t$, and φ and ψ are white-noise processes (assume that all shocks can be observed with a one-period lag). Assume the central bank's loss function is $E[y]^2$.

a. Under a money-supply operating procedure, derive the value of m_t that minimizes $E[y]^2$.

b. Under an interest-rate operating procedure, derive the value of i_t that minimizes $E[y]^2$.

c. Explain why your answers in parts a and b depend on ρ_u and ρ_v.

d. Does the choice between a money-supply procedure and an interest-rate procedure depend on the ρ_i's? Explain.

e. Suppose the central bank sets its instrument for two periods (for example, $m_t = m_{t+1} = m^*$) to minimize $E[y_t]^2 + \beta E[y_{t+1}]^2$ where $0 < \beta < 1$. How is the instrument-choice problem affected by the ρ_i's?

2. Solve for the δ_i's appearing in (9.11) and show that the optimal rule for the base is the same as that implied by the value of μ^* given in (9.10).

3. Suppose the money-demand relationship is given by $m = -c_1 i + c_2 y + v$. Show how the choice of an interest-rate versus a money-supply operating procedure depends on c_2. Explain why the choice depends on c_2.

10 Interest Rates and Monetary Policy

10.1 Introduction

Most central banks in the major industrialized economies implement policy by intervening in the money market to achieve a target level for a short-term interest rate.[1] In the United States, the Federal Reserve sets a target level for the federal funds rate and then influences the supply of bank reserves to maintain the funds rate at the targeted value. The funds rate serves as the operational target for policy, and, because it can be closely controlled, it can for most purposes be treated as the instrument of policy. Nevertheless, most theoretical models continue to treat policy as if it were implemented through the use of a money-supply operating procedure, or at least by some sort of policy rule oriented toward the control of a monetary aggregate. Treating the nominal money supply as the instrument of monetary policy is the approach taken in most undergraduate textbooks in which financial-market equilibrium is summarized by an LM curve.[2] This perspective emphasizes the role of money-demand disturbances in affecting the link between the money supply, interest rates, and real economic activity.

If the central bank can directly control short-term interest rates, the predictability (or unpredictability) of money demand becomes less relevant. Instead, the linkages between the very short-term interest rate the central bank controls and the broad range of market interest rates that affect investment and consumption spending, as well as the link between interest rates and exchange rates, become of critical importance.

In this chapter, we examine the implications of using an interest rate as the short-run operational target of monetary policy. The actual policy instrument of central banks is usually the supply of reserve assets, but these can be adjusted to maintain close control of a short-term rate such as the interbank overnight rate. Under the assumption that components of aggregate spending are more closely linked to movements in long-term interest rates, monetary policy actions affecting short-term interest rates are linked to the aggregate economy through the term structure of interest rates. The term structure and the relationship between long-term rates and expected inflation become important in policy design. By treating an interest rate as the variable under the control of the central bank, one obtains a framework that more closely matches the way in which most policy makers view policy.

---

1. This statement is certainly true of the United States. As discussed in Bernanke and Mishkin (1992), Morton and Wood (1993), and Kasman (1993), the central banks in the major OECD countries also use short-term market interest rates as their instrument of policy (the chief exception is the Swiss National Bank).

2. See, for example, Hall and Taylor (1997), Abel and Bernanke (1995), and Mankiw (1997).

10.2   Interest-Rate Rules and the Price Level

In this section, we explore the implications for the price level of policies that focus on the interest rate. As the models of Chapters 2 and 3 showed, the steady-state real rate of interest is determined by the marginal product of capital and so, in the long run, monetary policy will have no effect on real rates of return.[3] Monetary policy can affect nominal rates, both in the short run and in the long run, but the Fisher relationship links the real rate, expected inflation, and the nominal rate of interest. Targets for nominal interest rates and inflation cannot be independently chosen, and controlling the nominal interest rate will have important implications for the behavior of the aggregate price level.

10.2.1   Price-Level Determinacy

Chapter 5 made use of a model of the following basic form:

$$y_t = y^c + a(p_t - E_{t-1}p_t) + e_t \tag{10.1}$$

$$y_t = \alpha_0 - \alpha_1 r_t + u_t \tag{10.2}$$

$$m_t - p_t = -ci_t + y_t + v_t \tag{10.3}$$

$$i_t = r_t + (E_t p_{t+1} - p_t) \tag{10.4}$$

where y, m, and p are the natural logs of output, the money stock, and the price level, and r and i are the real and nominal rates of interest. In chapter 5, the specification of the model was completed by treating the nominal money supply as the policy instrument; the only exception occurred in section 5.4.4. We want to change this treatment, returning to the approach of section 5.4.4, by assuming the nominal interest rate is the policy instrument. Given real output, the price level, and the nominal interest rate, the nominal money supply will be determined endogenously by the money-demand equation (10.3). Although central banks may closely control the nominal rate i, it is the expected real rate of interest r that influences consumption and investment decisions and therefore aggregate demand.[4] This distinction has important implications for the feasibility of an interest targeting rule.

Suppose that the central bank attempts to conduct policy by fixing the nominal interest rate equal to some targeted value:

$$i_t = i^T \tag{10.5}$$

---

3. If money is superneutral, this will certainly be the case; in models in which money is not superneutral, the simulations in Chapters 2 and 3 indicated that the effect of inflation on equilibrium real returns was small.

4. Term-structure considerations are postponed until section 10.3.

Under this policy rule, the basic aggregate-demand-and-supply system given by equations (10.1), (10.2), and (10.4) becomes

$$y_t = y^c + a(p_t - \mathrm{E}_{t-1}p_t) + e_t \tag{10.6}$$

$$y_t = \alpha_0 - \alpha_1 r_t + u_t \tag{10.7}$$

$$i^T = r_t + (\mathrm{E}_t p_{t+1} - p_t) \tag{10.8}$$

The money-demand equation (10.3) is no longer relevant because the central bank must allow the nominal money stock to adjust to the level of money demand at the targeted interest rate and the level of output.

Note that the price level only appears in the form of an expectation error (i.e., as $p_t - \mathrm{E}_{t-1}p_t$ in the aggregate-supply equation) or as an expected rate of change (i.e., as $\mathrm{E}_t p_{t+1} - p_t$ in the Fisher equation). This structure implies that the price *level* is indeterminate. That is, if the sequence $\{p_{t+i}^*\}_{i=0}^{\infty}$ is an equilibrium, so is any sequence $\{\hat{p}_{t+i}\}_{i=0}^{\infty}$ where $\hat{p}$ differs from p^* by any constant κ: $\hat{p}_t = p_t^* + \kappa$ for all t. Since κ is an arbitrary constant, $p_t^* - \mathrm{E}_{t-1}p_t^* = \hat{p}_t - \mathrm{E}_{t-1}\hat{p}_t$; hence, y_t is the same under either price sequence. From (10.7), the equilibrium expected real interest rate is equal to $[\alpha_0 - y_t + u_t]/\alpha_1$, so it too is the same. With expected inflation the same under either price sequence, the only restriction on the price path is that the expected rate of inflation be such that $i^T = \dfrac{[\alpha_0 - y_t + u_t]}{\alpha_1} + \mathrm{E}_t p_{t+1}^* - p_t^*$.

The indeterminacy of the price level is perhaps even more apparent if equations (10.6)–(10.8) are rewritten explicitly in terms of the rate of inflation. By adding and subtracting ap_{t-1} to the supply function, the equilibrium conditions become

$$y_t = y^c + a(\pi_t - \mathrm{E}_{t-1}\pi_t) + e_t$$

$$y_t = \alpha_0 - \alpha_1 r_t + u_t$$

$$i^T = r_t + \mathrm{E}_t \pi_{t+1}$$

These three equations can be solved for output, the real rate of interest, and the rate of inflation. Since the price level does not appear, it is formally indeterminate.[5]

---

5. Employing McCallum's minimum-state solution method (McCallum 1983a), the equilibrium inflation rate is $\pi_t = i^T + \dfrac{y^c - \alpha_0}{\alpha_1} + \dfrac{u_t - e_t}{a}$ when u and e are serially uncorrelated and the target nominal interest rate is expected to remain constant. In this case, $\mathrm{E}_t \pi_{t+1} = i^T + \dfrac{y^c - \alpha_0}{\alpha_1}$, so permanent changes in the target rate i^T do not affect the real interest rate: $r_t = i^T - \mathrm{E}_t \pi_{t+1} = \dfrac{\alpha_0 - y^c}{\alpha_1}$.

As stressed by McCallum (1986), the issue of indeterminacy differs from the problem of multiple equilibria. The latter involves situations in which multiple equilibrium price paths are consistent with a given path for the nominal supply of money. We saw one example of such a multiplicity of equilibria when studying models of hyperinflation in Chapter 4. With indeterminacy, neither the price level nor the nominal supply of money is determined by the equilibrium conditions of the model. If the demand for real money balances is given by equation (10.3), then the price sequence p^* is associated with the sequence $m_t^* = p_t^* + y_t - ci_t^T + v_t$ while $\hat{p}$ is associated with $\hat{m}_t = \hat{p}_t + y_t - ci_t^T + v_t = m^* + \kappa$. The price sequences p^* and $\hat{p}$ will be associated with different paths for the nominal money stock.

Intuitively, if all agents expect the price level to be 10% higher permanently, such an expectation is completely self-fulfilling. In order to peg the nominal rate of interest, the central bank simply lets the nominal supply of money jump by 10%. This stands in contrast to the case in which the monetary policy authority controls the nominal quantity of money; a jump of 10% in the price level would reduce the real quantity of money, thereby disturbing the initial equilibrium. Under a rule such as (10.5) that has the policy maker pegging the nominal interest rate, the central bank lets the nominal quantity of money adjust as the price level does, leaving the real quantity unchanged.[6]

Price-level indeterminacy is often noted as a potential problem with pure interest-rate pegs; if private agents don't care about the absolute price level—and under pure interest-rate control, neither does the central bank—nothing pins down the price level. However, this problem will not arise if the central bank's behavior does depend on any nominal quantity such as the nominal money supply.

For example, suppose the nominal money supply (or a narrow reserve aggregate) is the actual instrument used to effect control of the interest rate, and assume it is adjusted in response to interest-rate movements (McCallum 1986; Canzoneri, Henderson, and Rogoff 1983):

$$m_t = \mu_0 + m_{t-1} + \mu(i_t - i^T) \tag{10.9}$$

Under this policy rule, the central bank adjusts the nominal-money-supply growth rate, $m_t - m_{t-1}$, in response to deviations of the nominal interest rate from its target value. If i_t fluctuates randomly around the target i^T, then the average rate of money growth will be μ_0. As $\mu \to \infty$, the variance of the nominal rate around the targeted value i^T shrinks, but the price level can remain determinate.

6. See Patinkin (1965) for an early discussion of price-level indeterminacy.

To verify these claims, we need to solve for the equilibrium price level (verifying that a determinant solution exists) and then show that the variance of the nominal interest rate around i^T can be made arbitrarily small by increasing μ. Employing the method of undetermined coefficients, (see Sheffrin 1983, McCallum 1989, or Attfield, Demery, and Duck 1991), the model can be solved by first postulating candidate solutions for the price level and the nominal interest rate as linear functions of the form

$$p_t = b_{10} + b_{11}m_{t-1} + b_{12}e_t + b_{13}u_t + b_{14}v_t \qquad (10.10)$$

$$i_t = b_{20} + b_{21}m_{t-1} + b_{22}e_t + b_{23}u_t + b_{24}v_t \qquad (10.11)$$

where the b_{ij}'s are as-yet-unknown coefficients whose values we need to determine. Equations (10.10) and (10.11) express the equilibrium values of p_t and i_t as functions of the contemporaneous disturbances e_t, u_t and v_t, and the state variable m_{t-1}.

Using (10.1) and (10.2) to solve for r_t and substituting the result into (10.4) yields

$$i_t = \frac{\alpha_0 - y^c}{\alpha_1} - \frac{a}{\alpha_1}[p_t - E_{t-1}p_t] + \frac{1}{\alpha_1}[u_t - e_t] + [E_t p_{t+1} - p_t] \qquad (10.12)$$

while substituting (10.1) into (10.3) and using the policy rule (10.9) yields

$$p_t = \mu_0 + m_{t-1} + (\mu + c)i_t - \mu i^T - y^c - a[p_t - E_{t-1}p_t] - e_t - v_t \qquad (10.13)$$

This procedure gives two equations to solve for the equilibrium price level and nominal interest rate, but they both involve expectational variables. These can be evaluated using the assumed solutions (10.10) and (10.11):

$$E_{t-1}p_t = b_{10} + b_{11}m_{t-1}$$

and

$$
\begin{aligned}
E_t p_{t+1} &= b_{10} + b_{11}m_t \\
&= b_{10} + b_{11}[\mu_0 + m_{t-1} + \mu(i_t - i^T)] \\
&= b_{10} + b_{11}\mu_0 + b_{11}m_{t-1} - b_{11}\mu i^T \\
&\quad + b_{11}\mu[b_{20} + b_{21}m_{t-1} + b_{22}e_t + b_{23}u_t + b_{24}v_t]
\end{aligned}
$$

These expressions for expectations can be substituted into (10.12) and (10.13) to yield

$$
\begin{aligned}
i_t &= \frac{\alpha_0 - y^c}{\alpha_1} - \frac{a}{\alpha_1}[b_{12}e_t + b_{13}u_t + b_{14}v_t] + \frac{1}{\alpha_1}[u_t - e_t] + b_{11}\mu_0 - b_{11}\mu i^T \\
&\quad + b_{11}\mu[b_{20} + b_{21}m_{t-1} + b_{22}e_t + b_{23}u_t + b_{24}v_t] - b_{12}e_t - b_{13}u_t - b_{14}v_t
\end{aligned}
$$

and

$$p_t = \mu_0 + m_{t-1} - \mu i^T - y^c + (\mu + c)[b_{20} + b_{21}m_{t-1} + b_{22}e_t + b_{23}u_t + b_{24}v_t]$$
$$- a[b_{12}e_t + b_{13}u_t + b_{14}v_t] - e_t - v_t$$

Equating these to the trial solutions (10.10) and (10.11) implies the following values for the unknown b_{ij}'s:[7]

$$b_{10} = \mu_0 - \mu i^T - y^c + (\mu + c)b_{20}$$

$$b_{11} = 1$$

$$b_{12} = -\frac{\alpha_1(1 - \mu) + (\mu + c)}{\varphi}$$

$$b_{13} = \frac{\mu + c}{\varphi}$$

$$b_{14} = -\frac{\alpha_1(1 - \mu)}{\varphi}$$

$$b_{20} = \frac{\alpha_0 - y^c}{\alpha_1(1 - \mu)} + \frac{\mu_0 - \mu i^T}{1 - \mu}$$

$$b_{21} = 0$$

$$b_{22} = \frac{\alpha_1 - 1}{\varphi}$$

$$b_{23} = \frac{1 + a}{\varphi}$$

$$b_{24} = \frac{\alpha_1 + a}{\varphi}$$

where $\varphi \equiv \alpha_1(1 - \mu)(1 + a) + (\mu + c)(\alpha_1 + a)$.

Collecting these results, the equilibrium nominal interest rate is given by

$$i_t = b_{20} + \frac{1}{\varphi}[(\alpha_1 - 1)e_t + (1 + a)u_t + (\alpha_1 + a)v_t] \qquad (10.14)$$

---

7. There is a second solution with $b_{11} = 1/\mu$ and $b_{21} = (1 - \mu)/[\mu(\mu + c)]$. McCallum (1986) shows that the solution in the text is the minimal state-variable solution. See also McCallum (1983a).

The nominal rate will fluctuate around i^T if $b_{20} = i^T$ which occurs when $i^T = r + \mu_0$ where $r = [\alpha_0 - y^c]/\alpha_1$ is the average real rate of interest. As a result, i^T, the target nominal rate, and μ_0, the average money growth rate, cannot be chosen independently. Since $\lim_{\mu \to \infty} |\varphi| = \infty$, and $\lim_{\mu \to \infty} b_{20} = i^T$, equation (10.14) implies that the variance of the nominal rate around i^T goes to zero as μ becomes arbitrarily large. At the same time,

$$\lim_{\mu \to \infty} b_{10} = \mu_0 - y^c + \lim_{\mu \to \infty} \left[\mu(b_{20} - i^T) + cb_{20} \right]$$

$$= \mu_0 - y^c - \left(\frac{\alpha_0 - y^c}{\alpha_1} + \mu_0 - i^T \right) + ci^T$$

$$= \mu_0 + ci^T - y^c < \infty$$

It follows that

$$\lim_{\mu \to \infty} p_t = \mu_0 + ci^T - y^c + m_{t-1} - \frac{1}{a} \left[e_t - \frac{1}{1 - \alpha_1} u_t - \frac{\alpha_1}{1 - \alpha_1} v_t \right]$$

which remains well defined.

One property of (10.9) is that the nominal money stock is $I(1)$. That is, m_t is nonstationary and integrated of order 1. This property of m leads the price level to be nonstationary also.[8] One implication is that the error variance of price-level forecasts increases with the forecast horizon.

As McCallum (1986) demonstrates, a different equilibrium describing the stochastic behavior of the nominal interest rate and the price level is obtained if the money-supply process takes the trend-stationary form

$$m_t = \mu' + \mu_0 t + \mu(i_t - i^T) \tag{10.15}$$

even though (10.15) and (10.9) both imply that the average growth rate of money will equal μ_0. With the money-supply process (10.15), the equilibrium price level is trend stationary, and the forecast error variance does not increase without limit as the forecast horizon increases.

It is not surprising that (10.9) and (10.15) lead to different solutions for the price level. Under (10.9), the nominal money supply is a nontrend-stationary process; random target misses have permanent effects on the future level of the money supply and therefore on the future price level. In contrast, (10.15) implies that the nominal

---

8. In contrast, the nominal interest rate is stationary because both the real rate of interest and the inflation rate (and therefore expected inflation) are stationary.

money supply is trend stationary. Deviations of money from the deterministic growth path $\mu' + \mu_0 t$ are temporary, so the price level is also trend stationary.

This discussion leads to two conclusions. First, monetary policy can be implemented to reduce fluctuations in the nominal interest rate without leading to price-level indeterminacy. The Canzoneri, Henderson, and Rogoff (1983) and McCallum (1986) papers showed that by adjusting the money supply aggressively in response to interest-rate movements, a central bank can reduce the variance of the nominal rate around its target level while leaving the price level determinate. Monetary policy can effectively fix the nominal rate in the sense of driving its variance to zero. However, the level at which the nominal rate can be set is determined by the growth rate of the nominal money supply. The choice of i^T determines μ_0 (or, equivalently, the choice of μ_0 determines the feasible value of i^T). Targets for the nominal interest rate and rate of inflation cannot be independently determined.

Second, the underlying behavior of the nominal money supply is not uniquely determined by the assumption that the nominal rate is to be fixed at i^T; this target can be achieved with different money-supply processes. And the different processes for m will lead to different behavior of the price level. A complete description of policy, even under a nominal-interest-rate targeting policy, needs to specify the underlying money-supply process.

Models of interest-rate targeting are relevant for understanding actual policy. Barro (1989) analyzes interest-rate targeting under the assumption that the target for the nominal rate follows a random walk.[9] Based on U.S. data, Barro finds that the model's predictions for the time-series behavior of nominal rates, the money supply, and inflation are consistent with his interest-rate-targeting specification. Rudebusch (1995) provides an empirical model of changes in the federal-funds-rate target set by the Federal Reserve's FOMC and demonstrates how this target-setting behavior helps account for the behavior of longer-term interest rates.

10.2.2 Interest-Rate Smoothing

The previous subsection showed how price-level indeterminacy could arise under a pure interest-rate peg and how the equilibrium price path would depend on the exact nature of the rule governing the feedback response of the nominal money supply to nominal-interest-rate movements. The example of that section showed how non-stationarity of the nominal money supply would lead to a nonstationary price level.

---

9. Barro takes the actual policy instrument to be the nominal money supply with the feedback rule for m determined by the desire to minimize a loss function that depends on the variance of the nominal rate around its target and the variance of one-step-ahead price-level forecast errors.

This analysis treated the policy rule governing m_t as exogenous, deriving the equilibrium behavior of the nominal interest rate and the price level for given values of the key parameter μ.

This approach does not provide guidance as to how μ might be chosen. To do so requires that the objectives of the policy authority be specified; in this way, we can then determine the value of μ (or more generally, the parameters of a policy rule) that is optimal in the sense of maximizing the objective function of the policy maker.[10] In this section, we first discuss how a nonstationary price level might arise if the central bank's objectives include a concern for reducing market-interest-rate fluctuations. This case is of particular interest since central banks are commonly viewed as following policies designed to smooth financial-market fluctuations. Reducing seasonal fluctuations in market interest rates, for example, was a major objective behind the creation of the Federal Reserve in 1913, and Mankiw and Miron (1986) and Mankiw, Miron, and Weil (1987) document that the Fed succeeded in eliminating fluctuations in interest rates at seasonal frequencies.[11] Central banks have often been criticized, however, for smoothing interest rates. During the late 1960s and the 1970s, the Fed's attempts to prevent interest rates from rising in the face of increasing inflation served to exacerbate subsequent inflation. Thus, an understanding of the consequences of interest-rate smoothing is important.

Suppose the central bank uses the nominal money supply as its policy instrument, and suppose it desires to minimize interest-rate fluctuations. What are the implications for the time-series behavior of the price level? Goodfriend (1987) provides an answer to this question. He assumed that the central bank's objective was to minimize a loss function that depends on the variances of the interest rate, inflation forecast errors, and expected inflation:[12]

$$L = \alpha E[i_t - a_0]^2 + \beta E[\pi_t - E_{t-1}\pi_t]^2 + \gamma E[E_t \pi_{t+1}]^2 \qquad (10.16)$$

where $\alpha, \beta, \gamma \geq 0$. In the loss function, i_t is the time-t nominal rate of interest and the parameter a_0 is the expected real rate of interest. Goodfriend characterizes a central bank with pure price-smoothing objectives as setting $\alpha = 0$ so that only the variance of price-level (inflation) forecast errors and the variance of expected inflation enter

10. This was the approach to policy determination used in Chapter 8.

11. The findings of Mankiw et al. have been questioned by Fishe and Wohar (1990) and by Angelini (1994a, 1994b). See also the reply to Angelini by Mankiw, Miron, and Weil (1994), and also Mankiw and Miron (1991).

12. Since $\pi_t - E_{t-1}\pi_t = p_t - E_{t-1}p_t$, the second term in (10.16) is equal to the variance of price-level forecast errors. In equilibrium, expected inflation will fluctuate around an average value of zero (see 10.24); thus, the last term in (10.16) is the variance of expected inflation.

the loss function. A central bank engaged in interest-rate smoothing is characterized by $\alpha > 0$.

The actual real rate of interest is taken by Goodfriend to be exogenous, equal to a_0 plus a white-noise stochastic disturbance q_t with variance σ_q^2. While systematic monetary policy does have important and persistent effects on real interest rates, Goodfriend's assumption is convenient for illustrating how the behavior of the price level will be affected by the central bank's objective function. The nominal rate is then given by

$$i_t = a_0 + \mathrm{E}_t \pi_{t+1} + q_t \tag{10.17}$$

This implies that the loss function (10.16) can be written as

$$L = \beta \mathrm{E}[\pi_t - \mathrm{E}_{t-1}\pi_t]^2 + (\alpha + \gamma)\mathrm{E}[\mathrm{E}_t \pi_{t+1}]^2 + 2\alpha\mathrm{E}[q_t \mathrm{E}_t \pi_{t+1}] + \alpha\sigma_q^2$$

The difference between a central bank with pure price-smoothing objectives and one with interest-rate-smoothing objectives, then, arises due to the covariance term $\mathrm{E}[q_t \mathrm{E}_t \pi_{t+1}]$.[13] If $\alpha > 0$, the central bank can lower its loss function by inducing a negative covariance between real rate shocks (q_t) and expected inflation. To see how this is achieved, as well as to determine the implications for the price level, requires that the rest of the model be specified.

The presence of $\mathrm{E}[\pi_t - \mathrm{E}_{t-1}\pi_t]^2$ in the policy authority's loss function could be motivated by a desire to minimize the output effects of inflation disturbances, since output deviations may be affected by inflation surprises. To simplify the presentation here and focus on Goodfriend's main conclusions, output will be treated as equal to a fixed constant, normalized to zero. Finally, assume that policy is implemented by setting the nominal money supply, and inflation is given by

$$\pi_t = m_t - m_{t-1} + v_t - v_{t-1} \tag{10.18}$$

where v_t is a mean-zero, serially uncorrelated random disturbance to velocity.[14] It is assumed that v and q are uncorrelated. Finally, the policy rule is assumed to take the form

$$m_t = m_{t-1} + \theta_1(i_t - \mathrm{E}_{t-1}i_t) - \theta_2(m_{t-1} - \mathrm{E}_{t-2}m_{t-1}) \tag{10.19}$$

This policy rule captures the idea, emphasized in Poole's analysis, that the policy

13. Since the variance of q_t is an exogenous constant, its presence in the loss function has no effect on the optimal policy choice. This constant will be ignored in the rest of the analysis.

14. Equation (10.18) is obtained by first differencing $p_t = m_t + v_t$.

authority cannot respond directly to contemporaneous disturbances because of imperfect information. Instead, it is possible to monitor and respond to contemporaneous interest-rate movements. Policy is characterized by the choices of θ_1 and θ_2. To give them some interpretation, note that (10.19) implies that $m_{t-1} - \mathrm{E}_{t-2}m_{t-1} = \theta_1(i_{t-1} - \mathrm{E}_{t-2}i_{t-1})$, so (10.19) can be rewritten as

$$m_t = m_{t-1} + \theta_1(i_t - \mathrm{E}_{t-1}i_t) - \theta_1\theta_2(i_{t-1} - \mathrm{E}_{t-2}i_{t-1}) \qquad (10.20)$$

The parameter θ_1 determines the money-growth-rate response to innovations in the nominal interest rate, while θ_2 then determines the extent to which the money-growth-rate effects of the response at time $t-1$ are subsequently offset. The effect on m_t is completely offset in period t if $\theta_2 = 1$. Under rational expectations, $i_t - \mathrm{E}_{t-1}i_t$ will be a mean-zero, serially uncorrelated random variable (which will depend on v_t and q_t), so we can write the policy rule as $m_t - m_{t-1} = \varepsilon_t - \theta_2\varepsilon_{t-1}$ where $\varepsilon_t \equiv \theta_1(i_t - \mathrm{E}_{t-1}i_t)$. The growth rate of the nominal money supply is a first-order moving-average process; if $\theta_2 = 1$, $m_t = \varepsilon_t$ and the *level* of the money stock is a white-noise process. For any other value of θ_2, the money stock is a nonstationary, integrated-of-order-1 process.

From (10.18) and (10.20),

$$\pi_t = \theta_1(i_t - \mathrm{E}_{t-1}i_t) - \theta_1\theta_2(i_{t-1} - \mathrm{E}_{t-2}i_{t-1}) + v_t - v_{t-1}$$

This implies that

$$\mathrm{E}_t\pi_{t+1} = -\theta_1\theta_2(i_t - \mathrm{E}_{t-1}i_t) - v_t$$

From the definition of the nominal interest rate, $i_t = a_0 + \mathrm{E}_t\pi_{t+1} + q_t = a_0 - \theta_1\theta_2(i_t - \mathrm{E}_{t-1}i_t) - v_t + q_t$, from which it follows that

$$i_t - \mathrm{E}_{t-1}i_t = \frac{q_t - v_t}{1 + \theta_1\theta_2}$$

This can then be used to show that the equilibrium nominal interest rate, the price level, and the nominal money stock are given by

$$i_t = a_0 + \frac{q_t - v_t}{1 + \theta_1\theta_2} \qquad (10.21)$$

$$\pi_t = \frac{\theta_1(q_t - v_t)}{1 + \theta_1\theta_2} - \frac{\theta_1\theta_2(q_{t-1} - v_{t-1})}{1 + \theta_1\theta_2} + v_t - v_{t-1}$$

$$= \frac{\theta_1(q_t - \theta_2 q_{t-1})}{1 + \theta_1\theta_2} + \frac{[1 - \theta_1(1 - \theta_2)]v_t - v_{t-1}}{1 + \theta_1\theta_2}$$

$$m_t = m_{t-1} + \frac{\theta_1(q_t - v_t)}{1 + \theta_1\theta_2} - \frac{\theta_1\theta_2(q_{t-1} - v_{t-1})}{1 + \theta_1\theta_2} \tag{10.22}$$

Given these general solutions, we can evaluate the central bank's loss function and determine the optimal values of θ_1 and θ_2. To do so, note that the inflation forecast error is

$$\pi_t - \mathrm{E}_{t-1}\pi_t = \frac{\theta_1 q_t}{1 + \theta_1\theta_2} + \frac{[1 - \theta_1(1 - \theta_2)]v_t}{1 + \theta_1\theta_2} \tag{10.23}$$

while expected inflation equals

$$\mathrm{E}_t\pi_{t+1} = \frac{-\theta_1\theta_2 q_t - v_t}{1 + \theta_1\theta_2} \tag{10.24}$$

Letting $A \equiv \theta_1\theta_2$,

$$L = \frac{\beta}{(1 + A)^2}[\theta_1^2\sigma_q^2 + (1 - \theta_1 + A)^2\sigma_v^2]$$

$$+ \frac{(\alpha + \gamma)}{(1 + A)^2}[A^2\sigma_q^2 + \sigma_v^2] - \frac{2\alpha}{(1 + A)}[A\sigma_q^2] \tag{10.25}$$

What are the optimal values of θ_1 and θ_2? We can treat this question equivalently as a problem of finding the optimal θ_1 and A. Differentiating (10.25) with respect to the two policy parameters, the first-order condition for θ_1 implies

$$\theta_1^* = \frac{(1 + A)\sigma_v^2}{\sigma_q^2 + \sigma_v^2}$$

while that for A yields

$$A^* = \frac{\alpha}{\gamma} + \left(1 + \frac{\alpha}{\gamma}\right)\frac{\sigma_v^2}{\sigma_q^2}$$

Since $A = \theta_1\theta_2$,

$$\theta_2^* = \frac{A^*}{\theta_1^*} = 1 + \left(\frac{\alpha}{\alpha + \gamma}\right)\frac{\sigma_q^2}{\sigma_v^2}$$

and

$$\theta_1^* = \left(1 + \frac{\alpha}{\gamma}\right)\frac{\sigma_v^2}{\sigma_q^2}$$

The factors determining θ_1^*, the optimal response to interest-rate innovations, are similar to those highlighted in the earlier analysis of instrument choice (see section 9.3) in that the relative variances of the underlying disturbances are important. The parameter θ_2 governs whether the policy response to interest-rate innovations is allowed to permanently affect the level of m, and therefore the price level. If $\alpha = 0$, then $\theta_2^* = 1$, and any policy response to interest-rate movements is fully offset after one period so that the money stock and the price level follow stationary processes.[15] But if the central bank places any weight on interest-smoothing objectives so that $\alpha > 0$, then $\theta_2^* \neq 1$ and both m and p are not trend stationary.

Consider how policy responds in the face of a positive real-interest-rate shock ($q_t > 0$). From (10.22), the money supply is increased when q_t is positive. This increase raises p_t, but because i_t is the sum of the exogenous real rate and expected inflation, the nominal rate can be prevented from rising only by generating an expectation of a deflation. Thus, monetary policy acts to smooth the nominal rate in Goodfriend's model by raising p_t relative to p_{t+1} so that $E_t \pi_{t+1}$ falls (see equation 10.24).

VanHoose (1989) relates the issue of interest-rate smoothing and price-level non-stationarity to the intermediate target problem discussed in section 9.3.3. He shows that price-level nontrend stationarity can arise under an optimal policy that is concerned only with minimizing price-level forecast errors and the variance of inflation (i.e., when $\alpha = 0$ in Goodfriend's model). Suppose α is equal to zero in (10.16) but policy is implemented via an intermediate targeting procedure in which a reserve aggregate is set to achieve a target for the money supply. As VanHoose emphasizes, targeting the money supply is an inefficient policy procedure, for the reasons discussed in Chapter 9. The policy maker has one instrument to achieve two objectives, minimum price-level forecast error and minimum inflation variance. With one instrument and two targets, the policy maker must compromise, and allowing the price level to be nonstationary is the optimal response.

Barro (1989) has used a model similar to Goodfriend's to examine policy designed to achieve a target nominal rate of interest when the target follows a random walk. He also assumes that the (exogenous) real rate and demand for money are subject to permanent shifts. A permanent shift in the real rate requires a permanent but opposite shift in expected inflation in order to maintain the target nominal rate.

The links between policy and interest rates in these models, with nominal rates affected only through changes in expected inflation while the real rate remains exogenous, contrast with the links between policy and nominal rates in models that

---

15. If we had included a constant term in the money-supply rule, m and p would be *trend* stationary.

assume that monetary policy affects real interest rates in the short run. In a sticky-wage or -price model, a rise in the nominal money supply increases the real quantity of money. To maintain money-market equilibrium, the nominal interest rate must fall to increase the real demand for money, and this, at least partially, represents a fall in the real rate. In Barro's and Goodfriend's analyses, a rise in the nominal money supply reduces the nominal rate only because the rise in m_t induces expectations of deflation. Under rational expectations, this can only occur if the rise in m_t is expected to be at least partially offset in the future so that the nominal money supply is expected to decline.

While this link between changes in the nominal money supply and nominal interest rates represents a theoretical possibility, it relies on the assumption that the money supply is negatively serially correlated. Increases in m_t are followed by decreases. If this were not the case, rational agents would not expect the price decline required for expected deflation to lower nominal interest rates. As indicated earlier, equation (10.20) implies that the growth rate of money is negatively serially correlated whenever $\theta_2 > 0$ (since $m_t - m_{t-1} = \varepsilon_t - \theta_2\varepsilon_{t-1}$). At least for the United States, the growth rate of money has been positively serially correlated. Therefore, although the desire to smooth interest rates may play a role in explaining the nonstationarity of the money supply and the price level, the exact mechanism emphasized in Goodfriend's model is unlikely to explain the observed nonstationarity of the price level, at least in the United States.

In the United States the nontrend-stationary behavior of the money supply arose during periods of monetary targeting in the 1970s because the Fed engaged in a policy of base drift. If the actual path for money overshot its target, the Fed would simply shift up the subsequent target path so that it would begin at the new actual level of m. Rather than maintaining the previous target path and reducing money growth to bring the actual money supply back to the original path, the whole path would be shifted, impounding target misses permanently into the level of the money supply (Broaddus and Goodfriend 1984; U.S. President 1985).[16] While base drift imparts $I(1)$ behavior to the money stock, a policy of base drift, or more generally one in which the nominal money supply is nontrend-stationary, need not result in a nonstationary price level. Empirical evidence suggests that velocity is nonsta-

16. Base drift leads to a money process similar to (10.9) in which innovations to m_t are permanently incorporated into the level of the expected future money supply. Under a money targeting policy, rebasing after target misses need not yield nontrend-stationary behavior for the money supply if the subsequent target growth rate is adjusted to bring m_t back to its original target path. This would require that overshoots be followed by reductions in the target growth rate and undershoots by increases in the target growth rate. This was not done in the United States (see Walsh 1986). For a recent analysis of the period of U.S. monetary targeting, see B. Friedman and Kuttner (1996).

tionary.[17] Permanent shifts in real money demand require permanent shifts in real money supply, and these can be achieved either by permanent (i.e., nonstationary) price-level behavior or by permanent shifts in the nominal supply of money. Walsh (1986) assumes that the central bank can observe money-demand shocks but cannot determine whether they are permanent or temporary, and shows how the optimal degree of base drift depends on the relative variance of the temporary and permanent components. Thus, even under a policy designed to produce stationary price-level behavior, the nominal money supply may exhibit nonstationary behavior.

If interest-rate-smoothing behavior does lead to a nonstationary price level, should this outcome be of concern? In the models we have been using, the price level itself has no particular importance. This fact has been reflected in the loss functions we have typically used in which it is inflation, not the price level, that enters. Permanent shifts in the price level affect the loss function only by producing errors in the public's forecast of the inflation rate. In a multiperiod setting, agents may be very concerned with the predictability of the price-level several years in the future. The presence of a unit root in the price-level process implies that the forecast-error variance will increase with the forecast horizon.[18] If there are efficiency gains from the ability to write long-term nominal contracts, there would be value in reducing uncertainty about the future price level. This analysis is the basis for arguments that central banks should target price stability and not simply a zero rate of inflation.

10.3   Interest-Rate Policies in General Equilibrium Models

The analysis in the previous sections of this chapter employed models that were not derived directly from the assumption of optimizing behavior on the part of the agents in the economy. One disadvantage of these models is that there is no natural welfare measure that can be used to evaluate alternative policies. Assuming the central bank is concerned with output and inflation variability is probably reasonable, but to derive conclusions about optimal policies, one would like to be able to evaluate the welfare of the representative agent under alternative policies.

17. See Gould et al. (1978) and Nelson and Plosser (1982) for the United States; Kim (1985) presents evidence for the United Kingdom. Hoffman, Rasche, and Tieslau (1995) employ cointegration techniques to argue that the long-run demand for money is stable in the United States, United Kingdom, Canada, Japan, and Germany.

18. Consider the process $p_t = p_{t-1} + e_t - a e_{t-1}$. The n-step-ahead forecast-error variance is $[1 + (1 - a)^2 (n - 1)] \sigma_e^2$. If $a = 1$, p is a stationary process and the forecast-error variance is independent of the forecast horizon. If $a \neq 1$, p is nonstationary and the forecast-error variance increases linearly with the forecast horizon.

Among the more recent papers employing general equilibrium, representative agent models to study interest rate policies are Carlstrom and Fuerst (1995, 1997) and Woodford (1997). Carlstrom and Fuerst address welfare issues associated with interest rate policies. They employ a cash-in-advance framework in which consumption must be financed from nominal money balances. As we saw in Chapter 3, a positive nominal interest rate represents a distorting tax on consumption, affecting the household's choice between cash goods (i.e., consumption) and credit goods (i.e., investment and leisure). Introducing one-period price stickiness into their model, Carlstrom and Fuerst (1997) conclude that a constant nominal interest rate eliminates the distortion on capital accumulation, an interest-rate peg Pareto dominates a fixed money rule, and for any interest-rate peg, there exists a money growth process that replicates the real equilibrium in the flexible price version of their model. That is, an appropriate movement in the nominal money growth rate can "undo" the effects of the one-period price stickiness.

To illustrate the basic issues in a very simple manner, consider the following three equilibrium conditions for a cash-in-advance economy in the absence of uncertainty:

$$\frac{u_c(c_t)}{1+i_t} = \beta R_{t+1} \frac{u_c(c_{t+1})}{1+i_t}$$

$$m_t = f[i_t, u_c(c_t)]$$

$$1 + i_t = \frac{R_t P_t}{P_{t-1}}$$

where u_c is the marginal utility of consumption, β is the subjective rate of time preference, R is one plus the real rate of return, i is the nominal interest rate, P is the price level, and m is the level of real money balances. The first of these three equations can be derived from the basic model of section 3.3.1 by recalling that $u_c(c_t) = (1 + i_t)\lambda_t$, where λ_t is the time t marginal value of wealth (see equations 3.20 and 3.24). Since $\lambda_t = \beta R_t \lambda_{t+1}$ (see equation 3.21), it follows that $u_c(c_t)/(1 + i_t) = \lambda_t = \beta R_t u_c(c_{t+1})/(1 + i_{t+1})$. The second equation is a standard money demand equation, in which the real demand for money depends on the nominal rate of interest and the marginal utility of consumption. The third equation is simply the Fisher relationship linking nominal and real returns. For purposes of illustration, the supply of labor is taken as fixed; this eliminates one of the channels through which the cash-in-advance constraint can affect the real equilibrium. The second and third equations of this system, as Woodford (1997) emphasizes, are traditionally interpreted as determining the price level and nominal interest rate for an exogenous nominal money supply process.

In an economy without the distortions introduced by a cash-in-advance constraint, the Euler condition for the optimal intertemporal allocation of consumption is simply $u_c(c_t) = \beta R_t u_c(c_{t+1})$. Comparing this to the cash-in-advance Euler condition shows that the intertemporal allocation of consumption will be distorted if the nominal interest rate varies over time. Under a nominal rate peg, $i_s = i_t = \bar{i}$ for all s and t, and the Euler condition reduces to $u_c(c_t) = \beta R_t u_c(c_{t+1})$, the same condition applying in an economy not facing a cash-in-advance constraint. If output follows an exogenous process and all output is perishable, equilibrium requires that c_t simply equal output, and the Euler condition then determines the real rate of return.

As we saw in section 10.2, the price level is indeterminate under such an interest-rate pegging policy. However, assuming P_t is predetermined due to price level stickiness still allows the money demand equation and the Fisher equation to determine P_{t+1} and m_t (and so the implied nominal supply of money) without affecting the real equilibrium determined by the Euler condition. In that sense, Carlstrom and Fuerst (1997) conclude that there exists a path for the nominal money supply in the face of price stickiness that leads to the same real equilibrium under an interest-rate peg as would occur with a flexible price level.

The Euler condition and the Fisher equation can be combined and written as $u_c(c_t)/(1 + i_{t-1}) = \beta P_t u_c(c_{t+1})/P_{t+1}$, or

$$\frac{P_t(1 + i_{t-1})}{P_{t+1}} = \frac{u_c(c_t)}{\beta u_c(c_{t+1})} \equiv z_t$$

Following Woodford (1997), an interest rate policy can be written as

$$1 + i_t = \phi(P_t, z_t)$$

The function $\phi(P_t, z_t)$ specifies the setting for the policy instrument (the nominal rate i_t) as a function of the current price level and the variable z_t, which captures the real factors that determine the marginal utility of consumption. Woodford labels policies of this form "Wicksellian" policies. Under such a policy, equilibrium, if it exists, is a sequence for the price level that satisfies

$$P_t \phi(P_t, z_t) = P_{t+1} z_t$$

Carlstrom and Fuerst (1995) provide some simulation evidence to suggest nominal interest-rate pegs dominate constant money growth rate policies. While this suggests a constant nominal interest-rate peg is desirable within the context of their model, they do not explicitly derive the optimal policy. Instead, their argument is based on quite different grounds than the traditional Poole (1970) argument for an interest-rate-oriented policy. In Poole's analysis, stabilizing the interest rate served to insulate

the real economy from purely financial disturbances. In contrast, Carlstrom and
Fuerst appeal to standard tax smoothing arguments to speculate, based on intertemporal tax considerations, that an interest-rate peg might be optimal.

The tax smoothing argument for an interest-rate peg is suggestive, but it is unlikely
to be robust in the face of financial market disturbances. For example, in an analysis
of optimal policy defined as money growth rate control, Ireland (1996) introduces a
stochastic velocity shock by assuming the cash-in-advance constraint applies to only
a time-varying fraction v_t of all consumption. In this case, the cash-in-advance constraint takes the form $P_t v_t c_t \leq Q_t$, where Q is the nominal quantity out of which cash
goods must be purchased. It is straightforward to show that the Euler condition must
be modified in this case to become

$$\frac{u_c(c_t)}{q_t} = \beta R_{t+1} \frac{u_c(c_{t+1})}{q_{t+1}}$$

where $q_t \equiv 1 + v_t i_t$. If $v_t \equiv 1$, the case considered by Carlstrom and Fuerst is
obtained. If v_t is random, eliminating the intertemporal distortion requires that q be
pegged and that the nominal interest rate vary over time to offset the stochastic
fluctuations in v_t. The introduction of a stochastic velocity disturbance suggests an
interest-rate peg would not be optimal.

In general, the welfare properties of interest-rate rules remains a relatively un-
explored area, one that is particularly important to examine since these are the types
of policies now used by most central banks.

10.4   The Term Structure of Interest Rates

The distinction between real and nominal rates of interest is critical for understanding important monetary-policy issues, but another important distinction is that
between short-term and long-term interest rates. Because aggregate-spending decisions are generally viewed as more closely related to long-term interest rates, while
the opportunity costs of holding money are best represented by short-term interest
rates, the appropriate interest rates in the aggregate-demand relationship and the
money-demand relationship are not the same. Changes in the short-term interest rate
serving as the operational target for implementing monetary policy will only affect
aggregate-spending decisions if longer-term rates of interest are affected. While the
use of an interest-rate-oriented policy reduces the importance of money demand in
the transmission of policy actions to the real economy, it raises to prominence the
role played by the term structure of interest rates.

The exposition here will build on the expectations theory of the term structure. For a systematic discussion of the theory of the term structure, see Cox, Ingersoll, and Ross (1985), Shiller (1990), or Campbell and Shiller (1991). Our objective is to illustrate how the term structure will depend on the conduct of monetary policy. Under the expectations hypothesis of the term structure, long-term nominal interest rates depend on expectations of future nominal short-term interest rates. These future short rates will be functions of monetary policy, so expectations about future policy will play an important role in determining the shape of the term structure.

10.4.1   The Expectations Theory of the Term Structure

Under the expectations theory of the term structure, the n-period interest rate will be equal to an average of the current short-term rate and the future short-term rates expected to hold over the n-period horizon. For example, if $i_{n,t}$ is the nominal yield to maturity at time t on an n-period discount bond while i_t is the one-period rate, the pure expectations hypothesis in the absence of uncertainty would imply that[19]

$$(1 + i_{n,t})^n = \prod_{i=0}^{n-1}(1 + i_{t+i})$$

This condition ensures that the holding-period yield on the n-period bond is equal to the yield from holding a sequence of one-period bonds. Taking logs of both sides and recalling that $\ln(1 + x) \approx x$ for small x yields a common approximation:

$$i_{n,t} = \frac{1}{n}\sum_{i=0}^{n-1} i_{t+i}$$

Since an n-period bond becomes an $(n - 1)$–period bond after one period, these two relationships can also be written as

$$(1 + i_{n,t})^n = (1 + i_t)(1 + i_{n-1,t+1})^{n-1}$$

and

$$i_{n,t} = \frac{1}{n}i_t + \frac{n - 1}{n}i_{n-1,t+1}$$

These conditions will not hold exactly under conditions of uncertainty for two

---

19. A constant risk premium could easily be incorporated. A time-varying risk premium will be added to the analysis that follows.

reasons. First, if risk-neutral investors equate expected one-period returns, then the one-period rate $1 + i_t$ will equal $E_t \dfrac{(1 + i_{n,t})^n}{(1 + i_{n-1,t+1})^{n-1}}$, which, from Jensen's inequality, is not the same as $(1 + i_{n,t})^n = (1 + i_t)E_t(1 + i_{n-1,t+1})^{n-1}$.[20] Second, Jensen's inequality implies that $\ln E_t(1 + i_{n-1,t+1})$ is not the same as $E_t \ln(1 + i_{n-1,t+1})$. For illustrating the basic issues involving the term structure of interest rates and the role of monetary policy, however, we will ignore these issues, and it will be sufficient to simplify even further by dealing only with one- and two-period interest rates. Letting $I_t \equiv i_{2,t}$ be the two-period rate (the "long-term" interest rate), the term-structure equation becomes

$$(1 + I_t)^2 = (1 + i_t)(1 + E_t i_{t+1}) \tag{10.26}$$

and this will be approximated as

$$I_t = \tfrac{1}{2}(i_t + E_t i_{t+1}) \tag{10.27}$$

The critical implication of this relationship for monetary policy is that the current structure of interest rates will depend on current short rates *and* on market expectations of future short rates. Since the short rate is affected by monetary policy, I_t will depend on expectations about future policy.

The one-period-ahead forward rate is defined as

$$f_t^1 \equiv \frac{(1 + I_t)^2}{1 + i_t} - 1$$

If the pure expectations hypothesis of the term structure holds, equation (10.26) implies that f_t^1 is equal to the market's expectation of the future one-period rate. Hence, forward rates derived from the term structure are often used to gain information on expectations of future interest rates (see Dahlquist and Svensson 1996).

Equation (10.27) has a direct and testable empirical implication. Subtracting i_t from both sides, the equation can be rewritten as

$$I_t - i_t = \tfrac{1}{2}(E_t i_{t+1} - i_t)$$

If the current two-period rate is greater than the one-period rate (i.e., $I_t - i_t > 0$),

---

20. Suppose $P_{n,t}$ is the time-t price of an n-period discount bond. Then, $P_{n,t}^{-1} = (1 + i_{n,t})^n$. Since at time t this becomes an $(n - 1)$–period bond, the one-period gross return is

$$E_t P_{n-1,t+1}/P_{n,t} = E_t \frac{1}{(1 + i_{n-1,t+1})^{n-1}}(1 + i_{n,t})^n$$

then agents must expect the one-period rate to rise $(E_t i_{t+1} > i_t)$. Because we can always write $i_{t+1} = E_t i_{t+1} + (i_{t+1} - E_t i_{t+1})$, it follows that

$$\tfrac{1}{2}(i_{t+1} - i_t) = I_t - i_t + \tfrac{1}{2}(i_{t+1} - E_t i_{t+1})$$

$$= a + b(I_t - i_t) + \theta_{t+1} \qquad (10.28)$$

where $a = 0$, $b = 1$, and $\theta_{t+1} = \tfrac{1}{2}(i_{t+1} - E_t i_{t+1})$ is the error the private sector makes in forecasting the future short-term interest rate. Under the assumption of rational expectations, θ_{t+1} will be uncorrelated with information available at time t, so that (10.28) forms a regression equation that can be estimated consistently by least squares. Unfortunately, estimates of such equations usually reject the joint hypothesis that $a = 0$ and $b = 1$, generally obtaining point estimates of b significantly less than 1. Some of this empirical evidence is summarized in Rudebusch (1995, Table 1, p. 249) and McCallum (1994b, Table 1). As we will see, the observed relationship between long and short rates, as well as the way in which interest rates react to monetary policy, can depend on the manner in which policy is conducted.

10.4.2   Policy and the Term Structure

In this section, we use a simple model to illustrate how the behavior of nominal interest rates can depend on the money-supply process. Consider the following model:

$$R_t = q_t \qquad (10.29)$$

$$R_t = \tfrac{1}{2}[i_t - E_t \pi_{t+1} + E_t i_{t+1} - E_t \pi_{t+2}] \qquad (10.30)$$

$$m_t - p_t = -a i_t + v_t \qquad (10.31)$$

$$m_t = \gamma m_{t-1} + \varphi_t, \qquad 0 < \gamma < 1 \qquad (10.32)$$

where $\pi_t = p_t - p_{t-1}$.

We have assumed that output and the long-term (in this case, two-period!) real interest rate are exogenous, with the long-term real rate R_t equal to a stochastic, mean-zero random variable q_t. The variable R_t is equal to the average of the current real short-term rate $i_t - E_t \pi_{t+1}$ and the expected future real short rate $E_t i_{t+1} - E_t \pi_{t+2}$. The real demand for money is decreasing in the nominal short-term interest rate and is subject to a random shock v_t. Finally, the nominal money supply is assumed to follow a first-order autoregressive process, subject to a white noise control error φ_t. Note that this process implies that $E_t m_{t+1} = \gamma m_t$.

By using (10.31) to eliminate i_t and $E_t i_{t+1}$ from (10.30), this system of four equations implies that the equilibrium process for the price level must satisfy the following expectations difference equation:

$$2aq_t = (1+a)p_t + E_t p_{t+1} - aE_t p_{t+2} - (1+\gamma)m_t + v_t \qquad (10.33)$$

To find the solution for the short-term interest rate, we can employ the method of undetermined coefficients. Since the relevant state variables in (10.33) are m_t, q_t, and v_t, suppose we guess a solution of the form

$$p_t = b_1 m_t + b_2 q_t + b_3 v_t$$

This implies $E_t p_{t+1} = b_1 \gamma m_t$ and $E_t p_{t+2} = b_1 E_t m_{t+2} = b_1 \gamma^2 m_t$. Using these in (10.33), we find that the equilibrium solution for the price level is

$$p_t = \left[\frac{1}{1+a(1-\gamma)}\right] m_t + \frac{1}{1+a}[2aq_t - v_t] \qquad (10.34)$$

From the money-demand equation, $i_t = \dfrac{1}{a}(v_t + p_t - m_t)$, so, given the equilibrium process for p_t,

$$i_t = -\left[\frac{1-\gamma}{1+a(1-\gamma)}\right] m_t + \frac{1}{1+a}[2q_t + v_t] \qquad (10.35)$$

and the two-period nominal rate is

$$I_t = \tfrac{1}{2}(i_t + E_t i_{t+1})$$

$$= \tfrac{1}{2}\left\{-\left[\frac{1-\gamma^2}{1+a(1-\gamma)}\right] m_t + \frac{1}{1+a}[2q_t + v_t]\right\} \qquad (10.36)$$

Equation (10.36) illustrates how the long-term rate will depend on the money-supply process, where this process is characterized in this example by the parameter γ.

Because the current short-term interest rate depends on the current money supply and the expected future short rate, the current rate will depend on the expected future money supply. The effects of money-supply innovations on interest rates will depend on the way in which the money supply is being set. From equation (10.36), the impact of an innovation to m_t (i.e., a φ shock) on the current long rate is equal to

$$-\frac{1}{2}\left(-\frac{1-\gamma^2}{1+a(1-\gamma)}\right) < 0$$

which depends on the parameter γ. The greater is the degree of serial correlation in the money-supply process (the larger is γ), the smaller will be the effect on i_t of a change in m_t. The effect of a money innovation on slope of the term structure, $I_t - i_t$, is equal to $\frac{1}{2}(1 - \gamma)^2/[1 + a(1 - \gamma)]$, and this also depends to γ. To take the extreme case, suppose $\gamma = 1$; the nominal money supply follows a random walk with innovation φ_t. An innovation implies a permanent change in the *level* of the money supply. This causes a proportionate change in the price level (the coefficient on m_t in [10.34] is equal to one if $\gamma = 1$), but there is no impact on the expected rate of inflation. With the real rate exogenous, the nominal interest rate adjusts only in response to changes in expected inflation, so with $\gamma = 1$, changes in m have no effect on the nominal interest rate. If $\gamma < 1$, an unexpected increase in m causes the expectation of a subsequent decline in m and p. As in the model of the previous section, it is this expectation of a deflation that lowers the nominal rate of interest.

Similarly, the impact of real-interest-rate disturbances on nominal rates will depend on the money-supply process if policy responds to real disturbances. If, for example, the money-supply process is modified to become $m_t = m_{t-1} + \psi q_{t-1} + \varphi_t$ so that the growth rate of m_t depends on the real rate shock, it can be shown that the equilibrium short-term rate is

$$i_t = \left(\frac{2 + \psi}{1 + a}\right)q_t + \left(\frac{1}{1 + a}\right)v_t$$

If $\psi > 0$, an increase in the real rate ($q > 0$) induces an increase in the nominal money supply the following period. This increase implies that the money supply is expected to grow ($E_t m_{t+1} - m_t = \psi q_t > 0$), so expected inflation rises. This expectation increases the positive impact of q_t on the short-term nominal rate.

These results are illustrative, showing how interest-rate responses depend on expectations of the future money supply and, consequently, on the systematic behavior of m. The exact mechanism highlighted in these examples requires that a monetary innovation (i.e., $\varphi > 0$) generate an expected deflation in order for nominal rates to decline, since the real rate has been treated as exogenous. In fact, monetary policy does affect short-term real rates as well as expected inflation.

The dependence of interest rates and the term structure on monetary policy implies that the results of empirical studies of the term structure should depend on the operating procedures followed by the monetary authority. Recently, McCallum (1994b), Rudebusch (1995), Fuhrer (1996), and Balduzzi, Bertola, Foresi, and Klapper (1997) have examined the connection between the Fed's tendency to target interest rates, the dynamics of short-term interest rates, and empirical tests of the expectations model of the term structure.

This dependence can be seen most easily by employing a setup similar to that used by McCallum. Consider the following two-period model of nominal interest rates in which, as before, I is the two-period rate and i is the one-period rate:

$$I_t = \tfrac{1}{2}(i_t + E_t i_{t+1}) + \xi_t \qquad (10.37)$$

where ξ is a random variable that represents a time-varying term premium. Equation (10.27) implied that the pure expectations model of the term structure applied exactly, without error. The term premium ξ introduced in (10.37) allows for a stochastic deviation from the exact form of the expectations hypothesis. Variation in risk factors might account for the presence of ξ. Suppose further that the term premium is serially correlated:

$$\xi_t = \rho \xi_{t-1} + \eta_t \qquad (10.38)$$

where η_t is a white-noise process.

If we let $\varepsilon_{t+1} = i_{t+1} - E_t i_{t+1}$ be the expectational error in forecasting the future one-period rate, equation (10.37) implies that

$$\tfrac{1}{2}(i_{t+1} - i_t) = I_t - i_t - \xi_t + \tfrac{1}{2}\varepsilon_{t+1} \qquad (10.39)$$

which is usually interpreted to mean that the slope coefficient in a regression of one-half the change in the short rate on the spread between the long rate and the short rate should equal 1. We have previously noted that actual estimates of this slope coefficient have generally been much less than 1, and have even been negative.

The final aspect of the model is a description of the behavior of the central bank. Since many central banks use the short-term interest rate as their operational policy instrument, and since they often engage in interest-rate smoothing, McCallum assumes $i_t = i_{t-1} + \mu(I_t - i_t) + \zeta_t$.[21] However, problems of multiple equilibria may arise when policy responds to forward-looking variables such as I_t (see Bernanke and Woodford [1997]). To avoid this possibility, assume that policy adjusts the short-term rate directly in response to the exogenous disturbance ξ_t according to

$$i_t = i_{t-1} - \mu \xi_t + \zeta_t \qquad (10.40)$$

where ζ is a white-noise process and $|\mu| < 1$. According to (10.40), a rise in the risk premium in the long rate induces a policy response that lowers the short rate. Exogenous changes in risk that alter the term structure might also affect consumption or investment spending, leading the central bank to lower short-term interest

---

21. McCallum actually allows the coefficient on i_{t-1} in (10.40) to differ from 1.

rates to counter the contractionary effects of a positive realization of ξ_t. Because we have not introduced any real explanation for either ξ or why policy might respond to it, it is important to keep in mind that this is only an illustrative example that serves to suggest how policy behavior might affect the term structure.

Equations (10.37)–(10.40) form a simple model that can be used to study how policy responses to the term-structure risk premium (i.e., μ) affect the observed relationship between short-term and long-term interest rates. From (10.40), $E_t i_{t+1} = i_t - \mu\rho\xi_t$, so

$$I_t = \tfrac{1}{2}(i_t + E_t i_{t+1}) + \xi_t = i_t + \left(1 - \frac{\mu\rho}{2}\right)\xi_t$$

This implies that

$$\left(1 - \frac{\mu\rho}{2}\right)^{-1}(I_t - i_t) = \xi_t$$

Using this result, equation (10.39) can be written as

$$\tfrac{1}{2}(i_{t+1} - i_t) = I_t - i_t - \left(1 - \frac{\mu\rho}{2}\right)^{-1}(I_t - i_t) + \tfrac{1}{2}\varepsilon_{t+1}$$

or

$$\tfrac{1}{2}(i_{t+1} - i_t) = -\left(\frac{\mu\rho}{2 - \mu\rho}\right)(I_t - i_t) + \tfrac{1}{2}\varepsilon_{t+1} \tag{10.41}$$

so that we would expect the regression coefficient on $I_t - i_t$ to be $-\left(\dfrac{\mu\rho}{2 - \mu\rho}\right)$ and not 1. In other words, the estimated slope of the term structure, even when the expectations model is correct, will depend on the serial correlation properties of the term premium (ρ) and on the policy response to the spread between long and short rates (μ). The problem arises even though equation (10.39) implies $\tfrac{1}{2}(i_{t+1} - i_t) = a + b(I_t - i_t) + x_{t+1}$ with $a = 0$ and $b = 1$ because the error term x_{t+1} is equal to $-\xi_t + \tfrac{1}{2}\varepsilon_{t+1}$; since this is correlated with $I_t - i_t$, ordinary least squares is an inconsistent estimator of b.

Rather than employing an equation such as (10.40) to represent policy behavior, Rudebusch (1995) uses data from periods of funds-rate targeting (1974–1979 and 1984–1992) to estimate a model of the Federal Reserve's target for the funds rate. Using this model, he is then able to simulate the implied behavior of the term structure, using the expectations hypothesis to link funds-rate behavior to the behavior of longer-term interest rates. He finds that the manner in which the Fed has adjusted its target can account for the failure of the spread between long and short rates to have much predictive content for changes in long rates, at least at horizons of three to 12 months [that is, for the failure to obtain a coefficient of 1 (or even a significant coefficient) in a regression of $\frac{1}{2}(i_{t+1} - i_t)$ on $(I_t - i_t)$]. Thus, if the three-month rate exceeds the funds rate, equation (10.28) would appear to predict a rise in the funds rate. As Rudebusch demonstrates, the Fed tends to set its target for the funds rate at a level it expects to maintain. In this case, any spread between the funds rate and other rates has no implications for future changes in the funds rate (in terms of equation [10.40], $\mu \approx 0$). Only as new information becomes available might the target funds rate change.

Fuhrer (1996) provides further evidence on the relationship between the Fed's policy rule and the behavior of long-term interest rates. He estimates time-varying parameters of a policy reaction rule for the funds rate consistent with observed long-term rates. Agents are assumed to use the current parameter values of the policy rule to forecast future short rates.[22] Fuhrer argues that the parameters he obtains are consistent with general views on the evolution of the Fed's reaction function. Balduzzi, Bertola, Foresi, and Klapper (1997) find that during the 1989–1996 period of Fed funds rate targeting in the United States, the term structure was consistent with a regime in which changes in the target for the fund rate occur infrequently but are partially predictable.

10.4.3   Expected Inflation and the Term Structure

The term structure has played an important role in recent years as an indicator of inflationary expectations. Since market interest rates are the sum of an expected real return and an expected inflation premium, the nominal interest rate on an n-period bond can be expressed as

$$i_{n,t} = \frac{1}{n}\sum_{i=0}^{n} E_t r_{t+i} + \frac{1}{n} E_t \bar{\pi}_{t+n}$$

where $E_t r_{t+i}$ is the one-period real rate expected at time t to prevail at $t+i$ and $E_t \bar{\pi}_{t+n} \equiv E_t p_{t+n} - p_t$ is the expected change in log price from t to $t+n$. If real rates are stationary around a constant value $\bar{r}$, then $\frac{1}{n}\sum_{i=0}^{n} E_t r_{t+i} \approx \bar{r}$ and

22. As Fuhrer notes, this behavior is not fully rational because agents presumably learn that the policy rule changes over time. However, the time-varying parameters approximately follow a random-walk process, so using the current values to forecast future policy does not introduce large systematic errors.

$$i_{n,t} \approx \bar{r} + \frac{1}{n} E_t \bar{\pi}_{t+n}$$

In this case, fluctuations in the long rate will be caused mainly by variations in expected inflation. Based on a study of interest rates on nominal and indexed government bonds in the United Kingdom, Barr and Campbell (1996) conclude that "almost 80% of the movement in long-term nominal rates appears to be due to changes in expected long-term inflation." For this reason, increases in long-term nominal rates of interest are often interpreted as signaling an increase in expected inflation.

Figure 10.1 shows U.S. quarterly data on nominal interest rates of various maturity. FYFF is the federal funds rate, an overnight rate on bank reserves. FYGN3 is the rate on three-month Treasury securities, while FYGT10 is the rate on 10-year constant-maturity government bonds. FYBAAC is the rate on Baa-rated corporate bonds. The patterns exhibited by the rates are quite similar; therefore, most theoretical models focus on a single representative interest rate. All nominal interest rates rose during the 1960s and 1970s as inflation increased, reflecting the relationship between expected inflation and nominal interest rates. All rates trended downward during the 1980s as inflation, together with expected inflation, declined. Rates of

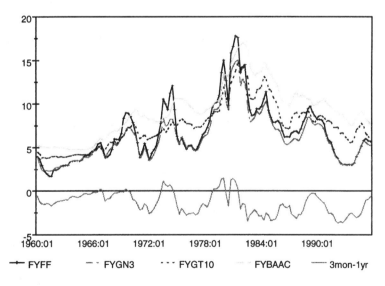

Figure 10.1
Short- and Long-Term Interest Rates

different maturity do display different behavior over shorter time intervals. The early 1990s provide one example of a period in which short rates declined much more than long rates.

Also shown in Figure 10.1 is the spread between the three-month Treasury bill rate and the 1-year government bond rate. This spread is normally negative, but its peaks have occurred at times typically associated with contractionary monetary policy; 1967, 1975, 1979–80, and 1990 are periods of economic slowdowns or recessions. Several authors have found that interest-rate spreads have predictive value for forecasting future output (Stock and Watson 1989; Bernanke and Blinder 1992; B. Friedman and Kuttner 1992). Friedman and Kuttner, for example, report that the spread between the commercial paper rate and the Treasury bill rate has predictive content for real output in the United States.

Short-run changes in long rates, particularly those following changes in monetary policy, are often interpreted as signaling the market's assessment of future inflation. Thus, a policy-induced rise in short rates that is accompanied by a decline in long rates would be interpreted as meaning the contractionary policy (the rise in short rates) is expected to lower future inflation, thereby lowering nominal long-term interest rates and future short-term rates. Conversely, a cut in the short-run policy rate that is accompanied by a rise in long rates would provide evidence that the central bank was following an inflationary policy. Goodfriend (1993) provides an interpretation of U.S. monetary policy in the period 1979–1992 based on the notion that long-term interest rates provide important information on market inflation expectations.

Buttiglione, Del Giovane, and Tristani (1996) have examined the impact of policy rate changes on forward rates in OECD countries. Under the hypothesis that changes in monetary policy do not affect the expected real interest rate far in the future, changes in the forward rates implied by the term structure should reflect the impact of the policy change on expected future inflation. The forward interest rate on a one-period discount bond, n periods in the future, can be derived from the rates on n- and $(n+1)$–period bonds and is equal to

$$f_t^n = \frac{(1 + i_{n+1,t})^{n+1}}{(1 + i_{n,t})^n} - 1 \approx (n+1)i_{n+1,t} - ni_{n,t}$$

Thus, if long-term expected real rates are constant, then for large n, $f_t^n \approx \bar{r} + E_t\bar{\pi}_{t+n+1} - E_t\bar{\pi}_{t+n} = \bar{r} + E_t[p_{t+n+1} - p_{t+n}]$, or $f_t^n \approx \bar{r} + E_t\pi_{t+n+1}$. The forward rate then provides a direct estimate of future expected rates of inflation.[23] Interestingly,

---

23. Söderlind and Svensson (1997) provide a survey of techniques for estimating market expectations from the term structure.

Buttiglione, Del Giovane, and Tristani find that a contractionary shift in policy (a rise in the short-term policy interest rate) lowered forward rates for some countries and raised them for others. The response of forward rates was closely related to a country's average inflation rate; for low-inflation countries, a policy action that increased short-term rates was estimated to lower forward rates. This response is consistent with the hypothesis that the increases in the short rate represented a credible policy expected to reduce inflation. In countries with high-inflation experiences, increases in short rates were not associated with decreases in forward rates.

A key maintained hypothesis in the view that movements in interest rates reveal information about inflation expectations is that the Fisher hypothesis, the hypothesis that nominal interest rates will incorporate a premium for expected inflation, holds. Suppose that the real rate is stationary around an average value of $\bar{r}$. Then, since $i_t = r_t + \pi_{t+1}^e = r_t + \pi_{t+1} + e_{t+1}$, where e_t is the inflation forecast error (which is stationary under rational expectations), we can write $i_t - \pi_{t+1} = v_t$ with v_t stationary. Thus, if the nominal interest rate and the inflation rate are nonstationary, they must be cointegrated under the Fisher hypothesis. This is the sense in which long-term movements in inflation should be reflected in the nominal interest rate. Mishkin (1992) has adopted this cointegrating interpretation of the Fisher relationship to test for the presence of a long-term relationship between inflation and nominal rates in the United States. If over a particular time period neither i nor π is integrated of order 1 but instead both are stationary, then there is no real meaning to the statement that permanent shifts in the level of inflation should cause similar movements in nominal rates because such permanent shifts have not occurred. If either i or π is $I(1)$, they should both be $I(1)$ and they should be cointegrated. Mishkin finds the evidence to be consistent with the Fisher relationship.

10.5 A Model for Policy Analysis

While the basic aggregate-supply, aggregate-demand model typified by equations (10.1) to (10.4) is widely used for policy analysis, it is too highly stylized and too heavily focused on the money supply as a policy tool to provide an adequate or completely satisfactory framework for policy analysis. Chapter 5 demonstrated how this simple framework could be derived as an approximation to a fully specified dynamic equilibrium model, but the impulse-response functions implied by that approximation failed to match the empirical evidence on the lags with which monetary-policy actions affect the real economy and inflation. And, by including only a single interest rate, the framework could not distinguish between the type of

short-term rate commonly employed by central banks as a policy instrument and
the longer-term rates relevant for consumption and investment decisions.

In this section, we review a model based on Fuhrer and Moore (1995a, 1995b) and
Fuhrer (1994a, 1997a) that incorporates a richer dynamic structure for price adjustment and a term structure of interest rates into a basic aggregate-supply, aggregate-
demand framework. Such a structure helps to bridge the gap between the simple
theoretical models used for gaining insights into policy questions and the large-scale
empirical models commonly employed by central banks. This particular model is
illustrative of others in the class; Taylor (1993b) has, for example, built upon similar
foundations to develop open-economy and multicountry models for policy analysis.
Other recent papers developing small models that could be used for policy analysis
are Yun (1996), King and Wolman (1998), McCallum and Nelson (1998), Rotemberg
and Woodford (1998), Rudebusch and Svensson (1998), Fuhrer (1979c), and Ireland
(1997).

10.5.1 A Closed-Economy Model

The model consists of four equations. The first relates aggregate spending to lagged
values of output and the long-term real interest rate; it corresponds to the aggregate
demand equation (10.2). The second equation is a term structure equation that links
the long-term rate to current and expected future values of the short rate. The third
equation is an inflation-adjustment equation in which current inflation depends on
lagged and expected future inflation and output; this equation will be based on the
specification discussed in section 5.5.4. The final equation is a policy-reaction function
that describes the evolution of the short-term interest rate, the latter assumed to be
the instrument of monetary policy.

The two critical components are the inflation-adjustment equation and the policy-
reaction function, so we can deal very briefly with the other two equations first. The
aggregate-spending relationship, corresponding to a traditional IS function, takes the
form

$$y_t = a_1 y_{t-1} + a_2 y_{t-2} - a_3 r_{t-1} + u_t \qquad (10.42)$$

where y is the deviation of log output from its steady-state level, r is the real interest
rate on long-term bonds, and u is an aggregate-demand shock, taken to follow a
first-order autoregressive process:

$$u_t = \rho u_{t-1} + \varepsilon_t$$

The parameters a_1 and a_2 will be important in governing the dynamic response of
output to shocks. Monetary policy will affect demand via r, so the assumption that

time-t spending depends on r_{t-1} will (partially) account for a lagged response of output to policy changes.

If equation (10.42) is compared to the aggregate spending equation (5.35) that was derived in section 5.4.1 from a model of optimizing agents, three important differences are apparent. First, (10.42) incorporates lagged values of output and the real, long-term interest rate. The presence of lagged variables will help the equation capture the dynamics in the data, but their presence is not motivated by any theoretical argument. Second, models of optimal consumption choice imply that current demand should depend on expected future income. Changes in current income that are expected to be permanent will have larger effects on spending than temporary changes will. Unless the lagged output terms are proxying for expected future output, this channel is absent from (10.42). Kerr and King (1996) discuss how the evaluation of interest rate policy rules can be affected by the role of expected future output, while McCallum and Nelson (1998) conduct an empirical evaluation of alternative policy rules using a small model in which current aggregate demand depends on expectations of future output. Finally, equation (10.42) is based on the assumption that the long-term bond rate is the interest rate that is important for aggregate consumption and investment decisions. The models developed in Chapter 5 contained only a single interest rate.

The long-term real rate is related, via the term structure, to the current short rate and expectations of future short rates. If expected real holding period yields are equalized on the long-term bond and the nominal federal funds rate i_t^f, then the two rates will be related by

$$r_t - D[E_t r_{t+1} - r_t] = i_t^f - E_t \pi_{t+1} \qquad (10.43)$$

where D is Macaulay's duration.[24] If $r_t > i_t^f - E_t \pi_{t+1}$, then expected real returns can be equal only if a capital loss is anticipated on the long-term bond. This implies $E_t r_{t+1} > r_t$; the long rate is expected to rise and the price of the long-term bond to fall. Conversely, expectations of a decline in the long rate, and a corresponding capital gain on long-term bonds, are consistent with the current long rate being less than the current expected real funds rate. Equation (10.43) can be solved forward to

---

24. See Shiller (1990) for a discussion of duration. A long-term coupon bond involving payments at different dates in the future can be viewed as a sequence of discount bonds, one associated with each coupon payment of the original bond. Payments further into the future have smaller value today because of discounting. Macaulay's duration provides a measure of the effective term of the original bond by taking a weighted average of the terms of these discount bonds, with each term weighted by a discount factor. For discount bonds, duration is equal to the term of the bond. For coupon bonds, duration is less than the term.

show that the current value of r_t depends on the current and expected future values of the real funds rate.

The most critical aspects of the model are those related to inflation adjustment and the setting of the policy instrument. Price and wage adjustment is based on the Fuhrer and Moore (1995a) model of multiperiod, overlapping nominal contracts that lead inflation to depend on both past inflation and expected future inflation (see section 5.5.4). For our example, assume contract prices x_t are set for two periods, with the aggregate price level p_t equal to a weighted average of contract prices set at times $t-1$ and t. Assuming half of all contracts are negotiated each period,

$$p_t = \tfrac{1}{2}(x_t + x_{t-1})$$

Define the real value of contracts negotiated at time t as $x_t - p_t \equiv z_t$. Define the index of average "real" contract prices negotiated in contracts still in effect at time t as

$$v_t \equiv \tfrac{1}{2}[z_t + z_{t-1}] \tag{10.44}$$

Fuhrer and Moore assume that in setting z_t, agents take two factors into account. First, they attempt to achieve a current real contract price equal to the expected average of the real contract index over the two-period life of the contract, $\tfrac{1}{2}(v_t + \mathrm{E}_t v_{t+1})$. Second, the contracted real price can deviate from this average expected index to reflect the current and expected state of the business cycle. This latter effect is taken to equal $\dfrac{\gamma}{2}(y_t + \mathrm{E}_t y_{t+1})$. Combining these assumptions with (10.44) yields

$$z_t = \tfrac{1}{2}(v_t + \mathrm{E}_t v_{t+1}) + \frac{\gamma}{2}(y_t + \mathrm{E}_t y_{t+1})$$

$$= \tfrac{1}{4}(z_{t-1} + 2z_t + \mathrm{E}_t z_{t+1}) + \frac{\gamma}{2}(y_t + \mathrm{E}_t y_{t+1})$$

$$= \tfrac{1}{2}(z_{t-1} + \mathrm{E}_t z_{t+1}) + \gamma(y_t + \mathrm{E}_t y_{t+1}) \tag{10.45}$$

Since $p_t = \tfrac{1}{2}(x_t + x_{t-1})$ and $x_t = z_t + p_t$, we can write the inflation rate as

$$\pi_t \equiv p_t - p_{t-1} = z_t + z_{t-1} \tag{10.46}$$

The inflation rate will depend on the real contract prices set at time t and $t-1$. The presence of z_{t-1} imparts a sluggishness to inflation adjustment in that new information that becomes available at the start of period t about current or future monetary policy can be reflected in z_t but not, by definition, in z_{t-1}. This fact limits the flexibility of current inflation to jump in response to new information. As shown in section 5.5.4, inflation can also be expressed as

$$\pi_t = \tfrac{1}{2}(\pi_{t-1} + \mathrm{E}_t\pi_{t+1}) + \gamma q_t + \eta_t \qquad (10.47)$$

where $\eta_t = -[\pi_t - \mathrm{E}_{t-1}\pi_t]$ and q_t depends on lagged, current, and expected future output.

The Fuhrer-Moore specification is closely related to, but distinct from, Taylor's original work on staggered, multiperiod overlapping contracts and aggregate-price adjustment. In the specific example studied in section 5.5.1, Taylor's model of price-level adjustment led to a reduced-form expression for the price level in which p_t depends on p_{t-1} and $\mathrm{E}_t p_{t+1}$. The backward-looking aspect of price behavior causes unanticipated reductions in the money supply to cause real output declines. Prices set previously are now "too" high relative to the new path for the money supply. Only as contracts expire can their real value be reduced to levels consistent with the new, lower money supply. However, the inflation rate depends on $\mathrm{E}_t \pi_{t+1}$, not π_{t-1}, so the inflation process does not display stickiness. As Ball (1994a) has shown, price rigidities based on backward-looking behavior in the price-level process need not imply that policies to reduce inflation by reducing the *growth rate* of money will cause a recession. Since m continues to grow, just at a slower rate, the real value of preset prices continues to be eroded, unlike the case of a level reduction in m. In the Fuhrer-Moore specification, the backward-looking nature of the *inflation* process implies that reductions in the growth rate of money will be costly in terms of output.

The final component of the Fuhrer-Moore model is a description of policy. The funds rate is taken to be the instrument of monetary policy, and the policy maker is assumed to respond to deviations of inflation from target, the output gap, and changes in output:

$$i_t^f = b_1 i_{t-1}^f + b_2(\pi_t - \pi^T) + b_3 y_t + b_4(y_t - y_{t-1}) + \varphi_t \qquad (10.48)$$

The parameters of the policy rule are all taken to be positive with $b_1 \le 1$. If inflation is above its target π^T, the funds rate is increased. Similarly, output above trend ($y_t > 0$) or an increase in output (even if the level is below trend) triggers funds-rate increases. In the terminology of Phillips (1957), the term $b_4(y_t - y_{t-1})$ represents a derivative response. The term φ_t is a mean-zero, serially uncorrelated random variable that represents a stochastic policy shock.[25]

---

25. Fuhrer (1996) reports estimates of a policy rule for the Fed similar to (10.48). He finds the parameters have evolved over time.

Table 10.1
Parameter Values (Baseline Case)

Coefficient	Value
a_1	1.53
a_2	−0.55
a_3	−0.35
b_1	0.84
b_2	0.27
b_3	0.11
b_4	0.42
γ	0.002

10.5.1.1 Policy Shocks Recall from Chapter 1 that monetary policy shocks, identified for the United States as shocks to the fed funds rate, produce a hump-shaped response in output that was spread over several quarters. The response of inflation was much more delayed. We can solve our modified Fuhrer-Moore policy model to see if it replicates these basic "facts." Doing so requires that specific values be assigned to the parameters of the model. Fuhrer (1994a) reports FIML estimates for a version of the model that incorporates a more complicated contracting specification than that of equation (10.45). Based on his estimates, Table 10.1 shows the baseline parameter values to be used for the model.

Figure 10.2 shows the response of output, the long-term real rate, and inflation to a shock to the policy instrument. The output response is much more consistent with empirical estimates of the impact of policy shocks than were the equilibrium models of Chapters 2 and 3 or the simple sticky-wage modification to a money-in-the-utility-function model of Chapter 5. The output response displays the hump-shaped pattern seen in estimated VARs for the United States and other industrial economies (Sims 1992; Taylor 1993b). The policy shock results in a rise in the short-term rate which, because $b_1 = 0.84$, displays a great deal of persistence and returns only gradually to the baseline. The policy shock leaves the funds rate (not shown) above the baseline for about eight quarters, and the figure shows that the long-term rate rises, but only about one-tenth as much as the funds rate. The long-rate increase, with a one-period lag, causes real output to decline. Output reaches its trough almost two years after the contractionary policy shock. Inflation declines temporarily, but it does not respond as sharply as output.

10.5.1.2 The Role of the Policy Rule The simple Fuhrer-Moore model captures some of the basic stylized facts of a monetary shock for the United States. Of more interest than the impact of exogenous "policy" shocks, however, is the role the parameters of the policy rule play in affecting the behavior of the economy. Policy

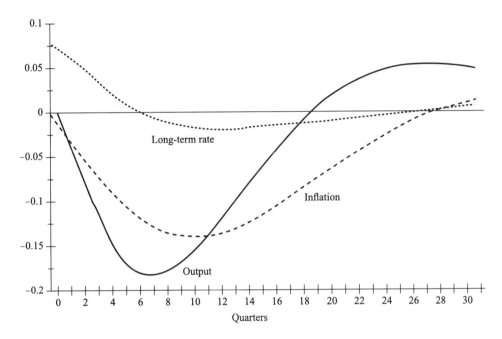

Figure 10.2
Response to a Policy Shock (Baseline Parameters)

makers can choose how to respond to inflation and output movements, and in the Fuhrer-Moore model these choices are captured by the parameters b_1 to b_4. The model can be used to examine how the response of long-term rates, output, and inflation to nonpolicy-originating disturbances might vary with alternative values of these parameters.

Figures 10.3 and 10.4 show the responses of output and inflation to a demand shock (ε_t) for different values of the policy parameters b_2 and b_3. The outcomes for three alternatives are shown. As revealed by Figure 10.3, the impact on output of an expansionary aggregate demand shock depends importantly on the parameters of the monetary policy rule for the funds rate. The solid line is based on the parameter values in Table 10.1. The alternatives represent stronger policy responses to either inflation, output, or both. Increasing the reaction to deviations of output from trend from 0.11 to 1.0 significantly dampens the impact of a demand shock on output. By moving the funds rate more aggressively, output is stabilized more effectively, and the standard deviation of output falls from 4.369 with the baseline parameters to 2.744.[26]

---

26. This is consistent with the argument of Ball (1997) that an increased response to output would provide better macroeconomic stabilization. See section 10.5.1.3.

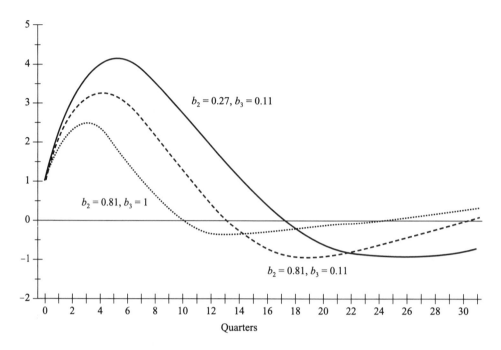

Figure 10.3
Output Response to Demand Shock under Alternative Policy Rules

For a given b_3, increases in b_2, the response to deviations of inflation from target, also act to stabilize output fluctuations, although the effects are small. Increasing b_2 by a factor of three, from 0.27 to 0.81, lowers the variance of output when $b_3 = 0.11$ but increases it (slightly) when $b_3 = 1$.

Figure 10.4 illustrates the effects of the policy-rule parameters on inflation. Aggregate-demand shocks lead to the greatest inflation responses for the baseline values. As with the output responses, increasing b_3 so that the funds rate is adjusted more strongly to output movements leads to significantly smaller inflation fluctuations.

The term structure behavior also is affected by the values of b_2 and b_3. A much more aggressive policy response to both inflation and output leads to greatly increased movements in the funds rate. The impact on long rates is much more muted, since the stronger response of the funds rate when $b_2 = 0.81$ and $b_3 = 1$ is offset by the faster return to zero. Under the baseline values, movements in the funds rate are much more persistent.

These experiments illustrate how a small model can be used to analyze the impact of alternative monetary-policy rules. The advantage of the model is the small number

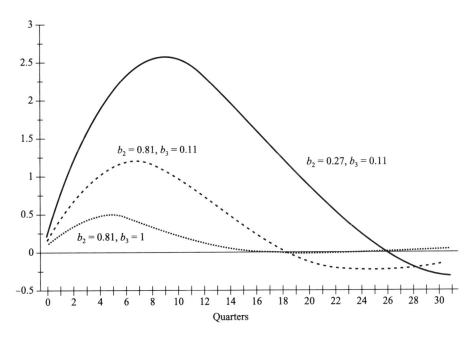

Figure 10.4
Inflation Response to a Demand Shock under Alternative Policy Rules

of parameters involved. These can be varied to gain insight into how changes in the systematic response of policy to economic conditions will alter the dynamic properties of output, inflation, and interest rates. As such, the model can serve as a laboratory for conducting policy experiments. Further examples of the use of small econometric models, as well as estimated VARs, for evaluating alternative policy rules include, in addition to the papers cited earlier, McCallum (1988) and Judd and Motley (1991, 1992). These last papers simulate the impacts of alternative policy rules, focusing on the use of various interest-rate and monetary-base feedback rules.

The disadvantage of this approach is the absence of a direct link from the decisions of agents in the economy to the relationships characterizing aggregate economic behavior. As Lucas (1976) long ago emphasized, changes in the policy regime have the potential to alter the decision rules agents follow, leading to changes in the empirical regularities on which models such as the one studied in this section are based.

10.5.1.3   Optimal Policy   While the previous subsection demonstrated the role of alternative policy parameter values through simulations, the linear structure of the model means that one can obtain analytic solutions when the central bank's objective function is quadratic. To illustrate, this subsection further simplifies the model to obtain a particularly tractable version. The simplifications involve dropping the distinction between the short-term interest rate and the long-term rate and ignoring the role of expected future inflation in the inflation-adjustment equation.[27] With these modifications, the model consists of the following two equations:

$$y_t = a_1 y_{t-1} + a_2 y_{t-2} - a_3(i_{t-1} - E_{t-1}\pi_t) + u_t \tag{10.49}$$

$$\pi_t = \pi_{t-1} + \gamma y_t + \eta_t \tag{10.50}$$

The disturbances u_t and η_t are taken to be serially uncorrelated with means equal to zero. Rudesbusch and Svensson (1997) estimate a model similar to (10.49) and (10.50) and derive the optimal policy rule. They also use the model to evaluate a large number of rules for setting the funds rate.

Policy actions (the setting of i_t) affect output and inflation with one-period lags in this formulation.[28] At time t, the choice of i_t affects y_{t+1} and π_{t+1}, but y_t and π_t are predetermined. Using the inflation equation, $E_t\pi_{t+1} = \pi_t + \gamma E_t y_{t+1}$, so period $t+1$ output will equal

$$y_{t+1} = a_1 y_t + a_2 y_{t-1} - a_3(i_t - \pi_t - \gamma E_t y_{t+1}) + u_{t+1}$$

Taking expectations of both sides, conditional on time t information, yields an expression for $E_t y_{t+1}$; using this expression to eliminate $E_t y_{t+1}$ gives

$$y_{t+1} = \frac{a_1 y_t + a_2 y_{t-1} - a_3(i_t - \pi_t)}{1 - a_3\gamma} + u_{t+1}$$

With y_t, y_{t-1}, and π_t all predetermined when i_t is chosen, it will prove convenient to define

$$\theta_t \equiv \frac{a_1 y_t + a_2 y_{t-1} - a_3(i_t - \pi_t)}{1 - a_3\gamma} \tag{10.51}$$

27. Fuhrer (1997b) has suggested based on U.S. data that forward-looking expectations may be unimportant empirically.

28. Svensson (1997a) has used a variant of this model in which the output variable in the inflation equation is lagged one period. This implies that policy affects output with a one-period lag and inflation with a two-period lag. The longer lag in the response of inflation is consistent with empirical evidence. McCallum (1997b) has shown, however, that the use of equation (10.50) in which lagged actual inflation appears with coefficient 1, can lead to problems of instability that would not arise if expectations of current or future inflation were included.

and treat this as the choice variable of the central bank. In terms of θ_t, then, the aggregate-demand and inflation equations become simply

$$y_{t+1} = \theta_t + u_{t+1} \tag{10.52}$$

and

$$\pi_{t+1} = \pi_t + \gamma\theta_t + v_{t+1} \tag{10.53}$$

where $v_{t+1} = \gamma u_{t+1} + \eta_{t+1}$.

Suppose the objective of the policy maker is to pick θ_t at each point in time to minimize expected loss given by[29]

$$L = \tfrac{1}{2}\mathrm{E}_t \sum_{i=1}^{\infty} \beta^i [\lambda y_{t+i}^2 + \pi_{t+i}^2] \tag{10.54}$$

The problem of minimizing expected loss subject to (10.52) and (10.53) is a simple problem in dynamic optimization. To solve it and obtain the optimal decision rule of the policy maker for setting θ_t (and therefore i_t), note that the only state variable at time t is π_t. We can therefore define the value function $V(\pi_t)$ as the expected present value of the policy maker's loss function if θ_{t+i} is set optimally. The value function satisfies

$$V(\pi_t) = \min \mathrm{E}_t\{\tfrac{1}{2}(\lambda y_{t+1}^2 + \pi_{t+1}^2) + \beta V(\pi_{t+1})\}$$

where the minimization is subject to (10.52) and (10.53). Substituting these two constraints into the value function yields

$$V(\pi_t) = \min \mathrm{E}_t\{\tfrac{1}{2}\lambda(\theta_t + u_{t+1})^2 + \tfrac{1}{2}(\pi_t + \gamma\theta_t + v_{t+1})^2 + \beta V(\pi_t + \gamma\theta_t + v_{t+1})\}$$

The first-order conditions are

$$(\lambda + \gamma^2)\theta_t + \gamma\pi_t + \gamma\beta\mathrm{E}_t V_\pi(\pi_{t+1}) = 0 \tag{10.55}$$

and, from the envelope theorem,

$$V_\pi(\pi_t) = \pi_t + \gamma\theta_t + \beta\mathrm{E}_t V_\pi(\pi_{t+1})$$

Multiplying the second of these by γ and adding it to the first implies $\gamma V_\pi(\pi_t) = -\lambda\theta_t$. Updating this one period and taking expectations, $\gamma\beta\mathrm{E}_t V_\pi(\pi_{t+1})$ can be eliminated from (10.55).

---

29. With y_t and π_t predetermined, the first term in the loss function is dated $t+1$.

$$(\lambda + \gamma^2)\theta_t + \gamma\pi_t - \beta\lambda E_t\theta_{t+1} = 0$$

Rearranging,

$$\theta_t = -\left(\frac{\gamma}{\lambda + \gamma^2}\right)\pi_t + \beta\left(\frac{\lambda}{\lambda + \gamma^2}\right)E_t\theta_{t+1} \tag{10.56}$$

Given the linear-quadratic structure of this problem, the optimal decision rule will be of the form $\theta_t = B\pi_t$. This in turn implies $E_t\theta_{t+1} = BE_t\pi_{t+1} = B(\pi_t + \gamma\theta_t)$. Substituting these into (10.56), one obtains the following quadratic whose solution yields the desired value of B:

$$\beta\lambda\gamma B^2 + (\beta\lambda - \lambda - \gamma^2)B - \gamma = 0$$

Because $\pi_{t+1} = \pi_t + \gamma\theta_t + v_{t+1} = (1 + \gamma B)\pi_t + v_{t+1}$, stability of the inflation process requires $|1 + \gamma B| < 1$, so it is the negative solution for B that is relevant.

Recall that θ_t was defined in equation (10.51) as $[a_1 y_t + a_2 y_{t-1} - a_3(i_t - \pi_t)]/(1 - a_3\gamma)$, so the optimal rule for the actual policy instrument i_t is

$$i_t = \left[1 - \frac{B(1 - a_3\gamma)}{a_3}\right]\pi_t + \frac{a_1}{a_3}y_t + \frac{a_2}{a_3}y_{t-1}$$

which calls for the nominal interest rate to be adjusted on the basis of inflation and output. For the parameter values given in Table 10.1 and $\beta = 0.989$, Figure 10.5 shows the coefficient on inflation for this optimal policy rule as a function of λ, the relative weight on output fluctuations in the loss function. For the case of equal weight on output and inflation ($\lambda = 1$), the policy rule becomes

$$i_t = 1.26\pi_t + 4.37y_t - 1.57y_{t-1}$$

Using the parameters proposed by Ball (1997) for a similar exercise, one obtains[30]

$$i_t = 1.46\pi_t + 0.8y_t$$

Both these rules for adjusting the nominal interest rate are similar to "Taylor rules." Taylor (1993a) has shown that a rule of the form $i_t = 1.5\pi_t + 0.5y_t$ provides a good fit to the behavior of the federal-funds rate in the United States. According to

30. Ball's model has only one lag of output in the aggregate-spending equation. He views his model as appropriate for annual data, so the numbers reported are based on $\beta = 0.96$. His other parameter values are $a_1 = 0.8$, $a_3 = 1.0$, and $\gamma = 0.4$. Note that this implies a much stronger response of inflation to output (γ) and of spending to the interest rate (a_3). These changes affect mainly the coefficient on output. Ball also assumes output enters with a lag in the inflation equation, so he actually has y_{t-1} in the policy rule.

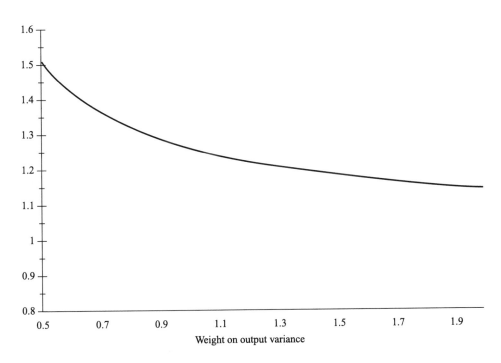

Figure 10.5
Inflation Coefficient in Interest-Rate Rule

the Taylor rule, the nominal rate is increased more than one-for-one with any increase in inflation. This policy ensures a real rate response that will act to lower inflation. For a given inflation rate, the real rate is also increased in response to output expansions. This rule, therefore, ensures that policy acts automatically to stabilize inflation and output.

In the model of this section, policy can affect the volatility of output and inflation. An efficient policy rule is one that minimizes the variance of inflation for each variance of output around the natural rate. This then provides an efficiency frontier that shows the feasible set of output and inflation variances that can be achieved. Along this frontier, acting to stabilize inflation more requires that output become more volatile. The relative weight placed on output and inflation volatility, the parameter λ in the loss function equation (10.54), then determines where on this frontier the central bank should locate. Examples of recent works that try to map out the efficiency frontier and evaluate alternative policy rules include Fuhrer (1994a, 1997) and Levin, Wieland, and Williams (1998) for the United States, de Brouwer and O'Regan (1997) for Australia, Amano, Coletti, and Macklem (1998) for Canada, and Batini and Haldan (1998) for the United Kingdom. Judd and Rudebusch (1997) show that the estimated parameters in a Taylor rule have varied with changes in the Fed chairmanship.

10.5.2 An Open-Economy Model

The basic Fuhrer-Moore model is a closed-economy model. Among recent analyses of interest-rate rules using calibrated and estimated small open-economy models are Svensson (1997d) and Batini and Haldan (1998). Taylor (1989, 1993b) has worked extensively with multicountry versions of similar small-scale, rational-expectations models designed to address policy issues.

To modify the Fuhrer-Moore model to incorporate open-economy considerations, the aggregate-spending equation (10.42) needs to incorporate the effect of the real exchange rate on foreign and domestic demand. For a two-country model, the IS specifications are assumed to take the form

$$y_t = a_y y_{t-1} - a_r r_{t-1} + a_\rho \rho_{t-1} + a_y^* y_t^* + u_t \tag{10.57}$$

$$y_t^* = a_y y_{t-1}^* - a_r r_{t-1}^* - a_\rho \rho_{t-1} + a_y^* y_t + u_t^* \tag{10.58}$$

where * denotes the foreign country, $\rho = s + p^* - p$ is the real exchange rate (where s is the nominal exchange rate), and we have simplified the dynamic structure by dropping the second lag of output. A rise in ρ, representing a depreciation of the home currency, shifts aggregate demand toward the home country ($a_\rho > 0$). Increases in income in either country increase aggregate demand in the other ($a_y^* > 0$).

Consumer prices in the home country are equal to $q_t = bp_t + (1-b)(s_t + p_t^*)$. Rewriting this as $q_t = p_t + (1-b)\rho_t$ and first differencing produces

$$\pi_t = p_t - p_{t-1} + (1-b)(\rho_t - \rho_{t-1})$$

$$= z_t + z_{t-1} + (1-b)(\rho_t - \rho_{t-1})$$

where domestic output price inflation is based on (10.46) and z_t is given by (10.45). A similar equation holds for foreign CPI inflation:

$$\pi_t^* = z_t^* + z_{t-1}^* - (1-b)(\rho_t - \rho_{t-1})$$

For each country, there is a term-structure equation of the form given by (10.43), while policy, in the form of a rule for the short-term nominal interest rate, will be represented by an equation of the form (10.48) for each country.[31]

---

31. An alternative would be to define policy in terms of a monetary-policy-conditions index of the type used, for example, in New Zealand. From equation (10.57), the real "MCI" would be equal to $-a_r r_{t-1} + a_\rho \rho_{t-1}$.

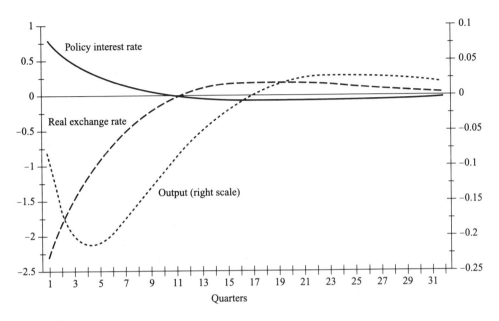

Figure 10.6
Response to a Home Policy Shock

This framework is similar to that used for multicountry policy analysis by Taylor (1993b). The major differences (besides dealing only with two countries) is the term-structure equation linking long-term and short-term interest rates, and the use of the Fuhrer-Moore inflation-adjustment model rather than Taylor's original price-level-adjustment model. To simulate the model we employ the same basic parameters as used for the closed-economy exercise with the exception that $a_y = 0.8$ and the new parameters introduced in the open-economy version are set at $a_p = 0.04$, $a_y^* = 0.1$, and $b = 0.8$.

Figure 10.6 illustrates the impact on domestic output and the real exchange rate of a domestic monetary-policy shock under the assumption that both home and foreign monetary policies are determined according to the policy rule (10.48). The rise in the short-term interest rate (the policy instrument) is followed by a decline in real output, with output following a typical hump-shaped pattern. The output decline is, from (10.57), induced by the rise in long-term rates and the real appreciation induced by the rise in interest rates. The real exchange rate does not overshoot; it falls below the baseline and then returns smoothly to its initial level. This behavior is consistent with the empirical evidence of Eichenbaum and Evans (1995) discussed in Chapter 6.

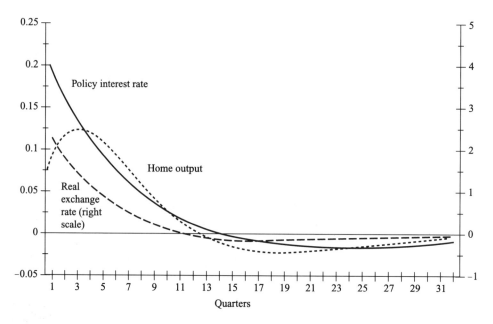

Figure 10.7
Response to a Foreign Policy Shock

Figure 10.7 illustrates the path followed by domestic real output, the real exchange rate, and the domestic monetary-policy instrument in response to a foreign monetary-policy shock. A contractionary foreign monetary policy induces a domestic output expansion. This occurs as a result of a domestic real depreciation that increases the demand for domestic output. The rise in the foreign short-term interest rate induces a rise in the domestic policy rate as well, and this dampens the domestic output expansion.

10.6 Summary

This chapter has examined a number of issues related to monetary policy. The general theme has been to focus on a short-term interest rate as the instrument of monetary policy and to move away from the traditional focus on monetary aggregates. Therefore, issues of price-level determinacy needed to be addressed, as well as the implications of interest-rate-smoothing behavior for the price level. With a short-term interest rate treated as the policy instrument, it is important also to incorporate term-structure considerations into a policy model to provide a link between the policy instrument and longer-term market interest rates that affect private-sector behavior.

The chapter concluded with simple examples of closed- and open-economy models that integrate simple aggregate-supply-and-demand frameworks with dynamics that capture the types of persistent adjustments to monetary shocks that characterize actual U.S. behavior. Despite some obvious weaknesses, models of this type provide one convenient means of simulating the effects of alternative policy rules. They are useful in giving insight into the possible effects of alternative policy rules, providing a useful compromise between highly stylized theoretical models and large-scale econometric models. To the extent that the Lucas (1976) critique is empirically relevant, the parameters of these models may be altered by changes in policy behavior. Unlike the models built directly on foundations derived from the decision problems of the agents in the economy, the models of this section are ad hoc. But unlike those earlier models, they provide useful approximations to the actual data-generating processes.

10.7   Problems

1. Suppose (10.1) is replaced by a Taylor sticky-price-adjustment model of the type studied in Chapter 5. Is the price level still indeterminate under the policy rule (10.5)? What if prices adjust according to the Fuhrer-Moore sticky-inflation model?

2. Derive the values of the unknown coefficients in (10.10) and (10.11) if the money-supply process is given by (10.15).

3. Suppose the money-supply process in section 10.4.2 is replaced with

$$m_t = \gamma m_{t-1} + \phi q_{t-1} + \xi_t$$

so that the policy maker is assumed to respond with a lag to the real rate shock, with the parameter ϕ viewed as a policy choice. Thus, policy involves a choice of γ and ϕ, with the parameter ϕ capturing the systematic response of policy to real-interest-rate shocks. Show how the effect of q_t on the one- and two-period nominal interest rates depends on ϕ. Explain why the absolute value of the impact of q_t on the spread between the long and short rates increases with ϕ.

4. Suppose the money-supply process in section 10.4.2 is replaced with

$$m_t = m_{t-1} + \xi_t - \gamma \xi_{t-1}$$

Does i_t depend on γ? Does I_t? Explain.

5. Show that equation (10.43) implies $r_t = \dfrac{1}{1+D} \displaystyle\sum_{i=0}^{\infty} \left(\dfrac{D}{1+D}\right)^i E_t(i_{t+i}^f - \pi_{t+1+i})$.

6. Ball (1997) uses the following two-equation model:

$$y_{t+1} = a_1 y_t - a_2 r_t + u_{t+1}$$

$$\pi_{t+1} = \pi_t + \gamma y_t + \eta_{t+1}$$

The disturbances u_t and η_t are taken to be serially uncorrelated. At time t, the policy maker chooses r_t, and the state variable at time t is $\pi_t + \gamma y_t \equiv \kappa_t$. Assume the policy maker's loss function is given by equation (10.54). The optimal policy rule takes the form $\theta_t = A\kappa_t$ where $\theta_t \equiv a_1 y_t - a_2 r_t$. Derive the optimal value of A.

References

Abel, A. B. 1985. "Dynamic Behavior of Capital Accumulation in a Cash-in-Advance Model." *Journal of Monetary Economics*, 16, no. 1 (July): 55–71.

Abel, A. B., and B. Bernanke. 1995. *Macroeconomics*, 2nd ed. Reading, MA: Addison-Wesley.

Abel, A. B., N. G. Mankiw, L. H. Summers, and R. Zeckhauser. 1989. "Assessing Dynamic Efficiency: Theory and Evidence." *Review of Economic Studies*, 56, no. 1 (January): 1–20.

Aiyagari, S. Rao, and Mark Gertler. 1985. "The Backing of Government Bonds and Monetarism." *Journal of Monetary Economics*, 16, no. 1 (July): 19–44.

Akerlof, G. A. 1970. "The Market for 'Lemons': Quality Uncertainty and the Market Mechanism." *Quarterly Journal of Economics*, 84, no. 3 (August): 488–500.

Akerlof, G. A., and J. L. Yellen. 1985. "Can Small Deviations from Rationality Make Significant Differences to Economic Equilibria?" *American Economic Review*, 75, no. 4 (September): 708–721.

Alchian, A. A. 1977. "Why Money?" *Journal of Money, Credit, and Banking*, 9, no. 1 (February, part 2): 133–140.

al-Nowaihi, A., and P. Levine. 1994. "Can Reputation Resolve the Monetary Policy Credibility Problem?" *Journal of Monetary Economics*, 33, no. 2 (April): 355–380.

al-Nowaihi, A., and P. Levine. 1996. "Independent but Accountable: Walsh Contracts and the Credibility Problem." CEPR Discussion Paper No. 1387.

Alesina, A. 1987. "Macroeconomic Policy in a Two-Party System as a Repeated Game." *Quarterly Journal of Economics*, 102, no. 3 (August): 651–678.

Alesina, A. 1988. "Macroeconomics and Politics." In S. Fischer (ed.), *NBER Macroeconomics Annual*, 11–55. Cambridge, MA: MIT Press.

Alesina, A., and R. Gatti. 1995. "Independent Central Banks: Low Inflation at No Cost?" *American Economic Review*, 85, no. 3 (May): 196–200.

Alesina, A., and N. Roubini. 1992. "Political Cycles in OECD Countries." *Review of Economics and Statistics*, 59, no. 4 (October): 663–688.

Alesina, A., and J. Sachs. 1988. "Political Parties and the Business Cycles in the United States: 1948–1984." *Journal of Money, Credit, and Banking*, 20, no. 1 (February): 63–82.

Alesina, A., and L. Summers. 1993. "Central Bank Independence and Macroeconomic Performance." *Journal of Money, Credit, and Banking*, 25, no. 2 (May): 157–162.

Amano, R., D. Coletti, and T. Macklem. 1998. "Monetary Policy Rules When Economic Behavior Changes." Research Department, Bank of Canada. February.

Ammer, J., and R. T. Freeman. 1995. "Inflation Targeting in the 1990s: The Experiences of New Zealand, Canada and the United Kingdom." *Journal of Economics and Business*, 47, no. 2 (May): 165–192.

Andersen, L., and J. Jordon. 1968. "Monetary and Fiscal Actions: A Test of Their Relative Importance in Economic Stabilization." Federal Reserve Bank of St. Louis *Review*, 50, November, pp. 11–24.

Andersen, T. M. 1989. "Credibility of Policy Announcements: The Output and Inflation Costs of Disinflationary Policies." *European Economic Review*, 33, no. 1 (January): 13–30.

Angelini, P. 1994a. "More on the Behavior of the Interest Rates and the Founding of the Fed." *Journal of Monetary Economics*, 34, no. 3 (December): 537–553.

Angelini, P. 1994b. "Testing for Structural Breaks: Trade-off between Power and Spurious Effects." *Journal of Monetary Economics*, 34, no. 3 (December): 561–566.

Asako, Kazumi. 1983. "The Utility Function and the Superneutrality of Money on the Transition Path." *Econometrica*, 51, no. 5 (September): 1593–1596.

Atkinson, A. B., and J. E. Stiglitz. 1972. "The Structure of Indirect Taxation and Economic Efficiency." *Journal of Public Economics*, 1, no. 1 (April): 97–119.

Attfield, C. L. F., D. Demery, and N. W. Duck. 1991. *Rational Expectations in Macroeconomics*, 2nd ed. Oxford: Blackwell.

Auernheimer, L. 1974. "The Honest Government's Guide to the Revenue from the Creation of Money." *Journal of Political Economy*, 82, no. 3 (May/June): 598–606.

Backus, D. K., and J. Driffill. 1985. "Inflation and Reputation." *American Economic Review*, 75, no. 3 (June): 530–538.

Backus, D. K., and P. J. Kehoe. 1992. "International Evidence on the Historical Properties of Business Cycles." *American Economic Review*, 82, no. 4 (September): 864–888.

Bade, R., and M. Parkin. 1984. "Central Bank Laws and Monetary Policy." Department of Economics, University of Western Ontario, London, Canada.

Bailey, M. J. 1956. "The Welfare Costs of Inflationary Finance." *Journal of Political Economy*, 64, no. 2 (April): 93–110.

Balduzzi, P., G. Bertola, S. Foresi, and L. Klapper. 1997. "Interest Rate Targeting and the Dynamics of Short-Term Rates." NBER Working Paper No. 5944, February.

Ball, L. 1991. "The Genesis of Inflation and the Costs of Disinflation." *Journal of Money, Credit, and Banking*, 23, no. 3, part 2 (August): 439–452.

Ball, L. 1993. "How Costly Is Disinflation? The Historical Evidence." Federal Reserve Bank of Philadelphia *Business Review*, November/December, pp. 17–28.

Ball, L. 1994a. "Credible Disinflation with Staggered Price-Setting." *American Economic Review*, 84, no. 1 (March): 282–289.

Ball, L. 1994b. "What Determines the Sacrifice Ratio?" In N. Gregory Mankiw (ed.), *Monetary Policy*. Chicago: University of Chicago Press.

Ball, L. 1995. "Time Consistent Inflation Policy and Persistent Changes in Inflation." *Journal of Monetary Economics*, 36, no. 2 (November): 329–350.

Ball, L. 1997. "Efficient Rules for Monetary Policy." NBER Working Paper No. 5952, March.

Ball, L., and D. Romer. 1991. "Sticky Prices as Coordination Failure." *American Economic Review*, 81, no. 3 (June): 539–552.

Bank of Canada. 1993. *Economic Behavior and Policy Choice under Price Stability*. Ottawa, Canada.

Barnett, W. A. 1980. "Economic Monetary Aggregates: An Application of Index Number and Aggregation Theory." *Journal of Econometrics*, 14, no. 1 (Summer): 11–48.

Barr, D. G., and J. Y. Campbell. 1996. "Inflation, Real Interest Rates, and the Bond Market: A Study of UK Nominal and Index-Linked Government Bond Prices." NBER Working Paper No. 5821, November.

Barro, R. J. 1974. "Are Government Bonds Net Wealth?" *Journal of Political Economy*, 82, no. 6 (November-December): 1095–1118.

Barro, R. J. 1976. "Rational Expectations and the Role of Monetary Policy." *Journal of Monetary Economics*, 2, no. 1 (January): 1–32.

Barro, R. J. 1977. "Unanticipated Money Growth and Unemployment in the United States." *American Economic Review*, 67, no. 1 (March): 101–115.

Barro, R. J. 1978. "Unanticipated Money, Output, and the Price Level in the United States." *Journal of Political Economy*, 86, no. 4 (August): 549–580.

Barro, R. J. 1979a. "On the Determination of the Public Debt." *Journal of Political Economy*, 87, no. 5, part 1 (October): 940–971.

Barro, R. J. 1979b. "Unanticipated Money Growth and Unemployment in the United States: Reply." *American Economic Review*, 69, no. 5 (December): 1004–1009.

Barro, R. J. 1981. *Money, Expectations, and Business Cycles*. New York: Academic Press.

Barro, R. J. 1986. "Reputation in a Model of Monetary Policy with Incomplete Information." *Journal of Monetary Economics*, 17, no. 1 (January): 3–20.

Barro, R. J. 1989. "Interest-Rate Targeting." *Journal of Monetary Economics*, 23, no. 1 (January): 3–30.

Barro, R. J. 1995. "Inflation and Economic Growth." Bank of England *Quarterly Bulletin*, May, pp. 39–52.

Barro, R. J. 1996. "Inflation and Growth." Federal Reserve Bank of St. Louis *Review*, 78, no. 3 (May/June): 153–169.

Barro, R. J., and D. B. Gordon. 1983a. "A Positive Theory of Monetary Policy in a Natural-Rate Model." *Journal of Political Economy*, 91, no. 4: 589–610.

Barro, R. J., and D. B. Gordon. 1983b. "Rules, Discretion, and Reputation in a Model of Monetary Policy." *Journal of Monetary Economics*, 12, no. 1: 101–121.

Barro, R. J., and R. G. King. 1984. "Time-Separable Preferences and Intertemporal-Substitution Models of Business Cycles." *Quarterly Journal of Economics*, 99, no. 4 (November): 817–839.

Barro, R. J., and M. Rush. 1980. "Unanticipated Money and Economic Activity." In S. Fischer (ed.), *Rational Expectations and Economic Policy*, 23–48. Chicago: University of Chicago Press.

Batini, N., and A. Haldan. 1998. "Forward-Looking Rules for Monetary Policy." Presented at the NBER Conference on Monetary Policy Rules. January. Islamorada, FL.

Batten, D. S., M. P. Blackwell, I. Kim, S. E. Nocera, and Y. Ozeki. 1990. "The Conduct of Monetary Policy in the Major Industrial Countries: Instruments and Operating Procedures." International Monetary Fund, Occasional Paper 70, July. Washington, DC.

Baumol, W. 1952. "The Transactions Demand for Cash." *Quarterly Journal of Economics*, 67, no. 4 (November): 545–556.

Bean, C. 1983. "Targeting Nominal Income: An Appraisal." *The Economics Journal*, 93 (December): 806–819.

Beaudry, P., and M. B. Devereux. 1995. "Monopolistic Competition, Price Setting, and the Effects of Real and Monetary Shocks." University of British Columbia Discussion Paper 93–94, Victoria, Canada.

Beetsma, R. W. J., and H. Jensen. In press. "Inflation Targets and Contracts with Uncertain Central Banker Preferences." *Journal of Money, Credit, and Banking*: forthcoming.

Benassy, Jean-Pascal. 1995. "Money and Wage Contracts in an Optimizing Model of the Business Cycle." *Journal of Monetary Economics*, 35, no. 2 (April): 303–315.

Bernanke, B. 1983. "Nonmonetary Effects of the Financial Crisis in the Propagation of the Great Depression." *American Economic Review*, 73, no. 3 (June): 257–276.

Bernanke, B. 1986. "Alternative Explanations of the Money-Income Correlation." *Carniege-Rochester Conference Series on Public Policy*, 25 (Autumn): 49–99.

Bernanke, B. S. 1993. "Credit in the Macroeconomy." Federal Reserve Bank of New York, *Quarterly Review*, 18, no. 1 (Spring): 50–70.

Bernanke, B. S., and A. S. Blinder. 1988. "Credit, Money, and Aggregate Demand." *American Economic Review*, 78, no. 2 (May): 435–439.

Bernanke, B. S., and A. S. Blinder. 1992. "The Federal Funds Rate and the Channels of Monetary Transmission." *American Economic Review*, 82, no. 4 (September): 901–921.

Bernanke, B. S., and M. Gertler. 1989. "Agency Costs, Net Worth, and Business Fluctuations." *American Economic Review*, 79, no. 1 (March): 14–31.

Bernanke, B. S., and M. Gertler. 1995. "Inside the Black Box: The Credit Channel of Monetary Policy Transmission." *Journal of Economic Perspectives*, 9, no. 4 (Fall): 27–48.

Bernanke, B. S., M. Gertler, and S. Gilchrist. 1996. "The Financial Accelerator and the Flight to Quality." *Review of Economics and Statistics*, 78, no. 1 (February): 1–15.

Bernanke, B. S., and C. Lown. 1992. "The Credit Crunch." *Brookings Papers on Economic Activity*, no. 2, pp. 205–239.

Bernanke, B. S., and I. Mihov. 1996. "Measuring Monetary Policy." Paper presented at the CEPR/SF Fed Conference, Stanford, CA, March.

Bernanke, B. S., and F. Mishkin. 1992. "Central Bank Behavior and the Strategy of Monetary Policy: Observations from Six Industrialized Countries." In O. J. Blanchard and S. Fischer (eds.), *NBER Macroeconomics Annual 1992*, 183–228. Cambridge, MA: MIT Press.

Bernanke, B. S., and M. Woodford. 1997. "Inflation Forecasts and Monetary Policy." *Journal of Money, Credit, and Banking*, 29, no. 4, part 2 (November): 653–684.

Bewley, Truman. 1983. "A Difficulty with the Optimum Quantity of Money." *Econometrica*, 51, no. 5 (September): 1485–1504.

Black, R., V. Cassino, A. Drew, E. Hansen, B. Hunt, D. Rose, and A. Scott. 1997. "The Forecasting and Policy System: The Core Model." Reserve Bank of New Zealand, Research Paper No. 43, August.

Blanchard, O. J. 1989. "A Traditional Interpretation of Economic Fluctuations." *American Economic Review*, 79, no. 5 (December): 1146–1164.

Blanchard, O. J. 1990. "Why Does Money Affect Output? A Survey." Chapter 15 in B. M. Friedman and F. H. Hahn (eds.), *Handbook of Monetary Economics, vol 2*, 778–835. New York: North-Holland.

Blanchard, O. J., and S. Fischer. 1989. *Lectures on Macroeconomics*. Cambridge, MA: MIT Press.

Blanchard, O. J., and C. M. Kahn. 1980. "The Solution of Linear Difference Models under Rational Expectations." *Econometrica*, 48, no. 5 (July): 1305–1311.

Blanchard, O. J., and N. Kiyotaki. 1987. "Monopolistic Competition and the Effects of Aggregate Demand." *American Economic Review*, 77, no. 4 (September): 647–666.

Blanchard, O. J., and D. Quah. 1989. "The Dynamic Effects of Aggregate Demand and Supply Disturbances." *American Economic Review*, 79, no. 4 (September): 655–673.

Blanchard, O. J., and M. W. Watson. 1986. "Are Business Cycles All Alike?" In R. J. Gordon (ed.), *The American Business Cycle: Continuity and Change*, 123–165. Chicago: University of Chicago Press.

Blinder, A. 1995. "Central Banking in Theory and Practice: Lecture II: Credibility, Discretion, and Independence." Marshall Lecture, University of Cambridge, May.

Bohn, H. 1991a. "Budget Balance through Revenue or Spending Adjustments? Some Historical Evidence for the United States." *Journal of Monetary Economics*, 27, no. 3 (June): 333–359.

Bohn, H. 1991b. "On Cash-in-Advance Models of Money Demand and Asset Pricing." *Journal of Money, Credit, and Banking*, 23, no. 2 (May): 224–242.

Bohn, H. 1991c. "Time Inconsistency of Monetary Policy in the Open Economy." *Journal of International Economics*, 30, nos. 3–4 (May): 249–266.

Bohn, H. 1991d. "The Sustainability of Budget Deficits with Lump-Sum and with Income-Based Taxation." *Journal of Money, Credit, and Banking*, 23, no. 3, part 2 (August): 580–604.

Bohn, H. 1992. "Budget Deficits and Government Accounting." *Carnegie-Rochester Conference Series on Public Policy*, 37, December, pp. 1–884.

Bohn, H. 1995. "The Sustainability of Budget Deficits in a Stochastic Economy." *Journal of Money, Credit, and Banking*, 27, no. 1 (February): 257–271.

Bonser-Neal, C., V. V. Roley, and G. H. Sellon, Jr. 1997. "Monetary Policy Actions, Intervention, and Exchange Rates: A Re-examination of the Empirical Relationships Using Federal Funds Rate Target Data." Federal Reserve Bank of Kansas City, March.

Borio, C. E. V. 1997. "The Implementation of Monetary Policy in Industrial Countries: A Survey." Bank for International Settlements Economic Papers, No. 47, July. Basle, Switzerland.

Boschen, J. F., and L. O. Mills. 1991. "The Effects of Countercyclical Monetary Policy on Money and Interest Rates: An Evaluation of Evidence from FOMC Documents." Working Paper 91–20, Federal Reserve Bank of Philadelphia, October.

Boschen, J. F., and L. O. Mills. 1995a. "The Relation between Narrative and Money Market Indicators of Monetary Policy." *Economic Inquiry*, 33, no. 1 (January): 24–44.

Boschen, J. F., and L. O. Mills. 1995b. "Tests of Long-run Neutrality Using Permanent Monetary and Real Shocks." *Journal of Monetary Economics*, 35, no. 1 (February): 25–44.

Brainard, W. 1967. "Uncertainty and the Effectiveness of Policy." *American Economic Review*, 57, no. 2 (May): 411–425.

Braun, R. A. 1991. "Comment on Optimal Fiscal and Monetary Policy: Some Recent Results." *Journal of Money, Credit, and Banking*, 23, no. 3, part 2 (August): 542–546.

Brayton, F., A. Levin, R. Tryon, and J. C. Williams. 1997. "The Evolution of the Macro Model at the Federal Reserve Board." Federal Reserve Board, Finance and Economics Discussion Series, 1997–29, May.

Brayton, F., and E. Mauskopf. 1985. "The Federal Reserve Board MPS Quarerly Econometric Model of the US Economy." *Economic Modelling*, 2, no. 3 (July): 170–292.

Brayton, F., E. Mauskopf, D. Reifschneider, P. Tinsley, and J. C. Williams. 1997. "The Role of Expectations in the FRB/US Macroeconomic Model." Federal Reserve *Bulletin*, 83, no. 4 (April): 227–246.

Brayton, F., and P. Tinsley. 1996. "A Guide to the FRB/US: A Macroeconomic Model of the United States." Federal Reserve Board, Finance and Economics Discussion Series, 1996–42, October.

Briault, C., A. Haldane, and M. King. 1997. "Independence and Accountability." In I. Kurodo (ed.), *Towards More Effective Monetary Policy*, 299–326. London: Macmillian.

Broaddus, A., and M. Goodfriend. 1984. "Base Drift and the Longer Run Growth of M1: Evidence from a Decade of Monetary Targeting." Federal Reserve of Richmond *Economic Review*, 70, no. 6 (November/December), pp. 3–14.

Brock, W. A. 1974. "Money and Growth: The Case of Long Run Perfect Foresight." *International Economic Review*, 15, no. 3 (October): 750–777.

Brock, W. A. 1975. "A Simple Perfect Foresight Monetary Model." *Journal of Monetary Economics*, 1, no. 2 (April): 133–150.

Brock, W. A., 1990. "Overlapping Generations Models with Money and Transaction Costs." In B. Friedman and F. Hahn (eds.), *The Handbook of Monetary Economics*, volume 1, 1990, 263–295. New York: North-Holland.

Brunner, K., and A. H. Meltzer. 1972. "Money, Debt, and Economic Activity." *Journal of Political Economy*, 80, no. 5 (September/October): 951–977.

Brunner, K., and A. H. Meltzer. 1988. "Money and Credit in the Monetary Transmission Process." *American Economic Review*, 78, no. 2 (May): 446–451.

Bruno, M., and S. Fischer. 1990. "Seigniorage, Operating Rules, and the High Inflation Trap." *Quarterly Journal of Economics*, 105, no. 2 (May): 353–374.

Bryant, R., P. Hooper, and C. Mann, eds. 1992. *Evaluating Policy Regimes: New Research in Empirical Macroeconomics*, Washington, DC: Brookings Institution.

Bullard, J., and J. W. Keating. 1995. "The Long-Run Relationship between Inflation and Output in Postwar Economies." *Journal of Monetary Economics*, 36, no. 3 (December): 477–496.

Buttiglione, L., P. Del Giovane, and O. Tristani. 1996. "Monetary Policy Actions and the Term Structure of Interest Rates: A Cross-Country Analysis." Paper presented at a Banca d'Italia, IGIER, and Centro Paolo Baffi workshop *Monetary Policy and the Term Structure of Interest Rates*, Università Bocconi, Milan, June.

Cagan, P. 1956. "The Monetary Dynamics of Hyperinflation." In M. Friedman (ed.), *Studies in the Quantity Theory of Money*. Chicago: University of Chicago Press.

Calvo, G. A. 1978. "On the Time Consistency of Optimal Policy in a Monetary Economy." *Econometrica*, 46, no. 6 (1978): 1411–1428.

Calvo, G. A. 1983. "Staggered Prices in a Utility-Maximizing Framework." *Journal of Monetary Economics*, 12, no. 3 (September): 983–998.

Calvo, G. A., and P. E. Guidotti. 1993. "On the Flexibility of Monetary Policy: The Case of the Optimal Inflation Tax." *Review of Economic Studies*, 60, no. 3 (July): 667–687.

Calvo, G. A., and L. Leiderman. 1992. "Optimal Inflation Tax Under Precommitment: Theory and Evidence." *American Economic Review*, 82, no. 1 (March): 179–194.

Campbell, J. Y. 1994. "Inspecting the Mechanism: An Analytical Approach to the Stochastic Growth Model." *Journal of Monetary Economics*, 33, no. 3 (June): 463–506.

Campbell, J. Y., and N. G. Mankiw. 1989. "Consumption, Income, and Interest Rates: Reinterpreting the Time Series Evidence." In O. J. Blanchard and S. Fischer (eds.), *NBER Macroeconomic Annual, 1989*, 185–216. Cambridge, MA: MIT Press.

Campbell, J. Y., and N. G. Mankiw. 1991. "The Response of Consumption to Income: A Cross-Country Investigation." *European Economic Review*, 35, no. 4 (May): 723–756.

Campbell, J. Y., and R. J. Shiller. 1991. "Yield Spreads and Interest Rate Movements: A Bird's Eye View." *Review of Economic Studies*, 58, no. 3 (May): 495–514.

Campillo, M., and J. Miron. 1997. "Why Does Inflation Differ Across Countries?" In C. D. Romer and D. H. Romer (eds.), *Reducing Inflation: Motivation and Strategy*. Chicago: University of Chicago Press.

Canzoneri, M. 1985. "Monetary Policy Games and the Role of Private Information." *American Economic Review*, 75, no. 4 (September): 1056–1070.

Canzoneri, M., and D. Henderson. 1989. *Noncooperative Monetary Policies in Interdependent Economies*. Cambridge, MA: MIT Press.

Canzoneri, M., D. Henderson, and K. Rogoff. 1983. "The Information Content of the Interest Rate and Optimal Monetary Policy." *Quarterly Journal of Economics*, 98, no. 4 (November): 545–566.

Canzoneri, M., C. Nolan, and A. Yates. 1997. "Mechanism for Achieving Monetary Stability: Inflation Targeting Versus the ERM." *Journal of Money, Credit and Banking*, 29, no. 1 (February): 46–60.

Cargill, Thomas. 1995a. "The Bank of Japan and the Federal Reserve: An Essay on Central Bank Independence." In K. Hoover and S. Sheffrin (eds.), *Monetarism and the Methodology of Economics*. Aldershot, Hants, England: Edward Elgar Publishing.

Cargill, Thomas. 1995b. "The Statistical Association between Central Bank Independence and Inflation." *Banca Nazionale del Lavoro Quarterly Review*, 48, no. 193 (June): 159–172.

Cargill, T. F., M. M. Hutchison, and T. Ito. 1997. *The Political Economy of Japanese Monetary Policy*. Cambridge, MA: MIT Press.

Carlson, K. M. 1978. "Does the St. Louis Equation Now Believe in Fiscal Policy?" Federal Reserve Bank of St. Louis *Review*, 60, no. 2 (February): 13–19.

Carlstrom, C. T., and T. S. Fuerst. 1997. "Interest Rate Rules in a Model with Sticky Prices." Federal Reserve Bank of Cleveland, March.

Carlstrom, C. T., and T. S. Fuerst. 1995. "Interest Rate Rules vs. Money Growth Rules: A Welfare Comparison in a Cash-in-Advance Economy." *Journal of Monetary Economics*, 36, no. 2 (November): 247–267.

Cecchetti, S. G. 1995. "Distinguishing Theories of the Monetary Transmission Mechanism." Federal Reserve Bank of St. Louis *Review*, 77, no. 3 (May/June): 83–97.

Chada, J. S., A. G. Haldane, and N. G. J. Janssen. 1998. "Shoe-Leather Costs Reconsidered." *The Economic Journal*, 108 (March): 363–382.

Champ, B., and S. Freemen. 1994. *Modeling Monetary Economies*. New York: J. Wiley.

Chari, V. V., L. J. Christiano, and M. Eichenbaum. 1995. "Inside Money, Outside Money and Short-Term Interest Rates." *Journal of Money, Credit and Banking*, 27, no. 4, part 2 (November): 1354–1386.

Chari, V. V., L. J. Christiano, and P. J. Kehoe. 1991. "Optimal Fiscal and Monetary Policy: Some Recent Results." *Journal of Money, Credit, and Banking*, 23, no. 3, part 2 (August): 519–539.

Chari, V. V., L. J. Christiano, and P. J. Kehoe. 1996. "Optimality of the Friedman Rule in Economies with Distorting Taxes." *Journal of Monetary Economics*, 37, no. 2 (April): 203–223.

Chari, V. V., P. J. Kehoe, and E. R. McGrattan. 1996. "Sticky Price Models of the Business Cycle: Can the Contract Multiplier Solve the Persistence Problem?" NBER Working Paper No. 5809, October.

Chiang, A. C. 1992. *Elements of Dynamic Optimization.* New York: McGraw-Hill.

Christiano, L. J. 1991. "Modelling the Liquidity Effect of a Money Shock." Federal Reserve Bank of Minneapolis *Quarterly Review* 15, no. 1 (Winter): 3–34.

Christiano, L. J., and M. Eichenbaum. 1992a. "Liquidity Effects and the Monetary Transmission Mechanism." *American Economic Review*, 82, no. 2 (May): 346–353.

Christiano, L. J., and M. Eichenbaum. 1992b. "Current Real Business Cycle Theories and Aggregate Labor-Market Fluctuations." *American Economic Review*, 82, no. 3 (June): 346–353

Christiano, L. J., and M. Eichenbaum. 1995. "Liquidity Effects, Monetary Policy and the Business Cycle." *Journal of Money, Credit and Banking*, 27, no. 4, part 1 (November): 1113–1136.

Christiano, L. J., M. Eichenbaum, and C. Evans. 1994. "Identification and the Effects of Monetary Policy Shocks." Working Paper WP–94–7, Federal Reserve Bank of Chicago, May.

Christiano, L. J., M. Eichenbaum, and C. Evans. 1996. "Sticky Price and Limited Participation Models of Money: A Comparison." Northwestern University, Evanston, IL, December.

Clarida, R., J. Galí, and M. Gertler. 1997. "Monetary Policy Rules in Practice: Some International Evidence." NBER Working Paper 6254, November.

Clarida, R., and M. Gertler. 1997. "How Does the Bundesbank Conduct Monetary Policy." In C. Romer and D. Romer (eds.), *Reducing Inflation*. Chicago: University of Chicago Press.

Clower, R. W. 1967. "A Reconsideration of the Microfoundations of Monetary Theory." *Western Economic Journal*, 6, no. 1 (December): 1–9.

Cogley, T., and J. M. Nason. 1995. "Output Dynamics in Real Business Cycle Models." *American Economic Review*, 85, no. 3 (June): 492–511.

Cole, H. L., and L. E. Ohanian. 1997. "Shrinking Money and Monetary Business Cycles." Mimeo, January. University of Pennsylvania, Philadelphia, PA.

Coleman, W. J., III. 1996. "Money and Output: A Test of Reverse Causation." *American Economic Review*, 86, no. 1 (March): 90–111.

Cook, T. (1989). "Determinants of the Federal Funds Rate, 1979–1982." Federal Reserve Bank of Richmond *Economic Review*, 75, no. 1 (January/February): 3–19.

Cook, T., and T. Hahn. 1989. "The Effect of Interest Rate Changes in the Federal Funds Rate Target on Market Interest Rates in the 1970s." *Journal of Monetary Economics*, 24, no. 3 (November): 331–351.

Cooley, T. F., ed. 1995. *Frontiers of Business Cycle Research.* Princeton, NJ: Princeton University Press.

Cooley, T. F., and G. D. Hansen. 1989. "The Inflation Tax in a Real Business Cycle Model." *American Economic Review*, 79, no. 4 (September): 733–748.

Cooley, T. F., and G. D. Hansen. 1995. "Money and the Business Cycle." Chapter 7 in T. F. Cooley (ed.), *Frontiers of Business Cycle Research*, 175–216. Princeton, NJ: Princeton University Press.

Cooley, T. F., and E. Prescott. 1995. "Economic Growth and Business Cycles." In T. F. Cooley (ed.), *Frontiers of Business Cycle Research*. Princeton, NJ: Princeton University Press.

Correia, I., and P. Teles. 1996. "Is the Friedman Rule Optimal When Money Is an Intermediate Good?" *Journal of Monetary Economics*, 38, no. 2 (October): 223–244.

Cosimano, T. F., and R. G. Sheehan. 1994. "The Federal Reserve Operating Procedure, 1984–1990: An Empirical Analysis." *Journal of Macroeconomics*, 16, no. 4 (Summer): 573–588.

Cover, J. P. 1992. "Asymmetric Effects of Positive and Negative Money Supply Shocks." *Quarterly Journal of Economics*, 107, no. 4 (November): 1261–1282.

Cox, J. C., J. E. Ingersol, and S. A. Ross. 1985. "A Theory of the Term Structure of Interest Rates." *Econometrica*, 53, no. 2 (March): 385–407.

Croushore, D. 1993. "Money in the Utility Function: Functional Equivalence to a Shopping-Time Model." *Journal of Macroeconomics*, 15, no. 1 (Winter): 175–182.

Cubitt, R. P. 1992. "Monetary Policy Games and Private Sector Precommitment." *Oxford Economic Papers*, 44, no. 3 (July): 513–530.

Cukierman, A. 1992. *Central Bank Strategies, Credibility and Independence*. Cambridge, MA: MIT Press.

Cukierman, A., P. Kalaitzidakis, L. H. Summers, and S. B. Webb. 1993. "Central Bank Independence, Growth, Investment, and Real Rates." *Carnegie-Rochester Conference Series on Public Policy*, 39 (December): 95–140.

Cukierman, A., and N. Liviatan. 1991. "Optimal Accomodation by Strong Policymakers under Incomplete Information." *Journal of Monetary Economics*, 27, no. 1 (February): 99–127.

Cukierman, A., and A. Meltzer. 1986. "A Theory of Ambiguity, Credibility, and Inflation under Discretion and Asymmetric Information." *Econometrica*, 54, no. 5 (September): 1099–1128.

Cukierman, A., S. B. Webb, and B. Neyapti. 1992. "Measuring the Independence of Central Banks and Its Effects on Policy Outcomes." *The World Bank Economic Review*, 6, no. 3 (September): 353–398.

Currie, D., and P. Levine. 1991. "The International Co-ordination of Monetary Policy: A Survey." In C. Green and D. Llewellyn (eds.), *Surveys in Monetary Economics*, vol. 1. Oxford, U.K.: Blackwell.

Dahlquist, M., and L. E. O. Svensson. 1996. "Estimating the Term Structure of Interest Rates for Monetary Policy Analysis." *Scandinavian Journal of Economics*, 98 (2): 163–183.

Debelle, G., and S. Fischer. 1994. "How Independent Should a Central Bank Be?" In J. C. Fuhrer (ed.), *Goals, Guidelines and Constraints Facing Monetary Policymakers*. Federal Reserve Bank of Boston.

de Brouwer, G., and J. O'Regan. 1997. "Evaluating Simple Monetary-Policy Rules for Australia." In P. Lowe (ed.), *Monetary Policy and Inflation Targeting*, 244–276. Reserve Bank of Australia, July.

de Haan, J., and G. J. van't Hag. 1995. "Variation in Central Bank Independence across Countries: Some Provisional Empirical Evidence." *Public Choice*, 85, nos. 3–4 (December): 335–351.

Demopoulos, G. D., G. M. Katsimbris, and S. M. Miller. 1987. "Monetary Policy and Central-Bank Financing of Government Budget Deficits." *European Economic Review*, 31, no. 5 (July): 1023–1050.

De Prano, M., and T. Mayer. 1965. "Tests of the Relative Importance of Autonomous Expenditures and Money." *American Economic Review*, 55, no. 4 (September): 729–752.

Diamond, P. 1983. "Money in Search Equilibrium." *Econometrica*, 52, no. 1 (January): 1–20.

Diamond, P. A., and J. A. Mirrlees. 1971. "Optimal Taxation and Public Production I: Production and Efficiency, and II: Tax Rules." *American Economic Review*, 61, no. 3 (June): 8–27, 261–278.

Diba, B. T., and H. I. Grossman. 1988a. "Rational Inflationary Bubbles." *Journal of Monetary Economics*, 21, no. 1 (January): 35–46.

Diba, B. T., and H. I. Grossman. 1988b. "Explosive Rational Bubbles in Stock Prices." *American Economic Review*, 78, no. 3 (June): 520–530.

Dixit, A. K. 1990. *Optimization in Economic Theory*, 2nd ed. Oxford: Oxford University Press.

Dornbusch, R. 1976. "Expectations and Exchange Rate Dynamics." *Journal of Political Economy*, 84, no. 6 (December): 1161–1176.

Dotsey, M., and P. Ireland. 1995. "Liquidity Effects and Transaction Technologies." *Journal of Money, Credit and Banking*, 27, no. 4, part 2 (November): 1441–1457.

Drazen, A. 1979. "The Optimal Rate of Inflation Revisited." *Journal of Monetary Economics*, 5, no. 2 (April): 231–248.

Drazen, A., and P. R. Mason. 1994. "Credibility of Policies versus Credibility of Policymakers." *Quarterly Journal of Economics*, 109, no. 3 (August): 735–754.

Driffill, J. 1988. "Macroeconomic Policy Games with Incomplete Information: A Survey." *European Economic Review*, 32, nos. 2–3 (March): 513–541.

Driffill, J., G. E. Mizon, and A. Ulph. 1990. "Costs of Inflation." In B. Friedman and F. Hahn (eds.), *The Handbook of Monetary Economics*, vol. 2, 1012–1066. New York: North-Holland.

Duguay, P. 1994. "Empirical Evidence on the Strength of the Monetary Transmission Mechanism in Canada." *Journal of Monetary Economics*, 33, no. 1 (February): 39–61.

Eichenbaum, M. 1992. "Comments: 'Interpreting the Macroeconomic Time Series Facts: The Effects of Monetary Policy' by Christopher Sims." *European Economic Review*, 36, no. 5 (June): 1001–1011.

Eichenbaum, M., and C. L. Evans. 1995. "Some Empirical Evidence on the Effects of Shocks to Monetary Policy on Exchange Rates." *Quarterly Journal of Economics*, 110, no. 4 (November): 975–1009.

Eichenbaum, M., and K. J. Singleton. 1986. "Do Equilibrium Real Business Cycle Theories Explain Postwar U.S. Business Cycles?" In S. Fischer (ed.), *NBER Macroeconomics Annual, 1986*, 91–135. Cambridge, MA: MIT Press.

Eijffinger, S. C. W., and Jakob de Haan. 1996. *The Political Economy of Central-Bank Independence*. Special Papers in International Economics, No. 19, Princeton University, Princeton, NJ, May.

Eijffinger, S., M. Hoeberichts, and E. Schaling. 1995. "Optimal Conservativeness in the Rogoff (1985) Model: A Graphical and Closed-Form Solution." CentER Discussion Paper No. 95121, December.

Eijffinger, S., and E. Schaling. 1993. "Central Bank Independence in Twelve Industrialized Countries." Banca Nazionale del Lavoro *Quarterly Review*, no. 184 (March): 49–89.

Eijffinger, S., and E. Schaling. 1995. "Optimal Commitment in an Open Economy: Credibility vs. Flexibility." CentER Discussion Paper No. 9579, July.

Engle, R., and C. Granger. 1987. "Cointegration and Error Correction: Representation, Estimation, and Testing." *Econometrica*, 55, no. 2 (March): 251–276.

Evans, G. W. 1991. "Pitfalls in Testing for Explosive Bubbles in Asset Prices." *American Economic Review*, 81, no. 4 (September): 922–930.

Faig, M. 1988. "Characterization of the Optimal Tax on Money When It Functions as a Medium of Exchange." *Journal of Monetary Economics*, 22, no. 1 (July): 137–148.

Fair, R. C. 1984. *Specification, Estimation, and Analysis of Macroeconometric Models*. Cambridge, MA: Harvard University Press.

Faust, J. 1996. "Whom Can You Trust? Theoretical Support for the Founders' Views." *Journal of Monetary Economics*, 37, no. 2 (April): 267–283.

Faust, J., and J. Irons. 1996. "Money, Politics and the Post-war Business Cycles." Federal Reserve Board, International Finance Discussion Papers Number 572, November. Washington, DC.

Federal Reserve Bank of New York. *Studies on Causes and Consequences of the 1989–92 Credit Slowdown*, February.

Federal Reserve System. 1981. *New Monetary Control Precedures*. Staff study.

Feenstra, R. C. 1986. "Functional Equivalence between Liquidity Costs and the Utility of Money." *Journal of Monetary Economics*, 17, no. 2 (March): 271–291.

Feldstein, M. 1978. "The Welfare Costs of Capital Income Taxation." *Journal of Political Economy*, 86, no. 2, part 2 (April): 529–551.

Feldstein, M. 1979. "The Welfare Costs of Permanent Inflation and Optimal Short-Run Economic Policy." *Journal of Political Economy*, 87, no. 4 (August): 749–768.

Feldstein, M. 1996. "The Costs and Benefits of Going from Low Inflation to Price Stability." NBER Working Paper No. 5469, February.

Feldstein, Martin, Jerry Green, and Eytan Sheshinski. 1978. "Inflation and Taxes in a Growing Economy with Debt and Equity Finance." *Journal of Political Economy*, 86, no. 2, part 2 (April): S53–S70.

Fischer, A. M. 1995. "New Zealand's Experience with Inflation Targets." In L. Leiderman and L. E. O. Svensson (eds.), *Inflation Targets*, 32–52. CEPR.

Fischer, A. M. 1996. "Central Bank Independence and Sacrifice Ratios." *Open Economy Review*, 7: 5–18.

Fischer, S. 1972. "Keynes-Wicksell and Neoclassical Models of Money and Growth." *American Economic Review*, 62, no. 5 (December): 880–890.

Fischer, S. 1974. "Money and the Production Function." *Economic Inquiry*, 12, no. 4 (November): 517–533.

Fischer, S. 1977. "Long-Term Contracts, Rational Expectations, and the Optimal Money Supply Rule." *Journal of Political Economy*, 85, no. 1 (February): 191–206.

Fischer, S. 1979a "Anticipations and the Nonneutrality of Money." *Journal of Political Economy*, 87, no. 2 (April): 225–252.

Fischer, S. 1979b. "Capital Accumulation on the Transition Path in a Monetary Optimizing Model." *Econometrica*, 47, no. 6 (November): 1433–1439.

Fischer, S. 1994. "Modern Central Banking." In F. Capie, C. Goodhart, S. Fischer, and N. Schnadt. *The Future of Central Banking*. Cambridge, U.K.: Cambridge University Press.

Fishe, R., and M. Wohar. 1990. "The Adjustment of Expectations to a Change in Regime: Comment." *American Economic Review*, 80, no. 4 (September): 968–976.

Fisher, I. 1896. *Appreciation and Interest*. New York: Macmillan.

Fisher, M. E., and J. J. Seater. 1993. "Long-Run Neutrality and Superneutrality in an ARIMA Framework." *American Economic Review*, 83, no. 3 (June): 402–415.

Flood, R., and P. Isard. 1988. "Monetary Policy Strategies." NBER Working Paper No. 2770, November.

Foley, D. K., and M. Sidranski. 1971. *Monetary and Fiscal Policy in a Growing Economy*. New York: Macmillian.

Frankel, J., and M. Chinn. 1995. "The Stabilizing Properties of a Nominal GNP Rule." *Journal of Money, Credit, and Banking*, 27, no. 2 (May): 318–334.

Fratianni, M., J. von Hagen, and C. Waller. 1997. "Central Banking as a Principal Agent Problem." *Economic Inquiry*, 35, no. 2 (April): 378–393.

Friedman, B. M. 1975. "Targets, Instruments and Indicators of Monetary Policy." *Journal of Monetary Economics*, 1, no. 4 (October): 443–473.

Friedman, B. M. 1977a. "Even the St. Louis Model Now Believes in Fiscal Policy." *Journal of Money, Credit, and Banking*, 9, no. 2 (May): 365–367.

Friedman, B. M. 1977b. "The Inefficiencies of Short-Run Monetary Targets for Monetary Policy." *Brookings Papers on Economic Activity*, 2: 293–335.

Friedman, B. M. 1990. "Targets and Instruments of Monetary Policy." In B. Friedman and F. Hahn (eds.), *The Handbook of Monetary Economics*, vol. 2, 1183–1230. New York: North-Holland.

Friedman, B. M., and K. N. Kuttner. 1992. "Money, Income, Prices and Interest Rates." *American Economic Review*, 82, no. 3 (June): 472–492.

Friedman, B. M., and K. N. Kuttner. 1996. "A Price Target for U.S. Monetary Policy? Lessons from the Experience with Money Growth Targets." *Brookings Papers on Economic Activity*, 1: 77–125.

Friedman, M. 1968. "The Role of Monetary Policy." *American Economic Review*, 58, no. 1 (March): 1–17.

Friedman, M. 1969. "The Optimum Quantity of Money." In his *The Optimum Quantity of Money and Other Essays*. Chicago: Aldine.

Friedman, M. 1977. "Nobel Lecture: Inflation and Unemployment." *Journal of Political Economy*, 85, no. 3 (June): 451–472.

Friedman, M., and D. Meiselman. 1963. "The Relative Stability of Monetary Velocity and the Investment Multiplier in the United States, 1897–1958." In *Stabilization Policies*, 165–268. Englewood Cliffs, NJ: Prentice Hall.

Friedman, M., and A. Schwartz. 1963a. "Money and Business Cycles." *Review of Economics and Statistics*, 45, no. 1, part 2 (February): 32–64.

Friedman, M., and A. Schwartz. 1963b. *A Monetary History of the United States, 1867–1960*. Princeton, NJ: Princeton University Press.

Froot, K. A., and R. H. Thaler. 1990. "Anomalies: Foreign Exchange." *Journal of Economic Perspectives*, 4, no. 3 (Summer): 179–192.

Froyen, Richard T., and Roger N. Waud. 1995. "Central Bank Independence and the Output-Inflation Tradeoff." *Journal of Economics and Business*, 47, no. 2 (May): 137–149.

Fudenberg, D., and E. Maskin. 1986. "Folk Theorems for Repeated Games with Discounting or with Incomplete Information." *Econometrica*, 54, no. 3 (May): 533–554.

Fuerst, T. S. 1995. "Monetary and Financial Interactions in the Business Cycle." *Journal of Money, Credit and Banking*, 27, no. 4, part 2 (November): 1321–1338.

Fuerst, T. S. 1992. "Liquidity, Loanable Funds, and Real Activity." *Journal of Monetary Economics*, 29, no. 1 (February): 3–24.

Fuhrer, J. C. 1994a. "Optimal Monetary Policy and the Sacrifice Ratio." In J. C. Fuhrer (ed.), *Goals, Guidelines, and Constraints Facing Monetary Policymakers*. Federal Reserve Bank of Boston Conference Series No. 38, June, 43–69.

Fuhrer, J. C. 1994b. "A Semi-classical Model of Price Level Adjustment: A Comment." In *Carnegie-Rochester Conference Series on Public Policy*, 41 (December): 285–294.

Fuhrer, J. C. 1996. "Monetary Policy Shifts and Long-Term Interest Rates." *Quarterly Journal of Economics*, 111, no. 4 (November): 1183–1209.

Fuhrer, J. C. 1997a. "Inflation/Output Variance Trade-offs and Optimal Monetary Policy." *Journal of Money, Credit and Banking*, 29, no. 2 (May): 214–234.

Fuhrer, J. C. 1997b. "The (Un)Importance of Forward-Looking Behavior in Price Specifications." *Journal of Money, Credit, and Banking*, 29, no. 3 (August): 338–350.

Fuhrer, J. C. 1977c. "Towards a Compact, Empirically-Verified Rational Expectations Model for Monetary Policy Analysis." *Carnegie-Rochester Conference Series on Public Policy*, 47 (December): 197–230.

Fuhrer, J. C., and G. R. Moore. 1995a. "Inflation Persistence." *Quarterly Journal of Economics*, 110, no. 1 (February): 127–159.

Fuhrer, J. C., and G. R. Moore. 1995b. "Monetary Policy Trade-offs and the Correlation between Nominal Interest Rates and Real Output." *American Economic Review*, 85, no. 1 (March): 219–239.

Galí, J. 1992. "How Well Does the IS-LM Model Fit the Postwar U.S. Data?" *Quarterly Journal of Economics*, 107, no. 2 (May): 709–738.

Garber, P. M., and L. E. O. Svensson. 1995. "The Operation and Collapse of Fixed Exchange Rate Systems." In G. M. Grossman and K. Rogoff (eds.), *Handbook of International Economics*, vol. 3. Amsterdam: North-Holland.

García de Paso, Jose I. 1993. "Monetary Policy with Private Information: A Role for Monetary Targets." Instituto Complutense de Analisis Economico Working Paper No. 9315, July.

García de Paso, Jose I. 1994. "A Model of Appointing Governors to the Central Bank." Instituto Complutense de Analisis Economico Working Paper No. 9416, October.

Garfinkel, M., and S. Oh. 1993. "Strategic Discipline in Monetary Policy with Private Information: Optimal Targeting Horizons." *American Economic Review*, 83, no. 1 (March): 99–117.

Gertler, M. 1988. "Financial Structure and Aggregate Activity: An Overview," *Journal of Money, Credit, and Banking*, 20, no. 3, part 2 (August): 559–588.

Gertler, M. 1995. "Comment on Monetary and Financial Interactions in the Business Cycle." *Journal of Money, Credit, and Banking*, 27, no. 4, part 2 (November): 1342–1353.

Gertler, M., and S. Gilchrist. 1993. "The Role of Credit Market Imperfections in the Monetary Transmission Mechanism: Arguments and Evidence." *Scandinavian Journal of Economics*, 95 (1): 43–64.

Gertler, M., and S. Gilchrist. 1994. "Monetary Policy, Business Cycles and the Behavior of Small Manufacturing Firms." *Quarterly Journal of Economics*, 109, no. 2 (May): 309–340.

Geweke, J. 1986. "The Superneutrality of Money in the United States: An Interpretation of the Evidence." *Econometrica*, 54, no. 1 (January): 1–22.

Giavazzi, F., and M. Pagano. 1988. "The Advantage of Tying One's Hands: EMS Discipline and Central Bank Credibility." *European Economic Review*, 32: 1055–1082.

Gillman, M. 1995. "Comparing Partial and General Equilibrium Estimates of the Welfare Costs of Inflation." *Contemporary Economic Policy*, 13, no. 4 (October): 60–71.

Goldfeld, S. M., and D. E. Sichel. 1990. "The Demand for Money." In B. Friedman and F. Hahn (eds.), *The Handbook of Monetary Economics*, vol. 1, 299–356. New York: North-Holland.

Goodfriend, M. 1983. "Discount Window Borrowing, Monetary Policy, and the Post–October 6, 1979 Federal Reserve Operating Procedure." *Journal of Monetary Economics*, 12, no. 3 (September): 343–356. Washington, DC.

Goodfriend, M. 1987. "Interest-Rate Smoothing and Price Level Trend-Stationarity." *Journal of Monetary Economics*, 19, no. 3 (May): 335–348.

Goodfriend, M. 1991. "Interest Rate Policy and the Conduct of Monetary Policy." *Carnegie-Rochester Conference Series on Public Policy*, 34 (Spring): 7–30.

Goodfriend, M. 1993. "Interest Rate Policy and the Inflation Scare Problem, 1979–1992." Federal Reserve Bank of Richmond *Economic Quarterly*, 79, no. 1 (Winter): 1–24.

Goodfriend, M., and D. Small, eds. 1993. *Operating Procedures and the Conduct of Monetary Policy: Conference Proceedings*, Finance and Economics Discussion Series, Working Studies 1, Parts 1 and 2, Federal Reserve System, March.

Goodhart, C. A. E., and J. Viñals. 1994. "Strategy and Tactics of Monetary Policy: Examples from Europe and the Antipodes." In J. C. Fuhrer (ed.), *Goals, Guidelines and Constraints Facing Monetary Policymakers*. Federal Reserve Bank of Boston.

Gordon, D. B., and E. M. Leeper. 1994. "The Dynamic Impacts of Monetary Policy: An Exercise in Tentative Identification." *Journal of Political Economy*, 102, no. 6 (December): 1228–1247.

Gordon, R. J. 1982. "Why Stopping Inflation May Be Costly: Evidence from Fourteen Historical Episodes." In R. E. Hall (ed.), *Inflation: Causes and Consequences*. Chicago: University of Chicago Press.

Gordon, R., and S. King. 1982. "The Output Costs of Disinflation in Traditional and Vector Autoregressive Models." *Brookings Papers on Economic Activity*, no. 1: 205–242.

Gould, J. P., et al. 1978. "The Stochastic Properties of Velocity and the Quantity Theory of Money." *Journal of Monetary Economics*, 4, no. 2 (April): 229–248.

Gray, J. A. 1978. "On Indexation and Contract Length." *Journal of Political Economy*, 86, no. 1 (February): 1–18.

Grier, Kevin B., and Howard E. Neiman. 1987. "Deficits, Politics and Money Growth." *Economic Inquiry*, 25, no. 2 (April): 201–214.

Grilli, V., D. Masciandaro, and G. Tabellini. 1991. "Political and Monetary Institutions and Public Financial Policies in the Industrial Countries." *Economic Policy*, 6, no. 2 (October): 341–392.

Grossman, S., and L. Weiss. 1983. "A Transactions-Based Model of the Monetary Transmission Mechanism." *American Economic Review*, 73, no. 5 (December): 871–880.

Guidotti, P. E., and C. A. Végh. 1993. "The Optimal Inflation Tax When Money Reduces Transactions Costs: A Reconsideration." *Journal of Monetary Economics*, 31, no. 2 (April): 189–205.

Guthrie, G., and J. Wright. 1998. "Market-Implemented Monetary Policy with Open Mouth Operations." University of Canterbury. February. Christchurch, N.Z.

Hahn, F. H. 1965. "On Some Problems of Proving the Existence of an Equilibrium in a Monetary Economy." In F. H. Hahn and F. P. R. Brechling (eds.), *The Theory of Interest Rates*, 126–135. London: Macmillan.

Hakkio, C., and M. Rush. 1991. "Is the Budget Deficit 'Too Large?'" *Economic Inquiry*, 29, no. 3 (July): 429–445.

Haldane, A. G., ed. 1995. *Targeting Inflation: A Conference of Central Banks on the Use of Inflation Targets*. Bank of England, March.

Haldane, A. G. 1997. "Designing Inflation Targets." In P. Lowe (ed.), *Monetary Policy and Inflation Targeting*. Reserve Bank of Australia, July, 76–112.

Hall, R. E., and N. G. Mankiw. 1994. "Nominal Income Targeting." In N. G. Mankiw (ed.), *Monetary Policy*. Chicago: University of Chicago Press.

Hall, R. E., and J. B. Taylor. 1997. *Macroeconomics*, 5th ed. New York: Norton.

Hamada, K. 1976. "A Strategic Analysis of Monetary Interdependence." *Journal of Political Economy*, 84, no. 4, part 1 (August): 677–700.

Hamilton, J. 1994. *Time Series Analysis*. Princeton, NJ: Princeton University Press.

Hamilton, J. 1996. "The Daily Market for Federal Funds." *Journal of Political Economy*, 104, no. 1 (February): 26–56.

Hamilton, J., and M. Flavin. 1986. "On the Limitations of Government Borrowing: A Framework for Empirical Testing." *American Econmic Review*, 76, no. 4 (September): 808–819.

Hansen, G. D., and E. C. Prescott. 1995. "Recursive Methods for Computing Equilibria of Business Cycle Models." Chapter 2 in T. F. Cooley (ed.), *Frontiers of Business Cycle Research*, 39–64. Princeton, NJ: Princeton University Press.

Hartley, P. 1988. "The Liquidity Services of Money." *International Economic Review*, 29, no. 1 (February): 1–24.

Havrilesky, T., and J. Gildea. 1991. "The Policy Preferences of FOMC Members as Revealed by Dissenting Votes." *Journal of Money, Credit and Banking*, 23, no. 1 (February): 130–138.

Havrilesky, T., and J. Gildea. 1995. "The Biases of Federal Reserve Bank Presidents." *Economic Inquiry*, 33, no. 2 (April): 274–284.

Herrendorf, B. 1995a. "Why Inflation Targets May Partly Substitute for Explicit Precommitment." University of Warwick, September.

Herrendorf, B. 1995b. "Transparency, Reputation, and Credibility under Floating and Pegged Exchange Rates." University of Warwick, mimeo.

Herrendorf, B. 1997. "Time Consistent Collection of Optimal Seigniorage: A Unifying Framework." *Journal of Economic Surveys*, 11, no. 1 (March): 1–46.

Herrendorf, B., and B. Lockwood. 1996. "Rogoff's 'Conservative' Central Banker Restored." *Journal of Money, Credit, and Banking*, 29, no. 4, part 1 (November): 476–495.

Herrendorf, B., and M. J. M. Neumann. 1997. "The Political Economy of Inflation and Central Bank Independence." University of Warwick, June.

Hoffman, D. L., R. H. Rasche, and M. A. Tieslau. 1995. "The Stability of Long-Run Money Demand in Five Industrial Countries. *Journal of Monetary Economics*, 35, no. 2 (April): 317–339.

Hoover, K. D. 1995. "Resolving the Liquidity Effect: Commentary." Federal Reserve Bank of St. Louis *Review*, 77, no. 3 (May/June): 26–32.

Hubbard, R. G. 1995. "Is There a Credit Channel for Monetary Policy?" Federal Reserve Bank of St. Louis *Review*, 77, no. 3 (May/June): 63–77.

Hutchison, M. M., and C. E. Walsh. 1992. "Empirical Evidence on the Insulation Properties of Fixed and Flexible Exchange Rates: The Japanese Experience." *Journal of International Economics*, 32, nos. 3–4: 241–263.

Hutchison, M. M., and C. E. Walsh. 1998. "Central Bank Institutional Design and the Output Cost of Disinflation: Did the 1989 New Zealand Reserve Bank Act Affect the Inflation-Output Tradeoff?" *Economics Journal* (May): 108.

Imrohoroglu, A. 1992. "The Welfare Costs of Inflation under Imperfect Insurance." *Journal of Economic Dynamics and Control*, 16, no. 1 (January): 79–91.

Ireland, P. N. 1996. "The Role of Countercyclical Monetary Policy." *Journal of Political Economy*, 104, no. 4 (August): 704–723.

Ireland, P. N. 1997. "A Small, Structural, Quarterly Model for Monetary Policy Evaluation." *Carnegie-Rochester Conference Series on Public Policy*, 47 (December): 83–108.

Jaffee, D., and T. Russell. "Imperfect Information, Uncertainty, and Credit Rationing." *Quarterly Journal of Economics*, 90, no. 4 (November): 651–666.

Jaffee, D., and J. E. Stiglitz. 1990. "Credit Rationing." In B. Friedman and F. Hahn (eds.), *The Handbook of Monetary Economics*, vol. 2. New York: North-Holland.

Johnson, D. R., and P. L. Siklos. 1994. "Empirical Evidence on the Independence of Central Banks." Wilfrid Laurier University, Waterloo, Canada, January.

Joines, David H. 1985. "Deficits and Money Growth in the United States, 1872–1983." *Journal of Monetary Economics*, 16, no. 3 (November): 329–351.

Jones, R. A. 1976. "The Origin and Development of Media of Exchange." *Journal of Political Economy*, 84, no. 4 (August): 757–775.

Jonsson, Gunnar. 1995. *Institutions and Incentives in Monetary and Fiscal Policy*. Ph.D. Dissertation, Institute for International Economic Studies, Stockholm University, Monograph Series No. 28.

Judd, J. P., and B. Motley. 1991. "Nominal Feedback Rules for Monetary Policy." Federal Reserve Bank of San Francisco *Economic Review*, Summer, pp. 3–17.

Judd, J. P., and B. Motley. 1992. "Controlling Inflation with an Interest Rate Instrument." Federal Reserve Bank of San Francisco *Economic Review*, Summer, pp. 3–22.

Judd, J. P., and G. D. Rudebusch. 1997. "A Tale of Three Chairmen." Federal Reserve Bank of San Francisco.

Judd, J. P., and J. Scadding. 1982. "The Search for a Stable Money Demand Function." *Journal of Economic Literature*, 20, no. 3 (September): 993–1023.

Judd, J. P., and B. Trehan. 1989. "Unemployment Rate Dynamics: Aggregate Demand and Supply Interactions." Federal Reserve Bank of San Francisco *Economic Review*, Fall, pp. 20–37.

Kareken, J. H., T. Muench, and N. Wallace. 1973. "Optimal Open Market Strategies: The Use of Information Variables." *American Economic Review*, 63, no. 1 (March): 156–172.

Kasa, K., and H. Popper. 1995. "Monetary Policy in Japan: A Structural VAR Analysis." Working Paper No. PB95–12, Federal Reserve Bank of San Francisco, December.

Kashyap, A. K., O. A. Lamont, and J. C. Stein. 1994. "Credit Conditions and the Cyclical Behavior of Inventories." *Quarterly Journal of Economics*, 109, no. 3 (August): 565–592.

Kashyap, A. N., J. C. Stein, and D. W. Wilcox. 1993. "Monetary Policy and Credit Conditions: Evidence from the Composition of External Finance." *American Economic Review*, 83, no. 1 (March): 78–98.

Kashyap, A. N., and J. C. Stein. 1993. "Monetary Policy and Bank Lending." NBER Working Paper No. 4317, April.

Kasman, B. 1993. "A Comparison of Monetary Policy Operating Procedures in Six Industrial Countries." In M. Goodfriend and D. Small (eds.), *Operating Procedures and the Conduct of Monetary Policy: Conference Proceedings*, Finance and Economics Discussion Series, Working Studies 1, Parts 1 and 2, Federal Reserve System, March. Washington, DC.

Keeton, W. 1979. *Equilibrium Credit Rationing*. New York: Garland Press.

Kerr, W., and R. King. 1996. "Limits on Interest Rate Rules in the IS Model." Federal Reserve Bank of Richmond *Economic Quarterly*, 82, no. 2 (Spring): 47–75.

Khoury, S. 1990. "The Federal Reserve Reaction Function." In T. Mayer (ed.), *The Political Economy of American Monetary Policy*, 27–49. Cambridge: Cambridge University Press.

Kiley, M. T. 1996. "The Lead of Output over Inflation in Sticky Price Models." Federal Reserve Board, Finance and Economics Discussion Series 96–33, August.

Kim, J. C. 1985. "Random Walk and the Velocity of Money: Some Evidence from Annual and Quarterly Data." *Economic Letters*, 18: 187–190.

Kimbrough, K. P. 1986a. "Inflation, Employment, and Welfare in the Presence of Transaction Costs." *Journal of Money, Credit and Banking*, 28, no. 2 (May): 127–140.

Kimbrough, K. P. 1986b. "The Optimum Quantity of Money Rule in the Theory of Public Finance." *Journal of Monetary Economics*, 18, no. 3 (November): 277–284.

King, R. G., and C. Plosser. 1984. "Money, Credit and Prices in a Real Business Cycle." *American Economic Review*, 74, no. 3 (June): 363–380.

King, R. G., and C. I. Plosser. 1985. "Money, Deficits, and Inflation." *Carnegie-Rochester Conference Series on Public Policy*, 22 (Spring): 147–196.

King, R. G., C. I. Plosser, and S. Rebelo. 1988. "Production, Growth and Business Cycles: I. The Basic Neoclassical Model." *Journal of Monetary Economics*, 21, nos. 2–3 (March/May): 195–232.

King, R. G., and M. W. Watson. 1996. "Money, Prices, Interest Rates and the Business Cycle." *Review of Economics and Statistics*, 78, no. 1 (February): 35–53.

King, R. G., and A. L. Wolman. 1996. "Inflation Targeting in a St. Louis Model of the 21st Century." Federal Reserve of St. Louis *Review*, 78, no. 3 (May/June): 83–107.

King, R. G., and A. L. Wolman. 1998. "What Should the Monetary Authority Do When Prices Are Sticky?" University of Virginia, January.

King, S. R. 1986. "Monetary Tranmission: Through Bank Loans or Bank Liabilities?" *Journal of Money, Credit, and Banking*, 18, no. 3 (August): 290–303

Kiyotaki, N., and J. Moore. 1997. "Credit Cycles." *Journal of Political Economy*, 105, no. 2 (April): 211–248.

Kiyotaki, N., and R. Wright. 1989. "On Money as a Medium of Exchange." *Journal of Political Economy*, 97, no. 4 (August): 927–954.

Kiyotaki, N., and R. Wright. 1993. "A Search-Theoretic Approach to Monetary Economics." *American Economic Review*, 83, no. 1 (March): 63–77.

Klein, M., and M. J. M. Neumann. 1990. "Seigniorage: What Is It and Who Gets It?" *Weltwirtschaftliches Archiv*, 126 (2): 205–221.

Kormendi, R. C., and P. G. Meguire. 1984. "Cross-Regime Evidence of Macroeconomic Rationality." *Journal of Political Economy*, 92, no. 5 (October): 875–908.

Kormendi, R. C., and P. G. Meguire. 1985. "Macroeconomic Determinants of Growth: Cross-Country Evidence." *Journal of Monetary Economics*, 16, no. 2 (September): 141–163.

Kreps, David, and Robert Wison. 1982. "Reputation and Imperfect Information." *Journal of Economic Theory*, 27, no. 2 (August): 253–279.

Krugman, P. R. 1979. "A Model of Balance of Payments Crises." *Journal of Money, Credit, and Banking*, 11, no. 3 (August): 311–325.

Krugman, P. R. 1991. "Target Zones and Exchange Rate Dynamics." *Quarterly Journal of Economics*, 106, no. 3 (August): 669–682.

Kydland, F. E., and E. C. Prescott. 1977. "Rules Rather Than Discretion: The Inconsistency of Optimal Plans." *Journal of Political Economy*, 85, no. 3 (June): 473–491.

Kydland, F. E., and E. C. Prescott. 1982. "Time to Build and Aggregate Fluctuations." *Econometrica*, 50, no. 6 (November): 1345–1370.

Kydland, F. E., and E. C. Prescott. 1990. "Business Cycles: Real Facts and a Monetary Myth." Federal Reserve Bank of Minneapolis *Quarterly Review*, 14 (Spring): 3–18.

Lacker, J. M. 1988. "Inside Money and Real Output." *Economic Letters*, 28 (1): 9–14.

Laidler, D. E. W. 1985. *The Demand for Money: Theories, Evidence, and Problems*, 3rd ed. New York: Harper & Row.

Laubach, T., and Adam S. Posen. 1997. "Disciplined Discretion: The German and Swiss Monetary Targeting Frameworks in Operation." Federal Reserve Bank of New York Research Paper No. 9707, January.

Leeper, E. M. 1991. "Equilibria under 'Active' and 'Passive' Monetary and Fiscal Policies." *Journal of Monetary Economics*, 27, no. 1 (February): 129–147.

Leeper, E. M. 1993. "Has the Romers' Narrative Approach Identified Monetary Policy Shock?" Federal Reserve Bank of Atlanta Working Paper No. 93–1, February.

Leeper, E. M., and D. B. Gordon. 1992. "In Search of the Liquidity Effect." *Journal of Monetary Economics*, 29, no. 3 (June): 341–369.

Leeper, E. M., C. A. Sims, and T. Zha. 1996. "What Does Monetary Policy Do?" *Brookings Papers on Economic Activity*, 2: 1–63.

Leiderman, L., and L. E. O. Svensson. 1995. *Inflation Targets*. London: CEPR.

LeRoy, S. 1984a. "Nominal Prices and Interest Rates in General Equilibrium: Money Shocks." *Journal of Business*, 57, no. 2 (April): 177–195.

LeRoy, S. 1984b. "Nominal Prices and Interest Rates in General Equilibrium: Endowment Shocks." *Journal of Business*, 57, no. 2 (April): 197–213.

Levhari, D., and D. Patinkin. 1968. "The Role of Money in a Simple Growth Model." *American Economic Review*, 58, no. 4 (September): 713–753.

Levin, A., J. Rogers, and B. Tryon. 1997. "A Guide to FRB/Global." Federal Reserve Board, June.

Levin, A., V. Wieland, and J. C. Williams. 1998. "Robustness of Simple Monetary Policy Rules under Model Uncertainty." Presented at the NBER Conference on Monetary Policy Rules. January. Islamorada, FL.

Lippi, F. 1996. *Central Bank Independence and Credibility: Essays on the Delegation Arrangements for Monetary Policy*. Ph.D. dissertation, Erasmus University, November. Rotterdam, The Netherlands.

Litterman, R., and L. Weiss. 1985. "Money, Real Interest Rates, and Output: A Reinterpretation of the Postwar U.S. Data." *Econometrica*, 53, no. 1 (January): 129–156.

Lockwood, B. 1997. "State-Contingent Inflation Contracts and Unemployment Persistence." *Journal of Money, Credit, and Banking*, 28, no. 3 (August): 286–299.

Lockwood, B., and A. Philippopoulos. 1994. "Insider Power, Employment Dynamics, and Multiple Inflation Equilibria." *Economica*, 61, no. 241 (February): 59–77.

Lohmann, S. 1992. "Optimal Commitment in Monetary Policy: Credibility versus Flexibility." *American Economic Review*, 82, no. 1 (March): 273–286.

Lowe, P., ed. 1997. *Monetary Policy and Inflation Targeting*. Reserve Bank of Australia, July.

Lucas, R. E., Jr. 1972. "Expectations and the Neutrality of Money." *Journal of Economic Theory*, 4, no. 2 (April): 103–124.

Lucas, R. E., Jr. 1973. "Some International Evidence on Output-Inflation Tradeoffs." *American Economic Review*, 63, no. 3 (June): 326–334.

Lucas, R. E., Jr. 1976. "Econometric Policy Evaluation: A Critique." *Carnegie-Rochester Conference Series on Public Policy*, 1: 19–46.

Lucas, R. E., Jr. 1980. "Two Illustrations of the Quantity Theory of Money." *American Economic Review*, 70, no. 5 (December): 1005–1014.

Lucas, R. E., Jr. 1990. "Liquidity and Interest Rates." *Journal of Economic Theory*, 50, no. 2 (April): 237–264.

Lucas, R. E., Jr. 1994. "The Welfare Costs of Inflation." CEPR Publication No. 394, Stanford University, Stanford, CA, February.

Lucas, R. E., Jr. 1996. "Nobel Lecture: Monetary Neutrality." *Journal of Political Economy*, 104, no. 4 (August): 661–682.

Lucas, R. E., Jr., and N. Stokey. 1983. "Optimal Fiscal and Monetary Policy in an Economy without Capital." *Journal of Monetary Economics*, 12, no. 1 (July): 55–93.

Lucas, R. E., Jr., and N. Stokey. 1987. "Money and Interest in a Cash-in-Advance Economy." *Econometrica*, 55, no. 3 (May): 491–514.

Maddala, G. S. 1992. *Introduction to Econometrics*, 2nd ed. New York: Macmillan.

Mankiw, N. G. 1985. "Small Menu Costs and Large Business Cycles: A Macroeconomic Model of Monopoly." *Quarterly Journal of Economics*, 101, no. 2 (May): 529–537.

Mankiw, N. G. 1987. "The Optimal Collection of Seigniorage: Theory and Evidence." *Journal of Monetary Economics*, 20, no. 2 (September): 327–341.

Mankiw, N. G. 1997. *Macroeconomics*, 3rd ed. New York: Worth.

Mankiw, N. G., and J. A. Miron. 1986. "The Changing Behavior of the Term Structure of Interest Rates." *Quarterly Journal of Economics*, 101, no. 2 (May): 211–228.

Mankiw, N. G., and J. A. Miron. 1991. "Should the Fed Smooth Interest Rates? The Case of Seasonal Monetary Policy." *Carnegie-Rochester Conference Series on Public Policy*, 39 (Spring): 41–69.

Mankiw, N. G., J. A. Miron, and D. N. Weil. 1987. "The Adjustment of Expectations to a Change in Regime: A Study of the Founding of the Federal Reserve." *American Economic Review*, 77, no. 3 (June): 358–374.

Mankiw, N. G., J. A. Miron, and D. N. Weil. 1994. "The Founding of the Fed and the Behavior of Interest Rates: What Can Be Learned from Small Samples?" *Journal of Monetary Economics*, 34, no. 3 (December): 555–559.

Mankiw, N. G., and L. H. Summers. 1986. "Money Demand and the Effects of Fiscal Policy." *Journal of Money, Credit, and Banking*, 18, no. 4 (November): 415–429.

Marshall, D. A. 1993. "Comment on 'Search, Bargaining, Money and Prices: Recent Results and Policy Implications.'" *Journal of Money, Credit, and Banking*, 25, no. 3, part 2 (August): 577–581.

Maskin, E., and J. Tirole. 1988. "Models of Dynamic Oligopoly I: Overview and Quality Competition with Large Fixed Costs." *Econometrica*, 56, no. 3 (May): 549–569.

Mattey, J., and R. Meese. 1986. "Empirical Assessment of Present Value Relationships." *Econometric Reviews*, 5 (2): 171–233.

McCallum, B. T. 1983a. "On Non-uniqueness in Rational Expectations Models: An Attempt at Perspective." *Journal of Monetary Economics*, 11, no. 2 (March): 139–168.

McCallum, B. T. 1983b. "The Role of Overlapping Generations Models in Monetary Economics." *Carnegie-Rochester Conference Series on Public Policy*, 18: 9–44.

McCallum, B. T. 1984a. "A Linearized Version of Lucas's Neutrality Model." *Canadian Journal of Economics*, 17, no. 1 (February): 138–145.

McCallum, B. T. 1984b. "On Low-Frequency Estimates of Long-Run Relationships in Macroeconomics." *Journal of Monetary Economics*, 14, no. 1 (July): 3–14.

McCallum, B. T. 1986. "Some Issues Concerning Interest Rate Pegging, Price Level Determinacy, and the Real Bills Doctrine." *Journal of Monetary Economics*, 17, no. 1 (January): 135–160.

McCallum, B. T. 1988. "Robustness Properties of a Rule for Monetary Policy." *Carnegie-Rochester Conference Series on Public Policy*, 29: 173–204.

McCallum, B. T. 1989. *Monetary Economics*. New York: Macmillan.

McCallum, B. T. 1990a. "Inflation: Theory and Evidence." Chapter 18 in B. Friedman and F. Hahn (eds.), *Handbook of Monetary Economics*, vol. 2, 963–1012. New York: North-Holland.

McCallum, B. T. 1990b. "Targets, Instruments, and Indicators of Monetary Policy." In W. S. Haraf and P. Cagan (eds.), *Monetary Policy for a Changing Financial Environment*, 44–70. Washington, DC: AEI Press.

McCallum, B. T. 1994a. "A Reconsideration of the Uncovered Interest Parity Relationship." *Journal of Monetary Economics*, 33, no. 1 (February): 105–132.

McCallum, B. T. 1994b. "Monetary Policy and the Term Structure of Interest Rates." NBER Working Paper No. 4938, November.

McCallum, B. T. 1994c. "A Semi-classical Model of Price Level Adjustment." *Carnegie-Rochester Conference Series on Public Policy*, 41 (December): 251–284.

McCallum, B. T. 1995. "Two Fallacies Concerning Central Bank Independence." *American Economic Review*, 85, no. 2 (May): 207–211.

McCallum, B. T. 1996. "Inflation Targeting in Canada, New Zealand, Sweden, the United Kingdom, and in General." NBER Working Paper No. 5579, May.

McCallum, B. T. 1997a. "Critical Issues Concerning Central Bank Independence." *Journal of Monetary Economics*, 39, no. 1 (July): 99–112.

McCallum, B. T. 1997b. "The Alleged Instability of Nominal Income Targeting." Reserve Bank of New Zealand Discussion Paper G97/6, August.

McCallum, B. T., and M. S. Goodfriend. 1987. "Demand for Money: Theoretical Studies." *The New Palgrave Dictionary of Economics*, London: Macmillan 775–781.

McCallum, B. T., and J. G. Hoehn. 1983. "Instrument Choice for Money Stock Control with Contemporaneous and Lagged Reserve Accounting: A Note." *Journal of Money, Credit, and Banking*, 15, no. 1 (February): 96–101.

McCallum, B. T., and E. Nelson. 1997. "An Optimizing IS-LM Specification for Monetary Policy and Business Cycle Analysis." NBER Working Paper No. 5875, January.

McCallum, B. T., and E. Nelson. 1998. "Performance of Operational Policy Rules in an Estimated Semi-Classical Structural Model." Presented at the NBER Conference on Monetary Policy Rules. January. Islamorada, FL.

McCandless, G. T., Jr., and W. E. Weber. 1995. "Some Monetary Facts." Federal Reserve Bank of Minneapolis *Quarterly Review*, 19, no. 3 (Summer): 2–11.

McKinnon, R., and K. Ohno. 1997. *Dollar and Yen: Resolving Economic Conflicts between the United States and Japan*. Cambridge, MA: MIT Press.

Meese, R. A., and K. Rogoff. 1983. "Empirical Exchange Rate Models of the Seventies: Do They Fit Out of Sample?" *Journal of International Economics*, 14, no. 1 (February): 3–24.

Metzler, L. 1951. "Wealth, Saving, and the Rate of Interest." *Journal of Political Economy*, 59, no. 2 (April): 93–116.

Meulendyke, A-M. 1989. *U.S. Monetary Policy and Financial Markets*. Federal Reserve Bank of New York.

Minford, P. 1995. "Time-Inconsistency, Democracy, and Optimal Contingent Rules." *Oxford Economic Papers*, 47, no. 2 (April): 195–210.

Mino, K., and S. Tsutsui. 1990. "Reputational Constraint and Signalling Effects in a Monetary Policy Game." *Oxford Economic Papers*, 42, no. 3 (July): 603–619.

Mishkin, F. S. 1982. "Does Anticipated Policy Matter? An Econometric Investigation." *Journal of Political Economy*, 90, no. 1 (February): 22–51.

Mishkin, F. S. 1992. "Is the Fisher Effect for Real? A Reexamination of the Relationship between Inflation and Interest Rates." *Journal of Monetary Economics*, 30, no. 2 (November): 195–215.

Mishkin, F. S., and A. S. Posen. 1997. "Inflation Targeting: Lessons from Four Countries." Federal Reserve Bank of New York, *Economic Policy Review*, 3, no. 3 (August): 9–110.

Modigliani, F. 1963. "The Monetary Mechanism and Its Interaction with Real Phenomena." *Review of Economics and Statistics*, 45, no. 1, part 2 (February): 79–107.

Modigliani, F., and A. Ando. 1976. "Impacts of Fiscal Actions on Aggregate Income and the Monetarist Controversy: Theory and Evidence." In J. L. Stein (ed.), *Monetarism*. Amsterdam: North-Holland.

Modigliani, F., R. Rasche, and J. P. Cooper. 1970. "Central Bank Policy, the Money Supply, and the Short-Term Rate of Interest." *Journal of Money, Credit, and Banking*, 2, no. 2 (May): 166–218.

Morton, J., and P. Wood. 1993. "Interest Rate Operating Procedures of Foreign Central Banks." In M. Goodfriend and D. Small (eds.), *Operating Procedures and the Conduct of Monetary Policy: Conference Proceedings*, Finance and Economics Discussion Series, Working Studies 1, Parts 1 and 2, Federal Reserve System, March. Washington, DC.

Mosser, P. C. 1994. "Influence of the Credit Crunch on Aggregate Demand and Implications for Monetary Policy." In *Studies on Causes and Consequences of the 1989–92 Credit Slowdown*. Federal Reserve Bank of New York, February, 259–299.

Motley, B. 1994. "Growth and Inflation: A Cross-Country Study." Paper prepared for the CEPR/SF Fed Conference on Monetary Policy in a Low-Inflation Environment, March. San Francisco, CA.

Muscatelli, A. 1998. "Inflation Contracts and Inflation Targets under Uncertainty: Why We Might Need Conservative Central Bankers." University of Glasgow Discussion Paper No. 9802, January.

Muscatelli, A. In press. "Optimal Inflation Contracts and Inflation Targets with Uncertain Central Bank Preferences: Accountability Through Independence?" *The Economic Journal*: forthcoming.

Mussa, M. 1981a. "Sticky Individual Prices and the Dynamics of the General Price Level." In *Carnegie-Rochester Conference Series on Public Policy*, 15: 261–296.

Mussa, M. 1981b. "Sticky Prices and Disequilibrium Adjustment in a Rational Model of the Inflationary Process." *American Economic Review*, 71, no. 5 (December): 1020–1027.

Nelson, C. R., and C. I. Plosser. 1982. "Trends and Random Walks in Macroeconomic Time Series: Some Evidence and Implications." *Journal of Monetary Economics*, 10, no. 2 (September): 139–162.

Nolan, C., and E. Schaling. 1996. "Monetary Policy Uncertainty and Central Bank Accountability." Bank Of England, London.

Obstfeld, M. 1985. "Floating Exchange Rates: Experience and Prospects." *Brookings Papers on Economic Activity*, 2: 369–450.

Obstfeld, M., and K. Rogoff. 1983. "Speculative Hyperinflations in Maximizing Models: Can We Rule Them Out?" *Journal of Political Economy*, 91, no. 4 (August): 675–687.

Obstfeld, M., and K. Rogoff. 1986. "Ruling Out Divergent Speculative Bubbles." *Journal of Monetary Economics*, 17, no. 3 (May): 349–362.

Obstfeld, M., and K. Rogoff. 1995. "Exchange Rate Dynamics Redux." *Journal of Political Economy*, 103, no. 3 (June): 624–660.

Obstfeld, M., and K. Rogoff. 1996. *Foundations of International Macroeconomics*. Cambridge, MA: MIT Press.

O'Flaherty, B. 1990. "The Care and Handling of Monetary Authorities." *Economics and Politics*, 2, no. 1 (March): 25–44.

Oh, S. 1989. "A Theory of a Generally Accepted Medium of Exchange and Barter." *Journal of Monetary Economics*, 23, no. 1 (January): 101–119.

Ohanian, L., and A. Stockman. 1995. "Resolving the Liquidity Effect." Federal Reserve Bank of St. Louis *Review*, 77, no. 3 (May/June): 3–25.

Oliner, S. D., and G. D. Rudebusch. 1995. "Is There a Bank Lending Channel for Monetary Policy?" Federal Reserve Bank of San Francisco *Economic Review*, Spring, pp. 3–20.

Oliner, S. D., and G. D. Rudebusch. 1996a. "Is There a Broad Credit Channel for Monetary Policy?" Federal Reserve Bank of San Francisco *Economic Review*, Winter, pp. 3–13.

Oliner, S. D., and G. D. Rudebusch. 1996b. "Monetary Policy and Credit Conditions: Evidence from the Composition of External Finance: Comment." *American Economic Review*, 86, no. 1 (March): 300–309.

Olson, M., Jr. 1996. "Big Bills Left on the Sidewalk: Why Some Nations Are Rich and Others Poor." *Journal of Economic Perspectives*, 10, no. 2 (Spring): 3–24.

Parsley, D. C., and S-J. Wei. 1996. "Convergence to the Law of One Price with Trade Barriers or Currency Fluctuations." *Quarterly Journal of Economics*, 111, no. 4 (November): 1211–1236.

Patinkin, Don. 1965. *Money, Interest, and Prices*, 2nd ed., New York: Harper & Row.

Pearce, D. 1993. "Discount Window Borrowing and Federal Reserve Operating Regimes." *Economic Inquiry*, 31, no. 4 (October): 564–579.

Peek, J., and E. Rosengren, eds. 1995. *Is Bank Lending Important for the Transmission of Monetary Policy?* Federal Reserve Bank of Boston Conference Series No. 39, June.

Peristiani, S. 1991. "The Model Structure of Discount Window Borrowing." *Journal of Money, Credit and Banking*, 23, no. 1 (February): 13–34.

Persson, T., and G. Tabellini, eds. 1990. *Macroeconomic Policy, Credibility and Politics*. Chur, Switzerland: Harwood Academic Publishers.

Persson, T., and G. Tabellini. 1993. "Designing Institutions for Monetary Stability." *Carnegie-Rochester Conference Series on Public Policy*, 39 (December).

Persson, T., and G. Tabellini, eds. 1994. *Monetary and Fiscal Policy, vol. 1: Credibility*, 53–84. Cambridge, MA: MIT Press.

Persson, T., and G. Tabellini. In press. "Political Economics and Macroeconomic Policy." In J. Taylor and M. Woodford, (eds.), *Handbook of Macroeconomics*.

Phelps, E. S. 1968. "Money-Wage Dynamics and Labor Market Equilibrium." *Journal of Political Economy*, 76, no. 4, part 2 (August): 678–711.

Phelps, E. S. 1973. "Inflation in the Theory of Public Finance." *Swedish Journal of Economics*, 75, no. 1 (March): 67–82.

Phillips, A. W. 1957. "Stabilisation Policy and the Time-Forms of Lagged Responses." *Economic Journal*, 67, no. 2 (June): 265–277.

Pollard, Patricia S. 1993. "Central Bank Independence and Economic Performance." Federal Reserve Bank of St. Louis *Review*, 75, no. 4 (July/August): 21–36.

Poloz, S., D. Rose, and R. Tetlow. 1994. "The Bank of Canada's New Quarterly Projections Model (QPM): An Introduction." *Bank of Canada Review*.

Poole, W. 1970. "Optimal Choice of Monetary Policy Instrument in a Simple Stochastic Macro Model." *Quarterly Journal of Economics*, 84, no. 2 (May): 197–216.

Posen, A. 1993. "Why Central Bank Independence Does Not Cause Low Inflation: There Is No Institutional Fix for Politics." In R.O'Brien (ed.), *Finance and the International Economy*, 7: 40–65. Oxford: Oxford University Press.

Posen, A. 1995. "Declarations Are Not Enough: Financial Sector Sources of Central Bank Independence." In B. Bernanke and J. Rotemberg (eds.), *NBER Macroeconomics Annual 1995*, 253–274.

Poterba, J. M., and J. J. Rotemberg. 1990. "Inflation and Taxation with Optimizing Governments." *Journal of Money, Credit and Banking*, 22, no. 1 (February): 1990, 1–18.

Ramey, V. 1993. "How Important Is the Credit Channel in the Transmission of Monetary Policy?" *Carnegie-Rochester Conference Series on Public Policy*, 39 (December): 1–45.

Ramsey, F. P. 1928. "A Mathematical Theory of Saving." *Economic Journal*, 38, no. 152 (December): 543–559.

Rasche, R. H. 1973. "A Comparative Static Analysis of Some Monetarist Propositions." Federal Reserve Bank of St. Louis *Review*, December, pp. 15–23.

Reichenstein, W. 1987. "The Impact of Money on Short-Term Interest Rates." *Economic Inquiry*, 25, no. 1 (January): 67–82.

Ritter, J. A. 1995. "The Transition from Barter to Fiat Money." *American Economic Review*, 85, no. 1 (March): 134–149.

Roberts, J. 1995. "New Keynesian Economics and the Phillips Curve." *Journal of Money, Credit and Banking*, 27, no. 4, part 1 (November): 975–984.

Roberts, J. 1997. "Is Inflation Sticky?" *Journal of Monetary Economics*, 39, no. 2 (July): 173–196.

Rogoff, K. 1985a. "Can International Policy Coordination Be Counterproductive?" *Journal of International Economics*, 18, nos. 3–4 (May): 199–217.

Rogoff, K. 1985b. "The Optimal Commitment to an Intermediate Monetary Target." *Quarterly Journal of Economics*, 100, no. 4 (November): 1169–1189.

Rogoff, K. 1989. "Reputation, Coordination, and Monetary Policy." In R. Barro (ed.), *Modern Business Cycle Theory*. Cambridge, MA: Harvard University Press.

Roley, V. V., and G. H. Sellon. 1996. "The Response of the Term Structure of Interest Rates to Federal Funds Rate Target Changes." Federal Reserve Bank of Kansas City, April.

Roley, V. V., and C. E. Walsh. 1985. "Monetary Policy Regimes, Expected Inflation, and the Response of Interest Rates to Money Anouncements." *Quarterly Journal of Economics*, 100, no. 5, Suppl.: 1011–1039.

Rolnick, A. J., and W. E. Weber. 1994. "Inflation, Money, and Output under Alternative Monetary Standards." Research Department Staff Report 175, Federal Reserve Bank of Minneapolis.

Romer, C. D., and D. H. Romer. 1989. "Does Monetary Policy Matter? A New Test in the Spirit of Friedman and Schwartz." In O. J. Blanchard and S. Fischer (eds.), *NBER Macroeconomics Annual, 1989*, 121–170. Cambridge, MA: MIT Press.

Romer, C. D., and D. H. Romer. 1990. "New Evidence on the Monetary Transmission Mechanism." *Brookings Papers on Economic Activity*, 1: 149–198.

Romer, D. 1993. "Openness and Inflation: Theory and Evidence." *Quarterly Journal of Economics*, 108, no. 4 (November): 869–903.

Romer, D. 1996. *Advanced Macroeconomics*. New York: McGraw-Hill.

Rotemberg, J. J. 1984. "A Monetary Equilibrium Model with Transaction Costs." *Journal of Political Economy*, 92, no. 1 (February): 40–58.

Rotemberg, J. J. 1987. "New Keynesian Microfoundations." In S. Fischer (ed.), *NBER Macroeconomics Annual, 1987*, 69–104. Cambridge, MA: MIT Press.

Rotemberg, J. J., and M. Woodford. 1995. "Dynamic General Equilibrium Models with Imperfectly Competitive Product Markets." In T. F. Cooley, (ed.), *Frontiers of Business Cycle Research*. Princeton, NJ: Princeton University Press.

Rotemberg, J. J., and M. Woodford. 1998. "Interest Rate Rules in an Estimated Sticky Price Model." Presented at the NBER Conference on Monetary Policy Rules. January. Islamorada, FL.

Rudebusch, G. D. 1995. "Federal Reserve Interest Rate Targeting, Rational Expectations, and the Term Structure." *Journal of Monetary Economics*, 35, no. 2 (April): 245–274.

Rudebusch, G. D. 1997. "Do Measures of Monetary Policy in a VAR Make Sense?" Federal Reserve Bank of San Francisco, June.

Rudebusch, G. D., and L. E. O. Svensson. 1997. "Policy Rules for Inflation Targeting." Paper prepared for the NBER Conference on Monetary Policy Rules. January. Islamorada, FL.

Samuelson, P. A. 1958. "An Exact Consumption-Loan Model of Interest with or without the Social Contrivance of Money." *Journal of Political Economy*, 66, no. 6 (December): 467–482.

Sargent, T. J. 1976. "The Observational Equivalence of Natural and Unnatural Rate Theories of Macroeconomics." *Journal of Political Economy*, 84, no. 3 (June): 631–640.

Sargent, T. J. 1982. "Beyond Supply and Demand Curves in Macroeconomics." *American Economic Review*, 72, no. 2 (May): 382–389.

Sargent, T. J. 1986. "The Ends of Four Big Inflations." In his *Rational Expectations and Inflation*, 40–109. New York: Harper & Row.

Sargent, T. J. 1987. *Dynamic Macroeconomic Theory*. Cambridge, MA: Harvard University Press.

Sargent, T. J., and N. Wallace. 1975. "'Rational' Expectations, the Optimal Monetary Instrument, and the Optimal Money Supply Rule." *Journal of Political Economy*, 83, no. 2 (April): 241–254.

Sargent, T. J., and N. Wallace. 1981. "Some Unpleasant Monetarist Arithmetic." Federal Reserve Bank of Minneapolis *Quarterly Review*, 5, no. 3, 1–17.

Sargent, T. J., and Wallace, N. 1985. "Some Unpleasant Monetarist Arithmetic." Federal Reserve Bank of Minneapolis *Quarterly Review*, 9, no. 1 (Winter): 15–31.

Schaling, E., M. Hoeberichts, and S. Eijffinger. 1998. "Incentive Contracts for Central Bankers under Uncertainty: Walsh-Svensson Non-Equivalence Revisited." CentER for Economic Research Discussion Paper No. 9811, Tilburg University, The Netherlands. February.

Schelde-Andersen, Palle. 1992. "OECD Country Experiences with Disinflation." In A. Blundell-Wignall (ed.), *Inflation, Disinflation and Monetary Policy*. Reserve Bank of Australia.

Schlagenhauf, D. E., and J. M. Wrase. 1995. "Liquidity and Real Activity in a Simple Open Economy Model." *Journal of Monetary Economics*, 35, no. 3 (June): 431–461.

Sheffrin, S. M. 1983. *Rational Expectations*. Cambridge: Cambridge University Press.

Sheffrin, S. M. 1995. "Identifying Monetary and Credit Shocks." In K. D. Hoover and S. M. Sheffrin (eds.), *Monetarism and the Methodology of Economics*, 151–163. Aldershot, U.K.: Edward Elgar.

Shi, S. 1995. "Money and Prices: A Model of Search and Bargaining." *Journal of Economic Theory*, 67, no. 2 (December): 467–496.

Shiller, R. J. 1981. "Do Stock Prices Move Too Much to be Justified by Subsequent Changes in Dividends?" *American Economic Review*, 71, no. 3 (June): 421–436.

Shiller, R. J. 1990. "The Term Structure of Interest Rates." In B. Friedman and F. Hahn (eds.), *The Handbook of Monetary Economics*, vol. 1, 626–722. New York: North-Holland.

Sidrauski, M. 1967. "Rational Choice and Patterns of Growth in a Monetary Economy." *American Economic Review*, 57, no. 2 (May): 534–544.

Sims, C. A. 1972. "Money, Income and Causality." *American Economic Review*, 62, no. 4 (September): 540–542.

Sims, C. A. 1980. "Comparison of Interwar and Postwar Business Cycles." *American Economic Review*, 70, no. 2 (May): 250–257.

Sims, C. A. 1988. "Identifying Policy Effects." In R. C. Bryant, D. W. Henderson, G. Holtham, P. Hooper, and S. A. Symansky (eds.), *Empirical Macroeconomics for Interdependent Economies*, 305–321. Washington, DC: Brookings Institution.

Sims, C. A. 1992. "Interpreting the Macroeconomic Time Series Facts: The Effects of Monetary Policy." *European Economic Review*, 36, no. 5 (June): 975–1000.

Sims, C. A. 1996. "Comments on Glenn Rudebusch's 'Do Measures of Monetary Policy in a VAR Make Sense?'" Yale University, New Haven, CT, July.

Small, D. H. 1979. "Unanticipated Money Growth and Unemployment in the United States: Comment." *American Economic Review*, 69, no. 5 (December): 996–1003.

Smith, B. 1983. "Limited Information, Credit Rationing, and Optimal Government Lending Policy." *American Economic Review*, 73, no. 3 (June): 305–318.

Söderlind, P., and L. E. O. Svensson. 1997. "New Techniques to Extract Market Expectations from Financial Instruments." *Journal of Monetary Economics*, 40, no. 2 (October): 383–429.

Soller, E. V., and C. J. Waller. 1997. "A Search Theoretic Model of Legal and Illegal Currency." Indiana University, July. Bloomington, IN.

Solow, R. 1956. "A Contribution to the Theory of Economic Growth." *Quarterly Journal of Economics*, 70, no. 1 (February): 65–94.

Spindt, P. 1985. "Money Is What Money Does: Monetary Aggregation and the Equations of Exchange." *Journal of Political Economy*, 93, no. 1 (February): 175–204.

Stein, J. 1969. "Neoclassical and Keynes-Wicksell Monetary Growth Models." *Journal of Money, Credit, and Banking*, 1, no. 2 (May): 153–171.

Stiglitz, J. E., and A. Weiss. 1981. "Credit Rationing in Markets with Imperfect Information." *American Economic Review*, 71, no. 3 (June): 393–410.

Stock, J. H., and M. W. Watson. 1989. "Interpreting the Evidence on Money-Income Causality." *Journal of Econometrics*, 40, no. 1 (January): 161–181.

Stockman, A. 1981. "Anticipated Inflation and the Capital Stock in a Cash-in-Advance Economy." *Journal of Monetary Economics*, 8, no. 3 (November): 387–393.

Strongin, S. 1995. "The Identification of Monetary Policy Disturbances: Explaining the Liquidity Puzzle." *Journal of Monetary Economics*, 35, no. 3 (August): 463–497.

Summers, L. H. 1981. "Optimal Inflation Policy." *Journal of Monetary Economics*, 7, no. 2 (March): 175–194.

Svensson, L. E. O. 1985. "Money and Asset Prices in a Cash-in-Advance Economy." *Journal of Political Economy*, 93, no. 5 (October): 919–944.

Svensson, L. E. O. 1986. "Sticky Goods Prices, Flexible Asset Prices, Monopolistic Competition, and Monetary Policy." *Review of Economic Studies*, 53, no. 3 (July): 385–405.

Svensson, L. E. O. 1996. "Price Level Targeting vs. Inflation Targeting: A Free Lunch?" NBER Working Paper No. 5719.

Svensson, L. E. O. 1997a. "Inflation Forecast Targeting: Implementing and Monitoring Inflation Targets." *European Economic Review*, 41, no. 6 (June): 1111–1146.

Svensson, L. E. O. 1997b. "Optimal Inflation Contracts, 'Conservative' Central Banks, and Linear Inflation Contracts." *American Economic Review*, 87, no. 1 (March): 98–114.

Svensson, L. E. O. 1997c. "Inflation Targeting: Some Extensions." NBER Working Paper No. 5962.

Svensson, L. E. O. 1997d. "Open-Economy Inflation Targeting." Institute for International Economic Studies, Stockholm, October.

Tabellini, G. 1988. "Centralized Wage Setting and Monetary Policy in a Reputational Equilibrium." *Journal of Money, Credit and Banking*, 20, no. 1 (February): 102–118.

Taylor, J. B. 1975. "Monetary Policy during a Transition to Rational Expectations." *Journal of Political Economy* 83, no. 5 (October): 1009–1021.

Taylor, J. B. 1979. "Staggered Wage Setting in a Macro Model." *American Economic Review*, 69, no. 2 (May): 108–113.

Taylor, J. B. 1980. "Aggregate Dynamics and Staggered Contracts." *Journal of Political Economy*, 88 (1): 1–24.

Taylor, J. B. 1983. "Comments on 'Rules, Discretion and Reputation in a Model of Monetary Policy' by R. J. Barro and D. B. Gordon." *Journal of Monetary Economics*, 12, no. 1 (July): 123–125.

Taylor, J. B. 1985. "What Would Nominal GNP Targeting Do to the Business Cycle?" *Carnegie-Rochester Conference Series on Public Policy*, 22: 61–84.

Taylor, J. B. 1989. "Policy Analysis with a Multicountry Model." In R. Bryant et al. (eds.), *Macroeconomic Policies in an Interdependent World*, 122–141. Washington, DC: Brookings Institution.

Taylor, J. B. 1993a. "Discretion versus Policy Rules in Practice." *Carnegie-Rochester Conferences Series on Public Policy*, 39 (December): 195–214.

Taylor, J. B. 1993b. *Macroeconomic Policy in a World Economy*. New York: W. W. Norton.

Taylor, J. B. 1996. "How Should Monetary Policy Respond to Shocks While Maintaining Long-Run Price Stability?—Conceptual Issues." In *Achieving Price Stability*, 181–195. Federal Reserve Bank of Kansas City.

Tobin, J. 1956. "The Interest Elasticity of the Transactions Demand for Cash." *Review of Economics and Statistics*, 38, no. 3 (August): 241–247.

Tobin, J. 1965. "Money and Economic Growth." *Econometrica*, 33, no. 4, part 2, (October): 671–684.

Tobin, J. 1969. "A General Equilibrium Approach to Monetary Theory." *Journal of Money, Credit, and Banking*, 1, no. 1 (February): 15–29.

Tobin, J. 1970. "Money and Income: Post Hoc Ergo Proctor Hoc?" *Quarterly Journal of Economics*, 84, no. 2 (May): 301–317.

Tobin, J., and W. Brainard. 1983. "Financial Intermediaries and the Effectiveness of Monetary Control." *American Economic Review*, 53: 383–400.

Tootell, G. 1991. "Are District Presidents More Conservative than Board Governors?" Federal Reserve Bank of Boston *New England Economic Review*, September-October, pp. 3–12.

Townsend, R. 1979. "Optimal Contracts and Competitive Markets with Costly State Verification." *Journal of Economic Theory*, 21, no. 2 (October): 265–293.

Trehan, B., and C. E. Walsh. 1988. "Common Trends, the Government's Budget Balance, and Revenue Smoothing." *Journal of Economic Dynamics and Control*, 12, no. 2/3 (June/September): 425–444.

Trehan, B., and C. E. Walsh. 1990. "Seigniorage and Tax Smoothing in the United States, 1914–1986." *Journal of Monetary Economics*, 25, no. 1 (January): 97–112.

Trehan, B., and C. E. Walsh. 1991. "Testing Intertemporal Budget Constraints: Theory and Applications to U.S. Federal Budget and Current Account Deficits." *Journal of Money, Credit and Banking*, 23, no. 2 (May): 206–223.

Trejos, A., and R. Wright. 1993. "Search, Bargaining, Money and Prices: Recent Results and Policy Implications." *Journal of Money, Credit, and Banking*, 25, no. 3, part 2 (August): 558–576.

Trejos, A., and R. Wright. 1995. "Search, Bargaining, Money and Prices." *Journal of Political Economy*, 103 (1): 118–141.

Uhlig, Harald. 1995. "A Toolkit for Analyzing Nonlinear Dynamic Stochastic Models Easily." Discussion Paper 101, Federal Reserve Bank of Minneapolis, June.

U.S. President. 1985. *Economic Report of the President*. Washington, DC.

VanHoose, D. 1989. "Monetary Targeting and Price Level Non-trend Stationarity." *Journal of Money, Credit and Banking*, 21, no. 2 (May): 232–239.

Vickers, J. 1986. "Signalling in a Model of Monetary Policy with Incomplete Information." *Oxford Economic Papers*, 38, no. 3 (November): 443–455.

Wallace, N. 1981. "A Modigliani-Miller Theorem for Open-Market Operations." *American Economic Review*, 71, no. 3 (June): 267–274.

Waller, C. J. 1989. "Monetary Policy Games and Central Bank Politics." *Journal of Money, Credit and Banking*, 21, no. 4 (November): 422–431.

Waller, C. J. 1990. "Administering the Window: A Game Theoretic Model of Discount Window Borrowing." *Journal of Monetary Economics*, 25, no. 2 (March): 273–287.

Waller, C. J. 1992. "A Bargaining Model of Partisan Appointments to the Central Bank." *Journal of Monetary Economics*, 29, no. 3 (June): 411–428.

Waller, C. J. 1995. "Performance Contracts for Central Bankers." Federal Reserve Bank of St. Louis *Review*, 77, no. 5 (September/October): 3–14.

Waller, C. J., and C. E. Walsh. 1996. "Central Bank Independence, Economic Behavior and Optimal Term Lengths." *American Economic Review*, 86, no. 5 (December): 1139–1153.

Walsh, C. E. 1982a. "Asset Substitutability and Monetary Policy: An Alternative Characterization." *Journal of Monetary Economics*, 9, no. 1 (January): 59–71.

Walsh, C. E. 1982b. "The Effects of Alternative Operating Procedures on Economic and Financial Relationships." *Monetary Policy Issues in the 1980s*, 133–163. Federal Reserve Bank of Kansas City.

Walsh, C. E. 1984. "Optimal Taxation by the Monetary Authority." NBER Working Paper No. 1375, June.

Walsh, C. E. 1986. "In Defense of Base Drift." *American Economic Review*, 76, no. 4 (September): 692–700.

Walsh, C. E. 1987. "Monetary Targeting and Inflation, 1976–1984." Federal Reserve Bank of San Francisco *Economic Review*, Winter, pp. 5–15.

Walsh, C. E. 1990. "Issues in the Choice of Monetary Policy Operating Procedures." In W. S. Haraf and P. Cagan (eds.), *Monetary Policy for a Changing Financial Environment*, 8–37. Washington, DC: AEI Press.

Walsh, C. E. 1992. "The New View of Banking." In J. Eatwell, M. Milgate, and P. Newman (eds.), *The New Palgrave Dictionary of Money and Finance*, 31–33. London: Macmillan.

Walsh, C. E. 1993. "What Caused the 1990 Recession?" Federal Reserve Bank of San Francisco *Economic Review*, Spring, pp. 33–48.

Walsh, C. E. 1994. "When Should Central Bankers Be Fired?" University of California, Santa Cruz.

Walsh, C. E. 1995a. "Optimal Contracts for Central Bankers." *American Economic Review*, 85, no. 1 (March): 150–167.

Walsh, C. E. 1995b. "Recent Central Bank Reforms and the Role of Price Stability as the Sole Objective of Monetary Policy." In B. Bernanke and J. Rotemberg (eds.), *NBER Macroeconomics Annual, 1995*, 237–252. Cambridge, MA: MIT Press.

Walsh, C. E. 1995c. "Is New Zealand's Reserve Bank Act of 1989 an Optimal Central Bank Contract?" *Journal of Money, Credit and Banking*, 27, no. 4, part 1 (November): 1179–1191.

Walsh, C. E. 1995d. "Central Bank Independence and the Short-Run Output-Inflation Tradeoff in the EC." In B. Eichengreen, J. Frieden and J. von Hagan (eds.), *Monetary and Fiscal Policy in an Integrated Europe*, 12–37. Berlin: Springer Verlag.

Walsh, C. E. 1996. "Announcements, Inflation Targeting, and Central Bank Incentives." University of California, Santa Cruz, October.

Walsh, C. E., and J. A. Wilcox. 1995. "Bank Credit and Economic Activity." In J. Peek and E. Rosengren (eds.), *Is Bank Lending Important for the Transmission of Monetary Policy?*, 83–112. Federal Reserve Bank of Boston Conference Series No. 39, June.

Wang, P., and C. K. Yip. 1992. "Alternative Approaches to Money and Growth." *Journal of Money, Credit and Banking*, 24, no. 4 (November): 553–562.

West, K. D. 1986. "Targeting Nominal Income: A Note." *The Economic Journal*, 96 (December): 1077–1083.

West, K. D. 1987. "A Specification Test for Speculative Bubbles." *Quarterly Journal of Economics*, 102, no. 3 (August): 553–580.

West, K. D. 1988. "Dividend Innovation and Stock Price Volatility." *Econometrica*, 56, no. 1 (January): 37–61.

Wilcox, D. W. 1989. "The Sustainability of Government Deficits: Implications of the Present-Value Borrowing Constraint." *Journal of Money, Credit and Banking*, 21, no. 3 (August): 291–306.

Williamson, S. D. 1986. "Costly Monitoring, Financial Intermediation and Equilibrium Credit Rationing." *Journal of Monetary Economics*, 18, no. 2 (September): 159–179.

Williamson, S. D. 1987a. "Costly Monitoring, Loan Contracts, and Equilibrium Credit Rationing." *Quarterly Journal of Economics*, 102, no. 1 (February): 135–145.

Williamson, S. D. 1987b. "Financial Intermediation, Business Failures, and Real Business Cycles." *Journal of Political Economy*, 95, no. 6 (December): 1196–1216.

Woodford, M. 1994. "Nonstandard Indicators for Monetary Policy: Can Their Usefulness Be Judged from Forecasting Regressions?" In N. G. Mankiw (ed.), *Monetary Policy*. Chicago: University of Chicago Press.

Woodford, M. 1995. "Price Level Determinacy without Control of a Monetary Aggregate." *Carniege-Rochester Conference Series on Public Policy*, 43: 1–46.

Woodford, M. 1996. "Control of the Public Debt: A Requirement for Price Stability?" Princeton University, Princeton, NJ, July.

Woodford, M. 1997. "Doing Without Money: Controlling Inflation in a Post-Monetary World." *Journal of Economic Dynamics and Control*: forthcoming.

Woolley, J. 1995. "Nixon, Burns, 1972, and Independence in Practice." University of California, Santa Barbara, May.

Yun, T. 1996. "Nominal Price Rigidity, Money Supply Endogeneity, and Business Cycles." *Journal of Monetary Economics*, 37, no. 2 (April): 345–370.

Author Index

Subject Index

A

Adaptive expectations
in Cagan's model, 153–154
hyperinflation and, 154–157
Ad hoc modeling, techniques of, 2
Adverse selection, imperfect information in credit markets, 289–292
Adverse shocks, broad credit channel, 318–319
Agency costs
broad credit channel, 318–319
credit markets, 288, 298–302
Aggregate demand
AS-IS-LM model, 208–213
bank lending channels, 305–307
closed-economy model of interest rates, 460–472
Federal Reserve operating procedures, 422–423
interest-rate policies, 214
intermediate targeting and, 396–403
monetary shocks and, 465–467
optimal policy and, 468–472
p-Bar model, 221–223
policy coordination in open economy models, 263–264
price-level determinacy, 433–438
small open-economy model, 270–272
term structure of interest rates, 448–451
Aggregate prices
multiperiod persistence, 199–202
nominal wage and inflation persistence, 216–226
Aggregate production function
MIU linear approximation, 88–91
optimizing agents in MIU model, 204–206
Aggregate spending
bank lending channels and, 315–317
closed-economy model of interest rates, 460–472
credit markets and, 285, 287
open-economy interest-rate rules, 472–475
real interest rates, 177–178
term structure of interest rates, 448–451
Aggregate supply
AS-IS-LM model, 208–211
central bank contracts and, 356–360
central bank objective function, 324–326
conservative central bankers and, 354–355
coordination and equilibrium in open economy models, 264–266
discretionary policy and economic activity, 327–329
equilibrium inflation and, 332–336
flexible targeting rules, 363–367
intermediate targeting and, 396–403
money multipliers, 404–406
noncoordination and equilibrium in open economy models, 268–269

price-level determinacy, 433–438
small open-economy models, 270n.22
strict targeting rules, 368–369
Alesina-Sachs political business cycle model, inflation bias and, 360–362
Announcements, discretionary policy and, 351
Asset accumulation
debt and money supply, 143–147
Tobin effect, 42–49
Asset pricing, cash-in-advance models, 101–107
Assets
bank lending channels, 304–307
credit channels and, 285
Kiyotaki-Moore credit model, 312–313
Asymmetric information
agency costs of credit markets, 301–302
central bank "types" and, 343–351
Atomistic agents, repeated game model, 341–343
Auditing probability, agency costs in credit markets, 301–302
Australia, inflation targeting in, 337n.9
Autonomous expenditures, time-series analysis with, 17
Autoregression coefficient, money-in-the-utility function, 74–75
Average inflation, central bank independence and, 375–381

B

Baa-rated corporate bonds, inflation expectations and term structure, 457–459
Backus-Driffill model, 343–347
Backward-looking expectations
closed economy model of interest rates, 463–464
inflation stickiness, 225–226
Ball model, 345–347
Bank lending channel, 286, 304–307, 315–317
Bank of Canada
price level policy, 326
structural econometric model, 34
Bank of England
independence of, 377
instrument independence, 379n.56
Bank of Italy, debt accommodation, 141
Bargaining, search theory and, 121–123
Barter, search theory and, 121–123
Base drift policy, interest-rate smoothing, 444–445
Baseline parameters
cash-in-advance (CIA) models, 110
closed economy model of interest rates, 464–467
Lucas islands model, 184–185
money-in-the-utility function, 74–77
Benchmark parameter values. *See* Baseline parameters

open economy version, 472-474
use for policy analysis, 460-467
Functional equivalence, transaction costs models,
    117–118
Future output, money-output correlation, 16

G
Game theory, monetary policy and, 4, 7
Gatherers, Kiyotaki-Moore credit model, 309–313
General equilibrium
    adverse selection in credit markets, 289n.3
    agency costs of credit markets, 299–302
    interest-rate policies, 445–448
    macroeconomic credit market models, 307–313
    monetary policy in, 41–91
    money-in-the-utility (MIU) function, 42, 49–79
    Tobin effect, 42–49
Germany
    conservative central banker model in, 354
    monetary demand, 445n.17
    operating procedures in, 423, 427
Goal independence, central banks and, 379–381
Goal variables and policy instruments, 386–387
Government budget constraints
    budget accounting, 132–138
    intertemporal budget balance, 138–140
    monetary and fiscal actions linked to, 147
    monetary policy and, 131–132
    partial equilibrium model of optimal seigniorage,
        158–162
Government deficits
    intertemporal budget balance, 139–140
    money supply and, 143–147
    seigniorage and, 147–148, 161–162
Government structures
    central bank preferences, 351–355
    contracts and optimal incentives, 356–360
    repeated game model of central banks, 341n.14
    reputational models, central bank "types,"
        344–351
Granger causality
    deficits and, 141
    money-output correlation, 18–19
Gross domestic product (GDP)
    detrended money and, 14–15
    interest rates and detrending of, 16–17
    monetary shocks and, 11
    reserve market model, 410–413
    short-run money-output correlations, 11–13
    vector autoregression (VAR) framework and, 28
    welfare costs of inflation, 63–64
Gross national product (GNP)
    Granger causality and, 19
    seigniorage and, 136–138

H
Heterogeneity
    credit channels, 285–286
    general equilibrium credit models, 308–313
    limited-participation models, 188n.19
High-powered money
    government budget constraints, 132–138
    seigniorage and, 136–138, 148–149
Hodrick-Prescott filter
    MIU correlations, 75n.33
    short-run money relationships, 11n.4
Homothetic preferences, Friedman's rule and CIA
    model, 165
Humphrey-Hawkins Act, 418–419
Hyperinflation
    disinflation and monetary policy, 37–39
    indeterminacy and, 433
    output costs, 224n.56
    seigniorage and, 154–157, 207n.48
    steady-state equilibrium, 60

I
Identification problem, bank lending channels,
    316–317
Imperfect competition
    Chari, Kehoe, and McGratten model, 242–244
    Obstfeld-Rogoff model, 242–244
    price setting and, 195–202
Imperfect information
    adverse selection in credit markets, 289–292
    central bank reputation and inflation bias, 338
    credit markets, 286, 288–302, 319
    interest-rate smoothing, 441–445
    Lucas islands model, 180–181, 227–231
    repeated game model, 341n.13
    short-run economic effects, 179–186
Implementability condition, Friedman's rule,
    169–170
Inada conditions, 43, 47n.6
Incentives
    central banks, 321–323
    contracts and, 355–360
    equilibrium inflation and, 332–336
    flexible targeting rules, 366–367
    institutional structures, 360–362
    relevance of inflation bias and, 370–375
Income expectations
    MIU sticky price model, 234–235
    noncoordinated policy, open economic models,
        269
Incomplete collateralization, agency costs of credit
    markets, 301–302
Independence
    conservative central bankers and, 353–355